# Plants That Merit Attention

Library of Congress Cataloging-in-Publication Data

Plants that merit attention / The Garden Club of America; Janet Meakin Poor, editor;
Nancy P. Brewster, photographic editor.
p.    cm.
Includes indexes.
Contents: v. 2. Shrubs
ISBN 0-88192-347-8
1. Landscape plants. 2. Plants, Ornamental. 3. Landscape plants—Pictorial works.
4. Plants, Ornamental—Pictorial works. I. Poor, Janet Meakin. II. Brewster, Nancy P.
III. Garden Club of America.
SB435.P6 1996                                                                              94-7957
635.9—dc20                                                                                  CIP

Published by

Timber Press, Inc.
The Haseltine Building
133 S.W. Second Avenue, Suite 450
Portland, Oregon 97204, U.S.A.

Printed in Hong Kong

With immense admiration and unending gratitude,
this volume is dedicated to

Dr. Theodore R. Dudley
Dr. Donald R. Egolf
Dr. Mildred E. Mathias

each of whom contributed in innumerable and significant ways
not only to this book and its predecessor publication
but also to the entire plant world.

These three internationally acknowledged and respected experts
epitomized unyielding excellence,
exceptional commitment,
and the relentless pursuit of perfection.

Their outstanding contributions to our horticultural heritage
have left us with a vibrant, living legacy
that we must cherish and nurture.

Were I to await for perfection,
my book would never be finished.

Tai T'ung
13th century

# CONTENTS

The greatest service which can be rendered to any country
is to add a useful plant to its culture.

Thomas Jefferson

# ACKNOWLEDGMENTS

The authorship of this book is unique. Hundreds of "authors" have contributed to this publication. In addition to Garden Club of America (GCA) members, others who have played an important role in the initial selection process and who have contributed invaluable information and photographs include professors, horticulturists, botanists, taxonomists, dendrologists, nursery professionals, and landscape architects. These interested and supportive individuals are dedicated to preserving diversity in the horticultural world.

Our immediate committee was composed of Garden Club of America members representing different regions of the United States. To collect and coordinate materials, each committee member worked with professionals from botanical gardens, arboreta, nurseries, and universities in her specific area. Each was responsible for obtaining research information and many of the color photographs, and for assuring a representative collection from each geographical region. This committee has been working diligently for almost seven years. A deep and grateful thank you to Alison Andrews, Patricia R. Bush, Jean Dozier, Rosemary T. Jones, Sally J. MacBride, Jan O. Pratt, Judith B. Sellers, Elizabeth A. Sharp, Louise G. Smith, Sally Squire, Peggy K. Thompson, and Louise Wrinkle.

Gerd Krüssmann's three-volume *Manual of Cultivated Broad-Leaved Trees & Shrubs* (1986) is the general reference authority for nomenclature in this volume. We have chosen to use the lowercase initial letter for all species, following the International Code of Botanical Nomenclature (Leningrad Edition, 1978) Article 73, Recommendation 73 F.1. The late Dr. Theodore R. Dudley, research botanist and taxonomist at the U.S. National Arboretum; the late Dr. Mildred E. Mathias, botanist and taxonomist at the Mildred E. Mathias Botanical Garden; and Floyd A. Swink, taxonomist at The Morton Arboretum, were the taxonomic advisors. Our most sincere gratitude to these knowledgeable taxonomists who have so ably served our project.

We are greatly appreciative of Graham Stuart Thomas, world-renowned plantsman and rosarian, and Stephen Scanniello, rosarian of the Brooklyn Botanic Garden, for their dedication, interest, and expertise in the rose section of this volume.

The botanical nomenclature in this publication is skillfully illustrated by the beautiful line drawings of the late artist-horticulturist Elizabeth T. Zimmerman. To further clarify the text, Mrs. Zimmerman and Dr. Ross Clark, curator of education at The Morton Arboretum, collaborated to write the botanical glossary. A sincere thank you to these dedicated contributors.

We are grateful for the long hours contributed by Noelle Hartley in compiling the nursery sources.

One of the most unusual aspects of this book is that so many interested individuals have generously shared their knowledge. There are no direct quotations; rather, the text is a compilation of the information gleaned from these willing participants. A most grateful thank you to these generous individuals who have spent countless hours answering questions, evaluating specific genera, and obtaining photographs:

Mrs. Jay L. Abbott, Litchfield, CT
Agriculture Canada, Morden Research Centre, Manitoba, Canada
Douglas Akerley, Manager, Martin Viette's Nurseries
William L. Ackerman, Ph.D., Ashton, MD
Eddie Aldridge, Aldridge Nurseries, Bessemer, AL
John H. Alexander, Curator of *Syringa* and Plant Propagator, The Arnold Arboretum

9

Gary Anderson, Ph.D., Chairman, Horticulture Division, Agricultural Technical Institute, Ohio State University

Thomas M. Antonio, Ph.D., Taxonomist, Chicago Botanic Garden

Johannes Apel, Director Emeritus, Hamburg Botanical Gardens

R. Armstrong

Kris Bachtell, Collections Department Supervisor, The Morton Arboretum

Bailey Nurseries, Minneapolis, MN

David P. Barnett, Ph.D., Director of Horticulture, Mt. Auburn Cemetery

Lynn R. Batdorf, Curator, U.S. National Arboretum

Mrs. George Beasley, Transplant Nursery

Ellie Bell, Englewood, NJ, GCA

Stephen Bender, Southern Living Magazine

Barbara Blackwell, St. Louis, MO

Nancy Bole, Cleveland, OH, GCA (d.)

Timothy Boland, Michigan State University

James Borland, Denver, CO

Carol Bornstein, Director of Horticulture, Santa Barbara Botanic Garden

Donald Brennan, Plant Introduction, Chicago Botanic Garden

Bruce Briggs, Briggs Nursery

Peter Bristol, Horticulturist, Holden Arboretum

Mary Stella Brosius, L.D., Descanso Gardens

Richard A. Brown, Director, The Bloedel Reserve

Hal Bruce, Director of Horticulture, Winterthur Gardens (d.)

Tamara Buchanan, The Sweetbriar

Al Bussewitz, The Arnold Arboretum (d.)

Lynn Callicott, Morden Research Station

Nancy Cammann, Darien, CT, GCA

Dr. Linda Campbell, High Country Rosarium (d.)

Ed Carman, Carman's Nursery

Paul Chandler

Anne Chatham, Stanleytown, VA, GCA

John Christiansen, former Horticulturist, Molbak's

Ross Clark, Ph.D., Curator of Adult Education, The Morton Arboretum

Horace Clay, Ph.D., Honolulu, HI (d.)

Yolanda Clay, Honolulu, HI, GCA

Sterling Cornelius, Cornelius Nursery

Elizabeth Platt Corning, Albany, NY, GCA (d.)

Paul Cox, Assistant Director, San Antonio Botanical Garden

Ann L. Crammond, Director, Atlanta Botanic Garden, GCA (d.)

James E. Cross, Environmentals

Carl Crumb, Mercer Island, WA

William L. Culberson, Sarah P. Duke Gardens, Duke University

Rick Darke, Curator of Plants, Longwood Gardens

Ray Daugherty, Green Acres Nursery

Campbell Davidson, Ph.D., Morden Research Center

Thomas Dilatush, Dilatush Nursery

Michael A. Dirr, Ph.D., Department of Horticulture, University of Georgia

Ruth Dix, Horticulturist, U.S. National Arboretum

George Dobbins, Sacramento, CA

Tom Dodd, Tom Dodd Nurseries

John Dourly, Rancho Santa Ana Botanical Garden

Kay Dresdner, Princeton, NY

Joyce Driemeyer, Landscape Architect

Bettina Dudley, Ph.D., Glendale, MD

Dick Dunmire, Senior Editor, Sunset Magazine

Ken Durio, Louisiana Nursery

Sue Dyckman, Skillman, NJ

Donald Egolf, Ph.D. (d.)

Linda Eirhart, Associate Curator, Winterthur Museum and Gardens

Gene Eisenbeiss, International Registrar of *Ilex*, U.S. National Arboretum

John Elsley, Horticultural Director, Wayside Gardens

David Ehrlinger, Cincinnati Botanic Garden

Fr. John L. Fiala, Syringa Hybridizer and Author of *Lilacs: The Genus Syringa* (d.)

Robert Fincham, Coenosium Gardens

William Flemmer, III, Princeton Nurseries

Harrison Flint, Ph.D., Professor of Horticulture, Purdue University

John Floyd, Southern Living Magazine

R. Roy Forster, Curator, Van Dusen Botanical Garden

Kathleen Freeland, Midwest Groundcovers

Monica Freeman, GCA Staff Administrator

Noreen Frink, Seattle, WA

Fred Galle, former Director of Horticulture, Callaway Gardens

Mary Gamble, former President, American Boxwood Society

Galen Gates, Manager of Horticulture Collections, Chicago Botanic Garden

Gary Gerlach, Director, Birmingham Botanical Garden

Thomas Green, Ph.D., Plant Pathologist, The Morton Arboretum

Harold Greer, Greer Gardens

Edward R. Hasselkus, Ph.D., Professor Emeritus, University of Wisconsin Landscape Arboretum; Curator, Longenecker Gardens

Richard Hawke, Plant Evaluator, Chicago Botanic Garden

Thomas Hawkins, Albany, NY

Robert Hays, Propagator, Brooklyn Botanic Garden

Robert S. Hebb, Ph.D.

M. Heger, Minnesota Landscape Arboretum

Happy Hieronimus, Portland, OR, GCA

William Hendricks, Lake County Nursery

James Henrich, Director of Horticulture, Denver Botanic Gardens

Ginger Henrichs, Librarian, Chicago Botanic Garden

Craig Hibben, Ph.D., Research Plant Pathologist, Brooklyn Botanic Garden, retired

Polly Hill, Vineyard Haven, MA, GCA

Merwin Hiller, Highland Park, IL

Duncan Himmelman, Instructor of Horticulture, Olds College

Robert T. Hirano, Harold L. Lyon Arboretum, University of Hawaii

Timothy Hohn, Curator, Plant Collections, University of Washington, Washington Park Arboretum

Charles Holetich, Ph.D., Arboriculturist, Royal Botanical Gardens, Ontario

Betty Hotchkiss, American Camellia Society

Clarence E. Hubbuch, Jr., Bernheim Forest Arboretum

Jean Iseli, Iseli Nursery (d.)

Japanese Consulate, Honolulu, HI

Kris Jarantoski, Director, Chicago Botanic Garden

Richard Jaynes, Ph.D., Broken Arrow Nursery

Karen Jennings, Park Seed Company, Greenwood, SC

Gordon E. Jones, Stanley, NY

Betty Kassab, Wallingford Rose Gardens

Panayoti Kelaidis, Curator, Rock Alpine Collection, Denver Botanic Gardens

Paul Kingsley, Meadowside Gardens

T. Kipping

Roy Klehm, President, Klehm Nursery

Joanne Knapp, Planting Fields Arboretum, retired

Gary Koller, Senior Horticulturist, The Arnold Arboretum

Harold Koopowitz, Ph.D., Director, University of California Arboretum, Irvine

Cornelia Kraft, Islip, NY, GCA

Susan Lammert, St. Louis, MO, GCA

Fred Lang, Landscape Architect, South Laguna, CA

V. Lauritzen, Kailua, HI

Eric Lautzenheiser, Director, San Antonio Botanical Garden

Lawrence Lee, Castro Valley, CA

Charles A. Lewis, former Research Fellow in Horticulture, The Morton Arboretum, retired

Richard W. Lighty, Ph.D., Director, Mt. Cuba Center

Grace Elizabeth Lotowycz, Locust Valley, NY

Cary Luria (d.)

Alex MacBride, Woodside, CA

William MacKentley, St. Lawrence Nursery

Denise Magnani, Director of Landscape, Winterthur Museum and Gardens

Ray Maleike, Ph.D., Extension Horticulturist, Western Washington Research and Extension Center

Sylvester March, Chief Horticulturist, U.S. National Arboretum

Claire Martin, Rosarian, Huntington Botanical Gardens

Elizabeth Martin, St. Louis, MO, GCA

Susan Martin, Curator, Gottelli Collection, U.S. National Arboretum

Peter Mazzeo, Taxonomist, U.S. National Arboretum

Megan McCarthy-Bilow, Chicago Botanic Garden

Elizabeth McClintock, Ph.D., San Francisco, CA

Deb McCown, Knight Hollow Nursery

Carolyn McGregor, Milwaukee, WI, GCA

Shirley Meneice, Pebble Beach, CA, GCA

Frederick Meyer, Ph.D., Botanist, U.S. National Arboretum, retired

Elizabeth Miller, Seattle, WA, GCA (d.)

P. Moe, Minnesota Landscape Arboretum

Gary Moller, Moller's Nursery

Edmond O. Moulin, Director of Horticulture, Brooklyn Botanic Garden, retired

Margaret Mulligan, Kirkland, WA

Kathy Musial, Botanist, Huntington Botanical Gardens

Peter Nelson, Brooklyn Botanic Garden

Rob Nicholson, The Arnold Arboretum

Philip Normandy, Brookside Gardens

Peter J. Olin, Director, Minnesota Landscape Arboretum

M. Olser, Minnesota Landscape Arboretum

Elwin R. Orton, Jr., Ph.D., Rutgers University

Richard C. Page, Director, Cheekwood Botanical Gardens

C. W. Eliot Paine, Director, Holden Arboretum

Alan Patterson, Ph.D., Scotland

Thomas Patterson, Panfield Nurseries

Harold Pellett, Ph.D., University of Minnesota Landscape Arboretum

Richard Piacentini, Director, Rhododendron Species Foundation

Andrew Pierce, Denver Botanic Garden

Polly Pierce, Dedham, MA, GCA

Fern Pietsch, Waimea Arboretum & Botanic Garden, Waimea Falls Park, GCA

G. Pirzio-Biroli, Mercer Island, WA

Jan Pirzio-Biroli, former Naturalist, Washington Park Arboretum

Jane Platt, Portland, OR, GCA (d.)

Beatrice Postian, Financial Coordinator, GCA

James Pringle, Ph.D., Royal Botanical Gardens, Ontario

J. C. Raulston, Ph.D., Director, NCSU Arboretum, North Carolina State University

Peter Raven, Ph.D., Director, Missouri Botanical Garden
Sally Reath, Newtown Square, PA, GCA
Mary Anne Rennebohm, Heard Gardens
Warren G. Roberts, Superintendent, The University Arboretum, University of California, Davis
Owen M. Rogers, Ph.D., University of New Hampshire
Royal Botanical Gardens Staff, Ontario, Canada
Daniel K. Ryniec, Curator of Lilacs, Brooklyn Botanic Garden
John J. Sabuco, Landscape Architect, Chicago, IL
Charles Salter, Salter Tree Farm
Claire E. Sawyers, Director, The Scott Arboretum, Swarthmore College
Stephen Scanniello, Rosarian, Brooklyn Botanic Garden
Elizabeth Scholtz, Ph.D., Director Emeritus, Brooklyn Botanic Garden
Ray Schulenberg, The Morton Arboretum
Elizabeth A. Sharp, Coatesville, PA
Mr. Sherk, Sheridan Nurseries
Holly Shimizu, U.S. Botanic Garden
Bennie Simpson, Texas A & M University, Research and Extension Center
L. Snyder, Minnesota Landscape Arboretum
Winn Soldani, Pompano Beach, FL
Johnson Spink, St. Louis Garden Club
Russell Stafford, Lunenburg, MA
Geoffrey Stanford, Ph.D., Dallas Nature Center
Howard Stensson, Sheridan Nursery
Gerald B. Straley, Curator of Collections, University of British Columbia Botanical Gardens
Charles Straub, Associate Professor of Horticulture, New York State University Agricultural and Technical College
Mary Ann Streeter, Wenham, MA, GCA
Strybing Arboretum Society, Helen Crocker Russel Library
Eldon Studebaker, Studebaker Nurseries
Jane Symmes, Cedar Lane Farms, GCA
John Teas, Teas Nursery
Audrey Teasdale, Botanist, Monrovia Nursery
Graham Stuart Thomas, Woking, United Kingdom
Jean Thomas, Kaneohe, HI, GCA
Leonard Thomas, Spring Grove Arboretum
Nancy Stallworth Thomas, Houston, TX, GCA
David Thompson, Foxborough Nursery
Robert Tichnor, Oregon State University, North Willamette Experiment Station
Robert G. Titus, Huntington, NY
Carl F. Totemeier, Ph.D., former Director of Horticulture, The New York Botanical Garden
University of Washington, Seattle
Celeste VanderMey, Plant Records Supervisor, Chicago Botanic Garden
Joyce Van Etten, Brooklyn Botanic Garden (d.)
M. Vehr, Spring Grove Arboretum
J. D. Vertrees, Maplewood Nursery (d.)
K. Vogel, Minnesota Landscape Arboretum
Freek Vrugtman, Curator of Collections, Royal Botanical Gardens, Hamilton, Ontario, and the International Registration Authority for *Syringa* cultivars
Ira Walker, Curator of Conifers, Brooklyn Botanic Garden
Sally Walker, San Antonio, TX, GCA
Keith J. Warren, J. Frank Schmidt Nursery
Gayle Weinstein, Chicago, IL
Paul Weissich, Ph.D., Kaneohe, HI
Ned Wells, Wells-Medina Nursery
Sally Wenzlau, San Marino, CA, GCA
Chris Willemsen, Mendham, NJ, GCA
Douglas Williams, Director, Mercer Arboretum and Botanic Gardens
Diana S. Wister, Palm Beach, FL, GCA
Edsel Wood, Bonsai Village
Keith R. Woolliams, Director, Waimea Arboretum and Botanic Garden
Barry Yinger, Ph.D., Lewisberry, PA
Judith D. Zuk, President, Brooklyn Botanic Garden

Joanne Freeman prepared the manuscript, but as the book slowly evolved also became a most helpful editor, critic, and supporter.

We are most grateful for the help and enduring patience of our spouses, Edward King Poor III and Andre W. Brewster, and our caring families.

No one could have been more encouraging and supportive than Richard Abel, former president and publisher of Timber Press. It has been a privilege to work with both Mr. Abel and the current president and publisher of Timber Press, Robert B. Conklin.

The interest and cooperation of the Horticulture Committee and the hundreds of Garden Club of America participants cannot be measured in words. Without the devotion and support of these dedicated individuals, this book would not have become a reality. We are deeply grateful.

Janet Meakin Poor
Nancy Peterson Brewster

# INTRODUCTION

A myriad of valuable shrubs is available to enhance our landscape. However, those enjoying a high degree of popularity have already been well studied, documented, and photographed; consequently, they are widely known to the trade and readily available to the gardener.

*Plants That Merit Attention, Volume II—Shrubs* has a different focus, namely, a select group of little-known shrubs which, by virtue of their superior garden worthiness, deserve to be preserved, propagated, promoted, and planted—-shrubs that have been bypassed unintentionally in the parade of plants currently in vogue in our gardens. The mission of this publication is to enrich our horticultural heritage and foster the use of these largely overlooked plants by making them more familiar to the gardener, more available to the landscape architect, and more obtainable in the nurseries.

Many of the shrubs in this volume have been around for many years as established plants hidden in the corner of an old estate or growing in lonely splendor in a remote area of a botanic garden or arboretum. These superb plants are in imminent danger of being lost to our present horticultural vocabulary. Other shrubs are new cultivars which deserve more extensive use but, for a variety of reasons that do not include lack of merit, have never received proper exposure in the horticultural literature.

Whether established or relatively new, all species and cultivars included in this book were chosen with the following criteria in mind:

- They are unusual.
- They are not readily available in at least one major region of the United States.
- They beautify the landscape by their outstanding attributes (e.g., flower, fruit, bark, habit).
- They are pest- and disease-resistant.
- They are tolerant of a variety of environmental conditions (e.g., pH level, soil compaction, salt, wind, wet conditions, drought, sun, or shade).

Few plants can meet all these criteria; however, the shrubs selected for this publication must, at minimum, be unusual and not readily available in major areas, and must enhance the landscape in some way. Each additional criterion met makes the plant increasingly valuable and more truly deserving of the title "Plant That Merits Attention." The roses included in this volume were selected for their landscape attributes rather than their individual bloom.

Although ornamental rhododendrons play a prominent role in our gardens, space limitations in this volume would not permit justice to be done to the many rhododendrons that merit attention. There are more than 1000 species of evergreen and deciduous rhododendrons, which have been the source of many thousands of hybrids that extend climatic limitations and add to the beauty and color variety of flowers and foliage. Entire books have deservedly been devoted to this elegant garden shrub, and the reader is referred to them for further information.

This book has been written for all those who are committed to nurturing and preserving the variety, diversity, and beauty of our gardens. It is the culmination of years of diligent effort and study, a harvest of intelligence gathered through the combined efforts of hundreds of dedicated individuals around the world working to ensure a wider palette of worthy plants for future generations of gardeners.

To be worthy of a name,
a plant should be a notable improvement over already existing named cultivars.
The assessment of the true qualities of a [plant] should be based on
observations over a period of (at least) several years of bloom and trial
in different areas of cultivation.
To name a cultivar on the basis of color alone
simply does not take into consideration questions of
the plant's growth qualities, disease resistance, height,
and many other necessary garden features.

Fr. John Fiala


It is required that each cultivar name be registered
by an accepted and recognized system and horticultural authority.
The principles governing acceptance or rejection of cultivar names for registration
are laid down in the *International Code of Nomenclature of Cultivated Plants.*
This code of regulations for botanical names
is revised periodically by a world botanical body.

# GLOSSARY OF BOTANICAL TERMS

### LEAVES

Leaves may be simple or compound, depending on how the **blade** (the flattened part of the leaf) develops. In a **simple** leaf, the blade develops as a single unit, but in a **compound** leaf, the blade is divided into two or more smaller parts called **leaflets.** A leaf with three leaflets is **trifoliate.**

The leaves of some plants are subtended by leaflike **stipules.** In many plants, stipules are present only in the early states of a season's growth, drying up and falling off as the season advances.

Early in the season, the **bud** containing next year's leaf begins to develop where the base of the leaf stalk, the **petiole,** joins the twig; it reaches its full development in late summer and then remains as a bud until the following spring triggers the development of a new leaf. The stalk of a leaflet, the **petiolule,** connects the leaflet to the petiole or to the **rachis,** the extension of the petiole on a compound leaf.

When the margin of a simple leaf is uninterrupted, neither toothed nor lobed, the leaf is said to be **entire;** when it is composed of teethlike cuts, it is said to be **toothed** or **dentate;** and when it is divided into rounded segments, the leaf is said to be **lobed.** A simple leaf that is **palmately lobed** has three or more lobes originating from the same point. When the lobes of a simple leaf are arranged in two rows along the petiole, the leaf is said to be **pinnately lobed.**

A compound leaf in which the leaflets are arranged in two rows along the petiole is said to be **pinnate,** or feather-like. When a pinnate leaf has an odd number of leaflets, it is described as **odd-pinnate;** when the leaflets occur in pairs, the leaf is described as **even-pinnate.** A pinnate leaf in which the leaflets themselves are further divided into leaflets is said to be **bipinnate.** A compound leaf is **palmate,** or palmlike, when its leaflets originate from the same point, like fingers of a hand.

### Leaves of Conifers

A number of conifers have **scalelike** leaves that are very small, often not more than 0.1 inch wide or long, and closely adpressed to the twig in pairs of opposite leaves or in whorls of three or four leaves. Some conifers with scale-like leaves also have **awl-shaped,** or **subulate,** leaves, especially on young growth. Certain junipers, such as *Juniperus chinensis,* and a few other conifers display these very sharp leaves on new twigs.

Pines (*Pinus* sp.) have **needlelike** leaves in bundles of two to five leaves which are enclosed at the base in a papery sheath. Spruces (*Picea* sp.) have leaves borne singly on the twigs, each leaf arising from a small peglike structure that remains on the twig after the leaf falls, so that the part of the twig which has lost its leaves is rough. The leaves are square in cross section and more or less sharply pointed.

### Arrangement of Leaves

Leaves that are attached to the same place on the petiole in pairs are said to be **opposite.** When more than two leaves are attached to the same place on the petiole, the arrangement is ringlike, or **whorled.** When leaves are arranged in ranks along the petiole, they are said to be **alternate.** Clusters of leaves that appear to arise from a common point, such as those of *Pinus* species, are said to be **fascicled.**

### Venation of Leaves

When three or more veins radiate from the same point, the venation is **palmate.** Veins that form a network are said to be **netted** or **reticulate.** Veins that run lengthwise, or parallel to the leaf margin, are said to be **parallel.** Veins are described as **pinnate** when they are arranged featherlike, in two rows along the petiole.

### Leaf Shapes

Leaves come in many shapes, which may be useful in plant identification. Illustrations self-explanatory.

### Leaf Tips—Edges—Bases

Leaf tips, edges, and bases are also helpful in identifying shrubs. Illustrations self-explanatory.

## FLOWERS

The illustration, Flower Parts, is purely diagrammatic; there is no typical flower. The parts of a flower vary in shape, size, and number from species to species. In many flowers some of these parts are absent.

The **essential parts** of a flower are the **pistils,** one or more (female), and the **stamens** (male). Either the pistils or stamens may be absent or small and infertile in some flowers; such flowers are said to be **unisexual.** The female reproductive organ, the pistil, has a stigma, a style, and an ovary within which are one or more ovules. The ovules mature into seeds. The male reproductive organ, the stamen, consists of a pollen-bearing anther carried on a filament.

Petals, sepals, and receptacles are **accessory parts** of a flower. **Petals** are often brightly colored; taken as a whole, they are called the **corolla.** Although **sepals** are usually green, they may be colored like the petals; taken as a whole, sepals are called the **calyx.** The calyx and the corolla together constitute the **perianth.** In wind-pollinated plants, the entire perianth may be missing and the reproductive organs contained either in bracts or in cuplike structures, also called **receptacles.**

### Monoecious and Dioecious Plants

When staminate (male) and pistillate (female) flowers are found on a single plant, that species is described as being unisexual, or **monoecious** (meaning "one household"). When staminate flowers occur on one plant and pistillate flowers on another, that species is said to be **dioecious** (meaning "two households"). This information is important when planting shrubs: if a dioecious species, such as an *Ilex* species, is desired in the landscape, a staminate shrub should be planted in fairly close proximity to a pistillate shrub to ensure pollination and hence ample production of the desired fruit.

### Ovary Position

It is sometimes necessary to know the position of the ovary to identify plants correctly and to understand the structure of fruits.

**Hypogynous** flowers are those in which all the flower parts are seated on the receptacle beneath the pistil. The pistil is said to be **superior.**

**Perigynous** flowers are those in which the receptacle has developed into a cup, open at the top. Bases of the sepals, petals, and stamens are fused with the tissues of the enlarged receptacle. The resulting structure is called an **hypanthium.** When one or more pistils are free-standing within the hypanthium, the ovary is said to be **superior.**

**Epigynous** flowers are those in which the hypanthium is closed at the top, enclosing the ovary of the pistil completely. The tissues of the ovary wall are fused with those of the hypanthium. The ovary is now said to be **inferior,** since it is beneath the flower parts, which appear to arise from a position above it in the flower.

### Inflorescences

**Catkins,** also called **aments,** are spikelike inflorescences found on some shrub species. Flowers of catkins are very small, inconspicuous, and unisexual. **Staminate catkins** are usually flexible and dangling; the small staminate flowers are borne beneath the scales of the catkin. Pistillate flowers may be borne on shorter, more or less erect **pistillate catkins,** or they may be solitary or clustered in a scaly cuplike structure on the twig.

**Solitary** flowers are seen in *Dendromecon rigida* (Bush Poppy) and *Hibiscus rosa-sinensis* (Chinese or Tropical Hibiscus), for example.

A **spike** produces **sessile,** or stalkless, flowers on a central stem, or **rachis.** The lowest flower opens first.

A **raceme** is like a spike except that the flowers have stalks, or **pedicels.** Again, the lowest flower opens first.

A **corymb** is a flat-topped development of a raceme in which the outside flowers on elongated pedicels open first. In an **umbel** all the flowers arise from a single point at the top of the flowering shoot.

A **cyme** is a complex inflorescence in which the center flower at the top of the shoot opens first. Side branches develop beneath this flower and these may branch again, the center flowers always opening first. Some species of *Cornus* (Dogwood), such as *C. sericea,* have cymose inflorescences.

A **panicle** is a much-branched development of a raceme.

## FRUITS

A fruit always involves a ripened ovary or group of ovaries. It may include other floral parts. A seed is a ripened ovule.

**Dry indehiscent fruits** do not **dehisce** (break open) at maturity until weathering softens the hard coat or an animal breaks open the fruit. An **achene** is a hard, dry, one-celled fruit developed from an ovary that has one **locule**

(cell); the seed is fastened to the ovary wall at only one point. An example of a shrub that produces achenes is *Potentilla fruticosa* (Cinquefoil). A **samara** is a winged, dry fruit. A **nut** is a relatively large, one-seeded fruit with a hard ovary wall; often the nut is held in a cup or surrounded by a husk. Small nuts are called **nutlets**, and sometimes achenes are called nutlets. *Caryopteris* and *Comptonia* are examples of genera that produce nutlets.

**Dry dehiscent fruits** break open naturally at maturity to release their seeds.

A **follicle** is a one-celled fruit that splits on only one side. *Physocarpus* and *Sorbaria* produce follicles. A **legume** is like a follicle except that it splits open on two sides. An example is the genus *Genista*. A **capsule** develops from ovaries having several locules; it dehisces along the tissues dividing the locules or at the back of each locule. The genera *Aesculus* and *Kalmia* are examples.

There are three kinds of **fleshy fruits**. A **drupe** is a fleshy fruit that contains in its center one or more hard seedlike structures, each of which contains a seed. Two examples are *Callicarpa* and *Cornus*. In a **berry,** the entire ovary enlarges to become fleshy, with the seeds embedded in the flesh. *Ilex* and *Mahonia* species produce berries. A **pome** develops from epigynous flowers in which the hypanthium enlarges to become the fleshy part of the fruit; the membrane at the outer boundary of the core is the ovary wall, and the core is the ripened ovary that contains within its locules the ripened ovules (seeds). Examples of pomes among the shrubs are seen in *Aronia* and *Chaenomeles*.

## CONIFERS

Conifers belong to the subdivision of seed-bearing plants known as **gymnosperms** (meaning "naked seeds"). Such seeds develop from ovules not enclosed in an ovary. Conifers are monoecious (rarely dioecious), producing inconspicuous staminate flowers on small scaly aments and conspicuous pistillate seed cones. The naked seeds are borne beneath the scales of the cone.

Junipers (*Juniperus* sp.) have fleshy cone scales that coalesce and are called "Juniper berries." In reality, they are true cones, not berries.

An aril is a fleshy structure that more or less encloses a single hard-coated seed. *Taxus* (Yew) is a familiar example.

# ILLUSTRATIONS OF BOTANICAL TERMS

## LEAVES

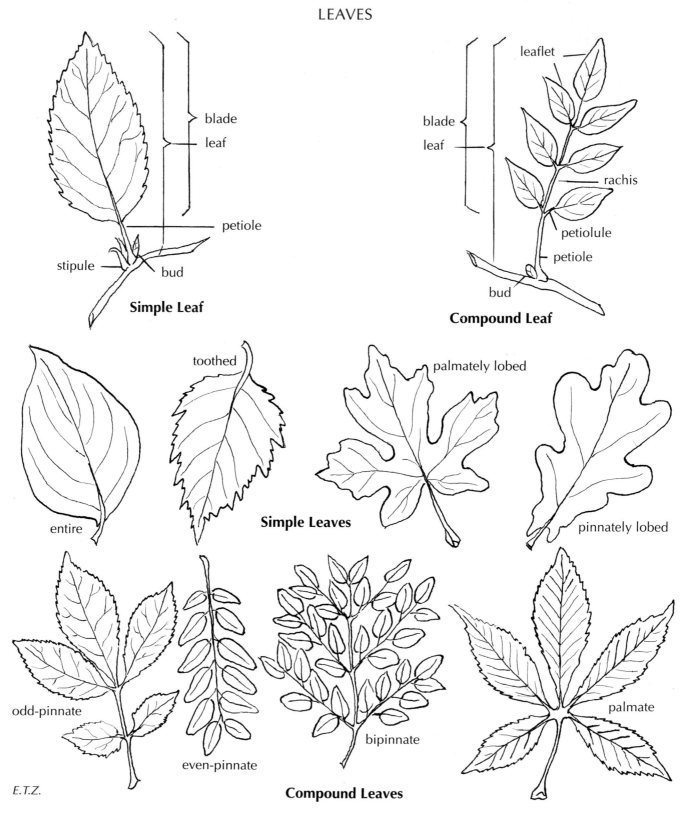

blade

leaf

leaflet

blade

leaf

petiole

rachis

stipule

bud

petiolule

petiole

bud

**Simple Leaf**

**Compound Leaf**

toothed

palmately lobed

entire

**Simple Leaves**

pinnately lobed

odd-pinnate

even-pinnate

bipinnate

palmate

E.T.Z.

**Compound Leaves**

## Leaves of Conifers

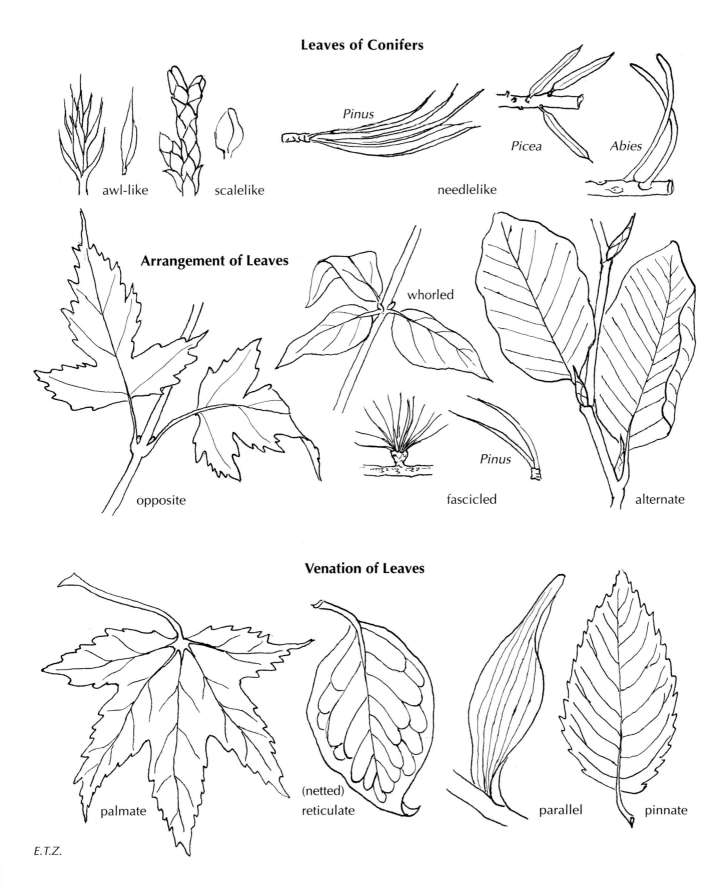

awl-like          scalelike

*Pinus*          *Picea*          *Abies*

needlelike

## Arrangement of Leaves

whorled

*Pinus*

opposite          fascicled          alternate

## Venation of Leaves

palmate          (netted) reticulate          parallel          pinnate

E.T.Z.

# LEAF SHAPES

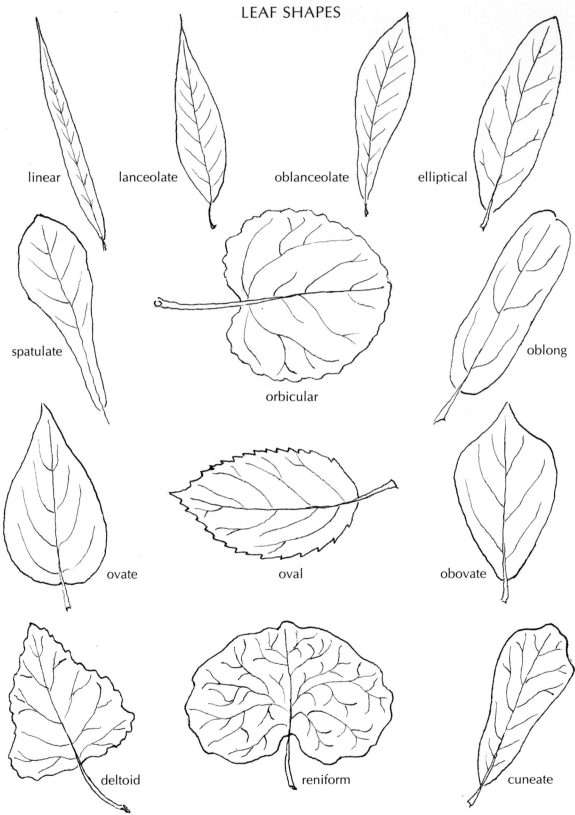

linear  lanceolate  oblanceolate  elliptical

spatulate

orbicular

oblong

ovate  oval  obovate

deltoid  reniform  cuneate

*E.T.Z.*

# LEAF TIPS—EDGES—BASES

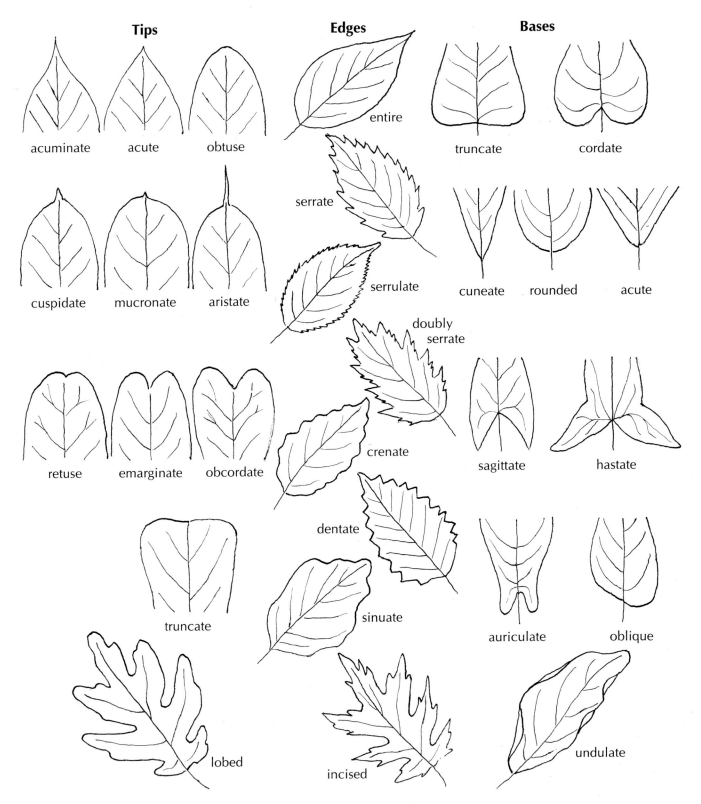

**Tips**

acuminate    acute    obtuse

cuspidate    mucronate    aristate

retuse    emarginate    obcordate

truncate

lobed

**Edges**

entire

serrate

serrulate

doubly serrate

crenate

dentate

sinuate

incised

**Bases**

truncate    cordate

cuneate    rounded    acute

sagittate    hastate

auriculate    oblique

undulate

E.T.Z.

# FLOWERS

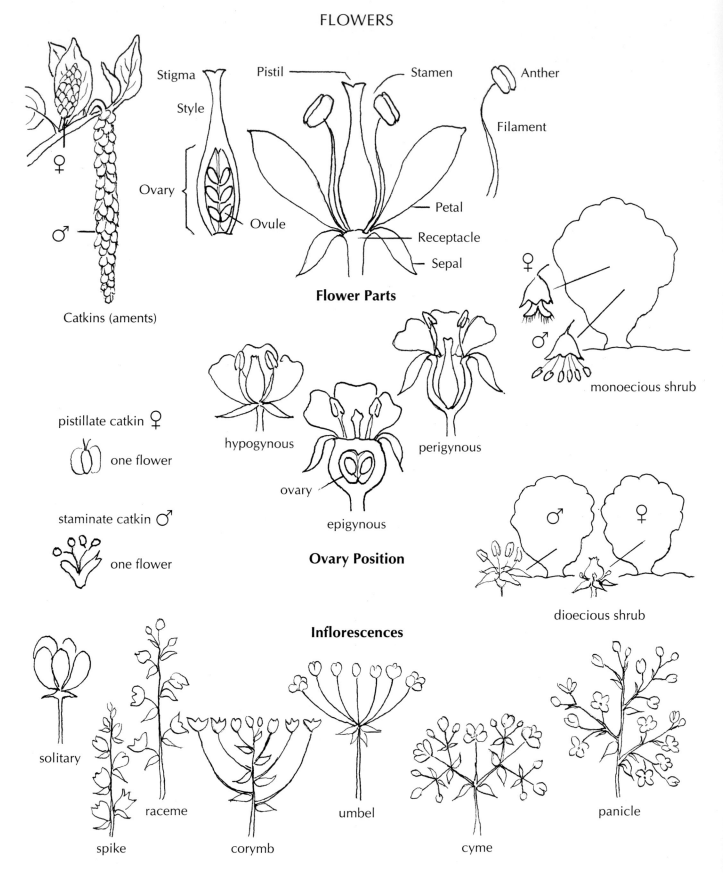

Catkins (aments)

Stigma

Style

Ovary

Ovule

Pistil

Stamen

Anther

Filament

Petal

Receptacle

Sepal

**Flower Parts**

pistillate catkin ♀

one flower

staminate catkin ♂

one flower

hypogynous

ovary

epigynous

perigynous

monoecious shrub

dioecious shrub

**Ovary Position**

**Inflorescences**

solitary

spike

raceme

corymb

umbel

cyme

panicle

*E.T.Z.*

# FRUITS

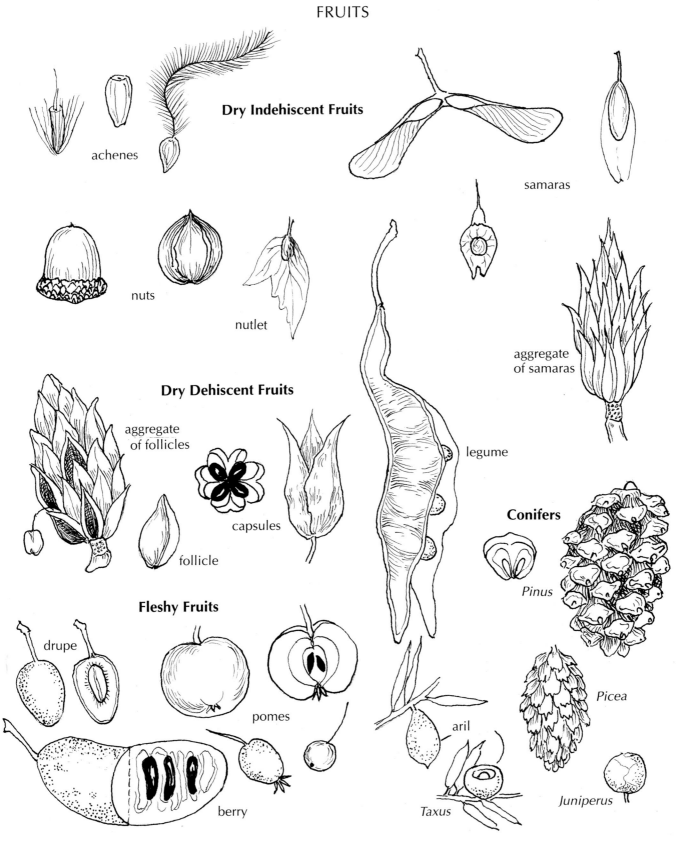

**Dry Indehiscent Fruits**

achenes

samaras

nuts

nutlet

aggregate
of samaras

**Dry Dehiscent Fruits**

aggregate
of follicles

capsules

follicle

legume

**Conifers**

*Pinus*

**Fleshy Fruits**

drupe

pomes

aril

*Picea*

berry

*Taxus*

*Juniperus*

E.T.Z.

# USDA HARDINESS ZONE MAP

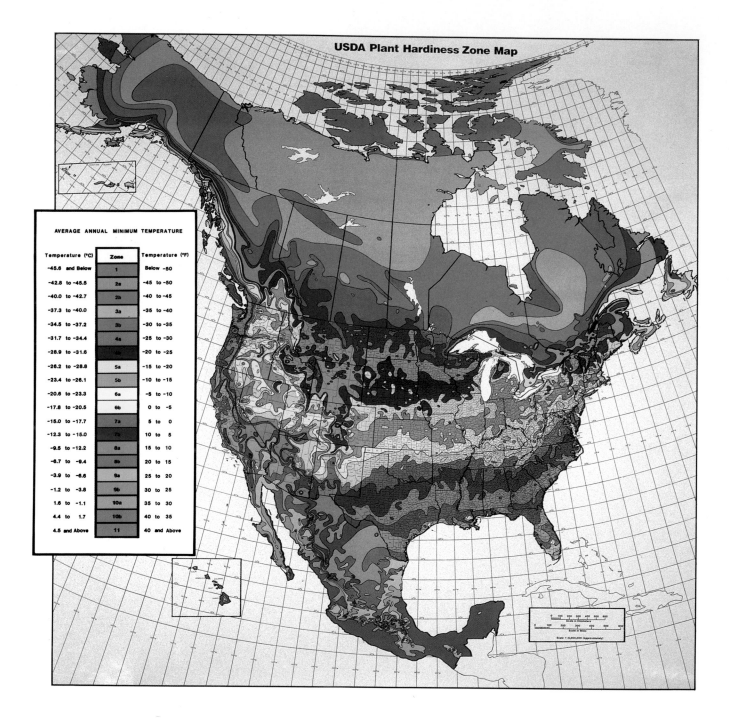

**USDA Plant Hardiness Zone Map**

### AVERAGE ANNUAL MINIMUM TEMPERATURE

| Temperature (°C) | Zone | Temperature (°F) |
|---|---|---|
| -45.6 and Below | 1 | Below -50 |
| -42.8 to -45.5 | 2a | -45 to -50 |
| -40.0 to -42.7 | 2b | -40 to -45 |
| -37.3 to -40.0 | 3a | -35 to -40 |
| -34.5 to -37.2 | 3b | -30 to -35 |
| -31.7 to -34.4 | 4a | -25 to -30 |
| -28.9 to -31.6 | 4b | -20 to -25 |
| -26.2 to -28.8 | 5a | -15 to -20 |
| -23.4 to -26.1 | 5b | -10 to -15 |
| -20.6 to -23.3 | 6a | -5 to -10 |
| -17.8 to -20.5 | 6b | 0 to -5 |
| -15.0 to -17.7 | 7a | 5 to 0 |
| -12.3 to -15.0 | 7b | 10 to 5 |
| -9.5 to -12.2 | 8a | 15 to 10 |
| -6.7 to -9.4 | 8b | 20 to 15 |
| -3.9 to -6.6 | 9a | 25 to 20 |
| -1.2 to -3.8 | 9b | 30 to 25 |
| 1.6 to -1.1 | 10a | 35 to 30 |
| 4.4 to 1.7 | 10b | 40 to 35 |
| 4.5 and Above | 11 | 40 and Above |

# USEFUL CONVERSION TABLES

## FAHRENHEIT/CELSIUS

| | |
|---|---|
| 45° | 7° |
| 40° | 4° |
| 35° | 2° |
| 32° | 0° |
| 30° | −1° |
| 25° | −4° |
| 20° | −7° |
| 15° | −9° |
| 10° | −12° |
| 5° | −15° |
| 0° | −18° |
| −5° | −21° |
| −10° | −23° |
| −15° | −26° |
| −20° | −29° |
| −25° | −32° |
| −30° | −34° |
| −35° | −37° |
| −40° | −40° |
| −45° | −43° |

## INCHES/MILLIMETERS

| | | |
|---|---|---|
| 0.04 | (1/24) | 1 mm |
| 0.06 | (1/16) | 1.5 mm |
| 0.07 | (1/15) | 1.7 mm |
| 0.08 | (1/12) | 2 mm |
| 0.1 | (1/8) | 3 mm |
| 0.2 | (1/6) | 4 mm |
| 0.25 | (1/4) | 6 mm |
| 0.3 | (1/3) | 8 mm |
| 0.3 | (5/16) | 8 mm |
| 0.4 | (3/8) | 10 mm |
| 0.4 | (7/16) | 10 mm |
| 0.5 | (1/2) | 13 mm |
| 0.6 | (9/16) | 16 mm |
| 0.6 | (3/5) | 16 mm |
| 0.6 | (5/8) | 16 mm |
| 0.7 | (2/3) | 17 mm |
| 0.75 | (3/4) | 19 mm |
| 0.8 | (4/5) | 20 mm |
| 0.8 | (13/16) | 20 mm |
| 0.9 | (7/8) | 22 mm |
| 1 | | 25 mm |

## INCHES/CENTIMETERS

| | |
|---|---|
| 1 | 2.5 cm |
| 1.5 | 4 cm |
| 2 | 5 cm |
| 2.5 | 6 cm |
| 3 | 8 cm |
| 3.5 | 9 cm |
| 4 | 10 cm |
| 4.5 | 11 cm |
| 5 | 13 cm |
| 5.5 | 14 cm |
| 6 | 15 cm |
| 6.5 | 16 cm |
| 7 | 18 cm |
| 7.5 | 19 cm |
| 8 | 20 cm |
| 8.5 | 21 cm |
| 9 | 23 cm |
| 9.5 | 24 cm |
| 10 | 25 cm |
| 11 | 28 cm |
| 12 | 31 cm |
| 13 | 33 cm |
| 14 | 35 cm |
| 15 | 38 cm |
| 16 | 40 cm |
| 17 | 43 cm |
| 18 | 45 cm |
| 19 | 48 cm |
| 20 | 50 cm |
| 25 | 63 cm |
| 30 | 75 cm |
| 35 | 88 cm |

## FORMULAS

$$°C = °F − 32 × 5 ÷ 9$$
$$cm = inches × 2.5$$
$$mm = inches × 25$$
$$cm = feet × 30$$
$$m = feet × 0.3$$

## FEET/METERS

| | |
|---|---|
| 1 | 0.3 m |
| 1.5 | 0.5 m |
| 2 | 0.6 m |
| 2.5 | 0.8 m |
| 3 | 1.0 m |
| 3.5 | 1.1 m |
| 4 | 1.2 m |
| 4.5 | 1.4 m |
| 5 | 1.5 m |
| 5.5 | 1.7 m |
| 6 | 1.8 m |
| 6.5 | 1.9 m |
| 7 | 2.0 m |
| 7.5 | 2.3 m |
| 8 | 2.4 m |
| 8.5 | 2.5 m |
| 9 | 2.7 m |
| 9.5 | 2.9 m |
| 10 | 3.0 m |
| 11 | 3.3 m |
| 12 | 3.6 m |
| 13 | 3.9 m |
| 14 | 4.2 m |
| 15 | 4.5 m |
| 16 | 4.8 m |
| 17 | 5.0 m |
| 18 | 5.4 m |
| 19 | 5.7 m |
| 20 | 6.0 m |
| 25 | 7.5 m |
| 30 | 9.0 m |
| 35 | 10.5 m |

## FEET/METERS

| | |
|---|---|
| 500 | 150 m |
| 1,000 | 300 m |
| 1,500 | 450 m |
| 2,000 | 600 m |
| 3,000 | 900 m |
| 4,000 | 1,200 m |
| 5,000 | 1,500 m |
| 6,000 | 1,800 m |
| 12,500 | 3,750 m |

The Royal Horticultural Society Award of Garden Merit,
reinstituted in 1992,
"recognizes plants of outstanding excellence
for garden decoration or use."

The Royal Horticultural Society Award of Merit
recognizes outstanding plants
that have been exhibited.

The Philadelphia Horticultural Society
Gold Medal (Styer Award) Program
"honors little-known and under-used plants of exceptional merit
and promotes their use."

# *Shrubs That Merit Attention A–Z*

# Abelia × grandiflora
## GLOSSY ABELIA

Parentage: *A. chinensis* × *A. uniflora*. Caprifoliaceae. USDA Zones (5)6–9. Introduced into cultivation in 1866 in Italy.

DESCRIPTION: Semi-evergreen shrub growing moderately fast to 3–6 ft. high (taller in warmer climates), with dense, spreading, multistemmed habit.
*Leaves:* Opposite, simple, ovate, borne in threes and fours, 1.5–2.5 in. long, shiny, dark green.
*Flowers:* White, with pale pink tinge, slightly fragrant; July–October.
*Fruit:* A leatherlike achene, not ornamental.
*Winter aspect:* Slender, arching branches.

CULTURE: Grows in full sun or partial shade; prefers well-drained, moist, acid soil.
*Disease and insect problems:* None serious; some mildew and root rot.
*Transplanting:* Easy.
*Propagation:* By softwood cuttings.

LANDSCAPE VALUE: A vigorous, semi-evergreen shrub with extremely attractive, glossy, dark green foliage and beautiful, profuse bloom over a long period. Hardiest and most floriferous of the abelias. May be used as hedge plant in warmer climates. Can grow far taller than average if grown on protected wall in mild climate. May die back to ground in northern regions, but grows back quickly in spring. Received RHS Award of Garden Merit.

Plant may be observed at AA, ABF, ATL, BBG, BC, BIR, BLO, BRK, BSG, CAL, FIL, FUL, HUN, LAC, LWD, MBG, MIS, MMA, MOR, MRT, NCS, NEW, OWG, PAL, PLF, RKEW, SPR, STG, STR, UBC, USN, VDG, WIS.

*Abelia* × *grandiflora* cultivars of interest:

*A.* × *grandiflora* 'Prostrata'. Compact, low growing, with smaller leaves; interesting burgundy-green winter color.
*A.* × *grandiflora* 'Sherwood'. More compact, reaching 3.5 ft. high and 4 ft. wide, with smaller leaves; interesting purple-green winter color. Lovely, small, dense shrub for massed plantings.

Related *Abelia* cultivar of interest:

*A.* 'Edward Goucher' (*A.* × *grandiflora* × *A. schumannii*). USDA Zones (5)6–9. Small shrub with bronze foliage turning glossy green, and orange-throated, lilac-pink flowers. Lovely for small garden. Described by H. Hillier as distinct in "having leaves in whorls of three." May freeze to the ground in Zone 5, but returns vigorously in spring; grows into substantial, attractive shrub in one season. Introduced in 1911 into the United States at Glenn Dale Plant Introduction Station, Maryland. Received RHS Award of Garden Merit.

Related *Abelia* species of interest:

*A. chinensis*. USDA Zones 8–9. Small, semi-evergreen shrub 3–5 ft. high, with spreading habit and abundant, fragrant, rose-tinted, white flowers in June–October. Prefers full sun. Native to China; discovered in 1817 by Clarke Abel.
*A. floribunda*. USDA Zones 8–9. Medium-sized, semi-evergreen shrub 6–10 ft. high, with profuse, tubular, bright pink-red to magenta flowers. Needs protection from wind; least hardy species, but said to be most beautiful of the genus. Good for warm wall in warmer climates, where it can reach 20 ft. high. Native to Mexico. Introduced into Europe in 1841. Received RHS Award of Garden Merit.

# Abeliophyllum distichum
## WHITE FORSYTHIA

Oleaceae. USDA Zones 5–8. Native to Korea. Introduced into cultivation in 1924.

DESCRIPTION: Deciduous shrub growing at moderate rate to 3–5 ft. high and 3–4 ft. wide, with multistemmed habit.
*Leaves:* Opposite, simple, medium green, little fall color but sometimes purple.
*Flowers:* White, with slight pink tinge, about 0.6 in. across, with 4 petals, on bare stems; March–April.
*Fruit:* A round capsule, similar to that of elm, not ornamental.
*Winter aspect:* Twiggy branching habit.

CULTURE: Needs warm sun to thrive and bloom well, but grows in light shade; prefers well-drained soil, but adapts to a variety of soil types; tolerates drought somewhat, but not wet conditions.
*Disease and insect problems:* None serious.
*Transplanting:* Easy.
*Propagation:* By softwood cuttings.

LANDSCAPE VALUE: An attractive shrub when in bloom in early spring. Valued for conspicuous, early flowers in the drab winter landscape; slightly fragrant blooms appear on bare branches before foliage unfolds. Not a specimen shrub when not in flower; thus, best planted in groups in shrub border for early spring effect. Related to *Forsythia*, but flower buds hardier than those of most *Forsythia* × *intermedia* types. Can become straggly; needs attentive pruning to maintain attractive habit.

Plant may be observed at AA, ABF, ATL, BBG, BC, BER, BF, BSG, CBG, CIN, DAW, DEN, DUK, GCC, HOL, HUN, LAC, LNG, LWD, MBG, MNL, MOR, MRT, MUN, NCS, NEB, NEW, PAL, PLF, RHO, RKEW, SKY, UBC, VDG.

*Abelia × grandiflora* (E. Neuman)

*Abeliophyllum distichum* (G. Koller)

*Abelia* 'Edward Goucher' (N. Frink)

*Abelia chinensis* (J. C. Raulston)

*Abeliophyllum distichum* 'Rosea' (G. Koller)

## *Acanthopanax sieboldianus* 'Variegatus'
### FIVE-LEAF ARALIA

Synonym: *A. pentaphyllus*. Araliaceae. USDA Zones 5–8. Species native to China and Japan; introduced into cultivation in 1874.

DESCRIPTION: Deciduous shrub growing rather quickly to 8 ft. high and as wide, with wide, arching branches.
*Leaves:* Alternate, compound, composed of 5 (sometimes 3 or 7) obovate-oblong leaflets 1–2.5 in. long and 0.5–1 in. wide, greenish white with white margins.
*Flowers:* Greenish white, dioecious, in dense, globose umbels; June–July.
*Fruit:* A black berry.
*Winter aspect:* Stems with short spines.

CULTURE: Grows in sun or shade; prefers well-drained soil, but adapts to all soils; tolerates pollution and drought.
*Disease and insect problems:* None serious; occasional leaf spot.
*Transplanting:* Easy.
*Propagation:* By seed or late-summer cuttings.

LANDSCAPE VALUE: A valuable foliage shrub for urban planting. Adaptable plant that withstands and remains attractive in diverse and adverse urban conditions. A good screen in sun or shade; spines create an effective pedestrian barrier. Withstands severe pruning; thus can be maintained as a compact plant.

Plant may be observed at AA, ABF, ATL, BBG, BRK, BSG, CBG, MIS, NCS, RKEW, UBC, USN.

## *Adina rubella*
### GLOSSY ADINA

Rubiaceae. USDA Zones 6–9. Native to southern China. Introduced into cultivation in 1969 by Kingsville Nursery, Maryland.

DESCRIPTION: Deciduous shrub growing at moderate rate to 5–6 ft. high (8–10 ft. in warmer climates) and 5–6 ft. wide, with spreading habit that is wider than high.
*Leaves:* Opposite, simple, elliptic, to 1 in. long, rich, deep, glossy green, similar to *Abelia* leaves, persisting into late fall, no fall color but bronze tinge in sun.
*Flowers:* White, with pink cast, 0.5–0.75 in. across, fragrant; June/July–October.
*Fruit:* Round, tiny, 0.25 in. across, not ornamental; dry seed head turns brown.
*Winter aspect:* Slender branches with red-brown, pubescent bark.

CULTURE: Grows in sun but best in partial shade; tolerates heavy clay or loam, wind, wet conditions, drought, and a wide pH range.
*Disease and insect problems:* None.
*Transplanting:* Easy; fibrous root system
*Propagation:* By softwood cuttings.

LANDSCAPE VALUE: A handsome, small shrub notable for its luxuriant, glossy green foliage, unique flower, and attractive habit. Little-known, easily grown plant that deserves wider attention. Can be used as dieback shrub in northern zones.

Plant may be observed at ABF, BBG, BF, CIN, DIN, HUN, MIS, NCS, USN.

## *Aesculus parviflora*
### BOTTLEBRUSH BUCKEYE

Hippocastanaceae. USDA Zones 5–8. Native to the United States, in Georgia and Alabama. Introduced into cultivation in 1785 by John Fraser.

DESCRIPTION: Deciduous shrub growing at moderate rate to 9–12 ft. high and 15 ft. wide, with spreading, multi-stemmed habit that usually is wider than high.
*Leaves:* Opposite, palmately lobed, 3–9 in. long, elliptic to oblong, tapering towards both ends, composed of 5–7 leaflets, medium dark green, turning yellow-green in fall, good fall color under ideal conditions.
*Flowers:* White, in cylindrical panicles, 8–12 in. long and to 4 in. wide; July–August.
*Fruit:* A glabrous, light brown capsule, 1–1.5 in.; much more fruit set in warmer climates.

CULTURE: Grows in sun or shade; adapts to a variety of soils, but prefers acid, well-drained humus.
*Disease and insect problems:* None serious.
*Transplanting:* Balled and burlapped or container-grown in early spring; shallow root system, stoloniferous but controllable.
*Propagation:* By root cuttings, softwood cuttings, division; seed rarely ripens except during hot, sunny summers.

LANDSCAPE VALUE: An outstanding specimen plant or excellent for massed plantings. Valued for summer flowering, shade tolerance, and interesting habit. Unusual, thin, pale pink stamens and red anthers stand out from white flowers. Vigorous, hardy grower, one of the best shrubs but often neglected. Grows in spreading, green billows and blooms midsummer in dappled shade. Can be rejuvenated by pruning to the ground. Received RHS Award of Garden Merit.

Plant may be observed at AA, ABF, ATL, BBG, BEA, BF, BIC, BLO, BRK, BSG, CAL, CBG, CHK, CIN, COX, CUH,

Acanthopanax sieboldianus 'Variegatus' (N. Brewster)    Acanthopanax sieboldianus 'Variegatus' (G. Koller)

Adina rubella (M. A. Dirr)

Adina rubella (M. A. Dirr)

Adina rubella (M. A. Dirr)

Aesculus parviflora (E. Hasselkus)

*Aesculus parviflora* continued

DAW, DEN, DIX, DUK, FIL, FUL, GCC, HOL, LAC, LNG, LWD, MBG, MIS, MMA, MNL, MOR, MRT, MTC, MUN, NCS, NEB, NEW, OWG, PAL, PLF, POW, RAN, RBC, RKEW, SBB, SEC, SKY, STG, STR, VDG, WIN, WIS.

*Aesculus parviflora* cultivar of interest:

*A. parviflora* 'Rogers'. Flowers later than species; has spectacular inflorescences, 18–30 in. long. Named for Dr. Rogers of Urbana, Illinois. Selection made by J. C. McDaniel, University of Illinois, from seedlings of *A. parviflora* f. *serotina*.

*Aesculus parviflora* form of interest:

*A. parviflora* f. *serotina*. Blooms 2–3 weeks after species, with longer (18–30 in.) inflorescences. Introduced in 1919 from Alabama.

Related *Aesculus* species of interest:

*A. californica*. California Horsechestnut. USDA Zones 8(9). Grows 9–12 ft. high, with bushy habit and broad, round crown. Leaves 3–5 in. long. White to pink, fragrant flowers are borne in dense, narrow panicles in May–June. Fruit is fig-shaped.

## *Amelanchier ovalis* 'Pumila'
## SERVICEBERRY

Rosaceae. USDA Zones 4–8. Native to south and central Europe. Introduced into cultivation in the late 16th century.

DESCRIPTION: Deciduous shrub growing at moderate rate to 3–4 ft. high and 2–3 ft. wide, with upright to arching habit.
*Leaves:* Elliptic to obovate, toothed margins, 1.5–2 in. long and 1.5 in. wide, with bluish cast, yellow with hints of orange in fall.
*Flowers:* White, in prominent, tight clusters in hairy, erect racemes; in May, with foliage.
*Fruit:* A red berry, ripening to blue-black.
*Winter aspect:* Gray, smooth bark; spreading branching habit.

CULTURE: Grows in full sun and shade in clay or loam; tolerates wind and soil pH to 7.8; needs little attention; likes a mulch but not necessary.
*Disease and insect problems:* None.
*Transplanting:* Easy.
*Propagation:* By division; not easy from cuttings.

LANDSCAPE VALUE: A handsome, easy-to-grow, small shrub seldom seen in the landscape. Excellent in massed plantings or as a striking specimen in a small, city garden. Good, low hedge for three seasons. Also effective in mixed perennial borders and planted in front of evergreens. Distinctive in that the five styles of its flowers are not joined at their bases as in other *Amelanchier* species. Should be pruned in late winter. A small gem that should be more readily available.

Plant may be observed at CBG, DEN, LNG.

## *Aralia elata* 'Aureovariegata'
## JAPANESE ANGELICA

Araliaceae. USDA Zones 4–9. Species native to Japan, Korea, Manchuria, and easternmost Russia; introduced into cultivation in 1830.

DESCRIPTION: Deciduous shrub growing slowly to 15 ft. high (30 ft. in the wild).
*Leaves:* 3–3.5 in. long, gray-green, with broad, irregular margins of strong yellow-gold.
*Flowers:* Small, soft creamy white, in large, terminal panicles 1–2 ft. long; August–September.
*Fruit:* Purple, globose.
*Winter aspect:* Flower stalks heavily covered with down.

CULTURE: Grows in sun and partial shade; prefers cool, well-drained, moist, fertile soil, but is remarkably tolerant of dry, wet, rocky, heavy, and acid to slightly alkaline soils.
*Disease and insect problems:* None serious.
*Transplanting:* Easy.
*Propagation:* By cuttings.

LANDSCAPE VALUE: A plant with all-season interest, valued for its handsome foliage and hardiness. Adaptable to a wide growing range, from Minnesota to Florida. Differs from the species in its gray-green foliage, splashed with yellow, which gives plant a misty appearance. Useful as a specimen or in groups in the shrub border. 'Aureovariegata', which is grafted on the species, and 'Variegata' are among the most striking and beautiful of all variegated shrubs; although distinct early in the growing season, both are variegated with silver-white as summer progresses. Received RHS Award of Garden Merit.

Plant may be observed at BBG, BF, MIS, NCS, WIS.

Other *Aralia elata* cultivars of interest:

*A. elata* 'Pyramidalis'. Narrowly upright, with smaller leaves than the species.
*A. elata* 'Variegata'. Attractive, similar to 'Pyramidalis', except for leaflets with creamy white blotches.

*Aesculus parviflora* 'Rogers'
(R. Klehm)

*Aesculus parviflora* f. *serotina* (G. Gates)

*Amelanchier ovalis* 'Pumila' (G. Gates)

*Amelanchier ovalis* 'Pumila' (G. Gates)

*Aralia elata* (Royal Botanical
Gardens, Ontario)

*Amelanchier ovalis* 'Pumila'
(G. Gates)

*Aralia elata* 'Aureovariegata' (J. C. Raulston)

33

## *Aralia spinosa*
### DEVIL'S WALKING STICK

Araliaceae. USDA Zones 5–9. Native to the United States, from southern Pennsylvania, Indiana, and eastern Iowa to Florida and eastern Texas. Introduced into cultivation in 1688.

DESCRIPTION: Deciduous shrub growing slowly to 10–20 (occasionally 30) ft. high, with heavy, coarse branches developing from the base to create a dense form.
*Leaves:* Alternate leaflets, 2–4 in. long, medium green, becoming subdued yellow in fall, at times purple.
*Flowers:* Handsome, large, off-white, in panicles 12–18 in. long, at the ends of branches, producing long-lasting veil effect over crown of plant; July–late August.
*Fruit:* A purple-black drupe, 0.25 in. long, in fall, attractive to birds.
*Winter aspect:* Coarsely branched, but interesting structure.

CULTURE: Grows in sun or partial shade; prefers cool, moist, well-drained, fertile soil, but tolerates rocky or heavy, dry soils; performs well in acid or slightly alkaline soils.
*Disease and insect problems:* None serious.
*Transplanting:* Easy.
*Propagation:* By seed or root cuttings.

LANDSCAPE VALUE: A tough plant that withstands urban conditions. Useful in the shrub border or as specimen. Very decorative and unusual with its thick, prickly stems and large, striking leaves.

Plant may be observed at AA, ABF, ABN, ATL, BBG, BC, BF, BLO, BRK, BSG, CAL, CIN, DAW, DUK, GCC, GIW, HOL, HOU, HUN, IES, LNG, MBG, MIS, MNL, MRT, MUN, NCA, NCS, NEB, NEW, PLF, RKEW, SKY, SPR, USN, ZOO.

Related *Aralia* species of interest:

*A. cordata* [*A. edulis*]. Spineless herb growing to 9 ft. high, with pinnate leaves, 2–3 in. long. Young shoots used for culinary purposes. Native to Japan; seldom used in the United States.

## *Arctostaphylos densiflora* 'Howard McMinn'
### MANZANITA

Ericaceae. USDA Zones 7–9. Native to the United States, in California.

DESCRIPTION: Broad-leaved evergreen growing at moderate rate to 5–6 ft. high and 7 ft. wide in 5 years, with mounded habit.
*Leaves:* Alternate, ovate, small, 0.5–1 in. long, leathery, glossy, dark green.
*Flowers:* Pink, fading to white, small, 0.25 in. or shorter, bell-shaped, in hanging clusters; February–April.
*Fruit:* Tiny, applelike (manzanita), in fall.
*Winter aspect:* Peeling, red-brown bark.

CULTURE: Grows in sun or light shade in a wide variety of lightly acid to alkaline soils; tolerates drought and wind and, when well established, salt, air pollution, and soil compaction; does not tolerate wet conditions except in well-drained soils; tip pruning encourages dense growth, but prostrate stems should not be pruned.
*Disease and insect problems:* Trouble-free in loose soil with good drainage.
*Transplanting:* Best in fall after first rain; fairly deep root system.
*Propagation:* By tip cuttings.

LANDSCAPE VALUE: A trouble-free shrub with handsome appearance year-round. Useful as high ground cover and hillside planting because of its drought resistance. Fruit is attractive to birds. Lower branches are susceptible to dieback in wet conditions. Frequent pinching helps control growth; prune tips after flowering to create dense shrub.

Plant may be observed at FUL, LAC, MIS, RAN, SBB, STR.

*Arctostaphylos densiflora* cultivar of interest:

*A. densiflora* 'Sentinel'. Grows to 6 ft. high and 8 ft. wide, with more upright habit than 'Howard McMinn'. Needs full sun for best growth. Susceptible to root rot and burn from salt.

*Aralia spinosa* (D. Ehrlinger)

*Aralia spinosa* (J. C. Raulston)

*Aralia cordata* (D. Brennan)

*Arctostaphylos densiflora* 'Howard McMinn' (A. MacBride)

*Arctostaphylos densiflora* 'Sentinel' (N. Brewster)

## *Arctostaphylos stanfordiana*
### STANFORD MANZANITA

Ericaceae. USDA Zones 7–9. Native to the United States, in California. Found in mountains at altitudes of 3000–5000 ft.

DESCRIPTION: Broad-leaved evergreen growing at moderate rate to 4–6 ft. high, with upright habit.
*Leaves:* Oblanceolate or narrow-ovate, 0.25–2.5 in. long and 1 in. wide, glossy, light green.
*Flowers:* White to pink, 0.25 in. wide, in terminal, elongated, pendulous panicles; spring.
*Fruit:* Bright red, 0.25 in. across, asymmetrical, in March–April.
*Winter aspect:* Smooth, red-brown bark; slender branching habit.

CULTURE: Grows in sun and partial shade; prefers porous, well-drained soil; does not tolerate wet conditions or soil compaction.
*Disease and insect problems:* Stem canker.
*Transplanting:* Difficult with large, field-grown plants; best with young plants in containers.
*Propagation:* By cuttings in late summer to fall.

LANDSCAPE VALUE: An excellent shrub for gardens in dry, mild climates. Attractive foliage, flower, and fruit. Effective as foundation, screen, or accent plant. Can be sheared for hedge or pinched to keep compact.

Plant may be observed at RAN, SBB, STR.

Related *Arctostaphylos* cultivar of interest:

*A. bakerii* 'Louis Edmunds'. USDA Zones 8–9. Grows 5–6 ft. high. Leaves ovate, elliptic, blunt, 1 in. long. Flowers pink, borne in drooping panicles. Fruit is brown. Species found at the mouth of Little Sur River, Monterey County, California. Finest of dwarf manzanitas but more tender.


## *Ardisia crenata*
### CORAL ARDISIA
### SPICEBERRY

Synonym: *A. crenulata.* Myrsinaceae. USDA Zone 10. Introduced into cultivation in 1809 from China and Malaya.

DESCRIPTION: Evergreen shrub growing slowly to 4–6 ft. high, with branches extending from straight trunk.
*Leaves:* Long-elliptic, tapering at both ends, thick, leathery, with crisped margins, shiny, dark green, young leaves redder.
*Flowers:* Reddish white; February–May.
*Fruit:* A globose, scarlet-red, waxy berry, in clusters, in February after flowers, ripening in winter.

CULTURE: Grows in sun and light shade in well-drained clay soil; tolerates moist conditions, but not salt, air pollution, or soil compaction.
*Disease and insect problems:* Scale.
*Transplanting:* Fairly easy.
*Propagation:* By seed and layering.

LANDSCAPE VALUE: Notable for handsome foliage, attractive red fruit, and lovely fragrance. Particularly suited for use in Oriental-style garden. Becomes leggy if not pinched when young.

Plant may be observed at ATL, BIR, BOK, CBG, DIN, FOU, LWD, MMA, MIS, RKEW.

Related *Ardisia* species of interest:

*A. crispa.* Native to Japan and China. Often confused with *A. crenata* but differs in foliage; leaves have about 8 pairs of lateral veins and margins are not crisped-undulate. Young twigs slightly hairy. Flowers fragrant, white or reddish, in June. Fruit is globose, red, ripening in winter.


## *Aronia arbutifolia* 'Brilliantissima'
### RED CHOKEBERRY

Rosaceae. USDA Zones 5–8. Native to eastern North America but cultivated in United Kingdom since 1700.

DESCRIPTION: Deciduous shrub growing slowly to 6–10 ft. high and 3–5 ft. wide, with upright, spreading, suckering habit.
*Leaves:* Alternate, elliptic to oblong, 1.5–3.5 in. long, margins serrated, tapering at both ends, dark green above, tomentose (covered with short, woolly hairs) and pale beneath, excellent red color in fall.
*Flowers:* Small, white to slightly pink, 0.5 in. across; late April–early May.
*Fruit:* A spectacular, red, pear-shaped pome, 0.25–0.4 in. across, in September–October, persisting into winter.

CULTURE: Grows in sun or partial shade, but needs full sun for best fruit and fuller plant; tolerates dry and moist conditions; prefers soil with good drainage, but grows in even poor soil.
*Disease and insect problems:* None serious: powdery mold, leaf spot.
*Transplanting:* Easy despite fibrous root system.
*Propagation:* By seed, softwood cuttings, and layering.

LANDSCAPE VALUE: This cultivar far exceeds the species in ornamental qualities: glorious brilliance of fall color, lustrous foliage, and depth of fruit color. A spectacular autumn plant, valued for its wide-ranging soil adaptability. Good border plant for massed plantings. May become leggy with age and in shade. Attractive to birds.

*Arctostaphylos stanfordiana* (Strybing Arboretum Society, Helen Crocker Russel Library)

*Arctostaphylos stanfordiana* (Strybing Arboretum Society, Helen Crocker Russel Library)

*Ardisia crenata* (A. Patterson)

*Ardisia crenata* (A. Patterson)

*Aronia arbutifolia* 'Brilliantissima' (G. Koller)

*Aronia arbutifolia* 'Brilliantissima' (G. Koller)

*Aronia arbutifolia* 'Brilliantissima' continued

Plant may be observed at AA, ATL, BBG, BF, BIC, BOE, CAL, CBG, CIN, DAW, DEN, DIX, DUK, GIW, HOL, LNG, LWD, MIS, MNL, MOD, MOR, MTC, NCS, NEB, NEW, PLF, SEC, SPR, UBC, USN, VDG.

Related *Aronia* species and variety of interest:

*A. melanocarpa.* Black Chokeberry. Similar to *A. arbutifolia* except smaller habit, growing to 3–5 ft. high; leaves glabrous with claret fall color; fruit purple-black and not persistent. Very adaptable to all soils.

*A. melanocarpa* var. *elata.* Much larger than species, growing to 9 ft. high, and with larger flowers and fruit.

# *Azara serrata*

Flacourtiaceae. USDA Zones 8–9. Native to Chile. Name commemorates J. N. Azara, a Spanish patron of botany. Introduced into cultivation in 1830.

DESCRIPTION: Broad-leaved evergreen growing at moderate rate to 8–10 ft. high, with upright habit.
*Leaves:* Alternate, ovate, glabrous, 2 in. long.
*Flowers:* Yellow, with abundant stamens and no petals, in globose, axillary umbels, 1.25–1.5 in. long, with a fragrance like mimosa; April–May.
*Winter aspect:* Red-brown twigs.

CULTURE: Best in partial shade; needs protection from hot afternoon sun; prefers deep, moist, well-drained, but not dry, humus soil; needs ample water and regular feeding.
*Disease and insect problems:* None serious.
*Transplanting:* Balled and burlapped or container-grown.
*Propagation:* By cuttings in late summer or early fall, with bottom heat and mist.

LANDSCAPE VALUE: A handsome evergreen with sweetly fragrant (chocolate or vanilla scent) blossoms. Inflorescence very distinct. A general purpose shrub for partially shaded locations. Can be pruned after blooming to control size.

Plant may be observed at: PAL, RAN, RKEW, STR.

Related *Azara* species of interest:

*A. dentata.* Flowers golden-yellow, fragrant, borne in short, branched clusters, in May–June. Grows 6–10 ft. high, with dense branching habit. Often confused with *A. serrata* but has smaller leaves, 1 in. long, fine-toothed, felted beneath. Needs considerable shade.

*A. petiolaris.* Flowers creamy white, with long stamens, in February–March. Grows 7–12 ft. high. Most ornamental *Azara,* with *Ilex*-like appearance; leaves dark green, leathery, tough, saw-toothed.

# *Bauhinia lunarioides*
## ANACACHO BAUHINIA

Synonym: *B. congesta.* Leguminosae. USDA Zones 8–10. Native to the United States, from southern Texas into northern Texas. Len Lowery of Texas called it Anacacho Orchid Tree in the 1970s.

DESCRIPTION: Deciduous shrub growing at moderate rate to 10–12 ft. high, with habit wider than high.
*Leaves:* Alternate, simple, divided to base into 2 leaflets, rounded, slightly wavy, 1–1.25 in. long and 0.25–0.9 in. wide, medium green.
*Flowers:* White to pink, 1 in. wide; March–April.
*Fruit:* A small, flat, dark brown bean, not conspicuous.
*Winter aspect:* Silver-gray, gnarled, contorted bark.

CULTURE: Needs full sun, intense light, and good drainage; prefers loamy soil; tolerates drought very well and a wide range of soil pH.
*Disease and insect problems:* None serious.
*Transplanting:* Balled and burlapped or container-grown.
*Propagation:* By seed.

LANDSCAPE VALUE: Attractive in flower and foliage. Creates a spectacular show in spring with a burst of blooms resembling a white cloud, then flowers occasionally throughout the season. Performs best in hot sun with brilliant light conditions. Amazingly tolerant of all pH levels. May be creatively planted against a wall where it receives full sun. Excellent examples of mature specimen at the University of Texas campus and younger shrubs at the San Antonio Botanical Garden. Genus names honors the 16th-century herbalists John and Casper Bauhin.

Plant may be observed at SAB.

*Aronia melanocarpa* var. *elata* (E. Hasselkus)

*Azara serrata* (N. Brewster)

*Aronia melanocarpa* var. *elata* (E. Hasselkus)

*Azara serrata* (Greer Gardens)

*Bauhinia lunarioides* (B. Simpson)

*Bauhinia lunarioides* (B. Simpson)

## *Berberis darwinii*
### DARWIN BARBERRY

Berberidaceae. USDA Zones 7–8. Native to Chile, Patagonia. Discovered by Charles Darwin when he served as naturalist on the famous voyage of the *Beagle*. Introduced into cultivation in 1849 by William Lobb for Messrs. Veitch.

DESCRIPTION: Evergreen shrub 6–10 ft. high, with very dense habit that is strong and upright when young but spreading with age.
*Leaves:* Obovate, 0.75–1.5 in. long, with 5-pointed edges, and 1–3 thorned teeth, tough, leathery, similar to *Ilex* leaves, dark green, glossy above and lighter, silver-green beneath.
*Flowers:* Golden-yellow, with reddish tinge, as many as 20 together, on pendulous racemes; April–May.
*Fruit:* Oval, blue-green-black, pea-sized, in clusters.
*Winter aspect:* Branchlets covered with red-brown pubescence.

CULTURE: Grows in sun and dappled shade; adapts to a wide range of soils, but prefers warm, loamy soil; dislikes very dry or water-logged conditions.
*Disease and insect problems:* None serious.
*Transplanting:* Easy.
*Propagation:* By seed, or by cuttings for colored-leaved varieties that do not come true from seed.

LANDSCAPE VALUE: A beautiful, useful shrub, at its peak in spring when it exhibits a profusion of golden blossoms. Also attractive in fall with its heavy crop of striking berries; occasionally reblooms lightly in fall. Can attain a great spread in mild, favorable conditions. Received RHS Award of Garden Merit.

Plant may be observed at CUH, LAC, MIS, RKEW, STR, UBC, VDG, WIS.

Related *Berberis* species of interest:

- *B. linearifolia.* USDA Zones 7–8. Attractive, evergreen to semi-evergreen shrub, with clusters of bright orange flowers, borne in profusion in mid- to late spring; fruit blue-black, ovate. Leaves 1.5 in. long, light to medium green, with silver cast beneath. Most often grown on the West Coast, particularly in the San Francisco area, and in United Kingdom.
- *B. verruculosa.* Warty Barberry. USDA Zones 6–8. Evergreen shrub 3–5 ft. high, with dense habit, golden-yellow flowers, and purple-black fruit. Small, dark green leaves turn burgundy in late fall. Introduced into cultivation in 1904 from western China.

## *Berberis koreana*
### KOREAN BARBERRY

Berberidaceae. USDA Zones 4–8. Native to Korea. Introduced into cultivation in 1905.

DESCRIPTION: Deciduous shrub growing at moderate rate to 3–6 ft. high and 2–4 ft. wide, with dense, oval habit.
*Leaves:* Alternate, simple, obovate to oval, serrate, dense, thorny, 1–2.5 in. long, medium to dark green, turning red-burgundy in fall.
*Flowers:* Yellow, small, 0.25 in. across, on arching racemes, 3–4 in. long; May.
*Fruit:* Waxy, red, ovate, 0.25 in. long.
*Winter aspect:* Spines on young, reddish twigs.

CULTURE: Prefers full sun, but grows in light shade; tolerates a wide range of soils, but does not like permanently wet soil.
*Disease and insect problems:* None serious.
*Transplanting:* Easy.
*Propagation:* By softwood cuttings.

LANDSCAPE VALUE: A very attractive, small, hardy shrub with showy, yellow flower clusters. Has larger leaves than most *Berberis* species; the handsome foliage is enhanced by autumn color and persistent, colorful fruit. Relatively trouble-free; requires only light pruning to maintain its shape. Note: Deciduous barberries are banned in Canada to help control black stem rust of wheat.

Plant may be observed at AA, ABF, BBG, BEA, BIC, BIR, BOE, BSG, CBG, DAW, IES, LAC, LNG, MRT, MUN, NEB, PLF, RKEW.

## *Berberis thunbergii*
### JAPANESE BARBERRY

Berberidaceae. USDA Zones 5–8. Native to southern Japan. Introduced into cultivation in 1864.

DESCRIPTION: Deciduous shrub growing at moderate rate to 3–6 ft. high and 4–6 ft. wide, with very dense, broad, rounded habit.
*Leaves:* Alternate, simple, bright green, with orange to claret fall color.
*Flowers:* Yellow, tinged with pink, with red calyx, cup-shaped, small, about 0.5 in. across, borne on pedicels; April–May.
*Fruit:* Elliptic, bright red.
*Winter aspect:* Persistent berries.

CULTURE: Grows in sun and light shade, though purple and variegated forms need full sun for best leaf color;

*Berberis linearifolia* (Greer Gardens)

*Berberis darwinii* (J. Apel)

*Berberis koreana* (G. Gates)

*Berberis koreana* (G. Gates)

*Berberis thunbergii* 'Atropurpurea' (J. C. Raulston)

*Berberis thunbergii* 'Bagatelle' (J. Elsley)

41

adapts very well; grows in wide variety of soils; tolerates urban conditions and drought, but not extremely wet conditions.

*Disease and insect problems:* Few; occasional leaf spot, anthracnose, root rot, rust, and wilt.

*Transplanting:* Easy.

*Propagation:* By seed and softwood cuttings for reliable retention of unusual characteristics.

LANDSCAPE VALUE: Used most often as a tough hedge or barrier planting, but a large number of cultivars possess attractive and diverse attributes that lend themselves to a variety of landscape situations. Performs well, but not as vigorously, in USDA Zone 8 or above. Occasional pruning of 3- to 4-year-old stems to ground level encourages new growth and stimulates leaf color. Received RHS Award of Garden Merit.

Plant may be observed at AA, ABF, ATL, BBG, BC, BIC, BOE, BRK, BSG, CAL, CBG, CIN, COX, DAW, DEN, DUK, FIL, GCC, HOL, HUN, IES, LNG, MBG, MIS, MNL, MRT, NCS, NEB, NEW, OWG, PAL, PLF, RBC, RKEW, SEC, SPR, VDG, WIS.

*Berberis thunbergii* cultivars of interest:

*B. thunbergii* 'Atropurpurea'. About the same size as species, with purple-tinged yellow flowers and red fruit. Needs sun for best foliage coloration; leaves are red-brown-purple. Comes relatively true to type from seed. Received RHS Award of Garden Merit.

*B. thunbergii* 'Bagatelle' (*B. thunbergii* 'Kobold' × 'Atropurpurea Nana'). Slow-growing, compact, dwarf cultivar, to 16 in. high. Twigs very short and dense; leaves strong, small, red-purple. Introduced in 1971 by K. W. Van Klaverin, Boskoop, Netherlands. Received RHS Award of Garden Merit.

*B. thunbergii* 'Bogozam'. Bonanza Gold. USDA Zones 4–7. Seedlings selected by Nicholas R. Moretti, Boskoop, Netherlands. Dwarf barberry growing to 18 in. high and 36 in. wide, with low, rounded, dense, spreading habit. Brilliant, golden foliage, creamy white flowers, and bright red fruit. Useful as miniature hedge, in border, or in massed plantings. Needs full sun for best color; resistant to sun scald.

*B. thunbergii* 'Globe'. Grows to 3 ft. high and 6 ft. wide, with globular habit. Dark green foliage turns red in fall. Patented selection; originated in 1971 by K. W. Van Klaverin, Boskoop, Netherlands. Received RHS Award of Garden Merit.

*B. thunbergii* 'Kobold'. Slow-growing dwarf form with broad, globose habit and dark green leaves; no fall color. Introduced in 1960 by K. W. Van Klaverin, Boskoop, Netherlands.

*B. thunbergii* 'Rose Glow'. Grows broadly upright, 5–6 ft. high; has small, white flowers and bright red-brown leaves with pink tones. Earliest of pink-tinged cultivars. Subsequent introduction 'Pink Queen' is perhaps superior. Introduced in 1957 by Spaargaren, Boskoop, Netherlands.

*B. thunbergii* 'Sparkle'. Dense shrub, with arching branches, growing to 3–4 ft. high. Attractive, leathery, dark green foliage turns orange-red in fall. Profuse yellow flowers and red fruit persist into winter. Introduced by Synnestvedt Nursery, Round Lake, Illinois.

Related *Berberis* species and cultivar of interest:

*B. × gladwynensis* 'William Penn' (*B. verruculosa × B. gagnepainii*). USDA Zones 7–9. Deciduous shrub, with dense, mounded habit and clear, yellow flowers, in April–May. Lustrous, dark green foliage turns attractive bronze in winter. Little known and extremely attractive, with perhaps the most handsome foliage of the barberries. Introduced by the Henry Foundation, Gladwyne, Pennsylvania.

*B. × wisleyensis* (*B. × carminea × B. × rubrostilla*). USDA Zones 6–8. Handsome evergreen shrub with graceful habit, 5–6 ft. high. Leathery leaves are thin, needle-tipped, 1–2 in. long, gray-green above with blue-green cast beneath. Yellow flowers bloom, in clusters, on slender stalks in May. Fruit is oblong. Red, angular twigs with numerous spines turn pale yellow in winter. Relatively tolerant of a range of soils. Often disseminated as *B. triacanthrophora*, which is not a true species. Native to central China; introduced in 1907 by E. H. Wilson.

# *Brugmansia arborea*
## ANGEL'S TRUMPET

Synonym: *Datura arborea*. Solanaceae. USDA Zone 10. Native to tropical America; long cultivated in Hawaii.

DESCRIPTION: Broad-leaved evergreen growing slowly to 15 ft. high, with compact habit.

*Leaves:* Pointed, ovate to oblong, downy, with entire margins, about 10 in. long.

*Flowers:* White to salmon-pink corollas, about 10 in. long, pendant, with 5 long, pointed lobes; long, tubular calyces split down one side; blooms most of year.

CULTURE: Grows in sun or shade; tolerates a wide variety of soils and adverse environmental conditions, including wind, drought, salt, and air pollution.

*Disease and insect problems:* None.

*Transplanting:* Easy.

*Propagation:* By cuttings.

*Berberis thunbergii* 'Bogozam' (Lake County Nursery)

*Berberis* × *wisleyensis* (N. Brewster)

*Berberis thunbergii* 'Rose Glow' (R. Klehm)

*Brugmansia arborea* (V. Lauritzen)

*Brugmansia arborea* (V. Lauritzen)

LANDSCAPE VALUE: The profusion of large, pendant, trumpet-shaped flowers that appear almost year-round make this a most striking ornamental plant. Its flowers and leaves are poisonous, and the entire plant contains a strong narcotic.

Plant may be observed at MUN, RKEW, WAI.

# *Brunfelsia australis*
## YESTERDAY, TODAY AND TOMORROW

Solanaceae. USDA Zones 9–10. Native to Argentina, Paraguay, southern Brazil.

DESCRIPTION: Evergreen shrub growing slowly to 8 ft. high, with bushy habit.
*Leaves:* Ovate, 2–3 in. long, shiny, dark green,
*Flowers:* White-eyed, violet, 5-lobed near base, gradually fading to white in about 3 days; corolla about 1.5 in. long, tube 1 in. long, calyx 3 in. long; year-round.

CULTURE: Grows in clay or loam with a pH of 5.5–6.5; tolerates wind, wet conditions, salt, and light shade.
*Disease and insect problems:* Sooty mold, scale, mealy bug.
*Transplanting:* Easy; shallow root system.
*Propagation:* By cuttings or seed.

LANDSCAPE VALUE: A good landscape shrub with shiny, dark green leaves and varying shades of flowers, which are produced throughout the year. Compact growth habit and pleasing fragrance add to its attractiveness. Freezes to the ground in USDA Zone 9.

Plant may be observed at BOK, HUN, LAC, MIS, MMA, NAT, RKEW, SEL, USN.

Related *Brunfelsia* species and variety of interest:

*B. latifolia.* Grows 1–3 ft. high. Light violet flowers have white eyes.
*B. pauciflora.* Grows 4–6 ft. high; well-branched, multi-stemmed from base. Glossy, green leaves are oval to elliptic. Salverform flowers are violet the first day, white the second.
*B. pauciflora* var. *calycina* 'Macrantha'. Flower calyces larger than those of species. Shrub grows in Hawaii only at cooler elevations; does not do well at sea level.

# *Buddleia alternifolia*
## BUTTERFLY BUSH

Loganiaceae. USDA Zones 5–6. Native to northwestern China. Introduced into cultivation in 1915.

DESCRIPTION: Deciduous shrub growing quickly to 6 ft. high and as wide, with arching, graceful branches that form a canopy.
*Leaves:* Alternate, lanceolate, 1.5–4 in. long, gray-green above, gray tomentose beneath, yellow in fall; no other member of the genus or the family has alternate leaves.
*Flowers:* Lilac-purple, trumpet-shaped, very fragrant, in dense clusters 0.75 in. across; mid- to late summer.
*Fruit:* A brown seed head, in winter.

CULTURE: Prefers sun, but grows in lightly dappled shade; tolerates some drought, clay, and dry gravel, but prefers rich, well-drained, loamy soil.
*Disease and insect problems:* None serious.
*Transplanting:* Easy.
*Propagation:* By softwood and hardwood cuttings.

LANDSCAPE VALUE: This graceful, arching shrub is particularly effective as a specimen plant. A single shoot can be trained into a weeping tree or espaliered fan-shaped on a wall. Thin out one-third of old wood after flowering; blooms appear on previous year's growth.

Plant may be observed at AA, ABF, ATL, BEA, DEN, MIS, NCS, PAL, PLF, RKEW, WIS.

*Buddleia alternifolia* cultivar of interest:

*B. alternifolia* 'Argentea'. Differs from species with silver-white, pubescent leaves.

# *Buddleia davidii*
## BUTTERFLY BUSH
## SUMMER LILAC

Synonym: *B. variabilis.* Loganiaceae. USDA Zones 5–9. Native to western China, Hupei and Sichuan Provinces. Introduced into cultivation in 1890 by E. H. Wilson.

DESCRIPTION: Deciduous shrub growing quickly to 10–15 ft. high, with arching habit.
*Leaves:* Opposite, simple, oval, lanceolate, 4–10 in. long and 1–3 in. wide, dark green above, white tomentose beneath, with overall gray-green effect; appearing late in spring leaves are tenacious in fall; no fall color.
*Flowers:* Lavender, fragrant, in upright or nodding panicles, usually 5–10 in. long; mid-July to frost.

*Brunfelsia australis* (V. Lauritzen)

*Brunfelsia australis* (V. Lauritzen)

*Buddleia alternifolia* (J. C. Raulston)

*Buddleia alternifolia* 'Argentea' (G. Koller)

*Buddleia davidii* 'Black Knight' (N. Brewster)

*Buddleia davidii* 'Black Knight' (E. Bell)

**Buddleia davidii** continued

CULTURE: Needs full sun; extremely adaptable to many conditions, but prefers well-drained, fertile, modified clay or loam; tolerates wind, but not wet conditions.
*Disease and insect problems:* None serious; sometimes nematodes in warmer areas.
*Transplanting:* Very easy; noninvasive root system.
*Propagation:* By seed (self-sown) or cuttings in June–July.

LANDSCAPE VALUE: A very long flowering summer shrub with branches arching to the ground. Superb as background in perennial border or rose garden. Attracts butterflies. Best used in massed plantings; not a specimen shrub. Most outstanding characteristic: spectacular inflorescences with lovely fragrance, 8–30 in. long and excellent for cutting. Purple color wonderful combined with yellow, dark red, and pink. Generally freezes back in USDA Zone 5, but after pruning emerges boldly with strong branches and profuse flowers. When cut to ground in spring can attain 5–7 ft. by autumn. Weedy and sparse if not grown in full sun. Flowers best if pruned to 1–2 ft. in early spring. Remove spent flowers to encourage new bloom but leave last ones for self-seeding. Many interesting cultivars of this species have been introduced since 1920.

Plant may be observed at ABF, ATL, BBG, BF, BOK, BRK, BSG, CAL, CBG, CIN, DEN, DUK, GCC, HUN, IES, LAC, LWD, NCS, NEB, NEW, PAL, PLF, POW, RBC, RKEW, SAB, SEC, STG, UBC, VDG, WIS.

*Buddleia davidii* cultivars of interest:

B. *davidii* 'Black Knight'. Deep purple-black flowers; 4–5 ft. high; vigorous and said to be hardier than other cultivars. Received RHS Award of Garden Merit.

B. *davidii* 'Charming'. Long (1–2 ft.) pink or lavender panicles; more upright than species.

B. *davidii* 'Dartmoor'. Deep lilac flowers, very fragrant, reminiscent of crushed blackberries; blooms early summer until fall; grows to 4–6 ft. high; produces large branched clusters for unique showy display. Received RHS Award of Merit and RHS Award of Garden Merit.

B. *davidii* 'Deep Lavender'. Large lavender flowers; 6 ft. high.

B. *davidii* 'Dubonnet'. Dark purple flowers with light orange throat rings; 5 ft. high.

B. *davidii* 'Empire Blue'. Violet-blue flowers with bronze eyes; best blue to date; strong grower with tighter habit than species. Received RHS Award of Garden Merit.

B. *davidii* 'Fascination'. Pink form, with wide panicles of strong lilac-pink; 5–6 ft. high; an old standard.

B. *davidii* 'Harlequin'. Variegated, maroon-red flowers; leaves with creamy white marks; lower growing.

B. *davidii* 'Pink Delight'. Best true pink form; introduced from Holland; perhaps best new addition to buddleias; compact habit; blooms over longer period than most cultivars. Received RHS Award of Garden Merit.

B. *davidii* 'Princeton Purple'. Purple flowers, wider than on most cultivars; dense, thick, textured leaves; 5 ft. high.

B. *davidii* 'Royal Red'. Warm purple-red flowers. Received RHS Award of Garden Merit.

B. *davidii* 'White Bouquet'. Pure white flowers with orange throat rings; low-growing.

B. *davidii* 'White Profusion'. Best white form, with long, stout panicles. Received RHS Award of Garden Merit.

## Buddleia globosa

Loganiaceae. USDA Zones 8–10. Native to Chile, Peru. Introduced into cultivation in 1774 by Kennedy and Lee.

DESCRIPTION: Semi-evergreen shrub 6–15 ft. high, with open, gaunt habit.
*Leaves:* Elliptic, ovate to lanceolate, 5–8 in. long, tapering at both ends, dark green and wrinkled, covered with tawny felt beneath.
*Flowers:* Bright yellow, fragrant, 0.75 in. wide; 8–10 globose heads arranged in terminal panicles, 6–8 in. long, in opposite pairs; mid-May in warmer climates.

CULTURE: Needs sun; prefers loamy, well-drained soil; grows in Hawaii only at elevations above 1000 ft.
*Disease and insect problems:* None serious.
*Transplanting:* Easy.
*Propagation:* By seed or cuttings.

LANDSCAPE VALUE: A handsome shrub, distinct among cultivated buddleias for its yellow flowers and their arrangement in globular heads. Flowers on previous season's wood; thus should not be pruned until after flowering. Best grown in a cool greenhouse in colder climates. Received RHS Award of Garden Merit.

Plant may be observed at BER, CAL, CIN, RKEW, VDG.

*Buddleia globosa* cultivar of interest:

B. *globosa* 'Lemon Ball'. Lemon-yellow flowers produced later than those of species.

*Buddleia davidii* 'Harlequin'
(J. C. Raulston)

*Buddleia davidii* 'Pink Delight' (N. Brewster)

*Buddleia davidii* 'White Profusion' (N. Brewster)

*Buddleia globosa* (J. C. Raulston)

*Buddleia globosa* (J. C. Raulston)

# Buddleia 'Lochinch'

Parentage: *B. fallowiana* × *B. davidii*. Loganiaceae. USDA Zones 7–9. Originated by the Earl of Stair in Lochinch, Scotland.

DESCRIPTION: Deciduous shrub 3–6 ft. high and as wide or wider, with compact, mounded growth habit; young shoots covered with a dense, white felt.
*Leaves:* Oblong-lanceolate, acuminate, from 2.5 in. long and 1 in. wide to 8–10 in. long and 2.5–3.5 in. wide, dark green and glabrous above, white tomentose beneath.
*Flowers:* Mauve to periwinkle-blue, August–September.

CULTURE: Needs full sun; extremely adaptable to many conditions, but prefers well-drained, fertile, modified clay or loam soil; tolerates wind, but not wet conditions.
*Disease and insect problems:* None serious.
*Transplanting:* Easy.
*Propagation:* By seed or cuttings.

LANDSCAPE VALUE: Hardier and more vigorous than *B. fallowiana*. Received RHS Award of Garden Merit.

Plant may be observed at ATL, CAL, CUH, NCS, RKEW, VDG.

Related *Buddleia* hybrid cultivars of interest:

*B.* 'Glasnevin' (*B. fallowiana* × *B. davidii*). USDA Zones 7–8. Dark lilac flowers; strong grower; leaves white tomentose on undersides. Hardier than *B. fallowiana*. Originated by the Earl of Stair in Lochinch, Scotland.

*B.* 'West Hill' (*B. fallowiana* × *B. davidii*). USDA Zones 7–8. Pale lilac flowers, very fragrant, August–October; very narrow panicles. Hardier than *B. fallowiana*. Originated by the Earl of Stair in Lochinch, Scotland; raised by Messrs. Hillier.

Related *Buddleia fallowiana* cultivar of interest:

*B. fallowiana* 'Alba'. USDA Zones 8–9. Very attractive with milk-white flowers. More tender but finer garden plant than any white-flowered form of *B. davidii*. Received RHS Award of Garden Merit.

# Buxus 'Green Mountain'
## BOXWOOD

Parentage: *B. sempervirens* 'Suffruticosa' × *B. microphylla* var. *koreana*. Buxaceae. USDA Zones 5–8. Native to Korea. Seedlings grown by Sheridan Nurseries, Georgetown, Ontario; introduced into cultivation in 1966.

DESCRIPTION: Broad-leaved evergreen to 5 ft. high and 3 ft. wide at base, with pyramidal habit.
*Leaves:* Elliptic, 0.75 in. long and 0.25 in. wide, dark green.
*Flowers:* Very small, in axillary or terminal clusters, not showy.

CULTURE: Grows in sun or partial shade; tolerates a variety of soils, except rocky or very heavy clay, with a pH of 6.0; needs good drainage, does not tolerate wet conditions; tolerates some wind and air pollution, but not drought, salt, or soil compaction; can be kept to size or renovated by cutting back severely in late winter or early spring, then fertilizing, watering, and mulching.
*Disease and insect problems:* None serious.
*Transplanting:* Easy in fall, preferably balled and burlapped.
*Propagation:* By softwood and hardwood cuttings, layering, and division.

LANDSCAPE VALUE: A delightful, neat, strong shrub; taller than wide, with superior hardiness. Less prone to winter scalding and more dependable than 'Green Gem' or 'Green Velvet'. The best boxwood for hedges as it withstands formal shearing. The winter color of the rich green foliage is superior, even when exposed to winter sun. Deer-resistant, as are all *Buxus*.

Plant may be observed at ATL, BBG, BIC, BLO, BOE, BRK, CBG, CIN, COX, DIX, GCC, LNG, LWD, MRT, NCS, OWG, PAL, RBC, RKEW, SEC, SPR, USN, RKEW, VDG.

Related *Buxus* cultivars of interest from *B. sempervirens* 'Suffruticosa' × *B. microphylla* var. *koreana*: The two cultivars described below differ significantly from *B.* 'Green Mountain' only in growth habit. All three cultivars are outstanding in that they combine the aesthetic advantages of English Boxwood with the hardiness of Korean Boxwood to create a handsome, dependable, hardy shrub for northern climates. They vary greatly in adaptation from northerly climates to southerly climates; best to use material propagated from plants in local nurseries.

*B.* 'Green Gem'. Slow growing, with mounded habit and slightly darker green leaves than *B.* 'Green Mountain' or *B.* 'Green Velvet'. Needs no pruning.

*B.* 'Green Velvet'. Vigorous, full, rounded form. Useful for low hedges.

*Buddleia* 'Lochinch' (N. Brewster)

*Buddleia* 'Lochinch' (N. Brewster)

*Buxus* 'Green Mountain' (D. Brennan)

*Buxus* 'Green Gem' (E. Hasselkus)

## *Buxus microphylla* var. *japonica* 'Morris Midget'
### DWARF BOXWOOD

Buxaceae. USDA Zones 5–9. Native to Japan. Introduced into cultivation in 1951 by Henry Skinner.

DESCRIPTION: Broad-leaved evergreen growing 0.25–0.75 in. per year to 1.5 ft. high and 3 ft. wide, with dwarf, mounded habit.
*Leaves:* Notched, elliptic, with obtuse to retuse tips, 0.25–0.4 in. wide and 0.4–0.6 in. long, yellow-green.
*Flowers:* Very small, fragrant, in axillary or terminal clusters, not showy.

CULTURE: Grows in sun and partial shade; tolerates air pollution and some wind, but not wet conditions, drought, salt, or soil compaction; has some problems with sunscald and desiccation; can be kept to size or renovated by cutting back severely in late winter or early spring and then fertilizing, watering, and mulching.
*Disease and insect problems:* None serious; some leaf miner; less trouble with nematodes than other boxwoods.
*Transplanting:* Easy, balled and burlapped, in fall; add 2 oz. superphosphate to bushel.
*Propagation:* By softwood or hardwood cuttings.

LANDSCAPE VALUE: An attractive, compact shrub that withstands pruning and shearing. Performs better in the southerly latitudes than does *B. sempervirens* because it is more tolerant of heat. More consistent habit than that of *B. microphylla* 'Compacta' and hardier than the species. Deer-resistant.

Plant may be observed at AA, BBG, BF, BSG, CAL, CBG, CUH, DUK, LWD, MCG, MIS, MRT, NCS, NEW, PLF, RBC, SPR, USN.

Related *B. microphylla* cultivar of interest:

*B. microphylla* 'Compacta'. Kingsville Dwarf Boxwood. USDA Zones 6–9. Native to Japan and China. Found as a seedling in 1912 by Sam Appleby; registered in 1948 by Henry Hohman. Broad-leaved evergreen growing 0.25–0.75 in. per year, to 12 in. high and 20 in. wide when 25 years old; dwarf, mounded habit. Excellent, dark green leaves to 0.5 in. long and 0.25 in. wide. Small, fragrant, nonshowy flowers. Grows in sun and partial shade; withstands air pollution and some wind. Wet conditions cause root rot. Excellent as hedge plant, edging, or in the formal garden. Very tolerant of frost; withstands dryness. Do not prune or cultivate. Deer-resistant.

## *Buxus sempervirens* 'Graham Blandy'
### BOXWOOD

Buxaceae. USDA Zones 6–8. Native to southern Europe. Brought by John Baldwin, Jr., to Blandy Experimental Farm, Virginia, in 1969; distributed by the U.S. National Arboretum in 1982.

DESCRIPTION: Broad-leaved evergreen to 10 ft. high and 1 ft. wide, with narrow, columnar habit.
*Leaves:* Elliptic-ovate, with obtuse tips, 1 in. long and 0.5 in. wide, medium green.
*Flowers:* Very small, in axillary or terminal clusters, not conspicuous.

CULTURE: Grows in sun or partial shade in clay or loam with a pH of 6.0–7.2; tolerates wind, air pollution, and some drought, but not wet conditions or salt.
*Disease and insect problems:* Plant lice (Psyllidae).
*Transplanting:* Easy; balled and burlapped, in fall.
*Propagation:* By softwood and hardwood cuttings, layering, and root division.

LANDSCAPE VALUE: Excellent as an accent plant or in small areas. Its spectacular habit is strongly vertical; sides are parallel along the full height of the plant. Many straight, strong stems rise directly from base; there is no horizontal branching. Deer-resistant.

Plant may be observed at AA, ABF, BBG, BEA, BF, BOE, CAL, CIN, GCC, HOL, IES, LNG, LWD, MIS, NCS, OWG, PAL, PLF, RBC, SEC, USN, VDG, WIS.

Other *Buxus sempervirens* cultivars of interest:

*B. sempervirens* 'Elegantissima'. Silver Box. USDA Zones 6–9. Grows 5 ft. high and 3.5 ft. wide; dense, compact, pyramidal habit. Holds foliage to ground; good for topiary or hedge. Dark green leaves to 0.9 in. long and 0.4 in. wide, with irregular, creamy white margins. From Germany. Introduced in 1862 by Karl Koch.

*B. sempervirens* 'Pullman'. USDA Zone 5 with protection. Distinct in its disciplined form and very deep, dark green leaves. Breaks dormancy later in spring than do most *Buxus*. Originated by William Pullman, Lake Forest, Illinois.

*B. sempervirens* 'Vardar Valley'. English Boxwood. USDA Zones 5–8. Attractive, broad-leaved evergreen, grows 1–4 in. per year, to 6 ft. high and 10 ft. wide; upright, spreading, flat-topped habit. Has glossy, blue-green leaves to 0.6 in. long and 0.5 in. wide and inconspicuous clusters of small flowers. Hardy; has withstood −23°F without injury. Tolerates extremely dry conditions. Useful for hedge, topiary, and formal garden plantings. Leaves are toxic to animals. Native to Vardar River

*Buxus microphylla* var. *japonica* 'Morris Midget'
(N. Brewster)

*Buxus microphylla* var. *japonica* 'Morris Midget' (N. Brewster)

*Buxus sempervirens* 'Graham Blandy'
(N. Brewster)

*Buxus sempervirens* 'Elegantissima' (N. Brewster)

*Buxus sempervirens* 'Graham Blandy'
(N. Brewster)

Valley, Yugoslavia. Edgar Anderson brought back cuttings taken during the 1935 expedition sponsored by the Arnold Arboretum. Donald Wyman named and registered the plant in 1957.

Related *Buxus* cultivar of interest:

B. 'Glencoe' (*B. sinica* × *B. sempervirens*). Robust evergreen with uniform, broad-oval habit. Excellent hardiness. Maintains good winter color. Leaves elliptic, deep green. Tolerates deep shade but tends to be slower growing without sunlight. Tolerates −22°F with no damage.

# Callicarpa americana
## FRENCH MULBERRY
## AMERICAN BEAUTYBERRY

Verbenaceae. USDA Zones 7–9. Native to the United States, from Virginia to Texas, and to the West Indies. Introduced into cultivation in 1724.

DESCRIPTION: Deciduous shrub growing rapidly to 3–8 ft. high and 6 ft. wide, with loose, open habit.
*Leaves:* Elliptic-ovate to ovate-oblong, 6 in. long, toothed, pale green, softly pubescent above, tomentose beneath.
*Flowers:* Pale blue to white, small, in clusters at leaf axils; late spring–early summer.
*Fruit:* A violet drupe, 0.3 in. across, produced in profusion, borne closer to the stem than in any other *Callicarpa* species.
*Winter aspect:* Young twigs tomentose.

CULTURE: Grows in full sun and light shade; tolerates moisture and drought; prefers clay or sand enriched with organic materials to recreate the plant's natural forest floor habitat; thrives in a wide variety of conditions; roots can be killed by a hard ground freeze.
*Disease and insect problems:* None.
*Transplanting:* Easy.
*Propagation:* By cuttings and seed; if grown from seed, color may vary.

LANDSCAPE VALUE: An excellent shrub for naturalizing or for planting in groups in the shrub border; requires some space. Valued for spectacular fruit, which provides unique display of berries after foliage has fallen and attracts birds. Needs minimal care after roots are established. Light green foliage contrasts handsomely with evergreens. The coarsest of all *Callicarpa* species, it is found in moist thickets. Flowers are produced on new growth, so annual pruning to about 2 ft. less than desired size controls growth.

Plant may be observed at AA, ABF, ABN, ATL, BBG, BF, BIR, BSG, CAL, CBG, CIN, CUH, DEN, DIX, DUK, FIL, MIS, MTC, MUN, NCS, PAL, PLF, RKEW, SAB, STG, UBC, USN, VDG.

*Callicarpa americana* variety of interest:

*C. americana* var. *lactea*. White-fruited.

Related *Callicarpa* cultivar of interest:

*C. bodinieri* var. *giraldii* 'Profusion'. Bodinier Beautyberry. USDA Zones 6–8. Native to Sichuan Province, China; introduced into cultivation in United Kingdom in 1907. Grows to 6–10 ft. high. Leaves are elliptic to ovate-elliptic and often exhibit pink-purple cast in fall. Purplish flowers and mauve-purple fruit are borne in large, dense clusters. Useful as late-season plant; flowering occurs at the end of summer and fruiting in fall. Produces more abundant fruit than species; requires second plant for best fruit production. Needs full sun for best growth and ornamental value, but does not need as much heat as species to flower and fruit. Though the species is not often cultivated in America, in Britain it is considered to be the finest species in the genus. Received RHS Award of Garden Merit.

# Callicarpa japonica
## JAPANESE BEAUTYBERRY

Verbenaceae. USDA Zones 6–8. Native to Japan. Introduced into cultivation in 1845.

DESCRIPTION: Deciduous shrub growing quickly to 4–6 ft. high and as wide or wider, with erect, rounded habit and arching branches.
*Leaves:* Opposite, simple, elliptic to ovate, 2.5–5 in. long and 1–2 in. wide.
*Flowers:* Perfect, pink-white; July.
*Fruit:* A berrylike, violet drupe.

CULTURE: Grows in sun and light shade; requires well-drained soil.
*Disease and insect problems:* None serious; occasional leaf spot, black mold.
*Transplanting:* Easy.
*Propagation:* By softwood cuttings.

LANDSCAPE VALUE: An outstanding, showy fruit display in fall, when leaves have fallen, makes this shrub a handsome addition to the autumn landscape. Use in group plantings for greater impact. Plant is most attractive when cut back to 10–20 in. from the ground; best to prune to ground and treat as perennial in northern climates (USDA Zone 5).

Plant may be observed at AA, BBG, BF, BSG, CBG, DIN, HOL, LNG, MIS, NCS, NEB, NEW, PLF, RKEW, SAB, USN, VDG.

*Buxus* 'Glencoe' (G. Gates)

*Callicarpa americana* (G. Koller)

*Callicarpa americana* (G. Koller)

*Callicarpa bodinieri* var. *giraldii* 'Profusion' (J. Elsley)

*Callicarpa japonica* 'Luxurians' (N. Brewster)

*Callicarpa japonica* 'Leucocarpa' (G. Koller)

53

*Calliparpa japonica* continued

*Callicarpa japonica* cultivars of interest:

C. *japonica* 'Leucocarpa'. Excellent form with abundant, heavy, white fruit. Clusters of white flowers in July–August. Leaves lighter green than species, with yellow autumn color.

C. *japonica* 'Luxurians'. Beautiful shrub with large, open fruit clusters and larger leaves than species.

Related *Callicarpa* species of interest:

C. *dichotoma*. Purple Beautyberry. USDA Zones 6–8. Native to eastern and central China, Japan, and Korea; introduced into cultivation in 1857. Grows 4–5 ft. high and 6–8 ft. wide, with graceful, refined habit; long, slender branches ultimately arch and their tips touch the ground. Elliptic to obovate leaves are light green beneath, nearly glabrous. Pink-lavender flowers are borne in cymes, 8 in. across, in June–August. Excellent for planting in groups in the shrub border. Violet fruit begins to ripen in late August and provides fabulous display by September–October. Not as vigorous as C. *americana* or C. *japonica*. Received Pennsylvania Horticultural Society Gold Medal (Styer Award) in 1989.

Related C. *dichotoma* cultivars of interest:

C. *dichotoma* 'Albifructus'. Very good, vigorous, white-fruited cultivar. Yellow stems provide interest in the winter landscape.

C. *dichotoma* 'Issai'. Colorful, profuse display of violet fruit.

# Calluna vulgaris
## HEATHER

Ericaceae. USDA Zones 5–7. Native to Europe, Asia Minor. Naturalized by Hull in northeastern North America.

DESCRIPTION: Broad-leaved evergreen growing slowly to 4–24 in. high, spreading to 2 ft. or more.
*Leaves:* Small, opposite, overlapping, medium green in summer, green to bronze in winter.
*Flowers:* One-sided, spikelike racemes, corollas bell-shaped, not conspicuous; July–September.
*Fruit:* A 4-valved capsule, in fall, not ornamental.
*Winter aspect:* Reddish tint on some cultivars.

CULTURE: Grows in full sun (for fullest flowering) or partial shade, in acid, sandy soil; tolerates wind and drought.
*Disease and insect problems:* Few; occasional Japanese beetle, oystershell scale, two-spotted mite.
*Transplanting:* Easy; root system quite shallow.
*Propagation:* By seed sown on peat moss, by layering, or by softwood cuttings in peat-perlite medium under mist; roots in 2–3 weeks.

LANDSCAPE VALUE: Has been in cultivation for centuries. Adds color and interest to the garden in every season. Excellent in rock gardens. Easy to naturalize. Occasional pruning necessary to retain habit. Most attractive in late summer and autumn. Cover with pine boughs in winter in USDA Zone 5. More than 600 cultivars provide wide palette of colors, both in foliage (yellow-orange, bronze, brown to red, variegated white) and flowers (lilac to purple, pink to carmine, white).

Plant may be observed at BBG, DEN, HOL, LWD, NEW, PAL, PLF, RHO, RKEW, UBC, VDG, WIS.

*Calluna vulgaris* cultivars of interest:

C. *vulgaris* 'Alba Plena'. Large, white, double flowers, in September–October. Found on moor near Oldenburg, Germany. Introduced into cultivation in 1934 by A. Lamken.

C. *vulgaris* 'County Wicklow'. One of the finest double pink cultivars with inflorescences to 6 in. long; in mid-August; dark green foliage. Introduced by Maxwell and Beale. Received RHS Award of Garden Merit.

C. *vulgaris* 'Darkness'. Upright, densely spaced, carmine-purple flowers; dense growth. Introduced by Pratt.

C. *vulgaris* 'Gold Haze'. Long, pale, golden-yellow shoots of foliage throughout year; white flowers in August–September. Introduced by J. W. Sparker before 1963. Received RHS Award of Garden Merit.

C. *vulgaris* 'H. E. Beale'. Vigorous habit, 16–18 in. high; silver-cast foliage; double pink flowers, in September–October; last well as cut flowers. Introduced by Maxwell & Beale.

*Callicarpa dichotoma* 'Albifructus' (N. Brewster)

*Callicarpa dichotoma* 'Issai' (D. Brennan)

*Calluna vulgaris* 'Alba Plena' (J. Apel)

*Calluna vulgaris* 'County Wicklow' (J. Apel)

*Calluna vulgaris* 'Darkness' (J. Apel)

*Calluna vulgaris* 'Gold Haze' (J. Apel)

# Calycanthus floridus
## CAROLINA ALLSPICE
## SWEET SHRUB

Calycanthaceae. USDA Zones 5–8. Native to south-central Pennsylvania and from southern Ohio to Florida and Mississippi. Introduced into cultivation in 1726.

DESCRIPTION: Deciduous shrub growing slowly to 6–8 ft. high and 6–12 ft. wide, with dense, bushy, rounded habit.
*Leaves:* Opposite, entire, ovate to elliptic, to 5 in. long, clear yellow fall color.
*Flowers:* Red-brown, large, 2 in. wide; May and sporadically until September.
*Fruit:* Brown, urn-shaped, similar to a rose hip.
*Winter aspect:* Gray-brown stems, flattened at nodes; aromatic bark.

CULTURE: Grows well in sun and shade, but becomes taller in full sun; adapts to a variety of soils, but prefers acid, loamy, moist soil.
*Disease and insect problems:* None.
*Transplanting:* Easy.
*Propagation:* By seed, cuttings, division, and layering. Seed germinates without stratification if collected and sown before dry.

LANDSCAPE VALUE: An extremely ornamental shrub with unusual blooms and sweet fragrance varying from strawberry to banana to pineapple; takes on aroma of cider at maturity. Attractive in shrub border but desirable close to an entrance where scent may be appreciated. Prune immediately after flowering since most flowers grow on previous year's wood. Bark has been used as cinnamon substitute. Known since colonial days. Often confused with *C. fertilis,* Pale Sweet Shrub, though the latter has less pubescent leaves and flowers with no fragrance, is a generous fruiter, and is less hardy.

Plant may be observed at AA, ABF, ATL, BC, BEA, BF, BIC, BIR, BOK, BRK, CAL, CBG, CHK, CIN, COX, CUH, DAW, DIX, DUK, GCC, GIW, HOL, HUN, IES, LAC, LNG, LWD, MBG, MIS, MNL, MOR, MRT, MTC, MUN, NCA, NCS, NEB, OWG, PAL, PLF, RKEW, STG, USN, VDG, WIN, ZOO.

*Calycanthus floridus* cultivars of interest:

*C. floridus* 'Athens'. Yellow-green flowers, extremely fragrant; 3–10 ft. high, lustrous, dark green foliage; larger than the species; urn-shaped fruit.

*C. floridus* 'Edith Wilder'. Abundant, burgundy flowers, with strong scent of pineapple and strawberry. Valued for its long bloom period of 3–4 weeks, mid-May to mid-June. Grows to 10 ft. high and as wide; often needs pruning to maintain a more compact shape. From Edith Wilder's garden in Pennsylvania.

# Camellia japonica
## JAPANESE CAMELLIA

Theaceae. USDA Zones 8–9. Native to Japan, China. Introduced into cultivation in 1742.

DESCRIPTION: Broad-leaved evergreen growing slowly to 10–15(20) ft. tall and 5–10 ft. wide, with rather tight and formal habit (some forms with a more relaxed habit).
*Leaves:* Alternate, simple, ovate, serrate, 2–4 in. long, leathery, deep green.
*Flowers:* Wide range of subtle color combinations of white, pink, and red; forms varying from semidouble to anemone-like to roselike; blooms 2–7 in. across, at the ends of branches, November–April.
*Fruit:* A woody capsule, 1 in. long.
*Winter aspect:* Blooms November–March in warmer climates or greenhouse.

CULTURE: Grows best in partial shade; can be burned by sun; flowers not as profuse or attractive in strong sun or deep shade; prefers moist, well-drained, rich, organic, acid soil; the taproot of container-grown plants is often severed; when grown in the garden, the taproot often reestablishes itself after a hard winter, which gives the plant cold tolerance.
*Disease and insect problems:* Flower blight in late winter/ early spring (serious), sooty mold on foliage and stems (not serious), leaf spot (rare), leaf blight, gall, dieback and stem canker (very serious in humid, warm climates), root rot, leaf variegation caused by virus (usually introduced for color variation and not a problem), tea and camellia scale, aphid on new growth in spring, spider mite when hot and dry, peony scale (can be very serious).
*Transplanting:* Easy, with young plants; best when plant is dormant.
*Propagation:* By cuttings, air layering, and grafting; seed results in new varieties, often with inferior flowers.

LANDSCAPE VALUE: A glorious shrub with full, beautiful blooms and handsome, lustrous, dark green foliage. A plant of great beauty for use as a specimen, in a border, or in massed plantings. Prune after flowering. Flower petals often turn brown at temperatures below 32°F. First *Camellia* species to be brought into cultivation in the West. More valued in Japan for oil from its seeds than for flowers; the oil is used for dressing women's hair and is of great commercial importance. Moderately hard, close-grained, light-colored wood, which takes on pink cast with exposure, is used for combs. Numerous cultivars selected for hardiness, habit, and attractive flowers.

Plant may be observed at ATL, BBG, BOK, BRK, CAL, DES, DIN, DUK, FIL, HUN, MAG, MID, MIS, MLG, PLF, RKEW, STG, STR, USN, VDG, WIS.

*Calycanthus floridus* (E. Hasselkus)

*Calycanthus floridus* 'Athens' (H. Shimizu)

*Calycanthus floridus* (E. Bell)

*Camellia japonica* (N. Brewster)

*Camellia japonica* 'Betty Sheffield Supreme' (J. Elsley)

*Camellia japonica* 'C. M. Wilson' (A. Patterson)

*Camellia japonica* continued

*Camellia japonica* cultivars of interest:

*C. japonica* 'Adolphe Audusson'. Dark red, large, semidouble flowers in midseason; average, compact growth. Introduced in 1875 by M. Audusson, France.

*C. japonica* 'Alaska'. Velvety white petals.

*C. japonica* 'Betty Sheffield Supreme'. White, medium to large flowers in midseason, with pink to red border on slightly wavy petals; semidouble to peony form. Average, compact growth. Introduced in 1960.

*C. japonica* 'C. M. Wilson' (sport of 'Elegans'). Pink, large to very large flowers. Introduced in 1949 by Mrs. A. E. Wilson, Pensacola, Florida. Received RHS Award of Garden Merit.

*C. japonica* 'Dahlohnega'. Canary-yellow, small to medium, formal double flowers midseason. Slow, open, upright growth. Introduced in 1986 by W. Homeyer.

*C. japonica* 'Eldorado'. Pale pink flowers.

*C. japonica* 'Elegans'. Rose-pink, large to very large, anemone-shaped flowers, with center petaloids often spotted white; early to midseason. Slow, spreading growth. Introduced in 1831 by A. Chandler, United Kingdom.

*C. japonica* 'Empress of Russia'. Dark coral-red petals with white blotches.

*C. japonica* 'Finlandia'. White, medium, semidouble flowers, with swirled, fluted petals; early to midseason. Compact growth. Introduced in 1910 to the United States from Japan.

*C. japonica* 'Guillio Nuccio'. Red flowers. Selected by Nuccio's Nursery, Altadena, California. Received RHS Award of Garden Merit.

*C. japonica* 'Holly Bright'. Red, semidouble flowers; unusual foliage like holly. Introduced in 1986 by Nuccio's Nursery, Altadena, California.

*C. japonica* 'Kumasaka'. Rose-pink, medium flowers, rose-form double to peony form; mid- to late season. Vigorous, compact growth. Introduced in 1896 to the United States from Japan.

*C. japonica* 'Lady Clare'. Deep pink, large, semidouble flowers; early to midseason. Vigorous, bushy growth. Introduced to United Kingdom from Japan in 1887.

*C. japonica* 'Magnoliaeflora'. Blush-pink, semidouble, medium flowers. Introduced in 1886 to Italy from Japan.

*C. japonica* 'Mansize'. White, miniature, midseason flowers with anemone form; upright growth. Introduced in 1961 to the United States by Wilson.

*C. japonica* 'Mathotiana'. Crimson, large to very large flowers, sometimes with purple cast, rose-form to formal double; mid- to late season. Vigorous, compact, upright growth. Introduced in 1840 to the United States from Europe.

*C. japonica* 'Nuccio's Gem'. White, formal double, early to midseason flowers; vigorous, compact, upright growth. Introduced in 1970 by Nuccio's Nursery, Altadena, California. Received RHS Award of Garden Merit.

*C. japonica* 'Otome'. Bright coral flowers with white flecks.

*C. japonica* 'Pink Perfection'. Shell-pink, small, formal double flowers; early to late season. Vigorous, upright growth. Introduced in 1875 to the United States from Japan.

*C. japonica* 'Pope Pius IX'. Vivid coral-red flowers.

*C. japonica* 'R. L. Wheeler'. Rose-pink, very large flowers, semidouble to anemone-form, with heavy outer petals and solid circle of stamens; early to midseason. Vigorous, upright growth. Introduced in 1949 by R. L. Wheeler, Macon, Georgia. Received RHS Award of Garden Merit.

*C. japonica* 'September Morn' [Yohei-Haku]. White to blush-pink, medium flowers, semidouble to peony to anemone form; very early bloomer, often in September. Introduced in 1936 to the United States from Japan as 'Chuguu'.

*C. japonica* 'Swan Lake'. White, large, rose-form double to loose peony; vigorous, compact, upright growth.

*C. japonica* 'Ville de Nantes' (sport of 'Donckelarii'). Unusual red and white, medium to large, semidouble flowers with fimbriated petals; introduced in 1910 from France by Heurtin, Nantes.

*Camellia* species of interest:

*C. chrysantha*. USDA Zone 9. Native to Guangxi Province, China. Introduced to the United States in 1980, when seeds were sent to several *Camellia* researchers. In 1975, a seedling was named '(Hu) Tuyama' by T. Tuyama of Japan; in 1984, a seedling C. 'Olympic Gold' was named by Meyer Piet, California. *Camellia chrysantha* was the first yellow *Camellia* to be brought into cultivation in the United States. Small, yellow blooms hang downward on pedicels from leaf nodes. Leaves are 3–5 in. long, very shiny, with heavy venation; new growth is red, turning bright to deep green. Rapid grower but not cold-hardy and of little landscape value; however, important to hybridizers as source of genes for yellow flower color. Since 1980, a number of other yellow-flowered species have been identified, most of these in China; they have not been released to the United States.

*Camellia japonica* 'Dahlohnega' (American Camellia Society)

*Camellia japonica* 'Empress of Russia' (Greer Gardens)

*Camellia japonica* 'Finlandia' (Greer Gardens)

*Camellia japonica* 'Guillio Nuccio' (P. K. Thompson)

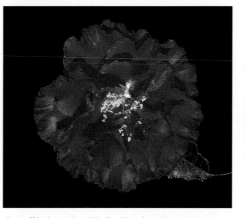

*Camellia japonica* 'Holly Bright' (American Camellia Society)

*Camellia japonica* 'Otome' (Greer Gardens)

*Camellia japonica* 'Pink Perfection' (Greer Gardens)

*Camellia japonica* 'R. L. Wheeler' (Greer Gardens)

*Camellia japonica* 'Swan Lake' (Monrovia Nursery)

# Camellia oleifera
## TEA-OIL CAMELLIA

Synonym: *C. oleosa*. Theaceae. USDA Zones 6–9. Native to China. Introduced into cultivation in 1803. Sent to United Kingdom from Canton by William Kerr, plant collector for the Royal Botanic Gardens, Kew.

DESCRIPTION: Broad-leaved evergreen growing vigorously to 12–15 ft. high and 12 ft. wide.
*Leaves:* Alternate, simple, elliptic, serrate, 1–3(5) in. long and 0.75–1.5 in. wide, glabrous, leathery, deep green.
*Flowers:* White, single, 2–2.75 in. across, fragrant; October–January.
*Fruit:* A brown capsule, to 1 in. across, with 1–3 seeds.
*Winter aspect:* Smooth, cinnamon-colored bark, sometimes with darker vertical strips.

CULTURE: Tolerates sun, but grows best in filtered shade in well-drained loam with a pH of 5.5–7.0; does not tolerate wet conditions.
*Disease and insect problems:* Peony scale in humid regions; flower petal blight; resistant to root rot.
*Transplanting:* Easy.
*Propagation:* By cuttings.

LANDSCAPE VALUE: A handsome shrub. One of the most common camellias in China, largely because the pressed seeds have long been used to produce oil. Do not plant in eastern exposure, where leaves tend to become cool and dewy in the early morning. Plants should gradually warm up before hot sun hits the foliage.

Plant may be observed at BIR, BRK, CAL, CAM, CBG, CIN, DIN, DOD, DUK, HUN, LAC, MBG, MCG, MIS, MLG, MOR, NCS, PLF, RKEW, STG, STR, USN, VDG.

*Camellia* hybrids of interest: Among the hardiest of camellias, *C. oleifera* has been used to impart cold hardiness to cultivars. Between 1979 and 1984, William Ackerman, U.S. National Arboretum, crossed *C. oleifera* with *C. sasanqua* and *C. hiemalis* cultivars to obtain compact hybrids with small, very shiny, dark green leaves and flowers of equal or better quality than those of *C. sasanqua*. These crosses bloom for 5–6 weeks in October–December. Flower forms are single, double, peonylike, anemonelike, and roselike, and range from white to pink to lavender. They are hardy in USDA Zones 6–8 and withstand temperatures of −10°F. Very early freezes burn flowers in bloom, but subsequent flowers are not affected. To date, these plants are free of die-back, root-rot, flower petal blight, and scale. They require only acid loam (pH 5.5–6.5) and a good mulch. Do not plant in eastern exposure; avoid over-fertilizing, which leads to loose, open growth.

*C.* 'Polar Ice' (*C. oleifera* × *C.* 'Frost Princess' (*C. hiemalis* × *C. oleifera*)). White, anemone-shaped flowers, 3.5 in. across, with golden-yellow anthers. Grows to 5.5 ft. in 10 years; more upright habit than *C.* 'Snow Flurry' and *C.* 'Winter's Hope'. Leaves obovate, 4 in. long and 1.75 in. wide, with crenate margins. Introduced in 1987.

*C.* 'Snow Flurry' (*C. oleifera* × *C.* 'Frost Princess' (*C. hiemalis* × *C. oleifera*)). White flowers, 2–3 in. across, with double, peony form. Grows to 6.5 ft. in 11 years with spreading habit. Leaves ovate, 3 in. long and 1 in. wide. Floriferous, very hardy shrub. Introduced in 1987.

*C.* 'Winter's Charm' (*C. sasanqua* 'Takara-awade' × *C. oleifera*). Lavender-pink, peony-form flowers. Grows to 6 ft. high and 4 ft. wide in 10 years, with upright habit. Leaves obovate, coarsely serrate, 3.5 in. long and 1.5 in. wide. Introduced in 1987.

*C.* 'Winter's Dream' (*C. hiemalis* 'Peach Puff' × *C. oleifera*). Pink, semidouble flowers, 3.75 in. across, with dark yellow anthers. Grows to 9 ft. high and 6 ft. wide in 12 years; pyramidal habit. Introduced in 1988.

*C.* 'Winter's Hope' (*C. oleifera* × *C.* 'Frost Princess' (*C. hiemalis* × *C. oleifera*)). White, semidouble flowers, 3.75 in. across, with yellow anthers. Grows to 7.75 ft. high and 7.5 ft. wide in 12 years; spreading habit. Leaves ovate, 3 in. long and 1.75 in. wide, with crenate margins. Introduced in 1987.

*C.* 'Winter's Interlude' (*C. oleifera* × *C.* sp. 'Pink Tea'). Pink flowers, 3 in. across, with anemone form; no anthers. Grows to 7 ft. high and 7–8 ft. wide; spreading habit. Introduced in 1991.

*C.* 'Winter's Rose' (*C. oleifera* × *C. hiemalis* 'Otome'). Shell-pink flowers with double rose form; very floriferous. Grows slowly to 4 ft. high in 10 years; compact, spreading habit with dropping branchlets. Leaves 2.75 in. long and 1 in. wide, with crenate margins. Introduced in 1987.

*C.* 'Winter's Star' (*C. oleifera* × *C. hiemalis* 'Showa-no-sakai'). Reddish purple flowers, 3.25 in. across, with white centers. Grows to 6 ft. high and 4.5 ft. wide in 12 years; upright habit. Semiglossy leaves are medium green, leathery, 3.75 in. long and 1.5 in. wide, with crenate margins. Introduced in 1988.

*C.* 'Winter's Waterlily' (*C. oleifera* × *C. sasanqua* 'Mini-no-Yuki'). Grows to 6–7 ft. high and 6 ft. wide, with globular habit. White flowers, 3.5 in. across, with anemone- to formal double form and yellow anthers. Introduced in 1991.

Related *Camellia* species of interest:

*C. rosaeflora*. USDA Zones 8–9. Native to China. Grows to 6–15 ft. high with open, sometimes pendulous habit. A showy addition to the landscape with its lovely single, pink, tubular blossoms, 1–2 in. across, which cover the plant January–March. Leaves are minutely crenate (crenulate) to serrulate, with obscure venation, 1–2 in. long, glabrous, dark green. Described by Hooker and

*Camellia oleifera* (Winterthur Gardens)

*Camellia oleifera* (J. C. Raulston)

*Camellia oleifera* (N. Brewster)

*Camellia* 'Snow Flurry' (W. Ackerman)

*Camellia* 'Winter's Rose' (W. Ackerman)

*Camellia* 'Winter's Hope' (W. Ackerman)

*Camellia* 'Winter's Star' (W. Ackerman)

*Camellia sinensis* (J. Apel)

introduced into cultivation by the Royal Botanic Gardens, Kew, in 1858, where it was long grown as *C. euryoides*; subsequently lost but rediscovered as a cultivated plant in Ceylon in 1935. Tolerates sun but prefers shade; can be propagated by cutting, grafting, and air layering.

*C. sinensis.* Tea Camellia. USDA Zones (7)8–9. Lovely, fall-flowering, broad-leaved evergreen reaching 4–6 ft. high, with vigorous habit. White, single flowers, with yellow stamens, 1 in. across, are borne on pedicels hanging from leaf nodes, in September–November. Flowers not as prominent as those of other camellias; often hidden by attractive, glabrous foliage. Lustrous, deep green leaves are alternate, simple, elliptic, serrate, 2–4 in. long, with heavy venation. Fruit is a capsule, 0.75 in. long, with 1–3 seeds. Performs best in shade, but grows well in full sun. More heat and drought tolerant than many other *Camellia* species, and hardier than *C. sasanqua;* can withstand temperatures to –12°F. Second *Camellia* species to be brought into cultivation in West; introduced from China in 1740 by the director of East India Company. Carl Linnaeus named the genus *Thea* in 1735 and the species *T. sinensis* in 1753. By the mid-1700s, *C. sinensis* played a significant role in the tea trade. It is the only species of the genus with major economic importance; however, it has never received proper recognition for its landscape value.

# Camellia × williamsii

Parentage: *C. japonica* × *C. saluenensis.* Theaceae. USDA Zones 8–9. Bred about 1930 by J. C. Williams, Caerhays Castle, Cornwall, United Kingdom.

DESCRIPTION: Broad-leaved evergreen to 15 ft. high and 7 ft. wide, with vigorous, dense habit.
*Leaves:* Elliptic to broad, with shallow, serrate margins, glossy, dark green above, lighter beneath.
*Flowers:* White to dark pink, single or semidouble; November–May.
*Fruit:* A seed pod, 1–1.5 in. across.

CULTURE: Adapts to both sun and cold; prefers slightly acid soil; requires good drainage, but soil should not be permitted to dry out.
*Disease and insect problems:* Flower blight in late winter/early spring (serious), sooty mold on foliage and stems (not serious), leaf spot (rare), leaf blight, gall, dieback and stem canker (very serious in humid, warm climates), root rot, leaf variegation caused by virus (usually introduced for color variation and not a problem), tea and camellia scale, aphid on new growth in spring, spider mite when hot and dry, peony scale (can be very serious).
*Transplanting:* Easy.
*Propagation:* By cuttings, air layering, and grafting.

LANDSCAPE VALUE: A most valuable, floriferous hybrid. Cultivars originating from this cross are excellent in form, beautiful, and free-flowering for a long period. Foliage resembles that of parent *C. japonica* and flowers those of parent *C. saluenensis.* Said to be more cold-hardy than either parent.

Plant may be observed at FIL, HUN, RKEW, STR, UBC, VDG.

*Camellia* × *williamsii* cultivars of interest:

*C.* × *williamsii* 'Anticipation'. Deep rose, large flowers, of very attractive peony form. Received RHS Award of Garden Merit.

*C.* × *williamsii* 'Donation' (*C. saluenensis* × *C. japonica* 'Donckelarii'). Clear pink, semidouble flowers; grows to 8 ft. high. Selected by Stephenson Clarke, Borde Hill, United Kingdom. Received RHS Award of Garden Merit.

*C.* × *williamsii* 'Hiraethyln'. Pale pink, perfect, single flowers; vigorous, compact, upright growth. Introduced at Bodnant, North Wales, in 1950. Received RHS Award of Garden Merit.

*C.* × *williamsii* 'J. C. Williams'. Lovely, medium pink flowers; long flowering season; vigorous habit with horizontal branches. First clone of *C.* × *williamsii* to be named. Selected at Caerhays Castle, Cornwall, United Kingdom, by J. C. Williams, in 1940. Received RHS Award of Garden Merit.

*C.* × *williamsii* 'Mary Christian'. Dark, clear pink, single flowers. One of the earliest cultivars of *C.* × *williamsii* to be selected at Caerhays Castle, Cornwall, United Kingdom; bred by J. C. Williams before 1942. Received RHS Award of Garden Merit.

*C.* × *williamsii* 'Salutation'. Pale pink flowers. Selected by Stephenson Clarke, Borde Hill, United Kingdom.

*C.* × *williamsii* 'St. Ewe'. Deep rose-pink, single flowers of medium size; vigorous, upright growth. Selected by J. C. Williams before 1947. Received RHS Award of Garden Merit.

*Camellia × williamsii* 'Donation' (L. Lee)

*Camellia × williamsii* 'Hiraethyln'
(N. Brewster)

*Camellia × williamsii* 'Mary Christian' (University of Washington)

*Camellia × williamsii* 'Mary Christian' (Greer
Gardens)

*Camellia × williamsii* 'Salutation' (N. Frink)

*Camellia × williamsii* 'St. Ewe' (L. Lee)

## *Caragana frutex* 'Globosa'
### RUSSIAN PEASHRUB

Fabaceae. USDA Zones 3–7. Native to southern Russia, Turkestan to Siberia. Introduced into cultivation in 1752.

DESCRIPTION: Deciduous shrub growing rather quickly to 2 ft. high and as wide, with dense, compact, globe-shaped habit.
*Leaves:* Elliptic to oblong, fine-textured, composed of 4 stalked leaflets, dark green, turning yellow-green in fall.
*Flowers:* Bright yellow, pealike flowers, 1 in. long.
*Fruit:* A pod, yellow-green, ultimately turning brown.

CULTURE: Needs sun; tolerates poor, alkaline soils, drought, salt, and wind.
*Disease and insect problems:* None serious; occasional damage from leafhopper; mite-resistant.
*Transplanting:* Easy.
*Propagation:* By seed.

LANDSCAPE VALUE: A tolerant shrub that should be used more in difficult growing conditions. Very hardy and extremely adaptable, although of limited ornamental value. Useful as hedge, screen, or windbreak in dry areas with tough growing conditions. Selected at Skinner Nursery, Dropmore, Manitoba.

Plant may be observed at AA, BBG, CBG, CIN, CUH, DEN, MOD, MNL, MRT, MUN, NEB, PAL, RBC, RKEW, SPR.

Related *Caragana* species of interest:

*C. aurantiaca.* Dwarf Peashrub. USDA Zones 5–7. Handsome small shrub with deep green foliage, growing to 4 ft. high. Rather graceful but bears triple spines. Golden flowers hang from underside of leaf stems. Initially cultivated in 1850 but lost and reintroduced in 1887.

*C. pygmaea.* Pygmy Peashrub. USDA Zones 4–7. Perhaps the most attractive of the peashrubs. Similar to *C. aurantiaca.* Yellow flowers bloom in May–June. Valued for its great tolerance of dry, alkaline soils. Introduced in 1751.

## *Carissa macrocarpa*
### NATAL PLUM

Synonym: *C. grandiflora.* Apocynaceae. USDA Zone 10. Native to South Africa.

DESCRIPTION: Broad-leaved evergreen growing at moderate rate to 8–18 ft. high, with bushy habit.
*Leaves:* Opposite, ovate, with 2-pronged spines to 1.5 in. and spurlike points to 3 in., short-stemmed, leathery, shiny, dark green, with milky juice.
*Flowers:* White, fragrant, with 5 petals, star-shaped, 1–2 in. across, in small clusters at branch tips; year-round.
*Fruit:* An ovoid to elliptic, scarlet berry, 1–2 in. long, with edible pulp.

CULTURE: Grows in sun or partial shade; not fussy about soil; tolerates drought, wet conditions, sand, salt; grows well on seacoast as well as inland.
*Disease and insect problems:* Tends to be insect-free in Hawaii; some mealy bug and scale in warm, humid areas.
*Transplanting:* Easy; shallow root system.
*Propagation:* By cuttings and seed.

LANDSCAPE VALUE: A handsome evergreen shrub outstanding for year-round white flowers with orange-blossom fragrance. Bloom followed by small, red, plumlike, cranberry-flavored, attractive fruit used for jellies, jams, and sauces, but eaten by birds as soon as it turns red. Often used in hedge plantings because of thick growth and sharp spines at branch nodes, which ward off dogs and cats. Do not plant too close to walks because of spines. Excellent hedge plant for seaside conditions and excellent accent plant. Gives Oriental feeling to garden when espaliered. Has many cultivars—some with larger flowers, some compact or dwarf, some without spines.

Plant may be observed at BOK, CBG, FAR, FOU, FUL, MMA, RKEW, WAI.

*Caragana frutex* 'Globosa' (Bailey Nurseries)

*Caragana frutex* 'Globosa' (G. Gates)

*Caragana pygmaea* (Bailey Nurseries)

*Carissa macrocarpa* (V. Lauritzen)

*Carissa macrocarpa* (V. Lauritzen)

*Carissa macrocarpa* (V. Lauritzen)

65

## *Carpenteria californica*
### BUSH ANEMONE

Saxifragaceae. USDA Zone 10. Native to California. Discovered by Colonel Fremont. Introduced to Europe in 1880.

DESCRIPTION: Broad-leaved evergreen to 3–6 ft. high, with many stems branching from base.
*Leaves:* 2–4.5 in. long, dark green above, whitish beneath.
*Flowers:* White, with 5 petals, anemonelike form, fragrant, with conspicuous yellow anthers, 1.5–3 in. wide, in terminal clusters of 3–7 flowers; May–August.

CULTURE: Grows in sun and light shade in a wide range of soils; tolerates salt air and, when established, drought, but not hot, dry sun.
*Disease and insect problems:* Few; occasional aphid; resistant to oak root fungus.
*Transplanting:* Deep root system.
*Propagation:* By seed (variable), by greenwood cuttings in summer, which root easily under mist, or by layering.

LANDSCAPE VALUE: One of the most splendid plants of the California flora, this handsome shrub is notable for its delightfully scented, large blossoms. Received RHS Award of Garden Merit.

Plant may be observed at BER, CUH, FUL, LAC, MIS, MMA, PAL, RAN, RKEW, SBB, STR, VDG, WIS.


## *Caryopteris* × *clandonensis*
### BLUEBEARD

Parentage: *C. incana* × *C. mongholica*. Verbenaceae. USDA Zones 5–8. Native to eastern Asia, China. Developed in 1933 by Arthur Simmonds, W. Clandon, United Kingdom.

DESCRIPTION: Deciduous shrub growing quickly to 2–3 ft. high, with full, to-the-ground, bushy habit.
*Leaves:* Opposite, ovate, 1.5 in. long and 0.5 in. wide, whitish beneath, thus appearing silver gray-green, no fall color.
*Flowers:* Blue, 0.75 in. long, in axillary or terminal cymes; August–frost.
*Fruit:* Dry, 4-valved, separating into winglike nutlets, not ornamental.
*Winter aspect:* Twiggy branching habit.

CULTURE: Needs full sun and well-drained, loose, modified clay to loam soil; tolerates some drought, but not wet conditions or soil compaction; should not be fertilized, which causes the plant to grow at the expense of flowering.
*Disease and insect problems:* None.
*Transplanting:* Easy.

*Propagation:* By softwood cuttings.

LANDSCAPE VALUE: A light, airy shrub excellent in perennial border or against rocks. Silvery foliage emits a subtle, pleasant fragrance when rubbed, and the true-blue flowers, which appear in late summer, attract butterflies. Dies to the ground in late spring as early budding out is generally killed by late frosts in USDA Zone 6. Blooms on new wood so can be cut back. Should be treated as herbaceous perennial in colder zones.

Plant may be observed at ABF, ATL, BBG, BC, BEA, BF, BIC, BSG, CAL, CBG, CIN, COX, CUH, DEN, FIL, GCC, HOL, LAC, LNG, LWD, MBG, MIS, MOR, MRT, NEW, OWG, PAL, PLF, RBC, RKEW, SPR, VDG, WIS, ZOO.

*Caryopteris* × *clandonensis* cultivars of interest:

*C.* × *clandonensis* 'Azure'. Bright azure-blue flowers.

*C.* × *clandonensis* 'Blue Mist'. Powder-blue flowers.

*C.* × *clandonensis* 'Dark Knight'. Deep blue-purple flowers.

*C.* × *clandonensis* 'Heavenly Blue'. Lovely pale blue flowers; more compact habit. Received RHS Award of Garden Merit.

*C.* × *clandonensis* 'Longwood Blue'. Spectacular, low mound of deep blue flowers enhanced by silver-gray foliage. Prolific bloomer; produces elegant, feathery, blue flowers in September. Smaller than species, sometimes reaching 3 ft. high and as wide. Prefers full sun and well-drained soil. Useful as low hedge or in rock garden. Superb for accenting borders. Uniform borders at Longwood Gardens perfect example of planting for best effect; Longwood staff chose best plant from original border of *Caryopteris* × *clandonensis* in 1983 and named it 'Longwood Blue.' Introduced into trade in 1987. Branches die back in winter; should be pruned severely in early spring.


## *Ceanothus* cultivars

Rhamnaceae. USDA Zones 7–8. Native to the United States. Introduced into cultivation in 1888.

DESCRIPTION: Broad-leaved evergreen growing at moderate rate to 2–5 ft. high and 10–12 ft. wide, with mounded habit.
*Leaves:* Alternate, oval, 1 in. long, dark green, with distinct venation.
*Flowers:* Medium to dark blue, in spikelike clusters 3–5 in. across; March–April/May.
*Fruit:* A 3-lobed capsule.

CULTURE: Grows in sun in a wide range of alkaline to neutral soils; tolerates drought and light wind; requires good drainage.
*Disease and insect problems:* Occasional whitefly and aphid

*Carpenteria californica* (University of Washington)

*Carpenteria californica* (University of Washington)

*Caryopteris* × *clandonensis* 'Longwood Blue' (J. Elsley)

*Caryopteris* × *clandonensis* 'Heavenly Blue' (J. C. Raulston)

*Ceanothus* 'Frosty Blue' (P. K. Thompson)

on new growth; root rot caused by water-mold organisms.
*Transplanting:* Not difficult; deep root system.
*Propagation:* By softwood cuttings in August, and by seed, given hot water treatment followed by 3 months stratification.

LANDSCAPE VALUE: An extremely attractive specimen, covered in spring by beautiful flowers in various shades of blue. Excellent as foundation shrub or as soft hedge when trimmed. Can be grown on a wall, where it reaches 8 ft. or more. Described as early as 1888 but little cultivated until the Santa Barbara Botanic Garden realized its value. A most satisfactory, handsome shrub, one of the hardiest of the evergreen species. Good for both seaside and dry areas. Often short-lived (10–12 years) and dies if watered too heavily in summer.

Plant may be observed at LAC, RAN, RKEW, SBB, WIN, WIS.

*Ceanothus* cultivars of interest: Most of these cannot be related to a species with any degree of certainty. Selected cultivars are sold in the trade under these names.

C. 'Concha'. Dark blue flowers borne in 1 in. clusters from red buds. Grows to 6–7 ft. high and 8–10 ft. wide, with dense habit and 1 in. long, dark green leaves. Attractive plant, hardy to 15°F.

C. 'Dark Star'. Dark blue-violet flowers in 1.5 in. clusters. Grows to 5–6 ft. high and 8–10 ft. wide, with dark green, 0.25 in. long leaves. Similar to 'Julia Phelps.'

C. 'Frosty Blue'. Sky-blue flowers, tinged with white, in 2.5–3 in. clusters. Grows to 10–12 ft. high and 12–20 ft. wide, with dark green, 2.5 in. long leaves. Sturdy stems permit this cultivar to be shaped as a small tree. Tolerates heavy soils.

C. 'Joyce Coulter'. Medium blue flowers in 3–5 in. clusters. Grows to 2–5 ft. high and 10–12 ft. wide, with medium green leaves and mounded habit.

C. 'Julia Phelps'. Dark indigo-blue flowers in 1 in. clusters. Good grower and bloomer, reaching 4.5–7 ft. high and 10–12 ft. wide, with medium green leaves. Densely and intricately branched.

C. 'Puget Blue'. Deep blue flowers borne in large, congested clusters. Blooms early, in March–April, with *Mahonia*, *Dendromecon*, and *Fremontodendron*. Grows to 6 ft. high, with open branching habit and dark green, deeply furrowed leaves. More tolerant of garden conditions than *C. impressus*. Originated before 1945 at the University of Washington, Seattle. Received RHS Award of Garden Merit.

Related *Ceanothus* hybrid of interest:

C. × *pallidus* (*C. delilianus* × *C. ovatus*) var. *roseus*. USDA Zones 6–8. Pale pink flowers in short panicles on long, leafy branchlets; leaves are ovate-oblong, obtuse at base, serrulate, 2.5–3.5 in. long, larger than those of other *Ceanothus* species. Shrub grows to 2–2.5 ft. high. Prune each spring to within 2–3 buds of previous year's wood since it flowers on current season's growth. Known in cultivation since 1830. A plant acquired by the Arnold Arboretum in 1889 from the Lemoine Nursery, Nancy, France.

# *Cephalotaxus harringtonia* 'Duke Gardens'
## JAPANESE PLUM YEW

Cephalotaxaceae. USDA Zones 6–9. Introduced into cultivation in Europe in 1861.

DESCRIPTION: Evergreen conifer growing slowly to 2–3 ft. high and 4–5 ft. wide, with spreading habit.
*Leaves:* Sharply acuminate, sickle-shaped, pointing upward, 1–2.5 in. long and 0.1 in. wide, dark green, very glossy above, with grayish bands beneath, aromatic to bitter odor.
*Winter aspect:* Gray, exfoliating bark; opposite, outspread, and somewhat nodding branches, borne in tiers.

CULTURE: Grows best in partial shade; tolerates sun, but color not as good; prefers moist, well-drained loam or sand with a pH of 6.5–7.5; tolerates drought when established, but not wind.
*Disease and insect problems:* None serious.
*Transplanting:* Easy, in container.
*Propagation:* By cuttings in December–March; difficult.

LANDSCAPE VALUE: A small, handsome shrub with good color year-round. A sport of *C. harringtonia* 'Fastigiata'; originated at Sarah P. Duke Gardens, Durham, North Carolina. Tolerant of heat; thus excellent for southern gardens. Its unique texture complements needled conifers; use in mixed groupings, massed plantings, or as an accent plant.

Plant may be observed at AA, ATL, BBG, BOK, BSG, CAL, CBG, CUH, DUK, LWD, MOR, NCS, NEW, RKEW, SAB, SKY, UBC, USN, VDG.

Other *Cephalotaxus harringtonia* cultivars of interest:

C. *harringtonia* 'Fastigiata'. Grows slowly to a sturdy 10 ft. high and 7 ft. wide; rotund, columnar habit, with branches steeply upright and needles spirally arranged.

C. *harringtonia* 'Prostrata'. Slow growing, with low, spreading habit; 30-year-old plant only 2–3 ft. high and as wide. Received Pennsylvania Horticultural Society Gold Medal (Styer Award) in 1994.

Ceanothus 'Joyce Coulter'
(Monrovia Nursery)

Ceanothus 'Julia Phelps' (E. Paine)

Ceanothus 'Puget Blue' (J. Elsley)

Ceanothus × pallidus var. roseus (J. C. Raulston)

Cephalotaxus harringtonia 'Duke Gardens' (N. Brewster)

Cephalotaxus harringtonia 'Duke Gardens' (N. Brewster)

## *Cercis chinensis* 'Alba'
CHINESE REDBUD

Fabaceae. USDA Zones 6–9. Species native to central China. Cultivar introduced in the 1980s from Japanese nurseries by Brookside Gardens, Wheaton, Maryland.

DESCRIPTION: Deciduous shrub growing slowly to 8–10 ft. high, with erect, multistemmed habit.
*Leaves:* Deeply cordate, 3–5 in. long and as wide, glossy, dark green above.
*Flowers:* White, 0.75 in. long, on naked stems; early spring.

CULTURE: Grows in sun and shade; prefers deep, fertile, moist, well-drained acid or alkaline soil, but adjusts to drier soils; tolerates wind, but not wet conditions.
*Disease and insect problems:* Canker, verticillium wilt.
*Transplanting:* Balled and burlapped, when young; resents moving when established.
*Propagation:* By softwood cuttings in summer or by grafting.

LANDSCAPE VALUE: Useful as specimen, in the shrub border, or naturalized in woodland with filtered sun. Attractive in informal settings or interplanted with Dogwoods. Can be pruned severely; produces new shoots from old wood. Blooms 10 days earlier than the native redbud, *C. canadensis.* Grows well in southern climates.

Related *C. chinensis* cultivar of interest:

*C. chinensis* 'Avondale'. USDA Zones 6–9. Selected seedling from Avondale, Auckland, New Zealand. Deep purple flowers appear on naked stems and on large limbs. Grows to 9–10 ft. high.

Related *Cercis* species and cultivar of interest:

*C. canadensis* subsp. *mexicana.* USDA Zones 6–9. Introduced into cultivation in eastern United States by Stephen Burns of Vine & Branch Nursery. Flowers lighter in color than those of *C. canadensis.* Fruit is a brown pod, appearing after leaves in fall; not ornamental. Useful for small gardens. Plant in containers in northerly latitudes. Tolerates hot, very dry weather.

*C. reniformis* 'Texas White'. USDA Zones 7–9. Seedling found near Fort Worth, Texas, in the late 1960s or early 1970s. Grows to 12–18 ft. high, with white flowers and glossy, rounded, thick-textured leaves. Tolerates hot, very dry weather.

## *Chaenomeles speciosa*
FLOWERING QUINCE

Rosaceae. USDA Zones 5–8. Native to eastern Asia.

DESCRIPTION: Deciduous shrub growing 1 ft. per year to 5–10 ft. high and as wide, with rounded, bushy, variable, spreading habit.
*Leaves:* Alternate, ovate to oblong, mostly glabrous, sharply serrated, 1.5–3 in. long, bronze when unfolding, then glossy, deep green.
*Flowers:* A wide range of colors, from white to pink to scarlet red depending on cultivar, bowl-shaped, 1–1.5 in. wide, with 5 petals and 20 or more stamens, before foliage; spring.
*Fruit:* A hard, quincelike, yellow-green pome, in fall, persisting until frost.
*Winter aspect:* Shiny, brown bark; dense branching habit.

CULTURE: Needs full sun; likes loamy soil; tolerates wind and drought, but not shade.
*Disease and insect problems:* Some leaf spot caused by overabundant rainfall; scale, mite (not usually a problem); chlorosis in soils with high pH.
*Transplanting:* Easy despite deep, invasive root system.
*Propagation:* By roots, cuttings of half-ripe wood, or seeds, stratified and sown in spring.

LANDSCAPE VALUE: A tough, hardy shrub useful for a dense hedge, specimen plant, or espalier. Early spring blooms are good for forcing and flower arranging. Dense habit makes it good bird shelter and screen. When grown in full sun, the profuse, colorful bloom creates a delightful flower display.

Plant may be observed at AA, BBG, BF, CAL, CBG, CIN, LNG, LWD, RKEW, VDG.

Other *Chaenomeles speciosa* cultivars of interest:

*C. speciosa* 'Moerloosi' ['Apple Blossom']. White with attractive pink edge. Received RHS Award of Garden Merit.

*C. speciosa* 'Rubra'. Deep, rich red flowers; more open habit than species.

*C. speciosa* 'Simonii'. Small, blood-red, semidouble flowers; semihorizontal habit.

*C. speciosa* 'Toyo-Nishiki'. Unusual combination of white, pink, and light red flowers on same branches; upright habit.

*Cercis chinensis* 'Alba' (L. Lee)

*Cercis chinensis* 'Avondale' (J. Elsley)

*Cercis canadensis* subsp. *mexicana* (J. C. Raulston)

*Cercis reniformis* 'Texas White' (J. Elsley)

*Chaenomeles speciosa* (G. Gates)

*Chaenomeles speciosa* 'Toyo-Nishiki' (J. Poor)

71

# *Chaenomeles* × *superba*
## FLOWERING QUINCE

Parentage: *C. japonica* × *C. speciosa*. Rosaceae. USDA Zones 5–8. Native to China. Discovered before 1880. Introduced into cultivation pre-1956 by Michael Dirr.

DESCRIPTION: Deciduous shrub growing at moderate rate to 5–6 ft. high, with dense, twiggy, suckering habit.
*Leaves:* Alternate, obovate, 1.5 in. long and 0.75 in. wide, shiny, dark green, shiny negligible fall color.
*Flowers:* From white to pink, orange, and crimson, single to double, 2 in. across; mid-April.
*Fruit:* Apple-shaped, larger than that of *C. japonica* and ripening later.
*Winter aspect:* Densely branched, twiggy, thorny habit.

CULTURE: Needs full sun or very light shade for best flowering; prefers modified clay soil; does not tolerate wet conditions, drought, or high pH.
*Disease and insect problems:* Typical rosaceous problems; can defoliate in too much rain but hard to kill.
*Transplanting:* Not difficult.
*Propagation:* By cuttings in August, or layering of suckers.

LANDSCAPE VALUE: Very attractive in spring with its lovely flowers, among largest of the Quince blooms. Excellent cut flowers, though blossoms appear mostly at branch axils. Occasionally blooms in fall. Can be planted as specimen, hedge, or border. Fine complement to taller shrubs. First cultivar developed about 1900 by O. Froebel, Zurich, Switzerland.

Plant may be observed at AA, BBG, BF, BIR, BRK, CAL, CBG, CHK, CIN, COX, CUH, DEN, DIX, HOL, HUN, IES, LNG, MBG, MIS, MRT, NEB, NEW, PAL, RKEW, STG, VDG.

*Chaenomeles* × *superba* cultivars of interest:

*C.* × *superba* 'Cameo'. Light apricot-pink, double flowers; more weatherproof than the single quinces.

*C.* × *superba* 'Fascination'. Very flat, deep scarlet red flowers; small applelike fruit; introduced in 1957 by J. Mosse.

*C.* × *superba* 'Fire Dance'. Glowing red, large single flowers; introduced in 1944 by Clarke.

*C.* × *superba* 'Jet Trail'. White flowers; low, mounded habit.

*C.* × *superba* 'Nicoline'. Crimson-red, large, single to semi-double flowers; introduced in 1954.

*C.* × *superba* 'Rowallane'. Bright, deep red, large, single flowers; introduced in 1920.

*C.* × *superba* 'Texas Scarlet'. Watermelon-red, large, flat, open, single flowers; introduced in 1951.

# *Chamaecyparis obtusa* 'Nana Gracilis'
## HINOKI FALSE CYPRESS

Cupressaceae. USDA Zones 4–8. Species native to Japan and Formosa. Cultivar introduced into United Kingdom in 1861 by J. G. Veitch.

DESCRIPTION: Evergreen conifer growing slowly to 6 ft. high and 3–4 ft. wide, with pyramidal habit when young becoming broadly conical with age.
*Leaves:* Blunt, thick, closely pressed, in 2 sizes: larger are 0.08 in. and bowl-shaped, smaller are 0.04 in.; shiny, dark green above, with glaucous (coated with a bloom) lines beneath.
*Fruit:* A round, brown cone, 0.5 in. diameter.
*Winter aspect:* Reddish brown, shredding bark.

CULTURE: Grows in sun and light shade; prefers good, moist loam with a neutral pH of 6.5–7.0; needs protection from wind.
*Disease and insect problems:* Occasional bagworm.
*Transplanting:* Easy, container-grown.
*Propagation:* By cuttings in September–January; difficult.

LANDSCAPE VALUE: A graceful shrub with cupped sprays of dark green foliage. Sufficiently diminutive for rock gardens; unique, rugged form makes it excellent for use as specimen. Hardy for containers if properly irrigated and fertilized. Clip tips of branches on older plants to induce denser branching. Yellow-needled cultivars of *C. obtusa* require partial shade; direct sun scalds leaves.

Plant may be observed at AA, ABF, ATL, BBG, BC, BEA, BF, BLO, BSG, CAL, CBG, CIN, COX, CUH, DAW, DEN, DUK, GCC, HOL, HUN, IES, LWD, MBG, MOD, MRT, NCS, NEW, OWG, PAL, PLF, RHO, RKEW, SEC, SPR, STG, STR, USN, VDG.

Other *Chamaecyparis obtusa* cultivars of interest:

*C. obtusa* 'Juniperoides'. Globose and open, with fan-shaped branches; to 1 ft. high. Introduced in 1923 by Rogers & Son.

*C. obtusa* 'Kosteri'. Light green, fine-textured foliage; to 5 ft. high, with conical habit and ascending branches. Introduced in 1915 by M. Koster and Zoom.

*C. obtusa* 'Nana'. Branches spreading and needles bright green, turning brownish in fall and winter; branchlets distinctive orange-brown. To 3 ft. high and as wide. Introduced in 1861 from Japan.

*C. obtusa* 'Nana Lutea'. Pure golden-yellow during entire season. Compact and open-branched, to 2.5 ft. high.

*Chaenomeles* × *superba* 'Cameo' (N. Brewster)

*Chaenomeles* × *superba* 'Cameo' (N. Brewster)

*Chaenomeles* × *superba* 'Jet Trail' (N. Brewster)

*Chaenomeles* × *superba* 'Rowallane'
(Winterthur Gardens)

*Chaenomeles* × *superba* 'Rowallane'
(Winterthur Gardens)

*Chamaecyparis obtusa* 'Nana Gracilis'
(N. Brewster)

*Chamaecyparis obtusa* 'Kosteri' (N. Brewster)

*Chamaecyparis obtusa* 'Nana Lutea' (S. Martin)

## *Chamaecyparis pisifera* 'Filifera Nana'
### THREADLEAF JAPANESE FALSE CYPRESS

Cupressaceae. USDA Zones 4–8. Species native to Japan. Cultivar grown before 1897 in Tharandt Forstgarten, Saxony.

DESCRIPTION: Evergreen conifer growing very slowly to 3 ft. high and 3–4 ft. wide, with dense, mounded habit.
*Leaves:* Scalelike, facial needles boat-shaped, sharply acuminate, filamentous, glossy, dark green with white, oblong marks beneath.
*Fruit:* A globose cone, 0.25 in. across, clustered, numerous.
*Winter aspect:* Smooth, reddish brown bark, peeling in thin strips; nodding habit with thin, drooping branchlets.

CULTURE: Grows in sun and partial shade; prefers loam with a pH of 6.5–7.0; tolerates drought when established, but not wet conditions; needs protection from drying winds; performs well in regions with high humidity.
*Disease and insect problems:* Few; occasional bagworm.
*Transplanting:* Easy, container-grown.
*Propagation:* By cuttings in October–December, rooted in sand and peat.

LANDSCAPE VALUE: An excellent shrub for rock gardens, small spaces such as terraces, and as accent in the shrub border. Exhibits complex, interesting foliage pattern. Many blue and yellow dwarf cultivars of *C. pisifera* are available.

Plant may be observed at AA, ATL, BC, BF, BSG, CBG, CUH, DEN, DIN, DUK, HOL, IES, LNG, MIS, MNL, MRT, NCS, NEW, OWG, PLF, RKEW, STG, STR, USN, VDG.

Other *Chamaecyparis pisifera* cultivars of interest:

*C. pisifera* 'Boulevard'. Blue in summer, gray-blue in winter; to 10 ft. or more high, with narrow, pyramidal habit.

*C. pisifera* 'Gold Spangle'. Light yellow with darker yellow filaments; to 9 ft. high, with conical habit. Introduced in 1900 by Zoster & Zonen Nursery, Boskoop, Netherlands.

*C. pisifera* 'Squarrosa Intermedia'. Needlelike, feathery, blue foliage, with dark green scales; to 6 ft. high, with loose, globose habit. Origin unknown.

## *Chimonanthus praecox*
### FRAGRANT WINTERSWEET

Calycanthaceae. USDA Zones 6–9. Native to China. Introduced into cultivation in 1766.

DESCRIPTION: Deciduous shrub growing slowly to 10–15 ft. high and 8–12 ft. wide (smaller in colder regions), with multistemmed habit.
*Leaves:* Lanceolate, apex acuminate, 2–5 in. long and 1–2.75 in. wide, glossy, green above, lighter beneath, turning yellow in fall.
*Flowers:* Transparent yellow, shading to brownish red at center, 0.75–1 in. across, very fragrant, on bare branches of previous summer's shoots; January–February in warmer regions, March in colder regions.
*Fruit:* Not ornamental.

CULTURE: Grows in sun and partial shade; prefers loam with good drainage; tolerates wet conditions.
*Disease and insect problems:* None serious.
*Transplanting:* Easy, balled and burlapped or container-grown.
*Propagation:* Easy, by seed in May–June; harder by cuttings in late July; can be layered.

LANDSCAPE VALUE: Valued for its very fragrant flowers and winter bloom; often in flower with snow on the ground. Can be used in shrub borders but is displayed to greatest advantage if grown as specimen or against background of low walls. Cut branches extremely attractive for indoor display. Prune old canes after blooming; leggy plants can be pruned to 8–12 in. from ground in late winter.

Plant may be observed at AA, ABF, ATL, BBG, BER, BIR, BRK, BSG, CAL, DIX, DUK, FIL, LAC, MCG, MIS, MOR, MUN, NCS, NEW, PAL, PLF, RKEW, STR, UBC, USN, VDG, WIS.

*Chimonanthus praecox* cultivar of interest:

*C. praecox* 'Luteus'. Unstained flowers of clear, waxy yellow, larger and opening later than those of species. Received RHS Award of Garden Merit.

Related *Chimonanthus* species of interest:

*C. nitens*. USDA Zone 8. White, solitary, axillary flowers. Leaves elliptic-lanceolate, with rounded base, 2.75–4 in. long and 1.25–1.5 in. wide. Introduced from Japan in 1930.

*Chamaecyparis pisifera* 'Filifera Nana' (E. Hasselkus)

*Chamaecyparis pisifera* 'Boulevard' (G. Koller)

*Chamaecyparis pisifera* 'Gold Spangle' (S. March)

*Chimonanthus praecox* (N. Frink)

*Chimonanthus praecox* 'Luteus'
(J. C. Raulston)

*Chimonanthus praecox* (B. Yinger)

# Choisya ternata
## MEXICAN ORANGE

Rosaceae. USDA Zones 8–9. Native to Mexico. Introduced into cultivation in 1866.

DESCRIPTION: Evergreen shrub growing at moderate rate when young, more slowly with age, to 6–9 ft. high, with dense, rounded, dome-shaped habit.
*Leaves:* Opposite, 3–6 in. long, usually composed of 3 obovate leaflets 1.5–3 in. long, rich green, pungent odor when crushed.
*Flowers:* White, fragrant, 1–1.5 in wide, in flat-topped clusters at the ends of stems; May–June.
*Fruit:* Not significant.
*Winter aspect:* Bright green stems.

CULTURE: Grows in full sun or shade; prefers light, acid loam; needs moist, well-drained soil and open but protected area with good air circulation.
*Disease and insect problems:* Few.
*Transplanting:* Easy.
*Propagation:* By cuttings.

LANDSCAPE VALUE: A good specimen in city plantings. Handsome in flower and foliage. Long bloom period and orange fragrance enhance attractiveness. May die back in harsh winters but usually rejuvenates itself the following spring; best to cut back to within 18 in. of ground after 3–4 years. Received RHS Award of Garden Merit.

Plant may be observed at ATL, BBG, FIL, HUN, NCS, RKEW, STR, VDG, WIS.

*Choisya ternata* cultivar of interest:

C. *ternata* 'Sundance'. USDA Zones 7–9. Notable for its fragrant, white flowers and golden foliage. Emerging foliage is brilliant yellow to chartreuse. Introduced in 1866 by Bressingham Gardens, United Kingdom. Received RHS Award of Garden Merit.

# Cistus × skanbergii
## ROCK ROSE

Parentage: *C. monspeliensis* × *C. parviflorus*. Cistaceae. USDA Zones 8–9. Native to the region around the Mediterranean Sea.

DESCRIPTION: Broad-leaved evergreen growing at moderate rate to 1.5 ft. high and as wide.
*Leaves:* Lanceolate, to 1.5 in. long and 0.4 in. wide, gray-green.
*Flowers:* Light pink to apricot-pink, saucer-shaped, 2 in. across; late spring.

CULTURE: Grows in sun in a variety of alkaline soils; tolerates drought, ocean winds, salt spray, and desert heat.
*Disease and insect problems:* None serious.
*Transplanting:* Easy; deep root system.
*Propagation:* By seed, layering, and cuttings under glass.

LANDSCAPE VALUE: A low, neat, unusually compact plant, excellent for sunny, dry, or wild areas. An ideal rock garden plant in the West, this drought-resistant shrub requires little care. Received RHS Award of Garden Merit.

Plant may be observed at FUL, HUN, LAC, RKEW, STR, VDG, WIS.

Related *Cistus* species of interest:

C. × *purpureus* (C. *ladanifer* × C. *villosus*). USDA Zone 8. Reddish purple flowers, 2.5–3 in. across, with spots of dark red at the base of petals, borne in terminal clusters, usually three together, in June. Best of its color in cultivation. Plant grows to 3–4 ft. high with rounded habit. Dull gray-green, obovate leaves, 1–2 in. long and 0.4–0.6 in. wide. Introduced before 1790. Received RHS Award of Garden Merit.

C. *salvifolius*. USDA Zone 8. White flowers, 1.5–2 in. across, with yellow stain at base of each petal, borne solitary or three together, in June. Grows to 2 ft. high, with compact habit. Leaves oval-ovate, 0.5–1.5 in. long and 0.5–1 in. wide, coated with down. Introduced in 1548.

Related *Cistus* cultivar of interest:

C. 'Silver Pink' (C. *laurifolius* × C. *villosus*). Grows to 2.5 ft. high, with neat, bushy habit. Raised by Hillier & Sons, it was first shown in 1919 and received an RHS Award of Merit. Flowers of pure silver pink, about 3 in. wide, with yellow stamens in center, distinct against dark green leaves. Grow in rich, well-drained soil for best results.

*Choisya ternata* (J. Apel)

*Choisya ternata* 'Sundance' (J. C. Raulston)

*Cistus* × *skanbergii* (P. K. Thompson)

*Cistus* × *skanbergii* (P. K. Thompson)

*Cistus salvifolius* (N. Brewster)

## *Clerodendrum trichotomum* var. *fargesii*
HARLEQUIN GLORY BOWER

Verbenaceae. USDA Zones 6–8. Native to Sichuan, China. Introduced to France by Père Farges; first raised by Maurice de Vilmorin in 1898.

DESCRIPTION: Deciduous shrub growing rapidly to 10–20 ft. high, with widespread habit.
*Leaves:* Opposite, ovate, coarse, with scattered hairs on both surfaces, purple-red when very young, turning glossy green.
*Flowers:* White, fragrant, small but numerous, in wide corymbs; July–September.
*Fruit:* Pale blue, ultimately black, 0.25 in. across, surrounded by a green, star-shaped calyx that turns pink and remains colorful after fruit drops.

CULTURE: Grows in sun and partial shade; prefers open, loamy, well-drained soil.
*Disease and insect problems:* Occasional whitefly, spider mite, mealy bug.
*Transplanting:* Easy.
*Propagation:* By seed in spring, root cuttings, or young suckers, which often originate from roots.

LANDSCAPE VALUE: A handsome, vigorous, late-flowering shrub with very dense foliage and effective, colorful fruit display. Not as showy as the species but hardier. Leaves have an unpleasant odor when crushed. Received RHS Award of Garden Merit.

Plant may be observed at BER, BSG, CBG, LWD, MOR, NEW, OWG, PAL, RKEW, VDG, WIS.

Related *Clerodendrum* species of interest:

C. *bungei*. USDA Zones 7–8. Lower growing, less cold-hardy; returns quickly following top-killing in winter; bright red flowers in clusters. Received RHS Award of Garden Merit.

C. *ugandense*. USDA Zone 9. Evergreen native to tropical Africa; can reach 10 ft. high; has glossy, dark green, elliptic leaves to 4.5 in. long; corollas with one violet-blue and three light blue lobes.

## *Clethra alnifolia*
SUMMERSWEET
SWEET PEPPER BUSH

Clethraceae. USDA Zones 5–8. Native to the United States, from Maine to Florida. Introduced into cultivation 1770.

DESCRIPTION: Deciduous shrub to 3–8 ft. high, with oval, round-topped, erect, suckering habit.
*Leaves:* Alternate, simple, obovate-oblong, 1.6–4 in. long and 0.5–2 in. wide, sharply serrate, glossy, deep green, turning yellow in fall.
*Flowers:* White, pink, or rose, depending on cultivar, in fragrant panicles, 2–6 in. long; July–August.
*Fruit:* A persistent spike of seed capsules.
*Winter aspect:* Brown, pubescent bark; seed capsules; upright, branching habit.

CULTURE: Grows in sun and shade in loam or sand with a pH of 4.5–7.0; tolerates wet conditions, drought, and salt.
*Disease and insect problems:* None serious; chlorosis when soil pH exceeds 7.5; spider mite may occur in very dry conditions.
*Transplanting:* Fairly easy; somewhat invasive root system.
*Propagation:* By cuttings in summer, rooted in sand and peat.

LANDSCAPE VALUE: An excellent plant of year-round interest for its showy, fragrant, late-summer flowers, fall color, and winter habit. Upright growth makes it ideal for narrow spaces, in perennial borders, and around foundations. Most effective in massed plantings and in prominent areas where its many attributes can be fully appreciated; excellent for container growing. Good as understory plant, but also does well in sun. Flourishes in moist areas and tolerates dry sites. Needs acid soil. Attracts rabbits in winter months, which should be considered when choosing this species for locations with large rabbit populations.

Plant may be observed at AA, ABF, ATL, BBG, BC, BEA, BER, BF, BIR, BSG, CAL, CBG, CIN, CUH, DAW, DEN, DIX, DUK, GCC, GIW, HOL, HOU, IES, LNG, LWD, MBG, MIS, MNL, MRT, MTC, MUN, NCS, NEW, OWG, PAL, PLF, POW, RBC, RHO, RKEW, SEC, SKY, SPR, STG, UBC, VDG, WIN, WIS.

*Clethra alnifolia* cultivars of interest:

C. *alnifolia* 'Hummingbird'. White-flowered shrub with attractive, glossy foliage. Flowers more heavily than other named cultivars. Delightfully fragrant, white flowers are produced freely July through August when little else is in bloom. Grows to 3–4 ft. high, with compact, full habit. Perfect for the small garden; unlike the species, 'Hummingbird' remains in low mound. The original plant, collected by Fred Galle, Callaway Gardens, on the

*Clerodendrum trichotomum* var. *fargesii* (J. Elsley)

*Clerodendrum trichotomum* var. *fargesii* (G. Gates)

*Clerodendrum trichotomum* var. *fargesii* (J. Apel)

*Clethra alnifolia* (G. Koller)

*Clethra alnifolia* 'Pink Spire' (Wayside Gardens)

*Clethra alnifolia* continued

banks of Hummingbird Lake, was less than 4 ft. high after 33 years. Propagation is extremely easy by softwood cuttings. Named and registered by Richard Feist of Ohio State University. Received Pennsylvania Horticultural Society Gold Medal (Styer Award) in 1994.

C. *alnifolia* 'Paniculata'. White flowers in terminal panicles, 6 in. long. Superior cultivar with greater vigor and showier flowers than species. Received RHS Award of Garden Merit.

C. *alnifolia* 'Pink Spire'. Pink Spire Summersweet, White Alder. Soft pink flowers open from buds that vary from pink to rose; blooms do not fade to white. Has darker buds and flowers than 'Rosea' and glossier foliage than the species.

C. *alnifolia* 'Rosea'. Dark pink flower buds open to pink blooms that fade to paler pink. Later bloom and glossier leaves than the species; blooms for 2 months in the proper conditions. Holds flower color better in shade.

Related *Clethra* species of interest:

C. *acuminata*. Cinnamon Bark Clethra. Native to the mountains of Virginia, Georgia, and Alabama; introduced into cultivation in 1806. Best in USDA Zones 6–7, but grows in USDA Zones 5 and 8 with some shade. Medium-sized shrub reaching 7–12 ft. high in cultivation (up to 20 ft. in the wild) and 4–8 ft. wide, with dark green foliage. White, fragrant flowers appear in slender, terminal racemes, 4–8 in. long. Very attractive, cinnamon-brown bark is sometimes exfoliating. Will grow in rocky, dry, gravelly soil.

# *Clethra barbinervis*
## TREE CLETHRA

Clethraceae. USDA Zones 7–8. Native to Japan. Introduced into cultivation in 1870.

DESCRIPTION: Deciduous shrub growing quickly when young to 30 ft. high.
*Leaves:* Obovate, acuminate, sharply serrate, pubescent, clustered at the ends of branches, to 5 in. long, red and yellow in fall.
*Flowers:* White, horizontally nodding, somewhat fragrant, in panicled racemes 4–6 in. long; summer–autumn.
*Fruit:* A persistent spike of seed capsules.
*Winter aspect:* Smooth, polished, exfoliating gray-brown bark; seed capsules; upright habit with horizontal branching.

CULTURE: Grows in shade in loam and sand; tolerates wet conditions. Needs ample moisture and fertile soil.
*Disease and insect problems:* None serious.

*Transplanting:* Fairly easy.
*Propagation:* By softwood cuttings and seed, which is easy to germinate.

LANDSCAPE VALUE: A large shrub or small tree best used as a specimen or in a tall hedge. Provides year-round interest with its uniquely formed flowers in late summer, red and yellow fall color, very ornamental bark, and candelabra-like branching habit, which accentuates striking appearance of flowers. Flowers more horizontal, more pendulous, and not as fragrant as those of *C. alnifolia*. Not fully hardy in northerly climates, where it dies back. Received RHS Award of Garden Merit.

Plant may be observed at AA, ABF, ATL, BBG, BF, BSG, CIN, DUK, GIW, HOL, LWD, MOR, MRT, MUN, NCS, NEW, RKEW, STR, VDG, WIS.

# *Comptonia peregrina*
## SWEET FERN

Myricaceae. USDA Zones 2–5. Native to North America from Nova Scotia south to North Carolina, Indiana, and Michigan. Introduced into cultivation in 1714.

DESCRIPTION: Deciduous shrub to 2–8 ft. high, with upright habit, spreading rapidly once established.
*Leaves:* Alternate, linear-oblong, deeply pinnately notched, 4.5 in. long, lustrous, dark olive-green.
*Flowers:* Yellow-green, not conspicuous.
*Fruit:* An olive-brown, burrlike nutlet.
*Winter aspect:* Slender, erect branches; rounded outline with age.

CULTURE: Grows in full sun or light shade; tolerates wind, drought, and wet conditions, including seashore; thrives in well-drained, acid loam or sand; fixes its own nitrogen, thus adapts to poor, infertile soils.
*Disease and insect problems:* None serious.
*Transplanting:* Difficult; shallow root system; best to use container-grown plants.
*Propagation:* By cuttings of young shoots (3 in. long), root cuttings in late winter or early spring, or division of clumps with large root balls; difficult by seed.

LANDSCAPE VALUE: Particularly suited for naturalistic areas and for use in holding banks and seashore plantings. The attractive foliage is wonderfully aromatic.

Plant may be observed at AA, ABF, ATL, BBG, CBG, CUH, DAW, DUK, GIW, HOL, IES, LNG, LWD, MRT, MTC, NCA, NCS, NEW, PLF, RBC, RKEW, SKY, USN.

*Comptonia peregrina* variety of interest:

C. *peregrina* var. *asplenifolia*. Unique foliage with deeper serrations than the species.

*Clethra barbinervis* (G. Koller)

*Clethra barbinervis* (B. Yinger)

*Comptonia peregrina* (D. Brennan)

*Comptonia peregrina* (E. Sharp)

*Comptonia peregrina* (A. Bussewitz)

## Cornus mas
### CORNELIAN CHERRY

Cornaceae. USDA Zones 5–8. Native to Europe and western Asia. Cultivated for centuries in United Kingdom.

DESCRIPTION: Deciduous shrub to 20 ft. high and 15 ft. wide, with rounded, multistemmed habit.
*Leaves:* Opposite, simple, ovate to elliptic, 2.5–4 in. long and 0.75–1.5 in. wide, deep green, with non-ornamental purple tinge in fall.
*Flowers:* Yellow, tiny; February–March in cool climates, earlier in warmer regions.
*Fruit:* A conspicuous, cherry-shaped drupe, bright red, edible but not delicious.
*Winter aspect:* Gray-brown bark.

CULTURE: Grows in shade, but prefers sun, where it is fuller and more attractive; likes well-drained soil with a pH of 6–8.
*Disease and insect problems:* None serious.
*Transplanting:* Easy.
*Propagation:* By seed and softwood cuttings.

LANDSCAPE VALUE: Valuable for its early bloom. Tiny, yellow, tufted flowers are produced profusely on bare stems, providing a mass of color when other shrubs are dormant. Very effective when planted in groups, but also useful as specimen. Fruit may be used for jams. Received RHS Award of Garden Merit.

Plant may be observed at AA, BBG, BEA, BIC, BOE, BSG, CBG, CIN, DEN, HOL, LNG, MBG, MCG, MIS, MOR, MRT, NCS, SEC, UBC, WIS.

*Cornus mas* cultivars of interest:

*C. mas* 'Aurea'. Gold foliage, more prominent early in season; fades somewhat in warmer weather. Smaller and less hardy than the species.
*C. mas* 'Flava'. Large, attractive, yellow fruit.
*C. mas* 'Golden Glory'. Yellow flowers in abundance in very early spring. Good shrub for cooler climates, flowering when little else is in bloom.
*C. mas* 'Variegata'. Handsome foliage bordered with creamy white margins; smaller and more free-fruiting than the species.

## Cornus sericea 'Silver & Gold'
### RED OSIER DOGWOOD

Synonym: *C. stolonifera*. Cornaceae. USDA Zones 3–8. Species native to the United States. Cultivar introduced in 1986 by Richard Lighty, Mt. Cuba Center, Greenville, Delaware.

DESCRIPTION: Deciduous shrub growing vigorously to 6–8 ft. high, with stoloniferous habit.
*Leaves:* Ovate to oblong-lanceolate, 2–5 in. long and 1–2.5 in. wide, with consistent, stable, creamy white variegations.
*Flowers:* Creamy white, in terminal cymes, 1.5–2 in. across; May–June.
*Fruit:* A short-lived, dark purple drupe.
*Winter aspect:* Yellow stems; loose, broad-spreading, multistemmed habit.

CULTURE: Grows in sun and shade, but color is better in sun; prefers light clay or loam with a pH of 4.0–6.5; tolerates wind, wet conditions, drought, air pollution, and some soil compaction; flourishes in moist sites similar to its native habitat.
*Disease and insect problems:* None.
*Transplanting:* Easy.
*Propagation:* By softwood cuttings.

LANDSCAPE VALUE: An attractive, colorful plant for the shrub border. Withstands heat and humidity in the Mid-Atlantic states better than variegated forms of the red-stemmed *C. alba*. Shows no leaf scorch when grown in full sun. Can be combined with other shrubby dogwoods with outstanding red or yellow stems for winter beauty. Received Pennsylvania Horticultural Society Gold Medal (Styer Award) in 1990.

Plant may be observed at AA, ATL, BBG, BOE, BRK, CBG, CIN, DAW, DEN, HOL, LNG, MOD, MNL, MTC, RKEW, SEC, VDG.

Other *Cornus sericea* cultivars of interest:

*C. sericea* 'Cardinal'. Glowing, almost iridescent, stems of seasonal-changing color. Stems are red in late fall, turning watermelon-pink in winter and pale chartreuse-green in spring. Not as tolerant of heat and humidity as 'Silver & Gold'.
*C. sericea* 'Isanti'. Red-stemmed; more compact form because of shorter internodes. Not as tolerant of heat and humidity as 'Silver & Gold'.

Cornus mas (J. C. Raulston)

Cornus mas (J. C. Raulston)

Cornus mas 'Flava' (Arnold Arboretum)

Cornus mas 'Golden Glory' (E. Hasselkus)

Cornus sericea 'Silver & Gold' (R. W. Lighty)

Cornus sericea 'Silver & Gold' (R. W. Lighty)

Cornus sericea 'Cardinal' (G. Gates)

## Correa reflexa
### AUSTRALIAN FUCHSIA

Rutaceae. USDA Zone 8. Native to Australia, Tasmania. Introduced into cultivation in 1804. Named for Portuguese botanist Jose Correa de Serra.

DESCRIPTION: Broad-leaved evergreen growing slowly to 3–8 ft. tall, with stiff, upright habit.
*Leaves:* Opposite, toothless, oval-cordate to oval-oblong, 0.5–1.5 in. long and 0.25 in. wide, leathery, dark green above, densely covered beneath with whitish hairs.
*Flowers:* Yellow-red, pendulous tube, 1 in. long and 0.25 in. wide, with protruding stamens, in clusters of 1–3 at the ends of short side branches; November–April.

CULTURE: Needs sun for good flowering in coastal areas, but prefers partial shade inland; does not like reflected heat from walls or pavement; tolerates poor, rocky soil with excellent drainage, as well as fertile, sandy peat; does not tolerate wet conditions, drought, overwatering, or overfertilizing.
*Disease and insect problems:* None serious.
*Transplanting:* Easy, container-grown.
*Propagation:* By cuttings in summer.

LANDSCAPE VALUE: An elegant shrub with long winter-blooming period; handsome, but not showy, flowers hang down along branches like small bells. Useful in massed plantings on banks or in shrub border; excellent in pots or in cool greenhouses in colder climates.

Plant may be observed at BBG, HUN, STR.

Related *Correa* cultivars and species of interest:

C. 'Carmine Bells' (*C. alba* × *C. backhousiana*). Bright red, tubular flowers, 1 in. long, tipped with yellow. Same habit as 'Ivory Bells'.

C. 'Ivory Bells' (*C. alba* × *C. backhousiana*). Creamy white, tubular flowers, 1 in. long. Grows to 2 ft. high, with densely branched habit.

C. × *harrisii* (*C. pulchella* × *C. reflexa*). Scarlet flowers, 1 in. long, with protruding yellow stamens. Grows to 2.5 ft. high; most compact of the correas.

## Corylopsis pauciflora
### BUTTERCUP WINTER HAZEL

Hamamelidaceae. USDA Zones 6–8. Native to Japan, Taiwan. Introduced in 1862 by Messrs. Veitch.

DESCRIPTION: Deciduous shrub to 4–6 ft. high, with spreading habit.
*Leaves:* Alternate, simple, ovate to broad-ovate, cordate to subcordate, with bristly margins, 1.5–3 in. long, smallest in genus, bright green above, silky beneath.
*Flowers:* Yellow, fragrant, 0.75 in. across, only 3 to a spike, but profuse; mid- to late April in cooler climates.
*Fruit:* A dehiscent capsule, not ornamental.
*Winter aspect:* Densely branched, graceful form.

CULTURE: Grows best in partial shade; does not tolerate full sun, which stunts plant and burns leaf margins; needs protection from strong, prevailing winds; likes well-drained, acid soil amended with peat moss or leaf mold.
*Disease and insect problems:* Almost trouble-free.
*Transplanting:* Best if balled and burlapped, in moist, well-drained soil.
*Propagation:* By softwood cuttings.

LANDSCAPE VALUE: A lovely, early blooming, dainty shrub with a profusion of bloom that creates a beautiful, showy, yellow pattern. Spikes shorter and fewer-flowered than those of *C. spicata* and others in the genus, but blossoms are larger, more open, and more attractive. Not as hardy as *C. spicata*. Name derived from Greek *korylos* ("hazelnut") and *opsis* ("like"). Received RHS Award of Garden Merit.

Plant may be observed at AA, ABF, ATL, BBG, BC, BEA, BER, BLO, BSG, CAL, CBG, CUH, DAW, DIX, DUK, FIL, GCC, LWD, MCG, MOR, MUN, NCS, NEW, PAL, PLF, RKEW, UBC, USN, VDG, WIN, WIS.

Related *Corylopsis* species of interest:

C. *platypetala*. USDA Zones 6–8. Introduced in 1907 by E. H. Wilson from western China. Reaches 8–10(20) ft. high and 10 ft. wide, with slender branches and erect habit. Leaves are alternate, simple, ovate to elliptic, 2.5–4 in. long, deep green above, glaucous beneath. Pale yellow, fragrant blooms are borne in racemes 1–2 in. long, with 10–20 flowers. Grows in full sun or light shade; prefers moist, acid, well-drained soil.

*Correa reflexa* (N. Brewster)

*Correa reflexa* (Strybing Arboretum Society, Helen Crocker Russel Library)

*Corylopsis pauciflora* (J. C. Raulston)

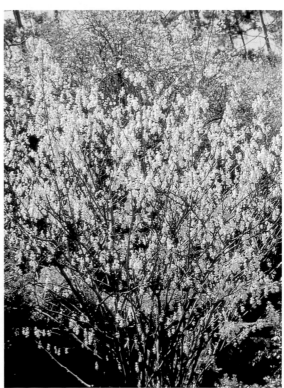

*Corylopsis platypetala* (Royal Botanical Gardens, Ontario)

*Corylopsis pauciflora* (J. C. Raulston)

## Corylopsis spicata
### SPIKE WINTER HAZEL

Hamamelidaceae. USDA Zones 6–9. Native to Japan. Introduced into cultivation in 1863 by Robert Fortune.

DESCRIPTION: Deciduous shrub 5–7 ft. high and 7–9 ft. wide, with layered habit.
*Leaves:* Alternate, ovate-round, cordate, serrate, purple-bronze when emerging, turning blue-green, then an unexciting yellow in autumn.
*Flowers:* Soft yellow, fragrant, with purple anthers, before foliage, in clusters of 6–12 on drooping racemes 1–2 in. long; early spring–April.

CULTURE: Grows in full sun or light shade, performing well even in half shade; likes fertile, acid or neutral soil.
*Disease and insect problems:* None serious.
*Transplanting:* Easy.
*Propagation:* By softwood cuttings, which root readily.

LANDSCAPE VALUE: Valued for its beautiful, early, pale yellow flowers when little else in the landscape is colorful. More delicate and subtle than forsythias; more open and spreading than *C. pauciflora*. Plant in locations not susceptible to late spring frosts, which damage early flowers.

Plant may be observed at AA, ABF, ATL, BBG, BER, BIR, BSG, CAL, CBG, CIN, CUH, DUK, GCC, LWD, MIS, MOR, MRT, MUN, NCS, NEW, OWG, PAL, PLF, RKEW, STR, UBC, USN, VDG, WIN, WIS.

Related *Corylopsis* species of interest:

*C. glabrescens.* Reaches 12 ft. tall, with dense, rounded habit. Hardy to −20°F.
*C. sinensis.* USDA Zones 6–9. Native to China. Pale primrose-yellow, fragrant flowers. Grows to 12 ft. high.
*C. sinensis* f. *veitchiana.* USDA Zones 7–9. Reaches 6 ft. high, with pale yellow bloom.

Related *Corylopsis* cultivars of interest:

*C. willmottiae* 'Spring Purple'. Fragrant Winter Hazel. USDA Zones 6–8. Introduced in 1908 by E. H. Wilson from western China. Said to be loveliest of the species, but has difficulty with cold spring weather. Grows to 12 ft. high with bright, plum-colored new growth, which changes to green. Fragrant, soft green-yellow flowers. Seldom seen in cultivation in the United States.
*C.* 'Winterthur' (*C. spicata* × *C. pauciflora*). Winter Hazel. USDA Zones 7–8. Combines fragrant flowers of *C. spicata* with the finer twigs and dense habit of *C. pauciflora*. Mature specimen is 10 ft. tall and twice as wide after 25 years. Foliage is handsome; pleated leaves are alternate, simple, toothed, strongly veined, to 3 in. long. Pendant spikes of pure, pale yellow, fragrant flowers bloom just before leaves appear in early spring. The profuse, delicate, cup-shaped flowers are beautiful on bare branches, especially during the cold days of March and early April; however, flowers can bloom so early in some years that there is danger of frostbite. Best flowering in sunny location, but grows well in shade; the delicate, light green leaves require light shade to maintain their freshness and beauty in southern zones. Good as understory planting. A refined shrub, it can be pruned to any size and shape. Will not tolerate drought; needs plenty of water during hot, dry summers. Prefers humus-rich soil. Developed at Winterthur Museum and Gardens. Henry Francis du Pont, creator of Winterthur, used this plant beautifully with *Rhododendron mucronulatum* to create a magical, pale yellow and lavender spring landscape.

## Cotoneaster horizontalis 'Robustus'
### ROCKSPRAY COTONEASTER

Rosaceae. USDA Zones 5–7. Species native to western China; introduced into cultivation in 1879. Cultivar discovered by Tips, Herk de Stad, Belgium; disseminated by Vuyk Van Nes.

DESCRIPTION: Semi-evergreen shrub growing slowly to 3 ft. high and 5 ft. wide, with broad, upright habit.
*Leaves:* Ovate, glossy, dark green above, lighter beneath, turning orange to scarlet in fall.
*Flowers:* Light pink, small, attractive but not strikingly conspicuous.
*Fruit:* A light red pome, abundant.
*Winter aspect:* Strong branching habit; persistent fruit.

CULTURE: Requires sun; prefers moist, well-drained soil but, when established, tolerates drought; tolerates salt and a wide variety of growing conditions, including heavy clay or sandy soil and high pH, but not wet conditions.
*Disease and insect problems:* Fire blight, mite.
*Transplanting:* Easy.
*Propagation:* By softwood cuttings.

LANDSCAPE VALUE: A small, robust shrub with shiny, attractive, deep green foliage and good fall color. Excellent for foundation planting or areas where low growth and wide spread is desired. Has year-round interest. More vigorous than the species.

Plant may be observed at AA, BBG, BEA, BER, BF, BIC, CBG, CIN, CUH, DAW, DEN, DOW, GCC, IES, LNG, LWD, MOD, MRT, OWG, PLF, POW, RBC, RKEW, SEC, STR, VDG.

Related *Cotoneaster* species and cultivars of interest:

*C. adpressus* 'Hessei'. USDA Zones 5–7. Very dwarf form to 1–1.5 ft. high and 5 ft. wide. Striking, with profuse fruit

*Corylopsis spicata* (J. C. Raulston)

*Corylopsis spicata* (N. Brewster)

*Cotoneaster adpressus* 'Hessei' (G. Gates)

*Corylopsis* 'Winterthur' (N. Brewster)

*Cotoneaster horizontalis* 'Robustus' (E. Hasselkus)

*Cotoneaster horizontalis* '**Robustus**' continued

and arching branches. Characteristics similar to those of
*C. horizontalis.*
*C. apiculatus.* USDA Zones 5–7; does not perform well in
warmer areas. Native to Sichuan Province, China; introduced into cultivation in 1910. Grows to 3 ft. high and
3–6 ft. wide. Similar to *C. horizontalis.*
*C. conspicuus* 'Decorus'. USDA Zones 7–8(9). Evergreen
shrub growing to 12–15 in. high, with matlike habit and
small, dense foliage. Bears profuse white flowers and
dark red fruit, which usually persists through the winter
and attracts birds. More tender than other cotoneasters
listed here.
*C. dammeri* 'Skogholm'. USDA Zones (6)7–9. Small, low-
growing, extremely attractive shrub with attributes similar to *C. horizontalis.* Ideal for massed plantings on
slopes. Shows great promise for cold hardiness. Possibly
a hybrid with *C. rotundifolius.*

## *Cotoneaster racemiflorus* var. *soongoricus*
REDBEAD COTONEASTER

Rosaceae. USDA Zones 4–7. Native to Central Asia, Dzun-
garia region. Introduced into cultivation in 1910 by E. H.
Wilson.

DESCRIPTION: Deciduous shrub to 8–15 ft. high and 10–15
ft. wide, with upright habit becoming almost weeping with
age.
*Leaves:* 0.75–2 in. long and 0.5–1.5 in. wide, dull blue-gray-
green, turning slightly yellow in fall.
*Flowers:* White, small; May.
*Fruit:* A deep pink-red pome, in August–October.
*Winter aspect:* Arching branches.

CULTURE: Requires sun and free air circulation; prefers
well-drained soil; thrives in dry, sandy soil with a pH of
6–7; does not tolerate permanently wet soil.
*Disease and insect problems:* More trouble-free than many
cotoneasters; occasional fire blight.
*Transplanting:* More difficult than many other *Cotoneaster*
species.
*Propagation:* By softwood cuttings.

LANDSCAPE VALUE: A distinctly graceful shrub with a
lovely display of profuse pink fruit. Foliage has a blue cast.
Flowers are very small, but beautiful in their abundance. A
good, hardy plant for numerous landscape uses. Perhaps
the best flowering and fruiting form among the larger
cotoneasters.

Plant may be observed at ABF, BBG, BEA, LNG, MOD,
MRT, PLF, STR, WIS.

Related *Cotoneaster* cultivar of interest:

*C.* × *watereri* 'Rothschildianus' (*C. frigidus* × *C. salicifolius*).
USDA Zones 7–9. Large shrub growing to 15 ft. high,
with distinct, spreading habit and conspicuous clusters
of creamy yellow fruit. Selected at the Rothschild estate,
Exbury, United Kingdom.

## *Cryptomeria japonica* '**Globosa Nana**'
DWARF JAPANESE CEDAR

Taxodiaceae. USDA Zones 6–8. Species native to China,
Japan. Cultivar described by Hornibrook in 1923.

DESCRIPTION: Evergreen conifer growing slowly to 2–5 ft.
high and 2.5–4.5 ft. wide, with compact, dome-shaped,
broadly conical habit.
*Leaves:* Four-angled, dagger-shaped, and curved inward,
0.25–0.75 in. long, bluish green in summer, rusty red in
winter.
*Fruit:* A terminal, globular cone, 0.5–1 in. long, dark brown.
*Winter aspect:* Reddish brown, exfoliating bark; spreading,
dense, irregular branching habit.

CULTURE: Grows best in light shade in deep, rich, acid soil
with a pH of 6.0–6.75; needs abundant moisture and shelter
from wind; can be damaged by winter sun and wet snow.
*Disease and insect problems:* Some leaf spot and branch
dieback.
*Transplanting:* Easy, container-grown.
*Propagation:* By cuttings in late summer–November, which
root in 2–3 months.

LANDSCAPE VALUE: A broadly conical, compact habit
makes this shrub an excellent choice for rock gardens and
for the front of the shrub border. Exhibits good color both
summer and winter. Do not plant in containers.

Plant may be observed at ABF, BRK, BSG, CAL, CUH,
DAW, DUK, LWD, NCS, PLF, SKY, STR, USN.

*Cotoneaster apiculatus* (R. Klehm)

*Cotoneaster conspicuus* 'Decorus' (Arnold Arboretum)

*Cotoneaster dammeri* 'Skogholm' (J. Apel)

*Cotoneaster racemiflorus* var. *soongoricus* (E. Hasselkus)

*Cotoneaster* × *watereri* 'Rothschildianus' (J. C. Raulston)

*Cryptomeria japonica* 'Globosa Nana' (S. March)

*Cryptomeria japonica* 'Globosa Nana' (N. Brewster)

## Cyrilla racemiflora
### LEATHERWOOD

Synonym: *C. parvifolia.* Cyrillaceae. USDA Zones 6–10. Native to southeastern United States. Introduced into cultivation in the West Indies in 1767.

DESCRIPTION: Deciduous to evergreen shrub (semi-evergreen in USDA Zone 7) growing at moderate rate to 10–15(25) ft. high and as wide, with large, spreading habit.
*Leaves:* Alternate, simple, shiny, green, persisting into late fall where deciduous, turning a glorious warm orange-red in fall.
*Flowers:* White, with 5 petals, slender, 3–6 in. long and 0.5–0.75 in. wide, in dangling racemes; July.
*Winter aspect:* Smooth, brown bark; twisted branches emerging from stout trunk.

CULTURE: Likes full sun and ample moisture (incorporate leaf mold or peat moss into existing soil to increase water retention); tolerates a wide range of soil types; grows in poorly drained to well-drained sites.
*Disease and insect problems:* None serious.
*Transplanting:* Easy
*Propagation:* By softwood cuttings.

LANDSCAPE VALUE: A spectacular shrub in all seasons. Flowers when few other shrubs are in bloom. Dark, glossy foliage is superb backdrop for the interesting midsummer display of long, thin, pendulous, white blooms. Outstanding, warm autumn color. Exhibits interesting form and blooms at young age. May be used as a specimen or in groupings. Plant with adequate space for growth. Often found in swamps and bogs.

Plant may be observed at AA, ABF, ATL, BBG, BF, BIR, CAL, CIN, CUH, DAW, DIX, DUK, GCC, HOU, MBG, MOD, MOR, NCS, PLF, RKEW, USN, WIN.

## Cytisus battandieri
### PINEAPPLE BROOM
### MOROCCAN BROOM

Leguminosae. USDA Zone 9. Native to Morocco, Atlas Mountains, at an altitude of 5000–6000 ft. Introduced in 1922.

DESCRIPTION: Deciduous shrub to 15 ft. high, with erect habit.
*Leaves:* Trifoliate, 1.5–3.5 in. long, silvery, hairy.
*Flowers:* Golden-yellow, 0.3–0.2 in. wide, in long panicles, closely spaced on upper half of racemes, 5 in. long, pineapple-scented.

*Fruit:* A small, green, stiff, hairy pea pod.
*Winter aspect:* Young shoots covered with silky down; strong, upright habit.

CULTURE: Needs sun and sandy, fertile, dry soil; adapts to a wide pH range, but stressed by thin and chalky soils.
*Disease and insect problems:* None serious; some leaf spot.
*Transplanting:* Difficult, unless balled and burlapped or container-grown.
*Propagation:* Self-seeding.

LANDSCAPE VALUE: A beautiful, interesting shrub with fragrant flowers, best suited for planting in groups in the open landscape; can also be used as a specimen on a protected wall. Grows in a protected site at the Royal Botanic Gardens, Kew. Foliage is among most attractive of the genus; large leaves are covered with silvery down. A vigorous grower that has proved hardier than originally thought. Needs renewal pruning; remove old growth after flowering. Received RHS Award of Garden Merit.

Plant may be observed at CUH, PAL, RKEW, UBC, VDG, WIS.

## Cytisus × praecox 'Allgold'
### WARMINSTER BROOM

Parentage: *C. purgans × C. multiflorus.* Leguminosae. USDA Zones 7–8. Introduced in 1963 by A. G. Brand, Boskoop, Netherlands.

DESCRIPTION: Deciduous shrub growing at moderate rate to 10 ft. high, with upright habit when young becoming arching with age.
*Leaves:* Simple, lanceolate to linear, gray-green to light green.
*Flowers:* Pure yellow, fading with age, 0.5–0.75 in. long, blooming along entire stem, very fragrant; spring.
*Fruit:* Not significant.
*Winter aspect:* Gray-green, nodding branches.

CULTURE: Grows best in full sun; adapts to most soils, but high pH may cause chlorosis; tolerates drought.
*Disease and insect problems:* Leaf spot, blight.
*Transplanting:* Best with container-grown plants, 15–24 in. high.
*Propagation:* By softwood cuttings in early summer.

LANDSCAPE VALUE: An outstanding small shrub with extremely attractive habit. Beautiful, long-lasting, yellow flowers are freely borne on graceful, arching stems. Received RHS Award of Garden Merit.

Plant may be observed at AA, ATL, BBG, GCC, LAC, PAL, PLF, RKEW.

*Cyrilla racemiflora* (E. Bell)

*Cyrilla racemiflora* (Planting Fields Arboretum)

*Cytisus battandieri* (J. C. Raulston)

*Cytisus battandieri* (University of Washington)

*Cytisus × praecox* 'Allgold' (J. Elsley)

Other *Cytisus × praecox* cultivars of interest:

*C. × praecox* 'Albus'. White flowers.

*C. × praecox* 'Hollandia'. Salmon-pink flowers; vigorous grower, to 4 ft. high. Received RHS Award of Garden Merit.

## Cytisus scoparius
### SCOTCH BROOM

Leguminosae. USDA Zones 6–8. Native to central and south Europe; found wild in Normandy in 1884.

DESCRIPTION: Deciduous shrub growing quickly when young, slower with age, to 6–10 ft. high and as wide, with broad, mounded habit and erect stems.
*Leaves:* Simple, trifoliate, oblanceolate, bright gray to deep green, pubescent when young, no fall color.
*Flowers:* Golden-yellow, large; May–June.
*Fruit:* A pod, 1.5–2 in. long.
*Winter aspect:* Branches pubescent when young; angular branching habit.

CULTURE: Best in full sun; prefers loamy, more fertile soils than other *Cytisus* species, but adapts to dry, sandy soil and a wide pH range.
*Disease and insect problems:* Leaf spot and blight can be troublesome.
*Transplanting:* Easier with container-grown plants.
*Propagation:* By seed and cuttings.

LANDSCAPE VALUE: A very attractive, spring-flowering shrub; creates spectacular color impact when used in massed plantings. Very useful and effective for roadside plantings. Deserves more widespread use despite being short-lived; usually needs replacement after 10–12 years. Extremely popular in Europe, especially in United Kingdom and Holland.

Plant may be observed at BBG, CAL, GCC, WIS.

*Cytisus scoparius* cultivars of interest:

*C. scoparius* 'Burkwoodii'. Carmine-red flowers and light green branches; strong, vigorous grower.

*C. scoparius* 'Lena'. Deep red flowers; free-flowering, vigorous, compact shrub. Received RHS Award of Garden Merit.

*C. scoparius* 'Lilac Time'. Small, lilac, early blooming flowers and gray-green branches; compact habit.

*C. scoparius* 'Luna'. Light yellow flowers and upright form. Received RHS Award of Garden Merit.

*C. scoparius* 'Moonlight'. Large, creamy white flowers and nodding habit.

## Danae racemosa
### ALEXANDRIAN LAUREL

Liliaceae. USDA Zones 8(9). Native to southwestern Asia, in Persia and Asia Minor. Introduced into cultivation in 1713.

DESCRIPTION: Broad-leaved evergreen growing at slow to moderate rate to 2–3 ft. high, with broad, arching habit.
*Leaves:* Alternate, oblong-lanceolate, tapering to apices, with cladophylls (green stems that function like leaves).
*Flowers:* Green-yellow, insignificant; late spring.
*Fruit:* An attractive, marble-sized, orange-red berry, in fall–winter.

CULTURE: Grows in half sun and half shade; prefers loam with a pH of 5–7; tolerates moist conditions and some drought.
*Disease and insect problems:* None serious.
*Transplanting:* Easy; fairly deep root system.
*Propagation:* By seed or division.

LANDSCAPE VALUE: An excellent, low evergreen with glossy leaves. Branches make lovely, long-lasting cuttings. Appears to tolerate extremes in weather. Difficult to obtain; seed has several inhibitors. Received RHS Award of Garden Merit.

Plant may be observed at ABF, ATL, BER, BIR, BSG, CAL, CUH, DIX, DUK, MBG, MCG, MUN, NCS, PAL, RKEW, STR, UBC, WIS.

## Daphne × burkwoodii
### DAPHNE

Parentage: *D. caucasica × D. cneorum*. Thymelaeaceae. USDA Zones 5–8. Introduced from Great Britain by Albert Burkwood.

DESCRIPTION: Semi-evergreen shrub growing vigorously to 3–4 ft. high, with compact, rounded, widespread habit.
*Leaves:* Oblong, 2 in. long, rich, gleaming green, no fall color; semi-evergreen foliage often remains on plant through November.
*Flowers:* Creamy white to flushed pink, fragrant, in dense, terminal clusters, 2 in. wide; May–June.
*Fruit:* A red berry, 0.3 in. diameter, in fall.

CULTURE: Grows in sun; prefers well-drained loam with a neutral pH, but adapts to a variety of soils; tolerates some shade but does not flower as profusely; does not like wet conditions or drought.
*Disease and insect problems:* Few; occasional wilt.
*Transplanting:* Best when small and container-grown.
*Propagation:* By softwood cuttings, seed, and layering.

*Cystus scoparius* 'Moonlight' (J. C. Raulston)

*Danae racemosa* (N. Brewster)

*Danae racemosa* (J. Elsley)

*Daphne × burkwoodii* 'Carol Mackie' (K. Freeland)

*Daphne × burkwoodii* 'Carol Mackie' (N. Brewster)

*Daphne* × *burkwoodii* continued

LANDSCAPE VALUE: A delightfully fragrant, free-flowering shrub. With a little warmth, blooms in the Pacific Northwest from midwinter to midspring. Once established, does not like to be moved. Received RHS Award of Merit in 1937. Albert Burkwood raised this hybrid of *D. caucasica* and *D. cneorum*, which resulted in only three seeds. One of two surviving plants was retained by Burkwood, and clones descended from it should be distinguished as 'Albert Burkwood'. The other plant, belonging to Burkwood's brother, is the original of the clone 'Somerset', which is hardier, more densely branched, and with a stronger growth habit than *D.* x *burkwoodii*. Both plants resemble *D. cneorum* in flower and foliage. This species and its cultivars are magnificent small shrubs that truly deserve more attention in today's gardens.

Plant may be observed at AA, ABF, BBG, CAL, CBG, CIN, DEN, GIW, HOL, LNG, LWD, MNL, MRT, MUN, NCS, NEW, PAL, PLF, RBC, RKEW, SEC, SPR, UBC, VDG.

*Daphne* × *burkwoodii* cultivars of interest:

*D.* × *burkwoodii* 'Carol Mackie'. Originated from a branch sport of 10-year-old plant of *D.* x *burkwoodii*. Named for owner Carol Mackie of Far Hills, New Jersey, and registered at Arnold Arboretum in 1969. Larger than 'Somerset', it has fragrant pink flowers and leaves with a dominant, attractive gold band around margins. Of great hardiness, this shrub has withstood temperatures of −40°F in Vermont. Needs good, aggressive pruning in early life to branch freely in maturity.

*D.* × *burkwoodii* 'Somerset'. Lovely, true pink in bud, opening to paler pink. Intensely fragrant and extremely hardy, with denser branching and stronger growth habit than species.

*D.* × *burkwoodii* 'Variegata'. Vigorous shrub with whitish pink flowers and lovely, delicate, white-edged foliage.

Related *Daphne* species of interest:

*D. caucasica*. One parent of *D.* × *burkwoodii*, this lovely shrub grows to 5 ft. high with mounded habit and withstands temperatures of −30°F. Fragrant, pink flowers bloom continuously from early spring until late fall. Perhaps the parent may prove an even better plant in that it is equally hardy, slightly taller, and produces profuse, delicately fragrant flowers over a longer season. Requires excellent drainage. Received Pennsylvania Horticultural Society Gold Medal (Styer Award) in 1990.

# *Daphne cneorum*
## GARLAND FLOWER
## ROSE DAPHNE

Thymelaeaceae. USDA Zones 5–8. Native to the mountains of central and southern Europe. Introduced into cultivation in 1752.

DESCRIPTION: Semi-evergreen shrub, sometimes evergreen, 1–3 ft. high and 2 ft. wide, with low, spreading habit.
*Leaves:* Narrow, lanceolate, 0.5–1 in. long, dark green, turning yellow in fall.
*Flowers:* Rose-pink, fragrant, in dense, terminal clusters; mid- to late spring and often again in late summer.
*Fruit:* Ovoid-oblong, light orange, turning to yellow-brown.

CULTURE: Grows in sun and light shade; prefers well-drained, moist, neutral to acid soil; does not tolerate drought; needs protection with evergreen boughs from winter sun and wind.
*Disease and insect problems:* Some crown rot in shady areas, aphid, mealy bug.
*Transplanting:* Not easy; does not like to be moved; shallow root system.
*Propagation:* By seed, layering, and softwood cuttings in early or late summer.

LANDSCAPE VALUE: One of the finest dwarf shrubs for the rock garden, an excellent border plant, and a beautifully compact, wonderfully fragrant addition to any garden; however, it is temperamental and slow to establish itself. Prune after established, preferably immediately after flowering.

Plant may be observed at AA, ABF, ATL, BBG, BER, CAL, CBG, DAW, DEN, DOW, GCC, HOL, MOD, MUN, NEW, PAL, PLF, RKEW, SKY, UBC, VDG.

*Daphne cneorum* cultivars of interest:

*D. cneorum* 'Alba'. White-flowered cultivar; less vigorous than species.
*D. cneorum* 'Eximia'. Best cultivar of the species, with deeper pink flowers and buds; more prostrate but with larger leaves and flowers than species.
*D. cneorum* 'Ruby Glow'. Dark pink flowers.

*Daphne × burkwoodii* 'Somerset' (J. Elsley)

*Daphne caucasica* (N. Brewster)

*Daphne cneorum* 'Eximia' (J. Elsley)

*Daphne cneorum* 'Ruby Glow' (E. Paine)

## *Daphne mezereum*
### FEBRUARY DAPHNE

Thymelaeaceae. USDA Zones 5–8. Native to Europe.

DESCRIPTION: Semi-evergreen to deciduous shrub 3–5 ft. high and as wide, with upright, rounded habit.
*Leaves:* Alternate, oblong, thin, hairless, 1.5–3.5 in. long and 0.3–1 in. wide, blue-green above, gray-green beneath.
*Flowers:* Lilac to rose-purple, fragrant; April.
*Fruit:* A pea-sized, poisonous red berry maturing in June.
*Winter aspect:* Upright branching habit.

CULTURE: Thrives in full sun, but tolerates shade and wet conditions; prefers cool, moist conditions and loamy soil with a neutral pH; needs protection from wind and constant water in the heat of summer.
*Disease and insect problems:* Some scale and virus.
*Transplanting:* Difficult; best moved in spring when small, balled and burlapped.
*Propagation:* By seed, which should be harvested as soon as fruit shows color.

LANDSCAPE VALUE: An early blooming, extremely fragrant, decorative shrub. A decoction of the bark, sold in drugstores under the name "Mezereum," is used as a stimulant and diuretic. Spring pruning should remove only dead or crossed branches.

Plant may be observed at AA, CUH, DEN, DOW, NEW, VDG.

*Daphne mezereum* form of interest:

D. *mezereum* f. *alba*. Creamy white flowers with yellow-amber fruit; grows more vigorously than the species.

*Daphne mezereum* f. *alba* cultivar of interest:

D. *mezereum* f. *alba* 'Bowles White'. Truer, purer white; reputedly best cultivar of the species.

Related *Daphne* species of interest:

D. *genkwa*. Lilac Daphne. USDA Zones 5–8. Introduced from China in 1843 by Fortune and later from Japan. Deciduous, 3–4 ft. high, with loose, sometimes straggly, habit. Leaves are lanceolate, 0.5 in. long and 0.5 in. wide, light green, silky beneath. Lilac-blue flowers appear before leaves in May on previous year's growth. A truly lovely shrub with coppery brown bark, claimed by some to be finest species of genus. Fruit is a white berry, not conspicuous. Grows in sun but likes partial shade. Somewhat tolerant of wet conditions but not drought-resistant. Appears to thrive best in areas with warm summer temperatures. Difficult to establish and somewhat tender and short-lived in cultivation, although the New York Botanical Garden has a specimen 10 ft. in diameter that has grown there for more than 30 years with no winter protection.

## *Daphne odora* 'Aureo-marginata'
### WINTER DAPHNE

Thymelaeaceae. USDA Zones 7–9. Native to China. Long cultivated in Japan. Introduced to Britain in 1771.

DESCRIPTION: Broad-leaved evergreen growing at moderate rate to 4–6 ft. high, with upright habit (more spreading in shade).
*Leaves:* Lanceolate, 3 in. long, deep green with creamy white to yellow margins.
*Flowers:* Fragrant, tubular, red-purple outside and paler (often white) inside; January–March.

CULTURE: Grows in sun, but performs well in shade in warm areas; does not tolerate drought; tolerates a variety of soils better than most daphnes.
*Disease and insect problems:* Few.
*Transplanting:* Does not like to be moved; best moved in spring when small, balled and burlapped.
*Propagation:* By cuttings, seed, and layering.

LANDSCAPE VALUE: A superior, early blooming shrub with dense, low habit. Very aromatic and hardier than species. Easiest daphne to grow. Flowers have good, long-lasting quality.

Plant may be observed at AA, BRK, BSG, CAL, DUK, FIL, MIS, NCS, PLF.

## *Daphne retusa*

Thymelaeaceae. USDA Zones 6–8. Introduced into cultivation in 1901 from western China by E. H. Wilson.

DESCRIPTION: Broad-leaved evergreen growing at moderate rate to 2–3 ft. high, with dense, compact habit.
*Leaves:* Oblong, lanceolate, 1–3 in. long, leathery, with rolled-under margins, shiny, dark green.
*Flowers:* Very fragrant, purple-pink outside, white with trace of pink inside, in dense terminal clusters 3 in. across; May, often with second bloom in late summer.
*Fruit:* Bright red, drupelike, attractive to birds.
*Winter aspect:* Dense branching habit.

CULTURE: Likes full sun and neutral, but not alkaline, soil; easy to grow.
*Disease and insect problems:* Few.
*Transplanting:* Difficult.
*Propagation:* Easy by cuttings, seed, and layering.

LANDSCAPE VALUE: A hardy, fragrant shrub attractive in all seasons. Much more tolerant of garden conditions than most daphnes. Rewarding shrub that is reliable, disease-resistant, and a superb specimen for the garden.

Daphne mezereum f. alba (J. Elsley)

Daphne mezereum (G. Koller)

Daphne genkwa (N. Brewster)

Daphne odora 'Aureo-marginata' (J. C. Raulston)

Daphne retusa (J. Elsley)

**Daphne retusa** continued

Plant may be observed at AA, BBG, BER, CUH, DUK, MUN, PAL, RBC, RHO, RKEW, UBC, VDG.

Related *Daphne* species of interest:

*D. giraldii.* Native to China. USDA Zone 6. Perhaps best yellow-flowered species, reaching 3–4 ft. high; easy to grow. Handsome red fruit.

*D. × mantensiana.* Outstanding cross of *D. × burkwoodii* 'Somerset' × *D. retusa.* USDA Zone 6. Excellent specimen or hedge; remains neat and manageable without pruning. No serious pests or diseases. Very fragrant, profuse, rose-purple flowers over exceedingly long period, except winter. Glossy, evergreen foliage similar to that of *Buxus.* Easy to cultivate; grows in full sun or partial shade. Brought into the trade in 1953 by Mantens Nursery, White Rock, British Columbia, Canada.

*D. tangutica.* Closely related to, but not as compact as *D. retusa.* Valued for continuous bloom and profusion of red fruit.

## Decaisnea fargesii

Lardizabalaceae. USDA Zones 6–8. Collected in the mountains of western China and sent to France in 1895 by Père Farges; later sent to the Royal Botanic Gardens, Kew, where it is hardy and grows well.

DESCRIPTION: Deciduous shrub to 9–15 ft. high, with upright habit.
*Leaves:* Alternate, pinnate, 2–3 ft. long, composed of 6–12 pairs of ovate, entire leaflets 3–6 in. long, blue-tinged when young, becoming deep green above and blue-green beneath.
*Flowers:* Yellow-green, on a thin stalk, in loose, drooping panicles 12–18 in. long; May–June.
*Fruit:* A metallic blue, cylindrical bean pod, 3–4 in. long and 0.75 in. wide, resembling a small sausage.
*Winter aspect:* Large winter buds; sparsely branched habit.

CULTURE: Grows in sun and semi-shade; prefers a rich, loamy, well-drained soil; needs protection from cold wind.
*Disease and insect problems:* None serious.
*Transplanting:* Easy.
*Propagation:* By seed.

LANDSCAPE VALUE: A fascinating, little-known shrub that flowers and fruits profusely. Striking for its fruit of unusual character; also an attractive foliage plant.

Plant may be observed at ABF, BBG, BF, BLO, CUH, CIN, MRT, MUN, RKEW, UBC, USN, VDG.

## Dendromecon rigida
BUSH POPPY

Papaveraceae. USDA Zone 9. Native to the United States, to Santa Cruz and to Santa Rosa Island, California. Discovered by David Douglas. Introduced into cultivation in 1854 by William Lobb.

DESCRIPTION: Broad-leaved evergreen growing slowly to 3–9 ft. high, with upright habit.
*Leaves:* Alternate, elliptic, lobeless, dense, entire, tough, 3 in. long and 1.5 in. wide, deep green.
*Flowers:* Bright yellow, fragrant, with 4 petals, 2 sepals, and numerous stamens, 2 in. across, poppylike, solitary, at tips of short side branches; March–June.
*Winter aspect:* Shredding yellow-gray or white bark; freely branched, stiff habit.

CULTURE: Needs sun and dry, well-drained, sandy soil; best in warm, dry summers; tolerates drought, but not wet conditions.
*Disease and insect problems:* None serious.
*Transplanting:* Easy.
*Propagation:* By cuttings of 3 nodes from well-ripened, firm summer shoots, placed in very sandy soil.

LANDSCAPE VALUE: A free-flowering evergreen that blooms March–June, with scattered bloom throughout the year. Flowers last for several days. Closely related to Matilija-poppy (*Romneya*). Pruning in spring should be restricted to cutting out weak or unwanted branches. Useful on banks or combined with other native shrubs.

Plant may be observed at FUL, RAN, SBB, STR.

## Deutzia gracilis 'Nikko'
SLENDER DEUTZIA

Saxifragaceae. USDA Zones 5–8. Introduced in 1975 from Japan.

DESCRIPTION: Deciduous shrub growing at moderate to fast rate to 2–4 ft. high and 4–5 ft. wide, with graceful, branching habit.
*Leaves:* Opposite, simple, oblong, small, rich green in summer, turning burgundy in fall.
*Flowers:* Pure white, perfect, abundant, in racemes; May–June.
*Fruit:* A small, brown capsule, not ornamental.

CULTURE: Grows in sun or light shade in a wide variety of soils and pH ranges, but prefers a good loam; tolerates high alkalinity and moist conditions, but not drought; needs adequate water supply.

*Decaisnea fargesii* (E. Sharp)

*Decaisnea fargesii* (J. Elsley)

*Decaisnea fargesii* (J. Apel)

*Dendromecon rigida* (P. K. Thompson)

*Deutzia gracilis* 'Nikko' (S. March)

*Dendromecon rigida* (P. K. Thompson)

*Deutzia gracilis* 'Nikko' (N. Brewster)

*Disease and insect problems:* None serious; aphid, leaf miner, leaf spot.
*Transplanting:* Easy; best in spring.
*Propagation:* By softwood cuttings.

LANDSCAPE VALUE: An attractive, dwarf, fine-textured shrub for a sunny hill or small garden site; best used in massed plantings combined with other deciduous, flowering shrubs. Prefers some shade in warmer climates. More compact than the species. Important to prune after blooming; cut older stems to ground every other year to promote new growth. Received Pennsylvania Horticultural Society Gold Medal (Styer Award) in 1989.

Plant may be observed at AA, ABF, ATL, BBG, BF, BSG, CHK, CIN, CUH, DAW, DEN, DUK, GCC, HOL, HUN, LNG, LWD, MIS, MOR, MRT, NEW, OWG, PAL, PLF, RKEW, SKY, UBC, USN, WIN.

Another *Deutzia gracilis* cultivar of interest:

*D. gracilis* 'Rosea'. Compact shrub with lovely, pink, bell-shaped flowers.

Related *Deutzia* species and cultivars of interest:

*D. chunii.* USDA Zones 6–8. Beautiful shrub reaching 6 ft. high, with oblong leaves and white-pink flowers. Late blooming; flowers appear in July. Not often found in cultivation but merits wider use. Introduced in 1935 from China.

*D.* × *hybrida* 'Magicien' (*D. discolor* × *D. longifolia*). Large, lovely, mauve-pink flowers with white edges; leaves elliptic.

*D. scabra* var. *candidissima*. Fuzzy Deutzia. USDA Zones 6–7. Popular in the 1940s. Large, coarse, vigorous shrub reaching 6–12 ft. high, with arching branches. White flowers with pink tinge borne in panicles 3–5 in. long; flowers later than *D. gracilis*. Tolerates a pH range of 6–8.

*D. scabra* 'Plena'. White, double flowers, tinged with rose-lavender on outside.

*D. scabra* 'Pride of Rochester'. USDA Zones 6–7. Flowers have rosy pink tinge; paler than species.

# *Diervilla sessilifolia*
## SOUTHERN BUSH HONEYSUCKLE

Caprifoliaceae. USDA Zones 5–8. Native to southeastern United States, from Virginia and Tennessee south to Georgia and Alabama. Introduced into cultivation in 1844.

DESCRIPTION: Deciduous shrub to 3–5 ft. high, with suckering habit.
*Leaves:* Opposite, ovate, heart-shaped at base, tapering to point, 2.5–7 in. long, glossy, deep green, with little fall color.
*Flowers:* Sulfur-yellow, about 3 in. across, in terminal clusters on current season's growth; June–August.
*Fruit:* A seed vessel, 0.5 in. long.

CULTURE: Better in sun, but tolerates shade; prefers cool, moist clay or loam soil; adapts to a wide pH range; tolerates wind.
*Disease and insect problems:* None.
*Transplanting:* Easy.
*Propagation:* By cuttings.

LANDSCAPE VALUE: A tough shrub for adverse conditions; very adaptable and easy to grow. Useful for planting on banks and in areas where thick groupings are desirable (e.g., sides of hills, mountains, and along stream banks). Should be pruned in early spring before new growth begins.

Plant may be observed at AA, ATL, BBG, BC, BEA, BIC, BRK, CAL, CBG, GIN, COX, DAW, DUK, GIW, IES, LNG, LWD, MIS, MNL, MOR, MRT, MUN, NCS, PAL, PLF, POW, RKEW, USN, WIN.

Related *Diervilla* species of interest:

*D. rivularis.* Georgia Bush Honeysuckle. USDA Zones 6–8. Lemon-yellow flowers, which may turn reddish, in July–August. Similar to *D. sessilifolia*, but leaves are downy, particularly on undersides, and seed is smaller. Grows to 3 ft. high. Also native to southeastern United States; introduced in 1902 at the Royal Botanic Gardens, Kew.

*D.* × *splendens* (*D. lonicera* × *D. sessilifolia*). Sulfur-yellow flowers. Leaves have short petiole and burgundy cast in fall. Cultivated since 1850s but origin unknown. More often seen in European gardens.

*Deutzia chunii* (L. Sharp)

*Deutzia chunii* (Winterthur Gardens)

*Deutzia scabra* 'Pride of Rochester' (Planting Fields Arboretum)

*Deutzia scabra* 'Plena' (Arnold Arboretum)

*Diervilla sessilifolia* (D. Brennan)

*Diervilla sessilifolia* (B. Blackwell)

*Diervilla rivularis* (G. Gates)

101

## Dipelta floribunda

Caprifoliaceae. USDA Zones 6–8. Native to central and western China. Found in the late 1800s but not introduced until 1902 when E. H. Wilson sent plants to Messrs. Veitch.

DESCRIPTION: Deciduous shrub growing at moderate rate to 7–10 ft. high (10–15 ft. in the wild).
*Leaves:* Opposite, ovate to oval, lanceolate, tapering at base, dull green, downy on both sides.
*Flowers:* Pale pink, with yellow throat, tubular, bell-shaped, fragrant, in terminal axillary clusters, 1.5 in. long and 1 in. wide, fragrant, nodding; May–June.
*Fruit:* A dry capsule, 0.75 in. long and 0.6 in. wide, surrounded by 2 bracts.
*Winter aspect:* Yellow-brown bark, shredding and peeling in long strips; multistemmed habit.

CULTURE: Requires sun.
*Disease and insect problems:* None serious.
*Transplanting:* Balled and burlapped.
*Propagation:* By cuttings in summer and hardwood cuttings in fall.

LANDSCAPE VALUE: A highly ornamental shrub with abundant, fragrant blooms. Resembles *Weigela* except in fruit and smaller flowers. A little known, seldom-used shrub valuable for the mixed border or massed to provide screening. Flowers borne on shoots of previous year's growth. Thinning out old and crowded branches keeps habit more attractive.

Plant may be observed at AA, BBG, CUH, MRT, MUN, RKEW.

## Disanthus cercidifolius

Hamamelidaceae. USDA Zones 6–8. Introduced in 1893 from Japan.

DESCRIPTION: Deciduous shrub growing at moderate rate to 6–12 ft. high, with open, upright habit.
*Leaves:* Alternate, cordate, 2–4.5 in. long, resembling unrelated *Cercis* leaves, dull blue-green, turning brilliant crimson and claret in fall.
*Flowers:* Dark purple, not conspicuous; fall.
*Fruit:* A nutlike capsule, not ornamental.
*Winter aspect:* Attractive branching habit.

CULTURE: Grows in sun and thrives in partial shade; does not tolerate wind, drought, or lime soils; prefers slightly acid loam.
*Disease and insect problems:* Vulnerable to fungus when grown in warm climates.
*Transplanting:* Relatively easy.
*Propagation:* By seed and cuttings.

LANDSCAPE VALUE: An interesting, unusual, medium-sized shrub with shapely leaves, late bloom, and magnificent fall color. The only species of genus; rarely found in nurseries. Requires no special care. Differs from other members of the Witch Hazel family, which have strong mid-vein; *Disanthus* has 5–7 main veins. Unpleasant odor to flower. Name derived from Greek *dis* (meaning "twice") and *anthos* (referring to 2-flowered heads); *cercidifolius* indicates leaves shaped like those of the well-known redbud. Received RHS Award of Garden Merit.

Plant may be observed at AA, ABF, BBG, BF, BER, BLO, BSG, CUH, FIL, LWD, MOR, MUN, RHO, RKEW, UBC, VDG, WIS.

## Duranta stenostachya
### BRAZILIAN SKY FLOWER

Verbenaceae. USDA Zone 10. Native to Brazil.

DESCRIPTION: Broad-leaved evergreen to 4–6 ft. high (15 ft. in ideal conditions), with neat, compact habit.
*Leaves:* Oblong-lanceolate, 3–8 in. long, arranged in pairs or whorls along stem, glossy, green.
*Flowers:* Lavender-blue, 0.5 in. across; summer.
*Fruit:* Yellow, 0.25–0.3 in. across, in clusters to 1 in. long.

CULTURE: Thrives in sun and hot conditions, but needs a constant level of moisture; likes loam or sandy soils; tolerates seaside conditions, wind, and drought.
*Disease and insect problems:* None.
*Transplanting:* Easy, if pruned hard when moved.
*Propagation:* By seed and cuttings in spring.

LANDSCAPE VALUE: Useful as a hedge or screen. Not as hardy as but neater and more compact than *D. repens*, with larger flowers and leaves. Lavender flowers attract butterflies in summer. Many plants sold as *D. stenostachya* are actually *D. repens*.

Plant may be observed at LAC, SAB.

*Dipelta floribunda* (G. Koller)

*Dipelta floribunda* (G. Koller)

*Disanthus cercidifolius* (G. Koller)

*Disanthus cercidifolius* (University of Washington)

*Duranta stenostachya* (R. Jones)

*Duranta stenostachya* (R. Jones)

*Duranta stenostachya* (R. Jones)

## Elaeagnus pungens
SILVER BERRY
RUSSIAN OLIVE
OLEASTER

Elaeagnaceae. USDA Zones 7–8. Introduced in 1820 from Japan.

DESCRIPTION: Broad-leaved evergreen growing vigorously to 12–15 ft. high, with wide, dense habit.
*Leaves:* Alternate, oblong, 1.5–4 in. long, crisped along margins, shiny, dark green above, dull white beneath and speckled with brown scales.
*Flowers:* Silver-white, pendulous, small, slightly fragrant; October–November.
*Fruit:* Drupelike, brown at first, turning red.
*Winter aspect:* Dense, spreading, somewhat thorny habit.

CULTURE: Likes sun; tolerates partial shade and drought; adapts to a wide range of soils.
*Disease and insect problems:* None serious; spider mite in warm, dry weather.
*Transplanting:* Very easy; fairly deep root system.
*Propagation:* By cuttings.

LANDSCAPE VALUE: Can be used as specimen, hedge, or espalier. Requires no special care.

Plant may be observed at ABF, ATL, BBG, BIR, BOK, BRK, BSG, CUH, DIX, FIL, FUL, HUN, LWD, MBG, MIS, MUN, NCS, NEW, PAL, PLF, RKEW, STR, UBC, VDG, WIS.

*Elaeagnus pungens* cultivars of interest:

*E. pungens* 'Aurea'. Similar to 'Variegata' but less effective.
*E. pungens* 'Aurea Dicksonii'. Similar to 'Variegata' but less effective.
*E. pungens* 'Fruitlandii'. Grows 8–10 ft. high, slightly larger than species, with soft green leaves and wavy margins.
*E. pungens* 'Hosoba-Fukurin'. Same habit and fragrant flowers as the species. Leaves with attractive cream margins do not sun-scorch as do those of some variegated cultivars.
*E. pungens* 'Maculata'. Grows slowly at first, then rapidly, to 8 ft. tall and as wide. Leaves ovate, 2.25–4.5 in. long, with puckered margins, yellow centers, and shiny upper surfaces that radiate sun in winter. Branches on which leaves have reverted to all-green should be removed. Received RHS Award of Garden Merit.
*E. pungens* 'Variegata'. Perhaps showiest of all hardy variegated shrubs; to 8 ft. high; soft green leaves have creamy white margins, each blade boldly colored down center with brilliant yellow.

Related hybrid of interest:

*Elaeagnus × ebbingei* (*E. macrophylla × E. pungens*). USDA Zone 8. Raised by Doorenbos at The Hague, Netherlands, in 1929. Favors *E. macrophylla* but more vigorous. Occasionally produces long, semiclimbing stems with narrower, longer leaves.

## Elliottia racemosa
GEORGIA PLUME

Ericaceae. USDA Zones (6)7–8. Native to the United States. Cultivated in 1813.

DESCRIPTION: Deciduous shrub growing quickly to 10–20 ft. high.
*Leaves:* Alternate, elliptic, 2–5 in. long and 0.75 in. wide, dull green above, paler and slightly pubescent beneath.
*Flowers:* White, slightly fragrant, with 4 petals and 8 stamens, in slender, terminal racemes; late summer.
*Fruit:* A 4- to 5-lobed capsule, 0.4 in. across, in fall.
*Winter aspect:* Lustrous, brown bark.

CULTURE: Grows best in sun in sandy, acid soil; tolerates some drought.
*Disease and insect problems:* None serious.
*Transplanting:* Difficult.
*Propagation:* By root cuttings or seed, though only 4 percent of seed is viable and thus few seedlings occur.

LANDSCAPE VALUE: A rare, large shrub that provides a magnificent display when showy, white flower panicles appear. Of interest strictly during flowering. Blooms June–July in southern climates; hardy in USDA Zone 6 once established. Suckers from roots to form colonies.

Plant may be observed at AA, BBG, BRK, BSG, CAL, CUH, DUK, MTC, NEW, NCS, RKEW.

*Elaeagnus pungens* (N. Brewster)

*Elaeagnus pungens* 'Hosoba-Fukurin' (N. Brewster)

*Elaeagnus pungens* 'Hosoba-Fukurin' (N. Brewster)

*Elaeagnus pungens* 'Variegata' (N. Brewster)

*Elliottia racemosa* (Arnold Arboretum)

*Elliottia racemosa* (G. Koller)

105

## Embothrium coccineum
### CHILEAN FIRE BUSH

Proteaceae. USDA Zones 8–9. Introduced in 1846 from Chile by William Lobb. Present-day plants grown from seed collected in 1926–1927 in the Andes by H. F. Comber.

DESCRIPTION: Broad-leaved evergreen 10–30 ft. high in milder regions, with erect habit.
*Leaves:* Alternate, occasionally somewhat opposite, simple, ovate, leathery, 2.5–4 in. long and 0.75–1.5 in. wide, deep green.
*Flowers:* Brilliant, orange-scarlet, tubular, about 2 in. long, in terminal and axillary racemes.
*Winter aspect:* Many-seeded follicles.

CULTURE: Needs sun; prefers moist, loamy, but not too heavy soil; does not like alkaline soil; tolerates wet conditions, but not wind.
*Disease and insect problems:* None serious.
*Transplanting:* Relatively easy.
*Propagation:* By seed, or by cuttings taken in August.

LANDSCAPE VALUE: A spectacular flowering shrub; prefers plenty of light but requires little care.

Plant may be observed at RKEW.

## Enkianthus campanulatus
### RED VEIN ENKIANTHUS

Ericaceae. USDA Zones 5–8. Introduced in 1870 from Japan.

DESCRIPTION: Deciduous shrub growing slowly to 6–8 ft. high (to 20 ft. high in warmer climates), with narrow, upright habit and distinct, multistemmed, layered branches.
*Leaves:* Alternate, simple, elliptic to obovate, 1–3 in. long and 0.5–1.25 in. wide, medium green, turning brilliant yellow, orange, and red in fall.
*Flowers:* Creamy yellow to light pink, bell-shaped, with red veins, in pendulous clusters; May–June.
*Fruit:* A dry, egg-shaped capsule, 0.75 in. long, borne upright.
*Winter aspect:* Bark reddish when young, turning brown with age.

CULTURE: Grows in full sun or partial light shade; prefers damp ground and well-drained, acid, loamy soil. Requires frequent watering in summer.
*Disease and insect problems:* None serious; occasional scale.
*Transplanting:* Difficult; roots take time to form.
*Propagation:* By seed and softwood cuttings.

LANDSCAPE VALUE: This attractive, little-known shrub deserves greater use for its interesting growth habit, spectacular fall color, and exceptionally lovely, delicate flowers like lily-of-the-valley that hang graciously in pendant clusters. The name of the genus means "pregnant flower." Integrates well with *Rhododendron, Kalmia,* and *Leucothoe.* Careful selection must be made for fall color, which is often variable. Early pruning helps to establish a good form early in life. Received RHS Award of Garden Merit.

Plant may be observed at AA, ABF, BBG, BC, BER, BF, BIR, BLO, BSG, CAL, CBG, CUH, DAW, DIX, DOW, DUK, GCC, GIW, HOL, HUN, IES, LWD, MIS, MOR, MRT, MUN, NCS, NEW, OWG, PAL, PLF, RBC, RHO, RKEW, SEC, SKY, UBC, USN, VDG, WIN, WIS.

*Enkianthus campanulatus* cultivars and variety of interest:

E. campanulatus 'Albiflorus'. Greenish white to pure white flowers with larger corollas than species. There may be as many as 15 blossoms on each panicle. Extremely attractive and much rarer than species.

E. campanulatus var. palibinii. Dark rose-red flowers, smaller than species. No record of origin of this hardy shrub brought from northern Japan to United Kingdom in 1889 by Charles Maries.

E. campanulatus 'Red Bells'. Base of corolla creamy yellow, with light red veins; flowers redder towards tip than species.

E. campanulatus 'Renoir'. Subdued, light yellow flowers with pink lobes. Selected by R. Nicholson.

E. campanulatus 'Showy Lantern'. Large, solid crimson flowers. Selected by the late Ed Mezitt, Weston Nurseries.

E. campanulatus 'Sikokianus'. Dark red-maroon buds opening to red, with streaks of shrimp-pink. Discovered at the University of Washington. Its distinctively colored blooms can be observed at the Barnard's Inn Farm, Vineyard Haven, Massachusetts.

Related *Enkianthus* variety of interest:

E. cernuus var. rubens. USDA Zones 6–8. Introduced from Japan in 1900. Outstanding, rich red, bell-shaped flowers, 0.25 in. long, in nodding racemes, in May. Unusually beautiful variety; smaller than the species in habit, leaf, and flower. Received RHS Award of Garden Merit.

Related *Enkianthus* species of interest:

E. chinensis. USDA Zones 7–8. Introduced in 1900 from China. Flowers 0.4 in. long, usually yellowish, veined with pink, but wide diversity in color—red, green-red, pale red, to white with lavender and a striped pattern. Chinese species less well known than Japanese; similar to *Pieris japonica* and resembles *E. campanulatus,* but leaves are elliptic to oblong, and there is variation in leaf size. Grows to 25 ft. high.

Embothrium coccineum (J. C. Raulston)

Embothrium coccineum (J. C. Raulston)

Enkianthus campanulatus (N. Brewster)

Enkianthus campanulatus (N. Brewster)

Enkianthus campanulatus 'Red Bells' (Greer Gardens)

*E. deflexus.* USDA Zones 6–7. E. H. Wilson, who called this "one of the most strikingly beautiful plants of the mountains of western China," collected seed in 1878 in the Himalayas; recorded as growing at altitudes to 12,500 ft. Larger flowers than *E. campanulatus*, 0.75 in. long, in wide color range of pink, red, pale yellow, white, or with red stripes, in May–June. Variable species.

## *Enkianthus perulatus*
### WHITE ENKIANTHUS

Ericaceae. USDA Zones 6–8. Introduced in 1859 from southwestern Japan.

DESCRIPTION: Deciduous shrub growing slowly to 6 ft. high and 9–12 ft. wide, with multistemmed habit about as wide as tall.
*Leaves:* Alternate, simple, elliptic-ovate to obovate, clustered at branch tips, finely serrate, 1–2 in. long, with outstanding scarlet-red fall color.
*Flowers:* White, lanternlike, 0.3 in. long, in profuse clusters of 3–10 florets, before foliage; May.
*Winter aspect:* Silvery bark; tiered branching habit.

CULTURE: Grows in full sun or partial light shade; prefers damp ground and well-drained, acid, loamy soil.
*Disease and insect problems:* None serious; occasional scale.
*Transplanting:* Difficult; roots take time to form.
*Propagation:* By cuttings in mid-June; not easy, but roots readily once roots take hold; careful over-wintering is the secret to successful production of rooted cuttings, according to Gossler Farms Nursery, Springfield, Oregon, which roots cuttings directly into 2.25 in. pots to minimize root disturbance and maintains young plants in the same container all winter at 35°F.

LANDSCAPE VALUE: Rarely planted in American gardens, this unique, delicate, fascinatingly attractive shrub exhibits a spectacular display of snowy white, showy flowers. Far less well known than *E. campanulatus*, to which it is closely related, this species differs in that it is smaller, 3–6 ft. high, with a more refined habit, a tiered branching pattern, a profusion of white flowers that appear before the leaves, and upright seed capsules. Foliage is bright green in summer, turning a brilliant scarlet in fall; most outstanding species of genus for fall color. In Japan is also used as a hedge plant. Perhaps one reason for the scarcity of this highly ornamental shrub is difficulty of propagation. Received RHS Award of Garden Merit.

Plant may be observed at AA, ABF, ATL, BBG, BER, BF, BRK, BSG, CUH, DUK, HOL, LWD, MOR, MUN, NCS, NEW, PLF, RKEW, UBC, WIN, WIS.

*Enkianthus perulatus* cultivar of interest:

*E. perulatus* 'Compactus'. Little-known cultivar, reaching about 18 in. high and 18–25 in. wide in 20 years. Very slow growing; takes many years to bloom. Attractive, twiggy habit in winter. Perfect for rock garden and a natural bonsai candidate.

## *Escallonia* × *exoniensis*
### ESCALLONIA

Parentage: *E. rosea* × *E. rubra*. Escalloniaceae (Grossulariaceae). USDA Zone 9. Named in honor of Escallon by his teacher, Spanish botanist Mutis. Native to South America. Introduced into cultivation in 1880s by Exeter Nurseries of Veitch & Sons.

DESCRIPTION: Evergreen shrub growing rapidly to 5–6 ft. high (18–20 ft. in milder climates), with graceful, open habit.
*Leaves:* Alternate, simple, margins usually dentate, 0.5–1.5 in. long, glossy green above, paler beneath.
*Flowers:* White-pink to rose, with 5 petals, in terminal racemes or panicles, 1.5–3 in. long; June–October and sometimes year-round.
*Fruit:* A capsule with numerous small seeds.

CULTURE: Needs full sun, but tolerates partial shade in hot interior valleys; tolerates wind, drought, salt air, and most soils, but prefers fertile, well-drained soil that is not too alkaline; may freeze at 10–15°F, but recovers quickly.
*Disease and insect problems:* None serious.
*Transplanting:* Easy, with container-grown plants.
*Propagation:* By cuttings of firm, but not hard, side shoots in August, rooted in sandy soil.

LANDSCAPE VALUE: A robust, vigorous shrub prized for its glossy foliage, graceful habit, continuous flowering, and tolerance of wind, drought, and salt. Superb hedge plant. Withstands direct coastal conditions.

Plant may be observed at FIL, HUN, LAC, LWD, STR, VDG, WIS.

*Escallonia* × *exoniensis* cultivars of interest:

*E.* × *exoniensis* 'Balfourii'. White flowers with bluish tint. Introduced into cultivation by Sir Isaac Bailey Balfour. Grows rapidly to 10–15 ft. high. Among hardiest of the species, this graceful plant makes a good hedge or windbreak. Tolerates lime and salt-laden wind.
*E.* × *exoniensis* 'Fradesii'. Pink to rose flowers in summer and later. Grows to a compact 5–6 ft. high. Origin unknown; may be a selection (cultivar) of *E. laevis*.

*Enkianthus perulatus* (N. Brewster)

*Enkianthus perulatus* (G. Koller)

*Enkianthus perulatus* (J. C. Raulston)

*Escallonia* × *exoniensis* (R. Jones)

*Escallonia* × *exoniensis* (R. Jones)

*Escallonia* × *exoniensis* 'Fradesii' (N. Brewster)

*Escallonia* × *exoniensis* continued

Related *Escallonia* species and cultivars of interest:

*E. bifida* [*E. montevidensis*]. Native to eastern South America, introduced in 1827. Pure white flowers bloom in large, flat, rounded panicles in September. Most attractive of white-flowering escallonias, with glossy, spatula-shaped leaves. Grows to 10 ft. or higher in mild climates; may be espaliered. Needs shelter in colder climates. Tolerates some shade; prefers loamy soil.

*E.* 'Pride of Donard' (*E. virgata* × *E. rubra*). Clear red flowers in June–August (almost year-round in milder areas). Introduced into cultivation by Slieve Donald Nursery, Newcastle, Ireland. Glossy, deep green leaves and dense, upright habit. Grows to 8 ft. or higher. Prefers sandy loam. Semi-evergreen in hard winters; will recover from frost damage. Received RHS Award of Garden Merit.

*E. rubra* 'C. F. Ball'. Crimson red flowers, 0.3 in. wide, in loose panicles, 2.5 in. long, in July–August. Vigorous grower to 6–15 ft. high, with upright habit. Lance-shaped leaves, 1–3 in. long, are aromatic when crushed. Tolerates most soils; likes some shade in hot areas. Variable in wild. Excellent as screen or hedge in coastal areas; withstands lime and salt air.

# *Euonymus alatus* 'Rudy Haag'
## RUDY HAAG BURNING BUSH

Celastraceae. USDA Zones 4–7. Native to the United States. Introduced into cultivation in 1963 by Kentucky nurseryman Rudy Haag.

DESCRIPTION: Deciduous shrub growing only 3 in. per year to 4–5 ft. high and as wide, with upright, spreading habit.
*Leaves:* Elliptic to obovate, 2–2.25 in. long and about 0.5 in. wide, dark green, turning bright red in fall.
*Flowers:* Not conspicuous.
*Fruit:* Not conspicuous.
*Winter aspect:* Interesting bark; strong branching habit.

CULTURE: Grows well in sun or heavy shade; tolerates wind, but not wet conditions; shows stress in very dry conditions.
*Disease and insect problems:* None.
*Transplanting:* Very easy; shallow, noninvasive root system.
*Propagation:* By softwood cuttings.

LANDSCAPE VALUE: A dense, low shrub with superb architectural habit, excellent form, and good fall color. Similar to *E. alatus* 'Compactus' but much more compact. Can be planted as specimen or grouped in front of larger shrubs and trees. One of the few plants of this size with a strong branching pattern. Withstands heavy pruning.

Plant may be observed at BF, BIC, BOE, CBG, DEN, LNG, MNL, MRT, OWG, SEC.

*Euonymus alatus* cultivars of interest:

*E. alatus* 'Nordine Strain'. Hardier, produces more fruit, and is more compact than the species, with branches close to the ground. Unique fruit production; after leaves drop, plant still has a whole season of glorious, persistent fruit. Named for Roy Nordine, former propagator at The Morton Arboretum.

*E. alatus* 'Timber Creek'. Chicago Fire Euonymus. Hardier than the species; grows to 8–10 ft. high and 6–8 ft. wide, with multistemmed habit. The corky wings, typical of the species, become less prominent as the plant matures, creating a more refined appearance. Young twigs and branches are mahogany-red. Dark green, somewhat leathery foliage is accented by reddish pink tints on new growth. Crimson-red fall color followed by red-orange fruit, remaining ornamentally effective into early winter. New release by the Chicagoland Grows Plant Introduction Program in 1995.

# *Euonymus europaeus* 'Redcap'
## EUROPEAN EUONYMUS

Celastraceae. USDA Zones 4–7. Native to Europe and western Asia. Selected by the University of Nebraska. Propagated by Interstate Nurseries, Hamburg, Iowa.

DESCRIPTION: Deciduous shrub growing at moderate to fast rate to 12–25 ft. high and 10–25 ft. wide, with upright, narrow habit when young becoming broad with age.
*Leaves:* Opposite, simple, ovate-elliptic to oblong, 1–3.5 in. long and 0.3–1.25 in. wide, dull green.
*Flowers:* Yellow-green, with yellow anthers, not showy; May.
*Fruit:* A pink to bright red, 4-lobed, dehiscent capsule with white seed and orange aril, borne abundantly and persistently.
*Winter aspect:* Angular, green branches with corklike stripes.

CULTURE: Grows in full sun or partial shade; tolerates moist soils, but needs good drainage; adapts to a wide pH range.
*Disease and insect problems:* Scale common, though dormant oil spray in spring, after temperature reaches 45°F, is a good preventative; timing of other sprays is very important since young crawlers move about only during a short period in spring. Euonymus caterpillar causes severe defoliation, but does not kill the plant.
*Transplanting:* Balled and burlapped.
*Propagation:* By cuttings.

*Euonymus alatus* 'Rudy Haag' (J. Poor)

*Euonymus alatus* 'Rudy Haag' (J. Poor)

*Euonymus alatus* 'Nordine Strain' (E. Hasselkus)

*Euonymus europaeus* 'Redcap' (R. Klehm)

*Euonymus oxyphyllus* (G. Koller)

111

LANDSCAPE VALUE: A handsome, relatively adaptable and tough shrub, useful for screens and massed plantings. One of the first shrubs to leaf out in the spring; foliage appears in April in the Midwest. A beautiful addition to the autumn landscape with its fall show of exceptionally colorful foliage and spectacular fuchsia-pink-orange fruit. Species used for centuries for screen plantings in Romania and the Czech Republic and to stabilize dunes in France.

Plant may be observed at BBG, BEA, BIC, DAW, FIL, GCC, HOL, LNG, MOD, MNL, MRT, SEC.

Related *Euonymus* species of interest:

*E. oxyphyllus.* USDA Zones 5–8. Native to Japan, China, and Korea. Introduced into United Kingdom in 1895. Handsome deciduous shrub growing slowly to 21 ft. high, with attractive, wine-glass habit and strong architectural branching pattern. Brownish green, non-ornamental flowers appear in May. Valued for its rich shades of red to purple-red-brown autumn color and showy, bright carmine-red, nearly globose fruit capsules, which also appear in the fall.

## *Exochorda giraldii* var. *wilsonii*
### REDBUD PEARLBUSH

Rosaceae. USDA Zones 6–8. Native to northern China. Introduced into cultivation in 1897.

DESCRIPTION: Deciduous shrub to 10–15 ft. high and as wide, with vigorous habit, more upright than the species.
*Leaves:* Alternate, simple, elliptic to oblong, 1–2.5 in. long and 0.5–1.5 in. wide, medium green, with no fall color.
*Flowers:* White, fragrant, 2 in. across, in clusters of 8–10 on racemes to 36 in. long; April–May in cooler climates, March in warmer climates.
*Fruit:* A green to yellow-brown capsule, ripening in October.
*Winter aspect:* Brown, glabrous stems.

CULTURE: Grows in sun or partial shade; prefers well-drained, loamy, acid soil, but tolerates a wide pH range.
*Disease and insect problems:* None serious.
*Transplanting:* Balled and burlapped or container-grown.
*Propagation:* By seed, or by cuttings in summer.

LANDSCAPE VALUE: An interesting, loosely branched shrub that becomes droopy with age. Best for shrub border or massed plantings. Beautiful in flower but not spectacular after bloom fades. A good, tough plant that tolerates heat and drought.

Plant may be observed at AA, CBG, CUH, DAW, HOL, MUN, PAL, RKEW, WIN, WIS.

Related *Exochorda* hybrid and cultivar of interest:

*E.* × *macrantha.* Less refined than *E.* × *macrantha* 'The Bride', a larger shrub growing to 12–15 ft. high.
*E.* × *macrantha* 'The Bride' (*E. korolkowii* × *E. racemosa*). USDA Zones 5–8. Grows to 4–6 ft. high. Gloriously beautiful in full bloom, with large, white, abundant flowers on pendulous branches. Flowers on previous year's growth. Withstands variable soil conditions. Developed in 1938 by Grootendorst. Received RHS Award of Garden Merit.

## *Feijoa sellowiana*
### PINEAPPLE GUAVA

Myrtaceae. USDA Zones 8–9. Native to South America. Introduced into cultivation in the Mediterranean region in 1890, in California in 1900, and in New Zealand in 1900–1925 by Hayward Wright.

DESCRIPTION: Broad-leaved evergreen growing rapidly to 10–15 ft. high (can reach 25 ft.); very widespreading habit.
*Leaves:* Opposite, oval, 2–3 in. long, glossy green above, silvery white beneath.
*Flowers:* Delicate, 1 in. wide, with 4 fleshy, white petals tinged purple on inner surfaces, sides, and tuft of large, red stamens; May–June.
*Fruit:* Oval, 1–4 in. long, grayish green, edible, with flavor reminiscent of pineapple.

CULTURE: Prefers sun and clay or loam soil; does not like wet conditions; tolerates drought, but needs summer moisture for fruit to develop to proper size.
*Disease and insect problems:* None serious.
*Propagation:* By cuttings and seed.

LANDSCAPE VALUE: An excellent shrub valued for its leaf color and for its unusual flowers and fruit, both of which are edible. Flower petals are used for salads, and the pineapple-flavored fruit can be eaten fresh, canned, or made into juice or jelly. Fruit being considered for use as commercial crop in California; New Zealand has already recognized its commercial value. May be trained into almost any shape; good for espalier. Can withstand severe pruning in late spring.

Plant may be observed at BOK, BRK, CAL, FIL, FUL, HUN, LAC, MBG, MMA, NAT, RBC, RKEW, SAB, SEL, STR, WAI.

*Feijoa sellowiana* cultivars of interest:

*F. sellowiana* 'Coolidge'. Widely used in landscaping. Self-fruiting; small fruit has mild flavor.
*F. sellowiana* 'Mammoth'. Bears large fruit.
*F. sellowiana* 'Triumph'. Preferred for commercial planting.

*Exochorda giraldii* var. *wilsonii* (G. Koller)

*Exochorda* × *macrantha* 'The Bride' (N. Brewster)

*Exochorda* × *macrantha* (J. C. Raulston)

*Exochorda* × *macrantha* 'The Bride' (N. Brewster)

*Feijoa sellowiana* (G. Dobbins)

*Feijoa sellowiana* (G. Dobbins)

## Forsythia × intermedia
### BORDER FORSYTHIA

Parentage: *F. suspensa* × *F. viridissima*. Oleaceae. USDA Zones 5–8. Described in 1885 by Hermann Zabel, director of the municipal garden, Munich, Germany. Introduced into cultivation circa 1900 by Späth Nurseries, Germany, and by the Arnold Arboretum in the 1940s.

DESCRIPTION: Deciduous shrub growing quickly to 8–10 ft. high and 10 ft. wide, with upright, loose, arching habit.
*Leaves:* Opposite, simple, 3–5 in. long, dark green above and lighter beneath, with tinge of burgundy in fall in warmer climates.
*Flowers:* Pale to deep yellow, borne on old wood; March–April.
*Fruit:* A brown capsule, 0.3 in. long.

CULTURE: Grows in sun or shade; needs sun for profuse bloom; prefers good, friable soil, but adapts to all soil types and pH ranges; tolerates urban conditions.
*Disease and insect problems:* None serious; occasional leaf spot, spider mite, crown gall, and Japanese weevil.
*Transplanting:* Easy, bare root or balled and burlapped.
*Propagation:* By seed, softwood cuttings, and hardwood cuttings.

LANDSCAPE VALUE: Valued for its colorful, early spring bloom when few trees and shrubs produce color. Buds often killed by cold in northern zones. Best in massed plantings and shrub border. Not a specimen plant; habit not particularly attractive. Tends to become rangy and needs frequent pruning to maintain shape. All forsythias should be pruned immediately after flowering; prune either by removing oldest stems and/or heading back to shape plant. Genus named after William Forsyth, an 18th-century British horticulturist.

Plant may be observed at AA, ABF, BBG, BC, BEA, BIC, BIR, BOE, BSG, CAL, CBG, CIN, CUH, DAW, DEN, DOW, FIL, GCC, HOL, HUN, LAC, LNG, LWD, MBG, MIS, MNL, MRT, MUN, NEB, NEW, OWG, PAL, PLF, RBC, RKEW, SEC, SKY, SPR, STG, VDG, WIS.

*Forsythia × intermedia* cultivars of interest:

*F. × intermedia* 'Gold Tide'. USDA Zones 5–9. New dwarf forsythia; a sport of *Forsythia x intermedia* 'Spring Glory'. Grows 20 in. high and 4 ft. wide. Heavy bloomer in early spring. Flowers, grapefruit-yellow and dense; foliage, clean moss-green. Tolerant of heat, drought, and urban conditions; superb for massed plantings on slope or trailing over walls.

*F. × intermedia* 'Lynwood'. Extremely bright, yellow flowers, upright growth. Originated in Lynwood garden of Miss Adair in northern Ireland. Introduced in 1935 by Slieve Donard Nursery, Newcastle, Ireland. Received RHS Award of Garden Merit.

*F. × intermedia* 'Spring Glory'. Abundant, sulfur-yellow flowers produced evenly along upright branches. Sport of *F. × intermedia* 'Primulina', found in a garden in 1930 by M. Horvath of Mentor, Ohio. Flowers paler and larger (to 2 in. across) than parent. Grows to 6–8 ft. high. Introduced in 1942 by Wayside Gardens.

## Forsythia 'Meadowlark'
### EARLY FORSYTHIA

Parentage: *F. ovata* × *F. europaea*. Oleaceae. USDA Zones 5–7. Introduced as a result of work at Arnold Arboretum and experimental stations in North and South Dakota.

DESCRIPTION: Deciduous shrub growing relatively quickly to 6–9 ft. high and as wide, with upright, spreading, semi-arching habit.
*Leaves:* Opposite, simple, ovate, medium to dark green.
*Flowers:* Brilliant yellow, 0.75 in. wide, borne profusely; March–April.
*Fruit:* Ovoid, 0.5 in. long, drawn to a slender apex before splitting.
*Winter aspect:* Pale, gray-brown bark.

CULTURE: Grows in sun or shade; needs sun for profuse bloom; prefers good, friable soil, but adapts to all soil types and pH ranges; tolerates urban conditions.
*Disease and insect problems:* None.
*Transplanting:* Easy.
*Propagation:* By seed, softwood cuttings, and hardwood cuttings.

LANDSCAPE VALUE: Great addition to northern gardens. Provides early yellow color in the somber landscape. After witch hazels, one of the first shrubs to bloom in spring. Probably hardiest cultivar for northern zones; extremely bud hardy, to −35°F.

Plant may be observed at AA, ABF, BBG, BIC, BOE, CBG, CIN, DAW, GCC, HOL, LNG, MOD, MRT, NEB, RKEW, SEC, SKY, SPR, RKEW, WIN, WIS.

Other cultivars of interest from *Forsythia ovata* × *F. europaea*:

*F.* 'Northern Gold'. Large-scale shrub with flowers of robust yellow hue. Grows 7–10 ft. high and 12 ft. wide. Useful for planting in parks and other spacious planting sites.

*F.* 'Northern Sun'. Spectacular yellow flowers, 0.75 in. long and 1 in. wide, in very early spring. Hardier than other *F. ovata* × *F. europaea* cultivars; recommended for northern cold zones to −30°F. Grows vigorously to 8–10 ft. high. Original plant grown from seed in 1957 at the University of Minnesota Landscape Arboretum.

*Forsythia × intermedia* 'Lynwood' (J. C. Raulston)

*Forsythia* 'Northern Gold' (R. Klehm)

*Forsythia* 'Meadowlark' (E. Hasselkus)

*Forsythia mandshurica* 'Vermont Sun' (N. Brewster)

*Forsythia* 'New Hampshire Gold' (N. Brewster)

Related *Forsythia* cultivars of interest:

*F. mandshurica* 'Vermont Sun'. USDA Zone 4. Large, soft yellow flowers, similar to those of *F. ovata*. One of the earliest forsythias to flower, blooming a week before *F. ovata*. Grows to 8 ft. high and as wide, with a distinct, erect, uniform, oval habit. Developed at the University of Vermont.

*F.* 'New Hampshire Gold' (*F. ovata* × *F.* × *intermedia* 'Lynwood'). Yellow, cold-hardy flowers. Grows to 5 ft. high, with mounded habit. Developed by Paul Joly, Windsor Road Nursery, Cornish, New Hampshire; result of a cross between *F.* × *intermedia* 'Lynwood', *F. ovata* 'Ottawa', and *F. europaea*.

*F.* 'Sunrise' (*F. ovata* × unknown parentage). Brilliant yellow flowers produced profusely on rather dense shrub to 5 ft. high. Hardy to −20°F. Introduced by Iowa State University.

*F. suspensa* var. *sieboldii*. Weeping Forsythia. USDA Zones (5)6–8. Yellow-gold flowers, 1 in. across, borne 1–3 along branches, in April. Does not flower as abundantly as *F.* × *intermedia*, but the long, trailing branches of yellow flowers provide graceful color to the spring landscape. Attractive espaliered or cascading over wall. Grown for its elegant, pendulous, arching habit. Reaches 8–10 ft. high (or higher if trained on wall). Medium to dark green leaves, which appear after flowers, are opposite, simple, oblong, with finely serrate margins, 4 in. long and 1–2 in. wide. Fruit is narrow-ovoid. Native to China and Japan; cultivated in Europe 1833 by Verkerk Pistorius. Introduced into Britain in 1857 as var. *sieboldii*.

*F. viridissima* var. *koreana* 'Ilgwang'. USDA Zones 4–8 (with shade in southernmost regions). New growth is pale yellow, with slightly darker, showy flowers. Oval leaves are chartreuse in shade and brighter yellow in sun, usually with dark blotch in center. Grows rapidly when young to reach 5–6 ft. high and as wide; rounded habit becomes more spreading with age. 'Ilgwang' (meaning sunlight in Korean) is one of the first plants to leaf out in the spring and holds its foliage late into fall—at times even into winter—making it especially valuable for cold climates. Tolerates wide range of conditions; only problem is leaf scorch in sunny sites.

*F.* 'Winterthur' (*F. ovata* × *F.* × *intermedia* 'Spring Glory'). USDA Zones 6–8. Flowers of lovely, delicate, pale yellow, similar to those of *Corylopsis* 'Winterthur', blend with other spring colors without dominating the landscape. Shrub combines compact habit of *F. ovata* and large flower size of *F.* × *intermedia*. Grows to 6 ft. high and blooms later than *F. ovata*. Origin is unknown, but plant has enhanced Winterthur Gardens for many years. Named and introduced to the trade in 1987 by Winterthur.

# *Fothergilla gardenii*
## WITCH ALDER

Hamamelidaceae. USDA Zones 5–8. Native to southeastern United States. Discovered by Dr. Garden of Charleston, South Carolina. Introduced into cultivation in 1770 by John Bartram.

DESCRIPTION: Deciduous shrub growing slowly to 2–3 ft. high, with compact, dense, mounded habit and spreading branches.
*Leaves:* Rounded or oblong, with several unequal teeth above middle of leaf margin, 1–2 in. long, leathery, medium green, turning brilliant yellow, orange, and crimson in fall.
*Flowers:* Cream-colored stamens, no petals, with yellow anthers, in terminal spikes, 1–2.5 in. long and 0.75–1.75 in. across, fragrant, before the leaves.
*Fruit:* A 2-seeded capsule, not ornamental, sparingly produced.
*Winter aspect:* Gray-brown, smooth bark; slender, often spreading habit.

CULTURE: Grows in sun and shade; best in moist, well-drained peat or sandy loam, with high organic content; prefers acid soil, but grows in alkaline soil; does not like heavy soil.
*Disease and insect problems:* None serious.
*Transplanting:* Moderately easy; best balled and burlapped.
*Propagation:* By seed, cuttings, and layering.

LANDSCAPE VALUE: A superb, little-used, small shrub with attractive inflorescences in bottlebrush-shaped spikes. Effective as foundation plant or combined with azaleas and rhododendrons. Spectacular autumn color. The species and its cultivar 'Blue Mist' have both received the Pennsylvania Horticultural Society Gold Medal (Styer Award). Genus name commemorates 18th-century gardener John Fothergill. Although he lived in Stratford-le-Bow, Essex, United Kingdom, Fothergill had one of the earliest and most extensive collections of American plants then in cultivation.

Plant may be observed at AA, ABF, ATL, BBG, BC, BEA, BER, BF, BIC, BLO, BRK, BSG, CBG, CIN, COX, CUH, DAW, DIX, DOW, DUK, GCC, GIW, HOL, LNG, LWD, MCG, MIS, MOR, MRT, MTC, NCS, NEW, PAL, PLF, RHO, SEC, STG, UBC, USN, VDG, ZOO.

*Fothergilla gardenii* cultivars of interest:

*F. gardenii* 'Blue Mist'. Very attractive, reaching 2–3 ft. high, with compact, mounded habit, and blue-green leaves. Does not produce vibrant fall color. Benefits from light shade. Original plant from the garden of John and Lydia Morris, which became the Morris Arboretum in 1932. Tom Dilatush, New Jersey nurseryman, acknowledged the value of this shrub and prompted the Morris

*Forsythia* 'Sunrise' (E. Hasselkus)

*Forsythia* 'Winterthur' (Winterthur Gardens)

*Forsythia viridissima* var. *koreana* 'Ilgwang' (J. C. Raulston)

*Fothergilla gardenii* (G. Koller)

*Fothergilla gardenii* (R. Klehm)

*Fothergilla gardenii* 'Blue Mist' (J. Elsley)

117

Arboretum staff to register the cultivar name in 1987. Received Pennsylvania Horticultural Society Gold Medal (Styer Award) in 1990.

*F. gardenii* 'Jane Platt'. Has more cascading habit than species, with more slender leaves and longer flowers. Grows to 3 ft. high, with lovely, vibrant, yellow-orange-red autumn color. Selected from the Portland garden of John and Jane Platt and introduced by Gossler Farms Nursery.

*F. gardenii* 'Mt. Airy'. USDA Zones 5–7. Handsome shrub reaching 3–5 ft. high with vigorous, upright habit, deep green foliage, profuse white flower spikes, and vibrant orange-red autumn color. Selected by Michael Dirr from the Mt. Airy Arboretum, Cincinnati, Ohio. Perhaps a hybrid of *F. gardenii* × *F. major*.

# Fothergilla major
## LARGE FOTHERGILLA

Hamamelidaceae. USDA Zones 5–8. Native to the United States—from Virginia to South Carolina. Introduced in 1780–1800, possibly by André Michaux. Grown in English gardens in 1780 but lost to cultivation until reintroduced by Arnold Arboretum in 1904.

DESCRIPTION: Deciduous shrub growing slowly to 6–10 ft. high, with pyramidal to rounded, multistemmed habit.
*Leaves:* Ovate to obovate, 2–4 in. long, dark green and leathery above, blue-green and pubescent beneath, turning golden-yellow, orange, red, and purple in fall.
*Flowers:* Creamy white stamens, yellow anthers, no petals, 2–3 in. long, in terminal spikes; April–May.
*Fruit:* A 2-valved, black capsule with explosive dehiscence, not ornamental.
*Winter aspect:* Smooth, gray bark; multistemmed habit varies from sparingly to freely branched.

CULTURE: Grows in sun and shade; prefers light shade in warmer climates; grows best in noncompacted peat or sandy loam with adequate year-round moisture; needs well-drained soil; tolerates alkaline soil better than widely believed.
*Disease and insect problems:* None serious.
*Transplanting:* Balled and burlapped.
*Propagation:* By seed, hardwood cuttings, and softwood cuttings; spreads profusely by underground stems.

LANDSCAPE VALUE: A good-sized, superior shrub. Similar to *F. gardenii* but larger and more upright, with denser and slightly coarser habit. Has same magnificent autumn color and interesting, attractive bottlebrush-shaped flowers, which, unlike those of *F. gardenii*, appear with foliage. Additional differences between the two species: *F. gardenii*

leaves are more pubescent on upper surfaces; *F. major* leaves are sometimes toothed nearly to the base, while *F. gardenii* leaves are not; *F. major* begins flowering after its leaves are nearly fully expanded, while *F. gardenii* begins flowering before the leaves expand in the spring. There is some controversy about whether location, climate, or species dictates simultaneous foliage and flower bloom and whether *F. gardenii* always blooms on bare branches and *F. major* blooms with the leaves. Received RHS Award of Garden Merit.

Plant can be observed at AA, ABF, ATL, BBG, BC, BEA, BER, BF, BIR, BLO, BRK, CAL, CBG, CIN, COX, CUH, DAW, DOW, DUK, GCC, GIW, HOL, IES, LNG, LWD, MBG, MOR, MRT, MTC, MUN, NCS, NEW, PAL, PLF, POW, RKEW, SKY, SPR, USN, VDG, WIS.

# Fouquieria splendens
## OCOTILLO

Fouquieriaceae. USDA Zones 8–10. Native to Mexico and southwestern desert regions of the United States.

DESCRIPTION: Deciduous shrub growing at moderate rate to 8–15(20) ft. high, with numerous, erect and leaning canes from base.
*Leaves:* Alternate, simple, oblong-obovate, fleshy, 0.5–1 in. long, appearing along the stems after rain but dropping as soon as ground moisture is exhausted.
*Flowers:* Orange-scarlet to scarlet, tubular, with recurved lobes, 0.75 in. long, with 5 sepals and 5 petals; petioles developing into stout spines borne in axils of the spine blades, 1.25 in. long; flowers crowded in terminal racemes, 4–10 in. long, before leaves, after spring/summer rains.
*Fruit:* An ovoid capsule, 0.3–0.75 in. long, with numerous flat, winged seeds.
*Winter aspect:* Gray, furrowed, thorny canes; stiff, whiplike stems.

CULTURE: Needs full sun and sand with excellent drainage; tolerates drought, but not overwatering; usually found on dry, rocky hillsides or desert flats; grows and flowers in hot, dry areas in Hawaii, especially on the dry side of mountains, at elevations of 500–1000 ft.
*Disease and insect problems:* None serious.
*Transplanting:* Easy.
*Propagation:* By cuttings rooted in soil.

LANDSCAPE VALUE: Valued for its unusual form and striking red flowers, this desert native is used ornamentally in cactus or succulent gardens, as an impenetrable hedge, screening, or silhouette against walls. Unlike cactus, does not store large amounts of water. Seemingly dead canes are leafless during rainless months but are transformed by

*Fothergilla major* (N. Brewster)

*Fothergilla major* (N. Brewster)

*Fothergilla major* (J. Apel)

*Fouquieria splendens* (S. Wenzlau)

*Fouquieria splendens* (S. Wenzlau)

rains into wands of bright, gray-green. Even when not in flower or leaf, dry canes are graceful and add an interesting dimension to the landscape. Most commonly called Ocotillo, but often called Slimwood, Jacob's Staff, Barda, or Ocote. Also called Candlewood because dry stems burn from one end like a candle; wood is hard, heavy, and burns easily. Flowers and seed pods sometimes eaten by Cahuilla Indians; beverage and cough medicine are made from flowers, and slender stems are used as walking sticks. Stout thorns are only unfavorable characteristic. Attractive to hummingbirds, which pollinate flowers. Genus name commemorates Edouard Fouquier, 19th-century French professor of medicine.

Plant may be observed at DEN, SAB.

## *Fremontodendron* 'California Glory'
### FLANNEL BUSH
### FREMONTIA

Parentage: *F. californicum* × *F. mexicanum*. Bombacaceae. USDA Zones 7–10. Native to the United States, in California and Arizona. Introduced into cultivation in 1851.

DESCRIPTION: Broad-leaved evergreen growing moderately fast to 6–20 ft. or higher, with upright, spreading habit.
*Leaves:* Alternate, simple, entire to slightly lobed, leathery, to 2 in. across, dark green above, covered with dense, gray-white, feltlike coating beneath.
*Flowers:* Deep, golden-yellow inside, red-orange tinge outside, saucer-shaped, to 3 in. across; spring–summer.
*Fruit:* A persistent, conical seed capsule, to 1.25 in. long, covered with rust-colored hairs, and with 2–3 brown seeds in each chamber.

CULTURE: Grows in sun or light shade in loam or sand; extremely drought resistant; tolerates air pollution but not wet conditions; needs little or no summer water; grows in Hawaii at higher, drier elevations of 2000–3000 ft.
*Disease and insect problems:* None known.
*Transplanting:* Fairly easy; shallow root system.
*Propagation:* By seed, soaked in hot water and stratified for 2–3 months, or by cuttings over heat.

LANDSCAPE VALUE: Stunning in flower in spring and summer, its leaves and branching pattern also give it year-round interest. Very prolific bloomer over long period. Pinch and prune to shape; can be espaliered. Hillside planting is best since it needs excellent drainage. May be short-lived. The hairy coating on leaves can cause an allergic reaction to those with sensitive skin. Attractive planted with *Ceanothus*.

Plant may be observed at LAC, RAN, SBB, WIS.

## *Gardenia taitensis*
### TIARE
### PINWHEEL GARDENIA

Rubiaceae. USDA Zone 10. Native to Society Islands. Introduced into cultivation prior to 1871 from Tahiti.

DESCRIPTION: Broad-leaved evergreen growing slowly to 8 ft. high, with bushy habit.
*Leaves:* Inverted ovate, about 4 in. long, shiny green.
*Flowers:* White, single, fragrant, with 5–6 lobes arranged like pinwheels around the corollas; year-round.

CULTURE: Grows in sun or shade; tolerates wind, wet conditions, salt, air pollution, and soil compaction, but not drought; needs adequate moisture; grows at sea level either on the coast or inland in Hawaii, but thrives at elevations of 1500 ft.
*Disease and insect problems:* Sooty mold, mealy bug, and scale.
*Transplanting:* Easy.
*Propagation:* By cuttings.

LANDSCAPE VALUE: An extremely attractive, useful shrub. Effective as a hedge; its shiny leaves and fragrant, pinwheeled, white flowers also make it valuable as an ornamental specimen.

Plant may be observed at LAC, NAT, WAI.

*Fremontodendron* 'California Glory' (J. Elsley)

*Fremontodendron* 'California Glory' (J. C. Raulston)

*Gardenia taitensis* (V. Lauritzen)

*Gardenia taitensis* (V. Lauritzen)

## Garrya elliptica 'James Roof'
### SILK TASSEL TREE

Garryaceae. USDA Zone 9. Native to southwestern United States, Mexico, and the West Indies. Species introduced into cultivation in 1828 by David Douglas.

DESCRIPTION: Evergreen shrub growing vigorously and rapidly to 12 ft., with densely branched, bushy habit. *Leaves:* Opposite, simple, oblong-elliptical, entire, with wavy margins, 1.5–3 in. long and half as wide, shiny, leathery, deep green above, woolly and gray beneath. *Flowers:* Yellow to green-yellow, thin, graceful catkins, 3–8 in. long in male; pale green, shorter (2.5–3 in. long) in female; dioecious, clustered flower tassels in winter; January–March. *Fruit:* A globose, dry, 2-seeded berry; female has purple fruit that persists June–September. *Winter aspect:* Very attractive catkins.

CULTURE: Grows in sun or partial shade in average and dry soil, but prefers good drainage; tolerates seaside exposure and atmospheric pollution very well; needs protection in cold areas; shoots of catkins can be damaged by hard frosts. *Disease and insect problems:* None serious. *Transplanting:* Not easy; best container-grown; does not like to be moved. *Propagation:* By cuttings.

LANDSCAPE VALUE: A handsome shrub that deserves wider use for its habit, tolerance of adverse conditions, attractive, evergreen foliage and ornamental winter bloom—conspicuous, long, silvery gray, tassel-like catkins, speckled with green anthers. Can be used as informal hedge, screen, or specimen. Male cultivar 'James Roof' is extremely attractive when its unusually long catkins open during the cold winter months; seedling of this cultivar selected before 1950 by Roof, director of Regional Parks Botanic Garden, Berkeley, California. Beautiful specimens of this shrub found in gardens in Cornwall and Devon, United Kingdom, where it grows much taller—to 16 ft. Only genus in the family. Received RHS Award of Garden Merit.

Plant may be observed at CUH, FIL, MMA, PAL, RAN, RKEW, SBB, STR, WIS.

*Garrya* hybrid of interest:

*G. × issaquahensis* (*G. elliptica × G. fremontii*). Attractive, large shrub noted for its dark green foliage, glossy above and glaucous, slightly hairy beneath. Originated in Seattle about 1957 in the garden of Mrs. Pat Ballard. Cultivar 'Pat Ballard', a male selection raised from this cross, is outstanding because of its brighter green, flat leaves, only slightly wavy at edges, and extremely long catkins, to 8–9 in., exhibiting a red-purple tinge.

## Genista pilosa
### SILKY LEAF WOADWAXEN

Leguminosae. USDA Zones 6–8. Native to Europe from Sweden to the Mediterranean regions. Introduced into cultivation in 1790.

DESCRIPTION: Deciduous shrub 1–1.5 ft. high, procumbent when young; mature plant forms low mass on twiggy shoots, which often grow erratically through one another. *Leaves:* Simple, obovate, narrow, 0.25–0.5 in. long, glabrous, deep green above, pubescent beneath. *Flowers:* Yellow, pealike, singly or in pairs, each on its own stalk forming a full raceme 2–6 in. long; May–July. *Fruit:* A silky pod, 0.75–1 in. long.

CULTURE: Needs sun and good drainage; likes sandy, gravelly, dry soil in alkaline range; tolerates poor soils. *Disease and insect problems:* None serious. *Transplanting:* Difficult because of deep root system. *Propagation:* Best by seed for healthier, longer-lived plants; also by cuttings in late July–August.

LANDSCAPE VALUE: A worthy, low shrub with a lovely mass of flowers in varying shades of yellow. Requires little maintenance. Excellent addition to rock gardens. Green stems give the appearance of an evergreen.

Plant may be observed at AA, ATL, BC, BER, CBG, CIN, CUH, DEN, LWD, MOD, MRT, NCS, NEW, PAL, RBC, RKEW, SKY, STR, UBC, VDG, WIS.

*Genista pilosa* cultivars of interest:

*G. pilosa* 'Goldilocks'. Numerous yellow flowers in May–June. Strong grower, taller and wider than species. Selected in Boskoop, Netherlands, by W. J. van der Laan in 1970.

*G. pilosa* 'Lemon Spreader'. Larger and deeper yellow flowers than species.

*G. pilosa* 'Vancouver Gold'. USDA Zones 6–9. Introduced by the University of British Columbia Botanical Garden. Handsome plant that grows to 1 ft. high and 3 ft. wide. Stems and leaves of this low-growing shrub are thin and small but densely massed, and are blanketed with bright, golden-yellow flowers in spring. Excellent for massed plantings. Grows in partial shade, but flowers best in full sun.

Related *Genista* species of interest:

*G. aethnensis*. Mount Etna Broom. USDA Zone 8. Golden-yellow, fragrant flowers profusely borne in loose, termi-

*Garrya elliptica* 'James Roof' (Strybing Arboretum Society, Helen Crocker Russel Library)

*Garrya elliptica* 'James Roof' (Strybing Arboretum Society, Helen Crocker Russel Library)

*Genista pilosa* 'Vancouver Gold' (University of British Columbia Botanical Garden)

*Genista lydia* (University of Washington)

*Genista sagittalis* (G. Koller)

*Genista pilosa* continued

nal racemes in July–August. Very popular in United Kingdom, this large, elegant shrub has thin, reedlike, leafless branches, which are nodding when young. Received RHS Award of Garden Merit.

G. *lydia*. USDA Zones (5)6–8. Golden-yellow flowers; very floriferous. Variable habit in the wild. Best planted on ledge in rock garden or at top of dry wall where graceful habit is displayed to best advantage. Introduced in 1926 by Dr. Turrill.

G. *sagittalis*. Arrow Broom. USDA Zones 5–7. Native to southeastern Europe; introduced into cultivation in 1588. Very attractive, hardy, vigorous, low-maintenance plant. Reaches 6–12 in. at maturity, with prostrate habit. Numerous, golden-yellow flowers bloom in June on racemes 0.5 in. long, creating a glorious yellow carpet in the landscape. Leaves are sparse, oval, 0.5–0.75 in. long, hairy. Likes full sun, although it tolerates light shade; grows in loam or sand in a wide pH range; tolerates dry, sandy soil, drought, and lime. Effective as edging plant for borders. Easily distinguished by its size from other *Genista* species. Probably cultivated as a medicinal plant.

## *Grevillea alpina*
### CATSCLAW MOUNTAIN GREVILLEA

Proteaceae. USDA Zone 9. Native to Australia. Introduced into cultivation before 1857.

DESCRIPTION: Evergreen shrub growing fairly rapidly once established to 5 ft. high, with prostrate habit (some forms have upright habit).
*Leaves:* Oval, about 1 in. long and 0.2 in. wide, medium green.
*Flowers:* Two-color combinations of white, orange, yellow, or red, in spiderlike clusters 1.5 in. across; year-round, but heaviest June–December.

CULTURE: Grows in sun or half shade in clay, loam, or sand with a pH of 5–7; tolerates some wind and, when established, drought; tolerates salt air but not saline soil; dislikes humidity.
*Disease and insect problems:* Root rot in heavy soils; stem mold and leaf spot in warm, humid weather; aphid, mealy bug.
*Transplanting:* Easy if not pot-bound; fairly shallow root system.
*Propagation:* By cuttings.

LANDSCAPE VALUE: A continuously blooming species that lends itself to use in shrub beds or rock gardens. Attractive to birds. Drought-tolerant and insect-resistant

when grown in proper conditions. Also frost-tolerant. Shape is improved with occasional light pruning. This species has produced some excellent hybrids, including 'Poorinda Wonder', 'Poorinda Tranquillity', and 'Poorinda Ruby'.

Plant may be observed at HUN, LAC, SCZ, STR, VDG.

*Grevillea alpina* cultivar of interest:

G. *alpina* 'Grampian's Gold'. Deep golden-yellow flowers with rusty brown hairs; good small to medium-size shrub which can be effectively used as a ground cover.

Related *Grevillea* cultivars of interest:

G. 'Canberra Gem' (G. *juniperina* × G. *rosmarinifolia*). Rounded shrub to 4.5 ft. high and as wide, with deeply indented leaves. Red flowers in small clusters. Received RHS Award of Garden Merit.

G. 'Robyn Gordon' (G. *banksii* 'Forster's' × G. *bipinnatifida*). Small, spreading shrub growing to 4.5 ft. high. Flowers are coral-red, spidery; large divided leaves.

Related *Grevillea* species of interest:

G. *victoriae*. Deep orange-red flowers; leaves entire, silver beneath, dropping. Grows to 6 ft. high and as wide.

## *Grevillea lavandulacea* 'Tanunda'
### LAVENDER GREVILLEA

Proteaceae. USDA Zone 9. Native to Australia.

DESCRIPTION: Broad-leaved evergreen growing at moderate rate to 6 ft. high and 4 ft. wide, with rounded, sprawling habit.
*Leaves:* Narrow, needlelike, 0.75 in. long, grayish green.
*Flowers:* Crimson and white, in spiderlike clusters 1 in. across; heaviest bloom November–June.
*Winter aspect:* Sprawling habit.

CULTURE: Grows in sun and partial shade in clay, loam, or sand with a pH of 5–7; tolerates some wind, some humidity, and frost.
*Disease and insect problems:* Root rot.
*Transplanting:* Best when young; shallow root system.
*Propagation:* By cuttings.

LANDSCAPE VALUE: A foreground shrub with good gray foliage color. Tolerant of a wider variety of soil and moisture conditions than most grevilleas. Blooms nearly all year. 'Victor Harbor' is possibly the best cultivar of the species.

Plant may be observed at FUL, HUN, STR.

*Grevillea alpina* (T. Kipping)

*Grevillea* 'Robyn Gordon' (Sunset Magazine)

*Grevillea alpina* (T. Kipping)

*Grevillea lavandulacea* 'Tanunda' (Sunset Magazine)

## Grevillea rosmarinifolia
### ROSEMARY GREVILLEA

Proteaceae. USDA Zone 9. Native to Australia. Introduced into cultivation in 1822 by Allan Cunningham.

DESCRIPTION: Broad-leaved evergreen growing at moderate rate to 4–6 ft. high and as wide or wider, with slender, loose, graceful habit.
*Leaves:* Alternate, closely set, linear, lanceolate, acute, narrow, stalkless, rough, 1.5 in. long and 0.1 in. wide, resembling rosemary leaves, dark green above, silvery beneath.
*Flowers:* Red with cream, 1–1.5 in. across, in dense, terminal clusters; fall–winter.
*Fruit:* A 1- or 2-seeded pod, not conspicuous.

CULTURE: Needs full sun and nonalkaline soil; tolerates poor, rocky, dry soil when established, drought, and heat, but not wet conditions.
*Disease and insect problems:* None serious.
*Transplanting:* Easy.
*Propagation:* By half-ripened shoots in July, rooted in peat with bottom heat; by seed, pushed into soil on edge, not flat.

LANDSCAPE VALUE: Noteworthy for its extremely attractive foliage, showy flowers, and tolerance of heat and drought. Scattered bloom appears throughout the year. Useful as clipped or unclipped hedge, in shrub beds, or as excellent container plant. Brittle wood subject to storm damage. Genus named for Charles Francis Greville, former vice-president of the Royal Society of London and a patron of horticulture and botany. Received RHS Award of Garden Merit.

Plant may be observed at BBG, FUL, RKEW, STR, WIS.

Another *Grevillea* species of interest:

*G. tridentifera.* Clusters of small, white, honey-scented flowers. Three-pronged leaves are needlelike, bright green. Useful as screen, hedge, or as bank cover. Broad-leaved shrub growing to 4–6 ft. high, with broader habit.

## Grewia occidentalis
### GREWIA

Tiliaceae. USDA Zone 10. Native to South Africa. Introduced into cultivation before 1690.

DESCRIPTION: Broad-leaved evergreen growing slowly to 8 ft. high, with compact habit.
*Leaves:* Ovate, toothed, about 2 in. long, with finely crenate margins.
*Flowers:* Light mauve, 2 in. across, with 5 narrow sepals and petals; April and later.

CULTURE: Grows in sun or light shade in sandy soil; tolerates wind, wet conditions, and salt, but not drought; flowers at low elevations in Hawaii, but prefers higher elevations of 1000–2000 ft.
*Disease and insect problems:* Mealy bug.
*Transplanting:* Quite easy; shallow root system.
*Propagation:* By cuttings.

LANDSCAPE VALUE: A most attractive ornamental with its full growth habit and large, mauve flowers. Excellent for topiary use.

Plant may be observed at BBG, FOS, FUL, HUN, LAC, LYO, RKEW.

## Hamamelis × intermedia
### WITCH HAZEL

Parentage: *H. japonica × H. mollis.* Hamamelidaceae. USDA Zones 5–8. Crossed in 1928 by Arnold Arboretum. Named in 1945 by Alfred Rehder.

DESCRIPTION: Deciduous shrub 15–20 ft. high, with upright, spreading habit, not densely branched.
*Leaves:* Large, obovate, resembling hazel-like foliage; fall color excellent, with red-flowering specimens often exhibiting redder foliage.
*Flowers:* Yellow to red, with strap-shaped petals; buds wormlike; late January–March in cooler climates.

CULTURE: Grows in sun or shade in moist, but not wet, acid soil; tolerates moderate urban pollution.
*Disease and insect problems:* None serious.
*Transplanting:* Best balled and burlapped.
*Propagation:* By cuttings in June–July; must be put on own roots to remain true to cultivar.

LANDSCAPE VALUE: A superb, strong, vigorous garden shrub with interesting, loose habit, winter flowering, and spectacular fall color. Generally problem-free, it has never received the widespread recognition it deserves. Its amazingly durable flowers bloom over a long period. North Carolina State Arboretum has one of the best collections. Witch hazel has been widely used for many years as a medicine for numerous ailments, ranging from hemorrhages to aching muscles, poison ivy, and sunburn. It is also an ingredient in cosmetics and soaps. Extract is made from leaves and bark of young stems and roots.

Plant may be observed at AA, ABF, ATL, BBG, BC, BEA, BER, BF, BLO, BRK, BSG, CAA, CAL, CBG, CHK, CIN, CUH, DEN, DUK, GCC, GIW, HOL, IES, ING, LNG, LWD, MIS, MOR, NCS, OWG, PAL, PLF, RBC, RKEW, SEC, SKY, STG, UBC, USN, VDG, WIN, WIS.

*Grevillea rosmarinifolia* (Strybing Arboretum Society, Helen Crocker Russel Library)

*Grevillea rosmarinifolia* (N. Brewster)

*Grewia occidentalis* (V. Lauritzen)

*Grevillea tridentifera* (Sunset Magazine)

*Grewia occidentalis* (V. Lauritzen)

*Hamamelis × intermedia* 'Arnold Promise' (B. Yinger)

*Hamamelis × intermedia* 'Diane' (E. Hasselkus)

127

*Hamamelis* × *intermedia* cultivars of interest:

*H.* × *intermedia* 'Arnold Promise'. Vigorous, wide-spreading, vase-shaped shrub, with downy, green-gray foliage. One of original seedlings raised at Arnold Arboretum from seed of *H. mollis*. Valued for its extra-large, lemon-yellow, fragrant blooms, 0.5–1 in. long, which persist up to 3 weeks. Received RHS Award of Garden Merit.

*H.* × *intermedia* 'Diane'. One of finest red-flowered cultivars, with blooms more copper than true red. Rich, orange-red fall color. Introduced in 1969 by Kalmthout Arboretum, Belgium. Received Pennsylvania Horticultural Society Gold Medal (Styer Award) in 1991. Received RHS Award of Garden Merit.

*H.* × *intermedia* 'Feuerzauber'. Vigorous plant with ascending branches, large, rounded leaves and copper-red, fragrant flowers with 0.75 in. long, kinked, and twisted petals.

*H.* × *intermedia* 'Jelena'. Each flower petal is red at base, orange in the middle and yellow at the tip; thus, shrub in bloom glows like copper. Warm apricot to red fall color. Vigorous shrub introduced by Kalmthout Arboretum, Belgium. Received RHS Award of Garden Merit.

*H.* × *intermedia* 'Primavera'. Primrose-yellow flowers in dense clusters; highly fragrant.

*H.* × *intermedia* 'Ruby Glow'. Red-copper flowers with long, thin, twisted petals mature to reddish brown. Foliage turns orange to scarlet in autumn. Somewhat erect in habit with medium-sized foliage. Developed in 1935 by Korl, Kalmthout Arboretum, Belgium.

# *Hamamelis mollis*
## CHINESE WITCH HAZEL

Hamamelidaceae. USDA Zones 6–8. Native to China. Introduced in 1879 by Charles Maries. Sent to the United States in 1907 via United Kingdom by E. H. Wilson.

DESCRIPTION: Deciduous shrub growing slowly to 10–15 ft. high and as wide, with oval to rounded, spreading habit.
*Leaves:* Alternate, simple, ovate to obovate, 3–6 in. long. medium gray-green in summer, turning an attractive, clear yellow in fall.
*Flowers:* Yellow, with red-brown calyx cups, delicately scented, persisting on bare branches; February–March.
*Fruit:* A dehiscent capsule, with 2 shiny, black seeds that burst forth at maturity.
*Winter aspect:* Handsome, smooth, gray bark.

CULTURE: Flowers best in full sun, but grows well in partial shade; prefers moist, well-drained, acid, organic soil, but has been observed in clay soil with a neutral pH; needs protection from wind.
*Disease and insect problems:* None serious.
*Transplanting:* Best balled and burlapped.
*Propagation:* By cuttings in June or by seed, requiring warm/cold treatment.

LANDSCAPE VALUE: A lovely, fragrant shrub that blooms early and deserves more frequent use. Has extremely attractive, fragrant flowers and many interesting cultivars. More compact and less hardy than *H.* × *intermedia* and *H. virginiana*. Received RHS Award of Garden Merit.

Plant may be observed at AA, ABF, ATL, BBG, BC, BEA, BER, BF, BLO, BSG, CAL, CBG, COX, CIN, CUH, DAW, DIX, DOW, DUK, GCC, HOL, IES, LWD, MIS, MOR, MRT, MUN, NCS, NEW, PAL, PLF, RKEW, SEC, SKY, STG, UBC, VDG, WIN, WIS.

*Hamamelis mollis* cultivars of interest:

*H. mollis* 'Brevipetala'. Upright shrub with profuse, fragrant, yellow flowers, red at bases and slightly twisted.

*H. mollis* 'Coombe Wood'. More spreading than species, with larger, deep yellow-gold, highly scented flowers.

*H. mollis* 'Pallida'. Green-yellow or sulfur-yellow, fragrant blooms, borne profusely. Grows to 15 ft. high with lustrous foliage; can be espaliered. Introduced by the Royal Horticultural Society. Received Pennsylvania Horticultural Society Gold Medal (Styer Award) in 1989. Received RHS Award of Garden Merit.

*Hamamelis* × *intermedia* 'Jelena' (B. Yinger)

*Hamamelis* × *intermedia* 'Jelena' (E. Hasselkus)

*Hamamelis* × *intermedia* 'Primavera' (N. Brewster)

*Hamamelis* × *intermedia* 'Ruby Glow' (B. Yinger)

*Hamamelis mollis* (J. C. Raulston)

*Hamamelis mollis* 'Brevipetala' (G. Gates)

## *Hamamelis virginiana*
### WITCH HAZEL

Hamamelidaceae. USDA Zones 4–8. Native to eastern North America from Nova Scotia to the mountains of Tennessee and the Carolinas. Introduced in 1736 by John Bartram of Philadelphia, Pennsylvania.

DESCRIPTION: Deciduous shrub 15–20 ft. high and almost as wide (30 ft. high and 20–25 ft. wide in the wild), with irregular, rounded, open habit.
*Leaves:* Alternate, simple, broadly ovate to obovate, round-toothed, 3–5 in. long and 2–3.5 in. wide, unequal at bases, turning yellow in fall.
*Flowers:* Tiny, fragrant, golden-yellow, ribbonlike; fall.
*Fruit:* A capsule, 0.5 in. long, that bursts, sending forth 2 glossy, black seeds.
*Winter aspect:* Gray-brown bark.

CULTURE: Grows in sun and shade; prefers good, moist, but not wet or heavy, soil; likes acid soil, but is more tolerant of pH variations than other *Hamamelis* species; tolerates smoke and urban pollution.
*Disease and insect problems:* Relatively trouble-free.
*Transplanting:* Best balled and burlapped.
*Propagation:* Not easy; by softwood cuttings or by seed, which takes 2 years to germinate.

LANDSCAPE VALUE: A marvelous understory shrub, long known but too infrequently used in the landscape. Attractive, easy-to-grow plant that requires little maintenance and has a sweet, heavenly, penetrating scent. Bloom often masked by foliage. Kalmthout Arboretum, Belgium, has raised seedlings of *H. virginiana* that flower after the leaves have fallen, producing a more effective fall blooming period. This shrub closes the blooming season before winter. Name "witch" comes from the Anglo-Saxon word *wych* ("to bend"); botanical name *Hamamelis* derives from the Greek *hama* ("together") and *mela* ("fruit"), because *H. virginiana* retains its fruit for an entire year before the seed ripens. Bark used for manufacture of the well-known medicinal witch hazel.

Plant may be observed at AA, ABF, ATL, BBG, BEA, BER, BF, BIC, BIR, BOE, BRK, BSG, CAL, CBG, CHK, CIN, COX, CUH, DAW, DEN, DIX, DOW, DUK, GCC, GIW, HOL, IES, LNG, LWD, MIS, MNL, MOR, MRT, MTC, MUN, NCA, NCS, NEB, NEW, PAL, PLF, RBC, RKEW, SAB, STG, STR, UBC, USN, VDG, WIN, ZOO.

Related *Hamamelis* species and form of interest:

*H. macrophylla.* Southern Witch Hazel. USDA Zones 7–9. Native to southeastern United States. Discovered in 1828. Introduced into cultivation in 1928. Rare species closely allied to *H. virginiana* but smaller in all respects.

Obovate, bright green leaves turn warm yellow in fall. Small to medium, pale yellow flower petals are narrow and crumpled. Shrub remains in flower until December in southerly latitudes.

*H. vernalis* f. *carnea.* Ozark Witch Hazel. USDA Zones 5–8. Collected in 1845 in Missouri by George Engelmann. Native to Missouri, Arkansas, and Louisiana; resembles Asian species in flowering on bare branches before foliage appears. Medium-sized to large shrub growing to 6–10 feet high, with greater spread. Blooms profusely in late winter. Has pungent scent, butter-yellow fall color, and interestingly colored flowers. Petals are red at base, graduating to apricot at tips; petals and calyces are pale, flesh-pink inside, kinked, and slightly twisted.

## *Heptacodium miconioides*
### SEVEN-SON FLOWER OF ZHEJIANG

Synonym: *H. jasminoides.* Caprifoliaceae. USDA Zones 5–7. Native to western China. Genus collected by E. H. Wilson in Hupei Province, China, in 1907. In 1916 Alfred Rehder of Arnold Arboretum described the new genus, which then disappeared but was rediscovered in 1980 by the Sino-American Botanic Expedition.

DESCRIPTION: Deciduous shrub growing rapidly and vigorously to 6–10 ft. in 6 years and ultimately to 15–20 ft., with erect, upright, multistemmed habit.
*Leaves:* Opposite, with pointed tips and rounded bases, 3–4 in. long and 2–2.25 in. wide, margins entire, with 3-nerved veins parallel to margins, dark green, turning muted purple in shade, persisting until November.
*Flowers:* Creamy white, jasminelike, small, single, sweetly fragrant, abundant, on tiered, 6-flowered whorls; early fall.
*Fruit:* Develops from flower, borne in large clusters in winter, showier than the flowers, green at first, turning rose and purple for several weeks, then turning tan.
*Winter aspect:* Arching branches; thin, light tan to brown bark, peeling off in small, paperlike strips.

CULTURE: Grows in full sun or partial shade, but flowers more abundantly in sun; prefers acid soil with excellent drainage and a pH of 5–6, but grows in alkaline soil; tolerates drought.
*Disease and insect problems:* None known.
*Transplanting:* Easy, balled and burlapped or container-grown.
*Propagation:* By single-node cuttings with mist.

LANDSCAPE VALUE: An exciting, almost unknown, rediscovered genus; no mature plants yet exist in North America. Flowers, fruit, and attractive bark provide multiseason interest. Apt to be leggy; needs to be pruned or topped out

*Hamamelis virginiana* (G. Koller)

*Hamamelis vernalis* f. *carnea* (K. Bachtell)

*Heptacodium miconioides* (N. Brewster)

*Heptacodium miconioides* (G. Koller)

*Heptacodium miconioides* (N. Brewster)

*Heptacodium miconioides* (N. Brewster)

131

*Heptacodium miconioides* continued

to keep in bounds and to better show off interesting bark. Potential tree for urban conditions. Received Pennsylvania Horticultural Society Gold Medal (Styer Award) in 1995.

Plant may be observed at AA, ATL, BBG, BEA, BF, BRK, CBG, CIN, DUK, HOL, MCG, MIS, MOR, MRT, NCS, PLF, RKEW, UBC, USN, WIN.

# *Heteromeles arbutifolia*
## CHRISTMAS BERRY
## CALIFORNIA HOLLY

Rosaceae. USDA Zone 8. Native to the United States, in southern California. Introduced into cultivation in 1796.

DESCRIPTION: Broad-leaved evergreen growing at moderate rate to 6–10 ft. high (25 ft. in the wild), with bushy, dense habit.
*Leaves:* Elliptic to oblong, short-stalked, sharply toothed, 2–4 in. long, thick, leathery, glossy, dark green.
*Flowers:* White, 0.25 in. across, in long, flattened terminal clusters; June–July.
*Fruit:* A berrylike pome, broadly egg-shaped, to 0.25 in. long, with ends incurved, bright cherry-red, rarely yellow, in loose clusters, in November–January.

CULTURE: Grows in sun or partial shade in any well-drained soil; tolerates some wind and drought, but thrives with water in summer; does not tolerate wet conditions.
*Disease and insect problems:* Prone to root rot and leaf fungus.
*Transplanting:* Easy, balled and burlapped.
*Propagation:* By seed or cuttings.

LANDSCAPE VALUE: A handsome evergreen, attractive year-round, with a splendid display of berries in winter. May be used as specimen, in groups, or on hillsides to control erosion. Fruit attractive to songbirds, pigeons, and quail. The only species in the genus, it is commonly found in the chaparral valleys of California.

Plant may be observed at FIL, FUL, LAC, MMA, MIS, RAN, RBC, SBB, STR, VDG.

# *Hibiscus rosa-sinensis*
## CHINESE HIBISCUS
## TROPICAL HIBISCUS

Malvaceae. USDA Zones 9–10. Native to China. Cultivated since 1730.

DESCRIPTION: Broad-leaved evergreen to 15 ft. high, with erect, glabrous habit.
*Leaves:* Coarse and obtuse, 2.5–3.5 in. long, glossy green.
*Flowers:* White to pink to red, yellow to orange, double and semidouble, 4–8 in. wide, solitary, in upper leaf axils.

CULTURE: Needs sun and protection from heat and winter frost; prefers clay or loam with a pH of 6–7; requires good drainage.
*Disease and insect problems:* Aphid; thrip can cause leaf edges and flower petals to curl and surfaces to become lumpy.
*Transplanting:* Easy.
*Propagation:* By softwood cuttings.

LANDSCAPE VALUE: One of the showiest flowering shrubs. Exhibits a great variety of color in flowers. Can be used for screen planting, as espalier, in container, or as greenhouse plant in areas where there is danger of frost. In warm inland areas, will grow best if partially shaded from the hot afternoon sun. Prune out one-third of old wood each spring, and pinch tips of stems during the summer to increase flowering.

Plant may be observed at DIN, MIS, PLF, RKEW.

*Hibiscus rosa-sinensis* cultivars of interest:

*H. rosa-sinensis* 'All Aglow'. Flowers have orange edges splashed with yellow and white center with pink halo;

*Hibiscus rosa-sinensis* (R. Jones)

*Heteromeles arbutifolia* (J. C. Raulston)

*Heteromeles arbutifolia* (J. C. Raulston)

*Hibiscus rosa-sinensis* 'All Aglow' (W. Soldani)

*Hibiscus rosa-sinensis* 'Fiesta' (Planting Fields Arboretum)

*Hibiscus rosa-sinensis* 'Cooperii' (J. Poor)

*Hibiscus rosa-sinensis* '5 Dimensions' (W. Soldani)

*Hibiscus rosa-sinensis* 'Tino Vietti' (Planting Fields Arboretum)

133

blooms of different size and configuration occur daily. A parent of 'Fiesta'.

*H. rosa-sinensis* 'Carolyn Coe'. Pale shrimp flowers with deep red eye.

*H. rosa-sinensis* 'Cooperii'. Pure red flowers with unusual white, pink, and green variegated foliage.

*H. rosa-sinensis* 'Fiesta'. Deep coral-orange flowers with white center and gold splashes.

*H. rosa-sinensis* '5 Dimensions'. Purple flowers.

*H. rosa-sinensis* 'Harvest Moon'. Beautiful, golden-yellow flowers, 4–9 in. across, with white center, and pink overlay, at times with orange spots; single blooms in cool weather, fully double in hot weather.

*H. rosa-sinensis* 'Herm Geller'. Lovely, orange flowers, 8–10 in. across, with a dark zinfandel-colored eye; lighter orange and yellow towards edges.

*H. rosa-sinensis* 'Tino Vietti' ['White Wings']. Pure white flowers with pale red center.

*H. rosa-sinensis* 'Tylene'. Abundant, single, gray-blue flowers with pink eye, 7–9 in. across.

# *Hibiscus syriacus* 'Diana'
## ROSE-OF-SHARON

Malvaceae. USDA Zones 5–8. Introduced into cultivation in 1971 by Donald Egolf of the U.S. National Arboretum.

DESCRIPTION: Deciduous shrub growing at moderate rate to 7.5 ft. high and 5 ft. wide, with dense, upright habit.
*Leaves:* Alternate, triangular, broad-cuneate or rounded at base, margins variously toothed and notched, palmately veined and lobed, 2.5–3.5 in. long and 1.5–2.5 in. wide, leathery, dark green.
*Flowers:* Pure white, solitary, ruffled and waxy, 4.5–6 in. across, with 5 distinct, wide, bell-shaped petals; late June/July–frost.

CULTURE: Grows best in sun in sandy loam with a pH of 5.5–7.0; tolerates wind, extreme heat, drought, air pollution, poor soil, and soil compaction.
*Disease and insect problems:* Japanese beetle.
*Transplanting:* Easy, balled and burlapped or bare root.
*Propagation:* By softwood or hardwood cuttings, which flower during their first season.

LANDSCAPE VALUE: An excellent, attractive plant for use as specimen, in shrub border, or as ornamental hedge. Needs full sun and spring pruning for heavier flowering and more compact growth. Because it is a triploid (tetraploid crossed with diploid), there is little or no seed produced as with the species, which has a short bloom sea-son, premature leaf drop and spontaneous seedings. The masses of blooms on *H. syriacus* 'Diana'—which often remain fully open for more than a day, even in hottest weather—drop immediately; thus, bud production is never inhibited, and the plant flowers freely for 3–4 months. Buds are not damaged by autumn frost. Received Pennsylvania Horticultural Society Gold Medal (Styer Award) in 1991. Also received RHS Award of Garden Merit.

Plant may be observed at AA, ABF, BBG, BF, BOK, BSG, CAL, CHK, CIN, DEN, FIL, HOL, LAC, MBG, MMA, MIS, MOR, NCS, NEW, OWG, PLF, RKEW, SEC, SPR, USN, VDG, WIN, WIS.

Other *Hibiscus syriacus* cultivars of interest:

*H. syriacus* 'Aphrodite'. Pink flowers with prominent, dark red eye spot.

*H. syriacus* 'Helene'. White flowers with prominent, dark red eye spot that radiates along veins to midpetal. 1981.

*H. syriacus* 'Lady Stanley'. White, semidouble flowers; petals marked at base with red, which occasionally streaks upward.

*H. syriacus* 'Minerva'. Lavender flowers with traces of pink overcast toward center and prominent, dark red eye spot. 1986.

*H. syriacus* 'Purpureus Variegatus'. Densely double, lilac-red flowers. Sparse bloomer; interesting primarily for white-variegated foliage. Strong grower. Descendent of 'Rubus', with larger flowers.

*H. syriacus* 'Woodbridge'. Single, deep red flowers with darker center. Descendent of 'Rubus', with larger and lighter flowers. Received RHS Award of Garden Merit.

Related *Hibiscus* cultivars of interest:

*H.* 'Lohengrin' (*H. paramutabilis* × *H. syriacus*). Pure white flowers, 5.5 in. wide, with a carmine-red center 2 in. wide; otherwise identical to 'Tosca'. A cross made by Hal Bruce, Winterthur.

*H.* 'Tosca' (*H. paramutabilis* × *H. syriacus*). Orchid-pink, saucer-shaped flowers, 5.5 in. wide, with carmine center 2 in. wide, July–frost. Large, maplelike, dark green leaves, to 8 in. wide. Shrub grows to 10 ft. in 4 years. Developed by Hal Bruce of Winterthur from an unknown clone of *H. syriacus* crossed with *H. paramutabilis*.

*Hibiscus syriacus* 'Diana' (L. Thomas)

*Hibiscus syriacus* 'Diana' (D. Egolf)

*Hibiscus syriacus* 'Purpureus Variegatus'
(J. C. Raulston)

*Hibiscus syriacus* 'Aphrodite' (D. Egolf)

*Hibiscus syriacus* 'Helene' (D. Egolf)

*Hibiscus* 'Lohengrin' (N. Brewster)

## *Hippophae rhamnoides*
### SEA BUCKTHORN

Elaeagnaceae. USDA Zones 3–7. Native to Europe and Asia.

DESCRIPTION: Deciduous shrub growing rapidly to 18–25 ft. high and 10 ft. wide, with loose, spreading, open habit.
*Leaves:* Alternate, sparsely stalked, tapered at both ends, linear, lanceolate, 1–3 in. long and 0.1–0.25 in. wide, dark gray-green above, glossy and silvery beneath.
*Flowers:* Yellow, in small clusters, before leaves, not conspicuous, not ornamental.
*Fruit:* Oval, rounded, 0.25–0.4 in. long, bright orange-yellow, juicy, clustered thickly on branches beginning in September, not attractive to birds, unisexual; female plant bears fruit.
*Winter aspect:* Divaricate (broadly spreading), thorny habit, with short stems.

CULTURE: Grows in sun; best in infertile, moist to dry gravel and sand; tolerates wet conditions and salt; often found near rivers.
*Disease and insect problems:* None serious.
*Transplanting:* Difficult to establish; use container plants.
*Propagation:* By root cuttings, division of suckers, and layering.

LANDSCAPE VALUE: Notable for its handsome winter aspect and attractive fruit borne from September throughout the winter. Excellent seashore plant; resists salt spray. Effective in massed plantings and borders. Cultivated for centuries and since 1940 for its vitamin-rich fruit. Stoloniferous; spreads by suckers. Dioecious; six females to one male plant suggested.

Plant may be observed at AA, ABF, BBG, DAW, LNG, MOD, MNL, MRT, MUN, RBC, RKEW, VDG, WIS.


## *Hydrangea arborescens* 'Annabelle'
### SMOOTH HYDRANGEA

Hydrangeaceae. USDA Zones 3–9. Native to eastern United States. Introduced into cultivation in 1962 by J. C. McDaniel of the University of Illinois.

DESCRIPTION: Deciduous shrub growing quickly to 3–5 ft. high and as wide, with clumpy, rounded habit.
*Leaves:* Serrate, with rounded base, 2.25–6 in. long and 1.75–5 in. wide, dark green above, tomentose beneath
*Flowers:* Light yellowish green, turning creamy white, with heads erect and symmetrical, in large, globose clusters 4–6 in. across, on new wood; late June–August.

CULTURE: Grows in sun with ample moisture, but prefers partial shade and rich, moist, well-drained, porous soil; adapts to a wide pH range; tolerates salt, but not drought.

*Disease and insect problems:* None serious; resistant to bud blight, leaf spot and mildew, to which other *Hydrangea* species are susceptible.
*Transplanting:* Easy; fibrous root system, best in early spring.
*Propagation:* By softwood cuttings in May–June.

LANDSCAPE VALUE: One of the finest and hardiest flowering shrubs, with large, very showy flowers and a long blooming period—up to one month in warmer climates and two months in colder regions. Spectacular in massed plantings, in shrub borders, or as informal hedge. Flowers are easily dried for indoor use. Cut to ground in late winter to produce new growth since flower buds form on new wood.

Plant may be observed at ABF, BBG, BF, BOE, BSG, CAL, CBG, CIN, COX, DEN, DIX, FIL, GCC, HOL, LNG, LWD, MBG, MNL, MIS, MOD, MOR, MRT, MUN, NEB, PAL, PLF, RHO, RKEW, STR, UBC, USN, VDG, WIS.

Related *Hydrangea* species of interest:

*H. aspera.* Grows to 12 ft. high and as wide or wider; shows a great variety in size, shape, and color of flowers. Sterile marginate flowers usually white; fertile flowers pink or blue, depending on pH of soil. One of the few hydrangeas that thrives in chalky soils but subject to late spring frosts.

*H. aspera* subsp. *aspera* [*H. villosa*]. USDA Zones 7–9. Blue or pink, flat blossoms borne in many-flowered cymes, 4–6 in. across, with sterile, white marginal florets, in June–July. Deciduous shrub grows to 3–9 ft. high. Leaves lanceolate to narrow-ovate, 4–7 in. long. Introduced from Nepal in 1825.

*H. sargentiana* [*H. aspera* subsp. *sargentiana*]. USDA Zones 7–9. Purplish blue flowers with sterile, white marginal florets. Grows to 6 ft. high, with very thick branches coated with mosslike hairs and bristles. Deciduous leaves ovate, 6–8 in. long, velvety, pubescent beneath. Useful for sheltered shrub border or woodland; requires light shade and protection from wind. Introduced from China in 1908.

*Hydrangea sargentiana* (University of British Columbia Botanical Garden)

136

*Hippophae rhamnoides* (University of Washington)

*Hippophae rhamnoides* (J. Apel)

*Hydrangea arborescens* 'Annabelle' (N. Brewster)

*Hydrangea aspera* (Royal Botanical Gardens, Ontario)

*Hydrangea arborescens* 'Annabelle' (N. Brewster)

*Hydrangea aspera* (B. Yinger)

## Hydrangea macrophylla
### BIGLEAF HYDRANGEA

Hydrangeaceae. USDA Zones 6–9. Native to Japan and China. First described in 1784 by Carl Thunberg in *Flora of Japan*. Brought from China to the Royal Botanic Gardens, Kew, in 1799 by Sir Joseph Banks.

DESCRIPTION: Deciduous shrub growing quickly to 3–8 ft. high, with rounded habit and erect, thick stems.
*Leaves:* Obovate to elliptic, coarsely serrate, cuneate at base, 4–8 in. long and 2.5–5 in. wide, lustrous green above, glabrous beneath.
*Flowers:* White, pink, or blue (depending on acidity and concentration of aluminum ions in soil), in clusters of fertile and sterile flowers, in umbellate panicles, 4–8 in. across, flat-topped with spherical heads.

CULTURE: Grows in sun and light shade; prefers well-drained, porous soil amended with peat moss or leaf mold; produces the bluest flowers in acid soils with a pH of 5.0–5.5, pink flowers in more alkaline soils with a pH of 6.0–6.5, and whiter flowers when pH exceeds 6.5; tolerates wet conditions, drought, and salt.
*Disease and insect problems:* None serious; aphid, red spider, leaf spot.
*Transplanting:* Easy, container-grown, in early spring.
*Propagation:* By softwood cuttings in May–July.

LANDSCAPE VALUE: Valued for its bold foliage and abundant flowering. Best for massed plantings, in the shrub border, or in large containers on patios or terraces. Excellent for seaside plantings. Prune immediately after flowering as buds form on previous season's growth. Plant is poisonous.

Plant may be observed at: BOE, BRK, BSG, CAL, CUH, DAW, LWD, NEW, RKEW, WIN, VDG, WIS.

*Hydrangea macrophylla* cultivars of interest: These cultivars can be divided into two groups. The largest group, the hortensia (H) type, are mop-headed hydrangeas growing to 4–6 ft. high or higher. Flowers are sterile and form large, globose heads. The second group, Lacecaps (L), are similar in habit but produce large, flattened corymbs of fertile flowers, surrounded by a showy ring of marginal florets.

*H. macrophylla* 'All Summer Beauty' (H). Abundant flowers of rich blue in acid soil, pink in neutral soil. Grows to compact 3–4 ft. high; flowers on new growth.
*H. macrophylla* 'Blue Billow' (L). Flattened clusters of fertile blue flowers with a ring of sterile blue flowers. Best blue-flowered cultivar; wide pH range; flowers produced for 3–4 weeks beginning in mid-June. Received Pennsylvania Horticultural Society Gold Medal (Styer Award) in 1990. Best grown in high shade with strong light in slightly acid soil. Has survived temperatures of −3°F with no bud damage. From a selected group of seeds of *H. macrophylla* brought back in 1966 from Mt. Halla, Korea, by Richard Lighty, director of Mt. Cuba Center in Delaware.
*H. macrophylla* 'Forever Pink' (H). Pink flowers, 4 in. across, in June, turning rose-red in fall. Compact shrub to 3 ft. high.
*H. macrophylla* 'Quadricolor' (L). Pale pink flowers. Grows to 4 ft. high; leaves unusually variegated with yellow, cream, sea-green, and deep green.
*H. macrophylla* 'Variegata Mariesii' (L). Rosy pink to rich blue, fertile flowers (depending on soil pH) surrounded by double ring of pink-red or light blue, sterile marginal florets. Grows to 3 ft. high, with leaves edged in creamy white. Brought from Japan in 1879.
*H. macrophylla* 'White Wave' (L). Blue or pink flowers with very large, pure white marginal florets with toothed sepals. Leaves acute-elliptic, thick. Grows to 3–3.5 ft. high. Raised in 1938 by Lemoine Nursery, Nancy, France, from *H. macrophylla* 'Variegata Mariesii'. Received RHS Award of Garden Merit.

Related *Hydrangea macrophylla* subsp. *serrata* cultivars of interest:

*H. macrophylla* subsp. *serrata* 'Bluebird'. Blue fertile flowers with large marginal florets of reddish purple or light blue, depending on soil acidity. Early flowering shrub to 5 ft. high, with thick branching habit. Received RHS Award of Garden Merit.
*H. macrophylla* subsp. *serrata* 'Preziosa'. Abundance of deep pink, mostly sterile flowers in flattened, globose clusters, turning to purple-red. Grows to 3–4 ft. high with red-brown branches. Leaves turn red in fall. A cross between *H. macrophylla* subsp. *serrata* and an hortensia. Developed by G. Arends of Wuppertal, West Germany, in 1961.

## Hydrangea paniculata 'Tardiva'
### PANICLE HYDRANGEA

Hydrangeaceae. USDA Zones 3–8. Native to Japan and China. Introduced into cultivation in 1861.

DESCRIPTION: Deciduous shrub growing quickly to 6–8 ft. high, with upright habit.
*Leaves:* Oval to ovate, cuneate at base, sometimes whorled, toothed, 3–6 in. long and 1.5–3 in. wide, dark green above, paler beneath.
*Flowers:* White sepals, 0.6–0.75 in. long, borne in fours rather than fives as in other *Hydrangea* species, in terminal panicles 6 in. long; August–late September.
*Winter aspect:* Coarsely spreading branching habit.

*Hydrangea macrophylla* (E. Hasselkus)

*Hydrangea macrophylla* 'Blue Billow' (Winterthur Gardens)

*Hydrangea macrophylla* subsp. *serrata* 'Preziosa' (T. Boland)

*Hydrangea macrophylla* 'Variegata Mariesii' (N. Brewster)

*Hydrangea paniculata* 'Tardiva' (G. Gates)

CULTURE: Grows in sun and partial shade in moist, well-drained soil amended with leaf mold; adapts to a wide pH range.
*Disease and insect problems:* None serious.
*Transplanting:* Easy, balled and burlapped or container-grown.
*Propagation:* By softwood cuttings in May–July.

LANDSCAPE VALUE: An asset in the shrub border or in massed plantings. Can also be pruned into a handsome tree form with a single trunk. One of the most cold-hardy of the genus, and the latest to bloom, producing panicles of white blossoms on arching branches when other shrubs have passed their peak. Flowers on new wood; prune in winter or early spring.

Plant may be observed at AA, BOE, BSG, CBG, CIN, COX, DAW, DIX, GCC, LNG, MBG, MNL, MIS, MRT, NCS, NEW, OWG, PAL, RKEW, SPR.

# *Hydrangea quercifolia*
## DOUBLE OAKLEAF HYDRANGEA

Hydrangeaceae (Saxifragaceae). USDA Zones 5–9. Native to the United States. Discovered in 1791 by John Bartram of Philadelphia, Pennsylvania.

DESCRIPTION: Deciduous, broad-leaved shrub growing 8–12 in. per year to 6–8 ft. tall and 6 ft. wide, with upright, vigorous habit and extensive branching.
*Leaves:* Large, 9 in. long and 6 in. wide, finely serrated, coarse, slightly leathery, with 3–7 lobes, green above, grayish green beneath, turning rose, claret, and burgundy in fall.
*Flowers:* White, semidouble, 1 in. wide, sterile, borne in large, bold, conical clusters 7–13 in. long; outer florets turn dusty rose as clusters age; May–July.
*Winter aspect:* Coarse, handsome, exfoliating bark, with cinnamon-colored stems.

CULTURE: Grows in sun or shade in clay or loam with a pH range of 4–7; tolerates brief drought, but not wet conditions, poor drainage, or salt.
*Disease and insect problems:* None.
*Transplanting:* Easy when dormant.
*Propagation:* By seed, layering, and cuttings of new growth in late May–June.

LANDSCAPE VALUE: An extremely attractive, hardy shrub with lobed, oaklike foliage and all-season interest. Foliage handsome throughout the growing season, varies in shape: some leaves are deeply lobed, while others are only slightly indented. Showy bloom in early summer can last for three months or more. Blooms are striking as outer florets of clusters turn pink while inner florets remain white. Bloom clusters almost too long and heavy to be held up without staking or proper pruning. There are probably more native *H. quercifolia* plants in Alabama than in all the rest of the world. Excellent planted with azaleas; good for massed plantings and shrub borders; shade-tolerant, so useful in woodland gardens or as understory plants. Plants may appear awkward at young age of 1 or 2 years; however, they grow quickly into spectacular, elegant shrubs. Received RHS Award of Garden Merit.

Plant may be observed at ABF, ATL, BBG, BEA, BF, BIR, BLO, BSG, CAL, CHK, CIN, DAW, DOW, FIL, GIW, HOL, MBG, MCG, MIS, MOR, MRT, MTC, NCS, NEB, OWG, PLF, RHO, RKEW, SEC, SKY, STG, WIS, ZOO.

*Hydrangea quercifolia* cultivars of interest:

*H. quercifolia* 'Snowflake'. Sterile cultivar with glorious, large flower panicles, 12–15 in. long, that remain on the shrub for months. Larger than species. Handsome claret-burgundy fall foliage. Introduced into cultivation in 1960 by Edgar G. and Loren L. Aldridge.
*H. quercifolia* 'Snow Queen'. Larger and more numerous sterile florets than species. Flower panicles remain upright on stiff stems and hold up better than those of the species, even after heavy rains. Mature flower heads turn russet before display of vibrant fall foliage. Introduced by Princeton Nurseries. Received Pennsylvania Horticultural Society Gold Medal (Styer Award) in 1989.

# *Hypericum patulum*
## GOLDEN CUP
## ST. JOHNSWORT

Hypericaceae. USDA Zones 6–8. Native to China, Himalayas, Japan. Introduced into cultivation from United Kingdom between 1920 and 1930.

DESCRIPTION: Semi-evergreen shrub 3 ft. high and as wide, with erect, compact habit.
*Leaves:* Opposite, oval, oblong or lanceolate, to 3 in. long, dark green above, glaucous beneath.
*Flowers:* Warm yellow, abundant, saucer-shaped, in terminal cymes, 2–3 in. across; continuously late June–October.

CULTURE: Grows in full sun or partial shade; adapts to a variety of soils, including poor, sandy ones.
*Disease and insect problems:* None serious.
*Transplanting:* Very easy, in spring.
*Propagation:* By seed and cuttings.

LANDSCAPE VALUE: An attractive shrub with bright yellow flowers. Cultivars are hardier and more vigorous than the species.

*Hydrangea quercifolia* 'Snowflake' (J. Poor)

*Hydrangea quercifolia* 'Snowflake' (L. Wrinkle)

*Hydrangea quercifolia* 'Snow Queen' (J. Elsley)

*Hypericum patulum* 'Hidcote' (J. C. Raulston)

*Hydrangea quercifolia* 'Snow Queen'
(N. Brewster)

**Hypericum patulum** continued

Plant may be observed at ATL, BBG, BC, BER, BF, BIC, BSG, CAL, CBG, CIN, CUH, DAW, DEN, GCC, HOL, HUN, LWD, MIS, MOR, MTC, NCS, PAL, PLF, RKEW, VDG, WIS.

*Hypericum patulum* cultivars of interest:

*H. patulum* 'Henryi'. USDA Zones 7–8. Dark yellow flowers to 2.5 in. across; larger than species. Introduced by A. Henry in 1898 and distributed by Messrs. Veitch. Treat as herbaceous perennial in northern climates.

*H. patulum* 'Hidcote'. USDA Zones 7–8. Fragrant, golden-yellow flowers; to 18 in. high and as wide. Possibly a garden hybrid of *H. forrestii* × *H. calycinum*. Received RHS Award of Garden Merit.

*H. patulum* 'Sungold'. Large, golden-yellow, fragrant flowers with conspicuous stamens.

Related *Hypericum* species and cultivars of interest:

*H. frondosum* 'Sunburst'. Golden St. Johnswort. USDA Zones 6–8. Native to southeastern United States. Introduced into cultivation in 1747. This seldom-seen semi-evergreen native is lower growing than the species, reaching an upright 3–4 ft. high. Handsome foliage has an interesting blue-green cast; leaves are 1–2.5 in. long. Good plant to face down smaller shrubs. Bright yellow flowers, 1–2 in. wide, appear in July, with stamens that form a dense brush 0.75 in. across. Attractive, although shrub holds dead flowers. 'Sunburst' has performed extremely well in Midwest evaluations; it prefers clay soil, and tolerates drought and soil compaction. Adds winter interest with its exfoliating red-brown bark and stout branches.

*H. hookeranum* 'Rowallane'. USDA Zone 9. Semi-evergreen shrub reaching about 2 ft. high, with erect habit. Oval leaves are 2–3 in. long, glossy green above, bluish beneath. Yellow flowers appear in small clusters, have flat, platelike corollas and nearly circular petals. Received RHS Award of Garden Merit.

*H. kalmianum*. USDA Zones (4)5–8. Dense-growing; very hardy evergreen shrub, to −40°F. Not as tall and with smaller flowers than those of *H. prolificum*.

*H. prolificum*. USDA Zones (4)5–8. Semi-evergreen hardy to −20°F, with narrow, shiny leaves, 1.25–3 in. long, and lustrous, exfoliating, brown bark in winter.

## Ilex cornuta 'Rotunda'
### CHINESE HOLLY

Aquifoliaceae. USDA Zones 7–9. Native to China, Korea. Introduced about 1941 by E. A. McIllhenny of Avery Island, Louisiana.

DESCRIPTION: Broad-leaved evergreen growing slowly to 3–4 ft. high and 6–8 ft. wide, with dense, compact, mounded habit.
*Leaves:* Strongly spiked, with 5–7 spines, somewhat rectangular, 1.25–3 in. long, leathery, glossy green.
*Fruit:* Red, occasional.

CULTURE: Grows in sun and partial shade; prefers loam with a pH of 5–6, but adapts to a wide pH range; tolerates some drought.
*Disease and insect problems:* Scale.
*Transplanting:* Easy, balled and burlapped or container-grown.
*Propagation:* By softwood cuttings in August–November.

LANDSCAPE VALUE: A handsome broad-leaved evergreen with very glossy leaves; useful as specimen, in borders, or as impenetrable hedge. Extremely tough, durable, and heat tolerant; widely used in southern climates.

Plant may be observed at BBG, BIR, CAL, NCS, STG.

Other *Ilex cornuta* cultivars of interest:

*I. cornuta* 'O. Spring'. Grows to 15 ft. high, with upright form. Leaves have creamy yellow margins; new foliage has purple tinge. Prefers partial shade. Introduced in 1968 by Tom Dodd, Semmes, Alabama.

*I. cornuta* 'Willowleaf'. Grows to 15 ft. high, with long, narrow, twisted leaves and an abundance of blood-red fruit that appears on very young plants. Introduced in 1953 by Cartwright Nursery, Collierville, Tennessee.

## Ilex crenata 'Beehive'
### JAPANESE HOLLY

Aquifoliaceae. USDA Zones 6–7. Native to Japan and Korea. Introduced in 1984 by Elwin Orton of Rutgers University.

DESCRIPTION: Broad-leaved evergreen growing slowly to 3.5 ft. high and 5 ft. wide, with dense, compact, mounded habit.
*Leaves:* Ovate to elliptic, 0.75 in. long and 0.25 in. wide, lustrous, dark green.
*Fruit:* (Male) None.

CULTURE: Grows in sun and partial shade in clay or loam with a pH of 5.5–6.0; tolerates wind, salt, and air pollution.
*Disease and insect problems:* Spider mite more serious in warm climates.

*Hypericum patulum* 'Hidcote' (G. Gates)

*Hypericum frondosum* 'Sunburst' (C. Ehrlinger)

*Ilex cornuta* 'Rotunda' (N. Brewster)

*Ilex cornuta* 'Rotunda' (N. Brewster)

*Ilex cornuta* 'Willowleaf' (N. Brewster)

*Ilex crenata* 'Beehive' (E. Orton)

*Transplanting:* Easy, balled and burlapped, year-round.
*Propagation:* By softwood cuttings in summer–November.

LANDSCAPE VALUE: A small, attractive shrub, with shape reminiscent of old-fashioned beehive; hence the name. An excellent, dwarf holly with unusually small, spineless leaves. A good rock garden plant; also useful as low hedge. Withstands pruning.

Plant may be observed at AA, ATL, BF, BRK, CAL, HOL, MIS, MOR, NCS, OWG, PLF, USN, VDG.

Other *Ilex crenata* cultivars of interest:

*I. crenata* 'Compacta'. Grows to 6 ft. high, with compact, globose habit. Leaves are 0.75 in. long, flat, lustrous, dark green. (Male)

*I. crenata* 'Delaware Diamond' ['Elfin']. USDA Zones 6–7. Introduced in 1970 by Norman Cannon, Greenwood, Delaware. Very dwarf, mounded habit with spreading branches and elliptic leaves. Grows 12 in. high and 18 in. wide. Excellent for rock garden. (Male)

*I. crenata* 'Dwarf Pagoda'. Introduced in 1972 by Elwin Orton, Rutgers University. Very slow growing (2 in. per year), with short internodes, heavy, coin-shaped foliage, and irregular branching habit. Grows to 10 ft. high. (Female)

*I. crenata* 'Glory'. Introduced in 1961 by J. Vermeulen, Neshanic, New Jersey. Grows to 5 ft. high and 8 ft. wide in 12 years. Dense, compact, globose habit; small, thick, glossy leaves are 0.25 in. long and 0.3 in. wide. One of hardiest cultivars in species; has withstood temperatures to −23°F. (Male)

*I. crenata* 'Golden Heller'. Introduced in 1972 by Lancaster Farms Nursery, Suffolk, Virginia. Grows to 4 ft. high and 5 ft. wide; leaves are 0.5 in. long, with yellow cast. (Female)

*I. crenata* 'Piccolo'. Introduced in 1979 by Norman Cannon, Greenwood, Delaware. Grows to 12 in. high and 8 in. wide in 8 years, with spherical, globose habit; foliage very tiny. (Female)

# *Ilex decidua* 'Warren's Red'
## POSSUMHAW

Aquifoliaceae. USDA Zones 5–9. Native to eastern United States. Originated in 1962 by the Otis Warren Nursery.

DESCRIPTION: Deciduous shrub growing at moderate rate to 18 ft. high and 15 ft. wide, with upright, vigorous habit, arching with age.
*Leaves:* Ovate to obovate, 3 in. long and 1.5 in. wide, unusually glossy, dark green.
*Fruit:* Red, 0.3 in. across, in fall–winter.

CULTURE: Grows best in sun; loses flowers and fruit when grown in shade; likes clay, loam, or sand with a pH of 4.5–6.5; tolerates wet conditions.
*Disease and insect problems:* None serious.
*Transplanting:* Easy.
*Propagation:* By softwood cuttings in late May–September, which root rapidly.

LANDSCAPE VALUE: Silver bark, unusually glossy leaves, and abundant red fruit that persists throughout winter months make this cultivar a striking addition to the winter landscape. Heavy fruiting develops an attractive, arched branching pattern in plant.

Plant may be observed at AA, ATL, BBG, BF, BIR, BRK, BSG, CAL, CBG, CUH, DAW, DUK, GIW, HOL, MBG, MIS, MOR, MTC, NCS, PLF, RKEW, SAB, SPR, USN, VDG, ZOO.

Other *Ilex decidua* cultivars of interest:

*I. decidua* 'Byer's Golden'. Grows to 15–20 ft. high, with upright, spreading, silver-gray branches and strongly multistemmed habit. Persisting, yellow fruit, 0.3 in. across, is clustered on short spurs on previous year's wood. Introduced in 1969 by Marcus Byers, Huntsville, Alabama.

*I. decidua* 'Council Fire'. Grows to 15 ft. high and 10 ft. wide, with upright to oval habit. Leaves are long, narrow, dark green. Colorful, showy, orange fruit to mid-March. Introduced in 1978 by J. Hartline, Anna, Illinois.

*I. decidua* 'Pocahontas'. Grows to 15–18 ft. high, with upright habit. The very glossy, red fruit, 0.3 in. across, does not persist as long as that of 'Council Fire'. Introduced in 1977 by J. Hartline, Anna, Illinois.

Related *Ilex* species of interest:

*I. amelanchier*. Swamp Holly. USDA Zones 7–9. Grows to 8 ft. high and 10 ft. wide; tends to become leggy. Found in sandy coastal plains from North Carolina to Florida and west to Louisiana. Like *I. decidua*, it develops fruit on side spurs and down stems. Outstanding for its almost iridescent, velvet red to cerise fruit, 0.25–0.5 in. across.

*Ilex crenata* 'Golden Heller' (J. C. Raulston)

*Ilex crenata* 'Piccolo' (P. Hill)

*Ilex decidua* 'Warren's Red' (N. Brewster)

*Ilex amelanchier* (N. Brewster)

*Ilex decidua* 'Byer's Golden' (G. Eisenbeiss)

*Ilex decidua* 'Council Fire' (C. Hubbuch)

## Ilex glabra 'Nordic'
### INKBERRY

Aquifoliaceae. USDA Zones (4)5–9. Native to North America—Nova Scotia to Florida, west to Missouri and Texas. Introduced into cultivation in 1987 by James Zampini, Lake County Nursery, Perry, Ohio. Patented under the name Chamzin; 'Nordic' is the trademark name.

DESCRIPTION: Broad-leaved evergreen growing slowly to 4 ft. high and as wide, with compact, rounded habit.
*Leaves:* Obovate to oblanceolate, slightly larger than species, 0.8–2 in. long and 0.3–0.6 in. wide, lustrous, dark green throughout winter.
*Fruit:* (Male) None.
*Winter aspect:* Multibranched, open habit.

CULTURE: Grows in sun and light shade in clay, loam, or sand with a pH of 5–6; survives in even heavy clay; tolerates salt, air pollution, and some wind, though bronzing may occur in very windy and sunny locations.
*Disease and insect problems:* None.
*Transplanting:* Easy, year-round.
*Propagation:* By softwood or hardwood cuttings and by transplanting suckering shoots around base.

LANDSCAPE VALUE: A good foundation plant, effective as hedge or in massed plantings. Tolerates pruning. Useful in damp areas and for tough urban environments. Hardy to −20°(−30°)F.

Plant can be observed at AA, ATL, BBG, BC, BF, BOE, BSG, CAL, CBG, CIN, CUH, DAW, DEN, DOW, DUK, GCC, HOL, IES, LWD, MCG, MIS, MOR, MRT, MTC, PLF, SAB, SEC, SPR, STG, USN, ZOO.

Other *Ilex glabra* cultivars of interest:

*I. glabra* 'Compacta'. Introduced in 1937 by William Flemmer, Princeton, New Jersey. Grows to 4 ft. high and 6 ft. wide, with compact, oval to round habit, and lustrous, jet black fruit. Needs pruning; tends to become leggy at base. (Female)

*I. glabra* 'Ivory Queen'. Introduced in 1961 by C. R. Wolf, Millville, New Jersey. Grows to 6 ft. high and 8 ft. wide; leaves are 2 in. long and 1.25 in. wide. Unusual, white-fruited cultivar, with black dot on apex of fruit. (Female)

*I. glabra* 'Nigra'. Grows to 5 ft. high in 30 years; not as leggy as most *I. glabra* cultivars; leaves are 1.25–1.75 in. long and 0.4–0.75 in. wide. Introduced before 1954 by Westbury Rose Co., Long Island, New York. (Male).

*I. glabra* 'Shamrock'. Introduced in 1977 by J. Tankard, Exmor, Virginia. Slower growing than 'Compacta' and 'Nordic'; grows to compact 5 ft. high and as wide. Holds lower leaves better than most cultivars; leaves are 1.5 in. long and 0.5 in. wide.

Related *Ilex* cultivars of interest:

*I. opaca* 'Clarendon Spreading'. USDA Zones 6–9. Developed in 1957 at Clarendon Gardens, North Carolina; not hardy north of Washington, DC. Attractive shrub with dense growth habit and large, spined leaves. Grows to 10 ft. high and as wide. Useful as specimen or high hedge.

*I. opaca* 'Maryland Dwarf'. American Holly. USDA Zones 5–9. Introduced in 1942 by E. Dilatush, Bunting's Nursery, Selbyville, Delaware. Broad-leaved evergreen growing slowly to 3 ft. high and 3 ft. wide, with rounded habit. Attractive, very low-spreading cultivar, often growing broader than tall. Sparse fruiting. Can withstand wind, air pollution, soil compaction as well as some wet conditions and drought.

## *Ilex* Interspecific Hybrids

The following are interspecific hybrid hollies, broad-leaved evergreens that are hardy in USDA Zones 7–8 unless otherwise indicated. They tolerate some shade and wind, but not wet conditions or drought. Other than mites, they have no serious disease or insect problems. They are easily transplanted, balled and burlapped or container-grown, and are propagated by softwood or hardwood cuttings. Plants can be pollinated by the male of the parental species.

*Ilex* 'Miniature' ((*I. aquifolium* × *I. cornuta*) 'Nellie R. Stevens' × *I. pernyi*). Introduced in 1993 by Gene Eisenbeiss, U.S. National Arboretum. Grows slowly to 5 ft. high and 6 ft. wide, with compact, broadly conical, semidwarf habit. Glossy, dark green leaves are square-shaped, with acute tips and broadly cuneate bases, 2 in. long and 0.75 in. wide. Red fruit is globose to subglobose, 0.4 in. across. A very colorful, showy shrub, with conspicuous fruit display. Excellent for use as accent plant. Small leaves give it fine-textured appearance. Needs sun; does not fruit well in shade. Prefers loam with pH of 5–6.

*Ilex* 'Rock Garden' (*I.* × *aquipernyi* × (*I. integra* × *I. pernyi* 'Accent')). USDA Zones 6–8. Introduced in 1985 by Elwin Orton, Rutgers University. Grows very slowly to 14 in. high and 22 in. wide; compact, dense, low-spreading, dwarf habit. Lustrous, green leaves are 1.6 in. long and 0.8 in. wide, with 3–4 moderately sized, flexible spines. Bright-red, globose fruit, 0.25 in. across, is borne in clusters. The only "typical" interspecific hybrid Holly (i.e., with spiny, prickly leaves). Suitable for rock gardens. Ideal for front of shrub border or areas where diminutive plant is needed. Requires a bit of extra care (i.e., winter protection and good drainage), but worth the effort.

*Ilex* 'September Gem' (*I. ciliospinosa* × (*I. aquifolium* × *I. pernyi*)). Introduced in 1978 by Gene Eisenbeiss, U.S. National Arboretum. Grows slowly to 6 ft. high and as

*Ilex glabra* 'Nordic' (N. Brewster)

*Ilex glabra* 'Compacta' (N. Brewster)

*Ilex glabra* 'Ivory Queen' (G. Eisenbeiss)

*Ilex glabra* 'Nigra' (N. Brewster)

*Ilex opaca* 'Maryland Dwarf' (C. Hubbuch)

*Ilex* 'Miniature' (N. Brewster)

147

wide, with compact, pyramidal habit. Glossy, dark green leaves are elliptic, narrowly ovate, finely pointed, 2 in. long and 0.5–0.75 in. wide, with 3 uniform, pointed spines. Abundant, bright red fruit is 0.4 in. across. Good semidwarf, fine-textured shrub for foundation or container planting or for use in large rock gardens. Distinctive for its early fruiting, as the name implies. Heat tolerant. Needs sun for compact growth. Remains compact without pruning.

Plant can be observed at ATL, BER, MBG, NCS, OWG, USN, VDG.

*Ilex* × *meserveae*. Blue Holly. No detailed information is included in this volume since these hollies are readily available; however, the following collection of *I.* × *meserveae* cultivars, hardy in USDA Zone 5, merits mention: 'Blue Angel' (USDA Zones 6–7), 'Blue Boy', 'Blue Girl', 'Blue Maid', 'Blue Prince', 'Blue Princess', and 'Blue Stallion'. Their outstanding characteristics include handsome, dark, bluish green foliage and attractive, red fruit (produced by female pistillate plants with feminine names). Hardy to −10° to −15°F. These Blue Holly cultivars are crosses of *I. aquifolium* × *I. rugosa* made by Kathleen K. Meserve, Long Island, New York. All are patented except one chance seedling, *I.* 'Pendleton Miller'; this cultivar, hardy to USDA Zone 7, grows to 1.5 ft. high and 7 ft. wide in 10 years.

Additional interspecific *Ilex* hybrids of interest:

*I.* 'China Boy' (*I. rugosa* × *I. cornuta*). Male.
*I.* 'China Girl' (*I. rugosa* × *I. cornuta*). Female.
*I.* 'Dragon Lady' (*I. pernyi* × *I. aquifolium*). Female.

These cultivars are often mistakenly referred to as Blue Hollies. They were also developed by Kathleen K. Meserve, then plant patents assigned to Conard Pyle Company. They are notable for their exceptional winter hardiness, heat tolerance, and compact, equally high and wide habit. Foliage of 'China Boy' and 'China Girl' is lighter green than that of 'Dragon Lady' or any of the Blue Hollies.

# *Ilex* 'Sparkleberry'
## WINTERBERRY

Parentage: *I. serrata* × *I. verticillata*. Aquifoliaceae. USDA Zones 5–9. Introduced in 1973 by Gene Eisenbeiss of the U.S. National Arboretum.

DESCRIPTION: Deciduous shrub growing more quickly than its parents to 12 ft. high and as wide, with upright habit and ascending branches.
*Leaves:* Elliptic, finely serrate, 3.75 in. long and 1.5 in. wide, bright red.
*Fruit:* Red, round, 0.4 in. diameter, glossy, in fall–March.
*Winter aspect:* Persistent fruit.

CULTURE: Needs full sun for best fruiting; grows in clay, loam, and sand with a pH of 4.5–6.5; tolerates wet conditions and some soil dryness.
*Disease and insect problems:* None serious.
*Transplanting:* Easy, balled and burlapped or container-grown.
*Propagation:* By softwood cuttings throughout the growing season.

LANDSCAPE VALUE: Provides effective contrast to snow or backgrounds of needled or broad-leaved evergreens with its spectacular display of particularly bright, glistening red fruit, which holds its color throughout the winter. Needs pollinator plant nearby for best fruiting. Excellent as specimen or in massed plantings. Received Pennsylvania Horticultural Society Gold Medal (Styer Award) in 1988.

Plant may be observed at AA, ATL, BBG, BC, BEA, BER, BSG, CBG, CIN, CUH, DAW, DUK, GCC, HOL, IES, LNG, LWD, MOR, NCS, PLF, POW, SPR, STG, USN, VDG.

Other *Ilex* cultivars of interest from *I. serrata* × *I. verticillata*:

*I.* 'Apollo'. Introduced in 1978 by U.S. National Arboretum. Grows to 10 ft. high and as wide. Received Pennsylvania Horticultural Society Gold Medal (Styer Award) in 1987. (Male)
*I.* 'Harvest Red'. Introduced in 1969 by Elwin Orton, Rutgers University. Grows to a well-shaped 9 ft. high and 10 ft. wide, with small, dark green leaves, which turn to burgundy in fall before dropping. Bright red fruit, 0.25 in. across, persists well into winter. Received Pennsylvania Horticultural Society Gold Medal (Styer Award) in 1991.
*I.* 'Raritan Chief'. Introduced in 1976 by Elwin Orton, Rutgers University. Grows to 6.5 ft. high and 12 ft. wide, with low, dense, spreading habit and brittle branches. Lustrous leaves are dark green. (Male)

Related *Ilex serrata* cultivars of interest:

*I. serrata* 'Bonfire'. Introduced in 1983 by Robert Simpson, Vincennes, Indiana. Grows to 12 ft. high and as wide,

*Ilex* 'Rock Garden' (N. Brewster)

*Ilex* 'Rock Garden' (E. Orton)

*Ilex* 'Sparkleberry' (N. Brewster)

*Ilex* 'Sparkleberry' (N. Brewster)

*Ilex* 'Harvest Red' (E. Orton)

*Ilex* 'Harvest Red' (E. Orton)

with rounded crown; broadly elliptic leaves are 5 in. long and 2 in. wide. Red fruit is 0.3 in. across.

*I. serrata* 'Sundrops'. Finetooth Holly. USDA Zones 5–9. Introduced into cultivation in 1991 by Gene Eisenbeiss, U.S. National Arboretum. Deciduous shrub growing at moderate rate to 6.5 ft. high and 12 ft. wide, with compact, spreading habit. Adds interest to the landscape with its abundant, pale yellow fruit and young twigs, which are tan to reddish brown in sunlight. The fine, white hairs covering the leaves give the plant a smooth appearance and velvetlike touch. Fruits well even in light shade.

# *Ilex verticillata*
## BLACK ALDER
## WINTERBERRY

Aquifoliaceae. USDA Zones 4–9. Native to eastern North America, from Canada to New England, west to Wisconsin and Missouri. Introduced into cultivation in 1736.

DESCRIPTION: Deciduous shrub growing at slow to moderate rate to 6–10(15) ft. high and as wide, with oval to rounded habit.
*Leaves:* Alternate, simple, elliptic or obovate, 1.5–3 in. long and 0.5–1 in. wide, deep green above, often pubescent beneath.
*Fruit:* Red, rounded, 0.25 in. diameter, in August, often persisting into midwinter.
*Winter aspect:* Persistent fruit retains color throughout winter.

CULTURE: Flourishes in sun; grows in partial shade, although fruit and flower production are reduced; prefers moist soil with a pH of 5.5–7.0; adapts to wet conditions and light and heavy soils; tolerates dry soils with ease.
*Disease and insect problems:* None serious; powdery mildew and leaf spot.
*Transplanting:* Easy, balled and burlapped or container-grown.
*Propagation:* By softwood cuttings in June–July.

LANDSCAPE VALUE: Hardiest of all hollies, this handsome shrub enlivens dull winter vistas with its lavish, arresting display of fruit, outstanding against snow, white-barked trees, or background of evergreens. Cut twigs last for months indoors without water. As with most hollies, female and male plants are necessary for pollination. Since fruiting occurs on current season's wood, shrub can be shaped by pruning. Cultivars adapt well to the Northwest and British Columbia. Cultivars can be divided into two distinct types: the "Northern" type is much slower grow-ing, lower in height, with smaller leaves and earlier blooms, while the "Southern" type is faster growing, with fewer but heavier stems, darker bark, later blooms, and larger, more leathery leaves with notched margins.

Plant may be observed at AA, ATL, BBG, BF, BIC, BIR, BRK, BSG, CBG, CIN, COX, CUH, DAW, DEN, DOW, DUK, GIW, HOL, IES, LNG, MIS, MNL, MOR, MRT, MTC, NCS, PLF, SEC, STG, USN, VDG.

*Ilex verticillata* cultivars of interest:

*I. verticillata* 'Afterglow'. Introduced in 1976 by Robert Simpson, Vincennes, Indiana. Grows slowly to 10 ft. high and as wide, with compact, globose, multistemmed habit. Leaves are smaller than those of most cultivars, 2.3 in. long and 1.5 in. wide, medium green. Orange-red fruit, 0.3 in. across, is clumped near tips of branches, from September–November,

*I. verticillata* 'Aurantiaca'. Grows to 4–5 ft. high, with medium green leaves. Orange fruit, 0.25–0.3 in. across, fades to orange-yellow; fruit fades easily in Zone 7 and below, turning black by January. Discovered in the wild in 1939 in Morris County, New Jersey, by Moldenke.

*I. verticillata* 'Maryland Beauty'. Introduced in 1970 by C. T. Jenkins, Mitchellville, Maryland. Grows to 12 ft. high and as wide; suckering at base creates compact, full-bodied appearance. Has lustrous, dark green leaves and tight clusters of shiny, red fruit.

*I. verticillata* 'Red Sprite'. Introduced in 1980 by Louis Sieboldi, Hampden Nurseries, Hampden, Massachusetts. One of the smallest cultivars, growing slowly to 3.5 ft. high and 4 ft. wide, with broadly rounded habit. Glossy, medium green leaves, 2.5 in. long and 1.5 in. wide, drop early in September, revealing excellent branching pattern and abundant display of fruit, 0.5 in. across, which covers branches thickly. Adaptable to small areas yet can hold prominent place in front of shrub border or in large rock gardens.

*I. verticillata* 'Scarlett O'Hara'. Introduced in 1990 by William Frederick, Houkessin, Delaware. Grows to 10 ft. high and 9 ft. wide; ascending habit with dense branching. Leaves elliptic, 2.75 in. long and 1.25 in. wide. Fruit abundant, orange-red, 0.4 in. across. Male: 'Rhett Butler'.

*I. verticillata* 'Shaver'. Introduced in 1972 by O. M. Neal, Morgantown, West Virginia. Grows to 5.5 ft. high and as wide, with upright, rounded habit and glossy, medium green leaves. Orange-red fruit, 0.4 in. across, is among largest fruit of *I. verticillata* cultivars; fruit is clustered profusely along stem and holds color for 2 months.

*I. verticillata* 'Sunset'. Introduced in 1983 by Robert Simpson, Vincennes, Indiana. Grows to 8 ft. high and 9 ft. wide, with multistemmed, spreading habit. Dark green leaves are elliptic, 4.75 in. long and 1.4 in. wide. Red fruit, 0.4 in. across, is borne abundantly.

*Ilex serrata* 'Sundrops' (N. Brewster)

*Ilex verticillata* 'Aurantiaca'
(E. Hasselkus)

*Ilex verticillata* 'Aurantiaca' (E. Paine)

*Ilex verticillata* 'Maryland Beauty'
(R. W. Lighty)

*Ilex verticillata* 'Red Sprite' (N. Brewster)

*Ilex verticillata* 'Winter Red' (N. Brewster)

151

*Ilex verticillata* continued

I. verticillata 'Tiasquam'. Introduced in 1984 by Polly Hill, Vineyard Haven, Massachusetts. Grows upright to 6 ft. high and 5 ft. wide. Leaves are elliptic to ovate, doubly serrulate, 2.75 in. long and 1.1 in. wide, glossy, medium green. Red fruit, 0.5 in. across, in mid-August–November. Extremely hardy and drought resistant. Name comes from only named river on Martha's Vineyard.

I. verticillata 'Winter Gold'. Sport of 'Winter Red', with same habit but golden-yellow fruit.

I. verticillata 'Winter Red'. Introduced in 1988 by Robert Simpson, Vincennes, Indiana. Grows to 9 ft. high and 8 ft. wide; erect, multistemmed habit, although tends to legginess in northerly latitudes. Leaves are elliptic, lanceolate, 4.5 in. long and 1.1 in. wide, and darker green than those of most cultivars. Intensely red fruit, 0.4 in. across, retains its color throughout winter; heaviest fruiting of I. verticillata cultivars, often causes branches to droop. Received Pennsylvania Horticultural Society Gold Medal (Styer Award) in 1995.

*Ilex verticillata* forms of interest:

I. verticillata f. chrysocarpa. Grows to 9 ft. high. The only true yellow cultivar, with fruit, 0.25 in. across, in September–November. Fruiting not as heavy as that of red cultivars or I. serrata 'Sundrops', and yellow fruit is less attractive than red to birds. Discovered in the wild in 1900 near New Bedford, Massachusetts, and named by B. L. Robinson.

## *Ilex vomitoria* 'Stokes Dwarf'
### YAUPON HOLLY

Aquifoliaceae. USDA Zones 8–10. Native to the United States, from Virginia south to Florida and west to Arkansas and Texas. Introduced in 1961 by the Southwestern Louisiana Institute.

DESCRIPTION: Broad-leaved evergreen growing slowly to 3 ft. high and 3–4 ft. wide, with dense, globe-shaped habit.
*Leaves:* Fine-toothed, glabrous, 0.5–1.5 in. long and 0.25–0.75 in. wide, lustrous, gray-green.
*Fruit:* (Male) None.

CULTURE: Grows in sun and shade in clay, loam, or sand with a pH of 5.5–6.2; tolerates wind, wet conditions, drought, and salt.
*Disease and insect problems:* None.
*Transplanting:* Easy, balled and burlapped or container-grown.
*Propagation:* By softwood cuttings in August–November.

LANDSCAPE VALUE: A small, closely branched shrub with tiny leaves and gray stems. One of the best hollies for southern climates. Makes excellent hedge or screen; also useful as accent or specimen. Requires close shearing and shaping.

Plant may be observed at BIR, BRK, CAL, LAC, MBG, MIS, NCS, SAB, USN, VDG.

Other *Ilex vomitoria* cultivars of interest:

I. vomitoria 'Dare County'. Orange-berried cultivar, discovered in the wild and selected in 1978 by Barton Bauers, Mann's Harbor, North Carolina.

I. vomitoria 'Jewel'. Globose, rounded, compact shrub with distinct branching habit. Excellent fruit production; whole twigs covered with red berries. Originated before 1954 by S. Solymosy.

## *Illicium floridanum*
### FLORIDA ANISE TREE

Illiciaceae. USDA Zones 8–9. Native to the United States, in Florida and Louisiana. Discovered in 1771 in Florida by John Bartram of Philadelphia, Pennsylvania.

DESCRIPTION: Broad-leaved evergreen growing at moderate rate to 5–10 ft. high, with upright, compact habit.
*Leaves:* Alternate, simple, elliptic-lanceolate, margins entire, 2.5–6 in. long, with red petioles, thick, leathery, dark green, glabrous above, paler beneath, aromatic when crushed.
*Flowers:* Burgundy, 1–2 in. across, with narrow petals; March–April/May.
*Fruit:* A green, 1-seeded, leathery, dehiscent follicle, in August–September, turning yellow and ultimately brown.

CULTURE: Prefers shade, but not heavy shade, and moist, well-drained rich, humic, peaty soil; adapts to a wide range of soils and grows well in difficult, shady, moist conditions; tolerates wet conditions.
*Disease and insect problems:* None serious.
*Transplanting:* Best balled and burlapped or container-grown.
*Propagation:* By seed and softwood cuttings.

LANDSCAPE VALUE: A glorious, aromatic, broad-leaved evergreen perfect for the shrub border or as a specimen plant. Often found in ravines and wet, deeply wooded areas. Adds immeasurably to the landscape with its unusual color and fragrance. Likes the shelter of a wall or similar winter protection. Foliage is stronger green and plant more attractive in deeper shade; foliage becomes droopy when temperature falls below freezing. Genus name *Illicium* means "allurement" and refers to the strongly but pleasantly fragrant, anise-scented foliage. Shrub requires regular pruning to maintain attractive shape. Seldom seen in gardens in the United States. *Illicium* species are not easily distinguished, so I. parviflorum is often sold as I. anisatum.

*Ilex verticillata* f. *chrysocarpa* (Arnold Arboretum)

*Ilex vomitoria* 'Stokes Dwarf' (N. Brewster)

*Ilex vomitoria* 'Stokes Dwarf' (N. Brewster)

*Illicium floridanum* (J. Elsley)

*Illicium floridanum* (N. Brewster)

*Illicium floridanum* continued

Plant may be observed at ABF, ATL, BBG, BIR, BOK, CAL, CUH, DIX, DUK, HUN, MIS, MTC, NCS, RKEW, SAB, STG, STR, UBC, USN, VDG.

*Illicium floridanum* cultivar of interest:

*I. floridanum* 'Halley's Comet'. Reflexed petals with redder color.

*Illicium floridanum* form of interest:

*I. floridanum* f. *album*. Lovely, white-flowered variation.

Related *Illicium* species of interest:

*I. anisatum.* Japanese Anise Tree. USDA Zones 7–8; introduced into cultivation in 1790 from Japan, China, and Taiwan. Pale, white-yellow-green flowers, 1 in. across, with about 30 very narrow petals, are profuse but not fragrant; in March–April, sometimes earlier in southerly latitudes. Grows 6–12(15) ft. high with somewhat pyramidal habit and gray-brown branches; more regular than other species. Lustrous, medium green leaves are alternate, simple, narrow, oval, 2–4 in. long and 1 in. wide, with green petioles and brown-spotted stems.

*I. henryi.* USDA Zones 8–9. Native to western China. Small, pink to deep red flowers, 0.5 in across, in April–May. Most attractive of all *Illicium* species in flower. Reaches 6–9(15) ft. high, with dense, pyramidal habit. Little known, but worthy of attention.

*I. mexicanum.* Mexican Anise. USDA Zone 8. Deep crimson flowers, 1–2 in. across. Relatively unknown, attractive, broad-leaved evergreen.

*I. parviflorum.* Small Anise. USDA Zones 8–9. Found mainly in Florida and southern Georgia. Perhaps the toughest of all the *Illicium* species included here. Often confused with other species, but there are definite differences: habit is less restrained—can grow 15–20 ft. high but often remains at about 10 ft.; foliage is olive-green; tolerates dry conditions as well as moist soils; grows in sun and shade; has smaller (0.5 in. across) flowers with 5–12 green-yellow petals, in May–June; often produces sporadic fall bloom.

# *Indigofera kirilowii*
## KIRILOW INDIGO

Leguminosae. USDA Zones 5–8. Native to northern China, Korea, southern Japan. Plants received at the Royal Botanic Gardens, Kew, and the Arnold Arboretum before 1914 from Maurice de Vilmorin.

DESCRIPTION: Deciduous shrub to 3 ft. high, with low, dense, suckering habit.
*Leaves:* Alternate, odd-pinnate, obovate-elliptic, 4–6 in. long, composed of 7–11 leaflets 0.25–1.25 in. long.
*Flowers:* Pink-lavender, in dense racemes, 4–5 in. long, often hidden by foliage; June/July–fall.
*Winter aspect:* Slightly hairy, erect stems when young, turning glabrous and angular with age.

CULTURE: Likes full sun; thrives in a variety of soils; adapts to calcareous soils and a wide pH range.
*Disease and insect problems:* None serious.
*Transplanting:* Easy.
*Propagation:* By cuttings.

LANDSCAPE VALUE: An attractive, small shrub with interesting, elegant foliage and lovely, bright almond-pink to lavender flowers. Blooms continuously throughout summer and fall. In colder climates needs to be pruned back to ground but will easily reestablish itself the next season. Older shrubs in warmer climates may need harsh pruning to achieve pleasing form.

Plant may be observed at ATL, BEA, BF, BRK, CBG, CIN, GCC, LNG, MRT, NCS, NEW, RKEW, SKY, USN, WIN.

*Illicium anisatum* (J. Elsley)

*Illicium anisatum* (B. Yinger)

*Indigofera kirilowii* (A. Bussewitz)

*Indigofera kirilowii* (A. Bussewitz)

# *Itea virginica*
## SWEETSPIRE

Iteaceae. USDA Zones 6–9. Native to the United States, from the pine barrens of New Jersey to Florida, Missouri, and Louisiana. Introduced into cultivation in 1744.

DESCRIPTION: Deciduous shrub growing at moderate rate to 3–5 ft. high and higher, with graceful, arching habit.
*Leaves:* Lustrous green, turning vibrant crimson to purple in fall.
*Flowers:* White, with 5 petals, to 0.25 in. across, in cylindrical racemes 2.5–6 in. long, at ends of branches; May–July.
*Fruit:* A 5-valved, pearl-like seed capsule.

CULTURE: Grows in full sun or light shade; tolerates deep shade, but is denser and produces better flowers and fall color in sun; prefers moist, fertile soil, but tolerates drought and wet conditions; adapts to all but extremely alkaline pH levels.
*Disease and insect problems:* None serious.
*Transplanting:* Easy.
*Propagation:* By seed, with no treatment, and by softwood cuttings.

LANDSCAPE VALUE: An attractive native shrub with charming, fragrant—although not spectacular—flowers, and splendid fall color. May be used in naturalistic plantings near water; combines well with broad-leaved evergreens; is especially suitable for planting along a border. Found in wild in large groups, typically along streams. Leaves often remain on plant until December. Pruning should remove older stems to give light and space for new growth; plant continually renews itself from base. Fruit attractive in flower arrangements.

Plant may be observed at AA, ABF, ABN, ATL, BBG, BC, BEA, BIC, BIR, BLO, BOK, BRK, BSG, CAL, CBG, CHK, CIN, CUH, DAW, DIX, DUK, GCC, GIW, HOL, HOU, LAC, LNG, LWD, MBG, MIS, MRT, MTC, MUN, NCS, NEW, PAL, PLF, RKEW, SAB, SPR, STG, STR, UBC, USN, VDG, WIN, WIS.

*Itea virginica* cultivars of interest:

*I. virginica* 'Beppu'. Collected in 1955 by John Creech. Handsome, fast-growing shrub reaching 2–2.5 ft. high. Foliage turns burgundy in autumn. Flowers smaller than species but with lovely fragrance.

*I. virginica* 'Henry's Garnet'. Excellent selection with large, fragrant flowers in early summer, and superb, brilliant, scarlet-purple fall color. Superior to species; retains neat, compact habit and changes strikingly from summer to fall. Grows in sun or partial shade and tolerates wet and dry soils. Will grow in swampy areas; found in bogs of New Jersey Pine Barrens. Grows well in heat; also cold-hardy to –20°F. Collected in 1954 in Georgia by Mary G. Henry, avid plant collector. Received Pennsylvania Horticultural Society Gold Medal (Styer Award) in 1988.

Related *Itea* species of interest:

*I. ilicifolia*. Holly Sweetspire. Introduced in 1895 from central China. One of the most attractive late-summer flowering shrubs. Evergreen, 6–12 ft. high, with holly-like, dark green, shiny leaves, 2–4 in. long and 1.5–2.75 in. wide. White flowers, with green cast, in July. Often seen in English gardens, this elegant shrub should be more widely used in North America. Received RHS Award of Garden Merit.

# *Ixora*
## IXORA

Rubiaceae. USDA Zone 10. Native to the East Indies.

DESCRIPTION: Broad-leaved evergreen 6 ft. high, with compact habit.
*Leaves:* Narrow to oblong, pointed, about 5 in. long, short-stemmed, shiny.
*Flowers:* Red, in clusters 4 in. across, calyces tiny, corollas 2 in. long, with 4 lobes; year-round.

CULTURE: Grows in sun in a variety of soils with a pH of 5.5–6.5; tolerates drought, wet conditions, wind, and some salt breezes, but should not be allowed to dry out.
*Disease and insect problems:* Sooty mold and scale.
*Transplanting:* Easy; shallow root system.
*Propagation:* By cuttings.

LANDSCAPE VALUE: With its bright red flower clusters and green leaves, *Ixora* is a much-used ornamental in gardens and public plantings. Can be pruned to desired shape and lends itself to use as a hedge, screen, or container plant. If allowed to grow naturally, it remains upright and bushy.

Plant may be observed at DIN, FAR, FHA, HOO, KOF, LWD, RKEW, WAI.

Note: The taxonomy of *Ixora* is confused, and the many hybrids available cannot easily be assigned to any particular species; often they are a mixture of hybrids of two or more species. Sturdy hybrids are available with flower colors ranging from pale and golden-yellow to pink, orange, and red. Dwarf forms are also available.

*Ixora* species and cultivar of interest:

*I. finlaysoniana*. Attractive, white-flowered species growing to 10 ft. high.

*I.* 'Nora Grant'. Clear, raspberry-pink bloom.

*Itea virginica* (G. Koller)

*Itea virginica* (J. C. Raulston)

*Itea ilicifolia* (J. C. Raulston)

*Ixora* sp. (V. Lauritzen)

*Ixora* sp. (V. Lauritzen)

157

## *Ixora odorata*
IXORA

Rubiaceae. USDA Zone 10. Native to Madagascar.

DESCRIPTION: Broad-leaved evergreen growing slowly to 7–10 ft. high, with upright habit.
*Leaves:* Ovate to narrow, 6 in. long, shiny green.
*Flowers:* White to yellowish, fragrant, 4 in. long, in large panicles, with long, 4-lobed corollas.

CULTURE: Grows in sun or light shade in loam or sand with a pH of 5–6; tolerates wet conditions, salt breezes, and soil compaction, but not drought.
*Disease and insect problems:* Mealy bug and scale.
*Transplanting:* Easy; shallow root system.
*Propagation:* By cuttings and root suckers.

LANDSCAPE VALUE: A valuable ornamental that bears its large, fragrant flowers intermittently throughout the year. Blooms provide lovely contrast to large, shiny leaves. Grows relatively close to the ocean. Excellent Hawaiian plant that grows from sea level to 1500 ft. elevation.

Plant may be observed at FHA, HOO, WAI.

Related *Ixora* species of interest:

*I. chinensis.* Lovely pale orange flowers. From Singapore.
*I. nienkui.* Chinese species with ivory flowers.


## *Juniperus chinensis* 'Echiniformis'
HEDGEHOG JUNIPER

Synonym: *J. sphaerica.* USDA Zones 2–6. Cupressaceae. Species native to North America, from New England to Pennsylvania and Nebraska. Cultivar introduced into cultivation in 1887 by Rinz of Frankfurt, Germany.

DESCRIPTION: Evergreen conifer growing very slowly to 2 ft. high and 2.5 ft. wide, with globose habit.
*Leaves:* Awl-shaped, tapering to spiny point, 0.6 in. long, needlelike, in whorls of 3, blue-green above, gray-green below.
*Winter aspect:* Steel-blue foliage; short, very dense twigs; reddish brown bark.

CULTURE: Needs sun; performs best in soil with a pH of 6.75–7.25, but grows in almost any soil, including those with lime; tolerates salt, wind, and drought, but not wet conditions.
*Disease and insect problems:* Relatively trouble-free; *Phomopsis* blight in very wet spring weather.
*Transplanting:* Easy, container-grown.
*Propagation:* By cuttings in December–March, after at least 2 hard freezes.

LANDSCAPE VALUE: One of the slowest growing junipers—a pincushion-shaped gem. Ideal for small rock gardens, troughs, and container plantings. Does not perform well in southerly latitudes.

Plant may be observed at AA, ABF, ATL, BBG, BF, BIC, BIR, BOE, BSG, CBG, CIN, COX, CUH, DAW, DEN, DUK, GCC, GIW, HOL, LNG, LWD, MIS, MOD, MNL, MRT, MUN, NCS, NEW, PAL, RBC, RKEW, SEC, USN, VDG.

Related *Juniperus* cultivars of interest:

*J. squamata* 'Blue Star'. Single Seed Juniper. USDA Zones 4–7. Species native to China and Taiwan; sport of 'Meyeri' introduced in 1964 by Hoogeveen Nursery, Netherlands. Grows slowly to 3 ft. high and 3–4 ft. wide, with broad, hemispherical habit. Striking silver-blue foliage holds its color throughout the winter; leaves are sharply acuminate, 0.06–0.1 in. long, curved, densely arranged in whorls of 3. Grows in sun and shade (requires shade in warmer areas) in well-drained loam with pH of 6.5–7.5. Tolerates drought and some wind. Does not like heat and humidity. Fungus and spider mite in hot, humid summers. Most attractive as a young plant. Excellent for rock gardens and containers. Recipient of Gold Medal in 1964, Boskoop, Netherlands.

*J. virginiana* 'Grey Owl'. Eastern Red Cedar. USDA Zones 2–8. Native to eastern and central North America; cultivar introduced in 1949 by F. J. Grootendorst, Boskoop, Netherlands. Elegant, ornamental shrub with excellent color, believed to be seedling of *J. virginiana* 'Glauca' × *J. × media* 'Pfitzerana'. Grows slowly to 3–6 ft. high and as wide, with stout, spreading habit. Fine-textured, soft silver-gray leaves are acuminate, scalelike, 0.4 in. long, whorled on terminal shoots. Female sets abundant, glaucous, globular cones, 0.07 in. across. Needs sun and prefers loam with pH of 6.0–7.0; tolerates wind and, when established, drought. Susceptible to bagworm. Ideal for use as specimen, hedge, windbreak, or topiary.

*Ixora odorata* (V. Lauritzen)

*Ixora odorata* (V. Lauritzen)

*Juniperus virginiana* 'Grey Owl' (N. Brewster)

*Juniperus chinensis* 'Echiniformis' (U.S. National Arboretum)

*Juniperus virginiana* 'Grey Owl' (N. Brewster)

# Kalmia latifolia
## MOUNTAIN LAUREL

Ericaceae. USDA Zones (4)5–8. Native to the United States. Introduced into cultivation in 1734.

DESCRIPTION: Broad-leaved evergreen growing 4–8 in. per year to 6–10 ft. high.
*Leaves:* Alternate, elliptic, entire, petioled, 2–5 in. long and less than 2 in. wide, leathery.
*Flowers:* Light pink buds open to near white; buds of cultivars white, deep pink, and red, with maroon-cinnamon inside corollas; late spring or early summer (May–June), after shoot growth has begun.
*Fruit:* A capsule, in clusters, in fall.
*Winter aspect:* Gray to cinnamon-colored bark; irregular, multistemmed habit.

CULTURE: Tolerates heavy shade, but grows in full sun in northerly latitudes; does not tolerate heavy or neutral to alkaline soils; likes loam or sand with a pH to 5.5; tolerates wind; roots need cool, mulched, moist soil.
*Disease and insect problems:* Black vine weevil, leaf spot and leaf blight, especially in humid areas.
*Transplanting:* Easy; shallow root system.
*Propagation:* Micropropagation, cuttings (some cultivars), seed, layering, grafting.

LANDSCAPE VALUE: One of the most attractive native evergreen shrubs, with gloriously beautiful, interesting blooms and handsome foliage year-round. Flowers have a lovely, intricate architecture in bud and when fully open. Each of the 10 anthers is held in a pocket. Bumblebees trip the anther filaments, so that pollen sticks to them and is transported to other plants, thereby assuring cross-pollination. Mountain Laurel is the state flower of Connecticut and Pennsylvania. Its fine-grained wood, used by Native Americans for spoons and small plates, is still used by craftspeople for candlesticks. A superb native plant with excellent cultivars, this species tends to be overlooked and under-used due to the difficulty of propagation. Tissue culture is now making these shrubs more readily available.

Plant may be observed at ABF, ATL, BBG, BC, BSG, CAL, CBG, DOW, DUK, GIW, HOL, MIS, MTC, NCS, NEW, OWG, PLF, RHO, RKEW, SEC, STG, UBC, VDG, WIS.

*Kalmia latifolia* cultivars of interest:

K. *latifolia* 'Alba'. Lovely, white flowers.
K. *latifolia* 'Bullseye'. This cultivar of banded form K. *latifolia* 'Fuscata' is distinguished by a broad, purplish cinnamon band of pigmentation on the inside of the corolla, with a white center and edge. Good grower, with new growth often a bronze-red; stems of new growth and petioles are purplish red on the side to the sun. Named and released by R. A. Jaynes at the Connecticut Agricultural Experiment Station in 1982. One of several banded cultivars.
K. *latifolia* 'Elf'. First miniature Mountain Laurel to be named. Leaf size and growth rate are about half that of the species, and leaves are more closely spaced on the stems. Flowers are only slightly smaller, light pink in bud, opening to nearly white. Young plants need to be pruned to develop a bushy, multistemmed habit. Older plants exhibit considerable grace and charm.
K. *latifolia* 'Freckles'. Arresting pink flowers with a band of purple spots around outer edges.
K. *latifolia* 'Fuscata'. White flowers with wide, purple-brown band on inner corolla.
K. *latifolia* 'Heart's Desire'. Combines the banded K. *latifolia* 'Fuscata' trait with red-pigmented buds. Flower is red in bud; when open, a cinnamon-red pigment almost fills the inside of the corolla, the lip and center of which are white. Flower truss is large and many-flowered, foliage is dark green, and the habit is broad and densely branched. Selected from a controlled cross and introduced in 1987.
K. *latifolia* 'Little Linda'. A miniature, somewhat lower and broader in stature than 'Elf'. Red buds open to medium pink flowers.
K. *latifolia* 'Minuet'. Another miniature, banded form with cinnamon-burgundy on inside of white flower. Noted for its dark, glossy green foliage.
K. *latifolia* 'Ostbo Red'. First red-budded Mountain Laurel to be named. Buds are intense, iridescent red when grown in sun. Undulate leaves are slightly smaller and more twisting than those of species. Petioles and stems of new growth are purplish red on the sun side. Selected in the 1940s; first propagated and named by J. Eichelser, Melrose Nursery, Olympia, Washington. Received RHS Award of Garden Merit. Other red-budded cultivars include 'Carol', 'Hearts of Fire', 'Olympic Fire', and 'Nipmuck'.
K. *latifolia* 'Peppermint'. Flower streaked with reddish pink, resembling peppermint candy. An attractive cultivar.
K. *latifolia* 'Pink Charm'. Deep pink to red flower buds open to a rich pink. Good grower with good habit. Unlike most Mountain Laurels, the cuttings are relatively easy to root. Stems of current season's growth are almost entirely purplish red; petioles are pigmented above. Other pink-flowered cultivars include 'Alpine Pink', 'Candy', 'Nancy', and 'Pink Surprise'.
K. *latifolia* 'Sarah'. Reddest selection to date. Flowers are red in bud, pink-red when open, and eye-catching in both stages. Foliage and habit are excellent. Petioles and young stems are purplish red. Other deeply pigmented selections include 'Richard Jaynes' and 'Sunset' from Weston Nurseries, and 'Raspberry Glow'.

*Kalmia latifolia* (R. Jaynes)

*Kalmia latifolia* 'Bullseye' (R. Jaynes)

*Kalmia latifolia* 'Ostbo Red' (Winterthur Gardens)

*Kalmia latifolia* 'Fuscata' (M. McCarthy-Bilow)

*Kalmia latifolia* 'Pink Charm' (R. Jaynes)

K. latifolia 'Silver Dollar'. Buds often blushed with pink, opening to white, with attractive pigment marks within the corollas. Flowers are 1.5 in. across, almost twice the normal diameter. Leaves are large, dark, leathery. Plants grow well in the field but may be a problem in containers. Other white-flowered cultivars include 'Snowdrift' and 'Stillwood', the former dense in habit.

K. latifolia 'Star Cluster'. Another cultivar of the banded *K. latifolia* 'Fuscata'. Has continuous, narrow, cinnamon-colored band inside the corolla. Foliage is dark green, and plant is broadly spreading. Apparently more tolerant of heavy soils than other *K. latifolia* cultivars. Has been propagated by cuttings. Selected and released by the Holden Arboretum, Mentor, Ohio.

Related *Kalmia* species, form, and cultivars of interest:

K. angustifolia. Sheep Laurel. USDA Zones 2–8. Native to the United States and Canada. A tough, very hardy, low-growing shrub reaching 2–3 ft. high, with upright, stoloniferous habit. Leaves, produced in whorls of 3, are somewhat leathery, oblong, 1–2.5 in. long; foliage pendant in fall. Flowers typically lavender-rose, but can be a rich, deep, red-wine color, or white. Dry capsules produced in fall. Good accent for larger shrubs. Grows in sun or light shade; prefers well-drained loam or sand in pH range of 4.5–6.0, but tolerates poor soil, wind, wet conditions (grows in and around swamps), and drought. Relatively insect-free except for occasional lacebug.

K. angustifolia f. candida. Has handsome white flowers and foliage with no red pigmentation.

K. angustifolia 'Hammonasset'. Selected by Richard Jaynes for its rich, blush-red flowers and strong growth habit. Grows to about 2 ft. high.

K. angustifolia 'Pumila'. Low-growing shrub cultivated mostly in United Kingdom. Blooms in June and sporadically in late summer. Flowers have a wide lavender band inside the corolla.

# *Kerria japonica* 'Picta'
## JAPANESE KERRIA

Rosaceae. USDA Zones 5–8. Native to western and central China. Introduced into cultivation in 1834. Named in honor of William Kerr, a gardener at the Royal Botanic Gardens, Kew, who was sent to China to obtain plants and who introduced the double-flowered form.

DESCRIPTION: Deciduous shrub growing slowly until established, then moderately to quickly, to 3–6 ft. high and 5–9 ft. wide, with upright, arching, rounded but twiggy habit.
*Leaves:* Alternate, simple, ovate, doubly serrate, 1.5–4 in. long and 0.5–4 in. wide, green with white margins, glabrous above, slightly pubescent and paler green beneath.
*Flowers:* Strong yellow, single, with 5 petals, at the ends of stems on the previous year's growth; May.
*Fruit:* An achene, not conspicuous.
*Winter aspect:* Yellow-green, thin, fine stems; dense, twiggy habit, becoming open and loose with age.

CULTURE: Grows in sun and shade in well-drained loam; needs protection from full sun in very exposed conditions; tolerates summer heat well if not in full sun.
*Disease and insect problems:* None serious; some leaf spot, twig blight, canker.
*Transplanting:* Balled and burlapped.
*Propagation:* By cuttings.

LANDSCAPE VALUE: A small, tough, adaptable shrub that enhances the landscape with attractive, margined leaves and its profusely borne, bright yellow flowers, which bloom over a long period. Useful in massed plantings (e.g., underplanting in shrub borders, in parking lots and public areas). Should be pruned after flowering.

Plant may be observed at AA, ABF, ATL, BBG, BC, BF, BSG, CBG, DAW, LNG, MIS, NCS, RKEW, SAB, VDG.

Another *Kerria japonica* cultivar of interest:

K. japonica 'Pleniflora'. Golden-yellow, double flowers, 1–2 in. across. Taller, more erect, and somewhat leggier than the species; however, its flowers are larger, more effective, and last longer than those of the species. Cultivated in Japan since the 1700s; introduced to Kew in 1804 by William Kerr.

*Kalmia latifolia* 'Silver Dollar' (R. Jaynes)

*Kalmia angustifolia* f. *candida* (J. C. Raulston)

*Kalmia angustifolia* 'Hammonasset' (R. Jaynes)

*Kerria japonica* 'Picta' (J. C. Raulston)

*Kerria japonica* 'Picta' (Royal Botanical Gardens, Ontario)

*Kerria japonica* 'Pleniflora' (G. Gates)

## Kolkwitzia amabilis
### BEAUTY BUSH

Caprifoliaceae. USDA Zones 5–8. Native to Hupei Province of central China. Introduced into cultivation in 1901 by E. H. Wilson.

DESCRIPTION: Deciduous shrub growing quickly to 6–10(15) ft. high, with erect, arching habit.
*Leaves:* Opposite, short-petioled, broadly ovate, sparsely serrate, dull green above, pubescent beneath.
*Flowers:* Small, pink, yellow-throated, bell-shaped flowers, in clusters of large, terminal corymbs on short, lateral shoots; May–June.
*Fruit:* Pinkish brown, bristly, persistent.
*Winter aspect:* Brown, flaking bark.

CULTURE: Needs sun; prefers well-drained, loamy, chalky soils; tolerates a wide pH range; has average water needs.
*Disease and insect problems:* None serious.
*Transplanting:* Easy.
*Propagation:* By cuttings.

LANDSCAPE VALUE: This outstanding bloomer deserves more frequent use in the landscape. Its profuse bloom creates a lovely array of pink flowers in spring. Not a specimen plant, as it is coarse and often unruly in a formal setting. Good as a windbreak. May become leggy with age; wise to prune older branches from base after flowering. Considered by E. H. Wilson to be one of his finest plant introductions.

Plant may be observed at AA, CBG, CHK, CIN, LNG, NCS, OWG, RKEW, WIS.

*Kolkwitzia amabilis* cultivars of interest:

*K. amabilis* 'Pink Cloud'. Flowers a stronger pink color. Developed in 1946 by the Royal Horticultural Society Gardens, Wisley, United Kingdom. Received RHS Award of Garden Merit.
*K. amabilis* 'Rosea'. Flowers redder in color. Introduced to the trade in 1960 by Ruys, Dedemsuaart, Netherlands.

## Lagerstroemia 'Acoma'
### DWARF CRAPE-MYRTLE

Parentage: *L. indica* × *L. fauriei*. Lythraceae. USDA Zones 7–9. Native to China, Korea. Introduced into cultivation in 1985 by Donald Egolf of the U.S. National Arboretum.

DESCRIPTION: Deciduous shrub growing slowly to 9 ft. high and 9.5 ft. wide in 14 years, with multistemmed, low spreading habit, semidwarf habit.
*Leaves:* Elliptic to obovate, acute at apex, obtuse at base, 1.5–2.5 in. long and 3–4 in. wide, dark green, turning dull red in fall.
*Flowers:* Pure white, anthers golden, 90–150 florets in pendulous, tapered panicles 6–7 in. long and 3–4 in. wide; July–September.
*Winter aspect:* Exfoliating bark; semipendulous branching habit; young branches red-purple, turning gray-brown, then light gray.

CULTURE: Grows best in sun in clay or loam with a pH of 5.0–6.5; tolerates some wind and soil compaction; needs moisture, but does not tolerate wet conditions.
*Disease and insect problems:* None serious; mildew-resistant.
*Transplanting:* Balled and burlapped or bare root, in late spring or early summer.
*Propagation:* By softwood cuttings under mist, which flower, although heavy flowering occurs during the second or third year.

LANDSCAPE VALUE: An extremely attractive specimen plant. Slow growth habit keeps it in scale in smaller gardens. Makes a good hedge with heavy pruning when dormant. Semidwarf cultivars tend to have smaller inflorescences than larger cultivars, but they have increased shoot growth, which initiates flower buds for persistent, recurrent bloom.

Plant may be observed at CHK, CIN, CUH, NCS, RKEW, USN.

Additional cultivars of interest from *Lagerstroemia indica* × *L. fauriei*:

*L.* 'Hopi'. Medium-pink florets (25–90) with crinkled petals. More compact than 'Acoma' and most cold-hardy of the listed cultivars.
*L.* 'Pecos'. Clear, light pink florets (140–350) with crinkled petals in globose panicles. Globose habit, with dark brown, exfoliating bark.
*L.* 'Zuni'. Medium lavender florets (50–75) in ovate panicles. Globose habit, with glossy, glabrous, featherlike leaves.

*Kolkwitzia amabilis* 'Pink Cloud' (J. Elsley)

*Kolkwitzia amabilis* 'Pink Cloud' (R. Klehm)

*Lagerstroemia* 'Acoma' (N. Brewster)

*Lagerstroemia* 'Acoma' (N. Brewster)

*Lagerstroemia* 'Acoma' (N. Brewster)

*Lagerstroemia* 'Hopi' (N. Brewster)

## Leiophyllum buxifolium
### BOX SANDMYRTLE

Ericaceae. USDA Zones 6–8. Native to eastern United States, from New Jersey south. Introduced in 1736 by Peter Collinson.

DESCRIPTION: Broad-leaved evergreen growing slowly to 1.5–3 ft. high, with compact, rounded habit, usually dense in cultivation.
*Leaves:* Usually alternate (may be opposite), boxlike, oblong, 0.3 in. long, leathery, glabrous, dark green above, paler beneath, turning bronze in fall.
*Flowers:* Deep pink buds open to clusters of white to pink-tinged flowers in terminal, umbel-like corymbs; May–June.
*Fruit:* A small, many-seeded, egg-shaped capsule.

CULTURE: Thrives in sun or partial shade; prefers acid loam or sand; does not like hot locations; does not tolerate drought.
*Disease and insect problems: Phytophthora* blight or honey fungus.
*Transplanting:* Not difficult; shallow root system.
*Propagation:* By seed, layering, and softwood and hardwood cuttings.

LANDSCAPE VALUE: Blends well with heaths, heathers, and azaleas. Especially effective in groups, but a single specimen enhances a small-scale rock garden. Also attractive in borders. Not easy to establish but worth the effort. Found mostly in the Pine Barrens of New Jersey. The only species in the genus.

Plant may be observed at AA, ATL, BBG, BER, CAL, DUK, GIW, HOL, MIS, MTC, MUN, NEW, RKEW, UBC.

A *Leiophyllum buxifolium* variety of interest:

*L. buxifolium* var. *hugeri.* More cushionlike habit than the species; grows to 1 ft. high. Leaves alternate and longer than species. Native to United States, from New Jersey to the Carolinas. Introduced in 1884. More commonly cultivated than the species.


## Leptodermis oblonga

Rubiaceae. USDA Zones 6–8. Native to northern China. Collected by William Purdom and others. Introduced into cultivation in 1905.

DESCRIPTION: Deciduous shrub growing at moderate rate to 5.5 ft. high and 5–6 ft. wide, with upright habit.
*Leaves:* Opposite, entire, ovate to oblong, acute or obtuse, varying from 0.1–2.5 in. long and 0.25–1 in. wide.
*Flowers:* Lavender, 0.75 in. long and 0.5 in. wide, clustered 15–20 in axils, tubular, resembling small lilac or daphne flowers; June, and again fall–frost.
*Fruit:* A gray-brown, nonshowy capsule, 0.75 in. long and 0.5 in. wide, in clusters, in October.
*Winter aspect:* Twiggy branching habit.

CULTURE: Grows best in a warm, dry site in full sun in well-drained soils; prefers loam; tolerates wind and drought, but not wet conditions.
*Disease and insect problems:* None noted.
*Transplanting:* Very easy; shallow root system.
*Propagation:* By seed, divisions, or softwood cuttings in early summer.

LANDSCAPE VALUE: A carefree, robust shrub with delicate, finely textured stems, leaves, and flowers, and low-growing, dense, twiggy habit. Flowers are lovely, soft lavender, with long season of bloom. Foliage is late to leaf out in spring. Plant is difficult to obtain; those now in cultivation in United Kingdom were probably raised from seed sent home by Reginald Farrer, who refers to *L. oblonga* as "a sturdy little shrub with panicles of Persian Lilac-like flowers in July." According to Farrer's *Plant Introductions,* shrub flowered at Highdown, Sussex, but died in winter of 1928–1929.

Plant may be observed at WIN.


## Leptospermum scoparium 'Red Damask'
### NEW ZEALAND TEA TREE

Myrtaceae. USDA Zones 9–10. Native to New Zealand. Raised in 1940 by W. E. Lamments of the University of California. Introduced into cultivation in 1955 by Slieve Donard Nursery, New Castle, Ireland.

DESCRIPTION: Broad-leaved evergreen growing at moderate rate to 6–8 ft. high, with narrow, upright habit.
*Leaves:* Lanceolate to elliptic, sharply pointed, linear, 0.25 in. long and 0.1 in. wide, bright green, with reddish dorsal side and margins.
*Flowers:* Deep cherry-red, circular, 1 in. across, fully double, at leaf axils or ends of short branches; midwinter to spring.

CULTURE: Grows in sun and partial shade; prefers moist, fertile, sandy and peaty loam with good drainage and a pH of 5.5–6.0; tolerates salt and, while dormant, drought, but not wet conditions.
*Disease and insect problems:* Root rot in poorly drained soil.
*Transplanting:* Easy, balled and burlapped or container-grown.
*Propagation:* By cuttings.

LANDSCAPE VALUE: A graceful, elegant, exceptionally free-flowering evergreen that blooms from December to

Leiophyllum buxifolium var. hugeri (H. M. Mulligan)

Leiophyllum buxifolium (J. Elsley)

Leptodermis oblonga (N. Brewster)

Leptodermis oblonga (E. Sharp)

Leptospermum scoparium 'Red Damask' (N. Brewster)

Leptospermum scoparium 'Helen Strybing' (N. Brewster)

**Leptospermum scoparium 'Red Damask'** continued

spring and sporadically year-round. Received RHS Award of Merit in 1955 and RHS Award of Garden Merit. Useful in mixed shrub border, as specimen, or as hedge. Hardier than other *Leptospermum* species. May be pruned by two-thirds to shape or contain growth. Pinch tips to produce denser plant. Called "tea tree" because Captain Cook brewed tea from its leaves to prevent scurvy among his crew.

Plant may be observed at BBG, FIL, LAC, LWD, MMA, RKEW, STR, WIS.

Other *Leptospermum scoparium* cultivars of interest:

*L. scoparium* 'Ash Burton Wax'. Creamy white flowers and dense habit; 7–9 ft. high.

*L. scoparium* 'Helen Strybing'. Deep pink flowers; 6–10 ft. high.

*L. scoparium* 'Martini'. Pale pink flowers; 7 ft. high and as wide.

*L. scoparium* 'Pink Cascade'. Pink, single flowers; 1 ft. high and 3–4 ft. wide, with weeping branches.

*L. scoparium* 'Snow White'. White, double flowers with green centers; 2 ft. high and 4 ft. wide, with spreading and compact habit.

Related *Leptospermum* species of interest:

*L. rotundifolium*. Flowers varying from white to deep purple-pink, 1 in. across. Shorter blooming period than that of *L. scoparium*. Leaves small and round, rather than needlelike. Grows to 6 ft. high and 9 ft. wide, with spreading, arching branching habit. Scarce and hard to propagate.

## *Lespedeza thunbergii* 'Alba'
## BUSH CLOVER

Fabaceae. USDA Zones 5–8. Native to China, Japan. Introduced into cultivation in Europe in 1837 by Philipp von Siebold.

DESCRIPTION: Deciduous shrub growing quickly to 4–8 ft. high and 4–5 ft. wide, with upright, semiwoody habit; dies back in winter.
*Leaves:* Oval or oval-lanceolate, 1.5–2 in. long, leaflets trifoliate, bluish green.
*Flowers:* White, pea-shaped, 0.5–0.6 in. long, in racemes 6 in. long, at leaf axils and at ends of shoots, forming loose panicles 2–2.5 ft. long; August–September.
*Winter aspect:* Long, nodding branches.

CULTURE: Grows in sun in any good garden soil with drainage; tolerates wind, but not wet conditions or air pollution.

*Disease and insect problems:* None serious.
*Transplanting:* Easy.
*Propagation:* By division of root clumps in April.

LANDSCAPE VALUE: Notable for its luxuriant annual growth of arching branches and profuse summer bloom when the bloom of other species has subsided. Excellent plant for shrub borders or in massed plantings. Do not plant as specimen since growth starts late in the season.

Plant may be observed at AA, BBG, BEA, BF, CIN, DUK, NCS, STG, USN, VDG.

Another *Lespedeza thunbergii* cultivar of interest:

*L. thunbergii* 'Gibraltar'. Rose-purple, pealike flowers, 0.5 in. long, in clusters 2 ft. long, in September. Glorious bloom in late season. A superior, vigorous plant that dies back each year after growing to 8 ft. high. Brought to public attention by William Frederick, Jr., Delaware. Found in 1950s on an old Wilmington estate, after which it was named.

## *Leucophyllum frutescens* 'Green Cloud'
## TEXAS SAGE
## CENIZA

Scrophulariaceae. USDA Zones 8–9. Native to the United States, in Texas, and to Mexico.

DESCRIPTION: Broad-leaved evergreen growing slowly to 5–8 ft. high and 4–6 ft. wide, with compact, loosely branched habit.
*Leaves:* Alternate, elliptic to obovate, lobeless, short-stalked, 0.5–1 in. long, deep green.
*Flowers:* Violet-purple, bell-shaped, 1 in. wide, axillary, tubular; summer.

CULTURE: Needs sun and heat; best in well-drained sand with a pH of 6.0–6.5; tolerates salt, wind, and drought.
*Disease and insect problems:* None serious.
*Transplanting:* Easy, balled and burlapped or container-grown.
*Propagation:* By cuttings.

LANDSCAPE VALUE: A valuable shrub for seaside or desert planting. Thrives with little water near the sea, but also needs heat to produce flowers. Tolerates desert dryness but needs very low humidity. Grown primarily for attractive foliage. Handsome plant that blends well with other plants tolerating dry conditions. Can be used as clipped hedge; withstands pruning and shearing for shape.

Plant may be observed at ATL, HUN, LAC, RAN, SAB.

*Leptospermum scoparium* 'Martini' (N. Brewster)

*Leptospermum scoparium* 'Snow White' (N. Brewster)

*Lespedeza thunbergii* 'Alba' (N. Brewster)

*Leucophyllum frutescens* 'Green Cloud' (B. Simpson)

*Lespedeza thunbergii* 'Alba' (N. Brewster)

Related *Leucophyllum frutescens* cultivars of interest:

*L. frutescens* 'Compactum'. Rose-purple flowers. Smaller and denser than *L. frutescens* 'Green Cloud'.

*L. frutescens* 'White Cloud'. White flowers and silvery foliage complement *L. frutescens* 'Green Cloud' or other plants with dark leaves.

## *Leucospermum cordifolium*
### NODDING PINCUSHION

Synonym: *L. nutans*. Proteaceae. USDA Zone 9. Native to South Africa.

DESCRIPTION: Broad-leaved evergreen growing at moderate rate to 4 ft. high and as wide, with sprawling habit.
*Leaves:* Oval, to 2.5 in. long, sessile, often 3-toothed at tips, medium green.
*Flowers:* Bright orange, in ball-shaped clusters, with tubular petals, to 4 in. across; late winter–early summer.

CULTURE: Grows in sun in alkaline to slightly acid loam or sand; likes wind; tolerates some drought.
*Disease and insect problems:* None.
*Transplanting:* Treat shallow roots with care.
*Propagation:* By seed or cuttings.

LANDSCAPE VALUE: An attractive and rewarding year-round plant with profuse, stunning flowers. The many, bright coral-orange, yellow-tipped, tubular petals resemble curved pins in a cushion; hence the name. The flowers are excellent for arrangements; they last 3 weeks in water and can be dried. Gophers can be a problem in some parts of the country; best to plant in wire baskets. Easier to grow than most proteas. A heavy bloomer and most rewarding plant.

Plant may be observed at HUN, RKEW, STR.

Related *Leucospermum* species of interest:

*L. reflexum*. Rocket Pincushion. Reaches 6–8 ft. tall and as wide. Unusual plant with stunning, ever-changing flowers, which begin as 3–4 in. wide balls of pinlike, orange, tubular petals, red-tipped with navy centers; petals reflex as they age to resemble a rocket. Blooms late winter through spring. Leaves are oval, sessile, 1 in. long, soft gray, crowded along stems. Treat roots with care when transplanting. Good filler or background shrub. Sprawling; not for small gardens. Plant usually dies after 10 years or so. Needs little water in summer, but demands good drainage to survive. Gophers can be a problem; planting in wire baskets is recommended.

Plant may be observed at RKEW, STR.

## *Leucothoe axillaris*
### COAST LEUCOTHOE

Ericaceae. USDA Zones 6–8. Native to southeastern United States, from Virginia south. Introduced into cultivation in 1765.

DESCRIPTION: Broad-leaved evergreen growing slowly to 2–4 ft. high and 1–2 ft. wide, with spreading habit and arching branches.
*Leaves:* Alternate, simple, ovate to lanceolate, 2–5 in. long and 1–1.5 in. wide, glossy, leathery, often bronze-green when emerging, turning dark green in summer, with bronze-purple cast in winter.
*Flowers:* White, 1–2.5 in. long, slightly fragrant, in axillary racemes; April–May.
*Fruit:* A capsule, not ornamental.

CULTURE: Prefers light shade, but grows in full sun with adequate moisture; likes moist, well-drained, organic, acid soil; does not tolerate drought or wind.
*Disease and insect problems:* Leaf spot, root rot.
*Transplanting:* Easy; best container-grown, in spring.
*Propagation:* By cuttings.

LANDSCAPE VALUE: A graceful, low-growing evergreen with interesting, lustrous foliage and beautiful, small, delicate flowers. Enhances rock gardens, poolsides, and slopes and is an attractive underplanting for larger plants (e.g., *Rhododendron*, *Pieris*). Similar to and often confused with *L. fontanesiana*, but its leaves are shorter, broader, and pointed at tips; its stalks are shorter; its sepals broader; and it is less hardy than *L. fontanesiana*.

Plant may be observed at AA, ABF, ATL, BBG, BC, BIR, BOK, BRK, BSG, CAL, CUL, DIX, DUK, GIW, HOL, MBG, MCG, MIS, MRT, MTC, MUN, NCS, NEW, PLF, UBC, USN, VDG.

Related *Leucothoe* species of interest:

*L. davisiae*. USDA Zone 9. Native to California, at high elevations of the Sierra Nevada, and parts of Oregon. Discovered and introduced by William Lobb in 1853 for Messrs. Veitch; subsequently found by N. J. Davis, for whom it was named. Small, neat, sturdy shrub with erect branches. Leaves rounded-ovate-oblong at base and short-pointed at apex, 1.25–2.5 in. long, lustrous, dark green. Creamy white flowers produced in clusters of erect racemes in late June.

*L. fontanesiana* 'Scarletta'. USDA Zones 6–8 (5 with protection). A handsome, graceful, truly dwarf shrub that grows to 2 ft. high and 3.5 ft. wide. Outstanding foliage unfurls a rich, glossy scarlet, turning deep, lustrous green, then a lovely burgundy in autumn and winter.

*L. keiskei*. Keisks Leucothoe. USDA Zones 6–8. Introduced in 1915 from Japan. Beautiful, dwarf, compact evergreen

*Leucophyllum frutescens* 'White Cloud' (B. Simpson)

*Leucospermum cordifolium* (J. Apel)

*Leucospermum reflexum* (N. Brewster)

*Leucospermum reflexum* (J. Apel)

*Leucothoe axillaris* (N. Brewster)

*Leucothoe axillaris* (N. Brewster)

with glossy, deep green foliage, 1.5–3 in. long and 0.5–1.5 in. wide; new growth has red cast, turns green in summer and a glorious red-burgundy in autumn. Lovely, large, white, cylindrical flowers bloom in short racemes in June–July.

## *Leucothoe populifolia*
### FLORIDA LEUCOTHOE

Synonym: *Agarista populifolia*. Ericaceae. USDA Zones 8–9. Native to the United States, from South Carolina to Florida. Introduced into cultivation in 1965.

DESCRIPTION: Broad-leaved evergreen 4–5 ft. high (12 ft. in wild), with arching, relaxed habit.
*Leaves:* Alternate, simple, glabrous, 1.25–4 in. long, red-purple when emerging, turning glossy green in summer, remaining green throughout winter.
*Flowers:* Ivory, pitcher-shaped, fragrant, pendulous, in axillary racemes.

CULTURE: Grows in shade in moist, rich, acid soils high in organic composition.
*Disease and insect problems:* None serious; not as susceptible to leaf spot as other *Leucothoe* species.
*Transplanting:* Easy.
*Propagation:* By cuttings in late summer.

LANDSCAPE VALUE: A most attractive, graceful, little-known evergreen shrub with profuse, fragrant blooms. Valuable along shady streams. Tends to sucker, but this can be useful for erosion control along banks. Lovely planted with larger leaved *Kalmia, Pieris,* and *Rhododendron*. May be pruned to keep smaller; remove one-third of oldest wood to ground level each spring on established plant to encourage growth of clean, handsome foliage.

Plant may be observed at ATL, BER, BIR, BLO, BSG, CAL, CUL, DIX, DUK, HOL, HUN, MBG, MTC, NCS, RKEW, STG, STR, UBC, USN.

## *Leycesteria formosa*
### HIMALAYAN HONEYSUCKLE

Caprifoliaceae. USDA Zones 7–8. Native from the Himalayas to western China. Introduced into cultivation in 1824.

DESCRIPTION: Deciduous shrub growing at moderate rate to 4–6 ft. high, with narrowly upright habit.
*Leaves:* Opposite, ovate, entire, with heart-shaped bases and long, tapered points, small teeth, erect and hollow stems, 2–7 in. long and 0.5 in. wide, deep green, grayish and downy beneath when young.
*Flowers:* Claret bracts in spikes, 1.5–4 in. long, at the ends of short shoots or at leaf axils; stalkless, arranged in tiers, bell-shaped, to 0.75 in. long, on current year's growth; July–September.
*Fruit:* A red-purple berry, 0.5 in. across, attractive to birds.
*Winter aspect:* Multibranched from base; sea-green stems.

CULTURE: Needs sun for best bract and fruit color; prefers rich, moist loam; tolerates wind, drought, and air pollution.
*Disease and insect problems:* None serious.
*Transplanting:* Easy, balled and burlapped or container-grown.
*Propagation:* By seed, which germinates easily in sandy peat; difficult by cuttings.

LANDSCAPE VALUE: A handsome native woodland shrub best in natural setting or shrub border. Needs sun for best flower and fruit color. May be pruned in spring. Partial dieback in winter not unusual; shrub rejuvenates the following growing season, often growing back successfully from roots. Named after William Leycester, Chief Justice in Bengal in the early 19th century.

Plant may be observed at ATL, BBG, BER, CIN, HUN, LAC, MMA, MIS, MUN, NCS, RBC, RKEW, UBC, VDG.

*Leucothoe davisiae* (Greer Gardens)

*Leucothoe keiskei* (J. C. Raulston)

*Leucothoe populifolia* (N. Brewster)

*Leycesteria formosa* (N. Brewster)

*Leycesteria formosa* (A. Patterson)

# Lindera benzoin
## SPICEBUSH

Lauraceae. USDA Zones 5–8. Native to North America, from Ontario and Maine south to Florida and Texas. Introduced into cultivation in 1683.

DESCRIPTION: Deciduous shrub to 6–12 ft. high and 15 ft. wide, with full, dense, rounded habit in cultivation (loose, open, wide-spreading habit in the wild).
*Leaves:* Ovate to lanceolate, 3–5 in. long, dark green, turning yellow in fall, but color is sporadic.
*Flowers:* Green-yellow, small, fragrant, dioecious, in axillary clusters on previous season's wood, 2–5 buds per node; April, lasting 3–4 weeks.
*Fruit:* An oblong, scarlet drupe, 0.5 in. wide, ripening August–October, attractive to birds; need male and female plants for effective fruit set.
*Winter aspect:* Slender, green-olive-brown stems.

CULTURE: Grows in deep shade, but flowers and fall color best in full sun; tolerates very moist or dry conditions, but prefers moist, acid, well-drained soils.
*Disease and insect problems:* None serious.
*Transplanting:* Difficult because of coarsely fibrous root system.
*Propagation:* By seed, with stratification; difficult by cuttings, although softwood and greenwood cuttings have been used.

LANDSCAPE VALUE: A handsome, interesting, little-used shrub for border or naturalizing. Grows in wooded areas. Spicily aromatic. When dried and powdered, fruits have been used as substitute for allspice. The young stems, fruit, and leaves are used to make an aromatic tea. Prune after flowers have faded.

Plant may be observed at AA, ABF, ATL, BBG, DOW, DUK, GCC, HOL, LAC, MIS, MOR, OWG, RKEW, SAB, UBC, USN, ZOO.

*Lindera benzoin* cultivars of interest:

*L. benzoin* 'Rubra'. Red, male-flowered selection from Hopkinton, Rhode Island.
*L. benzoin* 'Xanthocarpa'. Orange-yellow fruit; discovered at Arnold Arboretum in 1967 by Alfred Fordham.

Related *Lindera* species of interest:

*L. angustifolia.* Grows to 6–8 ft. high, with yellow flowers and black fruit; leaves 3–4 in. long, glossy green above, bluish green beneath, turning from yellow to orange to red in fall, sometimes persisting into winter.

# Lindera obtusiloba
## JAPANESE SPICEBUSH

Lauraceae. USDA Zones 6–8. Native to Japan, Korea, China. Introduced in 1880 by Charles Maries. Reintroduced from western China in 1907 by E. H. Wilson, who was collecting for the Arnold Arboretum.

DESCRIPTION: Deciduous shrub to 10–12 ft. high (20–30 ft. in the wild).
*Leaves:* Ovate, cordate at base, 4–6 in. long, varying from 3 lobes to none, rich green, turning brilliant bronze-yellow in October.
*Flowers:* Green-yellow, small, dioecious, less conspicuous and blooming 10 days earlier than those of *L. benzoin.*
*Fruit:* Globose, 0.25 in. wide, red, turning to black; need male and female plants for fruit.
*Winter aspect:* Yellow-gray to reddish bark.

CULTURE: Grows equally well in full sun or heavy shade; adapts to a variety of sites and acid soils; tolerates moist conditions, but needs good drainage.
*Disease and insect problems:* None.
*Transplanting:* Not easy.
*Propagation:* By softwood cuttings in mid-July and by seed, which requires a 3-month warm period, followed by a 3-month cold period.

LANDSCAPE VALUE: A good understory plant that can be effectively integrated into shrub border. Seldom found in the landscape. Handsome contrast of red-black fruit with yellow autumn foliage; good fall color even in shade. Compared to *L. benzoin*, the leaves of *L. obtusiloba* color in uniform pattern and remain on tree three weeks or longer; there is only one plump, reddish flower bud at each node; and leaves, buds, and stems are less aromatic.

Plant may be observed at AA, ABF, ATL, BBG, BRK, BSG, CIN, CUH, DAW, DUK, MIS, MOR, NEW, PAL, RHO, RKEW, UBC, VDG, WIS.

*Lindera benzoin* (Southern Living Magazine)

*Lindera angustifolia* (G. Koller)

*Lindera angustifolia* (G. Koller)

*Lindera obtusiloba* (G. Koller)

## Lonicera pileata
### PRIVET HONEYSUCKLE

Caprifoliaceae. USDA Zones 7–8. Native to China. Introduced into cultivation in 1900 by E. H. Wilson.

DESCRIPTION: Semi-evergreen shrub to 2–3 ft. high, with low, compact habit.
*Leaves:* Opposite, simple, ovate to oblong, small, 0.5–1.25 in. long and 0.2–0.5 in. wide, rich dark green, lustrous above, paler and slightly pubescent beneath. Young shoots purple, downy.
*Flowers:* Yellow-white, 0.5 in. long, in pairs, not very ornamental; May.
*Fruit:* A round, translucent, small, 0.25 in., violet berry, in clusters.
*Winter aspect:* Young shoots purple and downy; branching habit often horizontal.

CULTURE: Grows in sun, but prefers light shade; adapts to clay and loam in a wide pH range; does not tolerate hot, southern climates. Thrives by the sea. Needs good drainage.
*Disease and insect problems:* None serious.
*Transplanting:* Easy.
*Propagation:* By cuttings.

LANDSCAPE VALUE: A graceful, dwarf, semi-evergreen shrub with neat habit, branching pattern often horizontal, useful for under-planting, particularly in shade. Especially handsome in spring when new, bright green foliage appears among the older, darker green leaves. Does not like heat; elegant foliage not as attractive in warmer regions. Better known in Europe but could be utilized in U.S. gardens.

Plant may be observed at DOW.

Related *Lonicera* cultivars of interest:

*L.* 'Honey Rose' (*L.* 'Zabel' × *L. tatarica* 'Arnold Red'). USDA Zones 4–6. Introduced in 1993 by Minnesota Nurserymen's Research Corporation; bred for resistance to honeysuckle witches'-broom aphid. Grows rapidly to a compact 6–8 ft. high, with deep rose-red flowers, dark green foliage, and red fruit. Needs full sun; prefers loam but adapts to a variety of soils.

*L. pileata* 'Royal Carpet'. USDA Zones 7–8. Similar to *L. pileata.*

*L. xylosteum* 'Emerald Mound'. USDA Zones 4–6. One of the best low-growing, mounded honeysuckles with small, yellow-white flowers. Grows to about 3 ft. high and 4–5 ft. wide, with very attractive, blue-green foliage and deep red berries.

## Loropetalum chinensis

Hamamelidaceae. USDA Zone (8)9. Introduced into cultivation in 1880 from China.

DESCRIPTION: Evergreen shrub growing rapidly to 5–10(15) ft. high and as wide, with irregular habit.
*Leaves:* Alternate, simple, ovate, 1–2 in. long and 0.75–1.5 in wide, glossy, deep green above, gray-green and pubescent beneath.
*Flowers:* Creamy white, with narrow petals; April.
*Fruit:* A nutlike capsule.
*Winter aspect:* Brown bark; downy stems; arching habit.

CULTURE: Grows in sun and light shade; performs best when protected from full summer sun in hottest climates, and from sun and wind in colder climates; prefers well-drained, acid, organic soil; does not perform well in soils with a high pH.
*Disease and insect problems:* None serious.
*Transplanting:* Easy.
*Propagation:* By cuttings.

LANDSCAPE VALUE: A magnificent shrub in full flower—a glorious white and green display that lasts almost three weeks. A little-known plant that should attract more attention when made familiar to the gardener. Useful as a specimen or in massed plantings. Foliage may burn in winter in northern climates, but recovers quickly; if injured by frosts, it usually produces new growth. Withstands hard pruning.

Plant may be observed at AA, NCS, SHA.

Another *Loropetalum chinensis* cultivar of interest:

*L. chinensis* 'Rubra'. Striking plant with hot pink flowers and purple foliage; introduced by J. C. Raulston, North Carolina State Arboretum.

## Mahonia aquifolium
### OREGON HOLLY-GRAPE

Berberidaceae. USDA Zones (5)6–8. Native to the West Coast of North America, from Oregon to British Columbia. Introduced into cultivation in 1823.

DESCRIPTION: Broad-leaved evergreen growing slowly to 3–6 ft. high and 3–5 ft. wide, with upright, broad, sometimes dense habit.
*Leaves:* Alternate, odd-pinnate, composed of 5–9 ovate leaflets, spiny, with serrate margins and reddish stalks, bronze, turning to rich, deep, leathery green, becoming purple-bronze in winter.
*Flowers:* Yellow; March–April.
*Fruit:* A blue-black, grapelike berry, in August–September, persisting into winter.

*Lonicera pileata* (J. Elsley)

*Lonicera xylosteum* 'Emerald Mound' (E. Hasselkus)

*Loropetalum chinensis* (F. Galle)

*Loropetalum chinensis* (N. Brewster)

*Mahonia aquifolium* 'Mayhan Strain' (E. Hasselkus)

*Mahonia aquifolium* 'Apollo' (J. Elsley)

*Mahonia aquifolium* continued

CULTURE: Grows in full sun, but prefers light shade; needs moist, well-drained loose, acid loam or sand, although it also adapts to more alkaline soils with a pH of 6.5–7.3 but can develop chlorosis in high alkaline soil; does not tolerate desiccating winds, but can be grown in USDA Zone 5 with protection; foliage tends to scorch unless planted in protected site.
*Disease and insect problems:* Leaf scorch, rust, aphid, whitefly.
*Transplanting:* Best balled and burlapped.
*Propagation:* By stratified seed, cuttings in late fall, and division.

LANDSCAPE VALUE: A handsome evergreen foundation plant brought back by the Lewis and Clark expedition. Can be used as a specimen but better in groupings. Offers multi-season interest: yellow bloom in early spring, rich green foliage in summer, and deep bronze fall color enhanced by persistent, ornamental fruit. A sensitive plant that needs protection from wind. Has vigorous habit; increases by underground stolons (stems that root). Foliage similar to but softer than leaves of English Holly. Prune immediately after flowering, which occurs on previous year's wood.

Plant may be observed at AA, BOE, CAL, CIN, CUH, DAW, DEN, LNG, MMA, MIS, PAL, RAN, RKEW, SBB, STR, VDG, ZOO.

*Mahonia aquifolium* cultivars of interest:

*M. aquifolium* 'Apollo'. Outstanding cultivar with large, rich, golden-yellow to orange flowers in loose racemes, and large, glossy, handsome leaves. Broad, low habit. Received RHS Award of Garden Merit.
*M. aquifolium* 'Atropurpurea'. USDA Zones 5–8. Numerous yellow flowers and low, broad habit. Leaves turn purple-red in winter. Selected in Holland in 1915.
*M. aquifolium* 'Compacta'. USDA Zones 6–8. Very attractive small shrub growing to 2–3 ft. high.
*M. aquifolium* 'Golden Abundance'. USDA Zones 6–8. Vigorous handsome shrub with profuse yellow flowers, striking green leaves, abundant blue berries.
*M. aquifolium* 'Mayhan Strain'. USDA Zones 6–8. Small shrub growing to 30–40 in. high, with very attractive, glossy foliage. From Mayhan Nursery, Veradale, Washington.
*M. aquifolium* 'Moseri'. USDA Zones 5–8. Introduced into cultivation in 1895. Foliage opens bronze, turns first to rich green then deeper green as the season progresses.

Related *Mahonia* species of interest:

*M. nervosa* [*Berberis nervosa*]. Yellow flowers in terminal racemes to 9 in. long, longer than those of *M. aquifolium*. Leaves also longer, ovate to cordate, sometimes oblique;

deep green in spring and bright red in winter. Has more vibrant fall and winter color than other mahonias. Grows slowly to 2 ft. high. Culture identical to that of *M. aquifolium*.

## *Mahonia lomariifolia*
CHINESE MAHONIA
BURMESE MAHONIA

Berberidaceae. USDA Zone 9. Native to Myanmar (formerly Burma), western China, Taiwan. Introduced into cultivation in 1931 by seed from Tengyueh, Yunnan Province, China, by Major Johnson of Hidcote Manor, Gloucestershire, United Kingdom.

DESCRIPTION: Broad-leaved evergreen 8–12 ft. high (to 30 ft. in the wild), with multistemmed, erect habit.
*Leaves:* Lanceolate, odd-pinnate, 10–24 in. long, composed of 9–18 leaflets 1.5–4 in. long and 0.5–1 in. wide, glossy, rich green.
*Flowers:* Brilliant yellow, in erect, cylindrical spikes 4–8 in. long and 1 in. wide, fragrant; November–March.
*Fruit:* Oval, blue-black.

CULTURE: Grows in sun, but prefers shade and moist, well-drained soil; needs protection from desiccating winds.
*Disease and insect problems:* Leaf spot, scorch, whitefly, aphid.
*Transplanting:* Easy, balled and burlapped.
*Propagation:* By seed.

LANDSCAPE VALUE: Most handsome and stately of the mahonias, but not the hardiest. Imposing plant with striking characteristics: spectacular yellow flower spikes; medium-thick, erect branches; long, glossy, rich green leaves. Has received numerous awards in United Kingdom, including RHS Award of Garden Merit.

Plant may be observed at ATL, BIR, BLO, BRK, CUH, FIL, HUN, LAC, MMA, NCS, RKEW, STR, UBC, VDG.

Related *Mahonia* cultivars and species of interest:

*M.* 'Arthur Menzies' (*M. lomariifolia* × *M. bealei*). USDA Zones 7–8. Attractive, compact, medium-sized shrub with lemon-yellow flowers in long racemes in December–January, terminal clusters of bluish fruit, and handsome blue-green foliage, with 3–4 spines on each side of the leaflet. Upright, somewhat leggy habit. Grows in sun and partial shade in clay or loam. Not reliably hardy in cold weather; tends to die in temperatures below 0°F. Selected in 1964 at University of Washington Arboretum, Seattle; named after the supervisor of plant accessions at Strybing Arboretum, San Francisco, in whose garden this cross occurred.

*Mahonia aquifolium* 'Moseri' (J. Elsley)

*Mahonia lomariifolia* (J. C. Raulston)

*Mahonia lomariifolia* (University of Washington)

*Mahonia lomariifolia* (J. Elsley)

M. *fortunei*. An evergreen shrub growing to 5–6 ft. high. Yellow, dense flowers are borne on narrow, erect, cylindrical racemes, 2–3 in. long, in late fall. Compound, odd-pinnate leaves are 6–8 in. long, with lanceolate leaflets 3–4 in. long and 0.5 in. wide, tapering at both ends. Different from other mahonias in the dull green leaflets and slender racemes. Tender plant. Found in a Shanghai nursery by Robert Fortune, who introduced it in 1846.

M. × *media* 'Charity' (*M. japonica* × *M. lomariifolia*). Chinese Holly-Grape. USDA Zones 8–9. Superb, broad-leaved evergreen growing to 8–15 ft. high and as wide, with stately, vertical habit. Ovate leaves are 2.5–4.5 in. long and 1–1.5 in. wide, with 17–21 leaflets; glossy, rich green above, yellow-green below. Lemon-yellow, fragrant flowers, as many as 20 in a cluster, bloom in terminal racemes, 10–14 in. long, in January–February. Clusters of ovate, powdery blue-black fruit, 0.5 in. across, appear after flowers. One of the finest evergreen shrubs, it received the RHS Award of Merit in 1959 and the RHS Award of Garden Merit. Beautiful in foliage, flower, and fruit, and a vigorous grower. Needs partial shade to prevent yellowing; keep mulched. Prune stems to different lengths to induce branching. Native to China and Myanmar (Burma). Introduced in 1950 by Slieve Donard Nursery, Newcastle, Ireland; a seedling of *M. lomariifolia* selected by Sir Eric Saville from the nursery of L. R. Russell, Windelsham, Surrey, United Kingdom

# *Mahonia repens*
## CREEPING MAHONIA

Berberidaceae. USDA Zones 5–8. Native to the West Coast of North America, from British Columbia to California and northern Mexico. Originally discovered during the Lewis and Clarke expedition of 1804–1806.

DESCRIPTION: Broad-leaved evergreen growing slowly to 12 in. high and 2 ft. wide, with low, stoloniferous habit.
*Leaves:* Compound, odd-pinnate, composed of 3, 5, or 7 leaflets, ovate, pointed, spine-toothed, 1–2.5 in. long, dull, bluish green above and gray beneath, turning brilliant bronze-red in fall, with a purple cast in winter.
*Flowers:* Deep yellow, in racemes, 1.5–3 in. long, in clusters at the ends of branches; April–May.
*Fruit:* Blue-black, pruinose (with a white coating), 0.25 in. across, in clusters, in August–September.
*Winter aspect:* Stiff stems.

CULTURE: Grows in sun and partial shade; best in well-drained loam, but grows in clay; tolerates wind, but not wet conditions or drought.

*Disease and insect problems:* None serious.
*Transplanting:* Easy, balled and burlapped or container-grown; stoloniferous root system.
*Propagation:* By cuttings or division of stolons.

LANDSCAPE VALUE: A handsome small shrub that provides excellent evergreen cover for banks. Useful for erosion control, in foreground of shrub border, or in rock garden. Attractive fall color persists into midwinter. Not completely evergreen above USDA Zone 7.

Plant may be observed at AA, ABF, ATL, BC, BIC, CBG, CUH, CIN, DAW, DEN, GIW, LAC, LNG, MNL, MIS, MRT, NEB, NEW, RAN, RKEW, SAB, SBB, STR, UBC, VDG.

Another *Mahonia* species of interest:

M. *trifoliata*. USDA Zone 9. Native to Mexico and the United States. Introduced in 1839. Easily recognized by trifoliate leaves; leaflets are acutely ovate, blue-white beneath. Red fruit.

# *Medinilla magnifica*
## MEDINILLA

Melastomataceae. USDA Zone 10. Native to the Philippines, Java, tropical Africa, Southeast Asia. Introduced into cultivation in 1965.

DESCRIPTION: Broad-leaved evergreen growing at moderate rate to 8–10 ft. high, with thick, rangy habit.
*Leaves:* Opposite, ovate to ovate-oblong, large, to 1 ft. long, thick, pointed, stemless, dark green.
*Flowers:* Showy pink bracts, 1–4 in. long, with purple anthers, in handsome, pendulous, cone-shaped panicles 1 in. long; April–June.
*Fruit:* A berry.

CULTURE: Likes light shade and loam with a pH of 5.5–6.5; withstands wet conditions; somewhat tolerant of salt, air pollution, and soil compaction; prefers to be kept moist, with high humidity.
*Disease and insect problems:* Mealy bug.
*Transplanting:* Easy; shallow root system.
*Propagation:* By cuttings.

LANDSCAPE VALUE: Beautiful and most unusual, showy flowers make this a good ornamental. Also useful where thick growth is needed. Rain forest epiphyte in Philippines.

Plant may be observed at BIR, CBG, FAR, FHA, FIL, MIS, NAT, RKEW, WAI.

Mahonia 'Arthur Menzies' (J. C. Raulston)    Mahonia repens (E. Hasselkus)

Mahonia repens (N. Brewster)

Mahonia trifoliata (B. Simpson)

Medinilla magnifica (V. Lauritzen)    Medinilla magnifica (V. Lauritzen)

## Michelia figo
### BANANA SHRUB

Magnoliaceae. USDA Zone 10. Introduced in 1789 from China.

DESCRIPTION: Broad-leaved evergreen growing slowly to 6–10(15) ft., with dense habit.
*Leaves:* Alternate, simple, oval to slightly obovate, acute, cuneately tapered at base, leathery, 3 in. long, initially covered with tan pubescence but maturing to lustrous, dark green above, lighter beneath.
*Flowers:* Creamy yellow, shaded with brownish purple, 1.5 in. across, fragrant; March–May.
*Fruit:* A red seed, appearing after blooms fade.

CULTURE: Grows in sun, or partial shade in warmer climates; likes a rich, acid, well-drained soil, ideally sandy clay with a covering of leaf mold; requires ample water; performs best in Hawaii when grown at elevations of 1000–3000 ft.; easy to grow and maintain.
*Disease and insect problems:* None.
*Transplanting:* Not difficult.
*Propagation:* By cuttings of ripe wood, rooted under glass; seed seldom viable.

LANDSCAPE VALUE: An attractive, disease-free shrub for warm, wind-free spots. Flowers, which resemble small *Magnolia* blossoms, have a rich, fruity fragrance reminiscent of ripening melons or bananas. Effective in container or espaliered near entrances.

Plant may be observed at ATL, BBG, BIR, BOK, BRK, BSG, DIN, DUK, FIL, FUL, HUN, LAC, LWD, MIS, MMA, NAT, NCS, SEL, SHA, STG, UBC, WAI.

## Myrica pensylvanica
### BAYBERRY

Myricaceae. USDA Zones 3–7. Native to North America, from Florida to northeastern United States, into Canada and Nova Scotia. Introduced into cultivation in 1725.

DESCRIPTION: Deciduous to semi-evergreen in warmer zones, growing at moderate to fast rate to 6–10 ft. high, with upright, rounded habit.
*Leaves:* Alternate, simple, obovate-oblong, dentate to entire margin, pubescent on both sides, gray-green, aromatic.
*Flowers:* Not ornamental, borne in catkins, male stamens yellow-green, female stigmas stalkless, with no sepals or petals, before leaves; March–April.
*Fruit:* A small, 0.2 in. across, decorative, fragrant drupe, gray-white with waxy coat, covering branches and persisting into winter and spring.
*Winter aspect:* Young wood downy; dense branching habit.

CULTURE: Grows in sun and partial shade; prefers sandy, acid soil, but adapts to a wide pH range; tolerates dry, sandy soil and wind-swept seaside conditions, including salt spray.
*Disease and insect problems:* None serious.
*Transplanting:* Balled and burlapped.
*Propagation:* By seed and cuttings.

LANDSCAPE VALUE: A handsome shrub in all seasons, with pleasing habit. Lustrous, leathery, green foliage, aromatic when crushed, is attractive in spring and summer. Abundant, gray-white fruit on female appears in fall and persists into late winter, creating a striking appearance. Successfully used for erosion control; tends to sucker. Wax used for making highly aromatic bayberry candles.

Plant may be observed at ABF, BBG, BC, BEA, BF, BIC, BOE, BOK, BRK, BSG, CBG, CIN, COX, CUH, DAW, DEN, DOW, DUK, GCC, GIW, HOL, HUN, IES, LAC, LNG, LWD, MBG, MIS, MNL, MOR, MRT, MTC, MUN, NEB, NEW, OWG, PAL, PLF, POW, RBC, RKEW, SAB, SEC, SKY, SPR, STG, STR, VDG, ZOO.

Related *Myrica* species and variety of interest:

*M. cerifera.* Candleberry, Southern Waxmyrtle. USDA Zones 7–9. Beautiful southern evergreen, growing to 10–15 ft. high (35 ft. in wild). Leaves narrow, obovate, varying in size from 1.5 to 4 in. long and from 0.5 to 2 in. wide. Globose, gray fruit. Useful as screen, but may be pruned to expose handsome gray-white bark. Can also be used as specimen. Tolerates damp sites. Native to southeastern United States. Introduced in 1699.

*M. cerifera* var. *pumila.* USDA Zones 8–9. Lovely, small, southern shrub, often found in low woodlands and sandy pinelands of the Coastal Plain. Grows to 3–4 ft. high.

*M. gale.* Sweet Gale. USDA Zones 2–7. Low-growing, 2–4 ft. high, very hardy, deciduous shrub with dense habit and glossy, deep green foliage. Prefers moist, peaty areas. Often grown for its fragrance; leaves are aromatic when handled.

*Michelia figo* (Southern Living Magazine)

*Michelia figo* (S. Bender)

*Myrica pensylvanica* (University of Washington)

*Myrica pensylvanica* (G. Koller)

## Nandina domestica 'Alba'
### WHITE-BERRIED NANDINA

Berberidaceae. USDA Zones (6)7–9. Species native from India to China. Cultivar is an old one from Japan.

DESCRIPTION: Semi-evergreen shrub growing 6–12 in. per year when young, reaching 5–6 ft. high, with upright habit; flat-topped, spreading crown; few branches, but multiple stems form dense base.

*Leaves:* Alternate, 3-pinnate, leaflets subsessile (with a partial stalk), elliptic-lanceolate, generally more yellow than the species.

*Flowers:* White, star-shaped, 0.25–0.5 in. across, in dense, terminal panicles 8–12 in. long; early summer.

*Fruit:* Globular, 0.3 in. across, 2-seeded, creamy white to creamy yellow, forming during the summer, persisting through the winter.

*Winter aspect:* Interesting branching pattern.

CULTURE: Grows in sun or partial shade in a wide range of soils; tolerates wind, wet conditions, drought, and soil compaction.

*Disease and insect problems:* None serious.

*Transplanting:* Very easy; may defoliate if severely stressed (very rare) but recovers quickly.

*Propagation:* By cuttings, division of clumps, and tissue culture; seed yields high and true to type if parent plant isolated from red-fruited clones.

LANDSCAPE VALUE: A very handsome, multiseason plant for form, foliage, flowers, and fruit. Extremely tough and adaptable to varied light, soil, and moisture conditions. Depends on summer heat to ripen wood. Rare, but excellent alternative to red-fruiting types such as *N. domestica;* cream-colored fruit shows better under night lighting in landscape. Inflorescent stalks unattractive after fruit decline in late spring until covered by new leaves and flowers, but not a major drawback.

Plant may be observed at ATL, BBG, BIR, BRK, CAL, CBG, CHK, DEN, DUK, FIL, GCC, HUN, LAC, LWD, MBG, MIS, NCS, PLF, RKEW, SAB, SPR, STG, USN, VDG.

Other *Nandina domestica* cultivars of interest:

*N. domestica* 'Fire Power'. Reaches 1–2 ft. tall and 2 ft. wide, with dense, compact habit. Winter color is an interesting, attractive red.

*N. domestica* 'Gulf Stream'. Sport of *N.* 'Compacta Nana' at Hines Nursery, Houston, Texas. Grows to large, compact mound, 2.5–3.5 ft. high. Foliage is metallic blue-green in summer, intense red in winter.

*N. domestica* 'Harbor Dwarf'. One of the best compact forms. Grows to about 2–3 ft. high and as wide or wider, with graceful form and smaller flowers than species.

*N. domestica* 'Heavenly Bamboo'. More well known shrub with pink buds that open white with yellow anthers. Outstanding red berries ripening in September–October and persisting into winter. Spectacular. Introduced into cultivation from China in 1803.

*N. domestica* 'Royal Princess'. Leaflets smaller and narrower than those of species, creating graceful, feathery, fine-textured effect.

*N. domestica* 'San Gabriel'. Grows to 1–2 ft. high, with mounded habit. Very finely textured, feathery foliage. More tender than other *N. domestica* cultivars; best in USDA Zones 8–9.

*N. domestica* 'Umpqua Chief'. Medium-size shrub, growing to 5–6 ft. high. One of a series named for the Umpqua Indian tribe of the Pacific Northwest. Useful for uniformity in landscape plantings.

*N. domestica* 'Umpqua Princess'. Smallest of the Umpqua cultivars, growing to 3–4 ft. high and 2 ft. wide.

*N. domestica* 'Umpqua Warrior'. Largest of the Umpqua cultivars, reaching 6–8 ft. high, with large flowers and fruit.

*Nandina domestica* 'San Gabriel' (J. C. Raulston)

*Nandina domestica* (N. Brewster)

*Nandina domestica* (N. Brewster)

*Nandina domestica* (N. Brewster)

*Nandina domestica* 'Alba'
(J. C. Raulston)

*Nandina domestica* 'Fire Power' (J. C. Raulston)

*Nandina domestica* 'Harbor Dwarf' (N. Brewster)

## Neillia sinensis
### CHINESE NEILLIA

Rosaceae. USDA Zones 6–8. Native to Asia (China). Discovered by A. Henry. Introduced into cultivation in 1901 by E. H. Wilson.

DESCRIPTION: Deciduous shrub to 6 ft. high, with delicate, rounded habit.
*Leaves:* Alternate, simple, ovate, 2–4 in. long and 1.25–2.5 in. wide, sharply toothed, glabrous, rich green.
*Flowers:* Whitish pink, 12–20 in nodding racemes 1–2 in. long; May.
*Fruit:* An unwinged seed.
*Winter aspect:* Exfoliating bark, but not particularly interesting; young shoots glabrous and cylindrical.

CULTURE: Grows in sun and partial shade; prefers well-drained, moist, fertile soil, but tolerates less than ideal soil conditions.
*Disease and insect problems:* None serious.
*Transplanting:* Easy.
*Propagation:* By softwood cuttings or suckers in fall.

LANDSCAPE VALUE: A lovely, ornamental flowering shrub, similar to *Spiraea*. Little known but deserves wider use for long flowering period, graceful habit, ease of culture, and attractive foliage. Prune after flowering; mature plants enhanced by cutting older shoots at base.

Plant may be observed at AA, ABF, BBG, BSG, CBG, CIN, CUH, DUK, GCC, LWD, MIS, MOR, MRT, MUN, NCS, NEW, PLF, RKEW, SKY, STR, UBC, USN, WIN, VDG.

Other *Neillia* species of interest:

*N. affinis.* USDA Zones 6–8. Many pink flowers borne in spectacular, long racemes. Introduced in 1908 from China.

*N. thibetica.* USDA Zones 6–8. Numerous, slender spikes of rosy pink flowers borne in racemes 2–6 in. long, in May–June. More decorative than *N. sinensis.* Introduced in 1910.

## Neviusia alabamensis
### ALABAMA SNOWBREATH

Rosaceae. USDA Zones 5–8. Native to southeastern United States. Found in 1858 on the cliffs of Black Warrior River in Tuscaloosa, Alabama, and named by A. Gray after its discoverer, Reverend Nevius.

DESCRIPTION: Deciduous shrub growing at slow to moderate rate to 4–6 ft. high, with rounded habit, erect stems, and spreading branches.

*Leaves:* Alternate, doubly serrate, oval-oblong, 1–3.5 in. long.
*Flowers:* Tiny, white, on slender stalks, 0.75–1 in. long, with conspicuous cluster of white stamens but no petals; April–June.
*Winter aspect:* Delicate shoots, finely pubescent when young, turning glabrous with age; thin, arching branches.

CULTURE: Grows in sun or dappled shade in well-drained loam; requires ample moisture.
*Disease and insect problems:* None serious.
*Transplanting:* Easy.
*Propagation:* By softwood cuttings and seed; tendency to layer itself.

LANDSCAPE VALUE: A little-known shrub with robust habit, graceful arching branches, and a profusion of snowy white blossoms. Exceedingly stoloniferous. Smaller and more feathery than *Spiraea*. A vigorous grower that needs careful pruning to prevent a wild, shaggy look. Candidate for listing as endangered or threatened species by U.S. Fish & Wildlife Service.

Plant may be observed at AA, ABF, ATL, BBG, BEA, BF, BIC, BIR, BRK, CHK, CIN, CUH, DUK, GIW, HOL, LNG, MIS, MRT, MTC, NCS, NEW, RKEW, STR, USN.

## Osmanthus americanus
### DEVIL WOOD

Oleaceae. USDA Zones (6)7–9. Native to the United States. Introduced into cultivation in 1758.

DESCRIPTION: Broad-leaved evergreen to 15–25 ft. high, with bushy, upright habit.
*Leaves:* Lanceolate, with entire margins, dark, shiny green, not typical for the genus.
*Flowers:* White, small, 0.25 in. across, with 4 petals, in clusters, not conspicuous but strongly fragrant; spring.
*Fruit:* A blue-black drupe, 0.5 in. diameter, persisting from fall until spring.

CULTURE: Likes fairly dense shade, but grows in sun if soil is kept moist; more adaptable to a variety of soils than other species of *Osmanthus*, but prefers a pH of 4–6; tolerates wet conditions and salt air.
*Disease and insect problems:* None.
*Transplanting:* Easy.
*Propagation:* By cuttings.

LANDSCAPE VALUE: A fine evergreen for hedging in moist soil. Different from other *Osmanthus* species in that its loose, upright foliage does not have strong, hollylike spikes. Requires little maintenance, and is believed to be hardier than previously thought. Voles will eat roots.

*Neillia sinensis* (G. Koller)

*Neillia sinensis* (G. Koller)

*Neviusia alabamensis* (J. Spink)

*Neviusia alabamensis* (G. Koller)

*Osmanthus americanus* (M. Vehr)

*Osmanthus americanus* (F. Galle)

*Osmanthus americanus* continued

Plant may be observed at AA, ABF, ATL, BF, BIR, BRK, CAL, CUH, DUK, MOR, MTC, NCS, RKEW, SPR, STG, USN.

## Osmanthus delavayi
DELAVAY OSMANTHUS

Oleaceae. USDA Zones 9–10. Native to Yunnan and Sichuan Provinces, China. Introduced into cultivation in 1890 by Abbé Delavay.

DESCRIPTION: Evergreen shrub growing at slow to moderate rate to 6–20 ft. high, often wider than tall, with broad, spreading, rounded habit.
*Leaves:* Ovate, stiff, leathery, tapered at both ends, 0.5–1 in. long, finely and sharply dentate, dark, glossy green above, tiny dark spots beneath.
*Flowers:* Pure white, fragrant, in clusters of 4–8; April–May.
*Fruit:* Egg-shaped, blue-black.

CULTURE: Grows in sun or partial shade; prefers fertile, moist, well-drained, acid soil; grows at low elevations in Hawaii, but performs best at elevations of 2000–4000 ft.
*Disease and insect problems:* None serious.
*Transplanting:* Easy.
*Propagation:* By grafting on privet, but better and healthier when grown on own roots; summer cuttings root readily with bottom heat.

LANDSCAPE VALUE: One of the most beautiful white-flowered evergreens, with highly scented blossoms profusely displayed in April. Very distinct from the popular *O. heterophyllus* in having terminal and axillary flower clusters that open in April. Only one of the seeds sent to Maurice de Vilmorin in 1890 by Abbé Delavay germinated at the School of Arboriculture in Paris. Commercial stock was built up by grafting, with species available in French catalogs by 1911. Later reintroduced to Britain by Forrest. Received RHS Award of Garden Merit.

Plant may be observed at BIR, CAL, CUH, DUK, FIL, HUN, LAC, MIS, MMA, NCS, RKEW, STR, UBC, USN, VDG.

Related *Osmanthus* species and cultivar of interest:

*O.* × *burkwoodii* (*O. delavayi* × *Phillyrea decora*). USDA Zones 7–8. Attractive evergreen and hedge plant growing slowly to 6–9 ft. high and as wide, with dense, bushy habit. White, fragrant flowers, 5–7 in. across, bloom in terminal, axillary clusters of six or seven, in April–May. Leaves are ovate, elliptic, 1–2 in. long, slightly toothed, glossy, dark green. Developed before 1919 by Burkwood and Skipwith, Kingston-on-Thames, United Kingdom. Received RHS Award of Garden Merit.

*O. fragrans* 'Aurantiacus'. Sweet Olive. USDA Zones 8–9. Native to eastern Asia; introduced in 1856 from China. Useful shrub outstanding for its fragrant, orange flowers, which appear in autumn when few other shrubs are in bloom. The small, strongly scented flowers are often hidden by foliage; the Chinese use them for perfuming tea. Most fragrant of the species but the least hardy. Reaches 8–10 ft. high (can reach 20–30 ft. or more), with broad, dense, compact habit. Leaves, which are narrower and less glossy than those of species, are opposite, simple, ovate to elliptic-oblong, almost entire, 1–2.5 in. long and 1–1.5 in. wide, lustrous, dark green above, with yellow margins, pale yellow-green beneath. Fruit is a narrow, blue-black drupe, 0.4 in. long.

## Osmanthus heterophyllus
HOLLY TEA OLIVE
FALSE HOLLY

Synonym: *O. ilicifolius*. Oleaceae. USDA Zones 6–9. Native to Japan. Introduced into cultivation in 1856 by Thomas Lobb.

DESCRIPTION: Evergreen shrub growing at slow to moderate rate to 7–10(20) ft. high, with upright habit when young becoming wider with maturity.
*Leaves:* Opposite, simple, ovate to elliptic ovate, 1.5–2.5 in. long and 1–1.5 in. wide, leathery, dark green above, yellow-green beneath, margins becoming entire with age.
*Flowers:* White, with 4 petals, very fragrant; late September/October–early November.
*Fruit:* A long, blue-black drupe.

CULTURE: Grows in sun or light to medium shade; prefers well-drained, moist, fertile, acid soil, but adapts to a wide pH range; tolerates moderately harsh urban conditions.
*Disease and insect problems:* None serious.
*Transplanting:* Easy, container-grown.
*Propagation:* By cuttings.

LANDSCAPE VALUE: A handsome evergreen with deep green, glossy foliage. Useful as specimen or as screening hedge. Attractive all year. Hardiest of the Asian species. Foliage variable, so often confusing to identify; margins of maturing foliage can be entire, while younger foliage is coarsely spine-toothed. Becomes quite large, but withstands severe pruning well.

Plant may be observed at ABF, ATL, BBG, BC, BIR, BRK, BSG, CAL, DUK, HUN, LAC, LWD, MBG, PAL, PLF, RKEW, STG, UBC, USN, VDG, WIS.

*Osmanthus heterophyllus* cultivars of interest:

*O. heterophyllus* 'Aureomarginatus'. Yellow border on foliage.

*Osmanthus delavayi* (J. C. Raulston)

*Osmanthus* × *burkwoodii* (J. C. Raulston)

*Osmanthus* × *burkwoodii* (J. C. Raulston)

*Osmanthus fragrans* 'Aurantiacus' (J. C. Raulston)

*Osmanthus heterophyllus* 'Goshiki' (N. Brewster)

*Osmanthus heterophyllus* 'Sasaba' (N. Brewster)

**Osmanthus heterophyllus** continued

O. *heterophyllus* 'Goshiki'. Striking foliage with flecks and blotches of creamy white and various shades of green; predominantly white patterns on young foliage become less prominent with age. Unfolding leaves have pink cast. Grows to 10 ft. high. Name means "five colors" in Japanese. Introduced by Brookside Gardens.

O. *heterophyllus* 'Gulftide'. Foliage is strong, spiny, lobed, twisted, and glossy. Attractive shrub with dense habit. Grows to 10–15 ft. high. More cold-hardy than the species. Received RHS Award of Garden Merit.

O. *heterophyllus* 'Maculifolius'. Rare cultivar from Japan that exhibits spectacular variegation and is becoming more available.

O. *heterophyllus* 'Myrtifolius'. Slow-growing to 10–12 ft. high; compact habit and small, spineless leaves.

O. *heterophyllus* 'Rotundifolius'. Neat, compact habit with deep green, spineless, leathery leaves. Slow growing to 5–7 ft. high; less cold-hardy than the species.

O. *heterophyllus* 'Sasaba'. Deeply indented, shiny foliage, with pointed tips. Very slow growth to 4 ft. high. Introduced in 1989 by Barry Yinger. Its name, meaning "bamboo," refers to the leaves, which resemble bamboo.

O. *heterophyllus* 'Variegatus'. Handsome shrub to 8–10 ft. high; foliage accented with creamy white margins.

## *Pachystachys lutea*
## YELLOW LOLLIPOP PLANT
## YELLOW SHRIMP PLANT

Synonym: *Jacobinia lutea*. Acanthaceae. USDA Zone 10. Native to Brazil. Introduced in 1980.

DESCRIPTION: Evergreen shrub growing at moderate rate to 12 in. high, with spreading habit.
*Leaves:* Opposite, ovate, 4–5 in. long, medium green.
*Flowers:* Yellow flowers, with bracts 3 in. long, in compact clusters; most of the year.

CULTURE: Grows in sun and light shade; tolerates wind, wet conditions, some salt, air pollution, and soil compaction; likes loam with a pH of 5.5–6.5.
*Disease and insect problems:* Mealy bug and scale.
*Transplanting:* Very easy; shallow root system.
*Propagation:* By cuttings.

LANDSCAPE VALUE: Bright yellow "lollipop" flowers make this shrub valuable as an ornamental or an attractive hedge.

Plant may be observed at BBG, BIR, CIN, KOF, LAC, LWD, LYO, MMA, MIS, RKEW, SEL, WAI.

## *Paeonia suffruticosa*
## TREE PEONY

Paeoniaceae. USDA Zones 4–8. Native to Bhutan, Tibet, and China, but cultivated in Japan as early as the 6th century. Introduced to Europe in 1787 by Sir Joseph Banks. First Japanese varietal import into Europe by Philipp von Siebold in 1844.

DESCRIPTION: Deciduous, small, woody shrub growing relatively slowly to 6 ft. high and 4 ft. wide.
*Leaves:* Bipinnate, leaflets 2–4 in. long, deeply and incisedly divided, the apex of the lobes and teeth sharply acute, with a few hairs along the midrib.
*Flowers:* Pure white to white with purple inner flare, to all shades of pink and rose, to red and black-red, to yellow, peach, and ivory, with many bi-tone and tri-tone cultivars, 6–8 in. across, with 5 pistils, most varieties hermaphroditic; mid- to late spring.
*Fruit:* Round, about 0.25–0.4 in. diameter, shiny, purple-brown to black, in early fall.
*Winter aspect:* Coarsely branched with thick, glabrous twigs and prominent, dormant terminal and lateral buds; dramatic metamorphosis from winter dormancy to spring flowering.

CULTURE: Prefers a site with one-half to three-fourths sun, but grows well in full sun; noon shade prolongs blossom life; prefers deep, rich, well-drained soil with a slightly acid to neutral pH.
*Disease and insect problems:* None serious.
*Transplanting:* All season long if containerized; balled and burlapped in early spring and fall; bare root when dormant.
*Propagation:* By careful division of older plants, cutting, layering, grafting onto nursery root of herbaceous peony, and seed, which often requires double dormancy.

LANDSCAPE VALUE: An aristocratic, small shrub with bold, lush foliage. The elegant, lovely, large, mid- to late spring blooms are virtually unrivaled and come in a wide spectrum of colors. Valuable as a specimen or combined with other shrubs and perennials. A glorious plant that adds important architectural structure to herbaceous perennial gardens and should be given the adequate space it deserves. Requires little maintenance once established and can be a joy and marvel for generations. Plant becomes more ornamental each year as flower production increases; flowers often produced on 2- to 3-year-old plants. A portion of growth dies back each year to an overwintering bud, making the shrub semiherbaceous; its root system is completely woody. Prune in spring to thin unnecessary inner branchlets; remove spent blooms.

Plant may be observed at AA, BOE, DEN, GCC, MRT, PLF, RBC, VDG.

*Osmanthus heterophyllus* 'Gulftide' (N. Brewster)

*Pachystachys lutea* (V. Lauritzen)

*Paeonia suffruticosa* 'Hana Kisoi' (N. Brewster)

*Paeonia suffruticosa* 'Hana Kisoi' (R. Klehm)

*Paeonia suffruticosa* cultivars of interest:

*P. suffruticosa* 'Alhambra'. Bright golden-yellow, double blossoms with dark red basal flares. One of A. P. Saunders' hybrids.

*P. suffruticosa* 'Ariadne'. Alluring, peach-apricot flowers with rose-red petal fringes, fragrant; named for the daughter of Greek King Minos. Bred by Nassos Daphnis.

*P. suffruticosa* 'Companion of Serenity'. Delicate, ruffled flowers of softest pink, with slight red flares. Bred by William Gratwick.

*P. suffruticosa* 'Hana Kisoi'. Exotic, vivid pink, ruffled, airy blossoms. Name means "floral rivalry." Japanese origin.

*P. suffruticosa* 'Hephestos'. Deep, brick-red, fragrant, double flowers, with pointed, ruffled petals. Named for the Greek god of fire. Bred by Nassos Daphnis.

*P. suffruticosa* 'Joseph Rock'. Pure white, semidouble flowers accented with rich purple inner flares. A selected clone of *P. suffruticosa* subsp. *rockii.*

*P. suffruticosa* 'Leda'. Mauve-pink flowers highlighted with deep purple inner flares. Named for the Greek Queen of Sparta, mother of Castor and Pollux. Bred by Nassos Daphnis.

*P. suffruticosa* 'Renkaku'. Pure white, semidouble flowers. Name means "flight of the cranes." Japanese origin.

*P. suffruticosa* 'Shintenchi'. Cameo pink, large, tailored, semidouble, flowers. Name means "New Heaven and Earth." Japanese origin.

NOTE: A number of exceedingly beautiful tree peonies are available. Many are hybrids of Japanese origin, but are unfortunately mislabelled in the trade and therefore not true to name. Thus, they are not pictured or listed in this volume.

# *Pernettya mucronata*
## CHILEAN PERNETTYA

Ericaceae. USDA Zones 7–8. Native from Mexico to the Antarctic, New Zealand, and Tasmania. Introduced to Ireland by T. Davis in the late 19th century. Named for A. J. Pernetty, 1716–1801, who accompanied Bougainville on voyage around world.

DESCRIPTION: Broad-leaved evergreen growing relatively quickly to 2–5 ft. high, with compact habit in the sun, larger in the shade.
*Leaves:* Alternate, ovate-lanceolate to ovate, 0.75 in. long, sharp-pointed, lustrous, leathery green, turning bronzy in winter.
*Flowers:* White to pink, heathlike; May–June.
*Fruit:* A round berry, 0.5 in. across, colored white, pink, red, or lilac.
*Winter aspect:* Brightly colored fruit persists through fall and winter.

CULTURE: Grows in sun and some shade, but becomes larger and straggly in shade; likes moist, acid peat, but not alkaline or chalky conditions; tolerates wind and wet conditions.
*Disease and insect problems:* None.
*Transplanting:* Easy.
*Propagation:* By seed, softwood cuttings, layering, and rooted suckers.

LANDSCAPE VALUE: Adapts to many garden conditions. Dark brown foliage is wonderful foil for the bright berries, which remain on branches throughout winter. Plants flower but will not fruit unless several clones or varieties are present for cross-pollination.

Plant may be observed at CUH, FIL, HUN, MUN, PAL, RKEW, UBC, VDG.

*Pernettya mucronata* cultivars of interest:

*P. mucronata* 'Alba'. White flowers.
*P. mucronata* 'Coccinea'. Scarlet flowers.
*P. mucronata* 'Rosea'. Rosy pink flowers.
*P. mucronata* 'Rubra'. Dark red flowers.

*Paeonia suffruticosa* 'Ariadne' (R. Klehm)

*Paeonia suffruticosa* 'Leda' (R. Klehm)

*Paeonia suffruticosa* 'Renkaku' (R. Klehm)

*Paeonia suffruticosa* 'Shintenchi' (R. Klehm)

*Pernettya mucronata* (University of British Columbia Botanical Garden)

*Pernettya mucronata* 'Alba' (C. Crumb)

## *Philadelphus coronarius* 'Natchez'
### SWEET MOCK-ORANGE

Saxifragaceae. USDA Zones 4–8. Native to southeastern Europe and Asia Minor. Species thought to be introduced into cultivation in Italy from Caucasus in 1569. One of the first plants brought to the United States by the early settlers.

DESCRIPTION: Deciduous shrub growing quickly to 8–12 ft. high and 10–12 ft. wide, with rather stiff, upright habit.
*Leaves:* Simple, opposite, ovate, 1.5–3.5 in. long and 1–2 in. wide, deep green, no fall color.
*Flowers:* White, with 4 petals, extremely fragrant, in clusters of 5–7 per raceme; May–June.
*Fruit:* A persistent capsule.
*Winter aspect:* Exfoliating orange-brown bark.

CULTURE: Needs full sun for best bloom, but grows in partial shade; prefers moist, well-drained soil, but tolerates dry soil; adapts very well; needs little care except for assiduous pruning.
*Disease and insect problems:* Powdery mildew, rust, aphid, leaf miner, leaf spot; none serious but tend to create unattractive foliage.
*Transplanting:* Easy.
*Propagation:* By seed and softwood cuttings.

LANDSCAPE VALUE: Valued for its great fragrance and lovely, old-fashioned, white blooms. The most handsome *Philadelphus* in flower, but rather leggy and coarse except during the two weeks when in glorious, fragrant bloom. 'Natchez' should be planted in a location where its beautiful flowers can be appreciated but where the plant is not highly visible in all seasons. Attentive pruning is needed to keep plant in desirable shape; tends to become straggly. Prune immediately after flowering; cut old branches to the ground to rejuvenate plant. Related cultivars listed here have improved on the attributes of *P. coronarius*. Plants sold under the name *P. coronarius* are sometimes a hybrid of *P. inodorus,* with lovely flowers but little scent; thus, it is important to select plants while in bloom to be certain of fragrance.

Plant may be observed at AA, ABF, ATL, BBG, BC, BF, BIC, BRK, CBG, CHK, CIN, CUH, DEN, DOW, HOL, HUN, LNG, MBG, MIS, MOD, MNL, MRT, MUN, NEB, PLF, POW, RBC, SEC, SPR, STG, USN, VDG, WIN, WIS.

Another *Philadelphus coronarius* cultivar of interest:

*P. coronarius* 'Variegata'. USDA Zones 5–8. Leaves with creamy white margins. Cultivated since 1770. Received RHS Award of Garden Merit.

Related *Philadelphus* species of interest:

*P. × virginalis* (*P. × lemoinei × P. × nivalis* 'Plenus'). One of the most widely available hybrids. Semidouble to double, fragrant flowers in June, but scattered blooms appear all summer if plant is kept moist.

Related *Philadelphus × virginalis* cultivars of interest:

*P. × virginalis* 'Glacier'. USDA Zones 5–8. Very fragrant, double flowers, about 1.5 in. across. Grows to 5 ft. high. Introduced in 1918 by Lemoine Nursery, Nancy, France.

*P. × virginalis* 'Miniature Snowflake'. USDA Zones 5–8. White, double, fragrant flowers. Profuse bloom and disease-resistant, deep green foliage on a compact shrub growing to 3 ft. high.

*P. × virginalis* 'Minnesota Snowflake'. USDA Zones 4–8. White, double, fragrant flowers, 2 in. across. Grows to 8 ft. high, with arching branches. Hardy to –30°F. Introduced by G. D. Bush.

*P. × virginalis* 'Polar Star'. USDA Zones 5–9. White, semidouble, fragrant flowers, 2.5 in. wide, in May–June; bloom often recurs in fall. Seedling selected by the late Herbert Fischer of Illinois.

*Philadelphus × virginalis* 'Polar Star' (R. Klehm)

*Philadelphus coronarius* 'Natchez' (N. Brewster)

*Philadelphus coronarius* 'Variegata' (J. C. Raulston)

*Philadelphus coronarius* 'Natchez' (N. Brewster)

*Philadelphus × virginalis* 'Miniature Snowflake' (E. Hasselkus)

*Philadelphus × virginalis* 'Polar Star' (G. Gates)

## *Physocarpus opulifolius* 'Dart's Golden'
### COMMON NINEBARK

Rosaceae. USDA Zones 3–7. Native to North America, from Canada through Michigan to Tennessee and Virginia. Introduced into cultivation in 1687.

DESCRIPTION: Deciduous shrub growing at moderate to fast rate to 5–10 ft. high and as wide, with upright, spreading habit.
*Leaves:* Alternate, simple, 1.5–3 in. long and 0.75–1.5 in. wide.
*Flowers:* Pink-white, small, 0.3 in. across, in corymbs 1.5–2 in. across; May–June.
*Fruit:* A follicle.
*Winter aspect:* Glabrous, red-brown bark when young, becoming brown and exfoliating with age.

CULTURE: Grows in sun and partial shade in soils with a wide pH range; tolerates dry sites and tough urban conditions.
*Disease and insect problems:* None serious.
*Transplanting:* Easy.
*Propagation:* By softwood cuttings.

LANDSCAPE VALUE: More refined and compact than the species, with more attractive, longer lasting, yellow foliage. Not highly ornamental but useful in harsh, inhospitable climates and growing conditions where other plants will not survive. Seed capsules can be effective in the winter landscape. Cut to ground in winter to rejuvenate. Minnesota Landscape Arboretum has large collection. Received RHS Award of Garden Merit.

Plant may be observed at BF, BOE, CIN, DAW, MOD, MNL, RKEW, SEC, SPR.

## *Picea abies* 'Little Gem'
### DWARF NORWAY SPRUCE

Pinaceae. USDA Zones 3–7. Species native from central Europe to central Asia. Cultivar introduced before 1960 by F. J. Grootendorst, Boskoop, Netherlands.

DESCRIPTION: Evergreen conifer to 2 ft. high and 3.5 ft. wide, with flat, globose, cushionlike habit.
*Leaves:* Very thin and densely arranged, 0.3–0.75 in. long, bright green when young, turning deep, glossy green.
*Winter aspect:* Dense habit; very slender branches ascending obliquely from center outward.

CULTURE: Grows best in sun; prefers cool, moist, fertile loam (particularly in humid climates) with a pH of 6.5–7.5; tolerates wind.
*Disease and insect problems:* Red spider mite; fungal diseases in humid areas.
*Transplanting:* Easy, container-grown.
*Propagation:* By grafting.

LANDSCAPE VALUE: An attractive specimen with nest-like depression in center. Very dwarf form that may be used in shrub borders, rock gardens, or troughs.

Plant may be observed at AA, ABF, BC, BEA, BER, BF, BIC, BOE, BRK, BSG, CBG, COX, CUH, DAW, DEN, DOW, GCC, HOL, LNG, LWD, MIS, MNL, MOD, MOR, MRT, NCS, NEW, PAL, PLF, RBC, SEC, UBC, USN, VDG.

Other *Picea abies* cultivars of interest:

*P. abies* 'Nidiformis'. Broad and dense, with no central trunk; grows at rate of 1.5 in. per year to reach 4–6 ft. The most stable and reliable clone of *P. abies*.
*P. abies* 'Reflexa'. Weeping form, with branches plunging directly downward; grows 2 in. per year.

Related *Picea* cultivar of interest:

*P. omorika* 'Nana'. Dwarf Serbian Spruce. USDA Zones 4–7. Species native to Yugoslavia; found only near Drina and Lim Rivers. Cultivar introduced in 1930 by Goudkade, Boskoop, Netherlands. Grows to 7–8 ft. high, with broadly conical, very dense habit; branches are irregular in length. Leaves are flat needles, 0.4 in. long, radially arranged; dark green above, with 2 prominent, white, stomatal bands beneath. Fruit is a cylindrical cone 1.5–2 in. long. Prefers sun and deep, rich, moist, well-drained soil with pH of 6.5–7.5. Tolerates wind and heat. Does not withstand drought. Susceptible to aphid, but resistant to spider mite. Propagate by cuttings, December–March. Attractive as foundation plant, in rock garden, or in shrub border. More adaptable to cold and hot temperatures than other *Picea* species.

*Physocarpus opulifolius* 'Dart's Golden' (J. Elsley)

*Physocarpus opulifolius* 'Dart's Golden' (Greer Gardens)

*Picea abies* 'Little Gem' (J. Elsley)

*Picea omorika* 'Nana' (N. Brewster)

# Picea pungens 'Montgomery'
## DWARF COLORADO SPRUCE

Pinaceae. USDA Zones 2–7. Species native to western United States; discovered in 1862 by Dr. Parry. Cultivar obtained from Eastern Nursery by R. H. Montgomery of Coscob, Connecticut, and given to the New York Botanical Garden, where it is still growing.

DESCRIPTION: Evergreen conifer growing slowly to 6–8 ft. high and 10 ft. wide, with very compact, broadly conical habit.
*Leaves:* Four-sided, sharply pointed, 0.75–1 in. long, silver-blue with wax on needles.
*Winter aspect:* Rigid, horizontal branching habit.

CULTURE: Requires full sun, does not grow in shade; prefers a soil pH of 7.0–7.5; tolerates wind and tolerates drought better than other *Picea* species.
*Disease and insect problems:* Spider mite, gall.
*Transplanting:* Easy, container-grown.
*Propagation:* By cuttings and grafting.

LANDSCAPE VALUE: Attractive as accent shrub where bold color is desired; provides excellent contrast for green conifers or small-leafed maples. Retains its bright, silver-blue needles in summer and winter, as well as in maturity.

Plant may be observed at AA, BBG, BC, BEA, BF, BIC, BOE, BSG, CBG, CIN, COX, CUH, DAW, DEN, DOW, DUK, HOL, LNG, MOD, MNL, MRT, NEW, RBC, UBC, USN, VDG.

Other *Picea pungens* cultivars of interest:

*P. pungens* 'Compacta'. Needles dark green, branches flat and spreading; reaches 9 ft. high and 12 ft. wide in 75 years.

# Pieris floribunda 'Millstream'
## MOUNTAIN ANDROMEDA

Ericaceae. USDA Zones 5–7. Species native to southeastern United States, from Virginia to Georgia; introduced into cultivation in 1800s.

DESCRIPTION: Broad-leaved evergreen growing very slowly to 2–4 ft. high and as wide, with low, bushy, flat-topped or mounded habit.
*Leaves:* Ovate, pointed, 1–3 in. long and 0.5–1 in. wide, glossy, dark green.
*Flowers:* White, 2–4 in. across, fragrant, in dense, upright, terminal panicles; March–April, lasting 2–4 weeks.

CULTURE: Grows in sun in colder areas and in shade in southerly latitudes in moist, well-drained, acid soil; prefers a soil pH of 4.0–6.0, but grows in soil with a higher pH; does not tolerate wind, wet conditions, or drought.
*Disease and insect problems:* Leaf spot, mite.
*Transplanting:* Easy, balled and burlapped or container-grown.
*Propagation:* By seed sown as soon as ripe; cuttings difficult to root.

LANDSCAPE VALUE: A hardy and beautiful flowering evergreen with neat, bushy habit. Useful for planting in shrub borders, in groups, or in woodland gardens. More tolerant of alkaline soils than other *Pieris* and not afflicted with lacebug as is *P. japonica*.

Plant may be observed at AA, ABF, ATL, BBG, BC, BLO, CAL, CUH, DIX, DUK, GIW, HOL, HUN, LNG, NCS, NEW, PAL, PLF, RKEW, USN, WIS.

Related *Pieris* cultivars and species of interest:

*P.* 'Brouwer's Beauty' (*P. japonica* × *P. floribunda*). Dense, compact shrub. Flower buds are deep purplish red, and horizontal flower panicles are slightly arched. Leaves are very shiny; new growth is yellow-green. Susceptible to lacebug.

*P. formosa* var. *forrestii* 'Forest Flame'. Himalayan Pieris. Native to western China. Very compact, symmetrical shrub. Flower buds form in summer and are exposed all winter. Grows best in the western United States; needs cool, even climate. More tender than *P. floribunda* and *P. japonica*; USDA Zones 7–8. Received RHS Award of Merit in 1973 and RHS Award of Garden Merit.

*P. phillyreifolia*. USDA Zones 7–8. Native to the United States, in western Florida. Grows to 1.5–3 ft. high; elliptic habit with arching branches. Leaves are oblong to elliptic-oblong, 1–2 in. long, glossy, dark green, with margins somewhat involuted. White, bell-shaped flowers are borne in clusters of 4–12 on axillary racemes in January–February. A shade-tolerant evergreen with small, refined foliage and habit; useful as an understory shrub. Withstands wet conditions and salt better than other *Pieris*.

*P. taiwanensis*. USDA Zones 7–9. Introduced from Taiwan in 1918 by E. H. Wilson. Grows slowly to 3–7 ft. tall, with erect, rounded habit. Resembles *P. japonica* but has larger leaves. Young bronze to bronze-red foliage becomes dark to olive-green. White flowers, similar to Lily-of-the-Valley, appear in erect panicles 3–6 in. long, at the ends of shoots in March–April. Lateral branches are horizontal to pendulous. Excellent plant for woodland conditions where flowers and new growth are rarely harmed by early frosts. Received RHS Award of Merit in 1922.

*Picea pungens* 'Montgomery' (N. Brewster)

*Pieris floribunda* 'Millstream' (N. Brewster)

*Pieris floribunda* 'Millstream' (N. Brewster)

*Pieris* 'Brouwer's Beauty' (G. Gates)

*Pieris formosa* var. *forrestii* 'Forest Flame' (E. Paine)

*Pieris phillyreifolia* (F. Galle)

# Pieris japonica
## JAPANESE ANDROMEDA

Ericaceae. USDA Zones 5–8. Native to Japan. First recorded date of cultivation is 1870.

DESCRIPTION: Broad-leaved evergreen growing slowly to 10–12 ft. high and 6–8 ft. wide, with upright, bushy, dense habit.
*Leaves:* Obovate-oblong to oblanceolate-alternate, leathery, shallow-toothed, 1.25–3.5 in. long and 0.3–0.75 in. wide, rosettelike, new growth bronze-green to reddish becoming dark green above, lighter beneath.
*Flowers:* White, urn-shaped, waxy textured, 0.25 in. long, in 3- to 6-in. long terminal clusters of pendulous racemes; buds form in fall; April–May, lasting 1–2 weeks.
*Fruit:* A capsule, 0.25 in. long; should be removed after flowering.
*Winter aspect:* Brown, shredding bark; stiff, spreading habit.

CULTURE: Grows in sun or, in warmer climates, partial shade; likes moist, acid, very well drained soil; tolerates higher soil pH than other Ericaceae; does not tolerate wet conditions or drought; needs protection from wind, especially in winter; grows best in a sheltered spot with a western exposure.
*Disease and insect problems:* Leaf spot, lacebug, scale, mite.
*Transplanting:* Easy, balled and burlapped or container-grown.
*Propagation:* By cuttings in fall, rooted in peat-perlite mixture with rooting hormone.

LANDSCAPE VALUE: A handsome shrub with extremely attractive, glossy green foliage. Neat habit with branches to the ground. One of the hardiest varieties, useful in the shrub border, in massed plantings, or with other broad-leaved evergreens. Excellent in the woodland garden. Received RHS Award of Merit.

Plant may be observed at AA, ABF, ATL, BBG, BC, BIR, BSG, CAL, CBG, CUH, DAW, DEN, DUK, GCC, GIW, HOL, LWD, MCG, MIS, NCS, NEW, PAL, PLF, RBC, RKEW, SEC, STG, VDG, WIN, WIS.

*Pieris japonica* cultivars of interest:

P. *japonica* 'Bert Chandler'. White flowers; new foliage bright chartreuse to salmon-pink to cream to dark green; introduced in 1936 by Bert Chandler of Australia.
P. *japonica* 'Flamingo'. Rose-red flowers.
P. *japonica* 'Geisha'. Pure white flowers, with more slender leaves.
P. *japonica* 'Mountain Fire'. White flowers; new foliage brilliant red, the best red of the species. Received RHS Award of Garden Merit.
P. *japonica* 'Pygmaea'. Grows to compact 1–3 ft. high, with feathery appearance; leaves tiny, 0.5–1 in. long, needle-like.
P. *japonica* 'Red Mill'. White flowers, longer lasting than those of species; new growth bright red to mahogany-green; dense, bushy habit.
P. *japonica* 'Roslinda'. Pink flowers; new growth brownish red; grows to compact 4 ft. high and as wide.
P. *japonica* 'Valley Fire'. White flowers; new growth vivid red. More vigorous than many other P. *japonica* cultivars. Introduced by Robert Tichnor of Oregon State University. Received RHS Award of Garden Merit.
P. *japonica* 'Valley Rose'. Pale silvery pink flowers; tall shrub with open habit. Introduced by Robert Tichnor of Oregon State University.
P. *japonica* 'Valley Valentine'. Deep rose flowers, borne abundantly on dense, upright shrub. Introduced by Robert Tichnor of Oregon State University. Received RHS Award of Garden Merit.
P. *japonica* 'Variegata'. White flowers; narrow leaves with

*Pieris japonica* 'Valley Valentine' (J. Elsley)

*Pieris japonica* 'Variegata' (K. Freeland)

*Pieris japonica* 'Bert Chandler' (J. C. Raulston)

*Pieris japonica* 'Flamingo' (J. C. Raulston)

*Pieris japonica* 'Pygmaea' (J. C. Raulston)

*Pieris japonica* 'Valley Fire' (J. Elsley)

*Pieris japonica* continued

yellowish white margins. Grows slowly at first, reaching 12 ft. high at maturity.

*P. japonica* 'White Cascade'. Pure white flowers in long panicles; very floriferous, with bloom lasting 5 weeks. Introduced in 1942 by Vermeulen Nursery.

*P. japonica* 'White Pearl'. White flowers; extremely erect branches.

# *Pinus densiflora* 'Globosa'
## DWARF JAPANESE RED PINE

Pinaceae. USDA Zones 3–7. Species native to Japan and Korea; introduced into cultivation in Europe in 1854 by Philipp von Siebold.

DESCRIPTION: Evergreen conifer growing to 12 ft. high in 50 years, with rounded to hemispherical habit.
*Leaves:* Borne in twos, 1.5–2.5 in. long, apex acute, densely brushlike on shoots, lustrous dark green, needles only half as long as those of species, persisting 3 years.
*Fruit:* A cone, 0.75–1.5 in. long, solitary or grouped in whorls, directed downward.
*Winter aspect:* Horizontally spreading branching habit.

CULTURE: Prefers sun and well-drained soil with a pH of 6.0–7.5; does not tolerate wet conditions.
*Disease and insect problems:* Dry rot (*Diplodia*) in warmer climates.
*Transplanting:* Easy, balled and burlapped or container-grown.
*Propagation:* By grafting in November–March.

LANDSCAPE VALUE: A very slow growing, semiprostrate pine, useful for rock gardens, shrub borders, and bonsai. Trunk frequently crooked or leaning; crown is broad and flat.

Plant may be observed at CIN, DAW, HOL, MRT.

# *Pinus mugo* 'Mops'
## DWARF SWISS MOUNTAIN PINE

Pinaceae. USDA Zones 2–7. Species native to the Alps of central Europe. Cultivar introduced in 1951 by Hugo Hooftman, Boskoop, Netherlands.

DESCRIPTION: Evergreen conifer growing 1–2 in. per year to 3 ft. high and as wide, with globose habit and short branches.
*Leaves:* 2 per fascicle, 1–1.5 in. long, persisting 5–10 years, vivid dark green.

CULTURE: Best in full sun but grows in partial shade; prefers deep, moist loam with a pH of 6.5–7.5, but tolerates poor and calcareous soil.
*Disease and insect problems:* Rust, scale.
*Transplanting:* Easy; no tap root.
*Propagation:* By grafting.

LANDSCAPE VALUE: Excellent for rock gardens, shrub borders, banks, group plantings, or containers. Good color and dense, short-branched, dwarf habit.

Plant may be observed at AA, LNG, LWD, MIS, USN.

# *Pinus sylvestris* 'Beuvronensis'
## SCOTCH PINE

USDA Zones 3–7. Species native to North America, from Canada to the Allegheny Mountains. Cultivar discovered in 1871 as a witches'-broom; propagated by Transom Frères, Orleans, France.

DESCRIPTION: Evergreen conifer growing 1–2 in. per year to 3 ft. high and 4.5 ft. wide in 25 years, with broad, compact, dome-shaped habit.
*Leaves:* 0.75–1.25 in. long, bluish green.
*Winter aspect:* Dense, irregular branching habit.

CULTURE: Prefers full sun and clay or loam with a pH of 6.5–7.0; requires well-drained soil, but grows on poor, dry sites; tolerates some wind and drought when established.
*Disease and insect problems:* Blister rust; dry rot (*Diplodia*).
*Transplanting:* Easy, container-grown.
*Propagation:* By seed without stratification.

LANDSCAPE VALUE: One of the best pines for rock gardens or in front of shrub borders; can be used in trough gardens when kept in bounds. Shrub has ornamental, glossy, green twigs and reddish brown, very resinous buds.

Plant may be observed at AA, BC, DEN, DUK, LNG, LWD, MIS, MRT, RKEW, USN, VDG.

Another *Pinus sylvestris* cultivar of interest:

*P. sylvestris* 'Hillside Creeper'. Excellent for banks and rock gardens. Prostrate habit; grows to 2 ft. high and 8 ft. wide in 10 years. Attractive yellow-green color in winter.

*Pinus densiflora* 'Globosa' (Arnold Arboretum)

*Pinus mugo* 'Mops' (E. Hasselkus)

*Pinus sylvestris* 'Beuvronensis' (N. Brewster)

*Pinus sylvestris* 'Hillside Creeper' (N. Brewster)

# Potentilla fruticosa
## CINQUEFOIL

Rosaceae. USDA Zones 3–7. Native to the United States. Introduced into cultivation in 1700.

DESCRIPTION: Deciduous shrub growing slowly to 2–5 ft. high, with dense, upright, rounded habit.
*Leaves:* Alternate, compound, pinnate, composed of 3–7 leaflets, fine-textured, silky, grayish green to dark green; no fall color.
*Flowers:* With 5 petals, in single- or few-flowered cymes, about 1.25 in. across, predominantly yellow, but color varies from white to shades of yellow and red, depending on cultivar; June–frost;
*Fruit:* A persistent achene, not showy.
*Winter aspect:* Shiny, brown, exfoliating bark; dense, scraggly habit.

CULTURE: Likes full sun, but grows in some shade; prefers clay soil, but tolerates poor, dry, compacted soils; tolerates extreme cold.
*Disease and insect problems:* None serious; tends to mildew if evenings are wet; spider mite can be troublesome.
*Transplanting:* Easy; noninvasive root system.
*Propagation:* By softwood cuttings.

LANDSCAPE VALUE: A hardy, resilient shrub for the Midwest and urban conditions, with clean, fine-textured foliage and abundant, attractive color from summer until frost. Can be used for massed plantings, edging, and low hedge. Occasional pruning is necessary to avoid legginess; dense branching habit not particularly attractive in winter. Can tolerate less water than other species. One of the most floriferous plants throughout the growing season, particularly in hot, dry climates.

Plant may be observed at AA, BEA, BER, BIC, BOE, CBG, CIN, COX, CUH, DAW, DEN, GCC, HOL, LNG, LWD, MOD, MNL, MRT, NEB, NEW, PAL, PLF, RBC, RKEW, SEC, STG, UBC, VDG, WIS, ZOO.

*Potentilla fruticosa* cultivars of interest:

*P. fruticosa* 'Abbotswood'. Large, white flowers, and dark, bluish green foliage; considered one of the best of the whites. Received RHS Award of Garden Merit.
*P. fruticosa* 'Coronation Triumph'. Medium-bright yellow flowers. Very floriferous; tolerates extreme cold and drought.
*P. fruticosa* 'Day Dawn Viette'. Peach-pink flowers suffused with cream.
*P. fruticosa* 'Goldfinger'. Deep golden-yellow flowers, 1.75 in. across, and dark green foliage; best-performing *Potentilla* in Upper Midwest for heavy flowering and form. Introduced in 1970 by H. Knoll, Netherlands. Received RHS Award of Garden Merit.

*P. fruticosa* 'Katherine Dykes'. Lemon-yellow flowers 1–1.5 in. across; reaches 2–3 ft. high with medium green foliage and graceful, arching branches. Tends to become leggy with age. Received RHS Award of Garden Merit.
*P. fruticosa* 'Pink Queen'. Pink flowers.
*P. fruticosa* 'Primrose Beauty'. Pale yellow flowers, 1.4 in. diameter, and silvery green foliage; one of the finest performers. Introduced in 1955 by R. Cannegieter Hattam, Netherlands.
*P. fruticosa* 'Snowbird'. White, double flowers (12–15 petals) and dark green foliage; more floriferous than 'Abbotswood'. Introduced by University of Manitoba.
*P. fruticosa* 'Yellowbird'. Bright yellow, semidouble flowers (8–10 petals) and medium green foliage. Introduced by University of Manitoba.

# Prostanthera rotundifolia
## PEPPERMINT SHRUB

Labiatae. USDA Zones 9. Native to Tasmania and southeastern Australia. Introduced into cultivation in 1824.

DESCRIPTION: Broad-leaved evergreen growing at moderate rate to 4–10 ft. high and as wide, with dense, rounded habit.
*Leaves:* Clustered, nearly circular, obovate or ovate, with a few large teeth, 0.2–0.3 in. long and 0.25 in. wide, glossy, dark green above, dull below, strongly scented (as are the young branchlets).
*Flowers:* Purple-blue to deep lilac, bell-shaped, 0.5 in. long, with corolla 0.4 in. wide, short-stalked, in groups of 5 or more in axillary racemes; April–May.

CULTURE: Grows in full sun or light shade in slightly acid loam or sand; tolerates drought somewhat, but not wind.
*Disease and insect problems:* None serious.
*Transplanting:* Easy, balled and burlapped.
*Propagation:* By softwood cuttings.

LANDSCAPE VALUE: One of the most beautiful of all cultivated Tasmanian shrubs, with a well-mannered habit. Stunning in spring with profuse clouds of purple blooms covering the branches; flowers abundantly for two months. Foliage is strongly mint-scented. Useful as specimen, in massed plantings, or with other shrubs of contrasting color and texture. Very effective as a filler and may also be espaliered. Prune back hard immediately after flowering.

Plant may be observed at BBG, HUN, LAC, RKEW, UBC.

*Prostanthera rotundifolia* cultivar of interest:

*P. rotundifolia* 'Glen Davis'. Identical to the species except for larger, darker flowers.

*Potentilla fruticosa* 'Abbotswood' (E. Hasselkus)

*Potentilla fruticosa* 'Goldfinger' (B. Yinger)

*Potentilla fruticosa* 'Abbotswood' (E. Hasselkus)

*Potentilla fruticosa* 'Katherine Dykes' (N. Brewster)

*Prostanthera rotundifolia* 'Glen Davis' (P. K. Thompson)

*Prostanthera ovalifolia* (P. Nelson)

205

**_Prostanthera rotundifolia_ continued**

Related _Prostanthera_ species of interest:

_P. ovalifolia._ Similar but faster growing than _P. rotundifolia_, with lighter colored flowers and leaves and a slightly softer growth habit. Grows to 6 ft. high, with olive-green foliage. Flowers of soft lilac-mauve are borne on long, nodding shoots. USDA Zone 9.

# _Punica granatum_
## POMEGRANATE

Punicaceae. USDA Zones 8–10. Native to southeastern Europe and the Himalayas. Cultivated since the 16th century for its fruit.

DESCRIPTION: Deciduous shrub growing at moderate rate to 12–20 ft. high and as wide, with upright to oval habit.
_Leaves:_ Alternate, opposite or whorled, oval-lanceolate, new growth is bronze, turning stiff, glossy, dark green in summer and yellow-green in fall.
_Flowers:_ Coral to scarlet, with 5–7 crumpled petals, funnel-shaped, 1–1.5 in. across, in terminal or short side shoots, often in pairs; June–August.
_Fruit:_ Globose, red, 2–3 in. across, with a persistent calyx and many seeds, in September–October.
_Winter aspect:_ Angled branching habit.

CULTURE: Best in sun; grows in partial shade, but flowers poorly; prefers fertile, moist soils, but tolerates well-drained sand or clay soils; tolerates intense heat.
_Disease and insect problems:_ None serious, except in desert settings where leaf-footed plantbug may drill holes in fruit.
_Transplanting:_ Easy.
_Propagation:_ By softwood cuttings in September and by grafting.

LANDSCAPE VALUE: Valued for its brilliant flowers and colorful fruit. Excellent in shrub border, in groupings, or in containers in cooler climates. Grown outside in warmer regions, but easily grown in greenhouse. Flowers on new growth. Needs long, warm growing season.

Plant may be observed at BBG, BRK, DIN, FIL, LAC, MMA, PAL, RBC, RKEW, SAB, STR, USN.

_Punica granatum_ cultivars of interest:

_P. granatum_ 'Hizakuru'. Red, double, ruffled flowers.
_P. granatum_ 'Shiro Botan'. White, double flowers.
_P. granatum_ 'Toyosho'. Salmon-pink, double flowers.
_P. granatum_ 'Wonderful'. Red, single flowers, to 4 in. across; grows to fountain-shaped 10 ft. high. Best fruiting cultivar.

Additional, more compact _Punica granatum_ cultivars of interest:

_P. granatum_ 'Emperior'. Red, double flowers; grows to 14 in. high and 14 in. wide in 10 years.
_P. granatum_ 'Nana'. Orange-red, double flowers. Grows to compact 3 ft. high, with tiny leaves, 0.25–0.75 in. long; nearly evergreen in mild climates. Flowers followed by small fruit in summer; blooms when very small and bears fruit when only 12 in. high.
_P. granatum_ 'Peach Princess'. Apricot flowers with pink fruit.
_P. granatum_ 'Twisted Trunk'. Red flowers; grows to 3 ft. high with leaves 1.5 in. long and 0.5 in. wide. As plant matures, trunk twists into a spiral form.

# _Pyracantha_ 'Apache'
## FIRETHORN

Parentage: (_P. koidzumii_ 'Victory' × _P. koidzumii_ 'Rosedale') × _P. fortuneana_ 'Orange Glow'. Rosaceae. USDA Zones 7–8. Species native to southeastern Europe and central China. Cultivar introduced in 1986 by Donald Egolf of the U.S. National Arboretum.

DESCRIPTION: Semi-evergreen to evergreen shrub in warmer climates, growing slowly to 4 ft. high and 6 ft. wide, with compact, dwarf, low-spreading habit.
_Leaves:_ Alternate, entire, cuneate at base, 1.75–2.25 in. long and 0.25–0.75 in. wide, glossy, dark green above, yellow-green below.
_Flowers:_ Creamy white, 30–60 florets per corymb, 1.5 in. across, borne on spurs; May.
_Fruit:_ Glossy, bright red, 0.4 in. across, borne in clusters of 20–60; prolific display in late summer and fall.
_Winter aspect:_ Dense habit, with short internodes.

CULTURE: Requires sun; thrives in any good soil with a pH of 6.0–6.5; tolerates wind and some drought, but not wet conditions.
_Disease and insect problems:_ None serious; resistant to scab and fire blight.
_Transplanting:_ Easy, balled and burlapped or container-grown.
_Propagation:_ By softwood or hardwood cuttings in early summer–fall.

LANDSCAPE VALUE: Ideal as specimen, low hedge, in the shrub border, or as container plant. Valued for its nearly evergreen foliage, spring floral display, and abundant shiny, red fruit—ripening in August and persisting until December. Compact growth habit eliminates need for pruning.

Plant may be observed at BC, BF, DEN, GCC, MOR, NCS, USN.

*Punica granatum* 'Nana' (J. Apel)

*Punica granatum* 'Nana' (Brooklyn Botanic Garden)

*Pyracantha* 'Apache' (D. Egolf)

*Pyracantha* 'Apache' (D. Egolf)

## *Pyracantha* 'Navaho'
### SCARLET FIRETHORN

Parentage: *P. angustifolia* × *P.* 'Watereri'. Rosaceae. USDA Zones 7–9. Species native from southeastern Europe to central China. Cultivar introduced in 1978 by Donald Egolf of the U.S. National Arboretum.

DESCRIPTION: Semi-evergreen to evergreen shrub, growing at moderate rate to 6 ft. high and 7 ft. wide, with dense, compact, moundlike habit.
*Leaves:* Oblanceolate to elliptic, cuneate at base, 1–3 in. long and 0.4–0.6 in. wide, medium green above, gray-green beneath.
*Flowers:* Creamy white, bell-shaped, 0.25 in. across, in large trusses; spring.
*Fruit:* Depressed, globose, 0.25 in. across, 10–15 per inflorescence, smooth, waxy, maturing to red in October–November, persisting into late spring.
*Winter aspect:* Branches wide-spreading from base.

CULTURE: Grows in sun or partial shade, but needs full sun for best flowering and fruiting; prefers sandy loam with a pH of 6.0–6.5.
*Disease and insect problems:* None; resistant to scab and fire blight.
*Transplanting:* Balled and burlapped or container-grown, when young; more difficult when established.
*Propagation:* By softwood or hardwood cuttings, 6–8 in. long, in any potting medium; seed does not come true.

LANDSCAPE VALUE: A choice landscape plant. Attractive as specimen, foundation plant, espalier, barrier, or low hedge. Can be pruned at any time.

Plant may be observed at BC, CUH, DEN, LAC, MOR, NCS, USN.

Related *Pyracantha* cultivars of interest:

*P.* 'Fiery Cascade' (*P.* 'Watereri' × *P. crenulata* 'Kansuensis'). USDA Zones 7–9. Vigorous but dwarf habit growing to 3.5 ft. high and 5 ft. wide, with pendulous habit; long, slender, shiny, dark green leaves; and small (0.25 in. across) shiny, orange fruit in August, turning red by October. Exceptionally hardy; free of scab and fireblight. Introduced in 1979 by Elwin R. Orton, Jr., Rutgers University, New Jersey.

*P.* 'Gold Rush' (*P. angustifolia* × *P. crenata-serrata*). USDA Zones 7–8. Reaches 10 ft. high and as wide, with dense, spreading, intricately branched habit. Leaves are oblong to linear, 0.75–1.5 in. long and 0.4 in. wide, shiny dark green. Yellow-orange, flattened, globose fruit, 0.5 in. across, carried in dense clusters along branches. Selected in 1959 by Brian Mulligan of University of Washington Arboretum; named and introduced in 1975 by Joseph Witt.

## *Pyracantha* 'Pueblo'
### FIRETHORN

Parentage: *P. koidzumii* 'Belli' × *P. coccinea* var. *pauciflora*. Rosaceae. USDA Zones 7–9. Species native to southeastern Europe and central China. Cultivar introduced in 1987 by Donald Egolf of the U.S. National Arboretum.

DESCRIPTION: Semi-evergreen to evergreen shrub, growing at moderate rate to 6 ft. high and 10 ft. wide, with compact, spreading habit.
*Leaves:* Alternate, elliptic to obovate, 1.1–2.75 in. long and 0.4–0.9 in. wide, semiglossy, dark green.
*Flowers:* Creamy white, 20–45 florets per corymb, borne on spurs and short shoots along branches; early May.
*Fruit:* Depressed, globose, brilliant orange-red, 0.4–0.5 in. across, in clusters of 15–40, in August–frost.
*Winter aspect:* Dense, broadly horizontal branching habit.

CULTURE: Grows in sun; prefers good, sandy loam with a pH of 6.0–6.5; tolerates wind and some drought when established.
*Disease and insect problems:* None serious; resistant to scab and fire blight; needs no spraying.
*Transplanting:* Balled and burlapped or container-grown.
*Propagation:* By softwood or hardwood cuttings, which fruit heavily by the 2nd year.

LANDSCAPE VALUE: A superior *Pyracantha*, combining almost-evergreen foliage, compact habit, and persistent, brilliant, orange-red fruit. Spreading habit makes it ideal for massed plantings, informal or formal hedges, or as espalier against bare walls.

Plant may be observed at ABF, BBG, BSG, CUH, LWD, MOR, NCS, OWG, PLF, USN, VDG.

Related *Pyracantha* cultivars of interest:

*P.* 'Mohave' (*P. koidzumii* × *P. coccinea* 'Wyatt'). Grows to 12 ft. high and as wide, with upright habit. Provides magnificent display of large, waxy-textured, bright orange-red fruit, 20–40 per cluster, mid-August through

*Pyracantha* 'Mohave' (N. Brewster)

*Pyracantha* 'Navaho' (D. Egolf)

*Pyracantha* 'Fiery Cascade' (E. Orton)

*Pyracantha* 'Fiery Cascade' (E. Orton)

*Pyracantha* 'Pueblo' (D. Egolf)

*Pyracantha* 'Mohave' (D. Egolf)

*Pyracantha* 'Rutgers' (E. Orton)

winter. Disease-resistant. Hardy to Zone 6; has withstood temperatures of −5 ℉. Introduced in 1963 by Donald Egolf, U.S. National Arboretum.

*P.* 'Rutgers' (*P. coccinea* × *P. coccinea*). USDA Zones 6–9. Lowest growing *Pyracantha*. Grows to 4 ft. high and 7 ft. wide with low, spreading habit. Has excellent, glossy, dark green leaves and abundant orange berries that are larger than those of the species. Highly resistant to scab and fireblight. Introduced in 1980 by Elwin Orton of Rutgers University.

# *Pyracantha* 'Teton'
## FIRETHORN

Parentage: *P. fortuneana* 'Orange Glow' × *P. rogersiana* 'Flava'. Rosaceae. USDA Zones 6–9. Species native to southeastern Europe and central China. Cultivar introduced in 1976 by Donald Egolf of the U.S. National Arboretum.

DESCRIPTION: Semi-evergreen shrub depending on zone, growing at moderate rate to 12 ft. high and 9 ft. wide, with upright, columnar to pyramidal (in West) habit.
*Leaves:* Oblanceolate to elliptic, cuneate at base, 0.5–1.6 in. long and 0.4–0.6 in. wide.
*Flowers:* White, 1.5–2 in. across, densely borne on spurs or short shoots along branches; spring.
*Fruit:* Light yellow, maturing to medium yellow-orange in August–mid-October; more intense color in cooler climates.
*Winter aspect:* Branches strongly vertical from base.

CULTURE: Grows in sun and sandy loam with a pH of 6.0–6.5; tolerates some wind.
*Disease and insect problems:* Resistant to scab and fire blight.
*Transplanting:* Balled and burlapped or container-grown, when young; do not transplant when established.
*Propagation:* By softwood or hardwood cuttings.

LANDSCAPE VALUE: The first *Pyracantha* with a distinctly vertical growth habit. In the Pacific Northwest and cooler regions, it has a more pyramidal habit and more intensely colored orange fruit. Good landscape plant for restricted sites. Left unpruned, it can form a narrow hedge or screen. Among the most cold-hardy of the genus.

Plant may be observed at BRK, BSG, HOL, USN, VDG.

# *Rhamnus frangula* 'Asplenifolia'
## GLOSSY BUCKTHORN

Rhamnaceae. USDA Zones 2–7. Native to the United Kingdom. Developed from seed in 1888 in Maukau, Germany.

DESCRIPTION: Deciduous shrub growing slowly to 10–12 ft. high and 6–10 ft. wide, with upright, spreading habit.
*Leaves:* Margins irregularly notched and undulate, 1.5–2.25 in. long and 0.08–0.2 in. wide, dull, glazed dark green above, lighter and glossy beneath, turning yellow in fall.
*Flowers:* Creamy green, in clusters of 2–10 in leaf axils of young shoots, not conspicuous; May–June.
*Fruit:* Green to red to black, 0.25 in. across, in July–September.

CULTURE: Grows in sun and semishade in all types of well-drained soil.
*Disease and insect problems:* None serious; some fungus on winter-stressed shrubs.
*Transplanting:* Easy, balled and burlapped.
*Propagation:* By cuttings in June–July, or by seed, which germinates in 60 days in peat moss.

LANDSCAPE VALUE: A handsome cultivar noted for the fernlike texture of its leaves. Attractive in shrub border where its fine-textured foliage provides interesting contrast to that of broad-leaved evergreens. Bees love the flowers. Wood is used as charcoal in the manufacture of gunpowder.

Plant may be observed at AA, BF, BOE, CBG, CIN, CUH, DAW, DEN, GCC, LNG, MNL, MIS, NCS, SEC, SPR.

# *Rhodotypos scandens*
## JETBEAD
## WHITE KERRIA

Rosaceae. USDA Zones 5–8. Native to Japan and central China. Introduced into cultivation in 1866.

DESCRIPTION: Deciduous shrub growing moderately fast to 3–5 ft. high and 4–8 ft. wide, with openly branched, rounded, somewhat arching habit.
*Leaves:* Opposite, simple, ovate, 2.5–4 in. long, sharply serrate, medium green, glabrous above, lighter beneath, with little fall color change.
*Flowers:* White, with 4 petals, 1.5 in. wide, at ends of branches.
*Fruit:* Black, beadlike, 0.5 in. across, in threes or fours, persisting through winter.
*Winter aspect:* Branches green and glabrous when young, turning brown with age and streaked with gray.

CULTURE: Tolerates sun or shade, a variety of soils in a wide pH range, pollution, and environmental stress.

*Rhamnus frangula* 'Asplenifolia' (G. Koller)

*Pyracantha* 'Teton' (N. Brewster)

*Rhamnus frangula* 'Asplenifolia' (R. Klehm)

*Rhodotypos scandens* (G. Koller)

*Rhodotypos scandens* (G. Koller)

***Rhodotypos scandens*** continued

*Disease and insect problems:* None.
*Transplanting:* Easy.
*Propagation:* By root cuttings, when shrub is in leaf; seed requires acid scarification and cold stratification.

LANDSCAPE VALUE: A very hardy, easily propagated, flowering shrub. Valued for its adaptability, tolerance, and durability. Good choice for heavy shade and adverse environmental conditions. Also effective as a border plant. Leaves have a pleated look. Closely allied to *Kerria*.

Plant may be observed at AA, ABF, BBG, BC, BER, BF, BOE, CBG, CIN, DAW, DEN, DOW, GCC, HOL, LNG, LWD, MOR, MRT, MTC, NCS, NEW, OWG, PAL, PLF, POW, RKEW, SPR, USN, VDG, WIN.

# *Rhus aromatica* 'Gro-low'
## GRO-LOW SUMAC

Anacardiaceae. USDA Zones 4–8. Native to North America, from the northern Midwest region to Florida and Louisiana. Selected in the early 1970s by Synnestvedt Nursery, Round Lake, Illinois, from a group of seedlings.

DESCRIPTION: Deciduous shrub growing quickly to 2 ft. high and 6–8 ft. wide, with low, spreading habit.
*Leaves:* Alternate, ovate, trifoliate, coarsely toothed, medium green, with a bronze-orange to purple cast in fall.
*Flowers:* Yellow, small (female), not ornamental.
*Fruit:* A hairy, scarlet drupe, often persisting into winter.
*Winter aspect:* Low and spreading habit; lower branches turn up at tips.

CULTURE: Needs full sun for best fall color, but tolerates shade; prefers acid clay or loam, but grows in most soils.
*Disease and insect problems:* None serious; some rust, mite, scale, aphid.
*Transplanting:* Easy; often grown in containers because of deep, coarse, root system.
*Propagation:* By softwood cuttings.

LANDSCAPE VALUE: An excellent, practical small shrub for tough planting sites (e.g., in parking lots, as a fast cover for steep banks, and as an underplanting for the shrub border). Provides attractive foliage, habit, and handsome fall color when grown in full sun. Requires little maintenance. Responds well to heavy shearing. The Wisconsin highway department first used this shrub on banks along highways.

Plant may be observed at AA, ABF, ABN, ATL, BBG, BC, BEA, BF, BIC, BOK, CAL, CBG, CIN, COX, CUH, DAW, DEN, DOW, GCC, GIW, HOL, HOU, LNG, LWD, MIS, MOD, MNL, MOR, MRT, MTC, MUN, NCA, NCS, NEB, NEW, PLF, RBC, RKEW, SAB, SBB, SEC, SPR, STR, USN.

Related *Rhus* species, variety, and cultivar of interest:

*R. copallina*. Flameleaf Sumac. Native to eastern North America; introduced into cultivation in 1688. Small to medium-sized shrub with pinnate, lustrous leaves and dense, erect clusters of green-yellow flowers which are not highly ornamental. Notable for its spectacular, rich red and purple fall color.

*R. glabra* var. *cismontana*. Unusual variety used mainly in dry, cold environments. Valued for small size (4–5 ft. high) and hardiness (to USDA Zone 3); has more pyramidal-shaped, longer lasting scarlet seed plumes and lighter leaf undersides than species. Fruit excellent for attracting birds. Useful in sites similar to natural habitats—prairies, canyons, desert scrub and mountain bush areas, and open woodlands. Best in well-drained soils with neutral to high pH.

*R. trilobata*. Squawbush, Skunkbush. To USDA Zone 5. Native to Canada and the United States. Grows quickly to 3–5 ft. high and wider. Spring flowers yellowish, not conspicuous. Red or brilliant yellow fall color. Hairy leaves can accumulate dust, and some consider scent of bruised leaves unpleasant. Likes sun and clay soil; tolerates heat and drought. Use as windbreak, low hedge, covering for sunny slopes, or coarse ground cover for poor soils. Cultivated for timber in parts of the United States.

*R. trilobata* 'Autumn Amber'. Low-growing shrub with almost prostrate branches, to 1–1.5 ft. high. Good ground cover for soils with high pH.

# *Rhus chinensis* 'September Beauty'
## CHINESE SUMAC

Anacardiaceae. USDA Zones 6–8. Native to China, Japan, Korea, Manchuria, and Malaysia. Species introduced into cultivation in 1737. Cultivar introduced in 1985 by Elwin Orton of Rutgers University.

DESCRIPTION: Deciduous shrub to 20 ft. high, with loose, spreading, suckering habit.
*Leaves:* Compound, pinnate, coarsely toothed, 8–15 in. long, composed of 7–13 oval leaflets 2.5–4 in. long and half as wide, bright green in summer, turning bronze-orange-red in fall.
*Flowers:* Yellow-white, in large, terminal panicles; late summer.
*Fruit:* A small, pubescent, orange drupe.
*Winter aspect:* Downy winter buds; yellowish branchlets.

CULTURE: Grows in sun or shade; prefers well-drained soil, but adapts to a variety of soils with an average pH; tolerates drought and urban conditions, but not wet conditions.

*Rhus aromatica* 'Gro-low' (G. Gates)

*Rhus aromatica* 'Gro-low' (G. Gates)

*Rhus copallina* (E. Hasselkus)

*Rhus chinensis* 'September Beauty' (J. C. Raulston)

*Rhus chinensis* 'September Beauty' (J. Elsley)

*Disease and insect problems:* None serious; some rust, leaf spot, aphid, mite, and scale.
*Transplanting:* Easy.
*Propagation:* By cuttings.

LANDSCAPE VALUE: One of the most attractive of the late-flowering sumacs. Useful in spacious sites and naturalistic plantings. Valued for its tremendous flower panicles, which are superior to those of the species.

Plant may be observed at AA, ATL, BF, BSG, CIN, HOL, LNG, MOR, NCS, USN.

# *Rhus typhina* 'Dissecta'
# *Rhus typhina* 'Laciniata'
## STAGHORN SUMAC

Anacardiaceae. USDA Zones 4–8. Native to North America, from Canada south to Georgia and west to Iowa. Species introduced into cultivation in 1629. 'Dissecta' cultivated since the 1800s.

DESCRIPTION: Deciduous shrubs growing quickly to 15–25 ft. high and as wide or wider, with loose habit.
*Leaves:* Alternate, compound, pinnate, composed of 13–27 leaflets 2–5 in. long and 1–2 in. wide, bright green above, turning yellow, orange, or crimson in fall.
*Flowers:* Greenish yellow, female in dense, pubescent panicles 4–8 in. long, male in larger, more open panicles; June–July.
*Fruit:* A hairy, red, pyramidal drupe, very ornamental, very persistent.
*Winter aspect:* Red-brown, velvetlike pubescence on branches.

CULTURE: Grows in sun and shade; prefers well-drained soil, but adapts to a variety of soils; tolerates wind, drought, and urban conditions, but not wet conditions.
*Disease and insect problems:* Rust, aphid, mite, scale not serious; verticillium wilt noted.
*Transplanting:* Easy.
*Propagation:* By root cuttings.

LANDSCAPE VALUE: Handsome, large shrubs. Valued for their intense autumn color and very graceful, fernlike foliage. Used for massed plantings. Extremely tough; can be rejuvenated by cutting to ground in winter. Both cultivars have fine-textured, deeply lobed foliage, but leaves of 'Dissecta' more deeply divided than those of 'Laciniata'. Both plants are remarkably tolerant of air pollution. Fall colors of orange, vermillion, buttery yellow, or purple may be seen on the same shrub.

Plant may be observed at ATL, BBG, BF, BIC, BOE, BRK, CBG, CHK, CIN, COX, DAW, DEN, DOW, DUK, GCC, HOL, IES, LNG, MIS, MOD, MOR, MRT, NCS, NEB, NEW, PLF, RBC, RKEW, SEC, SKY, SPR, UBC, VDG.

# *Ribes alpinum* 'Green Mound'
## GREEN MOUND ALPINE CURRANT

Saxifragaceae. USDA Zones 3–7. Species introduced into cultivation from Europe in 1588.

DESCRIPTION: Deciduous shrub growing at moderate rate to 2–3 ft. high and as wide, with dense habit.
*Leaves:* Alternate, simple, round to ovate, 1–2 in. long, bright green in summer, turning yellow in fall.
*Flowers:* Green-yellow, small, not ornamental.
*Fruit:* A small, red berry, not often seen; male clones more dominant in cultivation.

CULTURE: Grows in sun and shade in clay or loam with a wide pH range; tolerates wind and most adverse urban conditions.
*Disease and insect problems:* Leaf spot, rust, currant aphid, scale, anthracnose; humidity and lack of air circulation can cause problems, but 'Green Mound' shows good resistance.
*Transplanting:* Easy.
*Propagation:* By softwood cuttings.

LANDSCAPE VALUE: A useful dwarf shrub for tough environmental conditions, particularly in urban areas. Grows well in calcareous soils, shade, and cold climates. Leafs out early in season.

Plant may be observed at AA, BBG, BER, BF, BIR, BLO, BOE, BSG, CBG, CIN, CUH, DAW, DEN, FIL, FUL, GIW, HOL, LAC, LNG, MIS, MMA, MNL, MOR, MRT, MUN, NEB, PAL, PLF, RAN, RBC, RKEW, SAB, SBB, SEC, SPR, STR, UBC, VDG.

Other *Ribes* species and cultivars of interest:

*R. aureum.* Golden Currant. USDA Zone 2. Native to western United States, from the plains to the Rocky Mountains. Introduced into cultivation in 1828. Blooms in May, producing many racemes of 1 in. long, yellow, tubular flowers, tipped in red, with a strong, spicy scent of clove. Usually found in riverside habitats. Leaves are 2 in. wide, resembling gooseberry leaves. Large, edible fruits are red, yellow, or black. Grows to 3–9 ft high with upright habit. Prefers full sun, which gives best orange-red fall color, but will grow in partial shade. Very adaptable to dry sites and poor soils.
*R. odoratum.* Clove Currant. USDA Zones 4–8. North American shrub introduced into cultivation in 1812. Valuable for its long seasons of interest and delicious clove scent.

*Rhus typhina* 'Dissecta' (E. Hasselkus)     *Rhus typhina* 'Laciniata' (Southern Living Magazine)

*Ribes alpinum* 'Green Mound' (G. Gates)

*Ribes alpinum* 'Green Mound' (M. Hiller)     *Ribes sanguineum* (Brooklyn Botanic Garden)

Yellow, fragrant flowers in spring are followed by purple, spice-scented berries in summer, which turn shiny black as they ripen; the edible fruit is highly attractive to birds and is used for preserves and pies. Foliage opens to blue-green and turns a warm, bronze-red in fall. A hardy, easily grown, adaptable plant that reaches 4–7 ft. high. Grows in sun or partial shade. Effective as hedge or windbreak. Requires little maintenance; prune out old wood after flowering to maintain an attractive, healthy habit. Shrub was popular in the 19th and early 20th centuries but lost favor because of its tendency to white-pine blister rust; new rust-resistant varieties have permitted its use in the landscape once again. Gardeners should check with the local Department of Agriculture or cooperative extension offices to determine the legality of planting in their respective regions.

*R. odoratum* 'Aureum'. Very hardy selection that can be grown in USDA Zone 2. Produces more profuse bloom than the species.

*R. sanguineum*. Winter Currant. USDA Zones 6–8. Introduced into cultivation in 1818. Primarily seen on the West Coast of North America. Two attractive cultivars are the white-flowered 'Alba' and red-flowered 'King Edward VII', lower growing than the species. Both cultivars grow to 5–6 ft. high; flowers appear in pendulous racemes 3 in. long, in April–May, and berries are 0.3 in. across. Grows in sun to light shade; tolerates some drought.

*R. speciosum*. Fuchsia-Flowered Gooseberry. Native to California and Mexico; grows in canyons near coast, in sage scrub. USDA Zones 8–9. Introduced into cultivation in 1828. Unlike most *Ribes* species, this semi-evergreen shrub is not fragrant, but is attractive for its rich red, drooping flowers, which bloom January–May; flowers with long, protruding stems resemble those of *Fuchsia*. Grows to 3–6 ft. high with spreading, twiggy habit and spiny, bristly stems. Thick, green leaves, 1 in. long, are similar to those of the fruiting gooseberry. Best in sun near coast and in partial shade inland; tolerates drought and heat when established.

# *Robinia hispida*
## ROSE ACACIA

Leguminosae. USDA Zones 5–8. Native to southeastern United States. Introduced into cultivation in 1743.

DESCRIPTION: Deciduous shrub growing rapidly when young to 6–8 ft., with lax, gaunt habit.
*Leaves:* Compound, odd-pinnate, 6–10 in. long, stalks hairy, composed of 7–13 oval to ovate leaflets 1.5–2.5 in. long, very dark green.
*Flowers:* Deep rose-pink, 1.25 in. long, with rounded petals and calyx 0.5–0.7 in. long; May–June.
*Fruit:* A pod, 1.5–2.5 in. long and 0.3 in. wide, thickly covered with gland-tipped bristles, rarely produced.

CULTURE: Grows in full sun; prefers deep, fertile, well-drained soil, but tolerates poor, dry soil.
*Disease and insect problems:* Canker, locust borer, leaf spot, leaf miner.
*Transplanting:* Prune severely when transplanting.
*Propagation:* By root cuttings and transplanted suckers.

LANDSCAPE VALUE: One of the most beautiful shrubs in flower. Exhibits lacy foliage and casts light shade. May be used as specimen or planted as screen. Good for stabilizing banks. Suckers and spreads underground in the wild, but in cultivation it is usually grafted on *R. pseudoacacia* to circumvent this characteristic. Brittle branches are often broken in storms.

Plant may be observed at AA, ABF, BBG, BIC, BIR, CAL, CIN, CUH, DUK, GIW, IES, LAC, LNG, LWD, MRT, MUN, NCA, NEB, NEW, RAN, RKEW, VDG.

*Robinia hispida* (Southern Living Magazine)

*Ribes speciosum* (J. Apel)

*Ribes sanguineum* 'Alba' (J. C. Raulston)

*Robinia hispida* (S. Bender)

217

## Rosa—Alba Roses

An extremely old group of roses, Albas were probably brought to the United Kingdom by the Romans. They were grown in the Middle Ages, most likely for medicinal purposes. *Rosa x alba* originated from a cross of *R. canina* × *R. damascena*.

The Albas are a small but important group and include some of the finest of the Old Roses. They are taller than most Old Roses, often reaching 6 ft. high; hence, their early name of Tree Roses. Dominant characteristics include gray-green foliage, pleasing fragrance, and limited flower color range—white, blush, light pink. All are dioecious. Although delicate and beautiful in appearance, they are tough plants that will grow under difficult conditions. They are among the most easily grown roses, even in partial shade.

*Rosa* × *alba* 'Celestial'. Fuller of flower and even lovelier than 'Semi Plena'.

*Rosa* × *alba* 'Semi Plena'. USDA Zones 5–8. Introduced from Kazanlic, Bulgaria. A luxuriant, lovely rose for the shrub border or as an individual specimen, it has long, arching canes and fine, gray-green foliage. Integrates well with other shrubs. This hardy rose has large, extremely fragrant, soft white to blush blooms. Excellent shrub for light shade and difficult positions. Received RHS Award of Garden Merit.

*Rosa* × *alba* 'White Rose of York'. Large, upright shrub, to 7 ft. high and 5 ft. wide. Fragrant, pure white, single flowers, with golden stamens. Gray-green foliage. Elongated, orange-red, autumn fruit. Tolerant of poor soils. Unknown parentage.

Plant may be observed at BBG, BOE, CBG, HUN, MNL, RBC, VDG, WIS.

## Rosa—Bourbon Roses

Named for the Ile de Bourbon, a small island in the Indian Ocean now known as Réunion, these roses, which are closely related to China Roses, represent the first real step towards the modern forms. They retain the robust and bushy growth of the Old Roses, while their foliage and stems resemble the Hybrid Tea. Most are good repeat bloomers. *Rosa* × *borboniana* originated from a cross of *R. chinensis* × *R. damascena*.

Knowledge of pruning is extremely important in growing Bourbon Roses. Main shoots should be cut back about one-third, and side shoots should be pruned back to three eyes. Dead growth should always be removed. Prune in late winter or early spring to encourage prolonged blooming. Flowering shoots should be cut when blooms are spent.

*Rosa* 'La Reine Victoria'. Introduced in 1872 from France by Schwartz. Grows to 4–6 ft. high and 3 ft. wide, with upright, vigorous habit. Fragrant, full-bodied, shell-like, deep pink (paler in center) flowers; petals incurve towards center. Soft green foliage. Especially valued for its fragrance, consistent bloom, and hardiness; flowers repeatedly. May be grown as climber and trained to posts. Also excellent as full, dense, colorful shrub. Severe pruning in dormancy, when shrub is 2–3 years old and established, enhances productivity. Some tendency to blackspot.

*Rosa* × *alba* 'White Rose of York' (J. Elsley)

*Rosa* 'La Reine Victoria' (Wayside Gardens)

*Rosa* 'Souvenir de la Malmaison'. Queen of Beauty and Fragrance. Early Bourbon named for Empress Josephine's famous rose garden at Malmaison near Paris, it is a cross between *R.* 'Madame Despres' and a Tea Rose. Introduced into cultivation in 1843 by J. Beluze. A vigorous grower and a constant repeat bloomer, its delicate ivory to flesh-pink flowers (deeper rose at center) are initially cupped, then become flat. Grows to 3–5 ft. high, with a 5 ft. spread. Has a strong fragrance similar to the Tea Rose and exhibits the virtue of "old blooms with great character." Can be a good climber, and there is a fine climbing sport. Dislikes wet conditions.

Plant may be observed at BBG, BC, BOE, FIL, HUN, LAC, MBG, MUN, NEW, PAL, RBC, SEC.

*Rosa* 'Souvenir de la Malmaison' (Wayside Gardens)

## *Rosa*—Centifolia and Moss Roses

Centifolia Roses were developed in the early 17th to the early 18th century by dedicated Dutch breeders, among them members of the founding fathers of the United States and many Dutch and Flemish artists. More than 200 hybrids and cultivars were introduced.

General characteristics of these roses include heavy flowers with numerous petals; graceful and luxuriant bloom; flowers usually in warm shades of pink that tend not to fade; large, rounded foliage; and a strong tendency to produce sports. Some pruning is required to maintain desired shape.

*Rosa centifolia* 'Rose de Meaux'. Said to have been developed in 1789 by Sweet. Charming, small shrub for small gardens, this lovely, miniature Centifolia with tiny foliage grows to about 3.5 ft. high and 3 ft. wide, with dense habit. Its pink, double flowers are exquisitely fragrant.

Plant may be observed at BBG, BOE, CBG, FIL, HUN, LAC, MRT, PAL.

MOSS ROSES are Centifolias with a mosslike growth on their sepals and, at times, down the flower stem, the result of a sport in the plant. These roses have a unique beauty and charm and an interesting, pinelike fragrance. The spreading, drooping foliage is vulnerable to mildew.

*R. centifolia* f. *muscosa* 'White Bath'. Shailer's White Moss Rose. Introduced in 1788 by Shailer. Grows slowly to 3–4 ft. high and 3 ft. wide, with dark green, glandular, fragrant foliage. The very double, white flowers that appear in June are tinged with blush and are fragrant, as are the calyces and canes when rubbed. One of the most beautiful of the small number of white Old Roses, 'White Bath' is lovely in the perennial border, where tall perennials can disguise its loss of foliage and wilted look in the heat of summer. Tolerates light shade and a variety of soils. Some mildew and blackspot. Received RHS Award of Garden Merit.

Plant may be observed at BBG, HUN, MNL, WIS.

*Rosa centifolia* 'Rose de Meaux' (Wayside Gardens)

## *Rosa*—Damask Roses

Damask Roses date back to ancient times and are of great historical interest; they were grown by the Persians—perhaps originating in the area of Damascus, Syria—and brought to Europe by the Crusaders.

This rose has two quite different parents: a natural hybrid of *Rosa gallica* and a wild species, *R. phoenicea*. Damask Roses are taller than Gallicas, usually reaching 5 ft. General characteristics include gray-green, elongated and pointed foliage that is downy beneath; long, thin hips; strong prickles; intense fragrance; and lovely, true pink blooms that differ completely from the deep purple-red Gallica shades.

219

There is no true species of *Rosa damascena;* rather there is a series of hybrids with strong influences of *R. gallica, R. canina,* and *R. phoenicea.* They have been valued and cultivated for centuries for both medicinal purposes and their fragrance.

*Rosa damascena* var. *bifera* 'Autumn Damask'. USDA Zones 5–8. Introduced in the 16th century to Italy and Spain.

*Rosa damascena* 'Madame Hardy' (N. Brewster)

*Rosa damascena* 'Madame Hardy' (N. Brewster)

Semidouble or double, white to pink flowers appear in spring and fall. This lovely, fragrant rose requires little maintenance and has few insect problems.

*Rosa damascena* 'Madame Hardy'. USDA Zones 5–8. Introduced in 1832 from France and named for the wife of the creator and curator of Empress Josephine's famous rose garden at Malmaison. Has tall, vigorous, spreading habit; grows quickly to 5–10 ft. high and as wide. Large, very double, white blooms with green "button eyes" appear in May. Has lovely, slightly lemony fragrance; used in perfumes, rose water, and a purgative liquor. Trains beautifully on a post or fence, or may be left free; very bushy. Cited as the best white Old Rose, this truly outstanding and exquisite rose requires little maintenance. Tolerates partial shade, some environmental stress, and a wide range of soils. Few disease problems, other than some blackspot. Following several years of growth, a hard pruning after flowering will stimulate flower production. Received RHS Award of Garden Merit.

Plant may be observed at BBG, BOE, CBG, DAW, FIL, HUN, IES, MNL, NEW, PAL, SEC, USN, WIS.

# *Rosa*—**Gallica Roses**

Gallica Roses (*Rosa gallica*) are the oldest garden roses. Native to southern and central Europe, or perhaps western Asia, they have been cultivated for centuries and were grown by both the Greeks and Romans. In the 1800s there were said to be more than 1000 cultivars. Most have been lost, but there remain more Gallicas than any other group of Old Roses, among them some of the most beautiful roses in the world.

General characteristics of the Gallicas include an exquisite, subtle mix of colors; glorious fragrance; height usually not exceeding 4 ft., with strong, upright growth pattern; numerous thorns; deep green foliage with rough texture; lush flowers in May–June, usually borne singly or in threes; tolerance of difficult growing conditions (i.e., poor, gravelly soil); extreme hardiness (surviving anywhere and thriving in very cold or hot climates). Gallicas require pruning only to thin, although an occasional hard pruning will stimulate bloom. Each Gallica has a unique blooming pattern.

*Rosa* 'Belle de Crécy'. Like 'Complicata', an outstanding cultivar of unknown parentage. One of the most attractive, free-flowering Gallicas. Summer flowers open in shades of cerise-pink, tinged with mauve to violet, and turn a softer lavender with age. Almost thornless. Grows to 4 ft. high and 3 ft. wide. Has a distinctive, potent fragrance. May be used as container plant. Received RHS Award of Garden Merit.

*Rosa* 'Complicata'. A rose of outstanding merit, whose origin is unknown. Has gray-green foliage, spectacular orange hips in fall, and large, single, pink flowers with colorful yellow centers. Needs cooler climate to maintain compact growth habit. Ideal for the smaller garden; beautiful as a climber or shrub. Tolerates partial shade and a variety of environmental stresses; disease-free. Received RHS Award of Garden Merit.

*Rosa gallica* var. *officinalis*. Apothecary's Rose. Historic rose said to be the "Red Rose of Lancaster," the emblem chosen by the House of Lancaster during the War of Roses. Appeared first in Europe, southeast of Paris, and used for making perfume in Provins, France. Said to date back to 1260 (referred to in a poem by Thibault IV, King of Navarre), this is the oldest cultivated form of the Gallica Rose and perhaps the best-known Gallica variety. Grown for centuries for medicinal purposes, thus the common name. Grown today for its superior garden qualities: low, branching growth; semidouble, light crimson, fragrant flowers accented with deep yellow stamens; dark green foliage. Blooms freely. May spread by suckering if grown on own roots. Can be used on banks where a good, substantial ground cover is needed. Grows to about 4 ft. high. Flower color varies according to growing conditions and climate; paler in warmer climates.

*Rosa* 'Versicolor'. A mutation of *R. gallica* var. *officinalis*, identical in growth, thorns, and foliage. An example of a Gallica with striped flowers, its distinct summer blooms are white, red, and pink, variously striped and spotted, with many yellow anthers.

Plant may be observed at BBG, BOE, CBG, CUH, FIL, HUN, IES, LAC, MNL, PAL, SEC, WIS.

## *Rosa*—Kordesii Roses

Meriting a separate category due to their origin, these roses are the result of extensive work done by W. Kordes in Germany beginning in 1925. The name *Rosa × kordesii* was given to a seedling by H. D. Wulff in 1951.

Kordesii Roses offer exceptional garden value. General characteristics include an upright, often climbing, growth habit; great freedom of bloom; and excellent resistance to winter frosts.

The Explorer Series consists of roses developed by the Ottawa Research Station in Ontario and named after early Canadian explorers.

*Rosa* 'Champlain'. Semidouble to double flowers of outstanding bright red, with slight fragrance. Reaches 2–3 ft. high, with shiny foliage. Moderate resistance to blackspot. (Explorer Series).

*Rosa* 'John Cabot'. Double, fragrant, red flowers. Derived from a cross of *R. × kordesii* with an unnamed seedling from open pollination. A vigorous grower with strong, arching branches; grows to 6–9 ft. high. Foliage is luxurious yellow-green. A valuable pillar or large bush rose, it flowers freely for 6–7 weeks in June–July and repeats sporadically in August–September. Survives winters in USDA Zones 4–5 with protection. Resistant to powdery mildew and blackspot. Propagated easily from softwood

*Rosa* 'Belle de Crécy' (Wayside Gardens)

*Rosa* 'John Cabot' (Agriculture Canada)

221

cuttings. Evaluated at Ottawa since 1970 and at 10 other test locations across Canada. Recipient of National Rose Society's Silver Medal in 1985.

*Rosa* 'John Davis'. Very fragrant, spicy, medium pink flowers with yellow bases. Bred by Felicitas Svejda, Ottawa Research Station; released 1986. Parentage: *R. × kordesii* × DO8 by open pollination; DO8 obtained from open pollination of seedling from *R.* 'Red Dawn' × *R.* 'Suzanne'. This hardy pillar rose flowers freely and intermittently throughout summer. Highly resistant to blackspot and mildew. Has dark yellow-green, glossy, leathery foliage. Easily propagated by softwood cuttings. (Explorer Series)

*Rosa* 'Henry Kelsey'. Bright red, fragrant, double flowers produced freely and repeatedly. Grows to 5–6 ft. high, with trailing growth habit. Performed well at Morden Research Station (USDA Zone 3), but in more severe climate dieback has occurred (50–80 percent), and flowering has been only fair to moderate. (Explorer Series)

*Rosa* 'William Baffin'. Deep pink-red flowers with abundant, glossy foliage; vigorous grower, with branches to 6–9 ft. long. Flowers freely and repeatedly. Highly resistant to blackspot and mildew. (Explorer Series)

Plant may be observed at BBG, BIC, BOE, CBG, HOL, LNG, MIS, MOD, MNL, NEW, RBC, VDG.

# *Rosa*—Rugosa Roses

*Rosa rugosa* is an extremely hardy wild rose of China, Russia, Japan, and Korea. Grown in the United States for more than 100 years, it is often called the Beach Rose because of its ability to tolerate harsh shoreline conditions. Rugosas need some pruning; removing old wood encourages new canes. The hips are a noted source of vitamin C.

General Rugosa characteristics are leathery, dark green foliage turning to yellow, orange, and red in the fall; disease resistance—no need for sprays or fertilizers; tolerance of a wide variety of soil conditions and environmental stresses—salt spray, drought, wind, and air pollution; best performance in full sun but tolerant of partial shade. Because of these unique characteristics, Rugosas have been used extensively by breeders to create hybrid cultivars. The Explorer Series consists of roses developed by the Ottawa Research Station in Ontario and named after early Canadian explorers.

*Rosa rugosa* 'Blanc Double de Coubert'. USDA Zone 3. Introduced in 1892. Grows to 5 ft. high; few hips. One of the finest Rugosas, its large flowers of pure white are tinged with blush when in bud; delicate petals open to semi-double form. Has strong fragrance. Breeder Cochet-Cochet of France describes this hybrid as a cross between *R. rugosa* and the exquisite Tea Rose *R.* 'Sombreuil.' Received RHS Award of Garden Merit.

*Rosa rugosa* 'Charles Albanel'. Introduced 1982 by Ottawa Research Station. Parentage: open pollination of a seedling in turn obtained from open pollination of *R. rugosa* 'Souvenir de Philemon Cochet'. This extremely hardy rose has medium red, fragrant flowers and abundant, yellow-green foliage. A dwarf shrub growing to about 3 ft. high, with a spreading habit, it makes a good ground cover. Very resistant to blackspot and mildew.

*Rosa* 'John Cabot' (Agriculture Canada)

*Rosa rugosa* 'Blanc Double de Coubert' (Wayside Gardens)

Easily propagated from softwood cuttings. (Explorer Series)

*Rosa rugosa* 'Fru Dagmar Hastrup' ['Frau Dagmar Hartopp']. Introduced in 1914 from Denmark; thought to be a seedling of *R. rugosa*. Grows to 4 ft. high. A good repeat bloomer, it has delicately beautiful, light pink flowers with cream-colored stamens. Blooms are followed by a large crop of deep red hips. Good for civic plantings since it is tough, attractive in massed plantings, and has a small, dense growth pattern that can tolerate harsh pruning without reduction in bloom. Received RHS Award of Garden Merit.

*Rosa rugosa* 'Henry Hudson'. Released in 1977 by Ottawa Research Station. Parentage: open pollination of a seedling, in turn obtained from open pollination of *R. rugosa* 'Schneezwerg'. Small shrub with double, fragrant, white flowers that have a pink hue and prominent yellow stamens; blooms freely throughout summer. May be used as a hardy flowering hedge or screen. Evaluated at Ottawa since 1967 and rated highly for hardiness (has performed well in USDA Zones 3–4), disease resistance, and flower form. Easily propagated from softwood cuttings. (Explorer Series)

*Rosa rugosa* 'Jens Munk'. Released in 1967 by Ottawa Research Station. Parentage: *R. rugosa* 'Schneezwerg' × *R.* 'Fru Dagmar Hastrup'. A vigorous shrub growing to 3–6 ft. high, it has medium pink flowers, is strongly armed with bristles, and has outstanding red hips in fall. Rated highly for hardiness, duration of flowering period, quantity of flowers, and resistance to blackspot and mildew. (Explorer Series)

*Rosa rugosa* 'Linda Campbell'. Introduced in 1991 by P. P. A. F. Moore, Wayside Gardens; named for respected Colorado rosarian. Brilliant crimson flowers produced in large clusters of 5–15 blooms. Grows to 5 ft. high and 8 ft. wide, with few thorns. Extremely hardy, heat-tolerant, and a good repeat bloomer with attractive, clean foliage.

*Rosa rugosa* 'Roseraie de l'Hay'. Bred in 1901 by Cochet-Cochet of France; named after the famous rose garden near Paris. Very reliable and attractive shrub rose with repeat bloom and few hips. Grows vigorously to 8 ft. high, with dense, spreading habit and good green foliage. Has large, double flowers of crimson-purple. Received RHS Award of Garden Merit.

*Rosa rugosa* 'Rubra'. Native of China; introduced into cultivation by Alfred Rehder. This vigorous, constant bloomer grows to 8–12 ft. high with upright, suckering habit; also creeps. Large, fragrant, single flowers of deep magenta-red appear from May until frost. Foliage is dark green, crinkled; stems turn golden-yellow to orange in fall. Large, showy, orange-red hips, from midsummer to winter, eventually shrivel and fall. Tolerant of most conditions, including seashore; thrives with neglect. Good in large borders in protected areas where it can spread; will overwhelm if not controlled. Can also be trimmed as a hedge. No disease problems. Received RHS Award of Garden Merit.

*Rosa rugosa* 'Sarah Van Fleet'. Introduced in 1926 by Dr. Van Fleet, one of America's greatest early rose hybridizers. A

*Rosa rugosa* 'Fru Dagmar Hastrup' (H. Shimizu)

*Rosa rugosa* 'Jens Munk' (Agriculture Canada)

questionable cross between *R. rugosa* and *R.* 'My Maryland', it is an excellent large shrub for the rear border; grows to 7–10 ft. high and as wide, with upright habit. Lovely, large, fragrant, China pink flowers with yellow stamens appear from mid-May until frost. Has typical good green Rugosa foliage with many thorns; young foliage is bronze-tinted. Thrives in cooler weather. Slightly sensitive to air pollution and high heat; susceptible to chlorosis and spider mite. Needs some pruning to keep thinned out.

*Rosa rugosa* 'Roseraie de l'Hay' (Wayside Gardens)

*Rosa rugosa* 'Sir Thomas Lipton'. A Van Fleet hybrid introduced in 1900 by Conard & Jones. This vigorous, rugged, trouble-free shrub grows to 6 ft. high and 4 ft. wide and thrives with little care. Tolerates wind, drought, and a wide pH range; often grows better in light shade since intense heat deters bloom. Perhaps the best white Rugosa cultivar, it has fabulously fragrant, double, pure white flowers, at times tinged slightly green. Blooms profusely in June and intermittently throughout summer and fall.

*Rosa rugosa* 'Therese Bugnet'. Introduced in 1950 from Canada by Bugnet. Grows to 5–6 ft. high and as wide, with vigorous, upright, spreading habit. Bred to withstand the rigors of northern winters and produce attractive blooms, it is prized for its large, flat, subtly fragrant 3–4 in. blossoms—dark red in bud, opening to a deep, clear pink. Following first flush in mid-June, some repeat bloom until frost. Requires little maintenance and has no major disease or insect problems. Tolerates partial shade, wind, and drought; does not like intense heat. Makes an excellent landscape shrub or can be trained on a pillar. One of the few privately developed, Canada-hardy roses; widely available in Canadian nurseries.

*Rosa rugosa* 'Topaz Jewel'. Introduced in 1988 by P. P. A. F. Moore, Wayside Gardens. A beautiful re-blooming, disease-resistant shrub growing to 5 ft. high and 7 ft. wide. Arching branches are covered with magnificent, fragrant, yellow blooms. Extremely hardy and trouble-free.

Plant may be observed at BBG, BIC, BOE, CBG, CIN, DAW, DOW, DUK, GCC, HUN, IES, LAC, LNG, LWD, MIS, MOD, MNL, MRT, NEW, PAL, PLF, RBC, RKEW, SEC, USN, VDG, WIS.

*Rosa rugosa* 'Topaz Jewel' (Wayside Gardens)

*Rosa rugosa* 'Sarah Van Fleet' (R. Armstrong)

# *Rosa*—Shrub Roses

Shrub Roses are useful garden plants that deserve a fresh evaluation of their outstanding attributes. These tough shrubs require little maintenance and produce profuse, colorful, fragrant flowers, providing a mass of color in the landscape.

The Explorer Series consists of roses developed by the Ottawa Research Station in Ontario and named after early Canadian explorers.

*Rosa* 'Carefree Beauty'. Grows well in all regions. Reaching 3–4 ft. high and 3 ft. wide, it is remarkably free of disease, requiring little spraying or maintenance. Has beautiful, double, pink blooms the entire flowering season and spectacular orange fruit in winter.

*Rosa* 'Carefree Wonder'. Introduced in 1990 by Conard Pyle. This maintenance-free shrub with medium green foliage grows to 4–5 ft. high and 4 ft. wide, with bushy habit. Produces medium-sized, semidouble, pink-white, free-form flowers nonstop from mid-May to frost. Hips form during blooming. Excellent massed as a hedge or as specimen or border plant. Tolerates partial shade, a wide variety of soils, drought, wind, and environmental stress. Care-free and disease-resistant.

*Rosa* 'Golden Wings' (Hybrid Tea *R.* 'Soeur Thérèse' × (*R. pimpinellifolia* × *R. xanthina*)). Introduced in 1956 by Shepard. Grows quickly to 6 ft. high and 4 ft. wide, with vigorous, bushy habit and light green foliage. Large yellow flowers, 4–5 in. across, bloom from late May until frost; golden-yellow to brown stamens persist after petals have fallen, adding another dimension of interest and beauty. Dark hips from midsummer to winter. Has some of the charm of a wild species. Grows in a wide range of soils; tolerates partial shade, wind, drought, and environmental stress. Some problems with blackspot and mildew. Received RHS Award of Garden Merit.

*Rosa* 'John Franklin'. A complex hybrid that grows to about 2–3 ft. high, with double, fragrant, red flowers throughout summer until fall. Slight blackspot by end of summer. Has performed well for eight years at the Morden Research Station in Canada. (Explorer Series, 1980)

*Rosa* 'A. MacKenzie'. Introduced in 1985, this complex hybrid has flowers that are superior to, although less hardy than, the *R. rugosa* and *R.* × *kordesii* hybrids. Requires pruning each spring. A vigorous shrub that grows to 3–6 ft. high and 2–3 ft. wide. Fragrant, double, red blooms produced prolifically throughout summer. Somewhat resistant to blackspot. (Explorer Series, 1985)

Plant may be observed at BBG, BOE, CBG, CIN, DAW, DEN, HUN, LNG, LWD, MBG, MIS, MNL, NEW, OWG, RBC, SEC, VDG, WIS.

*Rosa* 'Golden Wings' (G. Anderson)

*Rosa* 'Carefree Beauty' (N. Brewster)

*Rosa* 'Carefree Wonder' (E. Hasselkus)

ENGLISH SHRUB ROSES are not an officially recognized class but a group of roses created to combine the attributes of the glorious Old Shrub Roses with the qualities of disease resistance and repeat flowering needed for today's smaller gardens. According to famed English plantsman Graham Thomas, these hybrids of very mixed parentage—in the main bred by distinguished English rosarian David Austin—merit a separate subcategory within Shrub Roses.

Old Shrub Roses were prized for their unique character: vigor, double flowers, and distinctive fragrance. The Floribunda or Cluster Roses added the virtues of enhanced colors, glossy foliage, and the propensity for reliable repeat bloom.

Graham Stuart Thomas cites charm of shape and color among the prime attributes of the English Shrub Roses, pointing out that they display a grace not present in the stiff, upright growth habit and the often angular, stridently colored blooms preferred by today's breeders. General characteristics of the English Shrub Roses include vigorous, bushy, arching growth, whether large or small (2–8 ft. tall); varied but gently rounded shape to flowers, which reveal their greatest beauty when nearly full-blown; a wide range of strong fragrances, including the scent of myrrh; colors tending to soft pastel tints; delicate appearance; and repeat flowering.

The English Shrub Roses are not excessively hardy. Fertile soil, fertilizer, pruning, and moisture are necessary to assure best performance and the great asset of repeat bloom. Massed plantings are highly recommended to maximize their landscape value.

*Rosa* 'Bredon' (*R.* 'Wife of Bath' × *R.* 'Lilian Austin'). Introduced in 1984. Encompasses many of the qualities of a Floribunda. Short, to 5 ft. high and 3 ft. wide, vigorous shrub with numerous small blooms in large sprays; can be used for small hedges. Perfectly formed rosettes, about 2.5 in. across, are buff-yellow with paler edges. Has potent fragrance and small, leathery leaves.

*Rosa* 'English Garden' ((*R.* 'Lilian Austin' × unnamed seedling) × (*R.* 'Iceberg' × *R.* 'Wife of Bath')). Introduced in 1986 by Austin in Great Britain. Small, about 3 ft. high, with upright habit and light green foliage. Outstanding flower form, about 3.5 in. across, with numerous small petals; buff-yellow, paler towards edges. An almost perfect example of an Old Rose.

*Rosa* 'Gertrude Jekyll' (*R.* 'Wife of Bath' × *R.* 'Comte de Chambord'). Has the qualities of an Old Portland Rose. Introduced in 1986 by Austin. Flowers are large, deep pink, with beautiful precision of form. Has potent scent—a true Damask fragrance. Sometimes slow to repeat; thus, early winter pruning recommended to stimulate repeat flowering.

*Rosa* 'Graham Thomas' (*R.* 'Charles Austin' × (*R.* 'Iceberg' × unnamed English rose)). Introduced in 1982 by Austin. Perhaps the finest, most intensely yellow English Rose; deep, rich, yellow blooms are tinged with apricot and have a strong Tea Rose fragrance. A vigorous grower with smooth foliage of pleasant green, it grows to about 4 ft. high, although it has been reported to 10 ft. in South Africa. Received RHS Award of Garden Merit.

*Rosa* 'Heritage' (Unnamed English seedling × (*R.* 'Wife of Bath' × *R.* 'Iceberg')). Introduced in 1984 by Austin in Great Britain. Often cited as the most exquisite English Rose. Soft blush-pink flowers are of perfect formation and have a strong fragrance with a hint of lemon. A bushy, robust shrub of great beauty that grows to 4–5 ft. high.

*Rosa* 'Mary Rose' (*R.* 'Wife of Bath' × *R.* 'The Miller'). Introduced in 1983 at the Chelsea Flower Show. Has the modest charm of an Old Rose. Large, rose-pink, slightly fragrant flowers pale as the season progresses. Grows to about 4 ft. high with bushy habit. A tough plant that withstands pruning to stimulate further growth and bloom.

*Rosa* 'Perdita' (*R.* 'The Friar' × (unnamed seedling × *R.* 'Iceberg')). Introduced in 1983 by Austin. One of the best all-around cultivars, this small, full, slightly arching shrub grows to about 3.5 ft. high, with deep green foliage, potent fragrance, and double, apricot-blush flowers. Awarded the National Rose Society's Henry Edland Medal for fragrance in 1984.

*Rosa* 'Prioress'. Vigorous, upright shrub with dark green, glossy foliage and double, blush-white, fragrant flowers; good constant bloomer. Tolerates light shade, wind and a wide pH range. A rather care-free shrub, but some susceptibility to blackspot. Excellent as specimen or grouped in a border.

*Rosa* 'English Garden' (Wayside Gardens)

*Rosa* 'Gertrude Jekyll' (J. Elsley)

*Rosa* 'Graham Thomas' (Wayside Gardens)

*Rosa* 'Mary Rose' (Wayside Gardens)

*Rosa* 'Heritage' (J. Elsley)

*Rosa* 'Perdita' (Wayside Gardens)

*Rosa* 'Sir Walter Raleigh' (*R.* 'Lilian Austin' × *R.* 'Chaucer'). Introduced in 1985 by Austin. Grows to about 5 ft. high and 4 ft. wide, with erect, strong growth habit. A large rose with large leaves, its flowers are similar to those of the tree peony—pink, about 5 in. across, not quite fully double, with potent scent; good repeat flowering.

*Rosa* 'Wife of Bath' (Hybrid Tea *R.* 'Madame Caroline Testout' × (Floribunda *R.*' Ma Perkins' × *R.* 'Constance Spry')). Introduced in 1969 by Austin. Charming, small, bushy shrub growing to about 3 ft. high. Flowers begin as small, tight, pink buds, paling as they unfurl; strong scent and repeat bloom. Delicate in appearance but tough and reliable.

Plant may be observed at ATL, BBG, BOE, CIN, DAW, DEN, FIL, FUL, GCC, HUN, LWD, MBG, PAL, PLF, RBC, SEC, WIS.

MEIDELAND SHRUB ROSES, also known as Hybrid Shrub Roses from the House of Meilland, well-known French rose breeders, deserve mention but are not detailed in this volume because they are readily available. These versatile, disease-resistant shrubs are valuable additions to the landscape, displaying attractive foliage and blooming throughout the growing season with little care. Performance is superior even in relatively harsh climates. Ideal for hedges and massed plantings. Many cultivars, ranging in size from 2–5 ft. high and 3.5–6 ft. wide, provide multiseason interest with bright fruit and handsomely colored canes.

*Rosa* 'Bonica'. Among the loveliest cultivars in this group. Introduced the Meideland family in North America. Became an All American Rose Selection winner in 1987, the only Shrub Rose to be so honored. Profuse clusters of 3 in., fully double, shell-pink blooms are set off by the glossy, deep green foliage. Colorful hips add interest in late fall and winter. Received RHS Award of Garden Merit.

Plant may be observed at BBG, BOE, CBG, MNL, WIS.

PARKLAND SHRUB ROSES, a subset of Shrub Roses, include 10 cultivars that do not fit into existing categories and are best described as intermediate between Shrub and Floribunda Roses. All repeat bloom more freely than do Shrub Roses. They survive Canadian winters (USDA Zone 3) and are excellent choices for colder areas. Some, however, are subject to varying amounts of dieback, which results in a smaller plant habit. Although some plants die to near ground level during winter, in one growing season they will develop into attractive shrubs with an abundance of flowers. Not strongly fragrant.

*Rosa* 'Adelaide Hoodless'. Introduced in 1973. Red flowers.

*Rosa* 'Assiniboine'. Introduced in 1962. Red flowers.

*Rosa* 'Cuthbert Grant'. Introduced in 1967. Large, velvety, semidouble, crimson flowers. Selected as Manitoba's Centennial Rose; received RHS Award of Merit. Grows to 2–4 ft. high. Blooms late June to early July and again in late summer. Very resistant to blackspot.

*Rosa* 'Morden Amorette'. Introduced in 1977. Dark pink-red flowers.

*Rosa* 'Morden Blush' ((*R.* 'Prairie Princess' × *R.* 'Morden Amorette') × (*R.* 'Prairie Princess' × *R.* 'White Bouquet' × (*R. arkansana* × *R.* 'Assiniboine')). Introduced in 1988. Double, ivory-pink, slightly fragrant flowers with blush-pink center; produced from mid-June to first frost. Flower color more intense during cool weather. Grows to 2–3 ft. high, with upright habit. Tolerant of hot, dry conditions, resistant to mildew, and fairly resistant to blackspot.

*Rosa* 'Morden Blush' (Agriculture Canada)

*Rosa* 'Morden Centennial' (Agriculture Canada)

*Rosa* 'Morden Cardinette'. Introduced in 1980. Red flowers.

*Rosa* 'Morden Centennial' ((R. 'Prairie Princess' × R. 'White Bouquet') × (R. arkansana × R. 'Assiniboine')). Introduced in 1980. Lightly fragrant, medium pink flowers, borne singly or in clusters; heaviest bloom in late June to July and again in late August to September. Grows vigorously to 3–4 ft. high, with slightly glossy foliage. Moderate to good resistance to blackspot. Named for the centennial celebration of the town of Morden, Manitoba.

*Rosa* 'Morden Fireglow'. Introduced in 1989. Scarlet flowers.

*Rosa* 'Morden Ruby'. Introduced in 1977. Red flowers.

*Rosa* 'Winnipeg Parks'. Introduced in 1990. Dark pink-red flowers.

Plant may be observed at BBG, BOE, CBG, MNL, MOD.

## *Rosa*—Species Roses

The most ancient of all roses, Species Roses have been evolving for millions of years; many originated in central Asia. Unlike modern Hybrid Teas and Floribundas, Species Roses are true shrubs, growing to 4–6 ft. high, depending on the species. The flower form is also quite different in that the buds often open as small cups with small petals developing within, the flower reaching its full beauty upon expansion. These roses have suffered a long period of neglect but are finally reclaiming the attention they deserve.

General characteristics of the Species Roses are single flowers, usually with 5 petals, similar in appearance to apple blossoms; bloom once a year; first to bloom in spring; fragrant; tolerant of a wide temperature range—from the hot climates of Mexico and the Philippines to the cold arctic regions; tolerant of diverse soil conditions; sucker freely; need little pruning other than to control size; disease resistant—no need to spray or fertilize. These are excellent, attractive shrubs that require little attention and may be used for screens and borders in the landscape. Because of their care-free characteristics, they have been repeatedly used for hybridizing, creating new cultivars that have the ever-blooming characteristics of the modern rose.

*Rosa foetida* 'Bicolor'. Austrian Copper Rose. A favorite for centuries, this rose was found in a monastery garden in Europe in 1509. It proved to be a sport of *R. foetida*, the latter grown in the Arab world since the 12th century. Grows to 5–6 ft. high. Upper surfaces of its striking, single, 2–2.5 in. flowers are brilliant copper-red, with bright yellow beneath. Produces a spectacular show of blooms mid-May to mid-June, providing a splash of vibrant color in the landscape. Flowers not fragrant, but foliage has pleasant fragrance when crushed. Flowers often revert back to the pure yellow of *R. foetida*, and flowers of both colors may appear on same plant. Tends to suffer from blackspot and defoliates in heat, so best planted in sunny location where tall perennials can disguise its nakedness. Requires no care and only minimal pruning to thin.

*Rosa glauca* [*R. rubrifolia*]. Native to mountains of central and southern Europe; introduced into cultivation in 1830 by Pourret. Grows to 10–12 ft. high, with tall, wide, arching habit. Pink flowers with 5 petals, 1.5 in. across, appear from late May until the end of June, in groups of 1–3. Red hips persist from midsummer to autumn. Beautiful species for use as specimen or in border, with good form, lovely flowers, excellent red-green foliage, and colorful reddish canes. Too large for small gardens. Will grow in partial shade in a wide range of soils; tolerates wind, drought, and most environmental stresses. No

*Rosa glauca* (E. Hasselkus)

*Rosa glauca* (B. Yinger)

229

disease or insect problems. Received RHS Award of Garden Merit.

*Rosa hugonis.* Father Hugo's Rose. Originated 1899 in China; discovered by Hugh Scallan, introduced to commerce in 1908 by Veitch & Sons. Growing 3 ft. high, with spreading, arching habit and delicate, ferny foliage, this is one of the earliest roses to bloom; excellent for early spring border. Vibrant yellow flowers are 2.5 in. across and have 5–8 petals. Tolerates partial shade, drought, wind, and environmental stress, but grows much larger with good soil and light conditions. Needs to be thinned out after a few seasons. Received RHS Award of Garden Merit.

*Rosa xanthina.* An early bloomer with yellow flowers 2.5 in. across. Grows to 7–8 ft. high and 8–10 ft. wide at maturity. Tolerates drought, a variety of soils, and temperatures to –30°F. Resistant to the potato leafhopper, one of the most serious pest problems for roses. Received RHS Award of Garden Merit.

Plant may be observed at AA, BBG, BC, BER, BIC, BOE, CBG, CIN, CUH, DAW, DEN, DOW, FIL, FUL, HUN, IES, LAC, LNG, LWD, MIS, MNL, MRT, MUN, NEW, PAL, RBC, RKEW, SEC, UBC, VDG, WIS.

MOYESII ROSES, native to northwestern China, are among the finest selections of the Species Roses. They were introduced into cultivation by E. H. Wilson in 1903.

*Rosa* 'Geranium'. A seedling of *R. moyesii.* Grows to 8 ft. high. More compact than the species, with lighter, more abundant foliage and fewer thorns. Flowers are crimson-red with cream stamens. Has extremely attractive, large, orange-red fruit. Received RHS Award of Garden Merit.

*Rosa* 'Nevada'. Selected in Spain; introduced into cultivation in 1927 by Pedro Dot. Grows to 7–8 ft. high and as wide. Produces an abundance of large, single flowers with 12–15 petals that cover the plum-colored canes; blooms are white, sometimes tinged with pink, and stems are very yellow. Blooms from May until frost. Grows in partial shade and a wide range of soils; tolerates wind, drought, and environmental stress. Some blackspot. Exhibits many of the characteristics of its Chinese parent, *R. moyesii*—a graceful, shapely, dense, arching habit with thornless branches, light-green foliage, and sweet scent. Beautiful in the border or as a specimen. Can be trained as a climber. Lovely plum-colored canes provide winter color. Received RHS Award of Garden Merit.

Plant may be observed at BBG, BOE, CBG, CUH, HUN, IES, LWD, MNL, MUN, PAL, RBC, SEC, WIS.

*Rosa* 'Geranium' (B. Yinger)

*Rosa* 'Nevada' (S. Scanniello)

HYBRID SPECIES ROSES, a subcategory of Species Roses, include a number of lovely cultivars.

*Rosa* 'Buff Beauty'. Introduced in 1939 by A. Bentall. Significant for its beautiful buds, lovely flowers, and pattern of growth. Grows to 10 ft. high and 6 ft. wide, with tall, arching habit and small, dark green leaves; new growth is reddish green. Clusters of large, apricot-yellow, double flowers with Tea Rose fragrance from late May to frost; reliable, recurrent bloom. A lush, luxuriant beauty, this is considered one of the most exquisite yellow Shrub Roses. Good as a climber, for cascading over water, and as a container plant. Tolerates partial shade, wind, drought, environmental stress, and a wide range of soils. Some spider mite and blackspot. Received RHS Award of Garden Merit.

*Rosa* 'Canary Bird' (*R. hugonis* × *R. xanthina*). Famed for its deep yellow flower color, 3 in. flowers, graceful growth, and fernlike, gray-green foliage. Deep burgundy hips are not conspicuous. Grows to about 6 ft. high. Received RHS Award of Garden Merit.

*Rosa* 'Cantabrigiensis'. Named in 1931. Similar to *R. hugonis* but with sturdier growth; often grows to 8–10 ft. high. Large, saucer-shaped, pale yellow flowers appear in great profusion. Graceful shrub with dainty foliage and slight fragrance. A self-sown seedling.

Plant may be observed at BBG, BIR, BOE, CBG, CUH, DEN, HUN, LAC, MNL, NEW, PAL, RBC, VDG, WIS.

*Rosa* 'Canary Bird' (Planting Fields Arboretum)

PIMPINELLIFOLIA HYBRID ROSES, a subcategory of Hybrid Species roses, are characterized by prominent thorns. *Rosa pimpinellifolia* [*R. spinosissima*] is native to the British Isles, prevalent from Scotland to Cornwall; often called Scotch Rose. Also grown in Europe, western Asia, and North America.

A tough reliable shrub, the Pimpinellifolia hybrid survives poor conditions and sandy, seaside banks. Height varies with growing conditions; in wild, windswept regions, it remains very small, but in favorable soil it can grow to 6 ft. high; average garden height is 3 ft. Pimpinellifolia Roses have small, fernlike foliage and bloom in May–June. The shrub creates an attractive effect with little maintenance, making it a good choice for civic plantings.

*Rosa* 'Frühlingsduft' (*R.* 'Joanna Hill' × *R. pimpinellifolia* var. *altaica*). Introduced in Germany in 1947 by Kordes. This vigorous shrub grows to 10 ft. high and 6 ft. wide, with strong fragrance and soft yellow flowers flushed with pink. Received RHS Award of Garden Merit.

*Rosa* 'Frühlingsgold'. Bred in Germany; introduced into cultivation in 1937 by Kordes. Vigorous grower to 10 ft. high and 4 ft. wide. Large, single, richly fragrant flowers,

5–6 in. across, are yellow with hints of orange and red, fading to cream; profuse blooms in May do not repeat. One of the hardiest, most reliable and easily grown roses, with light gray-green, soft, crinkled foliage. Valuable in the border background or as a specimen. Becomes leggy in shade; best grown in sun and loamy soil with pH of 5.5–6.6. Susceptible to blackspot and other fungal problems; heat, lack of water, and disease cause defoliation.

*Rosa* 'Frühlingsmorgen'. Combination of *R. pimpinellifolia* var. *altaica* and a number of hybrid Tea Roses. A large shrub with enormous, fragrant, lavender-pink and yellow flowers, which bloom throughout June. Outstanding hips hang from canes.

*Rosa* 'Stanwell Perpetual'. Introduced in 1838 by Lee in Great Britain. A favorite Old Rose resulting from a chance crossing of *R. pimpinellifolia* and *R. damascena* 'Semperflorens' at a nursery in London. Grows to 5 ft. high and 8 ft. wide, with bushy, spreading habit. Very double, strongly fragrant, medium-sized flowers are blush-pink; the pale color deepens in cooler fall weather. Flowers May–frost, with a heavy flush of bloom in the spring followed by constant but somewhat fewer summer blooms, and a heavy proliferation again in autumn. The delicate, fernlike foliage and exquisite blush flowers are outstanding. Tolerates partial shade, a wide variety of soils, wind, drought, and environmental stress. Disease-free; foliage often becomes a discolored, mottled purple, but this does not affect the plant's health. Needs no care or pruning except for removal of dead wood. Gertrude Jekyll's favorite rose.

Plant may be observed at BBG, BOE, CBG, DEN, FIL, HUN, IES, LNG, LWD, MBG, MOD, MNL, MUN, NEW, PAL, RBC, SEC, VDG, WIS.

*Rosa* 'Stanwell Perpetual' (N. Brewster)

231

## Rosa—Tea Roses

A form of China Rose, *Rosa* × *odorata* is thought to have originated many centuries ago in China as a cross between *R. chinensis* and *R. gigantea*. Often described as "refined" and "aristocratic," perhaps because it is very tender. Tea Roses, like China Roses, continue growing and blooming into winter. A warm-climate rose that makes a beautiful landscape plant.

*Rosa* 'Duchesse de Brabant'. USDA Zones 7–9. Introduced in 1857 from France by Bernède. A lovely, relatively hardy Tea Rose suited to warmer regions; grows well in Texas and in Mediterranean climates. This extremely fragrant rose produces a prolific number of 2–3 in., very double, cupped blooms of soft, pinkish orange from April to November. Exhibits a strong, spreading shrub form in warmer climates only; in colder climates is grown as an annual. May be planted against a warm, sheltered wall and treated as a short climber. Objects to harsh pruning; prune only to thin out old growth and revive dead wood. Teddy Roosevelt's favorite rose; he wore it in his lapel.

Plant may be observed at BBG, BOE.

*Rosa* 'Duchesse de Brabant' (S. Scanniello)

## Rubus cockburnianus

Rosaceae. USDA Zones 5–8. Native to Sichuan Province, China. Introduced into cultivation in 1907 by E. H. Wilson.

DESCRIPTION: Deciduous shrub to 9 ft. high, with spreading, horizontally branched habit.
*Leaves:* Alternate, simple, composed of 7–9 leaflets, oblong, coarsely serrate, glabrous above, white tomentose beneath.
*Flowers:* Purple-pink, with numerous stamens, in small panicles; June.
*Fruit:* A black, 1-seeded drupe.

*Winter aspect:* Gray branches stand out against dark background or snow.

CULTURE: Grows in sun or shade; prefers moist conditions and acid soil, as well as moderate summer temperatures.
*Disease and insect problems:* None serious.
*Transplanting:* Best balled and burlapped or container-grown.
*Propagation:* By cuttings.

LANDSCAPE VALUE: Not grown for the beauty of its flower display but rather for the welcome color contrast it provides in the garden. Its gray branches and blue-gray, arching stems with attractive, fernlike leaves provide an effective contrast to darker plantings or walls and lend themselves well to the naturalized landscape. Received RHS Award of Garden Merit.

Plant may be observed at AA, BSG, CBG, CIN, MRT, MUN, NCS, RKEW, UBC, VDG, WIS.

## Rubus odoratus
### FLOWERING RASPBERRY
### THIMBLEBERRY

Rosaceae. USDA Zones 5–8. Native to eastern North America, from Nova Scotia, Quebec, and Ontario south to Michigan, North Carolina, Georgia, and Tennessee. Introduced into cultivation in 1770.

DESCRIPTION: Deciduous shrub growing fairly rapidly to 6 ft. high, with vigorous, suckering habit, and sparse, erect, thornless branches.
*Leaves:* Simple, broad-ovate, 3–5 lobed, finely serrate, large, 5–8 in. wide, heart-shaped, velvetlike texture, pubescent beneath, with good, red fall color in cooler climates.
*Flowers:* Purple-rose, fragrant, in branched clusters, 2 in. across; June–August.
*Fruit:* A flat, red, inedible berry, borne in small numbers in late summer.
*Winter aspect:* Shredding bark.

CULTURE: Grows in sun, but needs partial shade in southerly latitudes; prefers moist but not wet humus soil with a pH of 6.5–7.5 and moderate summer temperatures; does not tolerate high humidity, but in humid areas performs best in sun with good air circulation.
*Disease and insect problems:* None serious; some mildew, rust.
*Transplanting:* Easy, balled and burlapped or container-grown.
*Propagation:* By root cuttings and transplanted suckers.

LANDSCAPE VALUE: An excellent, trouble-free, understory plant for use in the naturalized landscape, where it

*Rubus cockburnianus* (J. C. Raulston)

*Rubus* 'Tridel' (R. Stafford)

*Rubus odoratus* (Brooklyn Botanic Garden)

*Rubus odoratus* (Brooklyn Botanic Garden)

233

*Rubus odoratus* continued

grows best. Requires little maintenance. Fragrant flowers are usually rose-purple but occasionally have whitish cast. Bloom not profuse, but flowers are attractive against the coarse, maple-leaf-shaped foliage.

Plant may be observed at AA, ABF, BBG, BER, CBG, CIN, DEN, DUK, GIW, HOL, IES, LAC, LWD, MRT, MTC, MUN, NCA, PAL, RBC, RKEW.

Related *Rubus* hybrid of interest:

*R.* 'Tridel' (*R. deliciosus* × *R. trilobus*). USDA Zones 5–7. Developed in 1950 by Collingwood Ingram of Beneden, Cranbrook, United Kingdom. Lovely roselike flowers, attractive foliage, and beautiful branching habit make this an outstanding shrub. White, round flowers, 2 in. across, appear in early summer. Very hardy and easy to grow; needs little maintenance. Reaches 3–6 ft. high, with loose, spreading habit and arching stems. Dark purple fruit in September, persisting into winter, is attractive to birds. Western relative of *R. odoratus* and similar to *R. deliciosus,* but pure white flowers are larger and more regular. One of the best in the genus.

## *Ruscus aculeatus*
### BUTCHER'S BROOM

Liliaceae. USDA Zones 8–9. Native to Europe, including southern United Kingdom, and North Africa. Introduced into cultivation in 1750.

DESCRIPTION: Deciduous shrub growing at slow to moderate rate to 1.5–3 ft. high, with mounded, erect habit.
*Leaves:* Ovate, 1.5 in. long and 0.5 in. wide, glossy, deep green; true leaves scalelike, with flattened stems (cladophylls).
*Flowers:* Off-white, small, 0.25 in. across, borne singly or in pairs, in leaf axils.
*Fruit:* An oblong, waxy, red berry, 0.3 in. long, ripening in early autumn, persisting through winter.
*Winter aspect:* Erect stems.

CULTURE: Tolerates deep shade; adapts to a variety of soils and pH levels; grows well by the seacoast.
*Disease and insect problems:* None serious.
*Transplanting:* Easy.
*Propagation:* By cuttings.

LANDSCAPE VALUE: An unusual, small shrub that survives in dense shade. The position of flowers and the persistent fruit create an interesting plant. Quite ornamental when laden with berries in fall. Plants are dioecious; male and female must be present to set fruit. Renews itself by suckers, which spring from base of shrub.

Plant may be observed at ABF, BBG, BRK, CAL, CUH, FIL, LAC, MMA, MIS, MUN, NCS, PAL, RKEW, STR, VDG.

## *Salix gracilistyla*
### ROSEGOLD PUSSY WILLOW

Salicaceae. USDA Zones 6–8. Native to China, Japan, Korea. Introduced into cultivation in 1900.

DESCRIPTION: Deciduous shrub to 3–9 ft. high, with erect, spreading, habit.
*Leaves:* Oval, 2–4 in. long and 1.25 in. wide, glabrous above, silky and hairy beneath, silver-gray when young, gray-green when mature, turning yellow in fall.
*Flowers:* Catkins 1.25 in. long, anthers rose and yellow, before leaves; early spring.
*Winter aspect:* Showy male catkins; stout, gray-green to gray-purple stems stand out in dull winter landscapes.

CULTURE: Grows in sun in clay or loam; tolerates damp conditions.
*Disease and insect problems:* Bacterial twig blight, canker, leaf spot, rust, mildew, aphid, scale.
*Transplanting:* Difficult; plant recovers slowly.
*Propagation:* By hardwood cuttings and rooting in water.

LANDSCAPE VALUE: An attractive shrub for small landscapes. Showy, well-shaped, pink-tinged, 1.25 in. male catkins are lovely in flower arrangements and much larger than the Pussy Willow common in the florist trade. Plant should be cut back to ground every 3–4 years to promote vigorous shoots and large catkins. Weak wood is subject to storm damage, and roots can damage foundations and invade water and septic systems.

Plant may be observed at AA, ABF, ATL, BBG, BER, BF, BLO, CBG, CIN, CUH, DAW, DEN, GIW, IES, LAC, LNG, MUN, NCS, NEW, PAL, PLF, RKEW, SKY, UBC, USN, VDG, WIS.

Related *Salix* species of interest:

*S. fargesii.* USDA Zone 6. Introduced in 1911 from W. Hupei, Sichuan Province, China. Attractive, slow-growing, small shrub, to 8 ft. high, with red-brown, polished stems and dark red winter buds. Large leaves, to 6 in. long, are deep, glossy green above with prominent purple veins, and lighter green and silky, pubescent beneath. Yellow catkins, 4–6 in. long, hang from goblet-shaped plant. Outstanding shrub.
*S. melanostachys.* Black Catkin Willow. USDA Zone 5. Native to Japan; introduced in 1950 by J. Spek, Boskoop, Netherlands. A most attractive shrub, growing rapidly to 10 ft. high and 6 ft. wide, with colorful stems, foliage, and flowers. Stems are purple-brown to green-brown; dark

*Ruscus aculeatus* (J. Elsley)

*Salix gracilistyla* (B. Yinger)

*Salix gracilistyla* (J. C. Raulston)

*Salix fargesii* (J. Elsley)

green leaves are ovate, toothed, with blue undersides. Deep purple-black, male catkins, with strong red anthers that turn yellow, are produced before leaves. Grows in sun in any soil; particularly suited to waterlogged areas since it requires a great amount of water. Useful for erosion control on banks. Received RHS Award of Garden Merit.

## *Salix lanata*
### WOOLLY WILLOW

Salicaceae. USDA Zones 2–4. Native to northern Europe and Asia. Introduced into cultivation in 1789.

DESCRIPTION: Deciduous shrub growing slowly to 3–4 ft. high, with low, twiggy, goblet-shaped habit.
*Leaves:* Alternate, simple, oval, 1–2 in. long and 0.75–1.5 in. wide, densely covered with silvery hairs on both surfaces.
*Flowers:* Catkins golden-yellow to gray, female 4 in. long, male 2 in. long; appearing with leaves in spring.

CULTURE: Grows in sun in clay or loam; tolerates damp conditions; needs cool climate.
*Disease and insect problems:* Blight, aphid, borer.
*Transplanting:* Difficult; plant recovers slowly.
*Propagation:* By hardwood cuttings and rooting in water.

LANDSCAPE VALUE: An extremely hardy, interesting plant. Catkins appear with the very attractive foliage. Can be grown at high altitudes. Attractive for rock gardens and water landscaping. Care must be taken because of invasive root system.

Plant may be observed at CUH, DEN, MNL, PAL, RKEW, UBC, VDG.

## *Sambucus racemosa* 'Plumosa Aurea'
### EUROPEAN RED-BERRIED ELDER

Caprifoliaceae. USDA Zones 5–8. Native to Europe and Asia Minor. Introduced into cultivation in 1895 by Messrs. Wezelenburg, Netherlands.

DESCRIPTION: Deciduous shrub growing slowly to 8–12 ft. high, with multistemmed, broad, rounded habit.
*Leaves:* Opposite, odd-pinnate, 6–9 in. long, composed of 5–7 finely cut leaflets 2–4 in. long, bright yellow; coarse teeth of leaflets extend almost to leaf centers.
*Flowers:* Rich yellow, in dense, terminal panicles 1.75–2.5 in. long; April–May.

*Fruit:* Scarlet-red, 0.25 in. diameter, packed tightly in panicles, in June–July.
*Winter aspect:* Spreading, arching branching habit.

CULTURE: Needs sun for foliage color; prefers moist soil, but tolerates dry conditions when established; tolerates a wide pH range and some drought, but not soil compaction.
*Disease and insect problems:* Borer, powdery mildew.
*Transplanting:* Easy, balled and burlapped or container-grown.
*Propagation:* Best by softwood cuttings; also by hardwood cuttings in late winter.

LANDSCAPE VALUE: One of the most attractive of the golden-leaved shrubs, enhanced by bright red fruits that are attractive to birds. Received RHS Award of Merit 1895. Can be cut back severely in late winter or early spring if overgrown or leggy; will renew itself from base.

Plant may be observed at CBG.

## *Sarcococca ruscifolia*
### FRAGRANT SARCOCOCCA

Buxaceae. USDA Zones 7–8. Native to China, Tibet. Introduced into cultivation in 1901.

DESCRIPTION: Broad-leaved evergreen growing 6 in. per year to 4–6 ft. high and 3–7 ft. wide, with compact, mounded habit.
*Leaves:* Ovate, 1.5–2.5 in. long, with wavy edge, densely set on branches, glossy, waxy, deep green.
*Flowers:* Milky white, small, 0.5 in. across, very fragrant, nearly hidden in axils of terminal leaves; early spring.
*Fruit:* Globose, 0.25 in. across, red, in December–March.
*Winter aspect:* Dense branching habit.

CULTURE: Best in partial shade; burns in full sun; prefers moist, well-drained, loose loam with a pH of 5.5; tolerates air pollution and some wind, but not drought or wet conditions.
*Disease and insect problems:* None serious.
*Transplanting:* Easy, container-grown.
*Propagation:* By seed, without pre-treatment; better and faster by cuttings in November–February.

LANDSCAPE VALUE: A handsome, small shrub with very fragrant flowers. Should be combined in shrub border with dwarf conifers and with contrasting textures. Excellent plant for light shade. Very effective as natural espalier against wall, with branches fanning out to form dark patterns.

Plant may be observed at ABF, ATL, BLO, CUH, FIL, HUN, LAC, MIS, NCS, PAL, RKEW, STR, UBC, VDG, WIS.

*Salix lanata* (University of British Columbia Botanical Garden)

*Salix lanata* (University of British Columbia Botanical Garden)

*Sambucus racemosa* 'Plumosa Aurea' (N. Brewster)

*Sambucus racemosa* 'Plumosa Aurea' (N. Brewster)

*Sarcococca ruscifolia* (N. Brewster)

*Sarcococca ruscifolia* (N. Brewster)

237

*Sarcococca ruscifolia* continued

Related *Sarcococca* species of interest:

*S. confusa.* USDA Zones 7–8. Grows to 3 ft. high and 5 ft. wide. Very similar to *S. ruscifolia* but with black fruit. Received RHS Award of Garden Merit.

# *Shepherdia argentea*
## SILVER BUFFALO BERRY

Elaeagnaceae. USDA Zones (2)3–6. Native to North America. Introduced into cultivation in 1918.

DESCRIPTION: Deciduous shrub 6–10(18) ft. high, with erect, rigid, spine-tipped branches and suckering habit.
*Leaves:* Narrowly oblong, 1 in. long.
*Flowers:* Not conspicuous, yellowish; male and female flowers on separate stems.
*Fruit:* An oval, pea-sized, red berry, tartly sweet, ornamental.
*Winter aspect:* Persistent fruit.

CULTURE: Likes sun and clay soil; tolerates wind and drought.
*Disease and insect problems:* None serious.
*Transplanting:* Deep root system.
*Propagation:* By root cuttings; by seed, stratified for 3 months at 40°F and not permitted to dry out beforehand.

LANDSCAPE VALUE: An extremely hardy shrub that can survive harsh winters, drought, salt, and high pH. Good hedge plant. Attracts birds. Fruit can be made into jelly. Not particularly ornamental, but of value for use along highways and for other tough growing conditions where other plants cannot survive. Needs no maintenance. An underused native shrub.

Plant may be observed at AA, ABF, BBG, CBG, CIN, DEN, GIW, HOL, LNG, MOD, MMA, MRT, MUN, NEB, PAL, RBC, RKEW, SBB, VDG.

Related *Shepherdia* species of interest:

*S. canadensis.* Russet Buffalo Berry. Smaller than *S. argentea.* Tough, easily grown plant that tolerates harsh growing conditions.

# *Skimmia japonica*
## JAPANESE SKIMMIA

Rutaceae. USDA Zones 6–8. Native to Japan, the Himalayas. Introduced into cultivation in 1838.

DESCRIPTION: Broad-leaved evergreen growing slowly to 3–4 ft. high and as wide (female wider), with dense, domed, spreading habit (male smaller and less open).
*Leaves:* Alternate, elliptic-oblong, toothless, short-stalked, in whorls, 2–5 in. long and 0.75–2 in. wide (leaves of female larger than those of male), glossy, bright, dark green above, yellow-green beneath, aromatic when crushed.
*Flowers:* Yellow-white, small, female flowers 0.3 in. across, male flowers slightly larger, in unisexual terminal panicles to 2 in. long and as wide; March–April.
*Fruit:* Globose to nearly flat, 0.3 in. across, red, appearing on female plants from midsummer through fall and winter.

CULTURE: Grows in partial to dense shade; full sun discolors foliage; prefers loam, but grows in a variety of moist soils with a pH of 5.0–5.75; does not tolerate wet conditions or drought, but tolerates wind in shade.
*Disease and insect problems:* Mite.
*Transplanting:* Easy, container-grown.
*Propagation:* By cuttings, rooted in water, in late summer–fall.

LANDSCAPE VALUE: A handsome plant for smaller city gardens, mixed evergreen plantings, and containers. Ideal as understory shrub since it tolerates deep shade. Excellent companion for shade-loving perennials in the woodland garden. Flower buds form in fall; flowers and fruit often appear on shrub at same time. Male habit more attractive, but female berries are showy; both male and female plants needed for fruiting. Burns

*Skimmia reevesiana* 'Rubella' (J. Apel)      *Skimmia reevesiana* 'Rubella' (J. C. Raulston)

*Sarcococca confusa* (N. Brewster)

*Sarcococca confusa* (N. Frink)

*Shepherdia argentea* (E. Hasselkus)

*Shepherdia argentea* (E. Hasselkus)

*Skimmia japonica* (N. Brewster)

*Skimmia japonica* (N. Brewster)

*Skimmia japonica* continued

badly in winter sun. In some cases, female plants are labeled "S. oblata" and male plants "S. fragrans" or "S. fragrantissima."

Plant may be observed at ABF, BBG, BC, BSG, CAL, CUH, DUK, LWD, MCG, MIS, MOR, NCS, NEW, OWG, PAL, PLF, RKEW, SKY, STR, UBC, USN, VDG, WIS.

*Skimmia japonica* cultivar and related cultivars of interest:

S. *japonica* 'Nymans'. Leaves oblanceolate; best fruiting of the skimmias. Received RHS Award of Garden Merit.

S. 'Formanii' (*S. japonica* × *S. reevesiana*). Grows vigorously to 2–3 ft. high and as wide, with broad-obovate leaves.

S. *reevesiana* 'Rubella'. Reeves Skimmia. Male, with large leaves, 3–4 in. long, and panicles of red buds throughout winter. Very fragrant in spring. Received RHS Award of Garden Merit.

# *Sorbaria sorbifolia*
## URAL FALSE SPIRAEA

Rosaceae. USDA Zones 2–10. Native to northern Asia. Introduced into cultivation in 1759.

DESCRIPTION: Deciduous shrub to 5–10 ft. high, with upright, coarse, suckering habit.
*Leaves:* Alternate, compound, pinnate, 8–10 in. long, composed of 13–23 lanceolate to lanceolate-ovate leaflets 2–4 in. long and more than 0.5 in. wide, acuminate, doubly serrate, almost glabrous, bright green.
*Flowers:* White, small, 0.3 in. across, in large, terminal panicles 4–10 in. long, covered with soft hairs, dense, upright, showy; late June–July.
*Fruit:* A dehiscent follicle.
*Winter aspect:* Upright, arching branching habit; flower heads turn brown and persist into winter.

CULTURE: Thrives in full sun, but grows vigorously in partial shade; prefers moist, well-drained loam with a pH of 6.0–7.5, but adapts to a wide range of moisture conditions, soil types, and pH variations; tends to be stunted in dry conditions; tolerates tough urban conditions.
*Disease and insect problems:* None serious.
*Transplanting:* Easy; fibrous roots spread profusely.
*Propagation:* By seed, with no stratification, or by root cuttings; spreads rapidly by suckers.

LANDSCAPE VALUE: A reliable summer-flowering shrub, valuable for feathery, attractive foliage and conspicuous white panicles, which bloom when little else is in flower. Best planted away from house because of peculiar, sometimes disagreeable, scent of flowers. New foliage is some-

what red when first emerging; fall color inconsequential. A robust spreader suited to larger gardens and broad, open landscapes. Suckers freely in light soils, where it requires room to move; fairly well behaved in heavier soils. Overcrowded or weak wood should be removed every few years. Prune in early spring before growth starts; flowers produced on current season's growth. Excellent for shrub border, massed plantings, screening, and bank cover.

Plant may be observed at AA, ABF, ATL, BBG, BER, BIC, BRK, CBG, CIN, COX, DAW, GCC, FIL, IES, LAC, LNG, MIS, MNL, MOD, MOR, MRT, MUN, NCS, NEB, NEW, PAL, PLF, RBC, RKEW, SPR, UBC, VDG.

Related *Sorbaria* species of interest:

S. *aitchisonii*. Kashmir False Spiraea. Introduced in 1895 from Afghanistan, Kashmir. Red shoots when young. Useful for highway plantings and other exposed areas where it can spread. Prune in early spring; flowers on new growth.

# *Sorbus reducta*
## DWARF MOUNTAIN ASH

Rosaceae. USDA Zones 6–8. Native to western China, Myanmar (formerly Burma). Introduced into cultivation in 1943.

DESCRIPTION: Deciduous shrub growing very slowly to 2–3 ft. high, with dense, bushy habit.
*Leaves:* Ovate to elliptic, coarsely serrate, 3 in. long, composed of 9–15 leaflets 0.75–1 in. long, dark green with red stems, turning dark bronze to red in fall.
*Flowers:* White, in dense heads in terminal clusters 0.6 in. wide; spring.
*Fruit:* Globose, 0.25 in. across, carmine, in open clusters, in fall.
*Winter aspect:* Slender, spreading branching habit.

CULTURE: Grows in sun and filtered shade; prefers loam with a pH of 5.5–6.5; tolerates some wind, but not wet conditions or drought.
*Disease and insect problems:* None serious.
*Transplanting:* Easy, container-grown.
*Propagation:* By underground roots.

LANDSCAPE VALUE: A good, small shrub for the woodland or rock garden. Striking, carmine-red fruit and bronze-red foliage in fall add to its landscape value. Underground suckering habit forms small thickets.

Plant may be observed at BER, CBG, MUN, PAL, RHO, RKEW, UBC, VDG.

*Sorbaria sorbifolia* (J. C. Raulston)

*Sorbaria sorbifolia* (J. Apel)

*Sorbus reducta* (N. Brewster)

*Sorbus reducta* (University of British Columbia Botanical Garden)

## *Spiraea* × *bumalda* 'Gold Flame'
### GOLD FLAME BUMALDA SPIRAEA

Parentage: *S. albiflora* × *S. japonica*. Rosaceae. USDA Zones 5–8. Introduced into cultivation by Shum's Nurseries, Rochester, New York.

DESCRIPTION: Deciduous shrub growing quickly to 2–3 ft. high, with rounded to irregular habit.
*Leaves:* Alternate, simple, finely toothed, 1–3 in. long, ovate to lanceolate; new growth red, copper, and orange, turning yellow to yellow-green in summer and fall.
*Flowers:* Rose-pink, in flat-topped corymbs 4–6 in. wide, on new growth; June–August.
*Fruit:* A brown follicle, with seed heads persisting into winter.
*Winter aspect:* Lined and ridged brown bark; persistent fruit calyces.

CULTURE: Grows in sun or light shade; prefers clay or loam with a pH of 6.0–7.5; tolerates drought, but not wet conditions.
*Disease and insect problems:* Many, but seldom fatal, including fire blight, leaf spot, powdery mildew, root rot, aphid.
*Transplanting:* Easy.
*Propagation:* By cuttings.

LANDSCAPE VALUE: With its ever-changing medley of foliage color, from russet-orange to bronze-red and yellow-green, this plant provides a welcome respite from the sea of green that dominates our landscapes. Like its close relatives 'Anthony Waterer' and 'Froebelii', 'Gold Flame' produces variegated foliage on rare occasions. Summer foliage color is determined by exposure and location: leaves are darker green in shade and in warmer areas and a brighter lime-green in sunny exposures and in northerly latitudes. Has a high tolerance for heat and performs admirably in southerly latitudes (USDA Zone 8). Good for massed plantings on slopes since it suckers from roots. Should be pruned in early spring before new growth appears. Received RHS Award of Garden Merit.

Plant may be observed at CBG, LNG, MRT, RKEW, WIS.

Another *Spiraea* × *bumalda* cultivar of interest:

*S.* × *bumalda* 'Golden Princess'. Arresting, attractive shrub with year-round interest. New growth in spring is bronze-yellow. The bright, golden foliage turns to soft, pale yellow-green in summer, contrasting with the flat corymbs of bright pink flowers that appear all summer. Foliage slightly smaller than that of *S.* × *bumalda* 'Gold Flame.' Grows to 2.5–3 ft. high. Habit not uniform on young plants and benefits from light pruning.

## *Spiraea* × *cinerea* 'Grefsheim'
### GREFSHEIM SPIRAEA

Parentage: *S. cana* × *S. hypericifolia*. Rosaceae. USDA Zones 4–8. Introduced 1949 by Grefsheim Nursery, Nes, Norway. Hybrid originated before 1884.

DESCRIPTION: Deciduous shrub growing at moderate rate to 5–6 ft. high, with dense, upright habit and arching stems.
*Leaves:* Narrow, elliptic or lanceolate, almost entire, 1.5–1.75 in. long, pubescent, soft dull green above, lighter beneath, turning a warm yellow-orange in fall.
*Flowers:* Pure white, abundant, small, fragrant, in dense spikes; April–May.
*Winter aspect:* Graceful, arching branches.

CULTURE: Grows in sun and some shade in clay or loam with a pH of 6.0–7.8; tolerates drought and all but very wet conditions.
*Disease and insect problems:* None serious.
*Transplanting:* Easy.
*Propagation:* By cuttings.

LANDSCAPE VALUE: An excellent, fragrant *Spiraea* with lovely, arching habit. It explodes with spring flowers that extend along leafless branches, covering them in white. The plant in flower is spectacular—a soft, lovely, white enhancement to the landscape. Flowers best in light shade. Received RHS Award of Garden Merit.

Plant may be observed at AA, CBG, CIN, HOL, LNG, MNL, MUN, PAL, RKEW, WIS.

## *Spiraea fritschiana*
### FRITSCH SPIRAEA

Rosaceae. USDA Zone 4. Native from central China to Korea. Introduced into cultivation in 1919.

DESCRIPTION: Deciduous shrub growing at moderate rate to 3–6 ft. high, with upright, mounded, full-bodied habit.
*Leaves:* Elliptic, serrate, 1.25–3 in. long, turning bright yellow to orange-red in full sun in fall.
*Flowers:* White, large, to 5 in. across, in flat-topped cymes; June.
*Fruit:* Seed capsules in July, persisting through winter.
*Winter aspect:* Lustrous, purple-brown, sharply angled, glabrous bark; persistent seed capsules.

CULTURE: Grows in sun and shade in a wide range of soils; prefers clay or loam with a pH of 6.0–7.5; performs well in both well-drained and heavier soils; tolerates wind, drought, and soil compaction.
*Disease and insect problems:* None.

*Spiraea* × *bumalda* 'Gold Flame' (J. Elsley)

*Spiraea* × *bumalda* 'Golden Princess' (J. Elsley)

*Spiraea* × *cinerea* 'Grefsheim' (G. Gates)

*Spiraea fritschiana* (G. Gates).

**Spiraea fritschiana** continued

*Transplanting:* Easy.
*Propagation:* By cuttings and seed.

LANDSCAPE VALUE: This fine shrub is unique among spiraeas in flower and fall color, performing equally well in high-maintenance landscapes and those receiving little or no care. It blooms in June, providing a contrast to other small-statured, pink-flowered spiraeas blooming at the same time. Maintains excellent, bright yellow fall color with only 4–5 hours of direct sunlight; in full sun foliage becomes a bright orange-red, much showier than the usual dark red fall color of most spiraeas. Very attractive to rabbits.

Plant may be observed at AA, BEA, CBG, DAW, LNG, MNL, MRT, RKEW.

## Spiraea japonica 'Shibori'
JAPANESE SPIRAEA

Synonym: *S. japonica* 'Shirobana'. Rosaceae. USDA Zones 3–8. Native to temperate East Asia. Introduced in 1963 from Japan.

DESCRIPTION: Deciduous shrub to 2–4 ft. high and 2.5–3 ft. wide in 10 years, with neat, dense, mounded habit.
*Leaves:* Alternate, simple, ovoid, doubly serrate, to 1 in. long, green, turning bronze in fall.
*Flowers:* In rounded corymbs of florets, 0.06 in. wide, with pink, rose, and white flowers blooming simultaneously; June–July.
*Fruit:* A small, brown, hard follicle.

CULTURE: Grows in full sun or light shade in acid, loamy soil; becomes chlorotic when soil pH reaches 7.5; tolerates wind and drought.
*Disease and insect problems:* None serious.
*Transplanting:* Easy; shallow root system.
*Propagation:* By cuttings.

LANDSCAPE VALUE: Uniquely interesting in that it produces white, pink, and rose flowers on same plant, in a refreshing, attractive floral display. Continues flowering sporadically throughout summer. Said to be clone of *S. japonica* 'Alpina' and retains the characteristics of the species. Its lustrous, deep green foliage is probably the most attractive of any *S. japonica* cultivar. Received RHS Award of Garden Merit.

Plant may be observed at AA, ATL, BC, BF, BSG, CBG, CIN, DOW, DUK, HOL, LNG, MOD, MNL, NCS, SEC, SPR, STG, USN, VDG, WIS.

## Spiraea nipponica
NIPPON SPIRAEA

Rosaceae. USDA Zones 5–8. Native to Shikoku Island, Japan. Introduced in 1885 by Philipp von Siebold.

DESCRIPTION: Deciduous shrub growing at moderate rate to 3–5 ft. high, with erect, densely branched habit.
*Leaves:* Alternate, simple, obovate to elliptic, crenate, broadly cuneate at base, 1–1.5 in. long and 0.5 in. wide, dark green above, bluish beneath.
*Flowers:* Small, white, in clusters of 8–12 on corymbs; May-June.
*Fruit:* A capsule, appearing in June, persisting into winter.

CULTURE: Best in full sun, but grows in partial shade; prefers soil with a pH of 6.0–7.5; tolerates wind and drought.
*Disease and insect problems:* None serious.
*Transplanting:* Easy.
*Propagation:* By cuttings.

LANDSCAPE VALUE: Among the best June-flowering shrubs, with abundant flowers and an erect, densely branched habit. A strong grower that performs well. Appears to be a superior substitute for *S.* x *vanhouttei*.

Plant may be observed at BBG, BC, BEA, BER, BF, BSG, CBG, CHK, CIN, COX, CUH, DAW, DEN, DOW, DUK, GCC, HOL, HUN, LWD, MIS, MOD, MNL, NEB, OWG, RBC, RKEW, SEC, SPR, STG, VDG, WIS.

*Spiraea nipponica* cultivars of interest:

*S. nipponica* 'Halward's Silver'. USDA Zones 3–6. Developed from seeds received in 1960 by the Royal Botanical Gardens, Hamilton, Ontario, from the Botanic Garden of the University of Copenhagen, Denmark. More compact and slower growing than species, with stiffly erect stems and numerous short, strongly ascending branches. Remains dense and compact without sacrifice of flower production. White flowers, larger than those of species, are lavishly produced on terminal, upward-facing corymbs, mostly concealing the foliage.

*S. nipponica* 'Snowmound'. USDA Zones 3–8. Cultivar selected in the United States. Excellent shrub reaching 3–5 ft. high and as wide, with neat, dense, mounded habit. Explodes with white flowers in May–June. Similar in habit and floral display to *S.* × *vanhouttei*, but smaller, with more attractive foliage; small, dark blue-green leaves remain handsome throughout the season. Useful as foundation plant or in perennial border. Unique in producing elongate, arching branches with secund corymbs (i.e., corymbs where all the leaves and flowers grow on one side). Handsome when grown in its natural form, which can be maintained with periodic pruning to renew shape. Received RHS Award of Garden Merit.

*Spiraea japonica* 'Shibori' (J. Elsley)

*Spiraea japonica* 'Shibori' (R. Klehm)

*Spiraea nipponica* 'Snowmound' (G. Gates)

245

## Stachyurus praecox
### EARLY SPIKETAIL

Stachyuraceae. USDA Zones 6–8. Native to Japan and the Himalayas. Cultivated since 1865.

DESCRIPTION: Deciduous shrub growing slowly to 6–10 ft. high, with upright habit.
*Leaves:* Ovate-lanceolate, tapered to sharp tip, toothed, 3–5 in. long and 1–1.7 in. wide, bright green, turning yellowish to rosy red in fall.
*Flowers:* Pale yellow, with 4 sepals and 4 petals, bell-shaped, 0.5 in. wide, in pendulous racemes, 3–4 in. long, in leaf axils; clusters of 12–20 unopened buds hang from branches during winter; February–March.
*Fruit:* Berrylike, green and yellow-red checked, in August–September.
*Winter aspect:* Chestnut-brown, slender, polished branches; spreading, arching habit.

CULTURE: Grows in full sun, but best in light shade in warmer climates; requires moist, well-drained, porous, acid peat; does not tolerate wet conditions; needs shelter in winter from heavy frost, which destroys buds.
*Disease and insect problems:* None serious.
*Transplanting:* Easy when small.
*Propagation:* By summer cuttings under mist, by layering, and by seed sown as soon as it is ripe.

LANDSCAPE VALUE: One of the finest winter-flowering shrubs; flowers appear when few plants are in bloom. Plant in front of dark background for striking display of reddish, leafless branches hung with yellow racemes. Usually needs no pruning, but can be pruned as soon as bloom is spent. Name from *stachys* ("spike") and *oura* ("tail"), alluding to racemes of flowers. Received RHS Award of Garden Merit.

Plant may be observed at AA, ABF, ATL, BBG, BSG, CAL, CUH, DUK, MRT, MUN, NCS, NEW, PAL, RKEW, STR, UBC, USN, VDG, WIS.


## Stephanandra incisa 'Crispa'
### CUTLEAF STEPHANANDRA

Rosaceae. USDA Zones 3–7. Found in 1920s in the nursery of A. M. Jensen, Holmstrup, Denmark. Introduced to the trade in 1949. Species native to Japan, Korea; cultivated as early as 1872.

DESCRIPTION: Deciduous shrub growing quickly to 1.5–3 ft. high, with dense, low, downward-bowed habit.
*Leaves:* Alternate, lobes incised and coarsely biserrate, triangular, ovate; fine leaves red-tinged when opening in spring, becoming bright green above, lighter and pubescent beneath in summer, then turning red-purple or red-orange in fall.
*Flowers:* Small, green-white, not ornamental; May–June.
*Fruit:* A follicle.
*Winter aspect:* Low, dense thicket of fine branches.

CULTURE: Grows in a variety of conditions; tips burn in winter in exposed areas, although plant comes back readily when pruned; prefers moist, acid, well-drained soil amended with peat moss or leaf mold; tolerates most soils, but develops chlorosis when pH is high.
*Disease and insect problems:* None serious.
*Transplanting:* Easy; roots where it touches the ground.
*Propagation:* By cuttings.

LANDSCAPE VALUE: Dense, fine texture and exceedingly wide spread create a graceful, arching plant. Effective as low hedge or ground cover. Excellent for massed plantings that need little maintenance. Also a substantial ground cover for bank plantings. Suckers from base.

Plant may be observed at AA, ATL, BBG, BC, BF, BOE, BSG, CBG, CIN, CUH, DAW, GCC, HOL, LNG, LWD, MIS, MNL, MRT, NCS, NEW, PLF, RBC, RKEW, SEC, USN.


## Streptosolen jamesonii
### MARMALADE BUSH

Solanaceae. USDA Zone 10. Native to Colombia, Ecuador.

DESCRIPTION: Deciduous, broad-leaved evergreen growing quickly to 6 ft. high and 10–15 ft. wide, with sprawling habit.
*Leaves:* Ovate, conspicuously veined and stalked, 1–1.25 in. long, bright green.
*Flowers:* Brilliant yellow-orange, 1 in. across, in clusters at branch ends, with 5 spreading petals of a deeper bright orange; April–October in cooler climates, year-round in warm climates.
*Fruit:* A leathery capsule.

CULTURE: Grows in sun and semishade in well-drained clay or loam; needs ample moisture, but does not tolerate wet conditions around roots; tolerates wind; performs best in warm, dry conditions; prefers cooler conditions in Hawaii.
*Disease and insect problems:* None.
*Transplanting:* Very easy.
*Propagation:* By cuttings, which root by themselves.

LANDSCAPE VALUE: A superb shrub with bright color display and easy care. Can be kept in container if well watered and fed, or trained as climber or espaliered. Effective as loose hedge. Becomes huge if not cut back and seems to like hard pruning; pruning should be done in late

*Stachyurus praecox* (G. Pirzio-Biroli)

*Stachyurus praecox* (B. Yinger)

*Stephanandra incisa* 'Crispa' (E. Hasselkus)

*Stephanandra incisa* 'Crispa' (Royal Botanical Gardens, Ontario)

*Streptosolen jamesonii* (R. Jones)

*Streptosolen jamesonii* (J. Apel)

*Streptosolen jamesonii* continued

winter and early spring. Must be placed so that its marvelous color will not clash with that of other plants. Used in Hawaii to make leis.

Plant may be observed at HUN, LAC, MIS, MMA, RKEW, STR.

# *Syringa*
## LILAC

There are about 30 species and more than 1600 cultivars in the genus *Syringa.* Specific attributes and distinguishing characteristics are provided for the species and cultivars selected for inclusion here. The following is a general overview of this large, varied, and deservedly popular genus, grown primarily for its enchanting flower display.

Lilacs are temperate region shrubs—although they can be grown with varying success in southerly latitudes, where dormancy must be induced by moisture deprivation rather than cold temperatures. Lilac performance is most assuredly not uniform. The same species and/or cultivars may vary in bloom color, quality, and quantity in different sites and demonstrate a greater or lesser degree of resistance to pests and diseases.

Most lilacs are evaluated in terms of growth—vigor and quality of foliage—and bloom—amount, distinction, color, size and form of floret, and thyrse (clusters on which the florets are borne). Fragrance, susceptibility to frost damage, and disease expression also have a bearing on evaluation.

Lilacs should be planted in early November or late April for best results, in an open, sunny location or in an area where they will receive at least 5.5 hours of direct sunlight each day. They prefer neutral or slightly alkaline soil with good drainage. In sandy soils, the cultivated area should be mulched with a decomposed organic mulch. In wet soils, it is desirable to build mounds 2 ft. high and 10 ft. wide to facilitate drainage.

Since buds for the following year's bloom are developed during the previous summer, it is advisable to water once every 3 weeks during dry periods, assuring water penetration to 5 in. To promote bud formation, apply high-phosphate fertilizer at the end of the blooming period. It is also advisable to cut off old blooms so that nutrients are not diverted from seed formation. Alternate-year blooming in lilacs is quite common. Lilac stems 1–2.5 in. thick produce the best-quality blooms in terms of size and color intensity. Single lilacs seem to be more fragrant than doubles. Cool springs with ample rain produce more intense fragrance.

Lilacs should be rejuvenated by pruning to create a shrub with 6–9 (12 at most) stems of varying thicknesses located within a 24–30 in. diameter, spaced so they do not rub. Such shaping may require 2–5 years. Rejuvenation is best done in December to February. If an existing shrub is already multistemmed, remove the largest stem, or any stem more than 5 in. in diameter, as close as possible to the ground. All but one or two replacement suckers should be removed 1 in. below ground level. Do not, however, remove more than 50% of the total mass of aboveground growth. Pruning should be done in June, at about the same time spent blooms are removed.

The lilacs included here have been selected not only for their desirable aesthetic characteristics but also for their resistance to pests and diseases. However, as noted earlier, resistance does vary with growing conditions and geographic location.

Two common lilac pests are lilac borer and oystershell scale. Since borers attack stems and branches of 1 in. diameter and larger, it is a good practice to remove older stems periodically as younger stems mature. Oystershell scales are sucking insects that attach to the bark of younger wood and can be chemically controlled.

Powdery mildew fungus is the most widespread and persistent lilac disease. Although it mars the appearance of the foliage, it usually does little damage to the plant. Another prevalent lilac disease, LRN (leaf roll necrosis) is likely caused by air pollution.

The most serious problem affecting *Syringa* is MLO, a microplasma-like organism first identified at The Morton Arboretum and subsequently in lilacs throughout the country. MLO manifests itself by reduced vigor, chlorosis, necrosis, premature fall coloring of foliage, witches'-broom (abnormal, dense clusters of stunted twigs), smaller blooms, remontant fall blooming, and suppressed buds. MLO can be latent in some plants and present no obvious symptoms; in others it can result in death. The late-blooming lilacs are especially susceptible; *S. vulgaris* and its cultivars are also susceptible but their reaction to the infection is far less severe.

The Royal Botanical Gardens, Hamilton, Ontario, with one of the largest and most representative collections of *Syringa,* is the International Registration Authority for *Syringa* cultivar names. Other major lilac collections include those at The Arnold Arboretum, Jamaica Plains, MA; Highland Park, Rochester, NY; and The Morton Arboretum, Lisle, IL. Additional collections of significance can be found at the following locations:

ARBORETA & BOTANICAL GARDENS

Bayard Cutting Arboretum, Long Island, NY
Bickelhaupt Arboretum, Clinton, IA
Boerner Botanical Gardens, Hales Corner, WI
Brooklyn Botanic Garden, Brooklyn, NY

Cary Arboretum, Millbrook, NY
Central Botanical Garden, Ukrainian Academy of Science, Kiev
Chicago Botanic Garden, Glencoe, IL
Denver Botanic Garden, Denver, CO
Freilinghausen Arboretum, Morris Township, NJ
George Landis Arboretum, Esperance, NY
The Holden Arboretum, Mentor, OH
Howard Taylor Memorial Lilac Arboretum, Millbrook, NY
John J. Tyler Arboretum, Lima, PA
Longwood Gardens, Kennett Square, PA
Minnesota Landscape Arboretum, Minnesota State University, St. Paul, MN
The New York Botanical Garden, Bronx, NY
The Scott Arboretum, Swarthmore College, Swarthmore, PA
Tennessee Botanical Gardens, Nashville, TN
University of California Botanical Garden, Riverside, CA
University of Nebraska, Maxwell Arboretum, Lincoln, NE
University of Washington Arboretum, Seattle, WA
University of Wisconsin Arboretum, Madison, WI
U.S. National Arboretum, Washington, DC

LAND GRANT COLLEGES & AGRICULTURAL EXPERIMENT STATIONS

Alice Harding Memorial Lilac Walk, Rutgers University, New Brunswick, NJ
Harris Memorial Lilac Walk, Cornell Plantations, Cornell University, Ithaca, NY
Hidden Lake Arboretum, Michigan State University, Tipton, MI
Purdue University, Horticultural Building, Lafayette, IN
University of Maine, Plant & Soil Sciences, Deering Hall, Orono, ME
University of New Hampshire, Plant Sciences, Durham, NH

PUBLIC PARKS & WHOLE TOWN PRIVATE PLANTINGS

Camden, ME
Cooperstown, NY
Delhi, NY
Hulda Klager Lilac Gardens, Woodland, WA
Lilacia Park, Lombard, IL
Mackinaw City, Mackinac Island, MI
Portsmouth, NH
Wiscasset, ME
Woodstock, VT

PRIVATE COLLECTIONS & LILAC GARDENS

Barnard's Inn Farm, Polly and Julian Hill, Vineyard Haven, MA
Lilac Land, Estate of Mrs. A. E. Lumley, Pelham, MA
Lilac Manor Farm, Charlotte Bass, South LaPorte, IN
Shelburne Museum Estate, Shelburne, VT

## *Syringa* × *hyacinthiflora*
## AMERICAN LILAC

Parentage: *S. oblata* × *S. vulgaris*. Oleaceae. USDA Zones 3–7. Garden hybrids; introduced into cultivation 1878 by Lemoine Nursery, Nancy, France.

DESCRIPTION: Deciduous shrub growing 8–12 in. per year to 10–12 ft. high and 10 ft. wide; cultivars vary considerably but tend to be lower and broader than *S.* × *hyacinthiflora*.
*Leaves:* Broad, ovate, solid green; cultivars purple-tinged in fall.
*Flowers:* Double, pink, lavender, or white; April–May, 7–10 days before those of *S. vulgaris*.
*Fruit:* Not conspicuous, should be removed with bloom to channel energy into bud production for next year's bloom.

CULTURE: Thrives in cool climates with plentiful sun, but grows in partial shade in warm climates; likes good air circulation; prefers moist, rich soil, but tolerates all but the wettest and driest soils.
*Disease and insect problems:* None serious; good resistance to mildew and MLO.
*Propagation:* By softwood cuttings and tissue culture.
*Transplanting:* Balled and burlapped or container-grown in spring and fall; bare root in spring.

LANDSCAPE VALUE: An early flowering shrub with exquisite blooms. Panicles more open and appearing 1–2 weeks earlier than those of *S. vulgaris*. An enchanting specimen shrub; also lovely in massed plantings. Prone to frost injury due to early bloom, but tolerates some frost.

Plant may be observed at AA, BBG, CUH, DEN, HOL, IES, LAC, LNG, MOD, NEW, RBC, RKEW, WIN.

*Syringa* × *hyacinthiflora* cultivars of interest:

*S.* × *hyacinthiflora* 'Blanche Sweet'. Unusual Rochester hybrid; white-blue flowers have traces of pink. To 10 ft. high. Resistant to mildew.

*Syringa* × *hyacinthiflora* 'Maiden's Blush' (E. Hasselkus)

249

**Syringa × hyacinthiflora** continued

S. × hyacinthiflora 'Maiden's Blush'. Introduced in 1966 by Frank L. Skinner, Dropmore, Manitoba. Light to medium rosy pink, single florets. Flowers are delicate, pale pink in warmer climates; in cooler regions with heavy soil, blooms take on lavender cast. Outstanding cultivar; pink cultivars often have smaller blooms. Needs to be pruned heavily.

S. × hyacinthiflora 'Sister Justena'. Introduced in 1956 by Frank L. Skinner, Dropmore, Manitoba. Early blooming, single flowers are a beautiful, fresh white, which is even more pronounced at twilight. Rounded in habit; produces an abundance of blooms from nearly ground up. In the landscape, a variety of white blooms is exceedingly effective, and massed planting is recommended if space permits.

Additional *Syringa* hybrid of interest:

S. × henryi (S. josikaea × S. villosa). USDA Zones 2–7. Originated by Louis Henry, inspector of the botanical garden of Paris Museum of Natural History; named and described in 1910 by C. K. Schneider. Pale violet-purple flowers appear in panicles 10-12 in. long, in May–June. One of the finest late-blooming lilacs; grows to about 9 ft. high.

*Syringa × henryi* cultivars of interest:

S. × henryi 'Lutèce'. Large, pale violet-pink to almost white flower. Some MLO has been detected.

S. × henryi 'Summer White'. Superb, true white flower; better than the parent.

# Syringa × josiflexa

Parentage: *S. josikaea × S. reflexa*. Oleaceae. USDA Zones 5–7. Garden hybrid. Originated in the 1920s and 1930s by Isabella Preston of the Central Experimental Farm, Ottawa, Ontario, Canada.

DESCRIPTION: Deciduous shrub growing quickly to 20 ft. high.
*Leaves:* Large, bold-textured, with deep green color when soil nitrogen is adequate.
*Flowers:* White, pink, rose, or lavender plumes; May.
*Fruit:* A capsule, not conspicuous.
*Winter aspect:* Fairly upright, with straight, uniform shoots; more multistemmed than *S. vulgaris*.

CULTURE: Needs sun, but grows in partial shade in southerly latitudes; prefers moist, rich, well-drained soil, but tolerates all but the wettest and driest soils; needs open, sunny location with good air circulation; very responsive to soil and site.

*Disease and insect problems:* MLO, manifested as witches'-broom; resistant to mildew, depending on location; some oystershell scale, but not too serious; borers attack stems about 1 in. diameter, 1–3 ft. above ground.
*Transplanting:* Balled and burlapped in spring or fall, bare root in spring.
*Propagation:* By softwood cuttings.

LANDSCAPE VALUE: An extremely beautiful race of hybrids developed in Ottawa by the superb horticulturist, Isabella Preston. This attractive, late-blooming shrub has plumelike panicles of fragrant flowers and needs space to grow. Can reach 20 ft. high, depending on cultivar and cultural practices, but desirable to maintain at about 8–10 ft.

Plant may be observed at AA, BBG, BF, BIC, CBG, HOL, LNG, MOD, NEB, NEW, RBC, SEC, VDG.

*Syringa × josiflexa* cultivars of interest:

S. × josiflexa 'Agnes Smith'. USDA Zones 4–6. Originated by Owen M. Rogers, University of New Hampshire; introduced in 1970. Single, white flowers, blooming about two weeks later than most commonly grown lilac cultivars.

S. × josiflexa 'Anna Amhoff'. USDA Zones 3–6. Originated by Albert F. Yaeger, University of New Hampshire; introduced in 1961 by Dahliatown Nurseries. An exceedingly lovely white cultivar.

*Syringa × josiflexa* 'Anna Amhoff' (C. Holetich)

*Syringa* × *hyacinthiflora* 'Sister Justena' (C. Holetich)

*Syringa* × *henryi* (Winterthur Gardens)

*Syringa* × *josiflexa* 'James MacFarlane'
(C. Holetich)

*Syringa* × *josiflexa* 'Royalty' (E. Hasselkus)

*Syringa* × *josiflexa* continued

S. × *josiflexa* 'James MacFarlane'. USDA Zones 3–6. Originated by Albert F. Yaeger; introduced about 1963 by Dahliatown Nurseries. Single, true pink florets.

S. × *josiflexa* 'Royalty'. USDA Zones 3–6. Introduced in 1937 by Isabella Preston. Deep violet buds open to pink-lavender, becoming lighter with age. A dense grower and the darkest of all cultivars. Susceptible to MLO, manifested as witches'-broom.

Related *Syringa* cultivars of interest from S. × *josiflexa* × S. × *prestoniae*:

S. 'Minuet'. Originated by William A. Cumming, Morden Research Station, Manitoba; introduced in 1972. Single, China rose to clear pink florets.

S. 'Miss Canada'. Originated by William A. Cumming, Morden Research Station, Manitoba; introduced in 1967. Bright pink-lavender, single flowers; tends to become leggy.

# *Syringa* × *laciniata*
## CUT LEAF LILAC

Oleaceae. USDA Zones 5–7. Native to northwestern China. Introduced into Turkey in the 17th century.

DESCRIPTION: Deciduous shrub to 6–8 ft. high and 9 ft. wide or wider, with arching, broad habit and numerous small (0.4 in.) stems.
*Leaves:* Glabrous, variably pinnate, to 2.5 in. long, strong green; unique, delicate, compound foliage.
*Flowers:* Pale lilac, fragrant, loose, single, in lateral panicles to 3 in. long; late spring.
*Fruit:* A capsule, not conspicuous.

CULTURE: Needs sun, but grows in partial shade in southerly latitudes; prefers moist, rich, well-drained soil, but tolerates all but the wettest and driest soils.
*Disease and insect problems:* Relatively disease-free, but some MLO, manifested as witches'-broom.
*Transplanting:* Balled and burlapped or container-grown in spring and fall; bare root in spring.
*Propagation:* By softwood cuttings and tissue culture.

LANDSCAPE VALUE: A graceful, small, May-blooming shrub, with lovely foliage and flowers. Clusters of pale lilac flowers are produced toward the ends of branches. A handsome species often confused in the trade.

Plant may be observed at AA, ATL, BBG, CBG, DEN, HUN, IES, LAC, LNG, MOD, MOR, MRT, MUN, NEW, RBC, RKEW, WIN.

Related *Syringa* variety of interest:

S. *oblata* var. *dilatata*. Lovely shrub with very pale, lilac flowers. Grows to 8 ft. high and as wide, with mounded habit. Differs from species in looser inflorescences and more open form. Valuable for unusual fall color of maroon with yellow undertones. Good mildew resistance if planted in favorable conditions (i.e., sun, air circulation, and good drainage).

# *Syringa meyeri* 'Palibin'
## MEYER LILAC

Oleaceae. USDA Zones 4–7(8). Discovered in 1909 at Fengtai, near Beijing, China, by Frank N. Meyer, who sent cuttings to the USDA.

DESCRIPTION: Deciduous shrub growing slowly to 3–5 ft. high and 4–7 ft. wide, with dense, uniform, rounded, mounded habit.
*Leaves:* Opposite, simple, elliptic-ovate, small, 0.75–1.5 in. long, with wavy margins; young leaves burgundy, turning deep green; no fall color.
*Flowers:* Deep purple buds open pink-white to violet, in dense panicles, 4 in. long and 2.5 in. wide, less fragrant than those of S. *vulgaris;* May, with an occasional second bloom in September.
*Fruit:* A capsule 0.5–0.75 in. long.

CULTURE: Needs sun, but grows in light shade in southerly latitudes; needs well-drained soil; does not tolerate wet conditions; seedlings need protection during first winter since shallow root system is readily damaged by heavy freezing and rapid thawing; easy to cultivate.
*Disease and insect problems:* Relatively disease-free; resistant to powdery mildew.
*Transplanting:* Balled and burlapped or container-grown in spring and fall; bare root in spring.
*Propagation:* By seed (variable) and softwood cuttings, which are not easy but more reliable for the dwarf form.

LANDSCAPE VALUE: A delightful, small shrub; one of the most dwarf lilacs. A delicately textured plant, with tight, compact, neat habit. Good for massed plantings. Abundant flowers bloom before foliage, almost completely covering shrub. Flowers fragrant, but without the strong scent of the common lilac. Has been grown in United Kingdom for many years as a rock garden shrub. Quite resistant to common lilac diseases and insects and one of the most maintenance-free lilacs. Early flower buds can be injured by late frost. Judicious pruning after flowering is beneficial. Received RHS Award of Garden Merit.

Plant may be observed at AA, ABF, BBG, BC, BEA, BER, BIC, BOE, CBG, CIN, DEN, DUK, HOL, LNG, LWD, MNL,

*Syringa* 'Miss Canada' (E. Hasselkus)

*Syringa* 'Minuet' (C. Holetich)

*Syringa* × *laciniata* (E. Hasselkus)

*Syringa meyeri* 'Palibin' (N. Brewster)

*Syringa oblata* var. *dilatata* (K. Bachtell)

*Syringa meyeri* 'Palibin' continued

MOD, MRT, MUN, NEB, NEW, OWG, RBC, RKEW, SEC, SPR, WIN, WIS.

Related species and cultivar of interest:

*Syringa microphylla.* Little Leaf Lilac. USDA Zones 5–7(8). Similar in blossom to *S. meyeri* 'Palibin', but rose-pink blooms appear in May–early June (and sparsely in fall) in panicles 2–3 in. long and 1.5 in. wide. Has smaller leaves but is a taller plant, reaching about 6 ft. high and 9–10 ft. wide. Not well known due to difficulty in propagating by traditional methods. Requires little renewal pruning. Attractive when grown as a standard plant in the landscape. Good disease and insect resistance in proper sites.

*S. microphylla* 'Superba'. Zones 5–7. Introduced in 1910 by William Purdom. Deep pink blossoms appear later and are lighter than those of the species. Long flowering period, intermittently May–October.

# *Syringa patula* 'Miss Kim'
## MISS KIM LILAC

Oleaceae. USDA Zones 3–7. Species first collected in 1895 by Miss Sonntag of Russian Legation near Tap Tong, China, and then in 1914 by E. H. Wilson. The first-named cultivar, 'Miss Kim', was grown from seed collected in 1947 by E. M. Meader; selected and named in 1954 by Albert F. Yaeger, New Hampshire Agriculture and Experimental Station.

DESCRIPTION: Deciduous shrub growing slowly to 4–7 ft. high and 4–6 ft. wide, with habit more upright than wide.
*Leaves:* Opposite, simple, elliptic to oblong, 2–5 in. long and 0.5–2 in. wide, dark green, pubescent beneath, turning a good mauve-purple in fall.
*Flowers:* Lilac (sometimes lavender-pink, fading to ice-blue), fragrant, with ascending heads, abundant, billowy; May–June.
*Fruit:* A capsule, not conspicuous.
*Winter aspect:* Slender, erect branches; young stems downy, burgundy.

CULTURE: Needs sun, tolerates light shade in southerly latitudes; needs good air circulation; prefers moist, rich, well-drained, neutral soil, but tolerates all but the wettest and driest soils; easy to cultivate.
*Disease and insect problems:* Resistant to powdery mildew; not seriously affected by other lilac diseases and insects.
*Transplanting:* Balled and burlapped or container-grown in spring and fall; bare root in spring.
*Propagation:* By softwood cuttings and tissue culture.

LANDSCAPE VALUE: The feathery blossoms of this lovely shrub have the spicy fragrance of cloves. A reasonably heavy bloomer, although blooms are not large. Deep purple buds open to blue-lavender flowers after peak blooming season of *S. vulgaris*. One of its greatest merits is its slow-growing, dwarf stature. An excellent rock garden plant, and one of the few lilacs with fall color. Suggest planting in groups. Grows well in a warm climate; self-seeds abundantly and could be good parent for useful cultivars. Received RHS Award of Garden Merit.

Plant may be observed at AA, BBG, BF, BIC, CBG, CIN, CUH, DEN, DUK, HOL, LNG, LWD, MOD, MNL, MRT, MUN, NEB, NEW, OWN, RBC, RKEW, SEC, SPR, WIS.

# *Syringa* × *prestoniae*
## PRESTON HYBRID LILACS
## CANADIAN HYBRID LILACS

Parentage: *S. reflexa* × *S. villosa*. Oleaceae. USDA Zones 2–7. Originated in the 1920s and 1930s by Isabella Preston of the Central Experimental Farm, Ottawa, Ontario, Canada.

DESCRIPTION: Deciduous shrub generally growing at moderate rate to 10–12 ft. tall, with strong, vigorous, non-suckering habit.
*Leaves:* Elliptic to oblong, to 7 in. long.
*Flowers:* Pink to lavender-pink (white and deep purple on some newer cultivars), with abundant seed, in nodding inflorescences on current year's shoots; May–June.
*Fruit:* Not ornamental.

CULTURE: Needs sun, but grows in partial shade in southerly latitudes; prefers moist, rich, well-drained soil, but tolerates all but the wettest and driest soils; needs open, sunny location with good air circulation.
*Disease and insect problems:* MLO, manifested as witches'-broom.
*Transplanting:* Balled and burlapped or container-grown in spring and fall; bare root in spring.
*Propagation:* By cuttings.

LANDSCAPE VALUE: This beautiful, extremely hardy, late-blooming shrub is taller and notably different from *S. vulgaris* in flower, foliage, fragrance, and habit. Effective as specimen shrub in the small garden. Where space permits, grouping *S.* × *prestoniae* with other species and cultivars of *Syringa* allows appreciation and enjoyment of the fascinating variety of lilac attributes. Prune *S.* × *prestoniae* to 3–5 trunks when young to keep full growth; blooms as young plant. Rejuvenation more difficult than for *S. vulgaris*. An important shrub for North America because of its hardiness; however, caution must be observed because of its susceptibility to MLO.

*Syringa patula* 'Miss Kim' (N. Brewster)

*Syringa patula* 'Miss Kim' (R. Klehm)

*Syringa × prestoniae* 'Ethel M. Webster'
(C. Holetich)

*Syringa × prestoniae* 'Alice Rose Foster' (C. Holetich)

*Syringa × prestoniae* 'Nike' (C. Holetich)

*Syringa* × *prestoniae* continued

When Isabella Preston crossed *S. villosa* with pollen of *S. reflexa*, she created a whole new group of late-blooming lilacs. Many Preston hybrids, often named to honor Shakespearian women, are similar to each other and thus difficult to obtain absolutely true to name. Numerous other attractive cultivars—with similar attributes—were subsequently added by Skinner, Bugala, Cumming, Alexander, Yaeger, Rogers, and Fiala.

Plant may be observed at AA, BBG, CUH, DEN, HOL, LNG, LWD, NEW, RBC, SPR, WIN.

*Syringa* × *prestoniae* cultivars of interest:

*S.* × *prestoniae* 'Alice Rose Foster'. Introduced in 1968 by John H. Alexander of Dahliatown Nurseries. Single, pink flowers.

*S.* × *prestoniae* 'Ethel M. Webster'. Originated by Isabella Preston; introduced in 1951. Single, flesh-pink, medium-sized, compact flowers in wide, loose panicles, May–June.

*S.* × *prestoniae* 'Isabella'. Introduced in 1928 by Isabella Preston. Single, pink flowers.

*S.* × *prestoniae* 'Nike'. Originated by Wladyshaw Bugala. Single, violet flowers.

# Syringa vulgaris
## COMMON LILAC

Oleaceae. USDA Zones 4–7(8). Native to southeastern Europe. Introduced into cultivation in North America by early settlers.

DESCRIPTION: Deciduous shrub growing at moderate rate to 8–16(20) ft. high and 6–15 ft. wide, with upright, irregular habit, becoming leggy with age.
*Leaves:* Opposite, simple, broad-ovate (heart-shaped), 2.5–5 in. long, with smooth margins, dark gray-green to dark blue-green; no conspicuous fall color.
*Flowers:* From white, pink, lavender, lilac, purple, and magenta to subtle combinations of these colors; range from single to multipetaled blooms; florets 0.3 in. long, in erect pyramidal spikes 4–10 in. long; May in cooler climates, earlier in warmer climates.
*Fruit:* A dehiscent, leathery capsule, about 5–8 in. long, with winged seeds.
*Winter aspect:* Tannish gray bark; fruit persisting to spring.

CULTURE: Thrives in cool climates with plentiful sun, but grows in partial shade in southerly latitudes; likes good air circulation; prefers moist, rich, well-drained soil amended with leaf mold, but adapts to a variety of neutral and alkaline soil conditions, if not too wet or dry.
*Disease and insect problems:* Mildew on foliage is unsightly but not serious to the health of the plant; borer on stressed plants; scale; occasional leaf miner, twig blight, and bacterial blight.
*Transplanting:* Best in fall after leaves have fallen.
*Propagation:* By softwood cuttings and division of root stock.

LANDSCAPE VALUE: Perhaps no other shrub species, except for some of the *Rosa* species, has been as widely used as a parent in the making of cultivars. There are hundreds of *S. vulgaris* cultivars—valued for their dense, glorious, colorful blooms, as well as their strong fragrance and hardiness, although they tend to be less vigorous in southerly latitudes. They make exquisite specimen plants, extremely attractive massed plantings, and effective privacy screens; when tightly clipped, they create a formal hedge. Often picturesque in old age, with rough, spiral-patterned bark. Because of their suckering tendency, they need regular maintenance. Renewal prune all lilacs every year or two by removing oldest stems at base to open up center for air circulation and so reduce tendency to mildew. Old blooms should be removed as soon as they fade; flower buds for next year's bloom are initiated within weeks of the current year's bloom.

Plant may be observed at AA, BBG, BIC, BIR, BOE, CBG, COX, DEN, FUL, HOL, HUN, LAC, LNG, LWD, MOD, MRT, OWG, RBC, RKEW, VDG, WIN.

*Syringa vulgaris* cultivars of interest:

*S. vulgaris* 'Agincourt Beauty'. Introduced in 1973 by L. K. Slater. Of special value for its extremely large, deep purple florets.

*S. vulgaris* 'Albert F. Holden'. Unique, large, open panicles of flowers; petals are deep purple inside, silvery blush on reverse. In windy conditions, the colors move in waves. Moderately fragrant, with dark green, disease-resistant foliage; to 7 ft. high.

*S. vulgaris* 'Blue Skies'. Developed by Ralph Moore and introduced by Monrovia Nurseries, Azusa, California. Light lavender-blue flowers. Vigorous grower reaching 10–12 ft. high; tolerates drought. Unique in that it requires virtually no winter chilling and blooms as well in USDA Zones 9–10 as in northerly latitudes; tolerates temperatures to −30°F.

*S. vulgaris* 'Dwight D. Eisenhower'. Introduced in 1968 by R. A. Fenicchia. Multipetaled flowers are beautiful pale to medium blue, slightly tinged with lavender. Excellent annual bloomer.

*S. vulgaris* 'Edith Cavell'. Full, medium-sized shrub with exceptionally lovely double flowers. Pale, sulfur-yellow

*Syringa vulgaris* 'Edward J. Gardner' (E. Hasselkus)

*Syringa vulgaris* 'Krasavitsa Moskvy' (C. Holetich)

*Syringa vulgaris* 'Primrose' (Winterthur Gardens)

*Syringa vulgaris* 'Rochester' (E. Hasselkus)

*Syringa vulgaris* continued

buds open to cream-colored to pure white flowers, borne in heavy, open, lacelike clusters. Sweet fragrance.

*S. vulgaris* 'Edward J. Gardner'. Introduced in 1950 by Gardner. One of the most beautiful double pinks; a fragrant, glorious, pale selection that some authorities believe has no peer among the *S. vulgaris* cultivars. Reaches 4 ft. high; subject to frost damage. Highly recommended by The Morton Arboretum.

*S. vulgaris* 'Emile Lemoine'. Double, pink-lavender florets on smallish thyrse. Showy shrub reaching 7 ft. high.

*S. vulgaris* 'Krasavitsa Moskvy'. Beauty of Moscow. Introduced in 1947 by L. Kolesnikov, Russia. Buds, tinted a lavender-rose, open to spectacular, creamy white, fragrant, double florets, tinged with pale lilac. Finest of this group in the authors' opinion. Strong, upright grower reaching a robust 12–15 ft. high. Highly recommended by The Morton Arboretum.

*S. vulgaris* 'Lavender Lady' (*S. vulgaris* × *S. laciniata*). Introduced in 1954 by W. E. Lamments. Lavender-purple, single, fragrant flowers. Open habit. Heat-tolerant.

*S. vulgaris* 'Ludwig Spaeth'. Large, single, deep purple, fragrant florets on large, compound thyrse; outstanding display. Vigorous plant reaching 8 ft. high; subject to frost damage. Received RHS Award of Garden Merit.

*S. vulgaris* 'Marie Frances'. Single, shrimp-pink flowers; small-statured, upright shrub; only 5.5 ft. high after 15 years. Named for Fr. John Fiala's sister.

*S. vulgaris* 'Mieczta'. Russian introduction. Large violet florets; strong, upright grower; less susceptible than many to mildew and leaf necrosis.

*S. vulgaris* 'Miss Ellen Willmott'. Lovely, showy, very fragrant, double flowers of creamy white, nearly twice as large as those of other white lilacs. Grows to 6–12 ft. high, with upright habit. An old-time, proven favorite.

*S. vulgaris* 'Primrose'. Introduced in 1949 by G. Maarse, Netherlands. Green-yellow buds open to light primrose yellow flowers during early stage of bloom, but the color often fades. Considerable variation in depth of color. Compact, unusual shrub of unique color. Experts suggest that Albert Lumley and Holden strains appear to be best for true yellow color. Color range is strongly affected by spring climatic conditions.

*S. vulgaris* 'Rochester'. Introduced in 1971 by Grant; seedling of 'Edith Cavell'. Slow-growing, with single, lustrous, waxlike, white blooms; one of the loveliest. Easily distinguishable in that a high percentage of the flowers have a corolla with 5 or more petals.

*S. vulgaris* 'Sensation'. Introduced in 1939 by D. Eveleens Maarse, Netherlands; sport of 'Hugo de Vries'. Unique blossoms of smaller, bicolored, single florets; deep purple buds open to creamy-margined, purple flowers. Magnificent and effective. Later blooming.

*S. vulgaris* 'Slater's Elegance'. Introduced in 1983 by L. K. Slater. Huge panicles of flowers with tint of yellow mixed with creamy white; petals to 1 in. in diameter.

*S. vulgaris* 'Victor Lemoine'. Double, lavender-pink florets on large, compound thyrse. Showy display; beautiful even in bud. Grows to 8 ft. high; seems disease-tolerant.

*S. vulgaris* 'Wedgwood Blue'. Another good blue with *S.* 'Rochester' as a parent. Named for the blue background of Wedgwood pottery. Pink buds open to large, blue, wisteria-type panicles. Upright, rounded habit; disease-resistant foliage.

*S. vulgaris* 'Wonder Blue'. One of the most typical of the blue lilacs. Dwarf habit, about 3–4(5) ft. tall. Sold as cultivar 'Little Boy Blue', but registered as 'Wonder Blue'.

*S. vulgaris* 'Yankee Doodle'. One of the deepest and darkest of the purple lilacs; profuse bloomer with large panicles and individual flowers 1 in. across. From Fr. John L. Fiala's Falconskeape Gardens, Medina, Ohio.

# *Tabernaemontana divaricata*
## CREPE JASMINE
## PAPER GARDENIA

Synonym: *Ervatamia divaricata*. Apocynaceae. USDA Zone 10. Native to India.

DESCRIPTION: Broad-leaved evergreen growing slowly to 8–10 ft. high., with spreading habit.
*Leaves:* Thin, ovate, long-pointed, paired, 3–5 in. long.
*Flowers:* White, with tubular corollas 1 in. long and 5–6 broad, crepey lobes, in clusters at branch tips; year-round.

CULTURE: Grows in sun or shade in clay or loam; tolerates most adverse environmental conditions; not affected by salt and pollution.
*Disease and insect problems:* None serious.
*Transplanting:* Easy.
*Propagation:* By cuttings.

LANDSCAPE VALUE: A very pretty green shrub with white, crepelike flowers all year; fragrant at night. Can be pruned into a variety of attractive shapes; shows particularly well when trained in an Oriental manner.

Plant may be observed at BBG, BOK, HUN, LAC, LWD, MIS, RKEW, WAI.

*Syringa vulgaris* 'Sensation' (C. Holetich)

*Tabernaemontana divaricata* (V. Lauritzen)

*Syringa vulgaris* 'Slater's Elegance' (C. Holetich)

*Tabernaemontana divaricata* (V. Lauritzen)

## *Taxus baccata* 'Adpressa Fowle'
## DWARF BOXLEAF ENGLISH YEW

Taxaceae. USDA Zones 5–7. Species native to Europe, North Africa. Cultivar introduced by Weston Nurseries, Hopkinton, Massachusetts.

DESCRIPTION: Evergreen conifer growing very slowly to 7 ft. high and 16 ft. wide, with compact habit.
*Leaves:* Broadly ovate to oblong, heavy-textured, 0.5–0.75 in. long, very uniform, black-green above, paler beneath.
*Winter aspect:* Ascending, broad, bushy limbs of uneven length.

CULTURE: Grows in sun and shade in all but highly acid soil; prefers a pH of 7.0–7.5; tolerates wind and some drought, but not wet conditions.
*Disease and insect problems:* Rare.
*Transplanting:* Easy, balled and burlapped.
*Propagation:* Easy by cuttings in fall.

LANDSCAPE VALUE: A beautiful, textured shrub that tolerates more shade than any other conifer. Excellent as an evergreen hedge or an understory shrub. Regenerates well after pruning.

Plant may be observed at AA, BBG, BLO, CIN, DAW, DEN, DOW, FIL, LNG, NEW, OWG, PAL, PLF, RKEW, SEC, USN.

Other *Taxus baccata* cultivars of interest:

*T. baccata* 'Beanpole'. Resembles 'Fastigiata Robusta' but more fastigiate and leaves narrower.
*T. baccata* 'Fastigiata Robusta'. Excellent accent plant, with rigidly upright branches.

Related *Taxus* cultivar of interest:

*Taxus × media* 'Runyan' (*T. baccata × T. cuspidata*). Exceptionally dark green leaves and dense growth habit. Grows 15 in. per year to 4 ft. tall and 8 ft. wide. Very hardy.

## *Tecoma stans*
## YELLOWBELLS
## TRUMPET BUSH
## YELLOW ELDER

Bignoniaceae. USDA Zone 10. Native to Argentina and North America, from Florida south to Mexico. Introduced into cultivation in 1730.

DESCRIPTION: Broad-leaved evergreen growing quickly to 15 ft. high, with erect, bushy habit.
*Leaves:* Medium green, 4 in. long.
*Flowers:* Bright yellow, bell-shaped, 2 in. across; fall.

CULTURE: Likes sun, heat, ample moisture, and deep soil; performs best in sites with summer heat and moist soil; tolerates wind and salt air.
*Disease and insect problems:* None.
*Transplanting:* Deep root system.
*Propagation:* By cuttings and seed.

LANDSCAPE VALUE: A very showy shrub with clusters of wonderful trumpetlike, yellow blossoms. Useful for large borders and boundary planting. Needs heavy feeding. Cut faded flowers to prolong bloom. Does not like frost, but if frozen back may bloom again the next year from new wood at base of plant. Can become somewhat of a nuisance since it reseeds itself easily in warm climates.

Plant may be observed at MMA, RKEW, SAB, WAI.

*Tecoma stans* variety of interest:

*T. stans* var. *angustata*. Narrow, more deeply toothed leaves and more cold-resistant than the species. Grows in Arizona, Texas, and into Mexico.

*Taxus baccata* 'Adpressa Fowle' (N. Brewster)

*Taxus baccata* 'Fastigiata Robusta' (N. Brewster)

*Taxus* × *media* 'Runyan' (M. Vehr)

*Tecoma stans* var. *angustata* (B. Simpson)

*Tecoma stans* var. *angustata* (B. Simpson)

## *Thevetia thevetioides*
## LUCKY NUT

Apocynaceae. USDA Zones 9–10. Native to Mexico and the West Indies.

DESCRIPTION: Broad-leaved evergreen growing rapidly to 12–15 ft. high and 12 ft. wide, with full, rounded habit.
*Leaves:* Narrow, alternate and entire, linear-lanceolate, 3–6 in. long and 1–2 in. wide, leathery, dark green, similar to Oleander leaves but corrugated and heavily veined beneath.
*Flowers:* Yellow to yellow-orange, funnel-shaped, 2–4 in. across and 2–3 in. long, with 5 lobes, in terminal stalked clusters, mildly fragrant; June/July–early winter.
*Fruit:* Thin, triangular, fleshy, 1-seeded, 1 in. across, red, ripening to black, following bloom.
*Winter aspect:* Open branching habit.

CULTURE: Likes sun and well-drained, fertile, sandy soil; does well on the seacoast; foliage may burn in strong storms.
*Disease and insect problems:* None.
*Transplanting:* Easy, container-grown.
*Propagation:* By seed and cuttings.

LANDSCAPE VALUE: Provides an almost continuous show of brilliant yellow flowers, which appear in large clusters beginning in summer. Flowers have pleasing fragrance. Use as specimen or for screening. Handsome container plant for colder climates. Thrives in heat, although desert heat may wilt flowers in summer. In Hawaii has naturalized in dry areas. Tolerates light frost. All parts of shrub are very poisonous like those of the related *Nerium* (Oleander). Fruit, known as lucky nut, is carried as charm in West Indies. Remove overcrowded shoots. Genus name commemorates 16th-century French monk, André Thevet, who traveled in Brazil.

Plant may be observed at LAC, RAN, WAI.

## *Thujopsis dolabrata* 'Nana'
## FALSE ARBORVITAE

Cupressaceae. USDA Zones 5–7. Species native to Japan. Cultivar introduced to United Kingdom in 1861 by James G. Veitch.

DESCRIPTION: Evergreen conifer growing slowly to 4 ft. high and as wide, with flat-topped, dense, bushy habit, without central leader.
*Leaves:* Ovate, fan-shaped, 0.08 in. long, bright green in summer and in winter, with white marks beneath.
*Winter aspect:* Branchlets arranged in opposite rows.

CULTURE: Thrives in sun but tolerates shade; needs some shade in warmer regions with a high humidity; prefers rich loam with a pH of 6.5–7.0; needs protection from wind and drying winter winds, which can burn the plant.
*Disease and insect problems:* None serious.
*Transplanting:* Easy, container-grown.
*Propagation:* By cuttings in November.

LANDSCAPE VALUE: A beautiful, thick, spreading cushion for shrub borders or low beds. Smaller and more finely textured than species. Broader and flatter than *Thuja*, with larger leaves.

Plant may be observed at AA, ABF, BBG, BSG, CUH, DEN, GCC, MCG, MUN, NCS, UBC, USN, VDG.

## *Tsuga canadensis* 'Jeddeloh'
## CANADIAN HEMLOCK

Pinaceae. USDA Zones 3–7. Species native to North America, from Hudson's Bay to the Carolinas. Cultivar introduced in 1950 by J. D. zu Jeddeloh, Germany.

DESCRIPTION: Evergreen conifer growing slowly to 4 ft. high and 6 ft. wide, with graceful, hemispherical habit.
*Leaves:* 0.25–0.7 in. long and 0.08–0.1 in. wide, bright, dark green above, lighter green beneath, with gray-white stomatal bands.

CULTURE: Thrives in partial shade in fertile, heavy, moist, well-drained loam with a pH of 6.0–7.0; does not tolerate wind; very sensitive to drought.
*Disease and insect problems:* Leaf minor, scale, spider mite, woolly aphid; a dormant oil spray in winter is helpful.
*Transplanting:* Easy, container-grown.
*Propagation:* By cuttings and layering.

*Tsuga canadensis* 'Jeddeloh' (J. Elsley)

*Thevetia thevetioides* (N. Brewster)

*Thevetia thevetioides* (R. Jones)

*Thujopsis dolabrata* 'Nana' (N. Brewster)

*Thujopsis dolabrata* 'Nana' (N. Brewster)

*Tsuga canadensis* 'Jervis' (N. Brewster)

*Tsuga canadensis* 'Jervis' (N. Brewster)

*Tsuga canadensis* 'Jeddeloh' continued

LANDSCAPE VALUE: A magnificent, graceful plant with stable habit. Attractive in rock gardens and shrub borders; may be grown in containers if watered regularly. Branches arranged in unique spiral, creating funnel-like depression in center. Performs poorly in hot, dry, sunny locations or alkaline soils. Cannot compete with root systems of other woody plants.

Plant may be observed at AA, ATL, BBG, BF, CAL, CBG, DEN, HOL, LWD, MOR, NCS, NEW, PAL, PLF, UBC, USN, VDG.

Other *Tsuga canadensis* cultivars of interest:

*T. canadensis* 'Bennett'. Very compact, broader than high, with flat depression in center. Grows 6 in. per year to reach 4 ft. high. Introduced in 1920 by M. Bennett, Highlands, New Jersey.

*T. canadensis* 'Jervis'. One of the smallest cultivars, growing to 3 ft. high and as wide; compressed, dense, twiggy habit, with irregularly arranged branches.

# *Ungnadia speciosa*
## MEXICAN BUCKEYE

Sapindaceae. USDA Zones 6–10. Native to the United States and Mexico. Introduced into cultivation in 1850.

DESCRIPTION: Deciduous (USDA Zones 6–7) to semi-evergreen shrub (USDA Zones 8–10), growing 1–2 ft. per year to 15–25 ft. high, with multistemmed habit; new shoots rise from base every year, while old ones continue to grow actively.
*Leaves:* Compound, odd-pinnate, alternate, 6–12 in. long, composed of 5–7 ovate to lanceolate leaflets 3–5 in. long and 0.5 in. wide, leathery, dark green and lustrous above, paler and pubescent to glabrous below, turning bright yellow in fall.
*Flowers:* Pink to purple, about 1 in. wide, borne in pubescent fascicles; spring.
*Fruit:* A 3-lobed (rarely 4-lobed) nutlet; 2 of the black seeds drop to the ground in fall, the 3rd in spring; poisonous if eaten in quantity.
*Winter aspect:* Mottled, gray to brown, thin, smooth bark; multistemmed, multibranching habit; striking fruit persists on branches for 24 months.

CULTURE: Grows in sun and partial shade in alkaline clay, loam, or sand; tolerates wind and drought; usually found in limestone soils along stream banks, in moist canyons, or on bluffs.
*Disease and insect problems:* None.
*Transplanting:* Easy when grown in clay; deep, noninvasive root system.

*Propagation:* By seed, which is highly viable, or by green cuttings to increase an especially desirable variant.

LANDSCAPE VALUE: A little-known, little-used plant with year-round interest. Splendid as specimen, in massed plantings, or as hedge. Branches can be pruned to ground level to encourage fullness. Flowers, which appear about 10 days after those of *Cercis canadensis*, put on a 2-week display; they resemble peach blossoms or redbuds at a distance and are a source of honey.

Plant may be observed at ABF, ABN, BOK, BBG, DAL, HOU, HUN, NCS, RKEW, SAB, VDG.

# *Viburnum* × *burkwoodii* 'Conoy'
## BURKWOOD VIBURNUM

Parentage: *V.* × *burkwoodii* × *V.* × *carlcephalum*. Caprifoliaceae. USDA Zones 7–8. Introduced into cultivation in 1988 by Donald Egolf of the U.S. National Arboretum.

DESCRIPTION: Deciduous to semi-evergreen shrub to 4.5 ft. high and 6 ft. wide, with spreading habit.
*Leaves:* Elliptic to lanceolate, 1.5–2 in. long and 0.75 in. wide, dark, glossy green.
*Flowers:* Dark red buds open creamy white, slightly fragrant, 2–2.5 in. across, stellate, with 20–75 florets; spring.
*Fruit:* A bright red drupe, in mid-August, turning black in October.
*Winter aspect:* Dense branching habit.

CULTURE: Grows in partial to full sun in heavy loam with a pH of 6.0–6.5; tolerates wind.
*Disease and insect problems:* None serious.
*Transplanting:* Easy; finely branched root system.
*Propagation:* By softwood cuttings under mist in June, which produce flowers on terminal shoots the 1st year and profuse flowers by the 3rd or 4th year.

LANDSCAPE VALUE: Extremely attractive as specimen, hedge, or in massed plantings. Restricted annual growth allows easy maintenance. Small, glossy, leathery leaves create a texture like boxwood; leaves bronze slightly in severe cold. Red fruit persists 6–8 weeks. An outstanding *Viburnum* that deserves wider use. Grows in USDA Zone 6 but not as an evergreen.

Plant may be observed at AA, ATL, BEA, BER, BLO, BSG, CIN, CUH, DEN, FIL, GCC, HOL, MOR, MUN, NCS, NEW, OWG, PAL, PLF, RBC, RKEW, SPR, STR, UBC, USN, VDG, WIN, WIS.

Another *Viburnum* × *burkwoodii* cultivar of interest:

*V.* × *burkwoodii* 'Mohawk' (*V.* × *burkwoodii* × *V. carlesii*).
Compact shrub with abundant inflorescences of brilliant,

*Ungnadia speciosa* (G. Stanford)

*Ungnadia speciosa* (G. Stanford)

*Ungnadia speciosa* (G. Stanford)

*Viburnum* × *burkwoodii* 'Conoy' (N. Brewster)

*Viburnum* × *burkwoodii* 'Conoy' (D. Egolf)

*Viburnum* × *burkwoodii* 'Conoy' (D. Egolf)

dark red flower buds that open to white petals with red blotches on reverse side. Flowers have spicy, clove fragrance. Reaches 7–8 ft. high, with equal or wider spread. Brilliant orange-red foliage in fall. Useful as specimen or in shrub border. Introduced in 1953 by Donald Egolf, U.S. National Arboretum. Hardy to USDA Zone 5. Received Pennsylvania Horticultural Society Gold Medal (Styer Award) in 1993.

Related *Viburnum* cultivars of interest:

*V.* × *bodnantense* 'Dawn' (*V. farreri* × *V. grandiflorum*). Vigorous, hardy deciduous shrub with leaves like *V. grandiflorum* and rich, fragrant, deep pink buds opening to white flowers in spring. Species native to northern China; introduced in 1935 by Bodnant Gardens. Received RHS Award of Garden Merit.

*V.* × *bodnantense* 'Deben' (*V. farreri* × *V. grandiflorum*). Rose-pink buds open to fragrant, white flowers tinged with pink, borne in 1–2 in. panicled clusters; flowers in winter on the Northwest and Southeast coasts, and in April farther north. Glorious in bloom, combining best characteristics of the parents. Grows to 7.5–9 ft. tall, with stiff, divaricate (broadly spreading) habit. Leaves are 4 in. long and 1.5 in. wide, bronze to dark green beneath, turning reddish purple in autumn. Fall fruit not ornamental. Needs full sun for best flowering; tolerates wind, but not wet conditions or drought. Pest- and disease-free. Late spring frost can damage flowers. USDA Zones 6–8. Introduced in 1962 by Messrs. Notcutt. Received RHS Award of Garden Merit.

# *Viburnum carlesii* 'Compactum'
## KOREAN SPICE VIBURNUM

Caprifoliaceae. USDA Zones 5–9. Native to Korea. Introduced into cultivation in 1950 by C. Hoogendoorn, Newport, Rhode Island.

DESCRIPTION: Deciduous shrub growing slowly to 3–4 ft. high, with compact habit.
*Leaves:* Acute at base, usually rounded, 2–4 in. long and almost as wide, darker green than the species, turning dull red in fall.
*Flowers:* Pink buds open white, very fragrant, in cymes 2–3 in. across; late April–May.
*Fruit:* Blue-black, nonshowy, in late summer.

CULTURE: Grows in sun or partial shade; prefers loam with a pH of 5.5–6.5; tolerates wind and drought.
*Disease and insect problems:* None serious.
*Transplanting:* Balled and burlapped; does not tolerate root disturbance.

*Propagation:* By softwood cuttings in June–July (difficult); often grafted on *V. lantana*, which may overtake original plant.

LANDSCAPE VALUE: A very compact habit makes this an excellent plant for small gardens—as specimen or in shrub border. The flowers, like those of the species, have strong, clovelike fragrance.

Plant may be observed at AA, BBG, BEA, BF, BIC, BOE, BSG, CBG, CIN, COX, CUH, DOW, DUK, HOL, IES, LNG, LWD, MIS, MRT, MUN, PAL, PLF, STG, USN, VDG, WIN, WIS.

Other *Viburnum carlesii* cultivars of interest:

*V. carlesii* 'Aurora'. Intensely red buds open to pink, then white, very fragrant flowers. Reaches 4–8 ft. high. Received RHS Award of Garden Merit.
*V. carlesii* 'Charis'. Same characteristics as 'Aurora', but with more vigorous growth habit. Both 1950 selections by L. Slinger of Slieve Donard Nursery, Newcastle, Ireland.

Related *Viburnum* cultivars of interest: These three cultivars can withstand −10°F without injury, but will be deciduous at these low temperatures.

*V.* × *carlcephalum* 'Cayuga' (*V. carlesii* × *V. carlcephalum*). USDA Zones 5–8. Introduced in 1953 by Donald Egolf, U.S. National Arboretum. Compact, deciduous shrub growing at medium rate to 4–6 ft. high. An abundance of pink buds open to slightly fragrant, waxy white flowers in dense, compound-umbellate cymes, 5–6 in. across, in late April–May. Leaves have better color than those of the larger flowered *V.* × *carlcephalum*, but flowers not as fragrant as those of *V. carlesii*. Less susceptible to bacterial leaf spot and powdery mildew than *V. carlesii*.
*V.* 'Chippewa' (*V. japonicum* × *V. dilatatum* 'Catskill'). USDA Zones 6–10. Introduced into cultivation in 1973 by Donald Egolf, U.S. National Arboretum. Deciduous (semi-evergreen in Zones 7–10) shrub growing at medium rate to 8 ft. high and 10 ft. wide; multistemmed, globose habit. Flowers are creamy white in cymes 4–6 in. across. Glossy, dark green leaves turn rich, red-purple in fall. Dark red, ovoid fruit in August, persisting into early winter. May be used as specimen, in massed groupings, or as large, informal hedge. This shrub and the related *V.* 'Huron' are cross-compatible, resulting in spectacular fruiting.
*V.* 'Huron' (*V. lobophyllum* × *V. japonicum*). Exhibits same growth, flowering, and fruiting characteristics as 'Chippewa', but with a dull, more elliptic-obovate leaf.

*Viburnum × bodnantense* 'Dawn' (Planting Fields Arboretum)

*Viburnum carlesii* 'Compactum' (J. Poor)

*Viburnum × carlcephalum* 'Cayuga' (D. Egolf)

*Viburnum* 'Chippewa' (D. Egolf)

## Viburnum dilatatum 'Erie'
### LINDEN VIBURNUM

Caprifoliaceae. USDA Zones 5–8. Native to China, Japan. Introduced into cultivation in 1969 by Donald Egolf of the U.S. National Arboretum.

DESCRIPTION: Deciduous shrub to 6 ft. high and 9 ft. wide, with upright, dense habit.
*Leaves:* Short-acuminate, coarsely toothed, 3.5 in. long and 3 in. wide, dull green, turning a good yellow, orange, and red in fall.
*Flowers:* Creamy white, in flat-topped cymes 4–5.5 in. across; mid-May.
*Fruit:* A conspicuous, red, flattened drupe, in August after leaves fall, persisting, becoming coral-pink after the first frost.
*Winter aspect:* Erect, wide-spreading branching habit; abundant inflorescences of fruit persist into late winter.

CULTURE: Likes sun and heavy loam with a pH of 6.0–6.5; tolerates wind.
*Disease and insect problems:* None serious; highly resistant to diseases and insects.
*Transplanting:* Easy, balled and burlapped.
*Propagation:* By cuttings in July.

LANDSCAPE VALUE: An excellent, extremely hardy, heavily flowering and fruiting *Viburnum* that thrives in same areas as the species. Received Pennsylvania Horticultural Society Gold Medal (Styer Award) in 1993.

Plant may be observed at AA, ABF, BBG, BRK, BSG, CHK, CIN, CUH, DAW, DIX, GCC, HOL, LWD, MBG, PAL, PLF, POW, RBC, SEC, SPR, STG, STR, USN, VDG, WIN.

Related *V. dilatatum* cultivars of interest:

*V. dilatatum* 'Catskill'. Slower growing and more compact, reaching 4.5 ft. high and 6.5 ft. wide.

*V. dilatatum* 'Iroquois'. Larger than 'Erie', reaching 7.5 ft. high and 10.5 ft. wide, with unusually large, leathery leaves, heavy flowering, and globose habit; difficult to obtain.

*V. dilatatum* 'Michael Dodge'. Plant literally covered with yellow fruit.

## Viburnum 'Eskimo'

Parentage: *V. × carlcephalum* 'Cayuga' × *V. utile*. Caprifoliaceae. USDA Zones 6–8. Introduced into cultivation in 1982 by Donald Egolf of the U.S. National Arboretum.

DESCRIPTION: Semi-evergreen shrub growing to 4.5 ft. high and 5 ft. wide. in 12 years, with compact habit.
*Leaves:* Obovate-elliptic, apex acute, base obtuse, 3.5 in. long and 1.5 in. wide, dark green.
*Flowers:* Pale cream, with pink tinge on outer edge, globose, in cymes 3–4 in. across, with 80–175 florets; May.
*Fruit:* Dull red, elliptic, in August, turning black in fall.

CULTURE: Grows in full or partial sun in heavy loam with a pH of 6.0–6.5.
*Disease and insect problems:* None serious; resistant to bacterial leaf spot.
*Transplanting:* Easy, balled and burlapped.
*Propagation:* By softwood cuttings under mist, which flower profusely in the 3rd or 4th year.

LANDSCAPE VALUE: An extremely attractive, dense, compact, slow-growing shrub, ideal for the smaller garden. Outstanding display of glossy, dark green foliage and abundant snowball flowers. Flower buds can be frost-damaged in colder regions, although they do survive. Received Pennsylvania Horticultural Society Gold Medal (Styer Award) in 1992.

Plant may be observed at ATL, BSG, CHK, CIN, CUH, DAW, DUK, HOL, MBG, MOR, RBC, RKEW, SEC, SPR, STG, USN.

Related *Viburnum* cultivar of interest:

*V.* 'Chesapeake' (*V. × carlcephalum* 'Cayuga' × *V. utile*). Small flowers on compact shrub reaching 6 ft. high and 10 ft. wide. Not as hardy as 'Eskimo'. Glossy, dark green, leathery leaves turn red to orange in fall. Extremely tolerant of drought. Better suited to southern regions.

*Viburnum dilatatum* 'Erie' (N. Brewster)

*Viburnum dilatatum* 'Iroquois' (N. Brewster)

*Viburnum dilatatum* 'Michael Dodge' (N. Brewster)

*Viburnum* 'Eskimo' (N. Brewster)

## *Viburnum farreri* 'Candidissimum'
### FRAGRANT VIBURNUM

Caprifoliaceae. USDA Zones 6–8. Native to northern China. Introduced into cultivation in the early 20th century by William Purdom for Messrs. Veitch.

DESCRIPTION: Deciduous shrub growing at moderate rate to 8–10 ft. high, with tight, upright habit.
*Leaves:* Obovate, slightly toothed, 1.5–4 in. long and 1–2.75 in. wide, lighter green than species.
*Flowers:* White, in panicled clusters, fragrant, heliotrope-like, before leaves; November in warmer climates, April in cooler climates.
*Fruit:* A small, glossy, light yellow drupe, in August, turning black in fall.

CULTURE: Prefers sun and loam with a pH of 6.5–7.5; tolerates wind.
*Disease and insect problems:* None.
*Transplanting:* Easy, balled and burlapped.
*Propagation:* By softwood cuttings.

LANDSCAPE VALUE: An extremely fragrant shrub. The earliest *Viburnum* to bloom, but flowers may be browned by frost.

Plant may be observed at AA, BER, DAW, LNG, MUN, USN, VDG, WIN.


## *Viburnum lantana* 'Mohican'
### WAYFARING TREE

Caprifoliaceae. USDA Zones 4–8. Native to Europe, North Africa, Asia Minor. Introduced into cultivation in 1956 by Donald Egolf of the U.S. National Arboretum.

DESCRIPTION: Deciduous shrub growing at moderate rate to 7 ft. high and 9 ft. wide in 15 years, with dense, compact, vigorous, globose habit.
*Leaves:* Ovate to oblong-ovate, thick, 4–4.5 in. long and 2–2.5 in. wide, dark green.
*Flowers:* Creamy white, in flat-topped cymes 3–5 in. across; early May.
*Fruit:* A glabrous, orange and red drupe, in July.
*Winter aspect:* Compact branching habit.

CULTURE: Grows in sun and light shade; prefers loam with a pH of 4.5–7.0; tolerates calcareous and dry soils better than other *Viburnum* species.
*Disease and insect problems:* None serious; resistant to bacterial leaf spot.
*Transplanting:* Easy; fibrous-rooted.
*Propagation:* By softwood cuttings.

LANDSCAPE VALUE: An excellent, nonfragrant *Viburnum* for cooler regions. Entire plant is enveloped for 7–10 days in late April–early May by creamy white flowers and expanding green leaves. Fruit begins to ripen in July and remains 4 or more weeks. Original seed of *V. lantana* from Poland.

Plant may be observed at BBG, BEA, BF, BIC, BOE, BRK, BSG, CBG, CHK, CIN, COX, DAW, DOW, MNL, MRT, NEB, RBC, SEC, SPR, USN.


## *Viburnum nudum* 'Winterthur'
### SMOOTH WITHE-ROD

Caprifoliaceae. USDA Zones 5–9. Native to eastern North America. Clone collected in 1961 in southern Delaware by Hal Bruce of Winterthur Gardens.

DESCRIPTION: Deciduous shrub 6 ft. high in 20 years, with upright habit.
*Leaves:* Elliptic, laurel-like, 2.5–4.5 in. long and 1–2.25 in. wide, dark, glossy green, turning a vibrant red-purple in fall.
*Flowers:* Creamy white, uniform, in perfect cymes 2–4 in. across; June.
*Fruit:* An oval berry, white in late summer, turning pink and, ultimately, blue in fall.

CULTURE: Grows well in both wet, shaded spots and sunny, well-drained sites; prefers loam with a pH of 5–6; tolerates wind and wet conditions.
*Disease and insect problems:* None.
*Transplanting:* Easy, balled and burlapped or small bare-root.
*Propagation:* By softwood cuttings in summer.

LANDSCAPE VALUE: A handsome, shiny-leaved, free-flowering shrub, with more compact and refined habit than that of species. Received Pennsylvania Horticultural Society Gold Medal (Styer Award) in 1991. Abundance of fruit in fall accents the claret-colored leaves. Needs cross-pollination with species for good fruiting. Adapts to varied growing conditions.

Plant may be observed at AA, ABF, BEA, BSG, CBG, GCC, MTC, USN, WIN.

*Viburnum farreri* 'Candidissimum' (R. W. Lighty)

*Viburnum lantana* 'Mohican' (D. Egolf)

*Viburnum farreri* 'Candidissimum' (Arnold Arboretum)

*Viburnum nudum* 'Winterthur' (Winterthur Gardens)

*Viburnum nudum* 'Winterthur' (L. Eirhart)

*Viburnum nudum* 'Winterthur' (N. Brewster)

## Viburnum plicatum f. tomentosum 'Shasta'
## DOUBLEFILE VIBURNUM

Caprifoliaceae. USDA Zones 6–8. Introduced into cultivation in 1979 by Donald Egolf of the U.S. National Arboretum.

DESCRIPTION: Deciduous shrub to 6 ft. high and 11 ft. wide, with compact habit.
*Leaves:* Ovate to oblong-ovate, dentate-serrate, 3.5–5 in. long and 2–3 in. wide, dark green, glabrous above, stellate beneath, turning dull, purple-red in fall.
*Flowers:* White, flat, usually 7-rayed, 3.5–4 in. across, outer margin florets sterile, borne in 2 rows along branches; spring.
*Fruit:* A red drupe, maturing to black, in clusters of 70–100, ripening in early August.
*Winter aspect:* Vertical main trunk with tiered, horizontal branches.

CULTURE: Needs sun in northerly latitudes, light shade in southerly latitudes; likes clay or loam with a pH of 6.0–6.5.
*Disease and insect problems:* None serious.
*Transplanting:* Easy, balled and burlapped.
*Propagation:* By softwood cuttings under mist; small plants frequently flower during their 1st season.

LANDSCAPE VALUE: A strongly tiered, horizontal branching habit makes this shrub showy in winter as well as summer. Pure white, sterile marginal florets are half again as large as those of other cultivars and cover the shrub almost entirely in spring. Received Pennsylvania Horticultural Society Gold Medal (Styer Award) in 1991.

Plant may be observed at ABF, ATL, BBG, BC, BEA, BF, BSG, CBG, CHK, CIN, CUH, DAW, DEN, DUK, FIL, HOL, IES, MOR, MRT, NCS, NEB, NEW, RBC, SPR, STG, UBC, USN, VDG.

Other *Viburnum plicatum* f. *tomentosum* cultivars of interest:

*V. plicatum* f. *tomentosum* 'Shoshoni'. Diminutive plant with a dense habit, fine-textured foliage, masses of creamy white flowers, and an abundance of persistent, scarlet fruit. Suitable for foundation plantings, for the rock garden or border, and as an informal or clipped low hedge. This cultivar is a seedling of self-pollinated *Viburnum plicatum* f. *tomentosum* 'Shasta'; the parent has grown to 3.5 ft. high and 7 ft. wide in 17 years. Registered in 1980 by Donald Egolf, U.S. National Arboretum. Hardy in USDA Zones 5–9. May be propagated by softwood or hardwood cuttings.

*V. plicatum* f. *tomentosum* 'Summer Snowflake'. Named by the University of British Columbia Botanical Garden. More compact than the form. Flowers continually throughout summer, although blooms are small.

## Viburnum × rhytidophylloides 'Alleghany'
## LANTANAPHYLLUM VIBURNUM

*Parentage: V. lantana* 'Mohican' × *V. rhytidophyllum.* Caprifoliaceae. USDA Zones 5–8. Introduced in 1958 by Donald Egolf of the U.S. National Arboretum.

DESCRIPTION: Deciduous shrub growing vigorously to 11 ft. high and as wide, with dense, globose habit.
*Leaves:* Elliptic to ovate-lanceolate, 5.5–6.5 in. long and 2.5 in. wide, dark green, leathery.
*Flowers:* Yellowish white, in terminal cymes 3–4 in. across; May–June.
*Fruit:* Brilliant red, in September and October.
*Winter aspect:* Stout, upright habit.

CULTURE: Grows in sun and partial shade; performs best in loam with a pH of 6–7; tolerates wind.
*Disease and insect problems:* None serious.
*Transplanting:* Easy, balled and burlapped.
*Propagation:* By softwood cuttings.

LANDSCAPE VALUE: Provides an abundant display of yellowish white inflorescences above the very dark green foliage. Hardy as far north as USDA Zone 5, yet withstands the heat of USDA Zone 8. May be planted as specimen or screen.

Plant may be observed at AA, ABF, ATL, BBG, BIC, BOE, BSG, CBG, CHK, CIN, COX, DAW, DIX, HUN, LNG, MBG, MRT, MUN, NCS, NEB, NEW, PLF, POW, RBC, RKEW, SEC, SPR, STG, UBC, USN, WIN, WIS.

Related *Viburnum* cultivars of interest:

*V. rhytidophyllum* 'Cree'. USDA Zones 5–8. Deciduous to semi-evergreen shrub with densely branched, compact habit and superior, dark foliage, which remains evergreen in USDA Zone 6. White flowers open in clusters 2–3 in. across; blooms in May in USDA Zone 7. Introduced by Donald Egolf; has grown to 8.5 ft. high and 8 ft. wide in 13 years.

*V.* 'Willowwood' (*V. rhytidophylloides* × *V. lantana*). Outstanding in form, flowering, and fruiting. Second flowering in early autumn. In wide use in the U.S. Midwest; holds its foliage until first severe frost. Larger than 'Alleghany'.

Related *Viburnum* species of interest:

*V.* × *pragense* (*V. rhytidophyllum* × *V. utile*). Prague Viburnum. USDA Zones 6–8. Introduced into cultivation in 1959 by Joseph Vik, Municipal Nurseries, Prague. Broad-leaved evergreen growing quickly to 10 ft. high and 6 ft. wide; upright, oval habit. Flowers pink in bud, opening to creamy white, flat-topped, terminal cymes 3–5 in. across, in April–May. Smaller, glossy, dark green leaves and

*Viburnum plicatum* f. *tomentosum* 'Shasta' (D. Egolf)

*Viburnum plicatum* f. *tomentosum* 'Shasta' (N. Brewster)

*Viburnum × rhytidophylloides*
'Alleghany' (D. Egolf)

*Viburnum × rhytidophylloides*
'Alleghany' (D. Egolf)

*Viburnum × rhytidophylloides* 'Alleghany' (F. Vrugtman)

*Viburnum* 'Willowwood' (N. Brewster)

*Viburnum × pragense* (N. Brewster)

273

tighter habit than *V. rhytidophyllum;* leaves do not drop. Survives −10°F without foliage discoloration. Should be pruned to retain dense form and to keep within bounds. Received RHS Award of Garden Merit.

## *Viburnum rufidulum*
### SOUTHERN BLACK HAW

Caprifoliaceae. USDA Zones 5–9. Native to eastern North America. Introduced into cultivation in 1727.

DESCRIPTION: Deciduous shrub growing at moderate rate to 10–12 ft. high, with rigid growth habit.
*Leaves:* Ovate to obovate, 2–4 in. long and 1–1.5 in. wide, leathery, serrulate, dark green above, glabrous below, turning rich burgundy in fall.
*Flowers:* Pure white, in cymes 3.5–4.5 in. across; May–June.
*Fruit:* Dark blue, pruinose, abundant.
*Winter aspect:* Open branching habit.

CULTURE: Grows in sun and shade in clay with a wide pH range; grows on top of hills, as well as by stream beds.
*Disease and insect problems:* None.
*Transplanting:* Easy.
*Propagation:* By softwood cuttings.

LANDSCAPE VALUE: An extremely tolerant, tough shrub, similar to *V. prunifolium.* Reaches at least 30 ft. high in the wild. Not as attractive as many other viburnums; however, merits attention for its outstanding heat tolerance and its abundance of attractive, dark blue fruit. Valued in hot, dry climates where many other viburnums do not grow well.

Plant may be observed at DAL, SAB.

## *Viburnum sargentii* 'Onondaga'
### SARGENT VIBURNUM

Caprifoliaceae. USDA Zones 4–6. Native to northeastern Asia. Introduced into cultivation in 1966 by Donald Egolf of the U.S. National Arboretum.

DESCRIPTION: Deciduous shrub growing at moderate rate to 6 ft. high and as wide, with globose habit.
*Leaves:* Acuminate, irregular, dentate, base round, 4–4.5 in. long and 3.75 in. wide, dark maroon when young, turning green with reddish tint.
*Flowers:* Red buds open creamy white with pale pink tinge, in cymes 2.5–4 in. across, with sterile marginal florets; May.
*Fruit:* A red, glabrous drupe, not abundant, in August–September.

CULTURE: Grows in sun and shade; prefers loam, but grows in clay, with a pH of 6.0–6.5.
*Disease and insect problems:* None.
*Transplanting:* Easy, balled and burlapped.
*Propagation:* By softwood or hardwood cuttings.

LANDSCAPE VALUE: A small-statured plant adaptable to the smaller garden for use in shrub borders or massed background plantings. Creamy white, sterile, and fertile florets are effectively displayed against the dark-tinged foliage; the young, velvety, fine-textured, dark maroon foliage maintains its maroon tinge as it matures. Plants produce greater foliage display if pruned to induce dense branching. Received RHS Award of Garden Merit.

Plant may be observed at AA, ABF, BBG, BEA, BF, BOE, BSG, CAL, CBG, CHK, CIN, CUH, DAW, DEN, DIX, HOL, GCC, LNG, MOR, MRT, NCS, NEW, RBC, RKEW, SEC, SKY, SPR, USN, WIS.

Other *Viburnum sargentii* cultivars of interest:

*V. sargentii* 'Flavum'. Very light green foliage, yellow anthers, and yellow fruit.

*V. sargentii* 'Susquehanna'. Larger shrub, reaching 12–15 ft. high, with dark green foliage, and upright habit; abundant, yellow-green fruit turns deep red and persists until winter.

Related *Viburnum* cultivar of interest:

*V. setigerum* 'Aurantiacum'. Tea Viburnum. USDA Zones 5–8. Introduced into cultivation in 1931. Deciduous shrub growing at medium rate to 8–12 ft. high with upright, often leggy, multistemmed habit. White, 5-rayed flowers in flat-topped cymes, 1–2 in. across, in May. Puts on a spectacular fall display with its abundance of orange-yellow fruit, a characteristic of the species. Its leggy habit can be controlled with pruning in the fall.

*Viburnum rufidulum* (G. Stanford)

*Viburnum rufidulum* (G. Stanford)

*Viburnum rufidulum* (P. Cox)

*Viburnum sargentii* 'Susquehanna' (E. Hasselkus)

*Viburnum sargentii* 'Onondaga' (E. Hasselkus)

*Viburnum setigerum* 'Aurantiacum' (E. Paine)

## Vitex agnus-castus
### CHASTE TREE

Verbenaceae. USDA Zones 7–9. Native to southern Europe, western Asia. Introduced into cultivation in 1570.

DESCRIPTION: Deciduous shrub growing quickly to 3–4 ft. high in cooler climates (6–12 ft. high in warmer climates), with upright habit and almost vertical branches.
*Leaves:* Opposite, compound, palmate, composed of 5–7 leaflets 2–6 in. long, dark gray-green; no fall color.
*Flowers:* Lilac, fragrant, in racemes 3–6 in. long, borne in terminal panicles 6–12 in. long; June–July in warmer climates, August in cooler climates.
*Fruit:* A small, gray-bronze drupe.
*Winter aspect:* Blotched, grayish bark.

CULTURE: Grows best in full sun and moist, well-drained soil with a neutral pH; dislikes waterlogged soils; tolerates some drought; easy to grow.
*Disease and insect problems:* None serious.
*Transplanting:* Easy.
*Propagation:* Easy, by seed without pre-treatment and by softwood cuttings.

LANDSCAPE VALUE: A vigorous shrub best used as specimen or in massed plantings; can also be espaliered. Entire shrub is aromatic, with silvery leaves and attractive, long-lasting flowers. Blooming period lasts 4 weeks; removing spent blooms is conducive to second flowering. Good for dried arrangements. Romans ground the dried fruit as substitute for black pepper. Treat as herbaceous perennial in northern climates. Prune in late winter or early spring; blooms occur on new growth. May be cut back to 1 ft. if overgrown. Self-sowing; many seedlings occur around mature specimens.

Plant may be observed at ABF, BBG, BF, BRK, BSG, CAL, CBG, HOL, HUN, LNG, NCS, PLF, RKEW, SAB, USN.

*Vitex agnus-castus* cultivars of interest:

*V. agnus-castus* 'Alba'. White-flowered, with smaller leaves; less vigorous and not as cold-hardy as the species, but lovely bloom.
*V. agnus-castus* 'Rosea'. Pink-flowered.
*V. agnus-castus* 'Silver Spire'. Vigorous, white-flowered.

## Vitex negundo var. heterophylla
### CHASTE TREE

Verbenaceae. USDA Zones 6–9. Native to northern China, Mongolia, Korea. Introduced into cultivation in 1697.

DESCRIPTION: Deciduous shrub growing quickly to 3–5 ft. in cooler climates (15 ft. in warmer climates), with loosely branched habit.
*Leaves:* Opposite, oval, elliptic to lanceolate, many-lobed, fine-textured, gray-tomentose beneath.
*Flowers:* Light violet, fragrant, in loose clusters grouped into spikes, 6–9 in. long; July–August.
*Fruit:* A small drupe, not ornamental.

CULTURE: Prefers full sun, warm temperatures, and loose, moist, well-drained soil with a neutral pH.
*Disease and insect problems:* None serious; leaf spot and some root rot.
*Transplanting:* Best if container-grown.
*Propagation:* By softwood cuttings, which root easily.

LANDSCAPE VALUE: A graceful shrub with interesting leaf pattern and fragrant, late blooms on current season's wood. Extremely attractive addition to shrub border. Treat as herbaceous perennial in northern climates. Needs pruning to shape. Cut to about 1 ft. high in spring or back to live wood on old shrubs.

Plant may be observed at ATL, BBG, CBG, CIN, LNG, MRT, NCS, PAL, RKEW, VDG.

Related *Vitex* species of interest:

*V. rotundifolia*. Grows to 3 ft. high, with prostrate to ascending blue flowers.

*Vitex agnus-castus* (D. Brennan)

*Vitex agnus-castus* (D. Brennan)

*Vitex negundo* var. *heterophylla* (G. Gates)

*Vitex agnus-castus* 'Silver Spire' (N. Brewster)

*Vitex negundo* var. *heterophylla* (G. Gates)

277

## Weigela florida 'Variegata'
### OLD-FASHIONED WEIGELA

Caprifoliaceae. USDA Zones 5–8. Native to northern China, Korea, Japan. Introduced into cultivation in 1850.

DESCRIPTION: Deciduous shrub growing at moderate rate to 4–6 ft. high and 6–10 ft. wide, with dense, spreading habit and arching branches.
*Leaves:* Opposite, elliptic, 3–4 in. long and 1.5 in. wide, edged in light yellow-cream; no fall color.
*Flowers:* Deep pink-rose, bell-shaped, 1 in. across; May–June.
*Fruit:* A glabrous capsule, not ornamental.

CULTURE: Needs sun for flowering; adapts to a variety of clay and loam soils, but requires good drainage.
*Disease and insect problems:* None serious.
*Transplanting:* Easy; prune after transplanting since considerable dieback can occur.
*Propagation:* By seed and softwood cuttings in summer.

LANDSCAPE VALUE: Good for massed plantings in shrub border. Handsome when in bloom, although very attractive, variegated foliage is more striking than flowers. Coarse texture is revealed in winter, so plant where it is not a focal point for winter viewing. Needs pruning and shaping to remain attractive. Received RHS Award of Garden Merit.

Plant may be observed at AA, ABF, ATL, BBG, BF, CIN, COX, DAW, DEN, FIL, HUN, LNG, MRT, NCS, NEW, RBC, RKEW, SPR, WIS.

Other *Weigela florida* cultivars of interest:

*W. florida* 'Evita'. Red flowers; grows to 2–3 ft. high with dense, spreading habit; blooms profusely in May–June, often with a light recurrent bloom later in season.
*W. florida* 'Red Prince'. Strong, red flowers, resistant to fading. Upright habit when immature. Grows to 5–7 ft. tall. An Iowa State University introduction.

## Xanthorhiza simplicissima
### YELLOW ROOT

Ranunculaceae. USDA Zones 5–9. Native to the eastern United States, from New York to Florida. Introduced into cultivation in United Kingdom about 1776.

DESCRIPTION: Deciduous shrub growing at moderate rate to 2–3 ft. high, with low, dense, spreading habit.
*Leaves:* Compound, pinnate, sharply lobed or toothed, celery-shaped, composed of about 5 leaflets, with a purplish cast when young, turning rich purple and bronze in fall with yellow highlights.
*Flowers:* Not conspicuous, delicate, star-shaped, brown-purple, 0.2 in. across, borne in drooping racemes 2–4 in. long, before leaves; March–May.
*Fruit:* A follicle, not conspicuous.
*Winter aspect:* Yellow bark.

CULTURE: Grows in sun or partial shade in clay or loam; tolerates wet conditions but not drought; performs best in moist soils, but grows in heavy ones; thrives along streams.
*Disease and insect problems:* None serious.
*Transplanting:* Easy in spring or fall; invasive root system; increases rapidly by underground stolons.
*Propagation:* By seed and division in early spring or fall.

LANDSCAPE VALUE: A low, dense shrub, with neat, uniform shape. Suckers from roots, so spreads freely; should not be used in small areas unless restrained. Valued for handsome foliage and ability to thrive on moist, shady slopes. Requires little care. A genus with a single species, *Xanthorhiza* gets its name from the color under the bark of its roots, which is a source of yellow dye.

Plant may be observed at AA, ABF, ATL, BBG, BF, BIC, BIR, BRK, DUK, GIW, HOL, LWD, MOR, MTC, MUN, NCS, PAL, PLF, RKEW, UBC, USN, VDG.

*Weigela florida* 'Variegata' (J. Elsley)

*Weigela florida* 'Variegata' (J. Elsley)

*Weigela florida* 'Red Prince' (E. Hasselkus)

*Weigela florida* 'Red Prince' (E. Hasselkus)

*Xanthorhiza simplicissima* (Planting Fields Arboretum)

*Xanthorhiza simplicissima* (C. Sawyers)

# Zenobia pulverulenta
## DUSTY ZENOBIA

Ericaceae. USDA Zones 6–9. Native to southeastern United States, from Virginia to South Carolina. Introduced into cultivation in 1801.

DESCRIPTION: Semi-evergreen (USDA Zones 8–9) to deciduous shrub (USDA Zones 6–7), to 2–4 ft. high, with upright, irregular habit.
*Leaves:* Ovate, waxy smooth, 2–3 in. long and 0.75 in. wide, gray to grayish blue-green, turning burgundy in fall.
*Flowers:* Pure white, 0.5 in. wide, bell-shaped, at shoot tips, grouped into long, pendulous racemes; June–early July.
*Fruit:* A 5-valved flat globose capsule.
*Winter aspect:* Upright habit, bending over with age.

CULTURE: Grows in sun and semishade in lime-free, well-drained, sandy, acid soil; does not tolerate drought.
*Disease and insect problems:* None serious.
*Transplanting:* Easy.
*Propagation:* By softwood cuttings in early summer, layering, or division in early spring; seed unreliable.

LANDSCAPE VALUE: A useful ornamental with its elegant clusters of lovely white flowers that resemble very large Lilies-of-the-Valley and its powdery, grayish blue-green foliage that contrasts with greener foliage of other shrubs. Has gracefully arching pink-beige stems. Deep, rich, red-purple fall color adds prolonged seasonal interest. In some cases where grown in USDA Zones 6–7 loses leaves; in southerly latitudes remains evergreen. Blooms when few other shrubs are in flower, perfuming the garden with the scent of anise. Requires occasional pruning after flowering to maximize next season's bloom. Can be maintained at any desired height, from a heavily pruned 2 ft. to a lightly pruned 4–5 ft., thus increasing its versatility. May be used as low, informal hedge; particularly effective for an ericaceous planting. Only species in the genus; named after Zenobia, queen of ancient Palmyra.

Plant may be observed at AA, ABF, ATL, BBG, BC, BER, BIR, BRK, DUK, GIW, HOL, LWD, MOR, MTC, MUN, NCS, PAL, PLF, RKEW, UBC, USN, VDG.

*Zenobia pulverulenta* (G. Koller)

*Zenobia pulverulenta* (A. Bussewitz)

*Zenobia pulverulenta* (A. Bussewitz)

# APPENDIX I

# Directory of Arboreta, Botanical Gardens, Gardens, and Parks

This directory of arboreta, botanical gardens, gardens, and parks is provided so that readers may readily identify some locations where shrubs may be observed. The codes that appear in the text are identified below. In some cases, the listings in the text include only the title shrub. Where possible, the additional shrubs of interest are included.

ABN  Armand Bayou Nature Center
John Grimes, Director
8500 Bay Area Boulevard
P.O. Box 58828
Houston, TX 77258

ABF  Arboretum of the Barnes Foundation
Dr. Timothy Storbeck, Director
57 Lapsley Lane
Merion Station, PA 19066

AA  The Arnold Arboretum
Dr. Robert Cook, Director
Harvard University
125 Arborway
Jamaica Plain, MA 02130-3519

ATL  Atlanta Botanical Garden
P. Alston Glenn, Executive Director
Piedmont Parkway at S. Prado
P.O. Box 77246
Atlanta, GA 30357

BC  Bayard Cutting Arboretum
Daniel D. Tompkins, Director
P.O. Box 466
Oakdale, NY 11769

BEA  W. J. Beal Botanical Garden
Tom Kehler, Director, Campus Park & Planning
Michigan State University
East Lansing, MI 48824

BF  Bernheim Forest Arboretum
Clarence E. Hubbuch, Jr., Horticulturist
Highway 245
Clermont, KY 40110

BER  The Berry Botanic Garden
Dr. Linda McMahan, Executive Director
11505 S.W. Summerville Avenue
Portland, OR 97219

BIC  Bickelhaupt Arboretum
Robert and Frances Bickelhaupt, Co-directors
340 S. 14th Street
Clinton, IA 52732

BIR  Birmingham Botanical Gardens
Gary Gerlach, Director
2612 Lane Park Road
Birmingham, AL 35223

BLO  Bloedel Reserve
Richard A. Brown, Director
7571 N.E. Dolphin Drive
Bainbridge Island, WA 98110-1097

BOE  Boerner Botanical Gardens
William J. Radler, Director
5879 S. 92nd Street
Hales Corners, WI 53130

BOK  Bok Tower Gardens
Jonathan A. Shaw, Director
Burns Avenue & Tower Boulevard
P.O. Box 3810
Lake Wales, FL 33859-3810

BRK   Brookgreen Gardens
Gurdon L. Tarbox, Jr., Director
U.S. Highway 17
South Murrells Inlet, SC 29576

BBG   Brooklyn Botanic Garden
Judith D. Zuk, President
1000 Washington Avenue
Brooklyn, NY 11225-1009

BSG   Brookside Gardens
David Vismara, Director
1500 Glenallan Avenue
Wheaton, MD 20902

CAL   Callaway Gardens
Dr. William E. Barrick, Director
U.S. Highway 27
P.O. Box 2000
Pine Mt., GA 31822

CUH   University of Washington Arboretum
Dr. Clement W. Hamilton, Director
University of Washington
Seattle, WA 98195

CEN   Central Park Conservancy
Arthur Ross Pinetum
81st Street & Central Park West
New York, NY 10024

CHK   Cheekwood Botanical Gardens
Richard C. Page, Director
Forrest Park Drive
Nashville, TN 37205

CBG   Chicago Botanic Garden
Kris Jarantoski, Director
Lake Cook Road
P.O. Box 400
Glencoe, IL 60022

CIN   Cincinnati Zoo and Botanical Garden
David B. Ehrlinger, Director of Horticulture
3400 Vine Street
Cincinnati, OH 45220

COX   Cox Arboretum
Mel Fine, Director
6733 Springboro Pike
Dayton, OH 45449

DAL   Dallas Nature Center
Dr. Geoffrey Stanford
755 Wheatland Road
Dallas, TX 75232

DAW   Dawes Arboretum
Donald R. Hendricks, Director
7770 Jacksontown Road S.E.
Newark, OH 43055

DEN   Denver Botanic Gardens
Richard H. Daley, Executive Director
909 York Street
Denver, CO 80206

DES   Descanso Gardens
Mary Stella Brosius
1418 Descanso Drive
La Cañada, CA 91011

DIN   Dinghushan Arboretum
Yu Sianglin
P.O. Box 1127
Canton, China

DIX   Dixon Gallery and Gardens
John E. Buchanan, Jr., Director
4339 Park Avenue
Memphis, TN 38117

DOW   Dow Gardens
Douglas J. Chapman
1018 W. Main Street
Midland, MI 48640

DUK   Sarah P. Duke Gardens
Dr. William Louis Culberson, Director
Duke University
Box 90341
Durham, NC 27706

FAR   Fairchild Tropical Garden
10901 Old Cutler Road
Miami, FL 33156

FHA   Foster Airport
Hilo, HI 96720

FIL   Filoli Center
Anne Taylor-Morosoli, Executive Director
Cañada Road
Woodside, CA 94062

FOU   Four Arts Garden
Four Arts Plaza
Royal Palm Way
Palm Beach, FL 33480

FUL   Fullerton Arboretum
Dr. David L. Walkington, Director
California State University
Fullerton, CA 92634

GCC   The Garden Center of Greater Cleveland
Alexander A. Apanius, Director
11030 East Boulevard
Cleveland, OH 44106

GIW   Garden in the Woods
David Longland, Executive Director
New England Wildflower Society
180 Hemenway Road
Framingham, MA 01701

GOL   Golden Gate Park
Dr. Elizabeth McClintock
1335 Union Street
San Francisco, CA 94109

HER   Hershey Gardens
Pat McCann
Hotel Road
P.O. Box BB
Hershey, PA 17033

HOL   Holden Arboretum
C. W. Eliot Paine
9500 Sperry Road
Mentor, OH 44060

HOO   Ho'Omaluhia Garden
Kaneohe, Oahu, HI 96744

HOU   Houston Arboretum and Botanical Society
Tom Olson, Director
4501 Woodway
Houston, TX 77024

HUN   Huntington Botanical Gardens
Dr. James P. Folsom, Curator
1151 Oxford Road
San Marino, CA 91108

IES   Institute of Ecosystem Studies Arboretum
Dr. E. Gene Likens, Director
Box AB
Millbrook, NY 12545

JAF   Japan Forestry and Forest Parks
Dr. K. Doi
P.O. Box 16
Tsukuba Norin Kenkyu
Danchi-Nai
Ibaraki, 305 Japan

KOF   Koolau Farmers
45-580 Kam Highway
Kaneohe, HI 96744

LNG   Longenecker Gardens
University of Wisconsin Arboretum
Gregory D. Armstrong, Director
1207 Seminole Highway
Madison, WI 53711

LWD   Longwood Gardens
Frederick E. Roberts, Director
P.O. Box 501
Kennett Square, PA 19348-0501

LAC   Los Angeles County Arboreta and Botanic Gardens
Kenneth C. Smith, Director
301 N. Baldwin Avenue
Arcadia, CA 91007

LYO   Harold L. Lyon Arboretum
University of Hawaii
3860 Manoa Road
Honolulu, HI 86822

MAG   Magnolia Plantations and Gardens
Route 4
Charleston, SC 29407

MBG   Memphis Botanic Garden
George Wise, Director and Horticulturist
750 Cherry Road
Memphis, TN 38117

MCG   McCrillis Gardens
6910 Greentree Road
Bethesda, MD 20034

MER   Mercer Arboretum
Leann Toles, Director
22306 Aldine-Westfield Road
Humble, TX 77338

MID   Middleton Place
Route 4
Charleston, SC 29407

MIS   Missouri Botanical Garden
Dr. Peter Raven, Director
P.O. Box 299
St. Louis, MO 63166

MLG   Massee Lane Gardens
1 Massee Lane
Fort Valley, GA 31030

MMA   Mildred E. Mathias Botanical Garden
Gary Overstreet, Administrative Assistant II,
Biology Department
University of California at Los Angeles
405 Hilgard
Los Angeles CA 90024-1606

MNL  Minnesota Landscape Arboretum
     Peter J. Olin, Director
     3675 Arboretum Drive
     P.O. Box 39
     Chanhassen, MN 55317

MOD  Morden Research Center
     Reg Cucey, Director
     Agriculture Canada
     P.O. Box 3001
     Morden, Manitoba
     Canada R0G 1J0

MOR  Morris Arboretum
     University of Pennsylvania
     Paul Meyer, Director
     9414 Meadowbrook Road
     Philadelphia, PA 19118

MRT  The Morton Arboretum
     Dr. Gerard T. Donnelly, Director
     Route 53
     Lisle, IL 60532-1282

MTC  Mt. Cuba Center
     Dr. Richard W. Lighty, Director
     Box 3570
     Barley Mill Road
     Greenville, DE 19807-0570

MUN  München Botanischer Garten
     Dr. W. Engelhardt
     Menzinger Strasse 63
     D-8000 Munich 19, Germany

NAT  National Tropical Botanical Garden
     Dr. William McK. Klein, Jr., Director
     P.O. Box 340
     Lawai, Kauai, HI 96765

NEB  Nebraska Statewide Arboretum
     Arthur H. Ode, Director
     University of Nebraska
     Lincoln, NE 68583-0715

NEW  The New York Botanical Garden
     Gregory Long, President
     200th Street & Southern Boulevard
     Bronx, NY 10458

NCA  North Carolina Arboretum
     George Briggs, Director
     P.O. Box 6617
     Asheville, NC 28816-6617

NCB  North Carolina Botanical Garden
     Dr. Peter S. White, Director
     CB Box 3375

     Totten Center
     University of North Carolina
     Chapel Hill, NC 27599-3375

NCS  North Carolina State University Arboretum
     Dr. J. C. Raulston, Director
     Box 7609
     North Carolina State University
     Raleigh, NC 27695-7609

OWG  Old Westbury Gardens
     Nelson W. Sterner, Director of Horticulture
     P.O. Box 430
     Old Westbury, NY 11568

PAL  Palmengarten
     Dr. G. Schoser, Director
     Siesmayerstrasse 61
     6000 Frankfurt, Germany

PLF  Planting Fields Arboretum
     Planting Fields Road
     P.O. Box 58
     Oyster Bay, NY 11771

POW  Powell Gardens
     Eric N. Tschanz, Executive Director
     Rte. 1
     Box 90
     Kingsville, MO 64061

RAN  Rancho Santa Ana Botanic Garden
     Dr. Roy L. Taylor, Director
     1500 North College Avenue
     Claremont, CA 91711

RHO  The Rhododendron Species Foundation
     Scott G. Veregara, Director
     P.O. Box 3798
     Federal Way, WA 98063-3798

RBC  Royal Botanical Gardens
     Dr. Gary Watson, Director,
     P.O. Box 399
     Hamilton, Ontario
     Canada L8N 3H8

RKEW Royal Botanic Gardens, Kew
     Professor Ghillean T. Prance, Director
     Richmond
     Surrey TW9 3AB
     United Kingdom

RUT  Rutgers University
     Dr. Bruce Hamilton
     P.O Box 231
     New Brunswick, NJ 08903

SAB   San Antonio Botanical Garden
Eric Lautzenheiser, Director
555 Funston Place
San Antonio, TX 78209

SBB   Santa Barbara Botanic Garden
Dr. Edward L. Schneider, Director
1212 Mission Canyon Road
Santa Barbara, CA 93105

SCZ   Santa Cruz Arboretum
University of California
Bay and High Streets
Santa Cruz, CA 95064

SCT   The Scott Arboretum
Claire E. Sawyers, Director
Swarthmore College
500 College Avenue
Swarthmore, PA 19081-1397

SEC   Secrest Arboretum
Kenneth D. Cochran, Curator
Ohio State University
1680 Madison Avenue
Wooster, OH 44691

SEL   The Marie Selby Botanical Gardens
Larry G. Pardue, Executive Director
811 S. Palm Avenue
Sarasota, FL 34236

SHA   Shanghai Botanical Gardens
Zhang Lian-quan, Director
1100 Long Wu Road
Shanghai 200232, China

SHE   Sherman Library and Gardens
Wade Roberts, Director
247 East Coast Highway
Corona del Mar, CA 92625

SKY   Skylands—New Jersey State Botanical Garden
1304 Scoatsburg Road
Ringwood, NJ 07456

SPR   Spring Grove Arboretum
Thomas Smith
4521 Spring Grove Avenue
Cincinnati, OH 45232

STG   State Botanical Garden of Georgia
Dr. A. J. Lewis, Director
2450 S. Milledge Avenue
Athens, GA 30605

STR   Strybing Arboretum and Botanical Gardens
Walden Valen, Director
9th Avenue & Lincoln Way
San Francisco, CA 94117

UBC   University of British Columbia Botanical Garden
A. Bruce Macdonald, Director
6804 S.W. Marine Dr.
Vancouver, British Columbia
Canada V6T 1W5

UCI   University of California at Irvine
Dr. Harold Koopowitz, Arboretum Director
School of Biological Sciences
Irvine, CA 92717

USN   U.S. National Arboretum
Dr. Thomas S. Elias, Director
3501 New York Avenue N.E.
Washington, DC 20002

VDG   Van Dusen Garden/Vancouver Botanic Gardens
Roy Forster, Curator
525l Oak Street
Vancouver, British Columbia
Canada V6M 4H1

WAI   Waimea Arboretum and Botanical Garden
Keith R. Woolliams, Director
Waimea Falls Park
59-864 Kamehameha Highway
Haleiwa, HI 96712

WAV   Wave Hill
675 W. 252nd Street
Bronx, NY 10471

WIN   Winterthur Museum and Gardens
John Feliciani, Director, Garden Operations
Winterthur, DE 19735

WIS   Royal Horticultural Society Garden, Wisley
Woking
Surrey GU23 6QB
United Kingdom

WOR   Worcester Horticulture Society
John Trexler, Executive Director
Tower Hill Botanic Garden
Boylston, MA 01505

ZOO   ZooAmerica Wildlife Park
Troy Stump, Director
1000 W. Hershey Park Drive
Hershey, PA 17033

# APPENDIX II-A

# Shrub Index with Nursery Source Codes

This index is provided so that readers may locate selected sources for the shrubs presented in this volume. To identify sources for a particular shrub, find the name of the shrub in this index, note the nursery codes after the name, and then refer to Appendix II-B, Directory of Nursery Sources, to obtain the nursery's name and address.

*Abelia chinensis* FOF, HIL, SAN

*Abelia* 'Edward Goucher' AMM, APP, ARN, ATL, BYE, CAL, CAN, CAR, CED, COU, ESV, FOF, GRB, GRR, HIS, HIV, ING, LOU, OKI, MAO, MIT, MOB, MON, NPI, PLE, RSN, SAN, SBN, SPR, STY, SUN, TWO, WAT, WEM, WIG

*Abelia floribunda* MOB, SAN, WEM

*Abelia* × *grandiflora* ALD, ANG, APP, CAL, ESV, GRB, GRR, HOB, ING, KRA, LAK, LOU, LUS, MEL, MON, PRI, SYL, WAR, WES

*Abelia* × *grandiflora* 'Prostrata' MAO, MON, SMT

*Abelia* × *grandiflora* 'Sherwood' AMM, ARN, ATL, CAL, CAN, ENV, FOF, GRA, HIV, LIV, MIT, PLE, SAN, SMT, TWO

*Abeliophyllum distichum* BRS, BUS, CAL, CAM, CAN, CUM, DAY, EAS, ESV, FOF, GOS, GRR, HEO, HER, HIL, HOL, LOS, MAO, MUS, ROY, TWO, WAY, WFF, WIT, WON

*Acanthopanax sieboldianus* 'Variegatus' BIG, ESV, GLA, GRR, LOS, TWO, WES

*Adina rubella* APP, WOD

*Aesculus californica* BER, CAA, CAM, FOF, HIL, NAS, SAN, WOD, YUC

*Aesculus parviflora* CAL, EAS, ESV, HOB, KLE, LOS, MAO, SAL, SHR, SUP, TWO, WAY, WES, WOD, WON

*Aesculus parviflora* 'Rogers' KLE

*Aesculus parviflora* f. *serotina* KLE, SAL, WAY, WOD

*Amelanchier ovalis* 'Pumila' ESV

*Aralia elata* 'Aureovariegata' ESV, FOX

*Aralia elata* 'Variegata' ESV, GRR, HEO

*Aralia spinosa* DUT, EEI, ESV, HAL, HEO, HIL, KLE, LAK, LOU, LAW, LOU, MCL, SHR

*Arctostaphylos bakerii* 'Louis Edmunds' CFN, LAS, NAS, TRL

*Arctostaphylos densiflora* 'Howard McMinn' CFL, HEO, MAO, TRL

*Arctostaphylos densiflora* 'Sentinel' LAS, NAS, TRL

*Arctostaphylos stanfordiana* COL

*Ardisia crenata* ALD, GRA, LOG, LOU

*Ardisia crispa* CAT

*Aronia arbutifolia* 'Brilliantissima' ADA, AMM, APP, ATL, BAI, BCN, BIG, CAL, COC, CON, CUL, CWW, EAS, EIS, FOF, GAN, GRR, GVN, HER, HIN, HLS, HOB, HOO, KAN, KIN, KLE, LAK, LAW, LOT, LUS, MAO, MCK, MOB, MOU, OLD, ONA, PLH, SHE, SNC, SPV, STY, SYN, TEC, TIM, WAU, WEI, WEM, WES, WIL

*Aronia melanocarpa* BAI, BER, BET, BRE, BRK, EAS, ESV, FOF, GAN, GRR, HEO, HER, JWL, KIN, LAK, LAW, LIT, MAO, MCK, NON, PLH, SCA, SCR, SNC, SON, STU, SYN, TEC, WAG, WED, WES

*Azara dentata* ESV, SAR, SKL, SQL, SUC

*Azara petiolaris* BOD, HIL

*Azara serrata* GRR

*Bauhinia lunarioides* LOU, SAB, WOD, YUC

*Berberis darwinii* BRS, ESV, FOF, GRR, HIL, MOB, NAS, WEM

*Berberis* × *gladwynensis* 'William Penn' AMM, APP, CAL, CAN, FOF, HIH, HIS, HIV, LAK, LUS, MAO, MOB, MON, NPI, PLE, STY, SIE, WAT, WIG

*Berberis koreana* BAC, BAI, CRO, DUT, ESV, FOF, GAN, GVN, HEO, JWL, LAK, LIT, MCK, MIN, NON, SNC, TWO, WED, WES, WOD

*Berberis linearifolia* ESV, HIL

*Berberis thunbergii* BAI, BRS, COU, CWW, ESV, FOF, GAN, HAL, HOO, JWL, LAK, KEL, LAW, LIT, LOU, MCK, MEL, MIN, PLH, SNC, TRI, WEI

*Berberis thunbergii* 'Atropurpurea' APP, BAI, BET, BIG, COC, ENV, ESV, FOX, GUE, HIH, HIV, JWL, KDN, KED, LAK, LOT, LUS, MCG, MAO, MCK, MEL, MON, MOU, MUS, ONA, SNC, SPR, STY, TUS, WDL, WES, ZEL

*Berberis thunbergii* 'Bagatelle' BRS, ESV, STY

*Berberis thunbergii* 'Bogozam' MRT

*Berberis thunbergii* 'Globe' BAI, STY

*Berberis thunbergii* 'Kobold' AMM, BET, BRS, CED, ESV, FAI, FOF, GAN, GRR, GRV, GVN, HIL, HIS, HIV, JWL, KIN, LAK, LIT, MON, PLH, SCH, SCR, STY, TUR, TWO, WAU, WEM, WES

*Berberis thunbergii* 'Rose Glow' AMM, APP, BAI, BET, BIG, BRS, CAL, CON, CWW, ENV, ESV, FOF, FOX, GAN, GRR, HIH, HIS, HIV, JWL, KLE, LAK, LOS, LOT, LOU, MAO, MCK, MIT, MOU, MSS, ONA, PLE, PLH, ROY, SCA, SNC, SPV, STU, STY, TWO, VLL, WES, ZEL

*Berberis thunbergii* 'Sparkle' APP, BAC, CWW, FOF, MON, LAK, STY

*Berberis verruculosa* ESV, FOF, FLO, MAO, MCL, MON, PNF

*Berberis × wisleyensis* FOF, GRB, LUS, PNF, PRI

*Brugmansia arborea* LOU, SNS

*Brunfelsia australis* LOG

*Brunfelsia latifolia* LOG

*Brunfelsia pauciflora* MBN, LOU

*Brunfelsia pauciflora* var. *calycina* 'Macrantha' GRA, LOG, LOU, MON, NPI, SAN, WAY

*Buddleia alternifolia* ESV, FOF, GRR, LOU, WAY, WES, WIT

*Buddleia alternifolia* 'Argentea' CAL, HEO, HIL, LOG, WFF

*Buddleia davidii* BAI, FOF, HUD, JWL, LOU, MOU, SHR, SUN, WAY, WES, WIT

*Buddleia davidii* 'Black Knight' BRS, CAL, COC, CRN, CWW, ESV, FOF, GRR, HEO, HIL, KRA, LAK, LOU, MAO, SAN, SHA, SNC, SPR, STY, WAY

*Buddleia davidii* 'Charming' BAI, BLS, BUR, FOF, HIS, KRA, LOU, MOU, WAR, WAU

*Buddleia davidii* 'Deep Lavender' CAL

*Buddleia davidii* 'Dartmoor' WAY

*Buddleia davidii* 'Dubonnet' BAI, CWW, HIS, KEL, MOU, SYL

*Buddleia davidii* 'Empire Blue' ATL, CAL, COC, CWW, ESV, FOF, GAN, HIL, JWL, LAK, LOU, MNR, MOU, NON, SNC, STY, WAY, WES

*Buddleia davidii* 'Fascination' BLS, CWW, ESV, LAL, LOU, MNR, SNC

*Buddleia davidii* 'Harlequin' HOL, LOU, ROY, STY

*Buddleia davidii* 'Pink Delight' BRS, CAL, COC, CON, ESV, GRL, LAL, MEL, MON, SHA, SNC, SYL, TWO, VIE, WAY, WES

*Buddleia davidii* 'Princeton Purple' CAL, LAL, SNC

*Buddleia davidii* 'Royal Red' ATL, CAL, COC, COL, FOF, HIL, JWL, LOU, MAO, MEL, MOU, PLA, SNC, STY, VIE

*Buddleia davidii* 'White Bouquet' CAL, CRN, FOF, HIH, HEO, MOB, MON, STY, WAT

*Buddleia davidii* 'White Profusion' ARN, CAL, COC, CWW, KRA, LOU, MAO, PDN, PLA, PLD, ROY, SNC, STY, WAY, WES

*Buddleia fallowiana* 'Alba' HEO

*Buddleia* 'Glasnevin' HEO

*Buddleia globosa* FOF, HEO, LOU

*Buddleia globosa* 'Lemon Ball' ESV, WAY

*Buddleia* 'Lochinch' ESV, GLA, HOE, HOL, MNR, PLD, SNC

*Buddleia* 'West Hill' ESV

*Buxus* 'Glencoe' BET, BEV, HIN, MID, SCR, STU, WIL

*Buxus* 'Green Gem' APP, DAY, ESV, FOX, HOB, SCA, SHR, WES

*Buxus* 'Green Mountain' APP, GRV, HOB, MID, SCA, SHR, TWO, WES

*Buxus* 'Green Velvet' APP, BAI, ESV, FIO, LOT, KIN, MID, PLH, SCA, SHR, TWO, WES, WIL

*Buxus microphylla* 'Compacta' AMN, APP, CAL, DIL, ENV, ESV, GLA, MCL, OLI, RIE, SIS, SPR

*Buxus microphylla* var. *japonica* 'Morris Midget' APP, ARN, BOV, BRO, ENV, FOF, FOX, GRR, MCL, MIT, NIC, SIS, SPV

*Buxus sempervirens* 'Elegantissima' COL, CUM, ENV, ESV, FOX, MCL, SKY, WDL, WES, WOD

*Buxus sempervirens* 'Graham Blandy' ENV, FOX, GRR, HOE, MCL, MIT, ROY, SKY, TWO

*Buxus sempervirens* 'Vardar Valley' AMM, ANG, CAL, CED, COT, ENV, ESV, FOF, FOX, HIV, LIT, LOS, LUS, MAO, MCL, OLI, SCA, SHA, SPV, STY, TWO, WDL, WES

*Callicarpa americana* CAM, CED, LOU, WOD

*Callicarpa americana* var. *lactea* AME, CAM, CCS, EEI, FFN, FSG, MES, MHS, MNP, LOU, WOD

*Callicarpa bodinieri* var. *giraldii* 'Profusion' BRS, CAL, COT, ESV, FOF, GOS, GRR, HEO, ISE, LOU, MAO, MOB, MON, OLI, WAY, WEM, WES, WIT

*Callicarpa dichotoma* APP, BOB, CAL, CAM, CON, CRN, DAY, EAS, ENV, ESV, FOF, FOX, LAK, LOU, NIC, PRI, MOT, NTW, HEO, STY, SYL, WEN, WIT

*Callicarpa dichotoma* 'Albifructus' CAL, WIT

*Callicarpa dichotoma* 'Issai' COL, HIS, HIV, ROY, WIT

*Callicarpa japonica* ANG, BAI, CAM, EAS, ROY, WEN, SYL

*Callicarpa japonica* 'Leucocarpa' CAL, CAM, COL, CON, CRN, ENV, ESV, FOF, GRR, MAO, ROY, STY, TWO, WIT, WOD

*Calluna vulgaris* ATL, BET, BIG, BLU, BRS, BYE, CED, COL, CUM, DUT, EAS, ENV, FOF, FOS, GAR, GRB, GRR, HAL, HLS, HOB, HUD, ISE, LAK, ROY, SBN, SHR, WEM, WES, WFF, WOD, WON

*Calluna vulgaris* 'Alba Plena' EAS, ESV

*Calluna vulgaris* 'County Wicklow' ARN, BRS, CAL, CUM, DAY, ESV, FOF, FLO, FOX, HOL, SYL, WES, WFF

*Calluna vulgaris* 'Darkness' BRS, ESV

*Calluna vulgaris* 'Gold Haze' DAY, ESV, FOX, SYL, WES, WFF

*Calluna vulgaris* 'H. E. Beale' BRK, BRS, CUM, DAY, ESV, LAK, SYL

*Calycanthus floridus* AMM, APP, BCN, BET, BUL, BYE, CAL, CED, DUT, EAS, EIS, FOF, FOS, GIM, GRB, GRI, GRR, GRV, HAL, HER, HLS, HOB, LAM, LOU, LUS, KLE, LOU, MAO, ORC, ROY, SHR, SUP, TUS, TWO, WAU, WAY, WEM, WES, WOD

*Calycanthus floridus* 'Athens' CAL, LAM, WOD

*Calycanthus floridus* 'Edith Wilder' APP

*Camellia chrysantha* NUC

*Camellia japonica* BOB, CAM, GRR, LOU, MEL, MOB, NUC, SYL

*Camellia japonica* 'Adolphe Audusson' BRS, CAM, DOD, HIL, LOU, MOB, NUC

*Camellia japonica* 'Alaska' CAM, NUC

*Camellia japonica* 'Betty Sheffield Supreme' CAM, GRR, HIH, HIL, LOU, NUC

*Camellia japonica* 'C. M. Wilson' CAM, ROY

*Camellia japonica* 'Dahlohnega' NUC

*Camellia japonica* 'Eldorado' NUC

*Camellia japonica* 'Elegans' CAM, HIL

*Camellia japonica* 'Finlandia' FLO, GRR, ROY, WHI

*Camellia japonica* 'Guillio Nuccio' HIL, NUC

*Camellia japonica* 'Holly Bright' NUC

*Camellia japonica* 'Kumasaka' GRR, MON, NUC, ROY, WHI

*Camellia japonica* 'Lady Clare' CAM, HIL

*Camellia japonica* 'Magnoliaeflora' DOD, MON, NUC, WHI

*Camellia japonica* 'Mansize' COG

*Camellia japonica* 'Mathotiana' CAM, LOU, NUC

*Camellia japonica* 'Nuccio's Gem' GRR, HIH, MON, NUC

*Camellia japonica* 'Otome' CAM, GRR

*Camellia japonica* 'Pink Perfection' CAM, FLO, GRB, GRR, HIH, LOU, NUC

*Camellia japonica* 'Pope Pius IX' CAN, HIH, HIS, NUC

*Camellia japonica* 'R. L. Wheeler' CAM, HIS, LIV, NUC, ROY

*Camellia japonica* 'Swan Lake' MON, NUC

*Camellia japonica* 'Ville de Nantes' FLO, GRR, NUC

*Camellia oleifera* CAM, DOD, GRR, NUC, ROY, WOD

*Camellia* 'Polar Ice' CAM, ROY

*Camellia rosaeflora* NUC, WOD

*Camellia sinensis* CAM, CED, COL, FLB, HEO, LOU, NUC, ROY, WOD

*Camellia* 'Snow Flurry' CAM, ROY

*Camellia × williamsii* BOV, GRR, HOB, WES

*Camellia × williamsii* 'Anticipation' BRS, FLO, GRR, HIL

*Camellia × williamsii* 'Donation' BOV, BRS, GOS, GRR, HIL, HOB, WEM, WES, WHI

*Camellia × williamsii* 'Hiraethyln' ARD, BOD

*Camellia × williamsii* 'J. C. Williams' BOD, COG, FLO, GNW, HIL

*Camellia × williamsii* 'Mary Christian' GRR, HIL, HOB, MOB, WEM, WHI

*Camellia × williamsii* 'Salutation' BOD, COG, GNW

*Camellia × williamsii* 'St. Ewe' BOD, COG, GNW, HIL

*Camellia* 'Winter's Charm' CAM, ROY

*Camellia* 'Winter's Dream' CAM, ROY

*Camellia* 'Winter's Hope' CAM, ROY

*Camellia* 'Winter's Interlude' ROY

*Camellia* 'Winter's Rose' CAM, ROY

*Camellia* 'Winter's Star' CAM, ROY

*Camellia* 'Winter's Waterlily' CAM, ROY

*Caragana aurantiaca* SHR, UXB

*Caragana frutex* 'Globosa' AUB, BAI, BRG, CRO, FOX, GVN, LEE, MOU, SHR

*Caragana pygmaea* AUB, BAI, BRK, FOF, FOX, GVN, ISE, MIN, NON, WES

*Carissa macrocarpa* HIS, LOG, LOU, MEL, SCU

*Carpenteria californica* COL, COT, FOF, FOT, GOS, GRR, HIL, LAS, NAS, TRL

*Caryopteris × clandonensis* CAL, HOL, ROY, SPV, STY, TWO, WAY, WFF

*Caryopteris × clandonensis* 'Azure' BNI, CAL, MOU, SPV, WAY

*Caryopteris × clandonensis* 'Blue Mist' APP, ATL, BAI, BIG, COC, CUM, CWW, FHF, FOF, GRR, HIH, JWL, KED, LAK, MAO, MOB, ROY, SNC, STY, TWO, WAY, WES

*Caryopteris × clandonensis* 'Dark Knight' CAL, CON, FOF, JWL, MAO, POW, ROY, SNC, STY, TWO, WEN

*Caryopteris × clandonensis* 'Heavenly Blue' BLK, BRS, ESV, HIL, PLA, ROY, SPR

*Caryopteris × clandonensis* 'Longwood Blue' BAC, CAL, DAY, EAS, FHF, FOF, GRR, HIS, HIV, LAL, NIC, PLA, PLD, ROY, VIE, WAY, WEN

*Ceanothus* 'Concha' HIS, MON, OKI, SAN

*Ceanothus* 'Dark Star' CFN, FOF, SAN

*Ceanothus* 'Frosty Blue' CFL, MON, OKI

*Ceanothus impressus* FOF, GRR, MON, SAN, TRL

*Ceanothus* 'Joyce Coulter' CFL, MON, SAN

*Ceanothus* 'Julia Phelps' BOE, FOF, HIS, OKI, WEM

*Cornus mas* APP, BRK, CAM, CWW, DAY, ESV, FOF, GIR, GRR, HOO, LOS, LUS, KAN, KRA, MEL, NIC, OWE, SYL, SYN, WEI, WES, WIT

*Cornus mas* 'Aurea' BRS, FOT, FOX, SAR, TWO

*Cornus mas* 'Flava' SAR

*Cornus mas* 'Golden Glory' BAC, BAI, CAL, CRO, CUL, FIO, FOX, GRR, JWL, KIN, KLE, MAO, OLI, OWE, SCA, SHA, STU, SYN, TEC, TIM, TWO, WEM, WIL

*Cornus mas* 'Variegata' ESV, FOT

*Cornus sericea* 'Cardinal' BAC, BAI, BRG, CAL, CRN, CRO, JWL, KLE, MAO, MCK, PLH, ROY, SNC, TWO

*Cornus sericea* 'Isanti' BAC, BAI, BAN, BER, BET, CLA, CRO, CWW, FIO, FOF, GAN, GVN, HIN, JWL, KLE, KIN, KNI, LIT, MAO, MCK, MID, MIN, MOU, NON, OLI, ONA, OWE, PLH, SCH, SCR, SNC, SON, STU, SWE, SYN, TUR, WAG, ZEL

*Cornus sericea* 'Silver & Gold' BEV, CAL, FOF, FOX, ENV, GRR, HEO, HOL, KLE, MEL, MOT, NIC, ROY, STY, WAY

*Correa* 'Carmine Bells' NAS, ROE, SAN

*Correa* × *harrisii* MBN, NAS, SQL

*Correa* 'Ivory Bells' GOS, NAS, SAN

*Correa reflexa* ROE

*Corylopsis glabrescens* ARB, BRK, ESV, GRR, FOF, EAS, LOU, PRI, SHF

*Corylopsis pauciflora* CAL, COT, EAS, ENV, ESV, FOF, FOX, GOS, GRR, HEO, LEW, LOU, MOB, MPK, ROY, SWE, TWO, WAY, WEM, WIT

*Corylopsis platypetala* ARB, ESV, GOS, GRR, FOF, FOX, SHF, SWE, SWT, WIT, WOD

*Corylopsis sinensis* CAL, CAM, FOF, FOX, GOS, GRR, HEO, LOU, TWO, WEM

*Corylopsis sinensis* f. *veitchiana* FOF, FOX, HEO

*Corylopsis spicata* ENV, FOF, FOT, GOS, GRR, HEO, HIL, KDN, LOU, MAO, MOB, SWE, SWT, TWO, WAY, WEM, WIT, WOD

*Corylopsis willmottiae* 'Spring Purple' BRS, COT

*Corylopsis* 'Winterthur' APP, CAL, FOX, STY, WIN

*Cotoneaster adpressus* 'Hessei' BET, CAL, HIL, MID, MON, PLH, SCH

*Cotoneaster apiculatus* APP, ARN, BAI, CAL, CON, CWW, ENV, FOF, GAN, GRI, GRL, HIS, ING, JWL, KAN, KLE, LAK, LUS, MCK, MIT, PLH, PRI, TWO, WES, WON

*Cotoneaster conspicuus* 'Decorus' ESV, HIL

*Cotoneaster dammeri* 'Skogholm' CAR, CHE, ESV, FOX, HIL, HNU, KRA, LAK, LIT, LOU, MAO, PRI, SIE, STY, WOD, WON

*Cotoneaster horizontalis* 'Robustus' APP, EAS, GRL, MID

*Cotoneaster racemiflorus* var. *soongoricus* FOF

*Cryptomeria japonica* 'Globosa Nana' APP, CAM, CUM, EAS, ENV, FOX, FUR, MPK, RAR, SPR, SYL, YUC

*Cyrilla racemiflora* BUL, EEI, FOF, FOX, GIM, HER, KED, LOU, OLI, SAL, SHF, SPR, TNA, WOD

*Cytisus battandieri* ESV, HEO, HIL, WEM

*Cytisus* × *praecox* 'Albus' ENV, ESV

*Cytisus* × *praecox* 'Allgold' ATL, CAL, CWW, ENV, ESV, FOF, HIL, HIV, LIT, MON, SPR

*Cytisus* × *praecox* 'Hollandia' CAL, COU, ENV, ESV, FOF, FOX, MON, SPR, TWO, WDL, WEM

*Cytisus scoparius* FLB, SCU, LAW, SHF, WAR

*Cytisus scoparius* 'Burkwoodii' CAL, CRN, FOF, MAO, MUM

*Cytisus scoparius* 'Lena' CAL, STY

*Cytisus scoparius* 'Lilac Time' FOF, POW, STY

*Cytisus scoparius* 'Moonlight' CAL, FOF, HIS, HIV, KED, MAO, MEL, MON

*Danae racemosa* HEO, HIL, WOD

*Daphne* × *burkwoodii* BRS, FOF, FOX, HEO, HIL, MIT, MOB, WES

*Daphne* × *burkwoodii* 'Carol Mackie' ARN, ATL, CAL, COT, EAS, ENV, FOF, GIN, GOS, GRR, MAO, MIT, OLI, ROC, ROY, SIS, SPR, SPV, TWO, WAY, WES, WFF

*Daphne* × *burkwoodii* 'Somerset' ARN, CAL, CAM, ESV, FLO, FOF, FOX, GAN, GRR, HEO, KLE, MIT, MOB, RIE, ROY, SIS, SPV, TWO, WAY, WES, WFF, WON

*Daphne* × *burkwoodii* 'Variegata' FOT

*Daphne caucasica* ARN, BRO, CAL, CAM, CRN, DLW, EAS, ENV, ESV, FOF, MIT, ROY, SIS, WES

*Daphne cneorum* AUB, BIG, DAY, EAS, FOF, GRR, HIL, IMP, MAO, MIT, MOB, MOE, OLD, ROY, SBN, SHR, WAY, WEM, WES, WFF

*Daphne cneorum* 'Alba' GOS, OLI, SIS

*Daphne cneorum* 'Eximia' ARN, EAS, ENV, DAY, HIL, OLI, ROY, SIS, SPR, TWO, WES, WFF

*Daphne cneorum* 'Ruby Glow' ARN, CAL, COT, FOF, GRR, HER, HIL, HOB, MEL, MOB, RIE, ROY, SIS, SYL, TWO, WES

*Daphne genkwa* ENV, GOS, GRR, HIL, ROY, SIS, TWO, WAY

*Daphne giraldii* COD, ESV

*Daphne* × *mantensiana* FOT, ROY

*Daphne mezereum* f. *alba* EAS, ESV, GOS, TWO, WFF

*Daphne odora* 'Aureo-marginata' BOE, BRS, FOF, GOS, GRR, HIL, LOU, MOB, WAY, WEM

*Daphne retusa* ENV, GOS, HIL, ROY, SIS, SPR

*Daphne tangutica* ARN, EAS, FOT, GOS, ROY, SIS

*Decaisnea fargesii* EAS, ESV, FOF, GOS, GRR, HIL, HEO, NAS, SHF

*Dendromecon rigida* HIL, LAS, NAS, SKL, SON, TRL

*Deutzia chunii* HIL, WIT

*Deutzia gracilis* 'Nikko' APP, ATL, BRS, CAL, CAN, CON, CRN, CUM, ENV, FOF, GRR, HIV, HOL, LAK, LOU, LOS, MAO, MOT, PLD, RIE, ROY, SHA, SIS, SPV, STY, TWO, WAY, WIW

*Deutzia gracilis* 'Rosea' BET, CRO, CWW, EIS, HIL, KED, KIN, SIE, WES

*Deutzia* × *hybrida* 'Magicien'  BRS, FOT

*Deutzia scabra* var. *candidissima*  GRR

*Deutzia scabra* 'Pride of Rochester'  ADA, CAL, FOS, HAL, ING, MAO, MEL, TUS, WAR, WEM

*Diervilla rivularis*  ATL, BOV, ESV, HEO

*Diervilla sessilifolia*  ATL, BIG, ESV, HIN, KIN, LUS, MID, PRI, SHA, SIE, SYN, WAR, WOD

*Diervilla* × *splendens*  BRS, CAL

*Dipelta floribunda*  ESV, HIL

*Disanthus cercidifolius*  COT, EAS, GOS, GRR, HIL, ROY, SCU, TWO, WEM

*Duranta stenostachya*  LOG, SAN

*Elaeagnus* × *ebbingei*  CAN, DOD, FOF, GRL, HIH, MAO, MON, NPI

*Elaeagnus pungens*  BOE, ESV, FOF, GRB, HIL, LIV, LOU, STY, WAT

*Elaeagnus pungens* 'Fruitlandii'  ALD, BOE, CAN, FNN, HIH, MAO, MOB, MON, NPI, STY, WEM, WIG

*Elaeagnus pungens* 'Hosoba-Fukurin'  WOD

*Elaeagnus pungens* 'Maculata'  BRS, ESV, FOF, GLA, GRR, LOU, MOB, SEN, WEM

*Elaeagnus pungens* 'Variegata'  LOG, NPI

*Elliottia racemosa*  WOD

*Embothrium coccineum*  FOF, FOT, GOS, GRR

*Enkianthus campanulatus*  APP, BRK, BRS, CAL, CON, DAY, EAS, ENV, ESV, FOF, FOT, FOX, GIR, GRR, HOB, HOL, IMP, KLE, LOS, LOU, MAO, MEL, MOB, OWE, ROY, SCU, STY, SWE, WEM, WES, WIT

*Enkianthus campanulatus* 'Albiflorus'  WES

*Enkianthus campanulatus* var. *palibinii*  ARN, ESV, FOX, OWE, SCU, SHF

*Enkianthus campanulatus* 'Red Bells'  CAL, CON, FOF, FOX, GOS, GRR, MAO, ROY, STY, TWO, WAY

*Enkianthus campanulatus* 'Showy Lantern'  WES

*Enkianthus campanulatus* 'Sikokianus'  APP, CAM, HOL

*Enkianthus cernuus* var. *rubens*  ESV, GRR, ROY

*Enkianthus chinensis*  ESV

*Enkianthus perulatus*  COT, CUM, ENV, ESV, GOS, GRR, SHF, WIT

*Enkianthus perulatus* 'Compactus'  CUM

*Escallonia bifida*  ESV, SKL, SUC

*Escallonia* × *exoniensis*  GRR, HIS, MOB, RSN, WEM

*Escallonia* × *exoniensis* 'Fradesii'  BOE, COL, FOF, HIS, MOB, MON, NAS, RSN, SAN, SUC, WEM

*Escallonia* 'Pride of Donard'  ESV, MOB, HIL

*Escallonia rubra* 'C. F. Ball'  ESV, HIL

*Euonymus alatus* 'Nordine Strain'  SYN, WEI, WEM

*Euonymus alatus* 'Rudy Haag'  SHA, SPV

*Euonymus europaeus* 'Redcap'  FOF, INT, KLE

*Euonymus oxyphyllus*  CAM, COL, ESV

*Exochorda giraldii* var. *wilsonii*  ESV, HIL, SCU

*Exochorda* × *macrantha* 'The Bride'  ARN, BRS, CAL, ESV, FOF, GOS, GRR, HEO, HIL, LOU, RIE, SHR, VIE, WAY, WEM, WES, WIT, WON

*Feijoa sellowiana*  ALD, FOF, GRL, HIH, HIS, KIW, LOU, MEL, MON, NPI, OKI, PAF, WAY, WOD

*Feijoa sellowiana* 'Coolidge'  NTW

*Forsythia* × *intermedia*  BAI, FOF, LUS, STY, WIB

*Forsythia* × *intermedia* 'Gold Tide'  WAY

*Forsythia* × *intermedia* 'Lynwood'  AMM, BAI, BIG, BRK, CAL, COC, CRD, CWW, EBH, ESV, FAI, FOF, GAN, GIR, GRR, KED, JWL, LAK, LIT, LOT, LOU, MAO, MEL, MOU, MSS, MUS, ONA, PLH, SNC, SPR, STY, WDL, WES, ZEL

*Forsythia* × *intermedia* 'Spring Glory'  AMM, APP, ARN, BAI, BET, BIG, CAL, ESV, FAI, FIO, HIH, HIS, HIV, LIT, LUS, MIT, MOB, MOU, SNC, STY, TUS, WAU, WAY, WES

*Forsythia mandshurica* 'Vermont Sun'  BAI, CAL, JWL, MAO, WES

*Forsythia* 'Meadowlark'  AMM, BAC, BAI, BAN, BRG, CRO, CWW, FOF, JWL, KIN, LOT, MCK, MIN, SCH, SIE, SNC, SYN, WES, WFF, ZEL

*Forsythia* 'New Hampshire Gold'  ARB, JWL, WIS

*Forsythia* 'Northern Gold'  APP, AUB, BAI, FOF, GRL, GVN, HOB, KRA, MCK, MOE, SHR, SNC, SON, SYN, WIS, WOD, WON

*Forsythia* 'Northern Sun'  ADA, APP, BAC, BAI, BAN, BER, BIG, BRE, CRO, CWW, EAS, FOF, GAN, GVN, HOO, JWL, KIN, KLE, KNI, LIT, LOT, MCK, MIL, MOU, NON, PLH, SCH, SHE, SMT, SNC, SON, SWE, WAR, WEI

*Forsythia* 'Sunrise'  BAI, HOO, JWL, KLE, MCK, MOU, ONA, SCH, SNC

*Forsythia suspensa* var. *sieboldii*  APP, CAL, LAK, SIE, WES, WOD, WON

*Forsythia viridissima* var. *koreana* 'Ilgwang'  HIV, ROY

*Forsythia* 'Winterthur'  APP, HIL, WIT

*Fothergilla gardenii*  ARR, BLS, BRS, CAL, CAM, CON, ESV, FOF, FOX, GRR, HOL, KHN, LOS, LOU, LUS, MAO, NIC, PRI, ROY, SPV, STY, WAY, WEM, WES

*Fothergilla gardenii* 'Blue Mist'  BOB, BRI, BRK, CAL, CAM, CRN, CUM, DLW, EAS, EEI, ENV, FOF, FOX, GOS, GRR, KLE, LOU, MAO, MOT, OWE, ROY, SPV, STY, TWO, VIN, WAY, WES, WIW

*Fothergilla gardenii* 'Jane Platt'  GOS, GRR

*Fothergilla gardenii* 'Mt. Airy'  BRK, EAS, GRR, ROY

*Fothergilla major*  BIG, BRK, CAM, DAY, EAS, ENV, ESV, FOF, GOS, GRR, HSS, KHN, LOS, LOU, LUS, PRI, ROY, WES, WOD

*Fouquieria splendens*  SNS, YUC

*Fremontodendron* 'California Glory'  ESV, NAS, TRL

*Gardenia taitensis* COR

*Garrya elliptica* 'James Roof' BRS, COT, GOS, GRR, HIL, LAS, NAS, WEM

*Garrya* × *issaquahensis* HEO

*Genista aethnensis* COL, ESV, FLB, FOF, FOX, HUD

*Genista lydia* ARN, ESV, FOF, FLO, LAK, MIT, MON, NAS, POW, SIS, SYL, WEM

*Genista pilosa* ARN, FOF, FLO, HUD, MPK, SYL, WEM

*Genista pilosa* 'Goldilocks' ESV, HIL, MON

*Genista pilosa* 'Lemon Spreader' BRS, ESV

*Genista pilosa* 'Vancouver Gold' BRS, CAL, CON, FOF, GRR, HEO, LOT, MON, PLD, POW, PRI, ROY, SIS, SPR, WAY, WEM

*Genista sagittalis* CAL, DAY, ENV, ESV, FOF, HIL, OLI, RIE, SIS, SYL, WEM

*Grevillea alpina* HIL, UCA

*Grevillea alpina* 'Grampian's Gold' UCA

*Grevillea* 'Canberra Gem' FOF, HIS, MON, NAS, SAN

*Grevillea lavandulacea* 'Tanunda' SQL

*Grevillea* 'Robyn Gordon' NAS

*Grevillea rosmarinifolia* FOT, HIL, NAS, WOD

*Grevillea tridentifera* SQL

*Grevillea victoriae* NAS, SAN

*Grewia occidentalis* ESV, MON


*Hamamelis* × *intermedia* FOX, LOU, STY, WOD

*Hamamelis* × *intermedia* 'Arnold Promise' AMM, ARR, BIG, BRK, CAL, ENV, ESV, FOX, GIR, GOS, GRE, GRR, HES, LOS, MAO, MCD, MCL, OLI, PRI, ROY, SHR, SPV, STY, TWO, WAY, WEM, WES, WOD

*Hamamelis* × *intermedia* 'Dianc' BRS, CAL, DLW, EAS, ESV, FOX, GIR, GOS, GRR, HEY, HOL, HOM, LEW, LOS, LOU, MAO, MCL, MOT, OWE, ROY, SCH, SHR, TWO, WAY, WFF, WIW, WOD

*Hamamelis* × *intermedia* 'Feuerzauber' ESV, FOX, MCL, ROY

*Hamamelis* × *intermedia* 'Jelena' ARR, CAL, ESV, FOX, GIR, GOS, GRR, HIL, MAO, MCL, ROY, SHR, TWO

*Hamamelis* × *intermedia* 'Primavera' CAL, ESV, FOX, GOS, HOL, MCD, MCL, ROY

*Hamamelis* × *intermedia* 'Ruby Glow' CAL, FOX, GOS, GRR, HES, MCD, MCL, ROY, WOD

*Hamamelis macrophylla* ATL, FOF, LOS

*Hamamelis mollis* CAM, ESV, FOF, FOX, GOS, GRR, HOL, LAW, LOU, MOB, PRI, SCU, SHF, SYN, WEM, WES

*Hamamelis mollis* 'Brevipetala' WES

*Hamamelis mollis* 'Coombe Wood' FOX, GOS, GRR, HIL

*Hamamelis mollis* 'Pallida' BRS, CAL, DLW, EAS, ESV, FOF, FOX, FOT, GIR, GOS, GRR, HOL, LOU, MAO, MCD, MOT, OWE, ROY, SHR, STY, TWO, WEM, WOD

*Hamamelis vernalis* f. *carnea* BAI, BET, FOF, FOX, GIR, GRR, KIN, KLE, LOS, MAO, ONA, PLH, WAY, WES, WIL, WOD

*Hamamelis virginiana* ADA, AMM, APP, BAC, BAI, BAN, BCN, BER, BET, BIG, BRE, CLA, DUT, ESV, FOF, FOS, FOX, GAR, GIR, GRB, GRI, GRR, HER, HIN, HIS, HOB, KED, KIN, KLE, LAK, LAM, LAN, LAW, LIT, LOS, LOT, MAO, MCG, MCK, MOB, MSS, ONA, PLE, PRI, ROY, SCA, SCH, SCN, SCR, SHA, SHR, SNC, SPR, SON, STY, SYN, TUR, WAR, WOD, WES

*Heptacodium miconioides* BRK, FOF, HEO, SHF, WAY

*Heteromeles arbutifolia* CAA, COL, FOF, LAS, NAS, TRL

*Hibiscus* 'Lohengrin' CAL, WIT

*Hibiscus rosa-sinensis* ALD, CAN, HIH, LOG, MON, SOL

*Hibiscus rosa-sinensis* 'All Aglow' SOL

*Hibiscus rosa-sinensis* 'Cooperi' GLA, LOG, SOL

*Hibiscus rosa-sinensis* 'Fiesta' MON, SOL, WAY

*Hibiscus rosa-sinensis* 'Herm Geller' SOL

*Hibiscus rosa-sinensis* 'Harvest Moon' SOL

*Hibiscus rosa-sinensis* 'Tino Vietti' LOU, SOL

*Hibiscus rosa-sinensis* 'Tylene' SOL

*Hibiscus syriacus* 'Aphrodite' MON, ROY, SHA, TRI

*Hibiscus syriacus* 'Diana' ANG, APP, ATL, BAI, BOB, CAL, CAN, EAS, ESV, FOF, GAN, GRL, HER, HIH, HIL, HIS, HIV, LAK, LIT, LOU, MAO, MOB, MON, MOT, PRI, ROY, SCA, SCH, SHA, SPR, STY, WAY, WEM, WIW, WOD

*Hibiscus syriacus* 'Helene' AMM, APP, BLS, CAL, GLA, LOU, MAO, MON, WAY, WEM, WOD

*Hibiscus syriacus* 'Lady Stanley' ALD, GRL, HIL, LIT

*Hibiscus syriacus* 'Minerva' HIH, MON, ROY, SHA, WAY

*Hibiscus syriacus* 'Purpureus Variegata' NIC, PLD

*Hibiscus syriacus* 'Woodbridge' BAI, CAN, GAN, ESV, HIL, HIS, LIT, LOU, MOB, MON, SCH, SNC

*Hibiscus* 'Tosca' CAL, WIT

*Hippophae rhamnoides* AUB, BAI, DUT, ESV, FOF, HIL, HUD, KRA, LAW, LIT, NRT, SCH, SHR, WAY

*Hydrangea arborescens* 'Annabelle' AMM, ARN, AUB, BAI, BAN, BET, BIG, BRS, CAL, CED, COC, CON, CRD, CRO, EIS, ESV, FIO, FOF, GAN, GRV, GVN, HER, HIL, HIN, HOB, HOO, JWL, KAN, KED, KIN, KLE, KRA, LIT, LOS, LUS, MAO, MIT, NON, ONA, OWE, PLH, PNF, PRI, SCR, SHA, SHR, SIE, SMH, SNC, SPR, SWE, SYN, TEC, TUR, TWO, WAY, WEM, WES, WIL, ZEL

*Hydrangea aspera* subsp. *aspera* GRR, GOS, WOD

*Hydrangea macrophylla* BUR, CAL, GRB, SBN, OWE

*Hydrangea macrophylla* 'All Summer Beauty' APP, BAI, CAL, COC, CON, CRD, CWW, LAK, LON, MAO, MCG, PNF, ROY, SNC, WAY, WEM, WIT, ZEL

*Hydrangea macrophylla* 'Blue Billow' CAL, CRN, GRR, LOU, MOT, POW, ROY, STY, WIT

*Hydrangea macrophylla* 'Forever Pink' BLS, CAL, CWW, HER, LOS, LOU, MAO, SHR, TWO, WAY

*Hydrangea macrophylla* subsp. *serrata* 'Bluebird' ESV, GOS, HOM, WEM

*Hydrangea macrophylla* subsp. *serrata* 'Preziosa' BRS, CAL, COC, ESV, FOF, FOT, GOS, GRR, HOM, SYL

*Hydrangea macrophylla* 'Variegata Mariesii' LAK, ROY, WES

*Hydrangea macrophylla* 'White Wave' HIL

*Hydrangea paniculata* 'Tardiva' AMM, ARR, BAI, BRS, CAL, ESV, FIO, FOF, FOX, GRV, HER, HIL, HIN, KIN, LOS, MAO, ROY, SCR, SHA, SPR, SYN, TEC, TUR, TWO, WAG

*Hydrangea quercifolia* BRK, ESV, FOF, FOT, GRR, HIH, LOS, LOU, PLH, SPV, WES, YUC

*Hydrangea quercifolia* 'Snowflake' AGN, CAL, CON, DOD, GOS, GRR, LOU, MAO, OWE, ROY, STY, TWO, WOD

*Hydrangea quercifolia* 'Snow Queen' AGN, APP, BOB, BRI, BRK, BRS, CAL, CON, EAS, FOF, FOX, GRR, LOU, MAO, OWE, PRI, SPR, STY, TWO, VIN, WAY, WES, WIT, WOD

*Hydrangea sargentiana* GOS, GRR, HOM

*Hypericum frondosum* 'Sunburst' BAI, CAL, CON, GAN, HOB, JWL, LIT, MON, PLD, SHR, SYN, WNC, WOD

*Hypericum hookeranum* 'Rowallane' LOU, PLD

*Hypericum kalmianum* BAC, BAI, CON, ESV, FOF, GAN, JWL, KAN, KEL, LIT, WOD, ROY, UXB

*Hypericum patulum* CAL, JWL, HEO, MAO, SHF, STY

*Hypericum patulum* 'Henryi' CON, GNI, GRL, HEO, HUD, MON, OKI, SMT

*Hypericum patulum* 'Hidcote' AMM, APP, ATL, BIG, BRS, CAL, COC, CWW, ESV, GAN, GLA, GRR, HEO, HIL, HIS, HIV, KED, LAK, LIT, LOU, LUS, MAO, MON, MOU, PNF, SNC, SMT, STY, WDL, WEM, WES, WFF

*Hypericum patulum* 'Sungold' BIG, CAL, CON, FOF, MAO, SPR, STY, WOD

*Hypericum prolificum* BRS, CON, CUM, FLB, KIN, WOD

*Ilex amelanchier* DOD, FOX, WOD

*Ilex* 'Apollo' APP, FOX, GIR, GOS, GRB, HOL, LAK

*Ilex* 'China Boy' CON, ENV, GRL, HOB, LAK, LOS, ROY, WAY, WES

*Ilex* 'China Girl' CON, ENV, GRL, HOB, KAN, LAK, LOS, ROY, WAY, WES

*Ilex cornuta* 'O. Spring' CAN, DOD, MCL, ROY

*Ilex cornuta* 'Rotunda' CAN, DOD, GRB, GRL, LIV, LOU, MEL, MON, PLE, ROY, WAR

*Ilex cornuta* 'Willowleaf' MON, TRI

*Ilex crenata* 'Beehive' APP, ARN, ENV, FOX, GRL, GRR, MCL, OLI, PRI, ROY, SHA, SPV

*Ilex crenata* 'Compacta' BOB, CAN, COU, FOS, GRL, ING, LOU, MON, OWE, PRI, TRI, WES

*Ilex crenata* 'Delaware Diamond' ENV

*Ilex crenata* 'Dwarf Pagoda' ARN, CUM, DIL, DLW, EAS, ENV, FOX, GOS, MCL, MIT, OLI, ROY, SPR, STY

*Ilex crenata* 'Glory' AMM, MCL, MON, ROY, SHA, WES

*Ilex crenata* 'Golden Heller' APP, CON, ENV, MCL, TWO

*Ilex crenata* 'Piccolo' ARN, CUM, FOX, GLA, GOS, MCL, MIT, MOB, ROY, SPR, WEM

*Ilex decidua* 'Byer's Golden' FOX, LOU

*Ilex decidua* 'Council Fire' FOX, GRR, LOU, OWE, SHA

*Ilex decidua* 'Pocahontas' FOX, LOU, SHA, WOD

*Ilex decidua* 'Warren's Red' CAL, FOX, GOS, GRR, LOU, MAO, NIC, ROY, SHA, SIM, WOD

*Ilex* 'Dragon Lady' CON, IMP, TWO

*Ilex glabra* 'Compacta' AMM, ATL, BIG, BRK, CAL, CRD, EBH, FIO, FOF, FOX, HNU, ING, KED, LAK, LOS, LOU, MAO, MCL, MON, PLH, PRI, SHA, SHR, SPR, SPV, STU, STY, TWO, WES, WDL, WON

*Ilex glabra* 'Ivory Queen' CAL, EAS, ENV, FOX, LOU, MCL, ROY

*Ilex glabra* 'Nigra' HNU, MCL

*Ilex glabra* 'Nordic' AMM, APP, BAC, BAN, CAL, FOX, GRB, GVN, LAK, MCL, SHR, SON, STY

*Ilex glabra* 'Shamrock' APP, BRK, CAL, CED, FOX, MAO, MCL, STY, WOD

*Ilex* 'Harvest Red' BEV, EAS, FOX, LOS, MCL, MOT, OWE, ROY, SIM, VIN, WAY

*Ilex × meserveae* 'Blue Angel' CON, EAS, ENV, GRR, HOM

*Ilex × meserveae* 'Blue Boy' FOF, GIR, LAK, LIT, LUS, MEL, TWO

*Ilex × meserveae* 'Blue Girl' FOF, GIR, LAK, ROY, TWO

*Ilex × meserveae* 'Blue Maid' BRK, CON, ENV, LAK, LOS, WES, WON

*Ilex × meserveae* 'Blue Prince' BRK, ENV, GAN, HIH, LAK, LOS, PLH, WES, WON

*Ilex × meserveae* 'Blue Princess' BRK, CON, GRR, GAN, HIH, LAK, LOS, LUS, PLH, ROY, WAY, WON

*Ilex × meserveae* 'Blue Stallion' CON, IMP, ROY, WAY, WES

*Ilex* 'Miniature' DOD, PRI, SHA

*Ilex opaca* 'Clarendon Spreading' PAT

*Ilex opaca* 'Maryland Dwarf' CAL, EAS, FOX, MAO, MCL, ROY, WAY

*Ilex* 'Raritan Chief' FOX, LOS, MAO, MCL, ROY

*Ilex* 'Rock Garden' EAS, ROY

*Ilex* 'September Gem' APP, FOF, ROY

*Ilex serrata* 'Bonfire' ING, MAG, PRI, SHA, WES

*Ilex serrata* 'Sundrops' ING, MAG, PRI

*Ilex* 'Sparkleberry' ANG, APP, ARN, BOB, BRK, CAL, CAN, CON, CRN, DLW, ESV, FOF, FOX, GIR, GRL, GRR, HEO, HEY, HOL, LAK, LOS, LOU, MCL, MIT, MOT, OWE, ROY, SIM, STY, VIN, WEI, WES, WIW, WOD

*Ilex verticillata* CAL, FOX, WIT

*Ilex verticillata* 'Afterglow' BAC, BAI, CAL, EAS, FOF, FOX, GRL, HER, MCL, OWE, SIM, SON, TWO, WES

*Ilex verticillata* 'Aurantiaca' BAC, FOX, HER, KIN, MCL, SIM, SON, TEC, TUR, WEM, WES

*Ilex verticillata* 'Maryland Beauty' FOX

*Ilex verticillata* 'Red Sprite' BAC, BAN, BIG, BRK, CAL, ENV, EAS, FOX, LUS, MCL, OLI, ROY, SIM, SPR, SPV, TWO, WEM, WIG

*Ilex verticillata* 'Scarlett O'Hara' FOX

*Ilex verticillata* 'Shaver' FOX, MCL, SIM, WES

*Ilex verticillata* 'Sunset' EAS, FOX, HEO, HER, LOS, MCL, OWE, ROY, SIM, SON, TWO, WES

*Ilex verticillata* 'Winter Red' BIG, BRK, CAL, CON, FOF, FOX, GRR, HER, HIN, KIN, KLE, LOU, LOS, MAO, MCL, OWE, PLE, ROY, SHA, SIM, SMT, STY, TUR, TWO, WAY, WEM, WEN, WES, WIT, WOD

*Ilex verticillata* f. *chrysocarpa* FOX, MCL

*Ilex vomitoria* 'Jewel' DOD, LOU, MON

*Ilex vomitoria* 'Stokes Dwarf' DOD, HIH, HIS, LOU, MON

*Illicium anisatum* CAM, CED, CEO, COL, ESV, FOF, FOT, GOS, GRR, HIL, LOG, LOU, WIG, WOD

*Illicium floridanum* ANN, BUL, CAM, CED, CFN, DOD, EAS, EEI, FNN, GIM, HES, HIL, LOU, MNP, SAL, SUP, TNA, WAY, WOD

*Illicium floridanum* f. *album* FOF, HEO, LOU, WOD

*Illicium floridanum* 'Halley's Comet' ROY

*Illicium henryi* CAM, WOD

*Illicium mexicanum* LOU, WOD

*Illicium parviflorum* CAM, CAN, CED, DOD, FOF, LOU, WOD

*Indigofera kirilowii* ESV, ROY, WFF

*Itea ilicifolia* ESV, HIL, WOD, YUC

*Itea virginica* ANN, APP, BCN, BOV, BUL, CAL, CAM, CCS, CED, CFN CON, CUM, DOD, EEI, ESV, FNN, FOF, FOT, FSG, GIM, GIR, GRR, HIL, LAK, LAM, LOU, SHA, SPV, STY, SWT, TNA, TWO, WES, WOD

*Itea virginica* 'Beppu' GOS, GRR, LAK, MAO, SPV, WES, WOD

*Itea virginica* 'Henry's Garnet' APP, ATL, BOB, BRO, CAL, CAN, CON, COT, CRN, EAS, ENV, FOF, GRR, HEO, KHN, KLE, LOU, MOT, NIC, ROY, SHA, SPR, SPV, STY, TWO, WES, WIW, WOD

*Ixora* species MOR

*Ixora chinensis* MIS

*Ixora odorata* MOR

*Juniperus chinensis* 'Echiniformis' DIL, FOX, KRI, OLI, RAR, RIE

*Juniperus squamata* 'Blue Star' APP, ARN, ATL, BIG, BRK, CAL, CAM, CON, COT, FOF, FOX, GRR, HEO, KED, LOS, LOT, MAO, MCG, MCL, MIT, MOB, ONA, POW, ROY, SCA, SPR, SPV, TWO, VLL, WAS, WEM

*Juniperus virginiana* 'Grey Owl' ANG, APP, ARN, BAC, CAL, CAM, EVE, FOX, GIR, GRB, GRL, HOO, LAK, MCK, MIN, MIT, SPV, SYN, TWO

*Kalmia angustifolia* BRK, ROY

*Kalmia angustifolia* 'Hammonasset' BRK, EAS, ROY

*Kalmia angustifolia* 'Pumila' BRK, ENV, FOX, ROY, WHI

*Kalmia latifolia* BRI, BRK, CUM, ENV, FOF, LAM, LOS, PRI, STY, TWO, WAY

*Kalmia latifolia* 'Alba' BRK

*Kalmia latifolia* 'Bullseye' APP, BRI, BRK, CUM, EAS, FOF, GOS, GRR, KDN, KEL, KHN, MAO, MOB, ROY, SCN, SHR, STY, WAS, WAY, WEN, WFF

*Kalmia latifolia* 'Elf' BCN, BRI, BRK, CAL, CRL, CUM, ENV, FOF, FOT, FOX, GAR, GOS, GRR, KEL, KHN, MAO, MOB, ROY, STY, TWO, WAY, WHI

*Kalmia latifolia* 'Freckles' GRR, TWO, WAS, WHI

*Kalmia latifolia* 'Fuscata' BRK

*Kalmia latifolia* 'Heart's Desire' BRI, BRK, CAL, CUM, EAS, ENV, FOX, GRR, ROY, SON, WAS, WHI

*Kalmia latifolia* 'Little Linda' BRK, EAS

*Kalmia latifolia* 'Minuet' APP, BRI, BRK, CUM, EAS, ENV, FOX, GOS, GRR, ROY, SIS, TWO

*Kalmia latifolia* 'Ostbo Red' APP, ATL, BAI, BRK, BRS, CAL, CRL, CUM, EIS, ENV, ESV, FOF, FOX, GRR, LOU, LOS, MAO, MOB, ROY, SHR, SPR, STY, TWO, WAY, WEM, WHI, WIT

*Kalmia latifolia* 'Peppermint' BRK, EAS

*Kalmia latifolia* 'Pink Charm' BRI, BRK, CUM, ENV, FOT, FOX, GOS, GRR, KEL, KHN, MAO, MOB, OLI, ROY, STY, WAS, WAY, WHI

*Kalmia latifolia* 'Sarah' BCN, BRI, BRK, CAL, CUM, EAS, ENV, FOX, GOS, GRR, KEL, KHN, MAO, STY, TWO, WAS, WFF, WHI

*Kalmia latifolia* 'Silver Dollar' BRI, BRK, EAS, ENV, FOX, FOT, GOS, GRR, KHN, MAO, MOB, OLI, WAS, WHI

*Kalmia latifolia* 'Star Cluster' LOS, ROY

*Kerria japonica* 'Picta' ARB, ARN, ATL, BRK, CAL, COL, CRN, DAY, EAS, ESV, GLA, GRR, HEO, HOL, MAO, MIT, MNR, ROC, ROY, SHR, SPR, WES, WOD, WON

*Kerria japonica* 'Pleniflora' APP, FOF, GRR, LOU, POW, PRI, WAY, WES, WON

*Kolkwitzia amabilis* CAM, FOF, GRR, LAK, MON, PLH, WAY, WES, WIT

*Kolkwitzia amabilis* 'Pink Cloud' ARB, BRS, CAL, CED, ESV, FOF, GOS, GRL, GRR, HIL, KLE, MAO, SHA, TWO, WAY, WON

*Kolkwitzia amabilis* 'Rosea' JWL, SHA

*Lagerstroemia* 'Acoma' BYE, CAL, CRN, FOF, HIS, MAO, OWE, ROY, SHA

*Lagerstroemia* 'Hopi' BYE, CAL, CAN, DOD, ELM, FOF, ING, MAO, OWE, ROY, SHA

*Lagerstroemia* 'Pecos' CAL, CAN, DOD, ING, MAO, MON, OWE, ROY

*Lagerstroemia* 'Zuni' BYE, CAL, CAN, FOF, HIS, ING, MAO, MON, OWE, SPR

*Leiophyllum buxifolium* BRK, CUM, EAS, ENV, ESV, GRR, HIL, OLI, WES, WOD

*Osmanthus heterophyllus* 'Aureomarginatus' ESV, LOU, HIL

*Osmanthus heterophyllus* 'Goshiki' GLA, FOX, MCL, ROY

*Osmanthus heterophyllus* 'Gulftide' ESV, GRB, HIL, ING, LOU, MCL, ROY, SMT, WAT, WEM

*Osmanthus heterophyllus* 'Maculifolius' MCL

*Osmanthus heterophyllus* 'Myrtifolius' ESV, MCL

*Osmanthus heterophyllus* 'Rotundifolius' CED, ESV, GRB, LOU, MCL, MON, ROY

*Osmanthus heterophyllus* 'Sasaba' FOX

*Osmanthus heterophyllus* 'Variegatus' ARN, CAN, COU, ESV, FOF, GRR, HEO, LOG, MEL, MIT, MON, ROY, WOD

*Pachystachys lutea* DAV, LOG

*Paeonia suffruticosa* CAL, KLE, SCU, SHF, SYL

*Paeonia suffruticosa* 'Alhambra' KLE, REA

*Paeonia suffruticosa* 'Ariadne' KLE

*Paeonia suffruticosa* 'Companion of Serenity' KLE

*Paeonia suffruticosa* 'Hana Kisoi' BUS, KLE, SMI, WAY

*Paeonia suffruticosa* 'Hephestos' KLE

*Paeonia suffruticosa* 'Joseph Rock' KLE, WAY, WOD

*Paeonia suffruticosa* 'Leda' KLE, WAY

*Paeonia suffruticosa* 'Renkaku' KLE

*Paeonia suffruticosa* 'Shintenchi' KLE, WIT

*Pernettya mucronata* DAY, FOF, GRR, MOB, HIL, HEO, MOB, MON, ROY, SWT, WEM

*Pernettya mucronata* 'Alba' ESV, FOF, HEO

*Pernettya mucronata* 'Rosea' ESV, FOF

*Pernettya mucronata* 'Rubra' ESV, FOF, MON

*Philadelphus coronarius* 'Natchez' BAI, BRS, CED, ESV, GRV, HIH, HOB, KEL, KLE, LOU, MAO, MOB, MON, SCA, SHA, TWO, WEM

*Philadelphus* × *virginalis* BUR, COC, FOS, GIR, HAL, JWL, MEL, MON, PLH, PRI, WAY, WES, WON, YUC

*Philadelphus* × *virginalis* 'Glacier' BER, CAL, MOB, MOU, SNC, TEC, WAR, WEM

*Philadelphus* × *virginalis* 'Miniature Snowflake' ARN, BAI, BIG, BRE, BRK, BUR, CAL, FAR, GAN, GRV, GVN, HER, JWL, KNI, KRA, LIT, LUS, MCK, MIN, OLD, NPI, OKI, ONA, PLH, TEC, TWO, SCH, SWE, SYN, WAY, WEM, WES

*Philadelphus* × *virginalis* 'Minnesota Snowflake' BAC, BAI, BET, BIG, BOV, BUR, CAL, COC, CWW, FAR, FOS, GAN, GRR, GVN, HIV, HLS, HOB, IMP, JWL, KEL, KIN, KRA, LAK, LIT, LOT, MCG, MCK, MIN, MOU, OLD, NPI, PLH, SBN, SCA, SNC, SPV, SWE, WAN, WAV, WAY, WED, WES, WFF, WNC, WON, ZEL

*Philadelphus* × *virginalis* 'Polar Star' BUR, KLE, WAY, WES

*Physocarpus opulifolius* 'Dart's Golden' APP, AUB, BAC, BAI, BAN, BRS, CAL, COC, CRO, CWW, FAR, FNN, FOF, GAN, GVN, HIL, JWL, KAN, KIN, KLE, KNI, KRA, LAK, LIT, LOT, MCK, MIN, MON, MOU, NON,

ONA, ROY, SCA, SCH, SHA, SHR, SNC, SWE, WED, WES, WOD, WON, ZEL

*Picea abies* 'Little Gem' ARN, BRK, BRS, CAL, CAM, CON, COT, DAY, EAS, ENV, FOF, FOX, FUR, GOS, GRR, GVN, ISE, KED, KLE, KRI, LAK, LOS, MAO, MCG, MIT, MOB, OKI, OLI, RAR, RIE, ROY, RSN, RUN, SIS, SPR, SPV, WAS, WAY, WEM

*Picea abies* 'Nidiformis' ADA, APP, ARN, ATL, BIG, BRS, CON, FOF, GRR, GUE, HER, HNU, ISE, KED, LAK, LOS, MAO, MID, MIT, MOB, MSS, OKI, OLI, PLH, RID, RSN, SHR, SPR, SPV, STY, TWO, WAS, WES, WON

*Picea abies* 'Reflexa' APP, AUB, BAI, BET, CAL, CRO, EIS, FLO, FNN, FOX, FUR, GIR, GRB, GRR, GVN, HOB, IMP, KRI, MIN, MON, NON, NPI, RIE, ROC, SBN, SPR, SWE, VLL, WAS, WDL, WOD, WTN

*Picea omorika* 'Nana' BIG, CAL, COT, DIL, EAS, FOX, HES, ISE, KLE, KRI, LAS, MAO, RAR, RIE, ROY, RUN, SCA, SHR, SPR, SPV, TWO, WDL, WES

*Picea pungens* 'Compacta' FOX, ISE, LAN, STU, WES

*Picea pungens* 'Montgomery' AMM, APP, BIG, CAL, CON, CUM, DAY, ENV, EAS, FLO, FOX, GRR, GVN, KRI, MIT, MOB, MON, PLH, RIE, ROC, ROY, RSN, RUN, SHR, SIS, SPR, SPV, STY, TWO, WAS, WEM, WES

*Pieris* 'Brouwer's Beauty' BRK, DAY, EAS, FOX, HNU, MAO, ROY, OLI, WES

*Pieris floribunda* 'Millstream' APP, CAR, DAY, GRR, ROY

*Pieris formosa* var. *forrestii* 'Forest Flame' AMM, BRS, ENV, ESV, FOX, GRR, HER, MIT, MOB, MON, ROY, ROY, SBN, SPR

*Pieris japonica* APP, BRK, COU, GRR, FLO, GIR, GRB, HUD, IMP, LAK, LOS, LOU, MEL, MON, PRI, ROY, SCU, SHF, SKY, SYL, WAY, WES

*Pieris japonica* 'Bert Chandler' BRS, EAS, ESV, FLO, GOS, GRR, MCL, POW, ROY

*Pieris japonica* 'Flamingo' APP, ARN, CAM, CUM, ESV, FLO, FOF, FOX, GRR, HIL, MCL, MIT, OLI, ROY, SBN, SPR, WEM

*Pieris japonica* 'Geisha' CUM, ESV, FOX, HER, MCL

*Pieris japonica* 'Mountain Fire' APP, ARN, ATL, BCN, BRI, BRK, CAL, CAM, CUM, ENV, ESV, FLO, FOF, FOX, FUR, GRR, HER, HIL, KED, LOU, MAO, MCG, MCL, MIT, MOB, MON, MUS, OLI, PLE, ROY, RSN, SMT, SPR, STY, WEM

*Pieris japonica* 'Pygmaea' ARN, CAL, CON, COT, DOD, EAS, ESV, FLO, FOF, FOX, FUR, GRR, HEO, MCL, MIT, POW, RIE, ROY, SIS, TWO

*Pieris japonica* 'Red Mill' BRS, CHE, CON, ESV, FOX, HER, LOS, MAO, MCL, ROY, STY, WAY

*Pieris japonica* 'Roslinda' ESV, MCL, ROY

*Pieris japonica* 'Valley Fire' ARN, ESV, FOF, FOX, FUR, GRR, MCL, MIT, SPR

*Pieris japonica* 'Valley Rose'  ARN, CUM, ENV, ESV, FLO, FOF, FOX, FUR, GRR, HER, HIL, LOU, MAO, MCL, MIT, MOB, PLE, ROY, WEM

*Pieris japonica* 'Valley Valentine'  ARN, ATL, BRK, CAM, ENV, ESV, FLO, FOF, FOX, FUR, GOS, GRR, HER, HIL, LOS, LOU, MCL, MIT, MOB, ROY, RSN, SPR, TWO, WAY, WEM

*Pieris japonica* 'Variegata'  APP, ARN, ATL, BOE, BRK, BRS, CAL, DAY, EAS, EIS, ENV, ESV, FLO, FOF, FOX, FUR, GOS, GRR, HER, HIL, LOU, MAO, MCL, MIT, MOB, MON, OLI, POW, ROY, RSN, SBN, SMT, TWO, WAY, WEM

*Pieris japonica* 'White Cascade'  BRI, ESV, FOX, GRR, HOM, MCL, MON, ROY, STY, WEM

*Pieris japonica* 'White Pearl'  MCL, ROY

*Pieris phillyreifolia*  DOD, EEI, WOD

*Pieris taiwanensis*  ESV, GIR, GRR, MAO, MIT, MOB, MON, POW, WEM

*Pinus densiflora* 'Globosa'  BRO, DLW, FOF, ISE, KRI, PAF, RAR, TWO

*Pinus mugo* 'Mops'  ARN, BRS, FOX, ISE, KRI, MIT, RAR, TWO

*Pinus sylvestris* 'Beuvronensis'  BRK, DLW, EAS, FOF, FOX, GVN, ISE, KRI, MIT, RAR, SPR, SPV, TWO, WES

*Pinus sylvestris* 'Hillside Creeper'  ATL, BRK, DLW, EAS, EAS, FOX, ISE, MIT, ROY, RUN, SPR, SPV, TWO

*Potentilla fruticosa*  GAN, JWL, KLE, LAW, LIT, PLT, SPV

*Potentilla fruticosa* 'Abbotswood'  AMM, APP, ARB, ARN, AUB, BAC, BAI, BAN, BET, BIG, BRE, BRG, BRS, CAL, CLA, COC, CON, CRO, CWW, EIS, ESV, FAR, FOF, FOX, GAN, GIR, GRV, GUE, GVN, HER, HIS, HIV, HNU, HOB, JWL, KAN, KDN, KLE, KNI, KRA, LAK, LAW, LIT, LOT, LMN, LUS, MAN, MAO, MAX, MCG, MCK, MEL, MID, MIL, MIN, MOB, MON, MOU, MSS, NON, NPI, ONA, ROC, RSN, SCA, SCH, SHR, SIE, SNC, SPR, SPV, SYN, TEC, TWO, WAR, WAY, WEM, WIL, WNC, WOD, WON, ZEL

*Potentilla fruticosa* 'Coronation Triumph'  HIL

*Potentilla fruticosa* 'Day Dawn Viette'  COC, CWW, FOF, LAK, MEL, MOU, WFF, VIE, WON, ZEL

*Potentilla fruticosa* 'Goldfinger'  APP, ARB, AUB, BAC, BAI, BAN, BER, BIG, BRE, BRG, BRS, CAL, CON, CRO, CWW, EAS, ESV, FUR, GAN, GRV, GUE, GVN, HER, HIN, HIS, HIV, HNU, HOB, HOO, ING, ISE, JWL, KAN, KIN, KLE, KRA, LAK, LAW, LEE, LIT, LMN, LOT, MAN, MAO, MCG, MCK, MIN, MOB, MOE, MON, NON, NPI, PLH, RSN, SCA, SCH, SHE, SHR, SNC, SPR, SPV, STU, SYN, TEC, TUR, TWO, WAY, WED, WEI, WIL, WNC, WOD, WON, ZEL

*Potentilla fruticosa* 'Katherine Dykes'  ARN, AUB, BAI, BRG, CRO, CWW, ESV, GAN, HOO, LOS, LUS, JWL, KIN, KRA, MOU, PRI, SNC, SYL, VIE, WAY, WES, WFF

*Potentilla fruticosa* 'Pink Queen'  REI, VIE

*Potentilla fruticosa* 'Primrose Beauty'  APP, ARN, ATL, BAC, BAI, BAN, CAL, CLA, CUM, CWW, DAY, EIS, ESV, FOF, FOX, FUR, GAN, GVN, HER, HIL, JWL, KAN, KIN, LAK, LIT, MAX, MCG, MEL, MID, MON, NON, NPI, PRI, SMH, SPR, SYN, TWO, WAR, WEM, WES, ZEL

*Potentilla fruticosa* 'Yellowbird'  HIL

*Prostanthera ovalifolia*  UCA

*Prostanthera rotundifolia*  BNI, HEO, HIL, LOG, SAO, SUC

*Prostanthera rotundifolia* 'Glen Davis'  UCA

*Punica granatum*  ALD, COL, FOF, HUD, LAW, MON, MPK, NPI, SAN, WOD

*Punica granatum* 'Emperior'  MPK

*Punica granatum* 'Hizakuru'  MPK

*Punica granatum* 'Nana'  BYE, FOF, GRL, HUD, LOG, MEL, MON, MPK, WOD

*Punica granatum* 'Peach Princess'  MPK

*Punica granatum* 'Shiro Botan'  MPK

*Punica granatum* 'Toyosho'  MPK, MON

*Punica granatum* 'Twisted Trunk'  MPK

*Punica granatum* 'Wonderful'  ALD, LOG, LOU, NTW, MON

*Pyracantha* 'Apache'  APP

*Pyracantha* 'Fiery Cascade'  APP, FOF, HIS, ING, PRI, ROY, WAY

*Pyracantha* 'Gold Rush'  HEO, WEM

*Pyracantha* 'Mohave'  APP, BIG, CAL, CAN, CRD, EAS, ESV, GIR, GRB, HIL, HIV, ING, LAK, LOT, LUS, MAO, MAX, MCL, MOB, MON, PRI, SMT, WAY, WEM, WES, WIG

*Pyracantha* 'Navaho'  CAL, GRB, HIL, MOB, PLE

*Pyracantha* 'Pueblo'  APP, MCL

*Pyracantha* 'Rutgers'  CAL, ING, MAO, MON, PRI, SMT

*Pyracantha* 'Teton'  APP, BOB, GRB, MEL, MOB, WES

*Rhamnus frangula* 'Asplenifolia'  AMM, ARB, BAC, BAI, BAN, FOF, GAN, GRV, HER, HOB, JWL, KLE, LIT, LOS, LOT, ONA, SCA, SNC, STU, TWO

*Rhodotypos scandens*  BIG, COL, FOF, FLO, GRB, GRR, HEO, HER, HIL, LAK, ONA, STY, WOD

*Rhus aromatica* 'Gro-low'  AMM, BAC, BAI, BAN, BET, FOF, FIO, GAN, GRV, GVN, HIN, HOO, JWL, KAN, KIN, KLE, KRA, LAK, LAN, LIT, LOS, MAN, MAO, MCK, MID, MIN, MOU, SCA, SCH, SCR, SHR, STU, SYN, TUR, WED, WES, WIL

*Rhus chinensis* 'September Beauty'  FOX, KLE, WAY

*Rhus copallina*  ARB, BIG, DUT, EEI, FOF, GAR, GIM, GRR, HIH, HIL, HLS, LUS, MEL, SHF, SYL, TNA, WAR

*Rhus glabra* var. *cismontana*  GAN, LIT, PRI, VAL

*Rhus trilobata*  FOF, GAN, HUD, LAS, LAW, LIT, LOU, MOZ, OLD, SCU, TRL, VAL, WOD

299

*Rhus trilobata* 'Autumn Amber' COL, FOF, GAN, LIT, LOU, NPI, OLD, SNS

*Rhus typhina* 'Dissecta' AMM, BAI, CAL, DAY, ESV, FIO, FOF, FOX, FUR, GRR, GRV, GVN, HIL, ISE, KLE, KRA, KRI, LAK, LAN, MAO, MCK, MOB, ONA, RIE, SCN, SHA, SHR, SIS, SNC, STU, SYN, TWO, WAY, WES, WIL, WOD

*Rhus typhina* 'Laciniata' BAI, CAL, CRO, FOF, GRR, HOB, HOO, JWL, MAO, MID, MOB, MON, MOU, SNC, WEI, WOD

*Ribes alpinum* 'Green Mound' BET, FIO, GRV, HIN, JWL, KIN, KLE, KNI, MID, MIN, SCA, SCH, SYN, TEC, TUR, WIL

*Ribes aureum* AUB, GRR, LAS, LAW, LIT, PLH, UXB, VAL

*Ribes odoratum* BAI, CAL, EVE, FOF, GVN, MEL, MIN, SNC, SWE

*Ribes odoratum* 'Aureum' HIL, SEA

*Ribes sanguineum* FOF, GRR, HEO, MON

*Ribes sanguineum* 'King Edward VII' ESV, FOF, GOS, GRR, NAS, REI, WEM

*Ribes speciosum* ESV, HIL, LAS, NAS, TRL

*Robinia hispida* ESV, FOF, GAR, LUS, MEL, TRH

*Rosa* 'Adelaide Hoodless' AUB, BAC, BAI, CAL, HOT, ING, JWL, KRA, LAK, LIT, MIN, MOE, SNC, SWE, VAL

*Rosa* × *alba* 'Celestial' GRM, LOW, PIC, WAY

*Rosa* × *alba* 'Semi Plena' LOW, PIC, WAY

*Rosa* × *alba* 'White Rose of York' HIL, HIR, ROS

*Rosa* 'A. MacKenzie' HOT, PIC, DOW

*Rosa* 'Assiniboine' HOT, KRA, VAL

*Rosa* 'Belle de Crécy' CAL, GRM, HCR, HIL, HIR, HOT, LOW, PIC, ROS, WAY

*Rosa* 'Bonica' BAC, BAI, BRE, BRG, CAL, CON, DOW, GRL, HOB, HOT, ING, KAN, LAK, LIT, MEL, MID, MIN, MOB, MOU, PLH, ROR, SWE, SYL, WAY, WEM, ZEL

*Rosa* 'Bredon' HOT, PIC, WAY

*Rosa* 'Buff Beauty' ARE, CNB, GRM, HIL, HIR, HOT, PIC, ROA, ROS, WAY

*Rosa* 'Canary Bird' HIL, HOT, MOB

*Rosa* 'Cantabrigiensis' HIL, PIC

*Rosa* 'Carefree Beauty' BAC, BAI, BAN, BGN, CAL, CON, HOT, KLE, KRA, LIT, MOB, MOU, PIC, ROR, SNC, SYL, TWO, WAY, WFF

*Rosa* 'Carefree Wonder' BAC, BGN, BRG, CAL, CON, DOW, ING, KLE, MOU, PLH, ROR, WAY

*Rosa centifolia* f. *muscosa* 'White Bath' HIL, HIR, HOT, LOW, PIC, WAY

*Rosa centifolia* 'Rose de Meaux' HIL, LOW, PIC, ROS, WAY

*Rosa* 'Champlain' AUB, BAC, BAI, CAL, DOW, EVE, HOT, KRA, PIC, SNC, SWE

*Rosa* 'Complicata' GRM, HCR, HEO, HOT, HRG, LOW, MOB, PIC, WAY

*Rosa* 'Cuthbert Grant' AUB, BAC, BAI, CAL, CRO, HOT, KRA, MOE, SWE, VAL

*Rosa damascena* var. *bifera* 'Autumn Damask' ARE, GRM, HRG, ROS

*Rosa damascena* 'Madame Hardy' BGN, CAL, GRM, HIL, HRG, LOW, PIC, ROS, WAY

*Rosa* 'Duchesse de Brabant' ARE, CNB, ROA, ROS

*Rosa* 'English Garden' BGN, HOT, PIC, ROA, ROR, WAY

*Rosa foetida* 'Bicolor' AUB, BAI, CAL, DOW, GAN, GRM, HIL, HIR, HOT, HRG, LAK, LIT, LUS, MEL, MOU, PIC, ROS, SNC, WAY

*Rosa* 'Frühlingsduft' WAY

*Rosa* 'Frühlingsgold' GRM, HCR, HIL, HIR, PIC, WAY

*Rosa* 'Frühlingsmorgen' GRM, HIL, LOW, WAY

*Rosa gallica* var. *officinalis* GRM, HIL, HIR, HRG, LOW, PIC, ROS, WAY

*Rosa* 'Geranium' HIL, HOT, PIC, WAY

*Rosa* 'Gertrude Jekyll' CAL, CNB, HOT, PIC, TWO, WAY, WIT

*Rosa glauca* ANG, BAI, FOF, GAN, GRM, HCR, HIR, HUD, KRA, LAW, PIC, ROS, SCU, UXB, WFF

*Rosa* 'Golden Wings' CNB, GOS, GRM, HCR, HIL, HIR, HIS, HOT, LOW, MOB, PIC, ROA

*Rosa* 'Graham Thomas' CON, GRM, HIL, HOT, PIC, PLH, ROR, ROS, WAY

*Rosa* 'Henry Kelsey' BAC, BAI, CAL, CNB, DOW, EVE, HOT, JWL, MOE, PIC

*Rosa* 'Heritage' BGN, CAL, CON, HIL, HOT, LOW, PIC, PLH, ROR, TWO, WAY, WIT

*Rosa hugonis* AMM, BIG, CAL, FOF, GRM, GRR, GVN, HCR, HER, HIR, HOT, LOS, MCK, OLD, WAY, WES, WON

*Rosa* 'John Cabot' ARE, AUB, BAC, BAI, CAL, DOW, HOT, KRA, PIC

*Rosa* 'John Davis' CAL, DOW, PIC, KRA

*Rosa* 'John Franklin' BAC, BAI, CAL, DOW, EVE, HOT, KRA, PIC

*Rosa* 'La Reine Victoria' HCR, HIL, HOT, ROS, WAY

*Rosa* 'Mary Rose' BGN, CAL, CON, HIL, HOT, PIC, PLH, ROA, ROR, WAY, WIT

*Rosa* 'Morden Amorette' HOT, VAL

*Rosa* 'Morden Blush' BAC, JWL, KRA, MOE

*Rosa* 'Morden Cardinette' KRA, MOE

*Rosa* 'Morden Centennial' AUB, BAC, BAI, CAL, HOT, LAK, MOE, SNC, SWE, WAY

*Rosa* 'Morden Fireglow' KRA, MOE

*Rosa* 'Morden Ruby' BAC, BAI, HOT, KRA, VAL

*Rosa* 'Nevada' GRM, HCR, HIL, HIR, HOT, PIC, WAY

*Rosa* 'Perdita' CNB, HOT, PIC, STY, WAY

*Rosa* 'Prioress' HOT

*Rosa rugosa* 'Blanc Double de Coubert' AUB, BGN, CAL, DOW, GRM, HCR, HIL, HOT, HRG, KRA, MOB, MOE, PIC, ROR, ROS, STY, WAY, WEM

*Rosa rugosa* 'Charles Albanel' BAC, BAI, CAL, DOW, LOW, KRA, PIC, TWO

*Rosa rugosa* 'Fru Dagmar Hastrup' ARE, BGN, CAL, CON, GRM, HIL, HOT, HRG, MOB, ROS, WAY

*Rosa rugosa* 'Henry Hudson' BAC, CAL, EVE, HOT, KRA, LOW, PIC, WFF

*Rosa rugosa* 'Jens Munk' ARE, AUB, BAC, BAI, CAL, DOW, EVE, HOT, KRA, LOW, PIC

*Rosa rugosa* 'Linda Campbell' CAL, PLH, ROR, WAY

*Rosa rugosa* 'Roseraie de l'Hay' BGN, GRM, HIL, HOT, LAK, LOW, ROS, WAY

*Rosa rugosa* 'Rubra' FLB, HIL, LAW, LOW, NTW, PIC, ROS, SYL, WAY

*Rosa rugosa* 'Sarah Van Fleet' ARE, CAL, HIR, LOW, PIC, WAY

*Rosa rugosa* 'Sir Thomas Lipton' BAI, CAL, CON, EVE, GAN, HCR, ING, LAK, LUS, MCK, MIN, MON, PIC, SYL, WAY

*Rosa rugosa* 'Therese Bugnet' AUB, CAL, CON, HCR, FOF, GAN, HOT, LOW, JWL, KHN, KRA, LAK, MIN, MOE, MON, PIC, PLH, ROR, ROS, SYL, TWO, WAY

*Rosa rugosa* 'Topaz Jewel' BAC, PLH, ROR, WAY

*Rosa* 'Sir Walter Raleigh' HIL, PIC, WAY

*Rosa* 'Souvenir de la Malmaison' ARE, CAL, GRM, HCR, HRG, HIL, HIR, LOW, PIC, ROR, ROS, WAY

*Rosa* 'Stanwell Perpetual' GRM, HCR, HIL, HIR, PIC

*Rosa* 'Versicolor' GRM, HIL, HIR, HOT, LOW, PIC, ROS

*Rosa* 'Wife of Bath' GRM, HOT, PIC, WAY

*Rosa* 'William Baffin' ARE, AUB, BAI, CAL, HOT, KRA, PIC, SWE

*Rosa* 'Winnipeg Parks' KRA, MOE

*Rosa xanthina* AUB, FOF, HIL, LAK, LAW, LIT, REI, SHF

*Rubus cockburnianus* FOF, HIL

*Rubus odoratus* BAI, ESV, FOF, GAR, GRI, HIL, UXB, WAV

*Rubus* 'Tridel' COT, GOS, GRR, HIL, LIT, WAY, WEM

*Ruscus aculeatus* HIL, WOD

*Salix fargesii* COL, GOS, HEO, HIL

*Salix gracilistyla* ESV, GRR, HIL, ROC, TRI, WAR, WIT

*Salix lanata* ESV, HIL

*Salix melanostachys* BAI, BOB, BOV, CAL, DAY, ESV, FOF, GLA, HEO, MEL, LIT, ROY, SYL, WAY, WEN, WES

*Sambucus racemosa* 'Plumosa Aurea' AUB, BRS, ESV, GRR, REI, WAY

*Sarcococca confusa* BRS, COL, ESV, FOT, HIL, SWT, THO, WAY, WOD

*Sarcococca ruscifolia* ALP, BEL, CMN, ESV, FOF, GRR, HAN, HEO, LOG, KRN, MON, NTW, RSN, SAN, SHF, WOD

*Shepherdia argentea* AUB, BAI, BRG, CRO, DUT, ENV, FAR, FOF, GAN, HER, JWL, KRA, LAW, LEE, LIT, LOT, MCK, MIN, NON, NPI, OLD, SCH, SHR, SLW, SNC, SWE, WES

*Shepherdia canadensis* BER, FOF, LAW, SCH, SCN, SNS, VAL

*Skimmia* 'Formanii' HIL

*Skimmia japonica* CAL, CUM, DAY, MAO, MCL, MON, RSN, SBN, STY, THO, WAY, WEM

*Skimmia japonica* 'Nymans' ESV, HIL

*Skimmia reevesiana* 'Rubella' CUM, ESV, FOF, HIL, LUS, MAO, MOB, WEM, WOD

*Sorbaria aitchisonii* ESV, HEO, HIL

*Sorbaria sorbifolia* ARB, BAC, BAI, BAN, CRO, ESV, FOF, GAN, GRR, GVN, JWL, KIN, KRA, LIT, MIN, NON, SCH, SHR, SNC, SYN, UXB, WEI, WON

*Sorbus reducta* ESV, FOF, GOS, GRR, HIL, REI, SHR

*Spiraea × bumalda* 'Golden Princess' BAI, BRS, CON, KLE, WAY

*Spiraea × bumalda* 'Gold Flame' ANG, APP, ARN, AUB, BAI, BRE, BRI, BRG, CAL, CAN, COU, ESV, FAI, GIR, GRB, GRR, HEO, HIV, HLS, JWL, KIN, KLE, KRA, LAK, LOU, MIT, MOE, PLH, POW, REI, ROY, SCR, SHA, SPV, SYL, SYN, VIF, WAY, WEI, WES, WON

*Spiraea × cinerea* 'Grefsheim' ARB, BAI, BRG, CON, ESV, EVE, FOF, GRV, HIL, HOO, HOT, JWL, KRA, LEE, MAX, PLH, SIE, SMT, SPV, WFF, WOD, WON

*Spiraea fritschiana* BAI, CRO, GVN, HOO, HOT, JWL, MCK, MIN, WAV, WAY

*Spiraea japonica* 'Shibori' AMM, BAI, BIG, BRS, CAL, COC, CON, CRN, CWW, ENV, ESV, FOF, FOX, GAN, GRR, GRV, HER, JWL, KDN, KED, KLE, KRA, LOS, LOT, MAO, PLE, POW, SCA, SHA, SHR, SMT, SNC, SPR, STY, WAY, WES, WON, ZEL

*Spiraea nipponica* APP, BAI, BIG, CAL, ESV, HOO, ISE, KLE, LAN, LIT, MID, MON, PLE, PRI, SHA, SNC, SPR, SYN, TWO, WES

*Spiraea nipponica* 'Halward's Silver' ARB, AUB, BAI, CAL, GVN, HOB, JWL, KRA, SHA, SHR, SNC, SYN, WES, WON

*Spiraea nipponica* 'Snowmound' AMM, APP, ATL, BAI, BET, BIG, BRS, CAL, COC, CRO, CWW, ESV, FAI, FIO, FOF, GAN, GRR, GUE, HNU, HOO, ISE, KED, KIN, KLE, LAK, LAN, LOS, LOT, MON, MOU, MSS, ONA, PLE, PLH, PRI, RID, SCA, SHA, SHR, SNC, SPR, STU, SYN, TEC, TWO, WAG, WES, WFF, WIL, WON, ZEL

*Stachyurus praecox* BRS, CAM, ESV, FOF, GOS, GRR, HIL, WEM, WOD, YUC

*Stephanandra incisa* 'Crispa' AMM, APP, ATL, BAI, BET, CAL, COT, ENV, ESV, FOF, GLA, HIL, JWL, KIN, LAK, MID, OLI, ONA, SCH, SCR, SHR, SNC, SPR, SYN, TUR, TWO, WAY, WEI, WEM, WES, WON

*Streptosolen jamesonii* LOG, MON, PAF

*Syringa × henryi* WIT

*Syringa × henryi* 'Lutèce' LAK

*Syringa × henryi* 'Summer White' WED

*Syringa × hyacinthiflora* BAI, CWW, GRR, HEA, JWL, WES, WIT

*Syringa × hyacinthiflora* 'Blanche Sweet' BAI, BEV, HEA, KHN, KLE, MEL, TWO

*Syringa* × *hyacinthiflora* 'Maiden's Blush' CAL, CON, CWW, EVE, HEA, LOS, WED

*Syringa* × *hyacinthiflora* 'Sister Justena' AUB, EVE, MOE, VAL, WED

*Syringa* × *josiflexa* WED

*Syringa* × *josiflexa* 'Agnes Smith' BOB, COU, HEA

*Syringa* × *josiflexa* 'Anna Amhoff' WED, WES

*Syringa* × *josiflexa* 'James MacFarlane' AMM, APP, BAC, BAI, BAN, BET, BRE, CAL, CRO, ESV, FAR, FOF, HEA, HIN, JWL, KAN, KIN, KLE, KNI, LAK, LEE, LIT, LUS, MAO, MCK, MIN, MOB, MOL, NON, ONA, PLH, SCA, SHR, SMH, STU, STY, SYN, TWO, WED, WES, ZEL

*Syringa* × *josiflexa* 'Royalty' AUB, BAC, CAL, ESV, JWL, KIN, LAK, LIT, MOE, MOU, ONA, MOE, PLH, SMH, SNC, SYN, WED, WEI, VAL

*Syringa* × *laciniata* ARB, CAL, CAN, CED, CWW, MOB, WAY

*Syringa meyeri* 'Palibin' AMM, APP, ATL, BAC, BAI, BER, BET, BEV, BOV, BRK, CAL, CLA, COC, CON, CUM, EAS, ENV, ESV, FOF, GAN, HEA, HER, HIN, HOB, HOO, IMP, JWL, KAN, KIN, KLE, LAK, LUS, MAN, MAO, MCG, MOL, NON, PLH, ROC, ROY, SCA, SCH, SCR, SHR, SNC, SPR, SWE, SYN, TWO, WES, WFF, WOD, WON, ZEL

*Syringa microphylla* HEA, KLE

*Syringa microphylla* 'Superba' APP, BAI, BRK, CAL, ESV, FOF, HEA, HER, HIL, KHN, KLE, LOS, MAO, WFF

*Syringa* 'Minuet' AUB, BAC, BAI, BAN, CAL, CRO, JWL, KRA, MIN, SNC, TWO, VAL, WED

*Syringa* 'Miss Canada' AUB, BAI, CAL, HEA, JWL, KRA, LIT, MIN, MOE, SNC, VAL, WED, WES

*Syringa oblata* var. *dilatata* HEA, JWL, WED

*Syringa patula* 'Miss Kim' AMM, APP, AUB, BAC, BAI, BAN, BER, BET, BEV, BIG, BRG, CAL, CON, CRO, CWW, DAY, EAS, ENV, FLO, FOF, GAN, GIR, GRR, GRV, GVN, HEA, HIN, HIS, HIV, HOB, JWL, KAN, KDN, KED, KIN, KLE, KNI, KRA, LIT, LMN, LOS, LOT, MAN, MAO, MCK, MOL, MOU, MSS, NON, ONA, OWE, ROY, SCA, SCH, SCR, SHA, SIE, SMH, SNC, SPR, STU, SWE, SYN, TWO, WAG, WAY, WED, WEM, WES, WFF, WIL, ZEL

*Syringa* × *prestoniae* CWW, HEA, KLE, LAK

*Syringa* × *prestoniae* 'Alice Rose Foster' SEL

*Syringa* × *prestoniae* 'Ethel M. Webster' LAK

*Syringa* × *prestoniae* 'Isabella' HIL, JWL, KLE, KRA, LAK, LIT, MOU, WED, WES

*Syringa* × *prestoniae* 'Nike' CWW

*Syringa vulgaris* AUB, BAI, BOB, BRG, CFS, COC, CWW, FOF, FOS, GAN, GRB, HES, HLS, HOB, JWL, KAN, KIN, KRA, LAK, LUS, MCK, MEL, MIN, PLH, PRI, SCU, SHF, SNC, SYL, SYN, WED, WEI, WNC

*Syringa vulgaris* 'Agincourt Beauty' BRI, CAL, GRR, JWL, KLE, SHR, WED

*Syringa vulgaris* 'Albert F. Holden' HEA, KHN, MEL, TWO, WED

*Syringa vulgaris* 'Blue Skies' GAN, HEA, LIT, MON

*Syringa vulgaris* 'Dwight D. Eisenhower' CWW, WES

*Syringa vulgaris* 'Edith Cavell' KLE, HEA, WED

*Syringa vulgaris* 'Edward J. Gardner' CAL, CWW, GRR, HEA, STY

*Syringa vulgaris* 'Emile Lemoine' CWW, WED

*Syringa vulgaris* 'Krasavitsa Moskvy' ARB, CAL, CON, CRO, CWW, FOF, HEA, HOO, KLE, WAY, WED

*Syringa vulgaris* 'Lavender Lady' AMM, BRI, CAL, GAN, HEA, HIS, LIT, MON, NPI, SMT, SPR, WAY

*Syringa vulgaris* 'Ludwig Spaeth' ARB, AUB, BAC, BAI, BRI, CWW, DOW, GRL, GRR, HEA, HOO, JWL, KRA, LOW, MOL, MOU, PLH, PRI, SNC, SYN, TWO, WAY, WED, WON, ZEL

*Syringa vulgaris* 'Marie Francis' HEA, KHN, MEL, WED

*Syringa vulgaris* 'Mieczta' SEL

*Syringa* 'Miss Ellen Willmott' EVE, HEA, JWL, MCK, PLH, WED

*Syringa vulgaris* 'Primrose' BAC, BAI, BRI, CAL, CWW, EVE, FOF, GRR, HEA, HIL, KLE, LAK, LOS, MEL, SIE, SWE, TWO, WAY, WED, WEM, WES, ZEL

*Syringa vulgaris* 'Rochester' BRI, CAL, CWW, WED

*Syringa vulgaris* 'Sensation' BAI, BEV, BRI, CAL, CON, CWW, EVE, FOF, GRL, GRR, HEA, HER, HIL, HIS, JWL, KAN, KLE, LAK, LOS, MCG, MCK, TWO, WAY, WED, WES

*Syringa vulgaris* 'Slater's Elegance' BRI, CAL, CWW, HEA, KLE, SHR, WED

*Syringa vulgaris* 'Victor Lemoine' BRI, GRR, HEA, WED

*Syringa vulgaris* 'Wedgwood Blue' KHN, MEL, WED

*Syringa vulgaris* 'Wonder Blue' WED

*Syringa vulgaris* 'Yankee Doodle' CWW, HEA, KHN, WED

*Tabernaemontana divaricata* LOG, LOU

*Taxus baccata* 'Adpressa Fowle' BRO, FOX, KRI, OLI, RAR, ROY, TWO, WES

*Taxus baccata* 'Beanpole' DLW, FOX, ROY, SON

*Taxus baccata* 'Fastigiata Robusta' APP, BIG, BRS, FOX, MAO, SBN, SON

*Taxus* × *media* 'Runyan' CRO, EVE, FIO, HOB, HOO, KLE, SCA, STU, ZEL

*Tecoma stans* ALD, GRL, HIH, HUD, LAW, LOG, LOU, SNS

*Tecoma stans* var. *angustata* LOG, MOZ

*Thevetia thevetioides* PAF, MON, SAN

*Thujopsis dolabrata* 'Nana' ARN, COT, CUM, DAY, FLO, FOF, FOX, GRR, ISE, MIT, MPK, ROY, SIS, SPR, SPV

*Tsuga canadensis* 'Bennett' ARN, BRO, CAM, DAY, EAS, ENV, FOF, FOX, FUR, GRR, ISE, KRI, LAK, LOW, MEL, MIT, ROY, SHR, SWT, WAS, WEM

*Tsuga canadensis* 'Jeddeloh' ARN, ATL, BRK, BRS, CAL, CON, CUM, DAY, ENV, FOX, FUR, GLA, GRR, HER, ISE, KED, KLE, KRI, LOS, MAO, MIT, MOB, OLI, RAR, RIE, ROC, ROY, RUN, SIS, SPV, SWT, TWO, WAS, WDL, WEM

*Tsuga canadensis* 'Jervis' ARN, CUM, DIL, EAS, FOX, GRR, HES, ISE, KRI, MAO, MIT, OLI, RUN, SPV, TWO, WAS

*Ungnadia speciosa* ALD, FOF, HUD, MOZ, SNS, WOD, YUC

*Viburnum × bodnantense* 'Dawn' BRS, ESV, FOF, GOS, GRR, HEO, HIL, HOM, ISE, MOB, MON, OWE, REI, ROY, STY, SYL, SWT, WAY, WEM, WES

*Viburnum × bodnantense* 'Deben' ESV, HEO

*Viburnum × burkwoodii* 'Conoy' ARN, BYE, CAL, FOF, FOX, MIT, ROY, SHA, STY

*Viburnum × burkwoodii* 'Mohawk' APP, ARN, BEV, BYE, CAL, DLW, FOF, FOX, HEY, HOB, HLS, LAK, LOS, LOU, KIN, MIT, MOT, OWE, SHA, STY, TWO, WAY, WIW, WOD

*Viburnum × carlcephalum* 'Cayuga' ARN, CAL, CED, FOF, FOX, GRL, KIN, KLE, LAK, LOS, MAO, MIT, ROY, SHA, STU, STY, SYN, TWO

*Viburnum carlesii* 'Aurora' ARB, BRS, FOT, HIL, ISE, KEL, LAK, MIT, ROY, WEM, WES, WIL

*Viburnum carlesii* 'Charis' FOT

*Viburnum carlesii* 'Compactum' ARB, BLS, CAL, DAY, EAS, ENV, FIO, FOF, GOS, HER, HOO, ISE, KIN, KHN, MOB, ROC, ROY, SYL, TIM, TUR, TWO, WAY, WEM

*Viburnum* 'Chesapeake' APP, ARN, FOF, FOX, MAO, MIT

*Viburnum* 'Chippewa' ARN, FOF, LOU, MIT, STY

*Viburnum dilatatum* 'Catskill' APP, ARN, ROY, STY

*Viburnum dilatatum* 'Erie' AMM, APP, ARN, BAI, BYE, CAL, FOF, FOX, HER, HEY, LAK, LOS, MAO, MIT, MOT, OWE, SHA, STY, SYL, WAY, WES, WIW

*Viburnum dilatatum* 'Iroquois' SHA, WES

*Viburnum dilatatum* 'Michael Dodge' CAL

*Viburnum* 'Eskimo' AMM, ARB, ARN, BCN, BYE, CAL, CED, FOF, FOX, GRB, GRL, GRR, HIL, HLS, HOB, LOS, LOU, MAO, MOT, OWE, ROC, ROY, SHA, STY, TRI, WAY, WIW, WOD

*Viburnum farreri* 'Candidissimum' ESV, FOF, WOD

*Viburnum* 'Huron' ARN, FOX, MIT, ROY

*Viburnum lantana* 'Mohican' APP, ARB, ARN, BAC, BAI, CAL, CON, DAY, FOX, HOO, JWL, KAN, KIN, KLE, LAK, LOS, LOT, MCG, MCK, MID, MIT, MSS, ONA, PLH, PRI, ROY, SCA, SHA, SNC, SPR, STY, SYN, TUR, TWO, WON, ZEL

*Viburnum nudum* 'Winterthur' CAL, CON, CRN, MOT, ROY, STY, WIT

*Viburnum plicatum* f. *tomentosum* 'Shasta' APP, ARN, BAI, BYE, CAL, CAM, CAN, CON, CRN, CWW, DAY, EAS, ENV, ESV, FOF, FOX, GRL, HEO, HLS, HOB, ISE, KLE,

LAK, LOS, LOU, MAO, MCG, MIT, MOT, OWE, PRI, ROY, SCA, SHA, SMT, SPR, STU, STY, TRI, TWO, WAY, WES, WIW, WOD, WON

*Viburnum plicatum* f. *tomentosum* 'Shoshoni' APP, ARN, EAS, ENV, MAO, MIT, ROC, ROY, SHA, STY, WES

*Viburnum plicatum* f. *tomentosum* 'Summer Snowflake' BRK, CAL, EAS, ESV, FOF, FOT, GOS, GRR, HEO, HIL, HOM, MAO, OWE, REI, ROY, SHR, STY

*Viburnum × pragense* AMM, APP, ARN, CAL, CED, COL, DAY, ESV, FOF, GAN, GRB, GOS, GTN, HER, HIV, LAK, LOU, MAO, MAX, MCL, MON, PLE, ROY, SHA, STY, SYL, TWO, WAT, WAY, WES, WIT

*Viburnum × rhytidophylloides* 'Alleghany' AMM, ANG, APP, ARN, BYE, CAL, CAN, CON, EIS, ESV, FLO, FOF, GRB, GRR, GRV, HIL, HLS, HOB, KLE, LAK, LOS, MAO, MIT, MON, NPI, PLE, ROY, SCA, SHA, STU, WES, WON

*Viburnum rufidulum* ARB, BUL, EEI, FOF, HOB, SHA, SHF, WOD

*Viburnum sargentii* 'Onondaga' AMM, ARN, BAC, BAI, BRS, FOF, FOT, FOX, GAN, HER, HIL, HOB, KLE, LAK, LOS, MIT, MON, RIE, ROY, SCA, SPR, SYN, WON

*Viburnum sargentii* 'Susquehanna' APP, ARN, ESV, FOF, GOS, KLE, LAK, LOS, MIT, TWO, WON

*Viburnum setigerum* 'Aurantiacum' MAO, SCU, SHF, WES

*Viburnum* 'Willowwood' ANG, ARB, ATL, FOF, HOB, LOS, KIN, MEL, MON, PRI

*Vitex agnus-castus* ATL, CAL, CRN, ESV, FOF, GRL, HIL, HUD, LOU, MAO, MON, MOZ, ROY, SHF, TWO, WES, WOD

*Vitex agnus-castus* 'Alba' FOF

*Vitex agnus-castus* 'Rosea' FOF

*Vitex agnus-castus* 'Silver Spire' CAM, ESV, LOU, ROY

*Vitex negundo* var. *heterophylla* CAL, FOF, LOU

*Vitex rotundifolia* FOF, NIC

*Weigela florida* 'Evita' ARN, CAL, CON, ESV, GOS, GRR, HIL, KRA, SHR

*Weigela florida* 'Red Prince' AMM, BAC, BAI, BAN, BRE, CAL, CRO, GVN, FOF, HOO, JWL, LIT, LON, MCK, MON, MOU, NON, ONA, PLH, SHA, SCN, SHR, SIE, SMH, SWE, ZEL

*Weigela florida* 'Variegata' APP, ARN, BAI, BIG, CAL, COC, CRD, CWW, GIR, GRR, GRV, GUE, HEO, HIL, JWL, KDN, KEL, KLE, KRA, LAK, LOT, LOU, MAO, MCG, MIT, MON, MOU, OWE, PLH, SNC, SHR, SPR, TWO, WAR, WES, WON, ZEL

*Xanthorhiza simplicissima* BIG, CAL, DAY, ESV, FOF, FOT, GAR, GRI, HIL, LUS, ROY, TRI, WES, WOD

*Zenobia pulverulenta* BOV, CUM, DOD, EAS, ESV, FOF, FOT, GOS, GRR, HIL, ROY, WES, WOD

# APPENDIX II-B

# Directory of Nursery Sources

This directory furnishes the names and addresses of nurseries listed in Appendix II-A, Shrub Index with Nursery Source Codes. Please note that this directory is not exhaustive; it includes only those nurseries which could be readily identified by the editorial group. Nurseries whose names are followed by (W) are wholesale growers only. Do not contact them directly, but rather furnish their name and address to your regular retail nursery center or to your landscape architect, who can then obtain the shrubs desired. Nurseries with both wholesale and retail sales are indicated by (W/R).

ADA  Adams Nursery, Inc.
Springfield Road, P.O. Box 606
Westfield, MA 01086

AGN  Aldridge Nurseries
2109 Montgomery Highway
P.O. Box 59683
Birmingham, AL 35259
(205) 939-0975

ALD  Aldridge Nursery, Inc. (W)
Route 1, Box 8
Von Ormy, TX 78073
(512) 622-3491

ALP  Alpha Nursery
5270 Hazel Green Road, N.E.
Salem, OR 97305

AME  American Native Products
P.O. Box 2703
Titusville, FL 32781
(407) 383-1967

AMM  Ammon Landscape Supply (W/R)
2141 Burlington Pike
Burlington, KY 41005
(606) 586-5200

AMN  American Nurseries
North Service Road
Dix Hills, NY 11746
(516) 673-2800

ANG  Angelica Nursery (W)
R.D. 1, Box 174
Kennedyville, MD 21645
(410) 928-3111

ANN  Apalachee Native Nursery
P.O. Box 204
Lloyd, FL 32337
(904) 997-8976

APP  Appalachian Gardens (W/R)
Box 82
Waynesboro, PA 17268-0082
(717) 762-4312

ARB  Arborvillage Farm Nursery
P.O. Box 227
Holt, MO 64084
(816) 264-3911

ARD  Ard Daraich Shrub Nursery
Ardgour, by Fort William
Invernesshire PH33 7AB
(08555) 248

ARE  Antique Rose Emporium (W/R)
Route 5, Box 143
Brenham, TX 77833
(409) 836-9051

ARN  Arrowhead Alpines
P.O. Box 857
Fowlerville, MI 48836
(517) 223-3581

ARR  Arrowhead Nursery
5030 Watia Road, Box 38
Bryson City, NC 28713

ATL  Atlantic Nurseries, Inc.
691 Deer Park Avenue
Dix Hills, NY 11746

AUB  Aubin Nurseries, Ltd.
Box 1089
Carman, Manitoba R0G 0J0
Canada
(204) 745-6703

BAC  Bachman's Nursery (W)
6877 235th Street W
Farmington, MN 55024
(612) 463-3288

BAN  Bachman's Nursery
6010 Lyndale Avenue S.
Minneapolis, MN 55419
(612) 861-7676

BAI  Bailey Nurseries, Inc. (W)
1325 Bailey Road
St. Paul, MN 55119
(612) 459-9744

BCN  Beaver Creek Nursery
7526 Pelleaux Road
Knoxville, TN 37938

BEV  Beaver Creek Nursery, Inc. (W)
6604 Randall Road
Poplar Grove, IL 61065
(815) 737-8758

BEL  Bell Family Nursery
6562 S. Zimmerman Road
Aurora, OR 97002

BER  Bernardo Beach Native Plant Farm
Star Route 7, Box 145
Veguito, NM 87062
(505) 345-6248

BET  Berthold Nursery (W/R)
434 E. Devon Avenue
Elk Grove Village, IL 60007
(847) 439-2600

BGN  Craig Bergmann's Country Garden
700 Kenosha Road, P.O. Box 424
Winthrop Harbour, IL 60096
(847) 746-0311

BIG  Bigelow Nurseries (W/R)
455 W. Main Street, P.O. Box 718
Northboro, MA 01532
(508) 845-2143

BLK  Kurt Bluemel, Inc.
2740 Greene Lane
Baldwin, MD 21013
(400) 557-7229

BLU  Blue Oak Nursery
2731 Mountain Oak Lane
Rescue, CA 95672
(916) 933-6692

BLS  Bluestone Perennials
7211 Middle Ridge Road
Madison, OH 44057
(216) 428-7535

BNI  Bluebird Nursery, Inc. (W)
515 Linden Street, P.O. Box 460
Clarkson, NE 68629
(402) 892-3457

BOB  Bobtown Nursery (W)
16212 Country Club Road
Melfa, VA 23410
(804) 787-8484

BOD  Bodnant Garden Nursery Ltd.
Tal-y-Cafn
Colwyn Bay, Clwyd LL28 5RE
Wales
United Kingdom
0492-650460

BOE  Boething Treeland Farms (W/R)
23475 Long Valley Road
Woodland Hills, CA 91367
(818) 883-1222

BOV  Bovees Nursery
1737 S.W. Coronado St.
Portland, OR 97219
(503) 244-9341

BRE  Brehm's Wondercreek Nursery
N6050 S. Crystal Lake Road
Beaver Dam, WI 53916
(414) 885-4300

BRG  Bergeson Nursery
Route 1, Box 184
Fertile, MN 56540
(218) 945-6988

BRI  Briggs Nursery, Inc. (W)
4407 Henderson Boulevard
Olympia, WA 98501
(206) 352-5405

BRK  Broken Arrow Nursery
13 Broken Arrow Road
Hamden, CT 06518
(203) 288-1026

BRO  Martin Brooks Rare Plant Nursery
(W/R)
235 Cherry Lane
Doylestown, PA 18901
(215) 348-4309

BRS  Bressingham Gardens
Bressingham, Diss,
Norfolk IP22 2AB
United Kingdom
0379-88464

BUL  Bullbay Creek Farm (W)
Route 2, Box 381
Tallahassee, FL 32301
(904) 878-6688

BUR  W. Atlee Burpee & Co.
300 Park Avenue
Warminster, PA 18974
(301) 848-5422

BUS  Busse Gardens (W/R)
5873 Oliver Avenue, S.W.
Cokato, MN 55321
(612) 286-2654

BYE  Byers Wholesale Nursery (W)
P.O. Box 560
Meridianville, AL 35759
(205) 828-0625

CAA  Calaveras Nursery (W)
1622 Highway 12
Valley Springs, CA 95252
(209) 772-1823

CAL  Carroll Gardens (W/R)
44 E. Main Street, P.O. Box 310
Westminster, MD 21157
(410) 876-7336

CAM  Camellia Forest Nursery
P.O. Box 291
125 Carolina Forest Road

Chapel Hill, NC 27516
(919) 967-5529

CAN  Carolina Nurseries (W)
739 Gaillard Road
Moncks Corner, SC 29461
(800) 845-2065

CAR  Carroll Nurseries
R.D. #4
Cochranton, PA 16314
(814) 425-8123

CAT  Carter Seeds
475 Mar Vista Drive
Vista, CA 92083
(800) 872-7711

CCS  Coastal Consulting Services
1844 S. Central Avenue
Flagler Beach, FL 32036
(904) 439-2493

CED  Cedar Lane Farms (W)
3790 Sandy Creek Road
Madison, GA 30650
(404) 342-2626

CFL  California Flora Nursery (W/R)
P.O. Box 3
Fulton, CA 95439
(707) 528-8813

CFN  Central Florida Native Flora
P.O. Box 1045
San Antonio, FL 33576
(904) 588-3687

CFS  Cascade Forestry Nursery
22033 Fillmore Road
Cascade, IA 52033
(319) 852-3042

CHE  Chesapeake Nurseries, Inc.
368 Pemberton Drive, R.F.D. 16
Salisbury, MD 21801
(410) 742-5622

CLA  Clavey's Woodstock Nursery (W)
6223 Alden Road
Woodstock, IL 60098
(815) 943-7778

CMN  Chehalem Mountain Nursery
Route 6, Box 412
Hillsboro, OR 97123
(503) 628-3765

CNB  Country Bloomers Nursery
Route 2, Box 33-B
Udall, KS 67146
(316) 846-7357

COC Concord Nurseries, Inc.
Mileblock Road N.
Collins, NY 14111
(800) 223-2211

COD Colorado Alpines, Inc.
P.O. Box 2708
Avon, CO 81620
(303) 949-6464

COG Coghurst Nursery
Ivy House Lane, Near Three Oaks
Hastings
East Sussex TN35 4NP
United Kingdom
0425-425371

COL Colvos Creek
1931 Second Avenue, #215
Seattle, WA 98101

CON Conard Pyle Nursery (W)
372 Rose Hill Road
West Grove, PA 19390
(800) 458-6559

COR Contemporary Landscaping
Company
41-758 Waikupanaha Street
Waimanalo, HI 96795

COT Collector's Nursery
1502 N.E. 162nd Avenue
Vancouver, WA 98684
(206) 256-8533

COU Country Gardens Nursery, Inc.
450 S. Service Road
Melville, NY 11747
(516) 694-0131

CRD Cooper Ridge Nurseries, Inc.
3348 E. Pleasant Drive
Hamburg, NY 14075

CRE Creative Native
P.O. Box 713
Perry, FL 32347

CRL Carlson's Garden Center (W/R)
P.O. Box 305
South Salem, NY 10590
(914) 763-5958

CRN Crownsville Nursery
P.O. Box 797
Crownsville, MD 21032
(410) 923-2212

CRO Cross Nurseries, Inc.
1977 Kenwood Trail
Lakeville, MN 55044
(612) 469-2414

CUL Cultra Nursery Co. (W)
E. Roosevelt Road, P.O. Box 126

Onarga, IL 60955
(815) 268-7211

CUM Cummins Garden
22 Robertsville Road
Marlboro, NJ 07746
(908) 536-2591

CWW Congdon & Weller (W)
Mile Block Road, P.O. Box 1507
North Collins, NY 14111
(800) 345-8305

DAR Darryl's Exotic Plant Nursery
6380 Via Real
Carpenteria, CA 93013
(805) 684-3911

DAV Davidson-Wilson Greenhouses
(W/R)
R.R. 2, P.O. Box 168
Crawfordsville, IN 47933
(317) 364-0556

DAY Daystar
Route #2, Box 250, Litchfield-
Hallowell
Litchfield, ME 04350
(207) 724-3369

DIL Dilatush Nursery
780 Route 130
Robbinsville, NJ 08691
(609) 585-5387

DLW Dilworth Nursery (W/R)
1200 Election Road
Oxford, PA 19363
(610) 932-0347

DOD Tom Dodd Nurseries, Inc. (W)
P.O. Drawer 45, US Highway 98
Semmes, AL 36575
(205) 649-1960

DOW Downham Nursery Inc.
626 Victoria Street
Strathroy, Ontario N7G 3C1
Canada
(519) 245-0220

DUT Dutch Mountain Nursery
7984 N. 48th Street, Route 1
Augusta, MI 49012
(616) 731-5232

EAS Eastern Plant Specialties
P.O. Box 226
Georgetown, ME 04548
(207) 371-2888

EBH H. Eberhard Nurseries, Inc. (W)
P.O. Box 486
East Moriches, NY 11940

EEI Environmental Equities, Inc.
1206 San Domingo Court
Clearwater, FL 34619
(813) 726-4908

EIS Eisler Nurseries
Route 422
Prospect, PA 16052
(412) 865-2830

ELM El Modena Garden Inc.
11911 Jeffrey Road
Santa Ana, CA 92701
(714) 559-1234

ENV Environmentals (W)
P.O. Box 730
Cutchogue, NY 11935
(516) 734-6439

ESV Esveld, Firma C.
Rijneveld 72
2771 XS Boskoop
Holland
011-31-1727-13289

EVE Evergreen Nursery Co. (W)
5027 County TT
Sturgeon Bay, WI 54235
(414) 743-4464

FAI Fairview Evergreen Nurseries, Inc.
(W)
7401 Water Street, P.O. Box E
Fairview, PA 16415
(814) 474-5712

FAR Farmer Seed & Nursery
818 N.W. Fourth Street
Faribault, MN 55021
(507) 334-1623

FFN Farnsworth Farms Nursery
7080 Hypoluxo Farms Road
Lake Worth, FL 33463
(407) 965-2657

FHF Friar's Head Farm
36 Sound Avenue
Riverhead, NY 11901

FIO Charles J. Fiore & Co. (W/R)
16606 W. Highway 22
Prairie View, IL 60069
(847) 913-1414

FLB Flowery Branch
P.O. Box 1330
Flowery Branch, GA 30542
(404) 536-8380

FLO Flora Lan Nursery
7940 N.W. Kansas City Road
Forest Grove, OR 97116
(503) 357-8386

FNN  Florida Natives Nursery
16018 Race Track Road
Odessa, FL 33556
(813) 920-5152

FOF  Forestfarm (R)
990 Tetherow Road
Williams, OR 97544-9599
(541) 846-6963

FOS  Forest Nursery Co. (W)
Route 2, Box 118-A
McMinnville, TN 37110
(615) 473-2133

FOT  Fortescue Garden Trust
The Garden House
Buckland Monachorum
Yelverton
Devon PL20 7LQ
United Kingdom
0822-854769

FOX  Foxborough Nursery (W)
3611 Miller Road
Street, MD 21154
(410) 836-7023

FSG  Florida Scrub Growers
730 Myakka Road
Sarasota, FL 34240
(941) 322-1915

FUR  Furr's Northwest Propagation
(W/R)
21601 S.E. Bornstedt Road
Sandy, OR 97055

GAN  Green Acres Nursery, Inc. (W/R)
4990 McIntyre
Golden, CO 80401
(303) 279-8204

GAR  Gardens of the Blue Ridge (W/R)
P.O. Box 10
Pineola, NC 28662
(704) 733-2417

GIL  Gilson Gardens (W/R)
3059 U.S. Route 20,
P.O. Box 277
Perry, OH 44081
(216) 259-4845

GIM  Green Images
1333 Taylor Creek Road
Christmas, FL 32709
(407) 282-1469

GIN  Grand Isle Nursery
S. Hero, VT 05486

GIR  Girard Nurseries (W/R)
6839 N. Ridge E., P.O. Box 428

Geneva, OH 44041-0428
(216) 466-2881

GLA  Glasshouse Works Greenhouses
Church Street, P.O. Box 97
Stewart, OH 45778-0097
(614) 662-2142

GNI  Greenbriar Nurseries, Inc.
P.O. Box 5189
Ocala, FL 32678
(904) 489-0133

GNW  Greenway Gardens
Churston Ferrers
Brixham
Devon TQ5 0ES
United Kingdom
0803-842382

GOS  Gossler Farms Nursery (W/R)
1200 Weaver Road
Springfield, OR 97478
(541) 746-3922

GRA  Grandview Nursery
Route 4, Box 44
Youngsville, LA 70592
(318) 856-5293

GRB  Greenbrier Farms, Inc.
201 Hickory Road W.
Chesapeake, VA 23322
(804) 421-2141

GRE  Greener 'n Ever Tree Nursery
8940 Carmel Valley Road
Carmel, CA 93921
(408) 624-2149

GRI  Griffey's Nursery
1670 Highway 25-70
Marshall, NC 28753
(704) 656-2334

GRL  Greenleaf Nursery Co. (W)
Highway 82 South
Park Hill, OK 74451
(918) 457-5172

GRM  Greenmantle Nursery
3010 Ettersburg Road
Garberville, CA 95440
(707) 986-7504

GRR  Greer Gardens (W/R)
1280 Goodpasture Island Road
Eugene, OR 97401-1794
(541) 686-8266

GRV  Green View Nursery
2700 Cedar Hills Drive
Dunlap, IL 61525
(309) 243-7761

GTN  Greentree Nurseries
5300 Crackersport Road
Allentown, PA 18104
(215) 395-6777

GUE  F.A. Guernsey & Co., Inc.
R.D. 1, Route 30, Box 294
Schoharie, NY 12157

GVN  Green Value Nursery
3180 Edgerton Street
Vadnais Heights, MN 55127
(612) 483-1176

HAL  H. G. Hallum Nursery Co.
Route 3
McMinnville, TN 37110
(615) 668-8504

HAN  Halladin Nursery (W/R)
16250 S.E. Highway 212
Clackamas, OR 97015

HCR  High Country Rosarium (W/R)
1717 Downing Street
Denver, CO 80218
(303) 832-4026

HEA  Heard Gardens, Ltd.
5355 Merle Hay Road
Johnston, IA 50131
(515) 276-4533

HEO  Heronswood Nursery (W/R)
7530 288th Street, NE
Kingston, WA 98346
(206) 297-4172

HER  R. Herbst, Wholesale Seed
Candlewood Isle, P.O. Box 108
New Fairfield, CT 06812
(203) 746-1842

HES  Hess's Nurseries (W)
Route 553, Box 326
Cedarville, NJ 08311
(609) 447-4213

HEY  Heasley's Nurseries, Inc. (W/R)
247 Freeport Road
Butler, PA 16001
(412) 287-1962

HIH  Hines Nurseries
P.O. Box 42284
Houston, TX 77242
(713) 342-1131

HIL  Hillier Nurseries Ltd. (W/R)
Ampfield House
Ampfield, Romsey
Hants SO51 9PA
United Kingdom
0794-68733

HIN Hinsdale Nurseries, Inc. (W)
7200 S. Madison Road
Hinsdale, IL 60521
(708) 232-1411

HIR Historical Roses
1657 W. Jackson Street
Painesville, OH 44077
(216) 357-7270

HIS Hines Nurseries (W)
P.O. Box 11208
Santa Ana, CA 92711
(800) 63-HINES

HIV Hines Nurseries (W)
P.O. Box 1449
Vacaville, CA 95696
(707) 446-4700

HLS Hillis Nursery Co., Inc.
Route 2, Box 142
McMinnville, TN 37110
(615) 668-4364

HNU Hansen Nurseries
P.O. Box 8
Sassamansville, PA 19472
(215) 754-7843

HOB C. M. Hobbs & Sons, Ltd. (W)
9300 W. Washington Street
P.O. Box 31227
Indianapolis, IN 46231
(317) 247-4478

HOL Holbrook Farm & Nursery (W/R)
115 Lance Road, P.O. Box 368
Fletcher, NC 28732
(704) 891-7790

HOM Homestead Nurseries, Ltd.
4262 Wright Road
Clayburn, B.C., V0X 1E0
Canada
(604) 859-3912

HOO Hooks Nursery, Inc.
P.O. Box 455
Lake Zurich, IL 60047
(708) 438-7198

HOT Hortico (W)
723 Robson Road, R.R. #1
Waterdown, Ontario L0R 2H0
Canada
(416) 689-6984

HRG Heritage Rose Gardens
16831 Mitchell Creek Drive
Ft. Bragg, CA 95437
(707) 984-6959

HSS Turk Hesselund Nursery
1255 Coast Village Road

Santa Barbara, CA 93108
(805) 969-5871

HST Hanchar's Superior Trees
R.D. 1, Box 118
Mahaffey, PA 15757
(814) 277-6674

HUD J. L. Hudson, Seedsman
P.O. Box 1058
Redwood City, CA 94064

IMP Imperial Nurseries
P.O. Box 120
Granby, CT 06035
(860) 653-4541

ING Ingleside Plantation Nurseries (W)
Box 1038
Oak Grove, VA 22443
(804) 224-7111

ISE Iseli Nursery, Inc. (W)
30590 S.E. Kelso Road
Boring, OR 97009
(800) 777-6202

INT Interstate Nurseries
P.O. Box 208
Hamburg, IA 51644
(800) 325-4180

JWL Jewell Nurseries (W)
Box 457
Lake City, MN 55041-0457
(800) 848-0933

KAN Kankakee Nursery Co.
P.O. Box 388
Aroma Park, IL 60910
(815) 937-9358

KDN Kelly Nurseries
P.O. Box 800
Dansville, NY 14437
(716) 335-2180

KED Keenan's Edgewood Nursery
3740 Stalker Road
Macedon, NY 14502

KEL Kelly Nurseries
410 8th Avenue, N.E.
Faribault, MN 55021
(507) 334-1623

KHN Knight Hollow Nursery, Inc. (W)
3333 Atom Road
Middleton, WI 53562
(608) 831-5570

KIN King Nursery
6849 Route 34
Oswego, IL 60543
(708) 554-1171

KIW Kiwi Developments
Route 3, S. Fimple Road, Box 61
Chico, LA 95926
(916) 345-0823

KLE Klehm Nursery (W/R)
Route 5, Penny Road, Box 197
South Barrington, IL 60010-9390
(847) 551-3710

KNI Knight's Creek Nursery
Route 5, Box 84A
Menomonie, WI 54751
(715) 664-8687

KRA V. Kraus Nurseries, Ltd.
Carlisle, Ontario L0R 1H0
Canada
(416) 689-4022

KRI Kristick Rare Plants
155 Mockingbird Road
Wellsville, PA 17365
(717) 292-2962

KRN Kraemer's Nursery
13523 Marquam Road, N.E.
Mt. Angel, OR 97362

LAK Lake County Nursery (W)
Route 84, Box 122
Perry, OH 44081-0122
(216) 259-5571

LAL Lamb Nurseries (W/R)
E. 101 Sharp Avenue
Spokane, WA 99202
(509) 328-7956

LAM Lamtree Farm (W/R)
Route 1, Box 162
Warrensville, NC 28693
(919) 385-6144

LAN Landscape Supply, Inc. (W)
24300 Brest Road
Taylor, MI 48108
(313) 946-7000

LAS Las Pilitas Nursery (W/R)
Star Route Box 23X
Santa Margarita, CA 93453
(805) 438-5992

LAW Lawyer Nursery (W)
950 Highway 200 W.
Plains, MT 59859
(406) 826-3881

LDN Landscape Nursery
1955 Apopka-Vin Road
Orlando, FL 32811
(407) 298-1703

LEE  Lee Nursery, Inc.
Route 2, Box 207
Fertile, MN 56540
(218) 574-2237

LEW  Lewis Nursery
1230 Route 313, Box 224
Fountainville, PA 18923

LIT  Little Valley Nurseries (W/R)
13022 E. 136th Avenue
Brighton, CO 80601
(303) 659-6708

LIV  Live Oak Gardens
284 Rip Van Winkle Road
New Iberia, LA 70560
(318) 367-3485

LMN  Lake Mills Nursery, Inc.
W7628 Conservation Road
Lake Mills, WI 53551
(414) 648-2034

LOG  Logee's Greenhouses
141 North Street
Danielson, CT 06239
(860) 774-8038

LON  Lone Star Growers
7960 Cagnon Road
San Antonio, TX 78227
(512) 677-8020

LOS  Herman Losely & Son, Inc.,
Nursery
3410 Shepard Road
Perry, OH 44081
(216) 259-2725

LOT  Land O'Trees
1042 Wehrle Drive
Williamsville, NY 14221

LOU  Louisiana Nursery
Route 7, Box 43
Opelousas, LA 70570
(318) 948-3696

LOW  Lowe's Own-Root Roses
6 Sheffield Road
Nashua, NH 03062
(603) 888-2214

LUS  Baier Lustgarten Farms and
Nurseries
1130 Middle Country Road
Middle Island, NY 11953
(516) 924-3444

MAG  Magnolia Gardens Nursery (W)
18810 Turtle Creek
Magnolia, TX 77355
(713) 356-1213

MAN  Manbeck Nurseries, Inc.
New Knoxville, OH 45871
(419) 753-2588

MAO  Manor View Farm
15601 Manor Road
Monkton, MD 21111
(410) 771-4700

MAP  Maple Leaf Nursery
4236 Greenstone Road
Placerville, CA 95667
(916) 622-2265

MAX  Maxalea Nurseries, Inc.
900 Oak Hill Road
Baltimore, MD 21239
(410) 377-7500

MBN  Monterey Bay Nursery (W)
Watsonville, CA 95077
(408) 724-6361

MCD  McDonald Nursery
Route 1, Box 113
Cameron, NC 28326
(919) 245-7618

MCG  A. McGill & Son
P.O. Box 70
Fairview, OR 97024
(503) 665-4156

MCK  McKay Nursery Co.
254 S. Jefferson Street
P.O. Box 185
Waterloo, WI 53594
(414) 478-2121

MCL  MacLean Nurseries (W/R)
9000 Satyr Hill Road
Baltimore, MD 21234
(410) 882-6714

MEL  Mellinger's, Inc.
2310 W. South Range Road
North Lima, OH 44452-9731
(216) 549-9861

MES  Mesozoic Landscapes, Inc.
7667 Park Lane West
Lake Worth, FL 33467
(407) 967-2630

MHS  Manatee Horticultural Services
P.O. Box 19021
W. Palm Beach, FL 33416-9021
(407) 439-1458

MID  Midwest Groundcovers (W)
P.O. Box 748
St. Charles, IL 60174
(708) 742-1790

MIL  J.E. Miller Nurseries, Inc.
5060 W. Lake Road
Canandaigua, NY 14424
(800) 836-9630

MIN  Minnesota Valley Wholesale, Inc.
14505 Johnson Memorial Drive
Shakopee, MN 55379
(612) 445-7120

MIS  Mist House
P.O. Box 3645
Boynton Beach, FL 33424
(407) 793-7376

MIT  Mitsch Nursery, Inc. (W)
6652 S. Lone Elder Road
Aurora, OR 97002-9399
(503) 266-9652

MNP  Mandarin Native Plants
13500 Mandarin Road
Jacksonville, FL 32223
(904) 268-2904

MNR  Montrose Nursery
P.O. Box 957
Hillsborough, NC 27278
(919) 732-7787

MOB  Molbak's
13625 N.E. 175th
Woodinville, WA 98072
(206) 483-5000

MOE  Morden Nurseries
P.O. Box 1270
Morden, Manitoba R0G 1J0
Canada
(204) 822-3311

MOD  Morden Research Center
Reg Cucey, Director
Agricultural Canada
P.O. Box 3001
Morden, Manitoba R0G IJ0

MOL  Moller's Nursery, Inc. (W)
34519 S.E. Lusted Road
Gresham, OR 97080
(800) 637-0777

MON  Monrovia Nursery Co. (W)
18331 E. Foothill Boulevard
Azusa, CA 91702-1336
(818) 334-9321

MOR  Moriwaki Nursery
Kahaluu, HI 96744

MOT  Robt. W. Montgomery Landscape
Nursery (W)
Route 113, Box 67
Chester Springs, PA 19425
(215) 644-3406

MOU Mount Arbor Nurseries
P.O. Box 129
Shenandoah, IA 51601
(712) 246-4250

MOZ Mountain States Nursery
P.O. Box 33982
Phoenix, AZ 85067
(602) 247-8509

MPK Miniature Plant Kingdom (W/R)
4125 Harrison Grade Road
Sebastopol, CA 95472
(707) 874-2233

MRT Moretti Nursery
Perry, OH 44801

MSS Moses Nurseries, Inc. (W)
2079 Lake Avenue
Lima, NY 14485

MUS Musser Forests (W/R)
P.O. Box 13
Indiana, PA 15701-0340
(412) 465-5685

NAS Native Sons Wholesale Nursery
379 W. El Campo Road
Arroyo Grande, CA 93420
(805) 481-5996

NIC Niche Gardens
1111 Dawson Road
Chapel Hill, NC 27516
(919) 967-0078

NON Northland Nursery
16700 Pueblo Boulevard
Jordan, MN 55352

NPI Native Plants, Inc.
417 Wakara Way
Salt Lake City, UT 84108
(801) 582-0144

NRT Northeast Nurseries
Country Road 48, Box 1158
Cutchogue, NY 11935

NTW Northwoods Nursery
27635 S. Oglesby Road
Canby, OR 97013
(503) 266-5432

NUC Nuccio's Nursery (W/R)
3555 Chaney Trail
P.O. Box 6160
Altadena, CA 91001
(818) 794-3383

OKI OKI Nursery Co. (W)
P.O. Box 7118
Sacramento, CA 95826
(916) 383-5665

OLD Old Farm Nursery (W/R)
5550 Indiana Street
Golden, CO 80403
(303) 278-0754

OLI Oliver Nurseries
1159 Bronson Road
Fairfield, CT 06430
(203) 259-5609

ONA Onarga Nursery Co.
Onarga, IL 60955
(815) 268-7244

ORC Orchid Gardens
2232-139th Avenue, NW
Andover, MN 55304
(612) 755-0205

OWE Owen Farms (W/R)
2951 Curve-Nankipoo Road
Route 3, Box 158-A
Ripley, TN 38063
(901) 635-1588

PAF Pacific Tree Farm (W/R)
4301 Lynwood Drive
Chula Vista, CA 92010
(619) 422-2400

PAT Patuxent Valley Nursery
11018 Berrypick Lane
Columbia, MD 21044
(301) 997-5689

PDN P&D Nursery
3940 S.W. Halcyon Road
Tualatin, OR 97062

PIC Pickering Nurseries
670 Kingston Road
Pickering, Ontario L1V 1A6
Canada
(416) 839-2111

PLA Plantage, Inc. (W)
P.O. Box 28
Cutchogue, NY 11935
(516) 734-6832

PLD Plant Delights Nursery
9421 Sauls Road
Raleigh, NC 27603
(919) 772-4794

PLE Pleasant Cove Nursery (W)
Route 3
Rock Island, TN 38581
(615) 686-2215

PLH Platt Hill Nursery, Inc.
222 W. Lake Street
Bloomingdale, IL 60108-1038
(708) 529-9394

PLT Plants of the Southwest
Agua Fria, Route 6, Box 11A
Santa Fe, NM 87501
(505) 471-2212

PNF Panfield Nurseries (W/R)
322 Southdown Road
Huntington, NY 11743
(516) 427-0112

POW Powell's Gardens (W/R)
Route 3, Box 21
Princeton, NC 27569
(919) 936-4421

PRI Princeton Nurseries (W)
P.O. Box 191
Princeton, NJ 08542
(609) 924-1776

QUA Quansett Nursery
794 Horseneck Road
South Dartmouth, MA 02748
(508) 636-6931

RAR Raraflora Nursery
16 Beverly Drive
Kintnersville, PA 18930
(610) 847-8208

REA Reath's Nursery (W/R)
County Road 577, Box 247
Vulcan, MI 49892
(906) 563-9777

REI Reid Collins Nurseries, Ltd.
2396 272nd Street, P.O. Box 430
Aldergrove, B.C. V0X 1A0
Canada
(604) 533-2212

RID Ridge Manor Nurseries
7925 N. Ridge E.
Madison, OH 44057

RIE Rice Creek Gardens
11506 Highway 65
Blaine, MN 55434
(612) 754-8090

ROA Rose Acres
6641 Crystal Boulevard
Diamond Springs, CA 95619
(916) 626-1722

ROC Rocknoll Nursery
7812 Mad River Road
Hillsboro, OH 45133
(513) 393-1278

ROE Rosendale Nursery (W)
2660 E. Lake Avenue
Watsonville, CA 95076
(408) 728-2599

ROR   Roses & Roses & Roses
      14985 Wadsworth Road
      Wadsworth, IL 60083
      (847) 338-1086

ROS   Roses of Yesterday & Today
      802 Brown's Valley Road
      Watsonville, CA 95076-0398
      (408) 724-2755

ROY   Roslyn Nursery (W/R)
      211 Burrs Lane
      Dix Hills, NY 11746
      (516) 643-9347

RSN   R&S Nursery
      Route 4, Box 1200
      Hillsboro, OR 97123

RUN   Ruslyn Nursery
      107 Mountain Rest Road
      New Paltz, NY 12561

SAL   Salter Tree Farm (W/R)
      Route 2, Box 1332
      Madison, FL 32340
      (904) 973-6312

SAN   San Marcos Growers (W)
      125 S. San Marcos Road
      P.O. Box 6827
      Santa Barbara, CA 93110
      (805) 964-5089

SAO   San Lorenzo Lumber Co. Nursery
      235 River
      Santa Cruz, CA 95060
      (408) 426-1020

SAR   Saratoga Horticultural Foundation
        (W)
      15185 Murphy Avenue
      San Martin, CA 95046
      (408) 779-3303

SBN   Sunny Border Nurseries, Inc.
      1709 Kensington Road
      P.O. Box 86
      Kensington, CT 06037
      (203) 828-0321

SCA   Scarff's Nursery, Inc.
      411 N. Dayton-Lakeview Road
      New Carlisle, OH 45344
      (513) 845-3821

SCH   J. Frank Schmidt & Son Co. (W)
      9500 S.E. 327th Avenue
      Boring, OR 97009
      (503) 663-4128

SCN   Schichtel's Nursery
      6745 Chestnut Ridge Road
      Orchard Park, NY 14127

SCR   Schroeder's Nursery
      23379 W. Route 66
      Grayslake, IL 60030
      (847) 546-9444

SCU   F. W. Schumacher Co., Inc. (W)
      36 Spring Hill Road
      Sandwich, MA 02563
      (508) 888-0659

SEL   Select Plus Nurseries
      1510 Pine Road
      Mascouche, Quebec J7L 2M4
      Canada
      (514) 477-3797

SHA   Shadow Nursery (W)
      Route 1, Box 37A
      Winchester, TN 37398
      (615) 967-6059

SHE   Shemin Nurseries, Inc. (W)
      4N755 Lombard Road
      P.O. Box 857
      Addison, IL 60101
      (708) 773-8090

SHF   Sheffield's Tree & Shrub Seed
      273 Auburn Road, Route 34
      Locke, NY 13092
      (315) 497-1058

SHR   Sheridan Nurseries (W)
      R.R. 4—10th Line
      Georgetown, Ontario L7G 4S7
      Canada
      (416) 873-2478

SIE   Siebenthaler Co. (W/R)
      3001 Catalpa Drive
      Dayton, OH 45405
      (513) 274-1154

SIM   Simpson Nursery Co. (W)
      1504 Wheatland Road
      P.O. Box 2065
      Vincennes, IN 47591
      (812) 882-2441

SIS   Siskiyou Rare Plant Nursery
      2825 Cummings Road
      Medford, OR 97501
      (541) 772-6846

SKL   Skylark Nursery
      6735 Sonoma Highway
      Santa Rosa, CA 95409
      (707) 539-1565

SKY   Skyline Evergreen Farm
      Bentonville, VA 22610
      (703) 635-4366

SLW   St. Lawrence Nurseries
      R.R. 5, Box 324
      Potsdam, NY 13676

SMH   Smith Nursery Co. (W/R)
      P.O. Box 515
      Charles City, IA 50616
      (515) 228-3239

SMI   Smirnow's Son
      11 Oakwood Drive W., Route #1
      Huntington, NY 11743
      (516) 421-0836

SMT   Smithfield Gardens
      Route 17, Crittenden Station
      Crittenden, VA 23433
      (804) 238-2511

SNC   Sherman Nursery Co. (W)
      1300 W. Grove Street
      Charles City, IA 50616
      (515) 228-1124

SNS   Southwestern Native Seeds
      P.O. Box 50503
      Tucson, AZ 85703

SOL   Winn Soldani's Fancy Hibiscus
        Nursery
      1442 S.W. 1st Avenue
      Pompano Beach, FL 33060-8706
      (305) 782-0741

SON   Shady Oaks Nursery
      700 19th Avenue N.E.
      Waseca, MN 56093
      (507) 835-5033

SPR   Sprainbrook Nursery, Inc. (W/R)
      448 Underhill Road
      Scarsdale, NY 10583
      (914) 723-2382

SPS   Spring Meadow Nursery, Inc.
      12601 120th Avenue
      Grand Haven, MI 49417
      (616) 846-4729

SPV   Springvale Farm Nursery, Inc.
      Mozier Hollow Road
      Hamburg, IL 62045
      (618) 232-1108

SQL   Soquel Growers
      3645 N. Main
      Soquel, CA 95073
      (408) 475-3533

STU   Studebaker Nurseries, Inc. (W)
      11140 Milton-Carlisle Road
      New Carlisle, OH 45344
      (513) 845-3816

STY   J. Franklin Styer Nurseries (W/R)
U.S. Route 1, Baltimore Pike
P.O. Box 98
Concordville, PA 19331
(215) 459-2400

SUC   Suncrest Nursery (W)
400 Casserly Road
Watsonville, CA 95076
(408) 728-2595

SUN   Sunlight Gardens
174 Golden Lane, CG4
Andersonville, TN 37705
(615) 494-8237

SUP   Superior Trees, Inc.
P.O. Box 9325
Lee, FL 32059
(904) 971-5159

SWE   Swedberg Nurseries, Inc.
P.O. Box 418
Battle Lake, MN 56515
(218) 864-5526

SWT   The Sweetbriar (W)
13825 132 Avenue NE
Kirkland, WA 98034
(206) 821-2222

SYL   Sylvan Nursery Inc.
1028 Horseneck Road
Westport, MA 02790
(508) 636-4573

SYN   Synnestvedt Nursery Co. (W/R)
24550 W. Highway 120
Round Lake, IL 60073
(847) 546-4700

TAY   Taylor's Nursery
3705 New Bern Avenue
Raleigh, NC 27610

TEC   Tecza & Sons Nurseries, Inc.
36 W730 McDonald
Elgin, IL 60123
(847) 742-3321

THO   Thomasville Nurseries, Inc.
P.O. Box 7
Thomasville, GA 31799
(912) 226-5568

TIM   Timber Creek Farms & Nurseries
(W)
10702 Allendale Road
Woodstock, IL 60098
(815) 648-4272

TNA   The Natives
2929 Carter Road
Davenport, FL 33837
(813) 422-6664

TRH   Treehaven Evergreen Nursery (W)
981 Jamison Road
Elma, NY 14059

TRI   Triangle Nursery (W)
Route 2
McMinnville, TN 37110
(615) 668-8022

TRL   Tree of Life (W)
33201 Ortega Highway
P.O. Box 736
San Juan Capistrano, CA 92693
(714) 728-0685

TRO   Tropic World (W/R)
26437 N. Center City Parkway
Escondido, CA 92026
(619) 746-6108

TUR   Matt Tures & Sons Nursery
9810 Dundee Road
Huntley, IL 60142
(847) 669-5024

TUS   Turner's Bend Nursery
Route 6, Box 175PL
McMinnville, TN 37110
(615) 668-4543

TWO   Twombly Nursery (W/R)
163 Barn Hill Road
Monroe, CT 06468
(203) 261-2133

UCA   University of California Arboretum
Santa Cruz, CA 95064
(408) 427-2998

UXB   Uxbridge Nurseries Ltd.
P.O. Box 400
Uxbridge, Ontario L9P 1M8
Canada
(416) 655-3379

VAL   Valley Nursery (W/R)
Box 4845
2801 N. Montana Avenue
Helena, MT 59604
(406) 442-8460

VIE   Martin Viette's Nurseries (W/R)
P.O. Box 10
Route 25A, Northern Blvd.
East Norwich, NY 11732
(516) 922-5530

VIN   Vine & Branch Nursery (W)
5 Hitching Rack Ct.
Durham, NC 27713
(919) 490-1866

VLL   Valley Gardens
Route 209, P.O. Box 76
Accord, NY 12404

WAG   Wagner Farms
9937 S. Route 59
Plainfield, IL 60544
(708) 904-0016

WAR   Warren County Nursery, Inc. (W)
Route 2, Box 204
McMinnville, TN 37110
(615) 668-8941

WAS   Washington Evergreen Nursery
Brooks Branch Road, P.O. Box 388
Leicester, NC 28748
(704) 683-5033

WAT   Watkin's Nursery (W)
15001 Midlothian Pike
Midlothian, VA 23113
(804) 379-8733

WAU   Waynesboro Nurseries, Inc. (W)
P.O. Box 987
Waynesboro, VA 22980
(540) 942-4141

WAV   Wavecrest Nursery (W/R)
2509 Lakeshore Drive
Fennville, MI 49408
(616) 543-4175

WAY   Wayside Gardens
1 Garden Lane
Hodges, SC 29695-0001
(800) 845-1124

WDL   Woodland Nursery
Johnson Road
Salisbury, MD 21801

WED   Wedge Nursery
Route 2, Box 114
Albert Lea, MN 56007
(507) 373-5225

WEI   Arthur Weiler, Inc.
12247 Russell Road
Zion, IL 60099
(847) 746-2393

WEM   Wells-Medina Nursery
8300 N.E. 24th Street
Bellevue, WA 98004
(206) 454-1853

WEN   We-Du Nurseries (W/R)
Route 5, Box 724
Marion, NC 28752
(704) 738-8300

WES   Weston Nurseries (W/R)
E. Main Street
Route 135, Box 186
Hopkinton, MA 01748-0186
(508) 435-3414

WFF  White Flower Farm
Route 63, P.O. Box 50
Litchfield, CT 06759-0050
(860) 496-9600

WHI  Whitney Gardens & Nursery
(W/R)
P.O. Box F, Highway 101
Brinnon, WA 98320-0080
(206) 796-4411

WIB  Willowbend Nursery
4654 Davis Road
Perry, OH 44081
(216) 259-3121

WIG  Wight Nurseries (W)
Box 390
Cairo, GA 31728
(912) 377-3033

WIL  Wilson Nurseries, Inc.
Route 1, Box 25
43W967 Route 72
Hampshire, IL 60140
(847) 683-3700

WIN  Winsel-Gibbs Nursery
31479 W. Pacific Coast Highway
Malibu, CA 90265
(213) 457-7672

WIS  Windsor Road Nurseries
Box 884
Cornish, NH 03745
(603) 543-3339

WIT  Winterthur Museum and Gardens
(W/R)
Route 52
Winterthur, DE 19735
(302) 888-4779

WIW  Willoway Nurseries, Inc. (W)
4534 Center Road
Avon, OH 44011
(216) 871-9494

WNC  Willis Nursery Co., Inc.
P.O. Box 530
5th & Cherry
Ottawa, KS 66067
(913) 242-2525

WOD  Woodlanders, Inc.
1128 Colleton Avenue
Aiken, SC 29801
(803) 648-7522

WON  Woodland Nurseries
2151 Camilla Road
Mississanga, Ontario L5A 2K1
Canada
(416) 277-2961

WTN  Whitman Nurseries, Inc.
326 Walt Whitman Road
Huntington Station, NY 11746
(516) 673-5021

YUC  Yucca Do Nursery
P.O. Box 655
Waller, TX 77484-0655
(409) 826-6363

ZEL  Zelenka Nursery, Inc. (W)
16127 Winans
Grand Haven, MI 49417
(616) 842-1367

# APPENDIX III

# Shrubs Grouped by Desirable Landscape Characteristics

## SHRUBS LISTED BY USDA HARDINESS ZONES

The hardiness of a plant cannot be determined solely by a definitive zone number. Often plant hardiness is affected by the plant's micro climate, which includes factors such as soil conditions, protection from wind, proximity to large bodies of water, sudden temperature variation, and so forth. The U.S. Department of Agriculture hardiness zone ranges presented here are suggested as a broad guide to planting. In some cases, the heat tolerance is unknown to date.

### ZONE 2

*Comptonia peregrina* 2–5
    *C. peregrina* var. *asplenifolia* 2–5
*Juniperus chinensis* 'Echiniformis' 2–6
    *J. virginiana* 'Grey Owl' 2–8
*Kalmia angustifolia* 2–8
    *K. angustifolia* f. *candida* 2–8
    *K. angustifolia* 'Hammonasset' 2–8
    *K. angustifolia* 'Pumila' 2–8
*Myrica gale* 2–7
*Picea pungens* 'Compacta' 2–7
    *P. pungens* 'Montgomery' 2–7
*Pinus mugo* 'Mops' 2–7
*Rhamnus frangula* 'Asplenifolia' 2–7
*Ribes aureum* 2–7
    *R. odoratum* 'Aureum' 2–8
*Salix lanata* 2–4
*Sorbaria aitchisonii* 2–10
    *S. sorbifolia* 2–10
*Syringa* × *henryi* 2–7
    *S.* × *henryi* 'Lutèce' 2–7
    *S.* × *henryi* 'Summer White' 2–7
    *S.* × *prestoniae* 2–7
    *S.* × *prestoniae* 'Alice Rose Foster' 2–7
    *S.* × *prestoniae* 'Ethel M. Webster' 2–7
    *S.* × *prestoniae* 'Isabella' 2–7
    *S.* × *prestoniae* 'Nike' 2–7

### ZONE 3

*Caragana frutex* 'Globosa' 3–7
*Cornus sericea* 'Cardinal' 3–8
    *C. sericea* 'Isanti' 3–8
    *C. sericea* 'Silver & Gold' 3–8
*Hippophae rhamnoides* 3–7
*Hydrangea arborescens* 'Annabelle' 3–9
    *H. aspera* subsp. *aspera* 3–9
    *H. paniculata* 'Tardiva' 3–8
    *H. sargentiana* 3–9
*Myrica pensylvanica* 3–7
*Picea abies* 'Little Gem' 3–7
    *P. abies* 'Nidiformis' 3–7
    *P. abies* 'Reflexa' 3–7
*Pinus densiflora* 'Globosa' 3–7
    *P. sylvestris* 'Beuvronensis' 3–7
    *P. sylvestris* 'Hillside Creeper' 3–7
*Physocarpus opulifolius* 'Dart's Golden' 3–7
*Potentilla fruticosa* 3–7
    *P. fruticosa* 'Abbotswood' 3–7
    *P. fruticosa* 'Coronation Triumph' 3–7
    *P. fruticosa* 'Day Dawn Viette' 3–7
    *P. fruticosa* 'Goldfinger' 3–7
    *P. fruticosa* 'Katherine Dykes' 3–7
    *P. fruticosa* 'Pink Queen' 3–7
    *P. fruticosa* 'Primrose Beauty' 3–7
    *P. fruticosa* 'Snowbird' 3–7
    *P. fruticosa* 'Yellowbird' 3–7
*Rhus glabra* var. *cismontana* 3–8
*Ribes alpinum* 'Green Mound' 3–7
*Rosa glauca* 3–8
    *R.* 'Henry Kelsey' 3–8
    *R. rugosa* 'Blanc Double de Coubert' 3–8
    *R. rugosa* 'Charles Albanel' 3–8
    *R. rugosa* 'Fru Dagmar Hastrup' 3–8
    *R. rugosa* 'Henry Hudson' 3–8

    *R. rugosa* 'Jens Munk' 3–8
    *R. rugosa* 'Linda Campbell' 3–8
    *R. rugosa* 'Roseraie de l'Hay' 3–8
    *R. rugosa* 'Rubra' 3–8
    *R. rugosa* 'Sarah Van Fleet' 3–8
    *R. rugosa* 'Sir Thomas Lipton' 3–8
    *R. rugosa* 'Topaz Jewel' 3–8
*Shepherdia argentea* (2)3–6
    *S. canadensis* (2)3–6
*Spiraea japonica* 'Shibori' 3–8
    *S. nipponica* 'Halward's Silver' 3–6
    *S. nipponica* 'Snowmound' 3–8
*Stephanandra incisa* 'Crispa' 3–7
*Syringa* × *hyacinthiflora* 3–7
    *S.* × *hyacinthiflora* 'Blanche Sweet' 3–7
    *S.* × *hyacinthiflora* 'Maiden's Blush' 3–7
    *S.* × *hyacinthiflora* 'Sister Justena' 3–7
    *S.* × *josiflexa* 'Anna Amhoff' 3–6
    *S.* × *josiflexa* 'James MacFarlane' 3–6
    *S.* × *josiflexa* 'Royalty' 3–6
    *S. patula* 'Miss Kim' 3–7
*Tsuga canadensis* 'Bennett' 3–7
    *T. canadensis* 'Jeddeloh' 3–7
    *T. canadensis* 'Jervis' 3–7

### ZONE 4

*Amelanchier ovalis* 'Pumila' 4–8
*Aralia elata* 'Aureovariegata' 4–9
    *A. elata* 'Pyramidalis' 4–9
    *A. elata* 'Variegata' 4–9
*Berberis koreana* 4–8
    *B. thunbergii* 'Bogozam' 4–7

*Caragana pygmaea* 4–7
*Chamaecyparis obtusa* 'Juniperoides' 4–8
  *C. obtusa* 'Kosteri' 4–8
  *C. obtusa* 'Nana' 4–8
  *C. obtusa* 'Nana Gracilis' 4–8
  *C. obtusa* 'Nana Lutea' 4–8
  *C. pisifera* 'Boulevard' 4–8
  *C. pisifera* 'Filifera Nana' 4–8
  *C. pisifera* 'Gold Spangle' 4–8
  *C. pisifera* 'Squarrosa Intermedia' 4–8
*Cotoneaster racemiflorus* var. *soongoricus* 4–7
*Euonymus alatus* 'Nordine Strain' 4–7
  *E. alatus* 'Rudy Haag' 4–7
  *E. alatus* 'Timber Creek' 4–7
  *E. europaeus* 'Redcap' 4–7
*Forsythia mandshurica* 'Vermont Sun' 4–7
  *F.* 'New Hampshire Gold' 4–7
  *F. viridissima* var. *koreana* 'Ilgwang' 4–8
*Hamamelis virginiana* 4–8
*Ilex verticillata* 4–9
  *I. verticillata* 'Afterglow' 4–9
  *I. verticillata* 'Aurantiaca' 4–9
  *I. verticillata* f. *chrysocarpa* 4–9
  *I. verticillata* 'Maryland Beauty' 4–9
  *I. verticillata* 'Red Sprite' 4–9
  *I. verticillata* 'Scarlett O'Hara' 4–9
  *I. verticillata* 'Shaver' 4–9
  *I. verticillata* 'Sunset' 4–9
  *I. verticillata* 'Tiasquam' 4–9
  *I. verticillata* 'Winter Gold' 4–9
  *I. verticillata* 'Winter Red' 4–9
*Juniperus squamata* 'Blue Star' 4–7
*Lonicera* 'Honey Rose' 4–6
  *L. xylosteum* 'Emerald Mound' 4–6
*Paeonia suffruticosa* 4–8
  *P. suffruticosa* 'Alhambra' 4–8
  *P. suffruticosa* 'Ariadne' 4–8
  *P. suffruticosa* 'Companion of Serenity' 4–8
  *P. suffruticosa* 'Hana Kisoi' 4–8
  *P. suffruticosa* 'Hephestos' 4–8
  *P. suffruticosa* 'Joseph Rock' 4–8
  *P. suffruticosa* 'Leda' 4–8
  *P. suffruticosa* 'Renkaku' 4–8
  *P. suffruticosa* 'Shintenchi' 4–8
*Philadelphus coronarius* 'Natchez' 4–8
  *P. × virginalis* 4–8
  *P. × virginalis* 'Minnesota Snowflake' 4–8
*Picea omorika* 'Nana' 4–7
*Rhus aromatica* 'Gro-low' 4–8
  *R. copallina* 4–8
  *R. typhina* 'Dissecta' 4–8
  *R. typhina* 'Laciniata' 4–8
*Ribes odoratum* 4–8
*Rosa* 'Adelaide Hoodless' (3)4–9
  *R.* 'A. MacKenzie' 4–9
  *R.* 'Assiniboine' (3)4–9

*R.* 'Carefree Beauty' 4–9
*R.* 'Carefree Wonder' 4–9
*R.* 'Cuthbert Grant' (3)4–9
*R.* 'Golden Wings' 4–9
*R.* 'John Franklin' 4–9
*R.* 'Morden Amorette' (3)4–9
*R.* 'Morden Blush' (3)4–9
*R.* 'Morden Cardinette' (3)4–9
*R.* 'Morden Centennial' (3)4–9
*R.* 'Morden Fireglow' (3)4–9
*R.* 'Morden Ruby' (3)4–9
*R. rugosa* 'Therese Bugnet' 4–8
*R.* 'Winnipeg Parks' (3)4–9
*Spiraea × cinerea* 'Grefsheim' 4–8
  *S. fritschiana* 4
*Syringa × josiflexa* 'Agnes Smith' 4–6
  *S. meyeri* 'Palibin' 4–7(8)
  *S. vulgaris* 4–7(8)
  *S. vulgaris* 'Agincourt Beauty' 4–7(8)
  *S. vulgaris* 'Albert F. Holden' 4–7(8)
  *S. vulgaris* 'Blue Skies' 4–10
  *S. vulgaris* 'Dwight D. Eisenhower' 4–7(8)
  *S. vulgaris* 'Edith Cavell' 4–7(8)
  *S. vulgaris* 'Edward J. Gardner' 4–7(8)
  *S. vulgaris* 'Emile Lemoine' 4–7(8)
  *S. vulgaris* 'Krasavitsa Moskvy' 4–7(8)
  *S. vulgaris* 'Lavender Lady' 4–7(8)
  *S. vulgaris* 'Ludwig Spaeth' 4–7(8)
  *S. vulgaris* 'Marie Francis' 4–7(8)
  *S. vulgaris* 'Mieczta' 4–7(8)
  *S. vulgaris* 'Miss Ellen Willmott' 4–7(8)
  *S. vulgaris* 'Primrose' 4–7(8)
  *S. vulgaris* 'Rochester' 4–7(8)
  *S. vulgaris* 'Sensation' 4–7(8)
  *S. vulgaris* 'Slater's Elegance' 4–7(8)
  *S. vulgaris* 'Victor Lemoine' 4–7(8)
  *S. vulgaris* 'Wedgwood Blue' 4–7(8)
  *S. vulgaris* 'Wonder Blue' 4–7(8)
  *S. vulgaris* 'Yankee Doodle' 4–7(8)
*Viburnum lantana* 'Mohican' 4–8
  *V. sargentii* 'Flavum' 4–6
  *V. sargentii* 'Onondaga' 4–6
  *V. sargentii* 'Susquehanna' 4–6

## ZONE 5

*Abeliophyllum distichum* 5–8
*Acanthopanax sieboldianus* 'Variegatus' 5–8
*Aesculus parviflora* 5–8
  *A. parviflora* 'Rogers' 5–8
  *A. parviflora* f. *serotina* 5–8
*Aralia cordata* 5–9
  *A. spinosa* 5–9
*Aronia arbutifolia* 'Brilliantissima' 5–8
  *A. melanocarpa* 5–8
*Berberis thunbergii* 5–8
  *B. thunbergii* 'Atropurpurea' 5–8
  *B. thunbergii* 'Bagatelle' 5–8

*B. thunbergii* 'Globe' 5–8
*B. thunbergii* 'Kobold' 5–8
*B. thunbergii* 'Rose Glow' 5–8
*B. thunbergii* 'Sparkle' 5–8
*Buddleia alternifolia* 5–6
  *B. alternifolia* 'Argentea' 5–6
  *B. davidii* 5–9
  *B. davidii* 'Black Knight' 5–9
  *B. davidii* 'Charming' 5–9
  *B. davidii* 'Deep Lavender' 5–9
  *B. davidii* 'Dubonnet' 5–9
  *B. davidii* 'Empire Blue' 5–9
  *B. davidii* 'Fascination' 5–9
  *B. davidii* 'Harlequin' 5–9
  *B. davidii* 'Pink Delight' 5–9
  *B. davidii* 'Princeton Purple' 5–9
  *B. davidii* 'Royal Red' 5–9
  *B. davidii* 'White Bouquet' 5–9
  *B. davidii* 'White Profusion' 5–9
*Buxus* 'Glencoe' 5–8
  *B.* 'Green Gem' 5–8
  *B.* 'Green Mountain' 5–8
  *B.* 'Green Velvet' 5–8
  *B. microphylla* var. *japonica* 'Morris Midget' 5–9
  *B. sempervirens* 'Vardar Valley' 5–8
*Calluna vulgaris* 5–7
  *C. vulgaris* 'Alba Plena' 5–7
  *C. vulgaris* 'County Wicklow' 5–7
  *C. vulgaris* 'Darkness' 5–7
  *C. vulgaris* 'Gold Haze' 5–7
  *C. vulgaris* 'H. E. Beale' 5–7
*Calycanthus floridus* 5–8
  *C. floridus* 'Athens' 5–8
  *C. floridus* 'Edith Wilder' 5–8
*Caragana aurantiaca* 5–7
*Caryopteris × clandonensis* 5–8
  *C. × clandonensis* 'Azure' 5–8
  *C. × clandonensis* 'Blue Mist' 5–8
  *C. × clandonensis* 'Dark Knight' 5–8
  *C. × clandonensis* 'Heavenly Blue' 5–8
  *C. × clandonensis* 'Longwood Blue' 5–8
*Chaenomeles speciosa* 5–8
  *C. speciosa* 'Moerloosi' 5–8
  *C. speciosa* 'Rubra' 5–8
  *C. speciosa* 'Simonii' 5–8
  *C. speciosa* 'Toyo-Nishiki' 5–8
  *C. × superba* 5–8
  *C. × superba* 'Cameo' 5–8
  *C. × superba* 'Fascination' 5–8
  *C. × superba* 'Fire Dance' 5–8
  *C. × superba* 'Jet Trail' 5–8
  *C. × superba* 'Nicoline' 5–8
  *C. × superba* 'Rowallane' 5–8
  *C. × superba* 'Texas Scarlet' 5–8
*Clethra alnifolia* 5–8
  *C. alnifolia* 'Hummingbird' 5–8

[*Clethra*]

  *C. alnifolia* 'Paniculata' 5–8

  *C. alnifolia* 'Pink Spire' 5–8

  *C. alnifolia* 'Rosea' 5–8

*Cornus mas* 5–8

  *C. mas* 'Aurea' 5–8

  *C. mas* 'Flava' 5–8

  *C. mas* 'Golden Glory' 5–8

  *C. mas* 'Variegata' 5–8

*Cotoneaster adpressus* 'Hessei' 5–7

  *C. apiculatus* 5–7

  *C. horizontalis* 'Robustus' 5–7

*Daphne* × *burkwoodii* 5–8

  *D.* × *burkwoodii* 'Carol Mackie' 5–8

  *D.* × *burkwoodii* 'Somerset' 5–8

  *D.* × *burkwoodii* 'Variegata' 5–8

  *D. caucasica* 5–8

  *D. cneorum* 5–8

  *D. cneorum* 'Alba' 5–8

  *D. cneorum* 'Eximia' 5–8

  *D. cneorum* 'Ruby Glow' 5–8

  *D. genkwa* 5–8

  *D. mezereum* 5–8

  *D. mezereum* f. *alba* 5–8

  *D. mezereum* f. *alba* 'Bowles White' 5–8

*Deutzia gracilis* 'Nikko' 5–8

  *D. gracilis* 'Rosea' 5–8

*Diervilla sessilifolia* 5–8

  *D.* × *splendens* 5–8

*Enkianthus campanulatus* 5–8

  *E. campanulatus* 'Albiflorus' 5–8

  *E. campanulatus* var. *palibinii* 5–8

  *E. campanulatus* 'Red Bells' 5–8

  *E. campanulatus* 'Renoir' 5–8

  *E. campanulatus* 'Showy Lantern' 5–8

  *E. campanulatus* 'Sikokianus' 5–8

*Euonymus oxyphyllus* 5–8

*Exochorda* × *macrantha* 'The Bride' 5–8

*Forsythia* × *intermedia* 5–8

  *F.* 'Gold Tide' 5–9

  *F.* × *intermedia* 'Lynwood' 5–8

  *F.* × *intermedia* 'Spring Glory' 5–8

  *F.* 'Meadowlark' 5–7

  *F.* 'Northern Gold' 5–7

  *F.* 'Northern Sun' 5–7

  *F.* 'Sunrise' 5–7

*Fothergilla gardenii* 5–8

  *F. gardenii* 'Blue Mist' 5–8

  *F. gardenii* 'Jane Platt' 5–8

  *F. gardenii* 'Mt. Airy' 5–7

  *F. major* 5–8

*Genista sagittalis* 5–7

*Hamamelis* × *intermedia* 5–8

  *H.* × *intermedia* 'Arnold Promise' 5–8

  *H.* × *intermedia* 'Diane' 5–8

  *H.* × *intermedia* 'Feuerzauber' 5–8

  *H.* × *intermedia* 'Jelena' 5–8

  *H.* × *intermedia* 'Primavera' 5–8

  *H.* × *intermedia* 'Ruby Glow' 5–8

  *H. vernalis* f. *carnea* 5–8

*Heptacodium miconioides* 5–7

*Hibiscus* 'Lohengrin' 5–8

  *H. syriacus* 'Aphrodite' 5–8

  *H. syriacus* 'Diana' 5–8

  *H. syriacus* 'Helene' 5–8

  *H. syriacus* 'Lady Stanley' 5–8

  *H. syriacus* 'Minerva' 5–8

  *H. syriacus* 'Purpureus Variegatus' 5–8

  *H. syriacus* 'Woodbridge' 5–8

  *H.* 'Tosca' 5–8

*Hydrangea quercifolia* 5–9

  *H. quercifolia* 'Snowflake' 5–9

  *H. quercifolia* 'Snow Queen' 5–9

*Hypericum kalmianum* (4)5–8

  *H. prolificum* (4)5–8

*Ilex* 'Apollo' 5–9

  *I.* 'China Boy' 5–7

  *I.* 'China Girl' 5–7

  *I. decidua* 'Byer's Golden' 5–9

  *I. decidua* 'Council Fire' 5–9

  *I. decidua* 'Pocahontas' 5–9

  *I. decidua* 'Warrens Red' 5–9

  *I.* 'Dragon Lady' 5–7

  *I. glabra* 'Compacta' 5–9

  *I. glabra* 'Ivory Queen' 5–9

  *I. glabra* 'Nigra' 5–9

  *I. glabra* 'Nordic' (4)5–9

  *I. glabra* 'Shamrock' 5–9

  *I.* 'Harvest Red' 5–9

  *I.* × *meserveae* 5–7

  *I.* × *meserveae* 'Blue Boy' 5–7

  *I.* × *meserveae* 'Blue Girl' 5–7

  *I.* × *meserveae* 'Blue Maid' 5–7

  *I.* × *meserveae* 'Blue Prince' 5–7

  *I.* × *meserveae* 'Blue Princess' 5–7

  *I.* × *meserveae* 'Blue Stallion' 5–7

  *I. opaca* 'Maryland Dwarf' 5–9

  *I.* 'Raritan Chief' 5–9

  *I. serrata* 'Bonfire' 5–9

  *I. serrata* 'Sundrops' 5–9

  *I.* 'Sparkleberry' 5–9

*Indigofera kirilowii* 5–8

*Kalmia latifolia* (4)5–8

  *K. latifolia* 'Alba' (4)5–8

  *K. latifolia* 'Bullseye' (4)5–8

  *K. latifolia* 'Elf' (4)5–8

  *K. latifolia* 'Freckles' (4)5–8

  *K. latifolia* 'Fuscata' (4)5–8

  *K. latifolia* 'Heart's Desire' (4)5–8

  *K. latifolia* 'Little Linda' (4)5–8

  *K. latifolia* 'Minuet' (4)5–8

  *K. latifolia* 'Ostbo Red' (4)5–8

  *K. latifolia* 'Peppermint' (4)5–8

  *K. latifolia* 'Pink Charm' (4)5–8

  *K. latifolia* 'Sarah' (4)5–8

  *K. latifolia* 'Silver Dollar' (4)5–8

  *K. latifolia* 'Star Cluster' (4)5–8

*Kerria japonica* 'Picta' 5–8

  *K. japonica* 'Pleniflora' 5–8

*Kolkwitzia amabilis* 5–8

  *K. amabilis* 'Pink Cloud' 5–8

  *K. amabilis* 'Rosea' 5–8

*Lespedeza thunbergii* 'Alba' 5–8

  *L. thunbergii* 'Gibraltar' 5–8

*Lindera angustifolia* 5–8

  *L. benzoin* 5–8

  *L. benzoin* 'Rubra' 5–8

  *L. benzoin* 'Xanthocarpa' 5–8

*Mahonia aquifolium* 'Atropurpurea' 5–8

  *M. aquifolium* 'Moseri' 5–8

  *M. repens* 5–8

*Neviusia alabamensis* 5–8

*Philadelphus coronarius* 'Variegata' 5–8

  *P.* × *virginalis* 'Glacier' 5–8

  *P.* × *virginalis* 'Miniature Snowflake' 5–8

  *P.* × *virginalis* 'Polar Star' 5–9

*Pieris* 'Brouwer's Beauty' 5–7

  *P. floribunda* 'Millstream' 5–7

  *P. japonica* 5–8

  *P. japonica* 'Bert Chandler' 5–8

  *P. japonica* 'Flamingo' 5–8

  *P. japonica* 'Geisha' 5–8

  *P. japonica* 'Mountain Fire' 5–8

  *P. japonica* 'Pygmaea' 5–8

  *P. japonica* 'Red Mill' 5–8

  *P. japonica* 'Roslinda' 5–8

  *P. japonica* 'Valley Fire' 5–8

  *P. japonica* 'Valley Rose' 5–8

  *P. japonica* 'Valley Valentine' 5–8

  *P. japonica* 'Variegata' 5–8

  *P. japonica* 'White Cascade' 5–8

  *P. japonica* 'White Pearl' 5–8

*Rhodotypos scandens* 5–8

*Rhus trilobata* 5–8

  *R. trilobata* 'Autumn Amber' 5–8

*Robinia hispida* 5–8

*Rosa* × *alba* 'Celestial'

  *R.* × *alba* 'Semi Plena' 5–8

  *R.* × *alba* 'White Rose of York' 5–8

  *R.* 'Belle de Crécy' 5–8(9)

  *R. bonica* 5–9

  *R.* 'Bredon' 5–9

  *R.* 'Buff Beauty' 5–9

  *R.* 'Canary Bird' 5–9

  *R.* 'Cantabrigiensis' 5–9

  *R. centifolia* f. *muscosa* 'White Bath' 5–9

  *R. centifolia* 'Rose de Meaux' 5–9

  *R.* 'Champlain' (4)5–8

  *R.* 'Complicata' 5–8(9)

  *R. damascena* var. *bifera* 'Autumn Damask' 5–8(9)

R. *damascena* 'Madame Hardy' 5–8(9)
R. 'English Garden' 5–9
R. *foetida* 'Bicolor' 5–8
R. 'Frühlingsduft' 5–8
R. 'Frühlingsgold' 5–8
R. 'Frühlingsmorgen' 5–8
R. *gallica* var. *officinalis* 5–8(9)
R. 'Geranium' 5–8
R. 'Gertrude Jekyll' 5–9
R. 'Graham Thomas' 5–9
R. 'Heritage' 5–9
R. *hugonis* 5–8
R. 'John Cabot' (4)5–8
R. 'John Davis' (4)5–8
R. 'La Reine Victoria' 5–9
R. 'Mary Rose' 5–9
R. 'Nevada' 5–8
R. 'Perdita' 5–9
R. 'Prioress' 5–9
R. 'Sir Walter Raleigh' 5–9
R. 'Souvenir de la Malmaison' 5–9
R. 'Stanwell Perpetual' 5–8
R. 'Versicolor' 5–8(9)
R. 'Wife of Bath' 5–9
R. 'William Baffin' (4)5–8
*Rubus cockburnianus* 5–8
R. *odoratus* 5–8
R. 'Tridel' 5–7
*Salix melanostachys* 5–7
*Sambucus racemosa* 'Plumosa Aurea' 5–8
*Spiraea* × *bumalda* 'Golden Princess' 5–8
S. × *bumalda* 'Gold Flame' 5–8
S. *nipponica* 5–8
*Syringa* × *josiflexa* 5–7
S. × *laciniata* 5–7
S. *oblata* var. *dilatata* 5–7
S. *microphylla* 5–7(8)
S. *microphylla* 'Superba' 5–7
S. 'Minuet' 5–7
S. 'Miss Canada' 5–7
*Taxus baccata* 'Adpressa Fowle' 5–7
T. *baccata* 'Beanpole' 5–7
T. *baccata* 'Fastigiata Robusta' 5–7
T. × *media* 'Runyan' 5–7
*Thujopsis dolabrata* 'Nana' 5–7
*Viburnum* × *burkwoodii* 'Mohawk' 5–8
V. × *carlcephalum* 'Cayuga' 5–8
V. *carlesii* 'Compactum' 5–9
V. *carlesii* 'Aurora' 5–9
V. *carlesii* 'Charis' 5–9
V. *dilatatum* 'Catskill' 5–8
V. *dilatatum* 'Erie' 5–8
V. *dilatatum* 'Iroquois' 5–8
V. *dilatatum* 'Michael Dodge' 5–8
V. *nudum* 'Winterthur' 5–9
V. *plicatum* f. *tomentosum* 'Shoshoni' 5–9

V. *plicatum* f. *tomentosum* 'Summer Snowflake' 5–9
V. × *rhytidophylloides* 'Alleghany' 5–8
V. × *rhytidophylloides* 'Cree' 5–8
V. *rufidulum* 5–9
V. *setigerum* 'Aurantiacum' 5–8
V. 'Willowwood' 5–8
*Weigela florida* 'Evita' 5–8
W. *florida* 'Red Prince' 5–8
W. *florida* 'Variegata' 5–8
*Xanthorhiza simplicissima* 5–9

## ZONE 6

*Abelia* 'Edward Goucher' (5)6–9
A. × *grandiflora* (5)6–9
A. × *grandiflora* 'Prostrata' (5)6–9
A. × *grandiflora* 'Sherwood' (5)6–9
*Adina rubella* 6–9
*Berberis verruculosa* 6–8
B. × *wisleyensis* 6–8
*Buxus microphylla* 'Compacta' 6–9
B. *sempervirens* 'Elegantissima' 6–9
B. *sempervirens* 'Graham Blandy' 6–8
B. *sempervirens* 'Pullman' (5)6–9
*Callicarpa bodinieri* var. *giraldii* 'Profusion' 6–8
C. *dichotoma* 6–8
C. *dichotoma* 'Albifructus' 6–8
C. *dichotoma* 'Issai' 6–8
C. *japonica* 6–8
C. *japonica* 'Leucocarpa' 6–8
C. *japonica* 'Luxurians' 6–8
*Camellia oleifera* 6–9
C. 'Polar Ice' 6–9
C. 'Snow Flurry' 6–9
C. 'Winter's Charm' 6–9
C. 'Winter's Dream' 6–9
C. 'Winter's Hope' 6–9
C. 'Winter's Interlude' 6–9
C. 'Winter's Rose' 6–9
C. 'Winter's Star' 6–9
C. 'Winter's Waterlily' 6–9
*Ceanothus* × *pallidus* var. *roseus* 6–8
*Cephalotaxus harringtonia* 'Duke Gardens' 6–9
C. *harringtonia* 'Fastigiata' 6–9
C. *harringtonia* 'Prostrata' 6–9
*Cercis canadensis* subsp. *mexicana* 6–9
C. *chinensis* 'Alba' 6–9
C. *chinensis* 'Avondale' 6–9
*Chimonanthus praecox* 6–9
C. *praecox* 'Luteus' 6–9
*Clerodendrum trichotomum* var. *fargesii* 6–8
*Clethra acuminata* (5)6–7(8)
*Corylopsis glabrescens* 6–9
C. *pauciflora* 6–8
C. *platypetala* 6–8

C. *sinensis* 6–9
C. *spicata* 6–9
C. *willmottiae* 'Spring Purple' 6–8
*Cryptomeria japonica* 'Globosa Nana' 6–8
*Cyrilla racemiflora* 6–10
*Cytisus scoparius* 6–8
C. *scoparius* 'Burkwoodii' 6–8
C. *scoparius* 'Lena' 6–8
C. *scoparius* 'Lilac Time' 6–8
C. *scoparius* 'Luna' 6–8
C. *scoparius* 'Moonlight' 6–8
*Daphne giraldii* 6–8
D. × *mantensiana* 6–8
D. *retusa* 6–8
D. *tangutica* 6–8
*Decaisnea fargesii* 6–8
*Deutzia chunii* 6–8
D. × *hybrida* 'Magicien' 6–8
D. *scabra* var. *candidissima* 6–7
D. *scabra* 'Plena' 6–7
D. *scabra* 'Pride of Rochester' 6–7
*Diervilla rivularis* 6–8
*Dipelta floribunda* 6–8
*Disanthus cercidifolius* 6–8
*Enkianthus cernuus* var. *rubens* 6–8
E. *deflexus* 6–7
E. *perulatus* 6–8
E. *perulatus* 'Compactus' 6–8
*Exochorda giraldii* var. *wilsonii* 6–8
*Forsythia suspensa* var. *sieboldii* (5)6–8
F. 'Winterthur' 6–8
*Genista lydia* (5)6–8
G. *pilosa* 6–8
G. *pilosa* 'Goldilocks' 6–8
G. *pilosa* 'Lemon Spreader' 6–8
G. *pilosa* 'Vancouver Gold' 6–9
*Hamamelis mollis* 6–8
H. *mollis* 'Brevipetala' 6–8
H. *mollis* 'Coombe Wood' 6–8
H. *mollis* 'Pallida' 6–8
*Hydrangea macrophylla* 6–9
H. *macrophylla* 'All Summer Beauty' 6–9
H. *macrophylla* 'Blue Billow' 6–9
H. *macrophylla* 'Forever Pink' 6–9
H. *macrophylla* 'Quadricolor' 6–9
H. *macrophylla* subsp. *serrata* 'Bluebird' 6–9
H. *macrophylla* subsp. *serrata* 'Preziosa' 6–9
H. *macrophylla* 'Variegata Mariesii' 6–9
H. *macrophylla* 'White Wave' 6–9
*Hypericum frondosum* 'Sunburst' 6–8
H. *patulum* 6–8
H. *patulum* 'Sungold' 6–8
*Ilex crenata* 'Beehive' 6–7
I. *crenata* 'Compacta' 6–7
I. *crenata* 'Delaware Diamond' 6–7

[*Ilex*]

*I. crenata* 'Dwarf Pagoda' 6–7
*I. crenata* 'Glory' 6–7
*I. crenata* 'Golden Heller' 6–7
*I. crenata* 'Piccolo' 6–7
*I. × meserveae* 'Blue Angel' 6–7
*I. opaca* 'Clarendon Spreading' 6–9
*I.* 'Rock Garden' 6–8
*Itea ilicifolia* 6–9
*I. virginica* 6–9
*I. virginica* 'Beppu' 6–9
*I. virginica* 'Henry's Garnet' 6–9
*Leiophyllum buxifolium* 6–8
*L. buxifolium* var. *hugeri* 6–8
*Leptodermis oblonga* 6–8
*Leucothoe axillaris* 6–8
*L. fontanesiana* 'Scarletta' (5)6–8
*L. keiskei* 6–8
*Lindera obtusiloba* 6–8
*Mahonia aquifolium* (5)6–8
*M. aquifolium* 'Apollo' (5)6–8
*M. aquifolium* 'Compacta' (5)6–8
*M. aquifolium* 'Golden Abundance' (5)6–8
*M. aquifolium* 'Mayhan Strain' (5)6–8
*M. nervosa* 6–8
*Neillia affinis* 6–8
*N. sinensis* 6–8
*N. thibetica* 6–8
*Osmanthus heterophyllus* 6–9
*O. heterophyllus* 'Aureomarginatus' 6–9
*O. heterophyllus* 'Goshiki' 6–9
*O. heterophyllus* 'Gulftide' 6–9
*O. heterophyllus* 'Maculifolius' 6–9
*O. heterophyllus* 'Myrtifolius' 6–9
*O. heterophyllus* 'Rotundifolius' 6–9
*O. heterophyllus* 'Sasaba' 6–9
*O. heterophyllus* 'Variegatus' 6–9
*Pyracantha* 'Mohave' 6–9
*P.* 'Rutgers' 6–9
*P.* 'Teton' 6–9
*Rhus chinensis* 'September Beauty' 6–8
*Ribes sanguineum* 6–8
*R. sanguineum* 'Alba' 6–8
*R. sanguineum* 'King Edward VII' 6–8
*Rosa xanthina* 6–8
*Salix fargesii* 6–8
*S. gracilistyla* 6–8
*Skimmia* 'Formanii' 6–8
*S. japonica* 6–8
*S. japonica* 'Nymans' 6–8
*S. reevesiana* 'Rubella' 6–8
*Sorbus reducta* 6–8
*Stachyurus praecox* 6–8
*Ungnadia speciosa* 6–10
*Viburnum × bodnantense* 'Dawn' 6–8
*V. × bodnantense* 'Deben' 6–8

*V.* 'Chesapeake' 6–8
*V.* 'Chippewa' 6–10
*V.* 'Eskimo' 6–8
*V. farreri* 'Candidissimum' 6–8
*V.* 'Huron' 6–10
*V. plicatum* f. *tomentosum* 'Shasta' 6–8
*V. × pragense* 6–8
*Vitex negundo* var. *heterophylla* 6–9
*V. rotundifolia* 6–9
*Zenobia pulverulenta* 6–9

## ZONE 7

*Arctostaphylos densiflora* 'Howard McMinn' 7–9
*A. densiflora* 'Sentinel' 7–9
*A. stanfordiana* 7–9
*Berberis darwinii* 7–8
*B. × gladwynensis* 'William Penn' 7–9
*B. linearifolia* 7–8
*Buddleia* 'Glasnevin' 7–8
*B.* 'Lochinch' 7–8
*B.* 'West Hill' 7–8
*Callicarpa americana* 7–9
*C. americana* var. *lactea* 7–9
*Ceanothus* 'Concha' 7–8
*C.* 'Dark Star' 7–8
*C.* 'Frosty Blue' 7–8
*C. impressus* 7–8
*C.* 'Joyce Coulter' 7–8
*C.* 'Julia Phelps' 7–8
*C. × pallidus* var. *roseus* 7–8
*C.* 'Puget Blue' 7–8
*Cercis reniformis* 'Texas White' 7–9
*Choisya ternata* 'Sundance' 7–9
*Clerodendrum bungei* 7–8
*Clethra barbinervis* 7–8
*Corylopsis sinensis* f. *veitchiana* 7–9
*C.* 'Winterthur' 7–8
*Cotoneaster conspicuus* 'Decorus' 7–8(9)
*C. dammeri* 'Skogholm' (6)7–9
*C. × watereri* 'Rothschildianus' 7–9
*Cytisus × praecox* 'Albus' 7–8
*C. × praecox* 'Allgold' 7–8
*C. × praecox* 'Hollandia' 7–8
*Daphne odora* 'Aureo-marginata' 7–9
*Elaeagnus pungens* 7–8
*E. pungens* 'Fruitlandii' 7–8
*E. pungens* 'Hosoba-Fukurin' 7–8
*E. pungens* 'Maculata' 7–8
*E. pungens* 'Variegata' 7–8
*Elliottia racemosa* (6)7–8
*Enkianthus chinensis* 7–8
*Fremontodendron* 'California Glory' 7–10
*Hamamelis macrophylla* 7–9
*Hydrangea aspera* subsp. *aspera* 7–9
*H. sargentiana* 7–9
*Hypericum patulum* 'Henryi' 7–8

*H. patulum* 'Hidcote' 7–8
*Ilex amelanchier* 7–9
*I. cornuta* 'O. Spring' 7–9
*I. cornuta* 'Rotunda' 7–9
*I. cornuta* 'Willowleaf' 7–9
*I.* 'Miniature' 7–8
*I.* 'September Gem' 7–8
*Illicium anisatum*
*Lagerstroemia* 'Acoma' 7–9
*L.* 'Hopi' 7–9
*L.* 'Pecos' 7–9
*L.* 'Zuni' 7–9
*Leycesteria formosa* 7–8
*Lonicera pileata* 7–8
*L. pileata* 'Royal Carpet' 7–8
*Mahonia* 'Arthur Menzies' 7–8
*Myrica cerifera* 7–9
*Nandina domestica* 'Alba' (6)7–9
*N. domestica* 'Fire Power' (6)7–9
*N. domestica* 'Gulf Stream' (6)7–9
*N. domestica* 'Harbor Dwarf' (6)7–9
*N. domestica* 'Heavenly Bamboo' (6)7–9
*N. domestica* 'Royal Princess' (6)7–9
*N. domestica* 'Umpqua Chief' (6)7–9
*N. domestica* 'Umpqua Princess' (6)7–9
*N. domestica* 'Umpqua Warrior' (6)7–9
*Osmanthus americanus* (6)7–9
*O. × burkwoodii* 7–8
*Pernettya mucronata* 7–8
*P. mucronata* 'Alba' 7–8
*P. mucronata* 'Coccinea' 7–8
*P. mucronata* 'Rosea' 7–8
*P. mucronata* 'Rubra' 7–8
*Pieris formosa* var. *forrestii* 'Forest Flame' 7–8
*P. phillyreifolia* 7–8
*P. taiwanensis* 7–9
*Pyracantha* 'Apache' 7–8
*P.* 'Fiery Cascade' 7–9
*P.* 'Gold Rush' 7–8
*P.* 'Navaho' 7–9
*P.* 'Pueblo' 7–9
*Rosa* 'Duchesse de Brabant' 7–9
*Sarcococca confusa* 7–8
*S. ruscifolia* 7–8
*Viburnum × burkwoodii* 'Conoy' 7–8
*Vitex agnus-castus* 7–9
*V. agnus-castus* 'Alba' 7–9
*V. agnus-castus* 'Rosea' 7–9
*V. agnus-castus* 'Silver Spire' 7–9

## ZONE 8

*Abelia chinensis* 8–9
*A. floribunda* 8–9
*Aesculus californica* 8(9)
*Arctostaphylos bakerii* 'Louis Edmunds' 8–9

*Azara dentata* 8–9
   *A. petiolaris* 8–9
   *A. serrata* 8–9
*Bauhinia lunarioides* 8–10
*Buddleia fallowiana* 'Alba' 8–9
   *B. globosa* 8–10
   *B. globosa* 'Lemon Ball' 8–10
*Camellia japonica* 8–9
   *C. japonica* 'Adolphe Audusson' 8–9
   *C. japonica* 'Alaska' 8–9
   *C. japonica* 'Betty Sheffield Supreme'
      8–9
   *C. japonica* 'C. M. Wilson' 8–9
   *C. japonica* 'Dahlohnega' 8–9
   *C. japonica* 'Eldorado' 8–9
   *C. japonica* 'Elegans' 8–9
   *C. japonica* 'Empress of Russia' 8–9
   *C. japonica* 'Finlandia' 8–9
   *C. japonica* 'Guillio Nuccio' 8–9
   *C. japonica* 'Holly Bright' 8–9
   *C. japonica* 'Kumasaka' 8–9
   *C. japonica* 'Lady Clare' 8–9
   *C. japonica* 'Magnoliaeflora' 8–9
   *C. japonica* 'Mansize' 8–9
   *C. japonica* 'Mathotiana' 8–9
   *C. japonica* 'Nuccio's Gem' 8–9
   *C. japonica* 'Otome' 8–9
   *C. japonica* 'Pink Perfection' 8–9
   *C. japonica* 'Pope Pius IX' 8–9
   *C. japonica* 'R. L. Wheeler' 8–9
   *C. japonica* 'September Morn' 8–9
   *C. japonica* 'Swan Lake' 8–9
   *C. japonica* 'Ville de Nantes' 8–9
   *C. rosaeflora* 8–9
   *C. sinensis* (7)8–9
   *C. × williamsii* 8–9
   *C. × williamsii* 'Anticipation' 8–9
   *C. × williamsii* 'Donation' 8–9
   *C. × williamsii* 'Hiraethyln' 8–9
   *C. × williamsii* 'J. C. Williams' 8–9
   *C. × williamsii* 'Mary Christian' 8–9
   *C. × williamsii* 'Salutation' 8–9
   *C. × williamsii* 'St. Ewe' 8–9
*Chimonanthus nitens* 8
*Choisya ternata* 8–9
*Cistus × purpureus* 8
   *C. salvifolius* 8
   *C.* 'Silver Pink' 8
   *C. × skanbergii* 8–9
*Correa* 'Carmine Bells' 8
   *C. × harrisii* 8
   *C.* 'Ivory Bells' 8
   *C. reflexa* 8
*Danae racemosa* 8(9)
*Elaeagnus × ebbingei* 8
*Embothrium coccineum* 8–9
*Feijoa sellowiana* 8

*F. sellowiana* 'Coolidge' 8
*F. sellowiana* 'Mammoth' 8
*F. sellowiana* 'Triumph' 8
*Fouquieria splendens* 8–10
*Genista aethnensis* 8
*Heteromeles arbutifolia* 8
*Ilex vomitoria* 'Dare County' 8–10
   *I. vomitoria* 'Jewel' 8–10
   *I. vomitoria* 'Stokes Dwarf' 8–10
*Illicium floridanum* 8–9
   *I. floridanum* f. *album* 8–9
   *I. floridanum* 'Halley's Comet' 8–9
   *I. henryi* 8–9
   *I. mexicanum* 8
   *I. parviflorum* 8–9
*Leucophyllum frutescens* 'Compactum' 8–9
   *L. frutescens* 'Green Cloud' 8–9
   *L. frutescens* 'White Cloud' 8–9
*Leucothoe populifolia* 8–9
*Mahonia × media* 'Charity' 8–9
*Myrica cerifera* var. *pumila* 8–9
*Nandina domestica* 'San Gabriel' 8–9
*Osmanthus fragrans* 'Aurantiacus' 8–9
*Punica granatum* 8–10
   *P. granatum* 'Emperior' 8–10
   *P. granatum* 'Hizakuru' 8–10
   *P. granatum* 'Nana' 8–10
   *P. granatum* 'Peach Princess' 8–10
   *P. granatum* 'Shiro Botan' 8–10
   *P. granatum* 'Toyosho' 8–10
   *P. granatum* 'Twisted Trunk' 8–10
   *P. granatum* 'Wonderful' 8–10
*Ribes speciosum* 8–9
*Ruscus aculeatus* 8–9

## ZONE 9

*Brunfelsia australis* 9–10
   *B. latifolia* 9–10
   *B. pauciflora* 9–10
   *B. pauciflora* var. *calycina* 'Macrantha'
      9–10
*Camellia chrysantha* 9
*Clerodendrum ugandense* 9
*Cytisus battandieri* 9
*Dendromecon rigida* 9
*Escallonia bifida* 9
   *E. × exoniensis* 9
   *E. × exoniensis* 'Balfourii' 9
   *E. × exoniensis* 'Fradesii' 9
   *E.* 'Pride of Donard' 9
   *E. rubra* 'C. F. Ball' 9
*Garrya elliptica* 'James Roof' 9
   *G. × issaquahensis* 9
*Grevillea alpina* 9
   *G. alpina* 'Grampian's Gold' 9
   *G.* 'Canberra Gem' 9
   *G. lavandulacea* 'Tanunda' 9

*G.* 'Robyn Gordon' 9
*G. rosmarinifolia* 9
*G. tridentifera* 9
*G. victoriae* 9
*Hibiscus rosa-sinensis* 9–10
   *H. rosa-sinensis* 'All Aglow' 9–10
   *H. rosa-sinensis* 'Carolyn Coe' 9–10
   *H. rosa-sinensis* 'Cooperi' 9–10
   *H. rosa-sinensis* 'Fiesta' 9–10
   *H. rosa-sinensis* 'Herm Geller' 9–10
   *H. rosa-sinensis* 'Harvest Moon' 9–10
   *H. rosa-sinensis* 'Tino Vietti' 9–10
   *H. rosa-sinensis* 'Tylene' 9–10
*Hypericum hookeranum* 'Rowallane' 9
*Leptospermum rotundifolium* 9–10
   *L. scoparium* 'Ash Burton Wax' 9–10
   *L. scoparium* 'Helen Strybing' 9–10
   *L. scoparium* 'Martini' 9–10
   *L. scoparium* 'Pink Cascade' 9–10
   *L. scoparium* 'Red Damask' 9–10
   *L. scoparium* 'Snow White' 9–10
*Leucospermum cordifolium* 9
   *L. reflexum* 9
*Leucothoe davisiae* 9
*Loropetalum chinensis* (8)9
   *L. chinensis* 'Rubra' (8)9
*Mahonia fortunei* 9
   *M. lomariifolia* 9
   *M. trifoliata* 9
*Osmanthus delavayi* 9–10
*Prostanthera ovalifolia* 9
   *P. rotundifolia* 9
   *P. rotundifolia* 'Glen Davis' 9
*Thevetia thevetioides* 9–10

## ZONE 10

*Ardisia crenata* 10
   *A. crispa* 10
*Brugmansia arborea* 10
*Carissa macrocarpa* 10
*Carpenteria californica* 10
*Duranta stenostachya* 10
*Gardenia taitensis* 10
*Grewia occidentalis* 10
*Ixora* sp. 10
   *I. chinensis* 10
   *I. finlaysoniana* 10
   *I. nienkui* 10
   *I.* 'Nora Grant' 10
   *I. odorata* 10
*Medinilla magnifica* 10
*Michelia figo* 10
*Pachystachys lutea* 10
*Streptosolen jamesonii* 10
*Tabernaemontana divaricata* 10
*Tecoma stans* 10
   *T. stans* var. *angustata* 10

# DECIDUOUS SHRUBS

As a general rule, the plants included in this listing are deciduous in cold climates. However, the same shrub grown in warmer climates could be semi-evergreen.

*Abeliophyllum distichum*
*Acanthopanax sieboldianus* 'Variegatus'
*Adina rubella*
*Aesculus californica*
    *A. parviflora*
    *A. parviflora* 'Rogers'
    *A. parviflora* f. *serotina*
*Amelanchier ovalis* 'Pumila'
*Aralia cordata*
    *A. elata* 'Aureovariegata'
    *A. elata* 'Pyramidalis'
    *A. elata* 'Variegata'
    *A. spinosa*
*Aronia arbutifolia* 'Brilliantissima'
    *A. melanocarpa*
*Bauhinia lunarioides*
*Berberis* × *gladwynensis* 'William Penn'
    *B. koreana*
    *B. thunbergii*
    *B. thunbergii* 'Atropurpurea'
    *B. thunbergii* 'Bagatelle'
    *B. thunbergii* 'Bogozam'
    *B. thunbergii* 'Globe'
    *B. thunbergii* 'Kobold'
    *B. thunbergii* 'Rose Glow'
    *B. thunbergii* 'Sparkle'
*Buddleia alternifolia*
    *B. alternifolia* 'Argentea'
    *B. davidii*
    *B. davidii* 'Black Knight'
    *B. davidii* 'Charming'
    *B. davidii* 'Deep Lavender'
    *B. davidii* 'Dubonnet'
    *B. davidii* 'Empire Blue'
    *B. davidii* 'Fascination'
    *B. davidii* 'Harlequin'
    *B. davidii* 'Pink Delight'
    *B. davidii* 'Princeton Purple'
    *B. davidii* 'Royal Red'
    *B. davidii* 'White Bouquet'
    *B. davidii* 'White Profusion'
    *B. fallowiana* 'Alba'
    *B.* 'Glasnevin'
    *B.* 'Lochinch'
    *B.* 'West Hill'
*Callicarpa americana*
    *C. americana* var. *lactea*
    *C. bodinieri* var. *giraldii* 'Profusion'
    *C. dichotoma*
    *C. dichotoma* 'Albifructus'
    *C. dichotoma* 'Issai'
    *C. japonica*
    *C. japonica* 'Leucocarpa'

*C. japonica* 'Luxurians'
*Calycanthus floridus*
    *C. floridus* 'Athens'
    *C. floridus* 'Edith Wilder'
*Caragana aurantiaca*
    *C. frutex* 'Globosa'
    *C. pygmaea*
*Caryopteris* × *clandonensis*
    *C.* × *clandonensis* 'Azure'
    *C.* × *clandonensis* 'Blue Mist'
    *C.* × *clandonensis* 'Dark Knight'
    *C.* × *clandonensis* 'Heavenly Blue'
    *C.* × *clandonensis* 'Longwood Blue'
*Cercis canadensis* subsp. *mexicana*
    *C. chinensis* 'Alba'
    *C. chinensis* 'Avondale'
    *C. reniformis* 'Texas White'
*Chaenomeles speciosa*
    *C. speciosa* 'Moerloosi'
    *C. speciosa* 'Rubra'
    *C. speciosa* 'Simonii'
    *C. speciosa* 'Toyo-Nishiki'
    *C.* × *superba*
    *C.* × *superba* 'Cameo'
    *C.* × *superba* 'Fascination'
    *C.* × *superba* 'Fire Dance'
    *C.* × *superba* 'Jet Trail'
    *C.* × *superba* 'Nicoline'
    *C.* × *superba* 'Rowallane'
    *C.* × *superba* 'Texas Scarlet'
*Chimonanthus nitens*
    *C. praecox*
    *C. praecox* 'Luteus'
*Clerodendrum bungei* (semi-evergreen)
    *C. trichotomum* var. *fargesii*
*Clethra acuminata*
    *C. alnifolia*
    *C. alnifolia* 'Hummingbird'
    *C. alnifolia* 'Paniculata'
    *C. alnifolia* 'Pink Spire'
    *C. alnifolia* 'Rosea'
    *C. barbinervis*
*Comptonia peregrina*
*Cornus mas*
    *C. mas* 'Aurea'
    *C. mas* 'Flava'
    *C. mas* 'Golden Glory'
    *C. mas* 'Variegata'
    *C. sericea* 'Cardinal'
    *C. sericea* 'Isanti'
    *C. sericea* 'Silver & Gold'
*Corylopsis glabrescens*
    *C. pauciflora*

*C. platypetala*
*C. sinensis*
*C. sinensis* f. *veitchiana*
*C. spicata*
*C. willmottiae* 'Spring Purple'
*C.* 'Winterthur'
*Cotoneaster adpressus* 'Hessei'
    *C. apiculatus*
    *C. dammeri* 'Skogholm'
    *C. horizontalis* 'Robustus'
    *C. racemiflorus* var. *soongoricus*
    *C.* × *watereri* 'Rothschildianus'
*Cyrilla racemiflora* (evergreen in warmer areas)
*Cytisus battandieri*
    *C.* × *praecox* 'Albus'
    *C.* × *praecox* 'Allgold'
    *C.* × *praecox* 'Hollandia'
    *C. scoparius*
    *C. scoparius* 'Burkwoodii'
    *C. scoparius* 'Lena'
    *C. scoparius* 'Lilac Time'
    *C. scoparius* 'Luna'
    *C. scoparius* 'Moonlight'
*Daphne* × *burkwoodii* (semi-evergreen)
    *D.* × *burkwoodii* 'Carol Mackie'
    *D.* × *burkwoodii* 'Somerset'
    *D.* × *burkwoodii* 'Variegata'
    *D. caucasica*
    *D. genkwa*
    *D. mezereum* (semi-evergreen)
    *D. mezereum* f. *alba*
    *D. mezereum* f. *alba* 'Bowles White'
*Decaisnea fargesii*
*Deutzia chunii*
    *D. gracilis* 'Nikko'
    *D. gracilis* 'Rosea'
    *D.* × *hybrida* 'Magicien'
    *D. scabra* var. *candidissima*
    *D. scabra* 'Plena'
    *D. scabra* 'Pride of Rochester'
*Diervilla rivularis*
    *D. sessilifolia*
    *D.* × *splendens*
*Dipelta floribunda*
*Disanthus cercidifolius*
*Elliottia racemosa*
*Enkianthus campanulatus*
    *E. campanulatus* 'Albiflorus'
    *E. campanulatus* var. *palibinii*
    *E. campanulatus* 'Red Bells'
    *E. campanulatus* 'Renoir'
    *E. campanulatus* 'Showy Lantern'

*E. campanulatus* 'Sikokianus'
*E. cernuus* var. *rubens*
*E. chinensis*
*E. deflexus*
*E. perulatus*
*E. perulatus* 'Compactus'
*Euonymus alatus* 'Nordine Strain'
*E. alatus* 'Rudy Haag'
*E. alatus* 'Timber Creek'
*E. europaeus* 'Redcap'
*E. oxyphyllus*
*Exochorda giraldii* var. *wilsonii*
*E. × macrantha* 'The Bride'
*Forsythia × intermedia*
*F. × intermedia* 'Lynwood'
*F. × intermedia* 'Spring Glory'
*F. mandshurica* 'Vermont Sun'
*F.* 'Meadowlark'
*F.* 'New Hampshire Gold'
*F.* 'Northern Gold'
*F.* 'Northern Sun'
*F.* 'Sunrise'
*F. suspensa* var. *sieboldii*
*F. viridissima* var. *koreana* 'Ilgwang'
*F.* 'Winterthur'
*Fothergilla gardenii*
*F. gardenii* 'Blue Mist'
*F. gardenii* 'Jane Platt'
*F. gardenii* 'Mt. Airy'
*F. major*
*Fouquieria splendens*
*Genista aethnensis*
*G. lydia*
*G. pilosa*
*G. pilosa* 'Goldilocks'
*G. pilosa* 'Lemon Spreader'
*G. pilosa* 'Vancouver Gold'
*G. sagittalis*
*Hamamelis × intermedia*
*H. × intermedia* 'Arnold Promise'
*H. × intermedia* 'Diane'
*H. × intermedia* 'Feuerzauber'
*H. × intermedia* 'Jelena'
*H. × intermedia* 'Primavera'
*H. × intermedia* 'Ruby Glow'
*Hamamelis macrophylla*
*H. mollis*
*H. mollis* 'Brevipetala'
*H. mollis* 'Coombe Wood'
*H. mollis* 'Pallida'
*H. vernalis* f. *carnea*
*H. virginiana*
*Heptacodium miconioides*
*Hibiscus* 'Lohengrin'
*H. syriacus* 'Aphrodite'
*H. syriacus* 'Diana'
*H. syriacus* 'Helene

*H. syriacus* 'Lady Stanley'
*H. syriacus* 'Minerva'
*H. syriacus* 'Purpureus Variegatus'
*H. syriacus* 'Woodbridge'
*H.* 'Tosca'
*Hippophae rhamnoides*
*Hydrangea arborescens* 'Annabelle'
*H. aspera* subsp. *aspera*
*H. macrophylla*
*H. macrophylla* 'All Summer Beauty'
*H. macrophylla* 'Blue Billow'
*H. macrophylla* 'Forever Pink'
*H. macrophylla* 'Quadricolor'
*H. macrophylla* subsp. *serrata* 'Bluebird'
*H. macrophylla* subsp. *serrata* 'Preziosa'
*H. macrophylla* 'Variegata Mariesii'
*H. macrophylla* 'White Wave'
*H. paniculata* 'Tardiva'
*H. quercifolia*
*H. quercifolia* 'Snowflake'
*H. quercifolia* 'Snow Queen'
*H. sargentiana*
*Ilex amelanchier*
*I.* 'Apollo'
*I. decidua* 'Byer's Golden'
*I. decidua* 'Council Fire'
*I. decidua* 'Pocahontas'
*I. decidua* 'Warren's Red'
*I.* 'Harvest Red'
*I.* 'Raritan Chief'
*I. serrata* 'Bonfire'
*I. serrata* 'Sundrops'
*I.* 'Sparkleberry'
*I. verticillata*
*I. verticillata* 'Afterglow'
*I. verticillata* 'Aurantiaca'
*I. verticillata* f. *chrysocarpa*
*I. verticillata* 'Maryland Beauty'
*I. verticillata* 'Red Sprite'
*I. verticillata* 'Scarlett O'Hara'
*I. verticillata* 'Shaver'
*I. verticillata* 'Sunset'
*I. verticillata* 'Tiasquam'
*I. verticillata* 'Winter Gold'
*I. verticillata* 'Winter Red'
*Indigofera kirilowii*
*Itea ilicifolia*
*I. virginica*
*I. virginica* 'Beppu'
*I. virginica* 'Henry's Garnet'
*Kerria japonica* 'Picta'
*K. japonica* 'Pleniflora'
*Kolkwitzia amabilis*
*K. amabilis* 'Pink Cloud'
*K. amabilis* 'Rosea'
*Lagerstroemia* 'Acoma'
*L.* 'Hopi'

*L.* 'Pecos'
*L.* 'Zuni'
*Leptodermis oblonga*
*Lespedeza thunbergii* 'Alba'
*L. thunbergii* 'Gibraltar'
*Leycesteria formosa*
*Lindera angustifolia*
*L. benzoin*
*L. benzoin* 'Rubra'
*L. benzoin* 'Xanthocarpa'
*L. obtusiloba*
*Lonicera* 'Honey Rose'
*L. pileata* 'Royal Carpet' (semi-evergreen)
*L. xylosteum* 'Emerald Mound'
*Myrica gale*
*M. pensylvanica*
*Neillia affinis*
*N. sinensis*
*N. thibetica*
*Neviusia alabamensis*
*Paeonia suffruticosa*
*P. suffruticosa* 'Alhambra'
*P. suffruticosa* 'Ariadne'
*P. suffruticosa* 'Companion of Serenity'
*P. suffruticosa* 'Hana Kisoi'
*P. suffruticosa* 'Hephestos'
*P. suffruticosa* 'Leda'
*P. suffruticosa* 'Joseph Rock'
*P. suffruticosa* 'Renkaku'
*P. suffruticosa* 'Shintenchi'
*Philadelphus coronarius* 'Natchez'
*P. coronarius* 'Variegata'
*P. virginalis*
*P. virginalis* 'Glacier'
*P. virginalis* 'Miniature Snowflake'
*P. virginalis* 'Minnesota Snowflake'
*P. virginalis* 'Polar Star'
*Physocarpus opulifolius* 'Dart's Golden'
*Potentilla fruticosa*
*P. fruticosa* 'Abbotswood'
*P. fruticosa* 'Coronation Triumph'
*P. fruticosa* 'Day Dawn Viette'
*P. fruticosa* 'Goldfinger'
*P. fruticosa* 'Katherine Dykes'
*P. fruticosa* 'Pink Queen'
*P. fruticosa* 'Primrose Beauty'
*P. fruticosa* 'Snowbird'
*P. fruticosa* 'Yellowbird'
*Punica granatum*
*P. granatum* 'Emperior'
*P. granatum* 'Hizakuru'
*P. granatum* 'Nana'
*P. granatum* 'Peach Princess'
*P. granatum* 'Shiro Botan'
*P. granatum* 'Toyosho'
*P. granatum* 'Twisted Trunk'
*P. granatum* 'Wonderful'

*Pyracantha* 'Apache' (semi-evergreen)
    *P.* 'Fiery Cascade' (semi-evergreen)
    *P.* 'Gold Rush' (semi-evergreen)
    *P.* 'Mohave' (semi-evergreen)
    *P.* 'Navaho' (semi-evergreen)
    *P.* 'Pueblo' (semi-evergreen)
    *P.* 'Rutgers' (semi-evergreen)
    *P.* 'Teton' (semi-evergreen)
*Rhamnus frangula* 'Asplenifolia'
*Rhodotypos scandens*
*Rhus aromatica* 'Gro-low'
    *R. chinensis* 'September Beauty'
    *R. copallina*
    *R. glabra* var. *cismontana*
    *R. trilobata*
    *R. trilobata* 'Autumn Amber'
    *R. typhina* 'Dissecta'
    *R. typhina* 'Laciniata'
*Ribes alpinum* 'Green Mound'
    *R. aureum*
    *R. odoratum*
    *R. odoratum* 'Aureum'
    *R. sanguineum*
    *R. sanguineum* 'Alba'
    *R. sanguineum* 'King Edward VII'
    *R. speciosum* (semi-evergreen)
*Robinia hispida*
*Rosa* 'Adelaide Hoodless'
    *R.* × *alba* 'Celestial'
    *R.* × *alba* 'Semi Plena'
    *R.* × *alba* 'White Rose of York'
    *R.* 'A. MacKenzie'
    *R.* 'Assiniboine'
    *R.* 'Belle de Crécy'
    *R.* 'Bonica'
    *R.* 'Bredon'
    *R.* 'Buff Beauty'
    *R.* 'Canary Bird'
    *R.* 'Cantabrigiensis'
    *R.* 'Carefree Beauty'
    *R.* 'Carefree Wonder'
    *R. centifolia* f. *muscosa* 'White Bath'
    *R. centifolia* 'Rose de Meaux'
    *R.* 'Champlain'
    *R.* 'Complicata'
    *R.* 'Cuthbert Grant'
    *R. damascena* var. *bifera* 'Autumn Damask'
    *R. damascena* 'Madame Hardy'
    *R.* 'Duchesse de Brabant'
    *R.* 'English Garden'
    *R. foetida* 'Bicolor'
    *R.* 'Frühlingsduft'
    *R.* 'Frühlingsgold'
    *R.* 'Frühlingsmorgen'
    *R. gallica* var. *officinalis*
    *R.* 'Geranium'
    *R.* 'Gertrude Jekyll'

*R. glauca*
*R.* 'Golden Wings'
*R.* 'Graham Thomas'
*R.* 'Henry Kelsey'
*R.* 'Heritage'
*R. hugonis*
*R.* 'John Cabot'
*R.* 'John Davis'
*R.* 'John Franklin'
*R.* 'La Reine Victoria'
*R.* 'Mary Rose'
*R.* 'Morden Amorette'
*R.* 'Morden Blush'
*R.* 'Morden Cardinette'
*R.* 'Morden Centennial'
*R.* 'Morden Fireglow'
*R.* 'Morden Ruby'
*R.* 'Nevada'
*R.* 'Perdita'
*R.* 'Prioress'
*R. rugosa* 'Blanc Double de Coubert'
*R. rugosa* 'Charles Albanel'
*R. rugosa* 'Fru Dagmar Hastrup'
*R. rugosa* 'Henry Hudson'
*R. rugosa* 'Jens Munk'
*R. rugosa* 'Linda Campbell'
*R. rugosa* 'Roseraie de l'Hay'
*R. rugosa* 'Rubra'
*R. rugosa* 'Sarah Van Fleet'
*R. rugosa* 'Sir Thomas Lipton'
*R. rugosa* 'Therese Bugnet'
*R. rugosa* 'Topaz Jewel'
*R.* 'Sir Walter Raleigh'
*R.* 'Souvenir de la Malmaison'
*R.* 'Stanwell Perpetual'
*R.* 'Versicolor'
*R.* 'Wife of Bath'
*R.* 'William Baffin'
*R.* 'Winnipeg Parks'
*R. xanthina*
*Rubus cockburnianus*
    *R. odoratus*
    *R.* 'Tridel'
*Ruscus aculeatus*
*Salix fargesii*
    *S. gracilistyla*
    *S. lanata*
    *S. melanostachys*
*Sambucus racemosa* 'Plumosa Aurea'
*Shepherdia argentea*
    *S. canadensis*
*Sorbaria aitchisonii*
    *S. sorbifolia*
*Sorbus reducta*
*Spiraea* × *bumalda* 'Golden Princess'
    *S.* × *bumalda* 'Gold Flame'
    *S.* × *cinerea* 'Grefsheim'

*S. fritschiana*
*S. japonica* 'Shibori'
*S. nipponica*
*S. nipponica* 'Halward's Silver'
*S. nipponica* 'Snowmound'
*Stachyurus praecox*
*Stephanandra incisa* 'Crispa'
*Streptosolen jamesonii*
*Syringa* × *henryi*
    *S.* × *henryi* 'Lutèce'
    *S.* × *henryi* 'Summer White'
    *S.* × *hyacinthiflora*
    *S.* × *hyacinthiflora* 'Blanche Sweet'
    *S.* × *hyacinthiflora* 'Maiden's Blush'
    *S.* × *hyacinthiflora* 'Sister Justena'
    *S.* × *josiflexa*
    *S.* × *josiflexa* 'Agnes Smith'
    *S.* × *josiflexa* 'Anna Amhoff'
    *S.* × *josiflexa* 'James MacFarlane'
    *S.* × *josiflexa* 'Royalty'
    *S.* × *laciniata*
    *S. meyeri* 'Palibin'
    *S. microphylla*
    *S. microphylla* 'Superba'
    *S.* 'Minuet'
    *S.* 'Miss Canada'
    *S. oblata* var. *dilatata*
    *S. patula* 'Miss Kim'
    *S.* × *prestoniae*
    *S.* × *prestoniae* 'Alice Rose Foster'
    *S.* × *prestoniae* 'Ethel M. Webster'
    *S.* × *prestoniae* 'Isabella'
    *S.* × *prestoniae* 'Nike'
    *S. vulgaris*
    *S. vulgaris* 'Agincourt Beauty'
    *S. vulgaris* 'Albert F. Holden'
    *S. vulgaris* 'Dwight D. Eisenhower'
    *S. vulgaris* 'Edith Cavell'
    *S. vulgaris* 'Edward J. Gardner'
    *S. vulgaris* 'Emile Lemoine'
    *S. vulgaris* 'Krasavitsa Moskvy'
    *S. vulgaris* 'Lavender Lady'
    *S. vulgaris* 'Ludwig Spaeth'
    *S. vulgaris* 'Marie Francis'
    *S. vulgaris* 'Mieczta'
    *S. vulgaris* 'Miss Ellen Willmott'
    *S. vulgaris* 'Primrose'
    *S. vulgaris* 'Rochester'
    *S. vulgaris* 'Sensation'
    *S. vulgaris* 'Slater's Elegance'
    *S. vulgaris* 'Victor Lemoine'
    *S. vulgaris* 'Wedgwood Blue'
    *S. vulgaris* 'Wonder Blue'
    *S. vulgaris* 'Yankee Doodle'
*Ungnadia speciosa* (semi-evergreen in
    warmer zones)
*Viburnum* × *bodnantense* 'Dawn'

*V.* × *bodnantense* 'Deben'
*V.* × *burkwoodii* 'Conoy' (semi-evergreen in warmer zones)
*V.* × *burkwoodii* 'Mohawk'
*V.* × *carlcephalum* 'Cayuga'
*V. carlesii* 'Aurora'
*V. carlesii* 'Charis'
*V. carlesii* 'Compactum'
*V.* 'Chesapeake'
*V.* 'Chippewa' (semi-evergreen in warmer zones)
*V. dilatatum* 'Catskill'
*V. dilatatum* 'Erie'
*V. dilatatum* 'Iroquois'
*V. dilatatum* 'Michael Dodge'

*V.* 'Eskimo' (semi-evergreen)
*V. farreri* 'Candidissimum'
*V.* 'Huron' (semi-evergreen in warmer zones)
*V. lantana* 'Mohican'
*V. nudum* 'Winterthur'
*V. plicatum* f. *tomentosum* 'Shasta'
*V. plicatum* f. *tomentosum* 'Shoshoni'
*V. plicatum* f. *tomentosum* 'Summer Snowflake'
*V.* × *rhytidophylloides* 'Alleghany'
*V.* × *rhytidophylloides* 'Cree' (semi-evergreen to evergreen in warmer zones)
*V. rufidulum*

*V. sargentii* 'Flavum'
*V. sargentii* 'Onondaga'
*V. sargentii* 'Susquehanna'
*V. setigerum* 'Aurantiacum'
*V.* 'Willowwood'
*Vitex agnus-castus*
*V. agnus-castus* 'Alba'
*V. agnus-castus* 'Rosea'
*V. agnus-castus* 'Silver Spire'
*V. negundo* var. *heterophylla*
*V. rotundifolia*
*Weigela florida* 'Evita'
*W. florida* 'Red Prince'
*W. florida* 'Variegata'
*Xanthorhiza simplicissima*

## EVERGREEN SHRUBS

Evergreens, plants that retain their foliage when dormant, are typically separated into two categories—needled and broad-leaved. Both remain evergreen *within the USDA zones specified*. However, microclimate factors, such as soil, wind, and temperature variations, will influence the limits of temperatures within which a plant will retain its foliage.

*Abelia chinensis*
*A.* 'Edward Goucher'
*A. floribunda*
*A.* × *grandiflora* (semi-evergreen)
*A.* × *grandiflora* 'Prostrata'
*A.* × *grandiflora* 'Sherwood'
*Arctostaphylos bakerii* 'Louis Edmunds'
*A. densiflora* 'Howard McMinn'
*A. densiflora* 'Sentinel'
*A. stanfordiana*
*Ardisia crenata*
*A. crispa*
*Azara dentata*
*A. petiolaris*
*A. serrata*
*Berberis darwinii*
*B. linearifolia*
*B. verruculosa*
*B.* × *wisleyensis*
*Brugmansia arborea*
*Brunfelsia australis*
*B. latifolia*
*B. pauciflora*
*B. pauciflora* var. *calycina* 'Macrantha'
*Buddleia globosa* (semi-evergreen)
*Buxus* 'Glencoe'
*B.* 'Green Gem'
*B.* 'Green Mountain'
*B.* 'Green Velvet'
*B. microphylla* 'Compacta'
*B. microphylla* var. *japonica* 'Morris Midget'
*B. sempervirens* 'Elegantissima'
*B. sempervirens* 'Graham Blandy'
*B. sempervirens* 'Pullman'
*B. sempervirens* 'Vardar Valley'

*Calluna vulgaris*
*C. vulgaris* 'Alba Plena'
*C. vulgaris* 'County Wicklow'
*C. vulgaris* 'Darkness'
*C. vulgaris* 'Gold Haze'
*C. vulgaris* 'H. E. Beale'
*Camellia japonica*
*C. japonica* 'Adolphe Audusson'
*C. japonica* 'Alaska'
*C. japonica* 'Betty Sheffield Supreme'
*C. japonica* 'C. M. Wilson'
*C. japonica* 'Dahlohnega'
*C. japonica* 'Eldorado'
*C. japonica* 'Elegans'
*C. japonica* 'Empress of Russia'
*C. japonica* 'Finlandia'
*C. japonica* 'Guillio Nuccio'
*C. japonica* 'Holly Bright'
*C. japonica* 'Kumasaka'
*C. japonica* 'Lady Clare'
*C. japonica* 'Magnoliaeflora'
*C. japonica* 'Mansize'
*C. japonica* 'Mathotiana'
*C. japonica* 'Nuccio's Gem'
*C. japonica* 'Otome'
*C. japonica* 'Pink Perfection'
*C. japonica* 'Pope Pius IX'
*C. japonica* 'R. L. Wheeler'
*C. japonica* 'September Morn'
*C. japonica* 'Swan Lake'
*C. japonica* 'Ville de Nantes'
*C. oleifera*
*C.* 'Polar Ice'
*C. rosaeflora*
*C. sinensis*

*C.* 'Snow Flurry'
*C.* × *williamsii*
*C.* × *williamsii* 'Anticipation'
*C.* × *williamsii* 'Donation'
*C.* × *williamsii* 'Hiraethlyn'
*C.* × *williamsii* 'J. C. Williams'
*C.* × *williamsii* 'Mary Christian'
*C.* × *williamsii* 'Salutation'
*C.* × *williamsii* 'St. Ewe'
*C.* 'Winter's Charm'
*C.* 'Winter's Dream'
*C.* 'Winter's Hope
*C.* 'Winter's Interlude'
*C.* 'Winter's Rose'
*C.* 'Winter's Star'
*C.* 'Winter's Waterlily'
*Carissa macrocarpa*
*Carpenteria californica*
*Ceanothus* 'Concha'
*C.* 'Dark Star'
*C.* 'Frosty Blue'
*C. impressus*
*C.* 'Joyce Coulter'
*C.* 'Julia Phelps'
*C.* 'Puget Blue'
*C.* × *pallidus* var. *roseus*
*Cephalotaxus harringtonia* 'Duke Gardens'
*C. harringtonia* 'Fastigiata'
*C. harringtonia* 'Prostrata'
*Chamaecyparis obtusa* 'Juniperoides'
*C. obtusa* 'Kosteri'
*C. obtusa* 'Nana'
*C. obtusa* 'Nana Gracilis'
*C. obtusa* 'Nana Lutea'
*C. pisifera* 'Boulevard'

[*Chamaecyparis*]
    *C. pisifera* 'Filifera Nana'
    *C. pisifera* 'Gold Spangle'
    *C. pisifera* 'Squarrosa Intermedia'
*Choisya ternata*
    *C. ternata* 'Sundance'
*Cistus* × *purpureus*
    *C. salvifolius*
    *C.* 'Silver Pink'
    *C.* × *skanbergii*
*Clerodendrum ugandense*
*Correa* 'Carmine Bells'
    *C.* 'Ivory Bells'
    *C.* × *harrisii*
    *C. reflexa*
*Cotoneaster conspicuus* 'Decorus'
*Cryptomeria japonica* 'Globosa Nana'
*Danae racemosa*
*Daphne cneorum* (semi-evergreen)
    *D. cneorum* 'Alba'
    *D. cneorum* 'Eximia'
    *D. cneorum* 'Ruby Glow'
    *D. giraldii*
    *D.* × *mantensiana*
    *D. odora* 'Aureo-marginata'
    *D. retusa*
    *D. tangutica*
*Dendromecon rigida*
*Duranta stenostachya*
*Elaeagnus pungens*
    *E. pungens* 'Fruitlandii'
    *E. pungens* 'Hosoba-Fukurin'
    *E. pungens* 'Maculata'
    *E. pungens* 'Variegata'
*Embothrium coccineum*
*Escallonia bifida*
    *E.* × *exoniensis*
    *E.* × *exoniensis* 'Balfourii'
    *E.* × *exoniensis* 'Fradesii'
    *E.* 'Pride of Donard'
    *E. rubra* 'C. F. Ball'
*Feijoa sellowiana*
    *F. sellowiana* 'Coolidge'
    *F. sellowiana* 'Mammoth'
    *F. sellowiana* 'Triumph'
*Fremontodendron* 'California Glory'
*Gardenia taitensis*
*Garrya elliptica* 'James Roof'
    *G.* × *issaquahensis*
*Grevillea alpina*
    *G. alpina* 'Grampian's Gold'
    *G.* 'Canberra Gem'
    *G. lavandulacea* 'Tanunda'
    *G.* 'Robyn Gordon'
    *G. rosmarinifolia*
    *G. tridentifera*
    *G. victoriae*

*Grewia occidentalis*
*Heteromeles arbutifolia*
*Hibiscus rosa-sinensis*
    *H. rosa-sinensis* 'All Aglow'
    *H. rosa-sinensis* 'Carolyn Coe'
    *H. rosa-sinensis* 'Cooperi'
    *H. rosa-sinensis* 'Fiesta'
    *H. rosa-sinensis* 'Herm Geller'
    *H. rosa-sinensis* 'Harvest Moon'
    *H. rosa-sinensis* 'Tino Vietti'
    *H. rosa-sinensis* 'Tylene'
*Hypericum frondosum* 'Sunburst' (semi-
    evergreen)
    *H. hookeranum* 'Rowàllane' (semi-
    evergreen)
    *H. kalmianum*
    *H. patulum* (semi-evergreen)
    *H. patulum* 'Henryi' (semi-evergreen)
    *H. patulum* 'Hidcote' (semi-evergreen)
    *H. patulum* 'Sungold' (semi-evergreen)
    *H. prolificum* (semi-evergreen)
*Ilex* 'China Boy'
    *I.* 'China Girl'
    *I. cornuta* 'O. Spring'
    *I. cornuta* 'Rotunda'
    *I. cornuta* 'Willowleaf'
    *I. crenata* 'Beehive'
    *I. crenata* 'Compacta'
    *I. crenata* 'Delaware Diamond'
    *I. crenata* 'Dwarf Pagoda'
    *I. crenata* 'Glory'
    *I. crenata* 'Golden Heller'
    *I. crenata* 'Piccolo'
    *I.* 'Dragon Lady'
    *I. glabra* 'Compacta'
    *I. glabra* 'Ivory Queen'
    *I. glabra* 'Nigra'
    *I. glabra* 'Nordic'
    *I. glabra* 'Shamrock'
    *I.* × *meserveae*
    *I.* × *meserveae* 'Blue Angel'
    *I.* × *meserveae* 'Blue Boy'
    *I.* × *meserveae* 'Blue Girl'
    *I.* × *meserveae* 'Blue Maid'
    *I.* × *meserveae* 'Blue Prince'
    *I.* × *meserveae* 'Blue Princess'
    *I.* × *meserveae* 'Blue Stallion'
    *I.* 'Miniature'
    *I. opaca* 'Clarendon Spreading'
    *I. opaca* 'Maryland Dwarf'
    *I.* 'Rock Garden'
    *I.* 'September Gem'
    *I. vomitoria* 'Dare County'
    *I. vomitoria* 'Jewel'
    *I. vomitoria* 'Stokes Dwarf'
*Illicium anisatum*
    *I. floridanum*

    *I. floridanum* f. *album*
    *I. floridanum* 'Halley's Comet'
    *I. henryi*
    *I. mexicanum*
    *I. parviflorum*
*Ixora* sp.
    *I. chinensis*
    *I. finlaysoniana*
    *I. nienkui*
    *I.* 'Nora Grant'
    *I. odorata*
*Juniperus chinensis* 'Echiniformis'
    *J. squamata* 'Blue Star'
    *J. virginiana* 'Grey Owl'
*Kalmia angustifolia*
    *K. angustifolia* 'Hammonasset'
    *K. angustifolia* 'Pumila'
    *K. latifolia*
    *K. latifolia* 'Alba'
    *K. latifolia* 'Bullseye'
    *K. latifolia* 'Elf'
    *K. latifolia* 'Freckles
    *K. latifolia* 'Fuscata'
    *K. latifolia* 'Heart's Desire'
    *K. latifolia* 'Little Linda'
    *K. latifolia* 'Minuet'
    *K. latifolia* 'Ostbo Red'
    *K. latifolia* 'Peppermint'
    *K. latifolia* 'Pink Charm'
    *K. latifolia* 'Sarah'
    *K. latifolia* 'Silver Dollar'
    *K. latifolia* 'Star Cluster'
*Leiophyllum buxifolium*
    *L. buxifolium* var. *hugeri*
*Leptospermum rotundifolium*
    *L. scoparium*
    *L. scoparium* 'Ash Burton Wax'
    *L. scoparium* 'Helen Strybing'
    *L. scoparium* 'Martini'
    *L. scoparium* 'Pink Cascade'
    *L. scoparium* 'Red Damask'
    *L. scoparium* 'Snow White'
*Leucophyllum frutescens* 'Compactum'
    *L. frutescens* 'Green Cloud'
    *L. frutescens* 'White Cloud'
*Leucospermum cordifolium*
    *L. reflexum*
*Leucothoe axillaris*
    *L. davisiae*
    *L. fontanesiana* 'Scarletta'
    *L. keiskei*
    *L. populifolia*
*Loropetalum chinensis*
    *L. chinensis* 'Rubra'
*Mahonia aquifolium*
    *M. aquifolium* 'Apollo'
    *M. aquifolium* 'Atropurpurea'

M. aquifolium 'Compacta'
M. aquifolium 'Golden Abundance'
M. aquifolium 'Mayhan Strain'
M. aquifolium 'Moseri'
M. 'Arthur Menzies'
M. fortunei
M. lomariifolia
M. × media 'Charity'
M. nervosa
M. repens
M. trifoliata
Medinilla magnifica
Michelia figo
Myrica cerifera
    M. cerifera var. pumila
Nandina domestica 'Alba' (semi-evergreen)
    N. domestica 'Fire Power' (semi-evergreen)
    N. domestica 'Gulf Stream' (semi-evergreen)
    N. domestica 'Harbor Dwarf' (semi-evergreen)
    N. domestica 'Heavenly Bamboo' (semi-evergreen)
    N. domestica 'Royal Princess' (semi-evergreen)
    N. domestica 'San Gabriel' (semi-evergreen)
    N. domestica 'Umpqua Chief' (semi-evergreen)
    N. domestica 'Umpqua Princess' (semi-evergreen)
    N. domestica 'Umpqua Warrior' (semi-evergreen)
Osmanthus americanus

O. × burkwoodii
O. delavayi
O. fragrans 'Aurantiacus'
O. heterophyllus
O. heterophyllus 'Aureomarginatus'
O. heterophyllus 'Goshiki'
O. heterophyllus 'Gulftide'
O. heterophyllus 'Maculifolius'
O. heterophyllus 'Myrtifolius'
O. heterophyllus 'Sasaba'
O. heterophyllus 'Variegatus'
Pachystachys lutea
Pernettya mucronata
    P. mucronata 'Alba'
    P. mucronata 'Coccinea'
    P. mucronata 'Rosea'
    P. mucronata 'Rubra'
Picea abies 'Little Gem'
    P. abies 'Nidiformis'
    P. abies 'Reflexa'
    P. omorika 'Nana'
    P. pungens 'Compacta'
    P. pungens 'Montgomery'
Pieris 'Brouwer's Beauty'
    P. floribunda 'Millstream'
    P. formosa var. forrestii 'Forest Flame'
    P. japonica
    P. japonica 'Bert Chandler'
    P. japonica 'Flamingo'
    P. japonica 'Geisha'
    P. japonica 'Mountain Fire'
    P. japonica 'Pygmaea'
    P. japonica 'Red Mill'
    P. japonica 'Roslinda'
    P. japonica 'Valley Fire'

P. japonica 'Valley Rose'
P. japonica 'Valley Valentine'
P. japonica 'Variegata'
P. japonica 'White Cascade'
P. japonica 'White Pearl'
P. phillyreifolia
P. taiwanensis
Pinus densiflora 'Globosa'
    P. mugo 'Mops'
    P. sylvestris 'Beuvronensis'
    P. sylvestris 'Hillside Creeper'
Prostanthera ovalifolia
    P. rotundifolia
    P. rotundifolia 'Glen Davis'
Sarcococca confusa
    S. ruscifolia
Skimmia formanii
    S. japonica
    S. japonica 'Nymans'
    S. reevesiana 'Rubella'
Tabernaemontana divaricata
Taxus baccata 'Adpressa Fowle'
    T. baccata 'Beanpole'
    T. baccata 'Fastigiata Robusta'
    T. × media 'Runyan'
Tecoma stans
    T. stans var. angustata
Thevetia thevetioides
Thujopsis dolabrata 'Nana'
Tsuga canadensis 'Bennett'
    T. canadensis 'Jeddeloh'
    T. canadensis 'Jervis'
Viburnum × pragense
Zenobia pulverulenta (semi-evergreen to evergreen)

## DWARF CONIFERS

With the considerable shrinking of suburban lots, dwarf conifers have become important landscape plants. They exhibit great diversity of texture and differ from the species not only in size but also in form—from mats and globes to spires—and color—from greens, blues, and golds to bronzes. They may be used as low hedges, container plants, or ground covers, and in rock gardens or in troughs and sinks. They are effective as background plants for other dwarf plantings, and provide an attractive contrast when combined with perennials or deciduous shrubs. Most dwarf conifers can withstand pruning. Pines can be dwarfed by removing one-half of new candle growth each spring, leaving lateral shoots intact.

Cephalotaxus harringtonia 'Duke Gardens'
    C. harringtonia 'Fastigiata'
    C. harringtonia 'Prostrata'
Chamaecyparis obtusa 'Juniperoides'
    C. obtusa 'Kosteri'
    C. obtusa 'Nana'
    C. obtusa 'Nana Gracilis'
    C. obtusa 'Nana Lutea'
    C. pisifera 'Boulevard'
    C. pisifera 'Filifera Nana'
    C. pisifera 'Gold Spangle'
    C. pisifera 'Squarrosa Intermedia'

Cryptomeria japonica 'Globosa Nana'
Juniperus chinensis 'Echiniformis'
    J. squamata 'Blue Star'
    J. virginiana 'Grey Owl'
Picea abies 'Little Gem'
    P. abies 'Nidiformis'
    P. abies 'Reflexa'
    P. omorika 'Nana'
    P. pungens 'Compacta'
    P. pungens 'Montgomery'
Pinus densiflora 'Globosa'

P. mugo 'Mops'
    P. sylvestris 'Beuvronensis'
    P. sylvestris 'Hillside Creeper'
Taxus baccata 'Adpressa Fowle'
    T. baccata 'Beanpole'
    T. baccata 'Fastigiata Robusta'
    T. × media 'Runyan'
Thujopsis dolabrata 'Nana'
Tsuga canadensis 'Bennett'
    T. canadensis 'Jeddeloh'
    T. canadensis 'Jervis'

# SHADE-TOLERANT SHRUBS

The plants listed here are, in varying degrees, shade tolerant. However, a shrub that produces conspicuous flowers, fruit, and fall color will perform best in the sun in colder climates. The same plants often need partial shade in warmer climates to prevent scorching and burning. Some shade-grown shrubs may become thin and leggy; other plants, however, prefer shade.

*Abelia chinensis*
   A. 'Edward Goucher'
   A. floribunda
   A. × grandiflora (partial)
   A. × grandiflora 'Prostrata'
   A. × grandiflora 'Sherwood'
*Abeliophyllum distichum* (partial)
*Acanthopanax sieboldianus* 'Variegatus'
*Adina rubella* (partial)
*Aesculus parviflora*
*Amelanchier ovalis* 'Pumila'
*Aralia cordata*
   A. elata 'Aureovariegata' (partial)
   A. elata 'Pyramidalis'
   A. elata 'Variegata'
   A. spinosa (partial)
*Arctostaphylos bakerii* 'Louis Edmunds'
   A. densiflora 'Howard McMinn' (partial)
   A. densiflora 'Sentinel'
   A. stanfordiana (partial)
*Ardisia crenata* (partial)
   A. crispa
*Aronia arbutifolia* 'Brilliantissima' (partial)
   A. melanocarpa
*Azara dentata*
   A. petiolaris
   A. serrata (best in partial shade)
*Brugmansia arborea*
*Brunfelsia australis* (partial)
*Buxus* 'Glencoe' (deep)
   B. 'Green Gem'
   B. 'Green Mountain' (partial)
   B. 'Green Velvet'
   B. microphylla 'Compacta'
   B. microphylla var. japonica 'Morris
      Midget' (partial)
   B. sempervirens 'Elegantissima'
   B. sempervirens 'Graham Blandy'
      (partial)
   B. sempervirens 'Pullman'
   B. sempervirens 'Vardar Valley'
*Callicarpa americana* (partial)
   C. americana f. lactea
   C. bodinieri var. giraldii 'Profusion'
   C. dichotoma
   C. dichotoma 'Albifructus'
   C. dichotoma 'Issai'
   C. japonica (partial)
   C. japonica 'Leucocarpa'
   C. japonica 'Luxurians'
*Calycanthus floridus*

*C. floridus* 'Athens'
*C. floridus* 'Edith Wilder'
*Camellia japonica* (best in partial shade)
   C. japonica 'Adolphe Audusson'
   C. japonica 'Alaska'
   C. japonica 'Betty Sheffield Supreme'
   C. japonica 'C. M. Wilson'
   C. japonica 'Dahlohnega'
   C. japonica 'Eldorado'
   C. japonica 'Elegans'
   C. japonica 'Empress of Russia'
   C. japonica 'Finlandia'
   C. japonica 'Holly Bright'
   C. japonica 'Kumasaka'
   C. japonica 'Lady Clare'
   C. japonica 'Magnoliaeflora'
   C. japonica 'Mansize'
   C. japonica 'Mathotiana'
   C. japonica 'Nuccio's Gem'
   C. japonica 'Otome'
   C. japonica 'Pink Perfection'
   C. japonica 'Pope Pius IX'
   C. japonica 'R. L. Wheeler'
   C. japonica 'September Morn'
   C. japonica 'Swan Lake'
   C. japonica 'Ville de Nantes'
   C. oleifera (best in filtered shade)
   C. 'Polar Ice'
   C. rosaeflora
   C. sinensis
   C. 'Snow Flurry'
   C. 'Winter's Charm'
   C. 'Winter's Dream'
   C. 'Winter's Hope'
   C. 'Winter's Interlude'
   C. 'Winter's Rose'
   C. 'Winter's Star'
   C. 'Winter's Waterlily'
*Carissa macrocarpa* (partial)
*Carpenteria californica* (partial)
*Cephalotaxus harringtonia* 'Duke Gardens'
      (best in partial shade)
   C. harringtonia 'Fastigiata'
   C. harringtonia 'Prostrata'
*Cercis canadensis* subsp. *mexicana*
   C. chinensis 'Alba'
   C. chinensis 'Avondale'
   C. reniformis 'Texas White'
*Chamaecyparis obtusa* 'Juniperoides'
   C. obtusa 'Kosteri'
   C. obtusa 'Nana'

*C. obtusa* 'Nana Gracilis' (partial)
*C. pisifera* 'Boulevard'
*C. pisifera* 'Filifera Nana' (partial)
*C. pisifera* 'Gold Spangle'
*C. pisifera* 'Squarrosa Intermedia'
*Chimonanthus praecox* (partial)
*Choisya ternata*
   C. ternata 'Sundance'
*Clerodendrum trichotomum* var. *fargesii*
      (partial)
*Clethra acuminata*
   C. alnifolia
   C. alnifolia 'Hummingbird'
   C. alnifolia 'Paniculata'
   C. alnifolia 'Pink Spire'
   C. alnifolia 'Rosea'
   C. barbinervis (best in shade)
*Comptonia peregrina* (partial)
*Cornus mas*
   C. mas 'Aurea'
   C. mas 'Flava'
   C. mas 'Golden Glory'
   C. mas 'Variegata'
   C. sericea 'Cardinal'
   C. sericea 'Isanti'
   C. sericea 'Silver & Gold'
*Correa* 'Carmine Bells'
   C. × harrisii
   C. 'Ivory Bells'
   C. reflexa (partial shade inland)
*Corylopsis glabrescens*
   C. pauciflora (partial)
   C. platypetala
   C. sinensis
   C. sinensis f. veitchiana
   C. spicata (partial to half shade)
   C. willmottiae 'Spring Purple'
   C. 'Winterthur' (grows well in
      shade)
*Cryptomeria japonica* 'Globosa Nana'
      (partial)
*Danae racemosa* (half shade)
*Decaisnea fargesii* (partial)
*Diervilla sessilifolia*
*Disanthus cercidifolius*
*Elaeagnus × ebbingei*
   E. pungens (partial)
   E. pungens 'Fruitlandii'
   E. pungens 'Hosoba-Fukurin'
   E. pungens 'Maculata'
   E. pungens 'Variegata'

*Enkianthus campanulatus* (partial)
  *E. campanulatus* 'Albiflorus'
  *E. campanulatus* var. *palibinii*
  *E. campanulatus* 'Red Bells'
  *E. campanulatus* 'Renoir'
  *E. campanulatus* 'Showy Lantern'
  *E. campanulatus* 'Sikokianus'
  *E. cernuus* var. *rubens*
  *E. chinensis*
  *E. deflexus*
*Escallonia bifida*
  *E. × exoniensis* (partial in hot interior
    valleys)
  *E. × exoniensis* 'Balfourii'
  *E. × exoniensis* 'Fradesii'
  *E.* 'Pride of Donard'
  *E. rubra* 'C. F. Ball'
*Euonymus alatus* 'Nordine Strain'
  *E. alatus* 'Rudy Haag'
  *E. alatus* 'Timber Creek'
  *E. europaeus* 'Redcap' (partial)
  *E. oxyphyllus*
*Fothergilla gardenii*
  *F. gardenii* 'Blue Mist'
  *F. gardenii* 'Jane Platt'
  *F. gardenii* 'Mt. Airy'
  *F. major*
*Fremontodendron* 'California Glory' (partial)
*Gardenia taitensis*
*Garrya elliptica* 'James Roof' (partial)
  *G. × issaquahensis*
*Grevillea alpina* (half shade)
  *G. alpina* 'Grampian's Gold'
  *G.* 'Canberra Gem'
  *G.* 'Robyn Gordon'
  *G. victoriae*
*Grevillea lavandulacea* 'Tanunda' (partial)
*Grewia occidentalis* (partial)
*Hamamelis × intermedia*
  *H. × intermedia* 'Arnold Promise'
  *H. × intermedia* 'Diane'
  *H. × intermedia* 'Feuerzauber'
  *H. × intermedia* 'Jelena'
  *H. × intermedia* 'Primavera'
  *H. × intermedia* 'Ruby Glow'
  *H. macrophylla*
  *H. mollis* (partial)
  *H. mollis* 'Brevipetala'
  *H. mollis* 'Coombe Wood'
  *H. mollis* 'Pallida'
  *H. vernalis* f. *carnea*
  *H. virginiana*
*Heptacodium miconioides* (partial)
*Heteromeles arbutifolia* (partial)
*Hibiscus rosa-sinensis* (partial)
  *H. rosa-sinensis* 'All Aglow'
  *H. rosa-sinensis* 'Carolyn Coe'

*H. rosa-sinensis* 'Cooperi'
*H. rosa-sinensis* 'Fiesta'
*H. rosa-sinensis* 'Herm Geller'
*H. rosa-sinensis* 'Harvest Moon'
*H. rosa-sinensis* 'Tino Vietti'
*H. rosa-sinensis* 'Tylene'
*Hydrangea arborescens* 'Annabelle'
  *H. aspera* subsp. *aspera*
  *H. macrophylla* (partial)
  *H. macrophylla* 'All Summer Beauty'
  *H. macrophylla* 'Blue Billow'
  *H. macrophylla* 'Forever Pink'
  *H. macrophylla* 'Quadricolor'
  *H. macrophylla* subsp. *serrata* 'Bluebird'
  *H. macrophylla* subsp. *serrata* 'Preziosa'
  *H. macrophylla* 'Variegata Mariesii'
  *H. macrophylla* 'White Wave'
  *H. paniculata* 'Tardiva' (partial)
  *H. quercifolia*
  *H. quercifolia* 'Snowflake'
  *H. quercifolia* 'Snow Queen'
  *H. sargentiana* (needs partial shade)
*Ilex cornuta* 'O. Spring'
  *I. cornuta* 'Rotunda' (partial)
  *I. cornuta* 'Willowleaf'
  *I. crenata* 'Beehive' (partial)
  *I. crenata* 'Compacta'
  *I. crenata* 'Delaware Diamond'
  *I. crenata* 'Dwarf Pagoda'
  *I. crenata* 'Glory'
  *I. crenata* 'Golden Heller'
  *I. crenata* 'Piccolo'
  *I. glabra* 'Compacta'
  *I. glabra* 'Ivory Queen'
  *I. glabra* 'Nigra'
  *I. glabra* 'Nordic' (partial)
  *I. glabra* 'Shamrock'
  *I. opaca* 'Clarendon Spreading'
  *I. opaca* 'Maryland Dwarf'
  *I.* 'Rock Garden' (partial)
  *I.* 'September Gem'
  *I. serrata* 'Sundrops' (light shade)
  *I. verticillata* (partial; lessens fruit
    production)
  *I. verticillata* 'Afterglow'
  *I. verticillata* 'Aurantiaca'
  *I. verticillata* f. *chrysocarpa*
  *I. verticillata* 'Maryland Beauty'
  *I. verticillata* 'Red Sprite'
  *I. verticillata* 'Scarlett O'Hara'
  *I. verticillata* 'Shaver'
  *I. verticillata* 'Sunset'
  *I. verticillata* 'Tiasquam'
  *I. verticillata* 'Winter Gold'
  *I. verticillata* 'Winter Red'
  *I. vomitoria* 'Dare County'
  *I. vomitoria* 'Jewel'

*I. vomitoria* 'Stokes Dwarf' (partial)
*Illicium anisatum*
  *I. floridanum* (heavy)
  *I. floridanum* f. *album*
  *I. floridanum* 'Halley's Comet'
  *I. henryi*
  *I. mexicanum*
  *I. parviflorum*
*Itea ilicifolia*
  *I. virginica* (partial)
  *I. virginica* 'Beppu'
  *I. virginica* 'Henry's Garnet'
*Juniperus squamata* 'Blue Star'
*Kalmia angustifolia* (partial)
  *K. angustifolia* 'Hammonasset'
  *K. angustifolia* 'Pumila'
  *K. latifolia* (heavy)
  *K. latifolia* 'Alba'
  *K. latifolia* 'Bullseye'
  *K. latifolia* 'Elf'
  *K. latifolia* 'Freckles'
  *K. latifolia* 'Fuscata'
  *K. latifolia* 'Heart's Desire'
  *K. latifolia* 'Little Linda'
  *K. latifolia* 'Minuet'
  *K. latifolia* 'Ostbo Red'
  *K. latifolia* 'Peppermint'
  *K. latifolia* 'Pink Charm'
  *K. latifolia* 'Sarah'
  *K. latifolia* 'Silver Dollar'
  *K. latifolia* 'Star Cluster'
*Kerria japonica* 'Picta'
  *K. japonica* 'Pleniflora'
*Leiophyllum buxifolium* (partial)
  *L. buxifolium* var. *hugeri*
*Leptospermum rotundifolium*
  *L. scoparium* 'Ash Burton Wax'
  *L. scoparium* 'Helen Strybing'
  *L. scoparium* 'Martini'
  *L. scoparium* 'Pink Cascade'
  *L. scoparium* 'Red Damask' (partial)
  *L. scoparium* 'Snow White'
*Leucothoe axillaris*
  *L. davisiae*
  *L. fontanesiana* 'Scarletta'
  *L. keiskei*
  *L. populifolia*
*Lindera angustifolia*
  *L. benzoin* (deep)
  *L. benzoin* 'Rubra'
  *L. benzoin* 'Xanthocarpa'
  *L. obtusiloba* (heavy)
*Lonicera* 'Honey Rose'
  *L. pileata* 'Royal Carpet' (partial)
  *L. xylosteum* 'Emerald Mound'
*Loropetalum chinensis* (partial)
  *L. chinensis* 'Rubra'

*Mahonia aquifolium*
  *M. aquifolium* 'Apollo'
  *M. aquifolium* 'Atropurpurea'
  *M. aquifolium* 'Compacta'
  *M. aquifolium* 'Golden Abundance'
  *M. aquifolium* 'Mayhan Strain'
  *M. aquifolium* 'Moseri'
  *M.* 'Arthur Menzies'
  *M. fortunei*
  *M. lomariifolia*
  *M. × media* 'Charity'
  *M. nervosa*
  *M. repens* (partial)
  *M. trifoliata*
*Medinilla magnifica* (partial)
*Michelia figo* (partial in warm climates)
*Myrica cerifera*
  *M. cerifera* var. *pumila*
  *M. gale*
  *M. pensylvanica* (partial)
*Neillia sinensis* (partial)
*Osmanthus americanus*
  *O. × burkwoodii*
  *O. delavayi* (partial)
  *O. fragrans* 'Aurantiacus'
  *O. heterophyllus* (partial)
  *O. heterophyllus* 'Aureomarginatus'
  *O. heterophyllus* 'Goshiki'
  *O. heterophyllus* 'Gulftide'
  *O. heterophyllus* 'Maculifolius'
  *O. heterophyllus* 'Myrtifolius'
  *O. heterophyllus* 'Rotundifolius'
  *O. heterophyllus* 'Sasaba'
  *O. heterophyllus* 'Variegatus'
*Pachystachys lutea* (partial)
*Pernettya mucronata* (partial)
  *P. mucronata* 'Alba'
  *P. mucronata* 'Coccinea'
  *P. mucronata* 'Rosea'
  *P. mucronata* 'Rubra'
*Pieris* 'Brouwer's Beauty'
  *P. floribunda* 'Millstream' (shade in South)
  *P. formosa* var. *forrestii* 'Forest Flame'
  *P. japonica* (partial)
  *P. japonica* 'Bert Chandler'
  *P. japonica* 'Flamingo'
  *P. japonica* 'Geisha'
  *P. japonica* 'Mountain Fire'
  *P. japonica* 'Pygmaea'
  *P. japonica* 'Red Mill'
  *P. japonica* 'Roslinda'
  *P. japonica* 'Valley Fire'
  *P. japonica* 'Valley Rose'
  *P. japonica* 'Valley Valentine'
  *P. japonica* 'Variegata'
  *P. japonica* 'White Cascade'

*P. japonica* 'White Pearl'
*P. phillyreifolia*
*P. taiwanensis* (woodland)
*Prostanthera ovalifolia*
  *P. rotundifolia* (partial)
  *P. rotundifolia* 'Glen Davis'
*Rhamnus frangula* 'Asplenifolia' (partial)
*Rhodotypos scandens*
*Rhus aromatica* 'Gro-low' (partial)
  *R. chinensis* 'September Beauty'
  *R. copallina*
  *R. glabra* var. *cismontana*
  *R. trilobata*
  *R. trilobata* 'Autumn Amber'
  *R. typhina* 'Dissecta'
  *R. typhina* 'Laciniata'
*Ribes alpinum* 'Green Mound'
  *R. aureum* (partial)
  *R. odoratum* (partial)
  *R. odoratum* 'Aureum'
  *R. sanguineum* (partial)
  *R. speciosum* (partial shade inland)
*Rubus cockburnianus*
  *R. odoratus* (partial shade in South)
  *R.* 'Tridel'
*Ruscus aculeatus* (dense)
*Sarcococca confusa*
  *S. ruscifolia* (best in partial shade)
*Skimmia* 'Formanii'
  *S. japonica* (partial to dense)
  *S. japonica* 'Nymans'
  *S. reevesiana* 'Rubella'
*Sorbaria aitchisonii*
  *S. sorbifolia* (partial)
*Sorbus reducta* (partial)
*Spiraea fritschiana* (partial)
*Stachyurus praecox* (partial in South)
*Streptosolen jamesonii* (partial)
*Syringa × henryi*
  *S. × henryi* 'Lutèce'
  *S. × henryi* 'Summer White'
  *S. × hyacinthiflora* (partial in South)
  *S. × hyacinthiflora* 'Blanche Sweet'
  *S. × hyacinthiflora* 'Maiden's Blush'
  *S. × hyacinthiflora* 'Sister Justena'
  *S. × josiflexa* (partial in South)
  *S. × josiflexa* 'Agnes Smith'
  *S. × josiflexa* 'Anna Amhoff'
  *S. × josiflexa* 'James MacFarlane'
  *S. × josiflexa* 'Royalty'
  *S. × laciniata* (partial in South)
  *S. meyeri* 'Palibin' (partial in South)
  *S. microphylla*
  *S. microphylla* 'Superba'
  *S.* 'Minuet'
  *S.* 'Miss Canada'
  *S. oblata* var. *dilatata*

  *S. patula* 'Miss Kim' (light in South)
  *S. × prestoniae* (light in South)
  *S. × prestoniae* 'Alice Rose Foster'
  *S. × prestoniae* 'Ethel M. Webster'
  *S. × prestoniae* 'Isabella'
  *S. × prestoniae* 'Nike'
  *S. vulgaris* (partial in South)
  *S. vulgaris* 'Agincourt Beauty'
  *S. vulgaris* 'Albert F. Holden'
  *S. vulgaris* 'Blue Skies'
  *S. vulgaris* 'Dwight D. Eisenhower'
  *S. vulgaris* 'Edith Cavell'
  *S. vulgaris* 'Edward J. Gardner'
  *S. vulgaris* 'Emile Lemoine'
  *S. vulgaris* 'Krasavitsa Moskvy'
  *S. vulgaris* 'Lavender Lady'
  *S. vulgaris* 'Ludwig Spaeth'
  *S. vulgaris* 'Marie Francis'
  *S. vulgaris* 'Mieczta'
  *S. vulgaris* 'Miss Ellen Willmott'
  *S. vulgaris* 'Primrose'
  *S. vulgaris* 'Rochester'
  *S. vulgaris* 'Sensation'
  *S. vulgaris* 'Slater's Elegance'
  *S. vulgaris* 'Victor Lemoine'
  *S. vulgaris* 'Wedgwood Blue'
  *S. vulgaris* 'Wonder Blue'
  *S. vulgaris* 'Yankee Doodle'
*Tabernaemontana divaricata*
*Taxus baccata* 'Adpressa Fowle'
  *T. baccata* 'Beanpole'
  *T. baccata* 'Fastigiata Robusta'
  *T. × media* 'Runyan'
*Thujopsis dolabrata* 'Nana'
*Tsuga canadensis* 'Bennett'
  *T. canadensis* 'Jeddeloh' (partial)
  *T. canadensis* 'Jervis'
*Ungnadia speciosa* (partial)
*Viburnum × carlcephalum* 'Cayuga' (partial)
  *V. carlesii* 'Aurora'
  *V. carlesii* 'Charis'
  *V. carlesii* 'Compactum' (partial)
  *V.* 'Chippewa'
  *V.* 'Eskimo' (partial in South)
  *V. lantana* 'Mohican'
  *V. nudum* 'Winterthur'
  *V. plicatum* f. *tomentosum* 'Shasta' (partial in South)
  *V. plicatum* f. *tomentosum* 'Shoshoni'
  *V. plicatum* f. *tomentosum* 'Summer Snowflake'
  *V. × rhytidophylloides* 'Alleghany' (partial)
  *V. rufidulum*
  *V. sargentii* 'Onondaga'
*Xanthorhiza simplicissima* (partial)
*Zenobia pulverulenta* (partial)

# SHRUBS FOR VARIOUS LEVELS OF SOIL MOISTURE

## MOIST TO WET CONDITIONS

*Adina rubella*
*Aralia cordata*
    *A. elata* 'Aureovariegata'
    *A. elata* 'Pyramidalis'
    *A. elata* 'Variegata'
    *A. spinosa*
*Arctostaphylos densiflora* 'Howard
    McMinn' (with good drainage)
    *A. densiflora* 'Sentinel'
*Brunfelsia australis*
    *B. latifolia*
    *B. pauciflora*
    *B. pauciflora* var. *calycina* 'Macrantha'
*Callicarpa americana*
    *C. americana* f. *lactea*
    *C. bodinieri* var. *giraldii* 'Profusion'
*Carissa macrocarpa*
*Cephalotaxus harringtonia* 'Duke Gardens'
    *C. harringtonia* 'Fastigiata'
    *C. harringtonia* 'Prostrata'
*Chimonanthus nitens*
    *C. praecox*
    *C. praecox* 'Luteus'
*Clethra acuminata*
    *C. alnifolia*
    *C. alnifolia* 'Hummingbird'
    *C. alnifolia* 'Paniculata'
    *C. alnifolia* 'Pink Spire'
    *C. alnifolia* 'Rosea'
    *C. barbinervis*
*Comptonia peregrina*
*Cornus sericea* 'Cardinal'
    *C. sericea* 'Isanti'
    *C. sericea* 'Silver & Gold'
*Cyrilla racemiflora*
*Daphne genkwa* (somewhat tolerant of wet
    conditions)
*Daphne mezereum*
    *D. mezereum* f. *alba*
    *D. mezereum* f. *alba* 'Bowles White'
    *Diervilla sessilifolia*
*Embothrium coccineum*
*Gardenia taitensis*
*Grewia occidentalis*
*Hippophae rhamnoides*
*Hydrangea macrophylla*
    *H. macrophylla* 'Blue Billow'
    *H. macrophylla* 'Forever Pink'
    *H. macrophylla* 'Quadricolor'
    *H. macrophylla* subsp. *serrata* 'Bluebird'
    *H. macrophylla* subsp. *serrata* 'Preziosa'
    *H. macrophylla* 'Variegata Mariesii'
    *H. macrophylla* 'White Wave'
*Ilex amelanchier*

*I.* 'Apollo'
*I. decidua* 'Byer's Golden'
*I. decidua* 'Council Fire'
*I. decidua* 'Pocahontas'
*I. decidua* 'Warren's Red'
*I.* 'Harvest Red'
*I.* 'Raritan Chief'
*I.* 'Sparkleberry'
*I. verticillata*
*I. verticillata* 'Afterglow'
*I. verticillata* 'Aurantiaca'
*I. verticillata* f. *chrysocarpa*
*I. verticillata* 'Maryland Beauty'
*I. verticillata* 'Red Sprite'
*I. verticillata* 'Scarlett O'Hara'
*I. verticillata* 'Shaver'
*I. verticillata* 'Sunset'
*I. verticillata* 'Tiasquam'
*I. verticillata* 'Winter Gold'
*I. verticillata* 'Winter Red'
*I. vomitoria* 'Dare County'
*I. vomitoria* 'Jewel'
*I. vomitoria* 'Stokes Dwarf'
*Illicium anisatum*
*I. floridanum*
*I. floridanum* f. *album*
*I. floridanum* 'Halley's Comet'
*I. henryi*
*I. mexicanum*
*I. parviflorum*
*Itea ilicifolia*
*I. virginica*
*I. virginica* 'Beppu'
*I. virginica* 'Henry's Garnet'
*Ixora* sp.
*I. chinensis*
*I. finlaysoniana*
*I. nienkui*
*I.* 'Nora Grant'
*I. odorata*
*Kalmia angustifolia*
    *K. angustifolia* 'Hammonasset'
    *K. angustifolia* 'Pumila'
*Lindera angustifolia*
    *L. benzoin*
    *L. benzoin* 'Rubra'
    *L. benzoin* 'Xanthocarpa'
*Medinilla magnifica*
*Nandina domestica* 'Alba'
    *N. domestica* 'Fire Power'
    *N. domestica* 'Gulf Stream'
    *N. domestica* 'Harbor Dwarf'
    *N. domestica* 'Heavenly Bamboo'
    *N. domestica* 'Royal Princess'
    *N. domestica* 'San Gabriel'

    *N. domestica* 'Umpqua Chief'
    *N. domestica* 'Umpqua Princess'
    *N. domestica* 'Umpqua Warrior'
*Osmanthus americanus*
*Pachystachys lutea*
*Pernettya mucronata*
    *P. mucronata* 'Alba'
    *P. mucronata* 'Coccinea'
    *P. mucronata* 'Rosea'
    *P. mucronata* 'Rubra'
*Pieris phillyreifolia*
*Salix fargesii*
    *S. gracilistyla*
    *S. lanata* (damp conditions/water
    landscaping)
    *S. melanostachys*
*Spiraea cinerea* 'Grefsheim' (all but very
    wet conditions)
*Ungnadia speciosa*
*Viburnum nudum* 'Winterthur'
*Xanthorhiza simplicissima*

## ARID CONDITIONS

*Acanthopanax sieboldianus* 'Variegatus'
*Adina rubella*
*Aralia cordata*
    *A. elata* 'Aureovariegata'
    *A. elata* 'Pyramidalis'
    *A. elata* 'Variegata'
    *A. spinosa*
*Arctostaphylos densiflora* 'Howard McMinn'
    *A. densiflora* 'Sentinel'
*Bauhinia lunarioides*
*Berberis × gladwynensis* 'William Penn'
    *B. thunbergii*
    *B. thunbergii* 'Atropurpurea'
    *B. thunbergii* 'Bagatelle'
    *B. thunbergii* 'Bogozam'
    *B. thunbergii* 'Globe'
    *B. thunbergii* 'Kobold'
    *B. thunbergii* 'Rose Glow'
    *B. thunbergii* 'Sparkle'
    *B. × wisleyensis*
*Brugmansia arborea*
*Buddleia alternifolia*
    *B. alternifolia* 'Argentea'
*Buxus* 'Glencoe'
    *B. microphylla* 'Compacta'
    *B. sempervirens* 'Elegantissima'
    *B. sempervirens* 'Graham Blandy'
    *B. sempervirens* 'Pullman'
    *B. sempervirens* 'Vardar Valley'
*Callicarpa americana*
    *C. americana* var. *lactea*
    *C. bodinieri* var. *giraldii* 'Profusion'

*Calluna vulgaris*
*Camellia sinensis* (more heat and drought
  tolerant than many other *Camellia*
  species)
*Caragana aurantiaca*
  *C. frutex* 'Globosa'
  *C. pygmaea*
*Carissa macrocarpa*
*Carpenteria californica*
*Caryopteris* × *clandonensis*
  *C.* × *clandonensis* 'Azure'
  *C.* × *clandonensis* 'Blue Mist'
  *C.* × *clandonensis* 'Dark Knight'
  *C.* × *clandonensis* 'Heavenly Blue'
  *C.* × *clandonensis* 'Longwood Blue'
*Cephalotaxus harringtonia* 'Duke Gardens'
  *C. harringtonia* 'Fastigiata'
  *C. harringtonia* 'Prostrata'
*Ceanothus* 'Concha'
  *C.* 'Dark Star'
  *C.* 'Frosty Blue'
  *C. impressus*
  *C.* 'Joyce Coulter'
  *C.* 'Julia Phelps'
  *C.* 'Puget Blue'
*Cercis canadensis* subsp. *mexicana* (very
  dry weather)
*Cercis reniformis* 'Texas White' (very dry
  weather)
*Chaenomeles speciosa*
  *C. speciosa* 'Moerloosi'
  *C. speciosa* 'Rubra'
  *C. speciosa* 'Simonii'
  *C. speciosa* 'Toyo-Nishiki'
*Chamaecyparis pisifera* 'Boulevard'
  *C. pisifera* 'Filifera Nana'
  *C. pisifera* 'Gold Spangle'
  *C. pisifera* 'Squarrosa Intermedia'
*Cistus* × *purpureus*
  *C. salvifolius*
  *C.* 'Silver Pink'
  *C.* × *skanbergii*
*Clethra acuminata*
  *C. alnifolia*
  *C. alnifolia* 'Hummingbird'
  *C. alnifolia* 'Paniculata'
  *C. alnifolia* 'Pink Spire'
  *C. alnifolia* 'Rosea'
*Comptonia peregrina*
*Cornus sericea* 'Cardinal'
  *C. sericea* 'Isanti'
  *C. sericea* 'Silver & Gold'
*Cotoneaster adpressus* 'Hessei'
  *C. apiculatus*
  *C. conspicuus* 'Decorus'
  *C. dammeri* 'Skogholm'
  *C. horizontalis* 'Robustus'

*C. racemiflorus* var. *soongoricus* (dry,
  sandy soil)
  *C.* × *watereri* 'Rothschildianus'
*Cytisus* × *praecox* 'Albus'
  *C.* × *praecox* 'Allgold'
  *C.* × *praecox* 'Hollandia'
  *C. scoparius* (dry, sandy soil)
  *C. scoparius* 'Burkwoodii'
  *C. scoparius* 'Lena'
  *C. scoparius* 'Lilac Time'
  *C. scoparius* 'Luna'
  *C. scoparius* 'Moonlight'
*Danae racemosa*
*Dendromecon rigida*
*Duranta stenostachya*
*Elaeagnus* × *ebbingei*
  *E. pungens*
  *E. pungens* 'Fruitlandii'
  *E. pungens* 'Hosoba-Fukurin'
  *E. pungens* 'Maculata'
  *E. pungens* 'Variegata'
*Escallonia exoniensis*
  *E. exoniensis* 'Balfourii'
  *E. exoniensis* 'Fradesii'
  *E.* 'Pride of Donard'
  *E. rubra* 'C. F. Ball'
*Exochorda* × *giraldii* var. *wilsonii*
  *E.* × *macrantha* 'The Bride'
*Feijoa sellowiana* (tolerates drought but
  needs summer moisture for fruit
  size)
  *F. sellowiana* 'Coolidge'
  *F. sellowiana* 'Mammoth'
  *F. sellowiana* 'Triumph'
*Fouquieria splendens*
*Fremontodendron* 'California Glory'
*Genista aethnensis*
  *G. lydia*
  *G. pilosa* (dry, gravelly soil)
  *G. pilosa* 'Goldilocks'
  *G. pilosa* 'Lemon Spreader'
  *G. pilosa* 'Vancouver Gold'
  *G. sagittalis*
*Grevillea alpina*
  *G. alpina* 'Grampian's Gold'
  *G.* 'Canberra Gem'
  *G.* 'Robyn Gordon'
  *G. rosmarinifolia*
  *G. tridentifera*
  *G. victoriae*
*Heptacodium miconioides*
*Heteromeles arbutifolia*
*Hibiscus* 'Lohengrin'
  *H. syriacus* 'Aphrodite'
  *H. syriacus* 'Diana'
  *H. syriacus* 'Helene'
  *H. syriacus* 'Lady Stanley'

  *H. syriacus* 'Minerva'
  *H. syriacus* 'Purpureus Variegatus'
  *H. syriacus* 'Woodbridge'
  *H.* 'Tosca'
*Hydrangea macrophylla*
  *H. macrophylla* 'Blue Billow'
  *H. macrophylla* 'Forever Pink'
  *H. macrophylla* 'Quadricolor'
  *H. macrophylla* subsp. *serrata* 'Bluebird'
  *H. macrophylla* subsp. *serrata* 'Preziosa'
  *H. macrophylla* 'Variegata Mariesii'
  *H. macrophylla* 'White Wave'
  *H. quercifolia* (brief drought)
  *H. quercifolia* 'Snowflake'
  *H. quercifolia* 'Snow Queen'
*Hypericum frondosum* 'Sunburst' (drought)
  *H. hookeranum* 'Rowallane'
  *H. kalmianum*
  *H. patulum* (poor, sandy soil)
  *H. patulum* 'Henryi'
  *H. patulum* 'Hidcote'
  *H. patulum* 'Sungold'
  *H. prolificum*
*Ilex* 'Apollo'
  *I. cornuta* 'O. Spring'
  *I. cornuta* 'Rotunda' (some drought)
  *I. cornuta* 'Willowleaf'
  *I.* 'Harvest Red'
  *I. opaca* 'Maryland Dwarf' (some
    drought)
  *I.* 'Raritan Chief'
  *I.* 'Sparkleberry' (some soil dryness)
  *I. verticillata* (tolerates dry soils with
    ease)
  *I. verticillata* 'Afterglow'
  *I. verticillata* 'Aurantiaca'
  *I. verticillata* f. *chrysocarpa*
  *I. verticillata* 'Maryland Beauty'
  *I. verticillata* 'Red Sprite'
  *I. verticillata* 'Scarlett O'Hara'
  *I. verticillata* 'Shaver'
  *I. verticillata* 'Sunset'
  *I. verticillata* 'Tiasquam' (tolerates
    drought)
  *I. verticillata* 'Winter Gold'
  *I. verticillata* 'Winter Red'
  *I. vomitoria* 'Dare County'
  *I. vomitoria* 'Jewel'
  *I. vomitoria* 'Stokes Dwarf'
*Illicium parviflorum*
*Itea ilicifolia*
  *I. virginica*
  *I. virginica* 'Beppu'
  *I. virginica* 'Henry's Garnet'
*Ixora* sp.
  *I. finlaysoniana*
  *I.* 'Nora Grant'

*Juniperus chinensis* 'Echiniformis'
    *J. squamata* 'Blue Star'
    *J. virginiana* 'Grey Owl'
*Kalmia angustifolia*
    *K. angustifolia* 'Hammonasset'
    *K. angustifolia* 'Pumila'
*Leptodermis oblonga*
*Leptospermum scoparium* 'Ash Burton Wax'
    *L. scoparium* 'Helen Strybing'
    *L. scoparium* 'Martini'
    *L. scoparium* 'Pink Cascade'
    *L. scoparium* 'Red Damask' (drought-
        tolerant while dormant)
    *L. scoparium* 'Snow White'
*Leucophyllum frutescens* 'Compactum'
    *L. frutescens* 'Green Cloud'
    *L. frutescens* 'White Cloud'
*Leucospermum cordifolium*
    *L. reflexum*
*Leycesteria formosa*
*Lindera angustifolia*
    *L. benzoin*
    *L. benzoin* 'Rubra'
    *L. benzoin* 'Xanthocarpa'
*Myrica pensylvanica*
*Nandina domestica* 'Alba'
    *N. domestica* 'Fire Power'
    *N. domestica* 'Gulf Stream'
    *N. domestica* 'Harbor Dwarf'
    *N. domestica* 'Heavenly Bamboo'
    *N. domestica* 'Royal Princess'
    *N. domestica* 'San Gabriel'
    *N. domestica* 'Umpqua Chief'
    *N. domestica* 'Umpqua Princess'
    *N. domestica* 'Umpqua Warrior'
*Philadelphus coronarius* 'Natchez' (dry soil)
    *P. coronarius* 'Variegata'
    *P. virginalis*
    *P. virginalis* 'Glacier'
    *P. virginalis* 'Miniature Snowflake'
    *P. virginalis* 'Minnesota Snowflake'
    *P. virginalis* 'Polar Star'
*Physocarpus opulifolius* 'Dart's Golden'
    (dry sites)
*Picea pungens* 'Compacta'
    *P. pungens* 'Montgomery' (more
        tolerant of drought than other *Picea*
        species)
*Pinus sylvestris* 'Beuvronensis' (some
    drought when established)
    *P. sylvestris* 'Hillside Creeper'
*Potentilla fruticosa* (poor, dry soil)
    *P. fruticosa* 'Abbotswood'
    *P. fruticosa* 'Coronation Triumph'
    *P. fruticosa* 'Day Dawn Viette'
    *P. fruticosa* 'Goldfinger'
    *P. fruticosa* 'Katherine Dykes'

    *P. fruticosa* 'Pink Queen'
    *P. fruticosa* 'Primrose Beauty'
    *P. fruticosa* 'Snowbird'
    *P. fruticosa* 'Yellowbird'
*Prostanthera rotundifolia* (somewhat
    drought tolerant)
*Punica granatum* (tolerates great heat and
    desert conditions)
    *P. granatum* 'Emperior'
    *P. granatum* 'Hizakuru'
    *P. granatum* 'Nana'
    *P. granatum* 'Peach Princess'
    *P. granatum* 'Shiro Botan'
    *P. granatum* 'Toyosho'
    *P. granatum* 'Twisted Trunk'
    *P. granatum* 'Wonderful'
*Pyracantha* 'Apache'
    *P.* 'Mohave'
    *P.* 'Pueblo'
    *P.* 'Rutgers'
*Rhus chinensis* 'September Beauty'
    *R. trilobata*
    *R. trilobata* 'Autumn Amber'
    *R. typhina* 'Dissecta'
    *R. typhina* 'Laciniata'
*Ribes aureum*
    *R. sanguineum*
    *R. speciosum*
*Robinia hispida* (poor, dry soil)
*Rosa* 'Buff Beauty'
    *R.* 'Carefree Wonder'
    *R. glauca*
    *R.* 'Golden Wings'
    *R. hugonis*
    *R.* 'Morden Blush' (hot, dry conditions)
    *R.* 'Nevada'
    *R. rugosa*
    *R.* 'Stanwell Perpetual'
    *R. xanthina*
*Sambucus racemosa* 'Plumosa Aurea'
    (some drought)
*Shepherdia argentea*
    *S. canadensis*
*Spiraea* × *bumalda* 'Golden Princess'
    *S.* × *bumalda* 'Gold Flame'
    *S.* × *cinerea* 'Grefsheim'
    *S. fritschiana*
    *S. japonica* 'Shibori'
    *S. nipponica*
    *S. nipponica* 'Halward's Silver'
    *S. nipponica* 'Snowmound'
*Streptosolen jamesonii* (best in warm, dry
    conditions)
*Syringa vulgaris* 'Blue Skies'
*Taxus baccata* 'Adpressa Fowle' (some
    drought)
    *T. baccata* 'Beanpole'

    *T. baccata* 'Fastigiata Robusta'
    *T.* × *media* 'Runyan'
*Ungnadia speciosa*
*Viburnum* × *carlcephalum* 'Cayuga'
    *V. carlesii* 'Aurora'
    *V. carlesii* 'Charis'
    *V. carlesii* 'Compactum'
    *V.* 'Chippewa'
    *V.* 'Huron'
    *V. setigerum* 'Aurantiacum' (some
        drought)
*Vitex agnus-castus*
    *V. agnus-castus* 'Alba'
    *V. agnus-castus* 'Rosea'
    *V. agnus-castus* 'Silver Spire'

## SEACOAST SHRUBS

*Brugmansia arborea* (wind/salt)
*Carissa macrocarpa*
*Carpenteria californica* (salt)
*Clethra alnifolia*
*Ceanothus* 'Concha'
    *C.* 'Dark Star'
    *C.* 'Frosty Blue'
    *C. impressus*
    *C.* 'Joyce Coulter'
    *C.* 'Julia Phelps'
    *C.* 'Puget Blue'
    *C.* × *pallidus* var. *roseus*
*Cistus* × *purpureus*
    *C. salviifolius*
    *C.* 'Silver Pink'
    *C.* × *skanbergii* (wind/salt)
*Comptonia peregrina*
*Correa* 'Carmine Bells'
    *C.* × *harrisii*
    *C.* 'Ivory Bells'
    *C. reflexa*
*Duranta stenostachya*
*Escallonia bifida*
    *E.* × *exoniensis*
    *E.* × *exoniensis* 'Balfourii'
    *E.* × *exoniensis* 'Fradesii'
    *E.* 'Pride of Donard'
    *E. rubra* 'C. F. Ball'
*Gardenia taitensis*
*Garrya elliptica* 'James Roof'
*Grewia occidentalis* (wind/wet/salt)
*Hippophae rhamnoides* (wet/salt)
*Hydrangea macrophylla*
    *H. macrophylla* 'Blue Billow'
    *H. macrophylla* 'Forever Pink'
    *H. macrophylla* 'Quadricolor'
    *H. macrophylla* subsp. *serrata* 'Bluebird'
    *H. macrophylla* subsp. *serrata* 'Preziosa'
    *H. macrophylla* 'Variegata Mariesii'
    *H. macrophylla* 'White Wave'

*Ixora* sp. (some salt/wet)
  *I. chinensis*
  *I. finlaysoniana*
  *I. nienkui*
  *I.* 'Nora Grant'
  *I. odorata*

*Leucophyllum frutescens* 'Compactum'
  *L. frutescens* 'Green Cloud'
  *L. frutescens* 'White Cloud'
*Medinilla magnifica*
*Osmanthus americanus* (wet/salt)
*Ribes speciosum* (best in sun near coast)

*Rosa rugosa*
*Ruscus aculeatus*
*Tecoma stans* (wind/salt)
  *T. stans* var. *angustata*
*Thevetia thevetioides*

# SHRUBS RESISTANT TO PESTS AND DISEASES

The plants listed below generally have proved resistant to pests or diseases when grown in conditions that are not highly stressful.

*Abeliophyllum distichum*
*Adina rubella*
*Aesculus californica*
  *A. parviflora*
  *A. parviflora* 'Rogers'
  *A. parviflora* f. *serotina*
*Amelanchier ovalis* 'Pumila'
*Aralia cordata*
  *A. elata* 'Aureovariegata'
  *A. elata* 'Pyramidalis'
  *A. elata* 'Variegata'
  *A. spinosa*
*Arctostaphylos densiflora* 'Howard McMinn'
*Azara dentata*
  *A. petiolaris*
  *A. serrata*
*Bauhinia lunarioides*
*Berberis darwinii*
  *B. koreana*
  *B. linearifolia*
  *B. verruculosa*
*Brugmansia arborea*
*Buddleia alternifolia*
  *B. alternifolia* 'Argentea'
  *B. globosa*
*Buxus* 'Green Gem'
  *B.* 'Green Mountain'
  *B.* 'Green Velvet'
*Callicarpa americana*
  *C. americana* var. *lactea*
  *C. bodinieri* var. *giraldii* 'Profusion'
*Calycanthus floridus*
  *C. floridus* 'Athens'
  *C. floridus* 'Edith Wilder'
*Caryopteris* × *clandonensis*
  *C.* × *clandonensis* 'Azure'
  *C.* × *clandonensis* 'Blue Mist'
  *C.* × *clandonensis* 'Dark Knight'
  *C.* × *clandonensis* 'Heavenly Blue'
  *C.* × *clandonensis* 'Longwood Blue'
*Cephalotaxus harringtonia* 'Duke Gardens'
  *C. harringtonia* 'Fastigiata'
  *C. harringtonia* 'Prostrata'
*Chaenomeles speciosa* 'Moerloosi'
*Chimonanthus nitens*
  *C. praecox*

*C. praecox* 'Luteus'
*Cistus* × *purpureus*
  *C. salvifolius*
  *C.* 'Silver Pink'
  *C.* × *skanbergii*
*Clethra barbinervis*
*Comptonia peregrina*
  *C. peregrina* var. *asplenifolia*
*Cornus mas*
  *C. mas* 'Aurea'
  *C. mas* 'Flava'
  *C. mas* 'Golden Glory'
  *C. mas* 'Variegata'
  *C. sericea* 'Cardinal'
  *C. sericea* 'Isanti'
  *C. sericea* 'Silver & Gold'
*Correa* 'Carmine Bells'
  *C.* 'Ivory Bells'
  *C.* × *harrisii*
  *C. reflexa*
*Corylopsis glabrescens*
  *C. pauciflora*
  *C. platypetala*
  *C. sinensis*
  *C. sinensis* f. *veitchiana*
  *C. spicata*
  *C. willmottiae* 'Spring Purple'
  *C.* 'Winterthur'
*Cyrilla racemiflora*
*Danae racemosa*
*Daphne* × *burkwoodii* (occasional wilting)
  *D.* × *burkwoodii* 'Carol Mackie'
  *D.* × *burkwoodii* 'Somerset'
  *D.* × *burkwoodii* 'Variegata'
  *D. caucasica*
  *D. giraldii*
  *D.* × *mantensiana*
  *D. odora* 'Aureo-marginata'
  *D. retusa*
  *D. tangutica*
*Decaisnea fargesii*
*Dendromecon rigida*
*Diervilla sessilifolia*
*Dipelta floribunda*
*Duranta stenostachya*
*Elliottia racemosa*

*Enkianthus campanulatus* (occasional scale)
  *E. campanulatus* 'Albiflorus'
  *E. campanulatus* var. *palibinii*
  *E. campanulatus* 'Red Bells'
  *E. campanulatus* 'Renoir'
  *E. campanulatus* 'Showy Lantern'
  *E. campanulatus* 'Sikokianus'
  *E. cernuus* var. *rubens*
  *E. chinensis*
  *E. deflexus*
  *E. perulatus* (occasional scale)
*Escallonia bifida*
  *E.* × *exoniensis*
  *E.* × *exoniensis* 'Balfourii'
  *E.* × *exoniensis* 'Fradesii'
*Euonymus alatus* 'Nordine Strain'
  *E. alatus* 'Rudy Haag'
*Exochorda giraldii* var. *wilsonii*
  *E.* × *macrantha* 'The Bride'
*Feijoa sellowiana*
  *F. sellowiana* 'Coolidge'
  *F. sellowiana* 'Mammoth'
  *F. sellowiana* 'Triumph'
*Forsythia mandshurica* 'Vermont Sun'
  *F.* 'Meadowlark'
  *F.* 'Northern Gold'
  *F.* 'Northern Sun'
  *F.* 'New Hampshire Gold'
  *F.* 'Sunrise'
  *F. suspensa* var. *sieboldii*
  *F. viridissima* var. *koreana* 'Ilgwang'
  *F.* 'Winterthur'
*Fothergilla gardenii*
  *F. gardenii* 'Blue Mist'
  *F. gardenii* 'Jane Platt'
  *F. gardenii* 'Mt. Airy'
  *F. major*
*Fouquieria splendens*
*Fremontodendron* 'California Glory'
*Garrya elliptica* 'James Roof'
  *G.* × *issaquahensis*
*Genista aethnensis*
  *G. lydia*
  *G. pilosa*
  *G. pilosa* 'Goldilocks'
  *G. pilosa* 'Lemon Spreader'

G. pilosa 'Vancouver Gold'
G. sagittalis
Grevillea rosmarinifolia
G. tridentifera
Hamamelis × intermedia
H. × intermedia 'Arnold Promise'
H. × intermedia 'Diane'
H. × intermedia 'Feuerzauber'
H. × intermedia 'Jelena'
H. × intermedia 'Primavera'
H. × intermedia 'Ruby Glow'
H. macrophylla
H. mollis
H. mollis 'Brevipetala'
H. mollis 'Coombe Wood'
H. mollis 'Pallida'
H. vernalis f. carnea
H. virginiana
Heptacodium miconioides
Hippophae rhamnoides
Hydrangea arborescens 'Annabelle'
H. aspera subsp. aspera
H. sargentiana
H. paniculata 'Tardiva'
H. quercifolia
H. quercifolia 'Snowflake'
H. quercifolia 'Snow Queen'
Hypericum frondosum 'Sunburst'
H. hookeranum 'Rowallane'
H. kalmianum
H. patulum
H. patulum 'Henryi'
H. patulum 'Hidcote'
H. patulum 'Sungold'
H. prolificum
Ilex amelanchier
I. 'Apollo'
I. decidua 'Byer's Golden'
I. decidua 'Council Fire'
I. decidua 'Pocahontas'
I. decidua 'Warren's Red'
I. glabra 'Compacta'
I. glabra 'Ivory Queen'
I. glabra 'Nigra'
I. glabra 'Nordic'
I. glabra 'Shamrock'
I. 'Harvest Red'
I. opaca 'Clarendon Spreading'
I. opaca 'Maryland Dwarf'
I. 'Raritan Chief'
I. serrata 'Bonfire'
I. serrata 'Sundrops'
I. 'Sparkleberry'
I. vomitoria 'Dare County'
I. vomitoria 'Jewel'
I. vomitoria 'Stokes Dwarf'
Illicium anisatum

I. floridanum
I. floridanum f. album
I. floridanum 'Halley's Comet'
I. henryi
I. mexicanum
I. parviflorum
Indigofera kirilowii
Itea ilicifolia
I. virginica
I. virginica 'Beppu'
I. virginica 'Henry's Garnet'
Juniperus chinensis 'Echiniformis'
Kalmia angustifolia (occasional lacebug)
K. angustifolia 'Hammonasset'
K. angustifolia 'Pumila'
Kolkwitzia amabilis
K. amabilis 'Pink Cloud'
K. amabilis 'Rosea'
Lagerstroemia 'Acoma'
L. 'Hopi'
L. 'Pecos'
L. 'Zuni'
Leptodermis oblonga
Lespedeza thunbergii 'Alba'
L. thunbergii 'Gibraltar'
Leucophyllum frutescens 'Compactum'
L. frutescens 'Green Cloud'
L. frutescens 'White Cloud'
Leucospermum cordifolium
L. reflexum
Leucothoe populifolia
Leycesteria formosa
Lindera angustifolia
L. benzoin
L. benzoin 'Rubra'
L. benzoin 'Xanthocarpa'
Lindera obtusiloba
Lonicera 'Honey Rose'
L. pileata 'Royal Carpet'
L. xylosteum 'Emerald Mound'
Loropetalum chinensis
L. chinensis 'Rubra'
Mahonia repens
M. trifoliata
Michelia figo
Myrica cerifera
M. cerifera var. pumila
M. gale
M. pensylvanica
Nandina domestica 'Alba'
N. domestica 'Fire Power'
N. domestica 'Gulf Stream'
N. domestica 'Harbor Dwarf'
N. domestica 'Heavenly Bamboo'
N. domestica 'Royal Princess'
N. domestica 'San Gabriel'
N. domestica 'Umpqua Chief'

N. domestica 'Umpqua Princess'
N. domestica 'Umpqua Warrior'
Neillia affinis
N. sinensis
N. thibetica
Neviusia alabamensis
Osmanthus americanus
O. × burkwoodii
O. delavayi
O. fragrans 'Aurantiacus'
O. heterophyllus
O. heterophyllus 'Aureomarginatus'
O. heterophyllus 'Goshiki'
O. heterophyllus 'Gulftide'
O. heterophyllus 'Maculifolius'
O. heterophyllus 'Rotundifolius'
O. heterophyllus 'Sasaba'
O. heterophyllus 'Variegatus'
Paeonia suffruticosa
P. suffruticosa 'Alhambra'
P. suffruticosa 'Ariadne'
P. suffruticosa 'Companion of Serenity'
P. suffruticosa 'Hana Kisoi'
P. suffruticosa 'Hephestos'
P. suffruticosa 'Joseph Rock'
P. suffruticosa 'Leda'
P. suffruticosa 'Renkaku'
P. suffruticosa 'Shintenchi'
Pernettya mucronata
P. mucronata 'Alba'
P. mucronata 'Coccinea'
P. mucronata 'Rosea'
P. mucronata 'Rubra'
Physocarpus opulifolius 'Dart's Golden'
Prostanthera ovalifolia
P. rotundifolia
P. rotundifolia 'Glen Davis'
Punica granatum (plantbug in desert)
P. granatum 'Emperior'
P. granatum 'Hizakuru'
P. granatum 'Nana'
P. granatum 'Peach Princess'
P. granatum 'Shiro Botan'
P. granatum 'Toyosho'
P. granatum 'Twisted Trunk'
P. granatum 'Wonderful'
Pyracantha 'Apache'
P. 'Fiery Cascade'
P. 'Gold Rush'
P. 'Mohave'
P. 'Navaho'
P. 'Pueblo'
P. 'Rutgers'
P. 'Teton'
Rhamnus frangula 'Asplenifolia' (some
fungus on winter-stressed shrubs)
Rhodotypos scandens

*Rosa* 'Bonica'
　*R.* 'Carefree Beauty'
　*R.* 'Complicata'
　*R. damascena* var. *bifera* 'Autumn Damask'
　*R. glauca*
　*R.* 'John Cabot'
　*R.* 'John Davis'
　*R.* 'Morden Blush'
　*R. rugosa* 'Charles Albanel'
　*R. rugosa* 'Henry Hudson'
　*R. rugosa* 'Jens Munk'
　*R. rugosa* 'Rubra'
　*R. rugosa* 'Therese Bugnet'
　*R. rugosa* 'Topaz Jewel'
　*R.* 'Stanwell Perpetual'
　*R.* 'William Baffin'
　*R. xanthina*
*Rubus cockburnianus*
*Ruscus aculeatus*
*Sarcococca confusa*
　*S. ruscifolia*
*Shepherdia argentea*
　*S. canadensis*
*Sorbaria aitchisonii*
　*S. sorbifolia*
*Sorbus reducta*
*Spiraea* × *cinerea* 'Grefsheim'
　*S. fritschiana*
　*S. japonica* 'Shibori'
　*S. nipponica*
　*S. nipponica* 'Halward's Silver'

　*S. nipponica* 'Snowmound'
*Stachyurus praecox*
*Stephanandra incisa* 'Crispa'
*Streptosolen jamesonii*
*Syringa* × *henryi*
　*S.* × *henryi* 'Lutèce'
　*S.* × *hyacinthiflora*
　*S.* × *hyacinthiflora* 'Blanche Sweet'
　*S.* × *hyacinthiflora* 'Maiden's Blush'
　*S.* × *hyacinthiflora* 'Sister Justena'
　*S. meyeri* 'Palibin'
　*S. patula* 'Miss Kim'
　*S. vulgaris* 'Albert F. Holden'
　*S. vulgaris* 'Mieczta' (resistant to
　　mildew and necrosis)
　*S. vulgaris* 'Victor Lemoine'
　*S. vulgaris* 'Wedgwood Blue'
*Tabernaemontana divaricata*
*Taxus baccata* 'Adpressa Fowle'
*Tecoma stans*
　*T. stans* var. *angustata*
*Thevetia thevetioides*
*Thujopsis dolabrata* 'Nana'
*Ungnadia speciosa*
*Viburnum* × *bodnantense* 'Dawn'
　*V.* × *bodnantense* 'Deben'
　*V.* × *burkwoodii* 'Conoy'
　*V.* × *burkwoodii* 'Mohawk'
　*V. carlesii* 'Aurora'
　*V. carlesii* 'Charis'
　*V. carlesii* 'Compactum'

　*V.* 'Chesapeake'
　*V.* 'Chippewa'
　*V. dilatatum* 'Catskill'
　*V. dilatatum* 'Erie'
　*V. dilatatum* 'Iroquois'
　*V. dilatatum* 'Michael Dodge'
　*V.* 'Eskimo'
　*V. farreri* 'Candidissimum'
　*V.* 'Huron'
　*V. lantana* 'Mohican'
　*V. nudum* 'Winterthur'
　*V. plicatum* f. *tomentosum* 'Shasta'
　*V. plicatum* f. *tomentosum* 'Shoshoni'
　*V. plicatum* f. *tomentosum* 'Summer
　　Snowflake'
　*V.* × *pragense*
　*V.* × *rhytidophylloides* 'Alleghany'
　*V. rufidulum*
　*V. sargentii* 'Flavum'
　*V. sargentii* 'Onondaga'
　*V. sargentii* 'Susquehanna'
　*V. setigerum* 'Aurantiacum'
　*V.* 'Willowwood'
*Vitex agnus-castus*
　*V. agnus-castus* 'Alba'
　*V. agnus-castus* 'Rosea'
　*V. agnus-castus* 'Silver Spire'
*Weigela florida* 'Evita'
　*W. florida* 'Red Prince'
　*W. florida* 'Variegata'
*Xanthorhiza simplicissima*

## SHRUBS WITH CONSPICUOUS BLOOM

**WHITE**

*Abelia chinensis*
　*A.* × *grandiflora*
　*A.* × *grandiflora* 'Prostrata'
　*A.* × *grandiflora* 'Sherwood'
*Abeliophyllum distichum* (pink cast)
*Acanthopanax sieboldianus* 'Variegatus'
*Adina rubella*
*Aesculus californica*
　*A. parviflora*
　*A. parviflora* f. *serotina*
*Amelanchier ovalis* 'Pumila'
*Aralia cordata*
　*A. elata* 'Aureovariegata'
　*A. elata* 'Pyramidalis'
　*A. elata* 'Variegata'
　*A. spinosa*
*Arctostaphylos stanfordiana* (white to pink)
*Ardisia crenata* (reddish white)
　*A. crispa*
*Aronia arbutifolia* 'Brilliantissima' (white
　to pink)

　*A. melanocarpa*
*Azara petiolaris*
*Bauhinia lunarioides* (white to pink)
*Berberis thunbergii* 'Bogozam'
　*B. thunbergii* 'Rose Glow'
*Brugmansia arborea* (white to salmon-pink)
*Buddleia davidii* 'White Bouquet'
　*B. davidii* 'White Profusion'
　*B. fallowiana* 'Alba'
*Callicarpa americana* var. *lactea*
　*C. japonica* 'Leucocarpa'
*Calluna vulgaris* 'Alba Plena'
　*C. vulgaris* 'Gold Haze'
*Calycanthus floridus*
　*C. floridus* 'Athens'
*Camellia japonica* 'Alaska'
　*C. japonica* 'Betty Sheffield Supreme'
　*C. japonica* 'Finlandia'
　*C. japonica* 'Mansize'
　*C. japonica* 'Nuccio's Gem'
　*C. japonica* 'September Morn' (white to
　　blush-pink)

　*C. japonica* 'Swan Lake'
　*C. japonica* 'Ville de Nantes' (red and
　　white)
*Camellia oleifera*
　*C.* 'Polar Ice'
　*C. sinensis*
　*C.* 'Snow Flurry'
　*C.* 'Winter's Hope
　*C.* 'Winter's Waterlily'
*Carissa macrocarpa*
*Carpenteria californica*
*Cercis chinensis* 'Alba'
　*C. reniformis* 'Texas White'
*Chaenomeles speciosa*
　*C. speciosa* 'Moerloosi' (pink edge)
　*C. speciosa* 'Toyo-Nishiki' (white/
　　pink/red on same branches)
　*C.* × *superba* 'Jet Trail'
*Chimonanthus nitens*
*Choisya ternata*
　*C. ternata* 'Sundance'
*Cistus salvifolius*

*Clerodendrum trichotomum* var. *fargesii*
*Clethra acuminata*
    *C. alnifolia* 'Hummingbird'
    *C. alnifolia* 'Paniculata'
    *C. barbinervis*
*Correa* 'Ivory Bells'
*Cotoneaster conspicuus* 'Decorus'
    *C. racemiflorus* var. *soongoricus*
    *C.* × *watereri* 'Rothschildianus'
*Cyrilla racemiflora*
*Cytisus* × *praecox* 'Albus'
    *C. scoparius* 'Moonlight'
*Daphne cneorum* 'Alba'
    *D. mezereum* f. *alba*
    *D. mezereum* f. *alba* 'Bowles White'
*Deutzia chunii* (white-pink)
    *D. gracilis* 'Nikko'
    *D. scabra* var. *candidissima*
    *D. scabra* 'Plena'
    *D. scabra* 'Pride of Rochester'
*Elaeagnus pungens*
    *E. pungens* 'Fruitlandii'
    *E. pungens* 'Hosoba-Fukurin'
    *E. pungens* 'Maculata'
    *E. pungens* 'Variegata'
*Elliottia racemosa*
*Enkianthus campanulatus* 'Albiflorus'
    *E. deflexus* (white/yellow to pink/red)
    *E. perulatus*
    *E. perulatus* 'Compactus'
*Escallonia bifida*
    *E.* × *exoniensis* 'Balfourii'
*Exochorda giraldii* var. *wilsonii*
    *E.* × *macrantha* 'The Bride'
*Feijoa sellowiana*
    *F. sellowiana* 'Coolidge'
    *F. sellowiana* 'Mammoth'
    *F. sellowiana* 'Triumph'
*Fothergilla gardenii*
    *F. gardenii* 'Blue Mist'
    *F. gardenii* 'Jane Platt'
    *F. gardenii* 'Mt. Airy'
    *F. major*
*Gardenia taitensis*
*Grevillea alpina* (two-tone combinations of
    white/orange/yellow/red)
    *G. tridentifera*
*Heptacodium miconioides*
*Heteromeles arbutifolia*
*Hibiscus* 'Lohengrin'
    *H. rosa-sinensis* (white to pink/red,
      yellow/orange)
    *H. rosa-sinensis* 'Tino Vietti'
    *H. syriacus* 'Diana'
    *H. syriacus* 'Helene'
    *H. syriacus* 'Lady Stanley'
*Hydrangea arborescens* 'Annabelle'

*H. macrophylla*
*H. paniculata* 'Tardiva'
*H. quercifolia*
*H. quercifolia* 'Snowflake'
*H. quercifolia* 'Snow Queen'
*Ilex* 'Harvest Red'
*Illicium anisatum* (white/yellow/green)
    *I. floridanum* f. *album*
*Itea finlaysoniana*
    *I. ilicifolia*
    *I. virginica*
    *I. virginica* 'Beppu'
    *I. virginica* 'Henry's Garnet'
*Ixora nienkui*
    *I. odorata*
*Kalmia angustifolia* (also lavender or red)
    *K. angustifolia* 'Pumila'
    *K. latifolia*
    *K. latifolia* 'Alba'
    *K. latifolia* 'Bullseye' (broad purplish
      band)
    *K. latifolia* 'Elf'
    *K. latifolia* 'Fuscata'
    *K. latifolia* 'Minuet'
    *K. latifolia* 'Silver Dollar'
    *K. latifolia* 'Star Cluster'
*Lagerstroemia* 'Acoma'
*Leiophyllum buxifolium*
    *L. buxifolium* var. *hugeri*
*Leptospermum rotundifolium* (white to
    purple-pink)
    *L. scoparium* 'Ash Burton Wax'
    *L. scoparium* 'Snow White'
*Lespedeza thunbergii* 'Alba'
*Leucophyllum frutescens* 'White Cloud'
*Leucothoe axillaris*
    *L. davisiae*
    *L. fontanesiana* 'Scarletta'
    *L. keiskei*
    *L. populifolia*
*Lonicera pileata* 'Royal Carpet'
    *L. xylosteum* 'Emerald Mound'
*Loropetalum chinensis*
*Nandina domestica* 'Alba'
    *N. domestica* 'Fire Power'
    *N. domestica* 'Gulf Stream'
    *N. domestica* 'Harbor Dwarf'
    *N. domestica* 'Heavenly Bamboo'
    *N. domestica* 'Royal Princess'
    *N. domestica* 'San Gabriel'
    *N. domestica* 'Umpqua Chief'
    *N. domestica* 'Umpqua Princess'
    *N. domestica* 'Umpqua Warrior'
*Neviusia alabamensis*
*Osmanthus* × *burkwoodii*
    *O. delavayi*
    *O. heterophyllus*

*O. heterophyllus* 'Aureomarginatus'
*O. heterophyllus* 'Goshiki'
*O. heterophyllus* 'Gulftide'
*O. heterophyllus* 'Maculifolius'
*O. heterophyllus* 'Myrtifolius'
*O. heterophyllus* 'Rotundifolius'
*O. heterophyllus* 'Sasaba'
*O. heterophyllus* 'Variegatus'
*Paeonia suffruticosa* 'Joseph Rock'
    *P. suffruticosa* 'Renkaku'
*Pernettya mucronata* 'Alba'
*Philadelphus coronarius* 'Natchez'
    *P. coronarius* 'Variegata'
    *P. virginalis*
    *P. virginalis* 'Glacier'
    *P. virginalis* 'Miniature Snowflake'
    *P. virginalis* 'Minnesota Snowflake'
    *P. virginalis* 'Polar Star'
*Pieris* 'Brouwer's Beauty'
    *P. floribunda* 'Millstream'
    *P. formosa* var. *forrestii* 'Forest Flame'
    *P. japonica*
    *P. japonica* 'Bert Chandler'
    *P. japonica* 'Geisha'
    *P. japonica* 'Mountain Fire'
    *P. japonica* 'Red Mill'
    *P. japonica* 'Valley Fire'
    *P. japonica* 'Variegata'
    *P. japonica* 'White Cascade'
    *P. japonica* 'White Pearl'
    *P. phillyreifolia*
    *P. taiwanensis*
*Physocarpus opulifolius* 'Dart's Golden'
*Potentilla fruticosa* 'Abbotswood'
    *P. fruticosa* 'Snowbird'
*Punica granatum* 'Shiro Botan'
*Pyracantha* 'Apache'
    *P.* 'Fiery Cascade'
    *P.* 'Gold Rush'
    *P.* 'Mohave'
    *P.* 'Navaho'
    *P.* 'Pueblo'
    *P.* 'Rutgers'
    *P.* 'Teton'
*Rhodotypos scandens*
*Rhus chinensis* 'September Beauty'
*Ribes sanguineum* 'Alba'
*Rosa* × *alba* 'Celestial' (white to blush)
    *R.* × *alba* 'Semi Plena' (white to blush)
    *R.* × *alba* 'White Rose of York'
    *R.* 'Carefree Wonder'
    *R. centifolia* f. *muscosa* 'White Bath'
    *R. damascena* var. *bifera* 'Autumn
      Damask' (white to pink)
    *R.* 'Morden Blush' (blush pink center)
    *R.* 'Nevada'
    *R.* 'Prioress'

[Rosa]
    *R. rugosa* 'Blanc Double de Coubert'
    *R. rugosa* 'Henry Hudson'
    *R. rugosa* 'Sir Thomas Lipton'
    *R.* 'Souvenir de la Malmaison' (ivory to flesh-pink)
    *R.* 'Versicolor' (white, red, and pink)
*Rubus* 'Tridel'
*Sarcococca confusa*
    *S. ruscifolia*
*Skimmia* 'Formanii'
    *S. japonica*
    *S. japonica* 'Nymans'
    *S. reevesiana* 'Rubella'
*Sorbaria aitchisonii*
    *S. sorbifolia*
*Sorbus reducta*
*Spiraea* × *cinerea* 'Grefsheim'
    *S. fritschiana*
    *S. japonica* 'Shibori' (also pink and rose)
    *S. nipponica*
    *S. nipponica* 'Halward's Silver'
    *S. nipponica* 'Snowmound'
*Syringa* × *henryi* 'Summer White'
    *S.* × *hyacinthiflora* 'Sister Justena'
    *S.* × *josiflexa* 'Agnes Smith'
    *S.* × *josiflexa* 'Anna Amhoff'
    *S.* × *prestoniae* (also pink and purple)
    *S. vulgaris*
    *S. vulgaris* 'Edith Cavell'
    *S. vulgaris* 'Krasavitsa Moskvy'
    *S. vulgaris* 'Miss Ellen Willmott'
    *S. vulgaris* 'Rochester'
    *S. vulgaris* 'Slater's Elegance'
*Tabernaemontana divaricata*
*Viburnum* × *bodnantense* 'Dawn'
    *V.* × *bodnantense* 'Deben'
    *V.* × *burkwoodii* 'Conoy'
    *V.* × *burkwoodii* 'Mohawk'
    *V.* × *carlcephalum* 'Cayuga'
    *V. carlesii* 'Aurora' (pink buds open white)
    *V. carlesii* 'Charis'
    *V. carlesii* 'Compactum'
    *V.* 'Chesapeake'
    *V.* 'Chippewa'
    *V. dilatatum* 'Catskill'
    *V. dilatatum* 'Erie'
    *V. dilatatum* 'Iroquois'
    *V. dilatatum* 'Michael Dodge'
    *V.* 'Eskimo'
    *V. farreri* 'Candidissimum'
    *V.* 'Huron'
    *V. lantana* 'Mohican'
    *V. nudum* 'Winterthur'
    *V. plicatum* f. *tomentosum* 'Shasta'

*V. plicatum* f. *tomentosum* 'Shoshoni'
*V. plicatum* f. *tomentosum* 'Summer Snowflake'
*V.* × *pragense*
*V.* × *rhytidophylloides* 'Alleghany'
*V.* × *rhytidophylloides* 'Cree'
*V. rufidulum*
*V. sargentii* 'Flavum'
*V. sargentii* 'Onondaga'
*V. sargentii* 'Susquehanna'
*V. setigerum* 'Aurantiacum'
*V.* 'Willowwood'
*Vitex agnus-castus* 'Alba'
    *V. agnus-castus* 'Silver Spire'
*Zenobia pulverulenta*

## BLUE TO VIOLET

*Brunfelsia australis*
    *B. latifolia*
    *B. pauciflora* (violet upon opening, turning white)
    *B. pauciflora* var. *calycina* 'Macrantha'
*Buddleia alternifolia*
    *B. alternifolia* 'Argentea'
    *B. davidii*
    *B. davidii* 'Black Knight' (deep purple-black)
    *B. davidii* 'Deep Lavender'
    *B. davidii* 'Dubonnet'
    *B. davidii* 'Empire Blue'
    *B. davidii* 'Princeton Purple'
    *B.* 'Glasnevin'
    *B.* 'Lochinch'
    *B.* 'West Hill'
*Callicarpa americana* (pale blue to white)
    *C. bodinieri* var. *giraldii* 'Profusion'
*Calluna vulgaris* 'Darkness'
*Camellia* 'Winter's Star'
*Caryopteris* × *clandonensis*
    *C.* × *clandonensis* 'Azure'
    *C.* × *clandonensis* 'Blue Mist'
    *C.* × *clandonensis* 'Dark Knight'
    *C.* × *clandonensis* 'Heavenly Blue'
    *C.* × *clandonensis* 'Longwood Blue'
*Ceanothus* 'Concha'
    *C.* 'Dark Star'
    *C.* 'Frosty Blue'
    *C. impressus*
    *C.* 'Joyce Coulter'
    *C.* 'Julia Phelps'
    *C.* 'Puget Blue'
*Cercis chinensis* 'Avondale'
*Cistus* × *purpureus*
*Clerodendrum ugandense*
*Cytisus scoparius* 'Lilac Time'
*Daphne genkwa*
    *D.* × *mantensiana*

*D. mezereum* (lilac to rose-purple)
*Duranta stenostachya*
*Garrya* × *issaquahensis*
*Grewia occidentalis*
*Hibiscus rosa-sinensis* 'Tylene'
    *H. syriacus* 'Minerva'
*Hydrangea aspera* subsp. *aspera* (blue or pink, white marginal florets)
    *H. macrophylla*
    *H. macrophylla* 'All Summer Beauty' (blue or pink)
    *H. macrophylla* 'Blue Billow'
    *H. macrophylla* 'White Wave' (blue or pink, white marginal florets)
    *H. macrophylla* subsp. *serrata* 'Bluebird'
    *H. sargentiana* (purplish blue, white marginal florets)
*Leptodermis oblonga*
*Leucophyllum frutescens* 'Compactum'
    *L. frutescens* 'Green Cloud'
*Prostanthera ovalifolia* (lilac-mauve)
    *P. rotundifolia*
    *P. rotundifolia* 'Glen Davis'
*Salix melanostachys* (deep purple-black)
*Syringa* × *henryi*
    *S.* × *hyacinthiflora* 'Blanche Sweet' (whitish blue, with pink traces)
    *S.* × *josiflexa* 'Royalty'
    *S. laciniata*
    *S.* 'Miss Canada'
    *S. patula* 'Miss Kim' (sometimes lavender-pink)
    *S.* × *prestoniae*
    *S.* × *prestoniae* 'Nike'
    *S. vulgaris*
    *S. vulgaris* 'Agincourt Beauty'
    *S. vulgaris* 'Albert F. Holden' (deep purple inside; blush outside)
    *S. vulgaris* 'Blue Skies'
    *S. vulgaris* 'Dwight D. Eisenhower'
    *S. vulgaris* 'Emile Lemoine'
    *S. vulgaris* 'Lavender Lady'
    *S. vulgaris* 'Ludwig Spaeth'
    *S. vulgaris* 'Mieczta'
    *S. vulgaris* 'Sensation'
    *S. vulgaris* 'Wedgwood Blue'
    *S. vulgaris* 'Wonder Blue'
    *S. vulgaris* 'Yankee Doodle'
*Vitex agnus-castus*
    *V. negundo* var. *heterophylla*
    *V. rotundifolia*

## YELLOW TO ORANGE

*Azara dentata*
    *A. serrata*
*Berberis darwinii*
    *B.* × *gladwynensis* 'William Penn'

B. koreana
B. linearifolia
B. thunbergii
B. thunbergii 'Atropurpurea'
B. thunbergii 'Bagatelle'
B. thunbergii 'Globe'
B. thunbergii 'Kobold'
B. thunbergii 'Sparkle'
B. verruculosa
B. × wisleyensis
Buddleia globosa
B. globosa 'Lemon Ball'
Caragana aurantiaca
C. frutex 'Globosa'
C. pygmaea
Camellia chrysantha
C. japonica 'Dahlohnega'
Chimonanthus praecox
C. praecox 'Luteus'
Cornus mas
C. mas 'Aurea'
C. mas 'Flava'
C. mas 'Golden Glory'
C. mas 'Variegata'
Corylopsis glabrescens
C. pauciflora
C. platypetala
C. sinensis
C. sinensis f. veitchiana
C. spicata
C. willmottiae 'Spring Purple'
C. 'Winterthur'
Cytisus battandieri
C. × praecox 'Allgold'
C. scoparius 'Luna'
Daphne giraldii
Dendromecon rigida
Diervilla rivularis
D. sessilifolia
D. × splendens
Enkianthus campanulatus (creamy yellow
to light pink)
E. campanulatus 'Red Bells' (red-
veined, reddish at tip)
E. campanulatus 'Renoir'
E. chinensis (usually yellowish veined
with pink but wide color range)
Forsythia 'Gold Tide' (grapefruit-yellow)
F. × intermedia
F. × intermedia 'Lynwood'
F. × intermedia 'Spring Glory'
F. mandshurica 'Vermont Sun'
F. 'Meadowlark'
F. 'New Hampshire Gold'
F. 'Northern Gold'
F. 'Northern Sun'
F. 'Sunrise'

F. suspensa var. sieboldii
F. viridissima var. koreana 'Ilgwang'
F. 'Winterthur'
Fremontodendron 'California Glory'
Garrya elliptica 'James Roof'
G. × issaquahensis
Genista aethnensis
G. lydia
G. pilosa
G. pilosa 'Goldilocks'
G. pilosa 'Lemon Spreader'
G. pilosa 'Vancouver Gold'
G. sagittalis
Grevillea alpina (two-tone combinations of
white, orange, yellow, red)
G. alpina 'Grampian's Gold'
Hamamelis × intermedia (yellow to red)
H. × intermedia 'Arnold Promise'
H. × intermedia 'Jelena' (red base,
orange middle, yellow tip)
H. × intermedia 'Primavera'
H. macrophylla
H. mollis
H. mollis 'Brevipetala' (red at base)
H. mollis 'Coombe Wood'
H. mollis 'Pallida'
H. virginiana
Hibiscus rosa-sinensis (white to pink to
red, yellow to orange)
H. rosa-sinensis 'All Aglow'
H. rosa-sinensis 'Fiesta'
H. rosa-sinensis 'Herm Geller'
H. rosa-sinensis 'Harvest Moon'
Hypericum frondosum 'Sunburst'
H. hookeranum 'Rowallane'
H. kalmianum
H. patulum
H. patulum 'Henryi'
H. patulum 'Hidcote'
H. patulum 'Sungold'
H. prolificum
Illicium anisatum (white-yellow-green)
I. parviflorum
Ixora chinensis
Kerria japonica 'Picta'
K. japonica 'Pleniflora'
Leucospermum cordifolium
L. reflexum
Lindera angustifolia
L. benzoin
L. benzoin 'Rubra'
L. benzoin 'Xanthocarpa'
L. obtusiloba
Mahonia aquifolium
M. aquifolium 'Apollo'
M. aquifolium 'Atropurpurea'
M. aquifolium 'Compacta'

M. aquifolium 'Golden Abundance'
M. aquifolium 'Mayhan Strain'
M. aquifolium 'Moseri'
M. 'Arthur Menzies'
M. fortunei
M. lomariifolia
M. × media 'Charity'
M. nervosa
M. repens
M. trifoliata
Michelia figo
Osmanthus fragrans 'Aurantiacus'
Pachystachys lutea
Paeonia suffruticosa 'Alhambra'
P. suffruticosa 'Ariadne'
Potentilla fruticosa 'Coronation Triumph'
P. fruticosa 'Goldfinger'
P. fruticosa 'Katherine Dykes'
P. fruticosa 'Primrose Beauty'
P. fruticosa 'Yellowbird'
Punica granatum 'Peach Princess' (apricot)
Rhus typhina 'Dissecta'
R. typhina 'Laciniata'
Rosa 'Bredon'
R. 'Buff Beauty'
R. 'Canary Bird'
R. 'Cantabrigiensis'
R. 'Duchesse de Brabant'
R. 'English Garden'
R. 'Frühlingsduft'
R. 'Frühlingsgold'
R. 'Frühlingsmorgen' (yellow and
lavender-pink)
R. 'Golden Wings'
R. 'Graham Thomas'
R. hugonis
R. 'Perdita'
R. rugosa 'Topaz Jewel'
R. xanthina
Salix fargesii
S. lanata
Sambucus racemosa 'Plumosa Aurea'
Stachyurus praecox
Syringa vulgaris 'Primrose'
Streptosolen jamesonii
Tecoma stans
T. stans var. angustata
Thevetia thevetioides

**PINK TO RED**

Abelia 'Edward Goucher'
A. floribunda
Arctostaphylos bakerii 'Louis Edmunds'
A. densiflora 'Howard McMinn'
A. densiflora 'Sentinel'
A. stanfordiana (white to pink)
Bauhinia lunarioides (white to pink)

*Buddleia davidii*
  *B. davidii* 'Charming'
  *B. davidii* 'Fascination'
  *B. davidii* 'Harlequin'
  *B. davidii* 'Pink Delight'
  *B. davidii* 'Royal Red'
*Callicarpa dichotoma*
  *C. dichotoma* 'Albifructus'
  *C. dichotoma* 'Issai'
  *C. japonica*
  *C. japonica* 'Luxurians'
  *Calluna vulgaris* 'H. E. Beale'
*Calycanthus floridus*
  *C. floridus* 'Edith Wilder'
*Camellia japonica*
  *C. japonica* 'Adolphe Audusson'
  *C. japonica* 'C. M. Wilson'
  *C. japonica* 'Eldorado'
  *C. japonica* 'Elegans'
  *C. japonica* 'Holly Bright'
  *C. japonica* 'Empress of Russia'
  *C. japonica* 'Guillio Nuccio'
  *C. japonica* 'Kumasaka'
  *C. japonica* 'Lady Clare'
  *C. japonica* 'Magnoliaeflora'
  *C. japonica* 'Mathotiana'
  *C. japonica* 'Otome'
  *C. japonica* 'Pink Perfection'
  *C. japonica* 'Pope Pius IX'
  *C. japonica* 'R. L. Wheeler'
  *C. japonica* 'September Morn' (white to
    blush-pink)
  *C. japonica* 'Ville de Nantes' (red and
    white)
  *C. rosaeflora*
  *C. × williamsii* 'Anticipation'
  *C. × williamsii* 'Donation'
  *C. × williamsii* 'Hiraethyln'
  *C. × williamsii* 'J. C. Williams'
  *C. × williamsii* 'Mary Christian'
  *C. × williamsii* 'Salutation'
  *C. × williamsii* 'St. Ewe'
  *C.* 'Winter's Charm'
  *C.* 'Winter's Dream'
  *C.* 'Winter's Interlude'
  *C.* 'Winter's Rose'
*Ceanothus × pallidus* var. *roseus*
*Cercis canadensis* subsp. *mexicana*
*Chaenomeles speciosa* 'Rubra'
  *C. speciosa* 'Simonii'
  *C. speciosa* 'Toyo-Nishiki'
    (white/pink/ red on same branch)
  *C. × superba*
  *C. × superba* 'Cameo'
  *C. × superba* 'Nicoline'
  *C. × superba* 'Rowallane'

*C. × superba* 'Texas Scarlet'
*Cistus* 'Silver Pink'
  *C. × skanbergii*
*Clerodendrum bungei*
*Clethra alnifolia* 'Pink Spire'
  *C. alnifolia* 'Rosea'
*Correa* 'Carmine Bells'
  *C. × harrisii*
  *C. reflexa*
*Cotoneaster adpressus* 'Hessei'
  *C. apiculatus*
  *C. dammeri*
  *C. horizontalis* 'Robustus'
*Cytisus × praecox* 'Hollandia'
  *C. scoparius* 'Burkwoodii'
  *C. scoparius* 'Lena'
*Daphne × burkwoodii* (pink to white)
  *D. × burkwoodii* 'Carol Mackie'
  *D. × burkwoodii* 'Somerset'
  *D. × burkwoodii* 'Variegata'
  *D. caucasica*
  *D. cneorum*
  *D. cneorum* 'Eximia'
  *D. cneorum* 'Ruby Glow'
  *D. odora* 'Aureo-marginata'
  *D. retusa*
  *D. tangutica*
*Deutzia × gracilis* 'Rosea'
  *D. × hybrida* 'Magicien'
*Dipelta floribunda*
*Embothrium coccineum*
*Enkianthus campanulatus* var. *palibinii*
  *E. campanulatus* 'Showy Lantern'
  *E. campanulatus* 'Sikokianus'
  *E. cernuus* var. *rubens*
*Escallonia × exoniensis*
  *E. × exoniensis* 'Fradesii'
  *E.* 'Pride of Donard'
  *E. rubra* 'C. F. Ball'
*Fouquieria splendens*
*Garrya × issaquahensis* (catkins with red-
    purple tinge)
*Grewia occidentalis*
*Grevillea alpina* (two-tone combinations of
    white/orange/yellow/red)
  *G.* 'Canberra Gem'
  *G.* 'Robyn Gordon'
  *G. rosmarinifolia*
  *G. victoriae*
*Hamamelis × intermedia* (yellow to red)
  *H. × intermedia* 'Diane'
  *H. × intermedia* 'Feuerzauber'
  *H. × intermedia* 'Ruby Glow'
  *H. vernalis* f. *carnea* (red base, apricot
    tip, flesh-pink inside)
*Hibiscus rosa-sinensis* (white to pink/red,

    yellow/orange)
  *H. rosa-sinensis* 'Carolyn Coe'
  *H. rosa-sinensis* 'Cooperi'
  *H. rosa-sinensis* 'Fiesta'
  *H. syriacus* 'Aphrodite'
  *H. syriacus* 'Purpureus Variegatus'
  *H. syriacus* 'Woodbridge'
  *H.* 'Tosca'
*Hydrangea aspera* subsp. *aspera* (blue or
    pink, white marginal florets)
  *H. macrophylla*
  *H. macrophylla* 'All Summer Beauty'
    (pink or blue)
  *H. macrophylla* 'Forever Pink'
  *H. macrophylla* 'Quadricolor'
  *H. macrophylla* subsp. *serrata* 'Preziosa'
  *H. macrophylla* 'Variegata Mariesii'
    (pink or blue)
  *H. macrophylla* 'White Wave' (pink or
    blue, white marginal florets)
*Illicium floridanum*
  *I. floridanum* 'Halley's Comet'
  *I. henryi*
  *I. mexicanum*
*Indigofera kirilowii*
*Ixora* sp.
  *I.* 'Nora Grant'
*Kalmia angustifolia* (also white)
  *K. angustifolia* 'Hammonasset'
  *K. latifolia* 'Freckles'
  *K. latifolia* 'Hearts Desire'
  *K. latifolia* 'Little Linda'
  *K. latifolia* 'Ostbo Red'
  *K. latifolia* 'Peppermint' (streaked with
    reddish pink)
  *K. latifolia* 'Pink Charm'
  *K. latifolia* 'Sarah'
*Kolkwitzia amabilis*
  *K. amabilis* 'Pink Cloud'
  *K. amabilis* 'Rosea'
*Lagerstroemia* 'Hopi'
  *L.* 'Pecos'
  *L.* 'Zuni'
*Leycesteria formosa*
*Leptospermum rotundifolium* (white to
    purple-pink)
  *L. scoparium* 'Helen Strybing'
  *L. scoparium* 'Martini'
  *L. scoparium* 'Pink Cascade'
  *L. scoparium* 'Red Damask'
*Lespedeza thunbergii* 'Gibraltar'
*Lindera benzoin* 'Rubra'
*Lonicera* 'Honey Rose'
*Loropetalum chinensis* 'Rubra'
*Medinilla magnifica*
*Neillia affinis*

N. sinensis
N. thibetica
Paeonia suffruticosa 'Companion of Serenity'
P. suffruticosa 'Hana Kisoi'
P. suffruticosa 'Hephestos'
P. suffruticosa 'Leda'
P. suffruticosa 'Shintenchi'
Pernettya mucronata 'Coccinea'
P. mucronata 'Rosea'
P. mucronata 'Rubra'
Pieris japonica 'Flamingo'
P. japonica 'Roslinda'
P. japonica 'Valley Rose'
P. japonica 'Valley Valentine'
Potentilla fruticosa 'Day Dawn Viette'
P. fruticosa 'Pink Queen'
Punica granatum
P. granatum 'Emperior'
P. granatum 'Hizakuru'
P. granatum 'Nana'
P. granatum 'Toyosho'
P. granatum 'Twisted Trunk'
P. granatum 'Wonderful'
Ribes sanguineum 'King Edward VII'
R. speciosum
Robinia hispida
Rosa 'Adelaide Hoodless'
R. 'A. MacKenzie'
R. 'Assiniboine'
R. 'Belle de Crécy'
R. 'Bonica'
R. 'Carefree Beauty'
R. centifolia 'Rose de Meaux'
R. 'Champlain'
R. 'Complicata'

R. 'Cuthbert Grant'
R. damascena var. bifera 'Autumn Damask' (white to pink)
R. foetida 'Bicolor'
R. 'Frühlingsmorgen' (lavender-pink and yellow)
R. gallica var. officinalis
R. 'Geranium'
R. 'Gertrude Jekyll'
R. glauca
R. 'Henry Kelsey'
R. 'Heritage'
R. 'John Cabot'
R. 'John Davis'
R. 'John Franklin'
R. 'La Reine Victoria'
R. 'Morden Amorette'
R. 'Morden Cardinelle'
R. 'Morden Centennial'
R. 'Morden Fireglow'
R. 'Morden Ruby'
R. rugosa 'Charles Albanel'
R. rugosa 'Fru Dagmar Hastrup'
R. rugosa 'Jens Munk'
R. rugosa 'Linda Campbell'
R. rugosa 'Roseraie de l'Hay'
R. rugosa 'Rubra'
R. rugosa 'Sarah Van Fleet'
R. rugosa 'Therese Bugnet'
R. 'Sir Walter Raleigh'
R. 'Souvenir de la Malmaison' (ivory to flesh pink)
R. 'Stanwell Perpetual'
R. 'Versicolor' (white, red, and pink)
R. 'Wife of Bath'

R. 'William Baffin'
R. 'Winnipeg Parks'
Rubus cockburnianus
R. odoratus
Salix gracilistyla
Spiraea × bumalda 'Golden Princess'
S. × bumalda 'Gold Flame'
S. japonica 'Shibori' (also white)
Syringa × henryi 'Lutèce'
S. × hyacinthiflora 'Maiden's Blush'
S. × josiflexa 'James MacFarlane'
S. meyeri 'Palibin'
S. 'Minuet'
S. microphylla
S. microphylla 'Superba'
S. oblata var. dilatata
S. × prestoniae (also white and deep purple)
S. × prestoniae 'Isabella'
S. vulgaris 'Edward J. Gardner'
S. vulgaris 'Marie Francis'
S. vulgaris 'Victor Lemoine'
Ungnadia speciosa
Vitex agnus-castus 'Rosea'
Weigela florida 'Evita'
W. florida 'Red Prince'
W. florida 'Variegata'

**GREEN**

Calycanthus floridus 'Athens' (yellow/green)
Decaisnea fargesii (yellow/green)
Garrya elliptica 'James Roof'
Illicium anisatum (white-yellow-green)
Rhamnus frangula 'Asplenifolia'

## SHRUBS TOLERANT OF ENVIRONMENTAL STRESS

In many cases, tolerance to environmental stress is unknown or not well documented. The plants listed below have exhibited considerable tolerance to such stress as air pollution, salt, general harsh urban conditions, and soil compaction.

Acanthopanax sieboldianus 'Variegatus' (pollution)
Aralia spinosa (urban conditions)
Arctostaphylos densiflora 'Howard McMinn' (air pollution/salt/soil compaction)
A. densiflora 'Sentinel'
Berberis thunbergii (urban conditions)
Brugmansia arborea (air pollution/salt)
Brunfelsia australis (salt/wind/wet conditions)
Buxus 'Glencoe'
B. 'Green Gem'
B. 'Green Mountain' (some air pollution)
B. 'Green Velvet'

B. microphylla 'Compacta' (air pollution)
B. microphylla 'Morris Midget' (air pollution)
B. sempervirens 'Elegantissima'
B. sempervirens 'Graham Blandy' (air pollution)
B. sempervirens 'Pullman'
B. sempervirens 'Vardar Valley'
Caragana aurantiaca
C. frutex 'Globosa' (salt/difficult growing conditions)
C. pygmaea
Carissa macrocarpa (salt/wet conditions)
Clethra alnifolia (salt/wet conditions)
Cornus sericea 'Cardinal'

C. sericea 'Isanti'
C. sericea 'Silver & Gold' (air pollution/some soil compaction)
Cotoneaster horizontalis 'Robustus' (some salt)
Diervilla sessilifolia (adverse conditions/wind/wide soil range)
Forsythia × intermedia (urban conditions)
F. × intermedia 'Lynwood'
F. × intermedia 'Spring Glory'
F. mandshurica 'Vermont Sun'
F. 'Meadowlark' (urban conditions)
F. 'New Hampshire Gold'
F. 'Northern Gold'
F. 'Northern Sun'

[Forsythia]
  F. 'Sunrise'
  F. suspensa var. sieboldii
  F. viridissima var. koreana 'Ilgwang'
  F. 'Winterthur'
Fremontodendron 'California Glory' (air pollution)
Gardenia taitensis (salt/air pollution/soil compaction)
Garrya elliptica 'James Roof' (air pollution)
Grewia occidentalis (salt/wet conditions/wind)
Hamamelis × intermedia (some pollution)
  H. × intermedia 'Arnold Promise'
  H. × intermedia 'Diane'
  H. × intermedia 'Feuerzauber'
  H. × intermedia 'Jelena'
  H. × intermedia 'Primavera'
  H. × intermedia 'Ruby Glow'
  H. virginiana (smoke, polluted city air)
Hibiscus 'Lohengrin'
  H. syriacus 'Aphrodite'
  H. syriacus 'Diana' (air pollution/soil compaction)
  H. syriacus 'Helene'
  H. syriacus 'Lady Stanley'
  H. syriacus 'Minerva'
  H. syriacus 'Purpureus Variegatus'
  H. syriacus 'Woodbridge'
  H. 'Tosca'
Hydrangea macrophylla (salt)
  H. macrophylla 'Blue Billow'
  H. macrophylla 'Forever Pink'
  H. macrophylla 'Quadricolor'
  H. macrophylla subsp. serrata 'Bluebird'
  H. macrophylla subsp. serrata 'Preziosa'
  H. macrophylla 'Variegata Mariesii'
  H. macrophylla 'White Wave'
Hypericum frondosum 'Sunburst' (soil compaction)
Ilex crenata 'Beehive' (air pollution)
  I. crenata 'Compacta'
  I. crenata 'Delaware Diamond'
  I. crenata 'Dwarf Pagoda'
  I. crenata 'Glory'
  I. crenata 'Golden Heller'
  I. crenata 'Piccolo'
  I. glabra 'Compacta'
  I. glabra 'Ivory Queen'
  I. glabra 'Nigra'

I. glabra 'Nordic' (salt/air pollution)
  I. glabra 'Shamrock'
  I. opaca 'Compacta'
  I. opaca 'Maryland Dwarf' (soil compaction)
  I. vomitoria 'Dare County'
  I. vomitoria 'Jewel'
  I. vomitoria 'Stokes Dwarf' (salt/wind/wet conditions)
Ixora chinensis
  I. nienkui
  I. odorata (soil compaction)
Juniperus chinensis 'Echiniformis' (salt)
Lagerstroemia 'Acoma' (some wind and soil compaction)
  L. 'Hopi'
  L. 'Pecos'
  L. 'Zuni'
Leptospermum scoparium 'Red Damask' (salt)
Leucophyllum frutescens 'Compactum'
  L. frutescens 'Green Cloud' (salt/wind/drought)
  L. frutescens 'White Cloud'
Leycesteria formosa (air pollution)
Medinilla magnifica (air pollution/soil compaction)
Nandina domestica 'Alba' (soil compaction/wind)
  N. domestica 'Fire Power'
  N. domestica 'Gulf Stream'
  N. domestica 'Harbor Dwarf'
  N. domestica 'Royal Princess'
  N. domestica 'Umpqua Chief'
  N. domestica 'Umpqua Princess'
  N. domestica 'Umpqua Warrior'
Osmanthus heterophyllus (moderate urban conditions)
  O. heterophyllus 'Aureomarginatus'
  O. heterophyllus 'Goshiki'
  O. heterophyllus 'Gulftide'
  O. heterophyllus 'Maculifolius'
  O. heterophyllus 'Myrtifolius'
  O. heterophyllus 'Rotundifolius'
  O. heterophyllus 'Sasaba'
  O. heterophyllus 'Variegatus'
Pachystachys lutea (air pollution/soil compaction/some salt, wind)
Physocarpus opulifolius 'Dart's Golden'
Pieris phillyreifolia (salt/wet conditions)

Potentilla fruticosa (soil compaction)
  P. fruticosa 'Abbotswood'
  P. fruticosa 'Day Dawn Viette'
  P. fruticosa 'Goldfinger'
  P. fruticosa 'Katherine Dykes'
  P. fruticosa 'Pink Queen'
  P. fruticosa 'Primrose Beauty'
Rhodotypos scandens (air pollution, environmental variations)
Rhus chinensis 'September Beauty' (urban conditions)
  R. typhina 'Dissecta' (urban conditions/air pollution)
  R. typhina 'Laciniata'
Ribes alpinum 'Green Mound' (urban conditions)
  R. aureum
  R. odoratum
  R. odoratum 'Aureum'
  R. sanguineum
  R. sanguineum 'Alba'
  R. sanguineum 'King Edward VII'
  R. speciosum
Rosa 'Buff Beauty' (wind/drought/stress)
  R. 'Carefree Wonder'
  R. 'Complicata'
  R. damascena 'Madame Hardy'
  R. glauca
  R. 'Golden Wings'
  R. hugonis
  R. 'Nevada' (wind/drought/stress)
  R. rugosa
  R. 'Stanwell Perpetual'
Rhus aromatica 'Gro-low' (tough planting sites)
  R. copallina
  R. glabra var. cismontana
  R. trilobata
  R. trilobata 'Autumn Amber'
Sarcococca confusa
  S. ruscifolia (air pollution)
Shepherdia argentea (tough growing conditions)
  S. canadensis
Sorbaria aitchisonii
  S. sorbifolia (tough city conditions)
Spiraea fritschiana (soil compaction/wind)
Tabernaemontana divaricata (adverse conditions)

## FRAGRANT SHRUBS

Abelia chinensis
  A. × grandiflora
Abeliophyllum distichum
Adina rubella

Aesculus californica
Ardisia crenata
  A. crispa
Azara dentata

A. petiolaris
  A. serrata
Brunfelsia australis
  B. latifolia

*B. pauciflora*
   *B. pauciflora* var. *calycina* 'Macrantha'
*Buddleia alternifolia*
   *B. davidii*
   *B. davidii* 'Black Knight'
   *B. davidii* 'Charming'
   *B. davidii* 'Deep Lavender'
   *B. davidii* 'Dubonnet'
   *B. davidii* 'Empire Blue'
   *B. davidii* 'Fascination'
   *B. davidii* 'Harlequin'
   *B. davidii* 'Pink Delight'
   *B. davidii* 'Princeton Purple'
   *B. davidii* 'Royal Red'
   *B. davidii* 'White Bouquet'
   *B. davidii* 'White Profusion'
   *B. globosa*
*Buxus microphylla* 'Compacta'
   *B. microphylla* var. *japonica* 'Morris Midget'
*Calycanthus floridus*
   *C. floridus* 'Athens'
   *C. floridus* 'Edith Wilder'
*Camellia oleifera*
   *C.* 'Polar Ice'
   *C. rosaeflora*
   *C.* 'Snow Flurry'
   *C.* 'Winter's Charm'
   *C.* 'Winter's Dream'
   *C.* 'Winter's Hope'
   *C.* 'Winter's Interlude'
   *C.* 'Winter's Rose'
   *C.* 'Winter's Star'
   *C.* 'Winter's Waterlily'
*Carissa macrocarpa*
*Carpenteria californica*
*Caryopteris* × *clandonensis* (foliage)
   *C.* × *clandonensis* 'Azure'
   *C.* × *clandonensis* 'Blue Mist'
   *C.* × *clandonensis* 'Dark Knight'
   *C.* × *clandonensis* 'Heavenly Blue'
   *C.* × *clandonensis* 'Longwood Blue'
*Cephalotaxus harringtonia* 'Duke Gardens'
   *C. harringtonia* 'Fastigiata'
   *C. harringtonia* 'Prostrata'
*Chimonanthus praecox*
*Choisya ternata* (foliage)
   *C. ternata* 'Sundance'
*Clerodendrum trichotomum* var. *fargesii*
*Clethra acuminata*
   *C. alnifolia*
   *C. alnifolia* 'Hummingbird'
   *C. alnifolia* 'Paniculata'
   *C. alnifolia* 'Pink Spire'
   *C. alnifolia* 'Rosea'
   *C. barbinervis*
*Comptonia peregrina* (foliage)

*Corylopsis glabrescens*
   *C. pauciflora*
   *C. platypetala*
   *C. sinensis*
   *C. sinensis* f. *veitchiana*
   *C. spicata*
   *C. willmottiae* 'Spring Purple'
   *C.* 'Winterthur'
*Cytisus battandieri*
   *C.* × *praecox* 'Albus'
   *C.* × *praecox* 'Allgold'
   *C.* × *praecox* 'Hollandia'
*Daphne* × *burkwoodii*
   *D.* × *burkwoodii* 'Carol Mackie'
   *D.* × *burkwoodii* 'Somerset'
   *D.* × *burkwoodii* 'Variegata'
   *D. caucasica*
   *D. cneorum*
   *D. cneorum* 'Alba'
   *D. cneorum* 'Eximia'
   *D. cneorum* 'Ruby Glow'
   *D. genkwa*
   *D. giraldii*
   *D. mantensiana*
   *D. mezereum* f. *alba*
   *D. mezereum* f. *alba* 'Bowles White'
   *D. odora* 'Aureo-marginata'
   *D. retusa*
   *D. tangutica*
*Dendromecon rigida*
*Dipelta floribunda*
*Elaeagnus pungens*
   *E. pungens* 'Fruitlandii'
   *E. pungens* 'Hosoba-Fukurin'
   *E. pungens* 'Maculata'
   *E. pungens* 'Variegata'
*Elliottia racemosa*
*Escallonia rubra* 'C. F. Ball' (foliage)
*Exochorda giraldii* var. *wilsonii*
   *E.* × *macrantha* 'The Bride'
*Fothergilla gardenii*
   *F. gardenii* 'Blue Mist'
   *F. gardenii* 'Jane Platt'
   *F. gardenii* 'Mt. Airy'
   *F. major*
*Gardenia taitensis*
*Hamamelis* × *intermedia*
   *H.* × *intermedia* 'Arnold Promise'
   *H.* × *intermedia* 'Diane'
   *H.* × *intermedia* 'Feuerzauber'
   *H.* × *intermedia* 'Jelena'
   *H.* × *intermedia* 'Primavera'
   *H.* × *intermedia* 'Ruby Glow'
   *H. macrophylla*
   *H. mollis*
   *H. mollis* 'Brevipetala'
   *H. mollis* 'Coombe Wood'

*H. mollis* 'Pallida'
*H. vernalis* f. *carnea*
*H. virginiana*
*Hypericum patulum* 'Hidcote'
   *H. patulum* 'Sungold'
*Illicium floridanum*
   *I. floridanum* f. *album*
   *I. floridanum* 'Halley's Comet'
*Itea ilicifolia*
   *I. virginica*
   *I. virginica* 'Beppu'
   *I. virginica* 'Henry's Garnet'
*Ixora* sp.
   *I. chinensis*
   *I. nienkui*
   *I. odorata*
*Leucothoe populifolia*
*Lindera angustifolia*
   *L. benzoin*
   *L. benzoin* 'Rubra'
   *L. benzoin* 'Xanthocarpa'
   *L. obtusiloba*
*Michelia figo* (foliage)
*Myrica cerifera*
   *M. cerifera* var. *pumila*
   *M. gale*
   *M. pensylvanica* (foliage)
*Osmanthus americanus*
   *O.* × *burkwoodii*
   *O. delavayi*
   *O. fragrans* 'Aurantiacus'
   *O. heterophyllus*
   *O. heterophyllus* 'Aureomarginatus'
   *O. heterophyllus* 'Goshiki'
   *O. heterophyllus* 'Gulftide'
   *O. heterophyllus* 'Maculifolius'
   *O. heterophyllus* 'Myrtifolius'
   *O. heterophyllus* 'Rotundifolius'
   *O. heterophyllus* 'Sasaba'
   *O. heterophyllus* 'Variegatus'
*Paeonia suffruticosa* 'Alhambra'
   *P. suffruticosa* 'Ariadne'
   *P. suffruticosa* 'Companion of Serenity'
   *P. suffruticosa* 'Hana Kisoi'
   *P. suffruticosa* 'Hephestos'
   *P. suffruticosa* 'Joseph Rock'
   *P. suffruticosa* 'Leda'
   *P. suffruticosa* 'Renkaku'
   *P. suffruticosa* 'Shintenchi'
*Philadelphus coronarius* 'Natchez'
   *P. coronarius* 'Variegata'
   *P. virginalis*
   *P. virginalis* 'Glacier'
   *P. virginalis* 'Miniature Snowflake'
   *P. virginalis* 'Minnesota Snowflake'
   *P. virginalis* 'Polar Star'

Prostanthera ovalifolia
P. rotundifolia
P. rotundifolia 'Glen Davis'
Ribes aureum
R. odoratum
R. odoratum 'Aureum'
Rosa × alba 'Celestial
R. × alba 'Semi Plena'
R. × alba 'White Rose of York'
R. 'A. MacKenzie'
R. 'Belle de Crécy'
R. 'Bredon'
R. 'Buff Beauty'
R. 'Canary Bird'
R. 'Cantabrigiensis'
R. 'Carefree Beauty'
R. 'Carefree Wonder'
R. centifolia 'Rose de Meaux'
R. centifolia f. muscosa 'White Bath'
R. 'Champlain'
R. damascena var. bifera 'Autumn
    Damask'
R. damascena 'Madame Hardy'
R. 'Duchesse de Brabant'
R. 'English Garden'
R. foetida 'Bicolor'
R. 'Frühlingsduft'
R. 'Frühlingsgold'
R. 'Frühlingsmorgen'
R. 'Gertrude Jekyll'
R. gallica var. officinalis
R. 'Golden Wings'
R. 'Graham Thomas'
R. 'Henry Kelsey'
R. 'Heritage'
R. 'John Cabot'
R. 'John Davis'
R. 'John Franklin'
R. 'La Reine Victoria'
R. 'Mary Rose'

R. 'Morden Blush'
R. 'Morden Centennial'
R. 'Nevada'
R. 'Perdita'
R. 'Prioress'
R. rugosa 'Blanc Double de Coubert'
R. rugosa 'Charles Albanel'
R. rugosa 'Henry Hudson'
R. rugosa 'Roseraie de l'Hay'
R. rugosa 'Rubra'
R. rugosa 'Sarah Van Fleet'
R. rugosa 'Sir Thomas Lipton'
R. rugosa 'Therese Bugnet'
R. rugosa 'Topaz Jewel'
R. 'Sir Walter Raleigh'
R. 'Souvenir de la Malmaison'
R. 'Stanwell Perpetual'
R. 'Versicolor'
R. 'Wife of Bath'
Rubus odoratus
Sarcococca confusa
S. ruscifolia
Skimmia japonica (foliage)
S. japonica 'Formanii'
S. japonica 'Nymans'
S. reevesiana 'Rubella'
Spiraea × cinerea 'Grefsheim'
Syringa × henryi
S. × henryi 'Lutèce'
S. × henryi 'Summer White'
S. × hyacinthiflora
S. × hyacinthiflora 'Blanche Sweet'
S. × hyacinthiflora 'Maiden's Blush'
S. × hyacinthiflora 'Sister Justena'
S. × josiflexa
S. × josiflexa 'Agnes Smith'
S. × josiflexa 'Anna Amhoff'
S. × josiflexa 'James MacFarlane'
S. × josiflexa 'Royalty'

S. laciniata
S. meyeri 'Palibin'
S. 'Minuet'
S. 'Miss Canada'
S. oblata var. dilatata
S. patula 'Miss Kim'
S. × prestoniae
S. × prestoniae 'Alice Rose Foster'
S. × prestoniae 'Ethel M. Webster'
S. × prestoniae 'Isabella'
S. × prestoniae 'Nike'
S. vulgaris
S. vulgaris 'Albert F. Holden'
S. vulgaris 'Edith Cavell'
S. vulgaris 'Edward J. Gardner'
S. vulgaris 'Krasavitsa Moskvy'
S. vulgaris 'Lavender Lady'
S. vulgaris 'Ludwig Spaeth'
S. vulgaris 'Miss Ellen Willmott'
S. vulgaris 'Sensation'
S. vulgaris 'Wedgwood Blue'
Tabernaemontana divaricata
Thevetia thevetioides
Viburnum × bodnantense 'Dawn'
V. × bodnantense 'Deben'
V. × burkwoodii 'Conoy'
V. × burkwoodii 'Mohawk'
V. × carlcephalum 'Cayuga'
V. carlesii 'Aurora'
V. carlesii 'Charis'
V. carlesii 'Compactum'
V. farreri 'Candidissimum'
Vilex ugnus-castus
V. agnus-castus 'Alba'
V. agnus-castus 'Rosea'
V. agnus-castus 'Silver Spire'
V. negundo var. heterophylla
V. rotundifolia
Zenobia pulverulenta

## SHRUBS WITH ORNAMENTAL FRUIT

Acanthopanax sieboldianus 'Variegatus'
Aesculus californica
A. parviflora
A. parviflora 'Rogers'
A. parviflora f. serotina
Amelanchier ovalis 'Pumila'
Aralia cordata
A. elata 'Aureovariegata'
A. elata 'Pyramidalis'
A. elata 'Variegata'
A. spinosa
Arctostaphylos bakerii 'Louis Edmunds'
A. densiflora 'Howard McMinn'

A. densiflora 'Sentinel'
A. stanfordiana
Ardisia crenata
A. crispa
Aronia arbutifolia 'Brilliantissima'
A. melanocarpa
Berberis darwinii
B. × gladwynensis 'William Penn'
B. koreana
B. linearifolia
B. thunbergii
B. thunbergii 'Atropurpurea'
B. thunbergii 'Bagatelle'

B. thunbergii 'Bogozam'
B. thunbergii 'Globe'
B. thunbergii 'Kobold'
B. thunbergii 'Rose Glow'
B. thunbergii 'Sparkle'
B. verruculosa
B. × wisleyensis
Callicarpa americana
C. americana f. lactea
C. bodinieri var. giraldii 'Profusion'
C. dichotoma
C. dichotoma 'Albifructus'
C. dichotoma 'Issai'

C. japonica
C. japonica 'Leucocarpa'
C. japonica 'Luxurians'
Calycanthus floridus
C. floridus 'Athens'
C. floridus 'Edith Wilder'
Carissa macrocarpa
Chaenomeles speciosa
C. speciosa 'Moerloosi'
C. speciosa 'Rubra'
C. speciosa 'Simonii'
C. speciosa 'Toyo-Nishiki'
C. × superba
C. × superba 'Cameo'
C. × superba 'Fascination'
C. × superba 'Fire Dance'
C. × superba 'Jet Trail'
C. × superba 'Nicoline'
C. × superba 'Rowallane'
C. × superba 'Texas Scarlet'
Clerodendrum bungei
C. trichotomum var. fargesii
C. ugandense
Clethra barbinervis
Cotoneaster adpressus 'Hessei'
C. apiculatus
C. conspicuus 'Decorus'
C. dammeri 'Skogholm'
C. horizontalis 'Robustus'
C. racemiflorus var. soongoricus
C. × watereri 'Rothschildianus'
Cryptomeria japonica 'Globosa Nana'
Danae racemosa
Daphne × burkwoodii
D. × burkwoodii 'Carol Mackie'
D. × burkwoodii 'Somerset'
D. × burkwoodii 'Variegata'
D. caucasica
D. cneorum
D. cneorum 'Alba'
D. cneorum 'Eximia'
D. cneorum 'Ruby Glow'
D. genkwa
D. giraldii
D. × mantensiana
D. mezereum
D. mezereum f. alba
D. mezereum f. alba 'Bowles White'
D. retusa
D. tangutica
Decaisnea fargesii
Dipelta floribunda
Duranta stenostachya
Elaeagnus × ebbingei
E. pungens
E. pungens 'Fruitlandii'
E. pungens 'Hosoba-Fukurin'

E. pungens 'Maculata'
E. pungens 'Variegata'
Elliottia racemosa
Euonymus alatus 'Nordine Strain'
E. alatus 'Timber Creek'
E. europaeus 'Redcap'
E. oxyphyllus
Feijoa sellowiana
F. sellowiana 'Coolidge'
F. sellowiana 'Mammoth'
F. sellowiana 'Triumph'
Fremontodendron 'California Glory'
Garrya elliptica 'James Roof'
Hamamelis mollis
H. mollis 'Brevipetala'
H. mollis 'Coombe Wood'
H. mollis 'Pallida'
H. virginiana
Heptacodium miconioides
Heteromeles arbutifolia
Hippophae rhamnoides
Ilex amelanchier
I. 'China Girl'
I. cornuta 'O. Spring'
I. cornuta 'Willowleaf'
I. decidua 'Byer's Golden'
I. decidua 'Council Fire'
I. decidua 'Pocahontas'
I. decidua 'Warren's Red'
I. 'Dragon Lady'
I. 'Harvest Red'
I. × meserveae
I. × meserveae 'Blue Angel'
I. × meserveae 'Blue Girl'
I. × meserveae 'Blue Maid'
I. × meserveae 'Blue Princess'
I. 'Miniature'
I. 'Rock Garden'
I. 'September Gem'
I. serrata 'Bonfire'
I serrata 'Sundrops'
I. 'Sparkleberry'
I. verticillata
I. verticillata 'Afterglow'
I. verticillata 'Aurantiaca'
I. verticillata f. chrysocarpa
I. verticillata 'Maryland Beauty'
I. verticillata 'Red Sprite'
I. verticillata 'Scarlett O'Hara'
I. verticillata 'Shaver'
I. verticillata 'Sunset'
I. verticillata 'Tiasquam'
I. verticillata 'Winter Gold'
I. verticillata 'Winter Red'
I. vomitoria 'Dare County'
I. vomitoria 'Jewel'
Juniperus virginiana 'Grey Owl'

Leycesteria formosa
Lindera angustifolia
L. benzoin
L. benzoin 'Rubra'
L. benzoin 'Xanthocarpa'
L. obtusiloba
Lonicera 'Honey Rose'
L. pileata 'Royal Carpet'
L. xylosteum 'Emerald Mound'
Mahonia 'Arthur Menzies'
M. aquifolium
M. aquifolium 'Apollo'
M. aquifolium 'Atropurpurea'
M. aquifolium 'Compacta'
M. aquifolium 'Golden Abundance'
M. aquifolium 'Mayhan Strain'
M. aquifolium 'Moseri'
M. fortunei
M. lomariifolia
M. × media 'Charity'
M. nervosa
M. repens
M. trifoliata
Medinilla magnifica
Michelia figo
Myrica cerifera
M. cerifera var. pumila
M. gale
M. pensylvanica
Nandina domestica 'Alba'
N. domestica 'Fire Power'
N. domestica 'Gulf Stream'
N. domestica 'Harbor Dwarf'
N. domestica 'Royal Princess'
N. domestica 'San Gabriel'
N. domestica 'Umpqua Chief'
N. domestica 'Umpqua Princess'
N. domestica 'Umpqua Warrior'
Osmanthus americanus
O. × burkwoodii
O. delavayi
O. fragrans 'Aurantiacus'
O. heterophyllus
O. heterophyllus 'Aureomarginatus'
O. heterophyllus 'Goshiki'
O. heterophyllus 'Gulftide'
O. heterophyllus 'Maculifolius'
O. heterophyllus 'Myrtifolius'
O. heterophyllus 'Rotundifolius'
O. heterophyllus 'Sasaba'
O. heterophyllus 'Variegatus'
Pernettya mucronata
P. mucronata 'Alba'
P. mucronata 'Coccinea'
P. mucronata 'Rosea'
P. mucronata 'Rubra'
Physocarpus opulifolius 'Dart's Golden'

*Picea omorika* 'Nana'
*Pieris japonica*
    *P. japonica* 'Bert Chandler'
    *P. japonica* 'Flamingo'
    *P. japonica* 'Geisha'
    *P. japonica* 'Mountain Fire'
    *P. japonica* 'Pygmaea'
    *P. japonica* 'Red Mill'
    *P. japonica* 'Roslinda'
    *P. japonica* 'Valley Fire'
    *P. japonica* 'Valley Rose'
    *P. japonica* 'Valley Valentine'
    *P. japonica* 'Variegata'
    *P. japonica* 'White Cascade'
    *P. japonica* 'White Pearl'
*Pinus densiflora* 'Globosa'
*Punica granatum*
    *P. granatum* 'Emperior'
    *P. granatum* 'Hizakuru'
    *P. granatum* 'Nana'
    *P. granatum* 'Peach Princess'
    *P. granatum* 'Shiro Botan'
    *P. granatum* 'Toyosho'
    *P. granatum* 'Twisted Trunk'
    *P. granatum* 'Wonderful'
*Pyracantha* 'Apache'
    *P.* 'Fiery Cascade'
    *P.* 'Gold Rush'
    *P.* 'Mohave'
    *P.* 'Navaho'
    *P.* 'Pueblo'
    *P.* 'Rutgers'
    *P.* 'Teton'
*Rhodotypos scandens*

*Rhus aromatica* 'Gro-low'
    *R. chinensis* 'September Beauty'
    *R. copallina*
    *R. glabra* var. *cismontana*
    *R. trilobata*
    *R. trilobata* 'Autumn Amber'
    *R. typhina* 'Dissecta'
    *R. typhina* 'Laciniata'
*Ribes alpinum* 'Green Mound'
    *R. aureum*
    *R. odoratum*
    *R. odoratum* 'Aureum'
    *R. sanguineum*
*Rosa* × *alba* 'White Rose of York'
    *R.* 'Bonica'
    *R.* 'Carefree Beauty'
    *R.* 'Carefree Wonder'
    *R.* 'Complicata'
    *R. damascena* var. *bifera* 'Autumn Damask'
    *R. damascena* 'Madame Hardy'
    *R.* 'Frühlingsmorgen'
    *R.* 'Geranium'
    *R. glauca*
    *R.* 'Golden Wings'
    *R. rugosa* 'Fru Dagmar Hastrup'
    *R. rugosa* 'Jens Munk'
    *R. rugosa* 'Rubra'
*Rubus cockburnianus*
    *R. odoratus*
    *R.* 'Tridel'
*Ruscus aculeatus*
*Sambucus racemosa* 'Plumosa Aurea'
*Sarcococca confusa*
    *S. ruscifolia*

*Skimmia japonica*
    *S. japonica* 'Formanii'
    *S. japonica* 'Nymans'
    *S. reevesiana* 'Rubella'
*Sorbus reducta*
*Stachyurus praecox*
*Streptosolen jamesonii*
*Ungnadia speciosa*
*Viburnum* × *burkwoodii* 'Conoy'
    *V.* × *burkwoodii* 'Mohawk'
    *V.* × *carlcephalum* 'Cayuga'
    *V.* 'Chesapeake'
    *V.* 'Chippewa'
    *V. dilatatum* 'Catskill'
    *V. dilatatum* 'Erie'
    *V. dilatatum* 'Iroquois'
    *V. dilatatum* 'Michael Dodge'
    *V.* 'Eskimo'
    *V. farreri* 'Candidissimum'
    *V.* 'Huron'
    *V. lantana* 'Mohican'
    *V. nudum* 'Winterthur'
    *V. plicatum* f. *tomentosum* 'Shasta'
    *V. plicatum* f. *tomentosum* 'Shoshoni'
    *V. plicatum* f. *tomentosum* 'Summer Snowflake'
    *V.* × *pragense*
    *V.* × *rhytidophylloides* 'Alleghany'
    *V. rufidulum*
    *V. sargentii* 'Flavum'
    *V. sargentii* 'Onondaga'
    *V. sargentii* 'Susquehanna'
    *V. setigerum* 'Aurantiacum'
    *V.* 'Willowwood'

## SHRUBS WITH CONSPICUOUS AUTUMN FOLIAGE

*Aesculus parviflora*
*Amelanchier ovalis* 'Pumila'
*Aralia cordata*
    *A. spinosa*
*Aronia arbutifolia* 'Brilliantissima'
    *A. melanocarpa*
*Berberis koreana*
    *B. thunbergii*
    *B. thunbergii* 'Atropurpurea'
    *B. thunbergii* 'Bagatelle'
    *B. thunbergii* 'Bogozam'
    *B. thunbergii* 'Globe'
    *B. thunbergii* 'Rose Glow'
    *B. thunbergii* 'Sparkle'
    *B. verruculosa*
*Buddleia alternifolia*
    *B. alternifolia* 'Argentea'
*Calycanthus floridus*
*Caragana aurantiaca*

    *C. frutex* 'Globosa'
    *C. pygmaea*
*Chimonanthus praecox*
*Clethra acuminata*
    *C. alnifolia*
    *C. alnifolia* 'Hummingbird'
    *C. alnifolia* 'Paniculata'
    *C. alnifolia* 'Pink Spire'
    *C. alnifolia* 'Rosea'
    *C. barbinervis*
*Cotoneaster adpressus* 'Hessei'
    *C. apiculatus*
    *C. conspicuus* 'Decorus'
    *C. dammeri* 'Skogholm'
    *C. racemiflorus* var. *soongoricus*
    *C.* × *watereri* 'Rothschildianus'
*Cyrilla racemiflora*
*Daphne cneorum*
    *D. cneorum* 'Alba'

    *D. cneorum* 'Eximia'
    *D. cneorum* 'Ruby Glow'
*Diervilla* × *splendens*
*Disanthus cercidifolius*
*Enkianthus campanulatus*
    *E. campanulatus* 'Albiflorus'
    *E. campanulatus* var. *palibinii*
    *E. campanulatus* 'Red Bells'
    *E. campanulatus* 'Renoir'
    *E. campanulatus* 'Showy Lantern'
    *E. campanulatus* 'Sikokianus'
    *E. cernuus* var. *rubens*
    *E. chinensis*
    *E. deflexus*
    *E. perulatus*
    *E. perulatus* 'Compactus'
*Euonymus alatus* 'Nordine Strain'
    *E. alatus* 'Rudy Haag'
    *E. alatus* 'Timber Creek'

*E. europaeus* 'Redcap'
*E. oxyphyllus*
*Fothergilla gardenii*
 *F. gardenii* 'Jane Platt'
 *F. gardenii* 'Mt. Airy'
 *F. major*
*Hamamelis* × *intermedia*
 *H.* × *intermedia* 'Arnold Promise'
 *H.* × *intermedia* 'Diane'
 *H.* × *intermedia* 'Feuerzauber'
 *H.* × *intermedia* 'Jelena'
 *H.* × *intermedia* 'Primavera'
 *H.* × *intermedia* 'Ruby Glow'
 *H. macrophylla*
 *H. mollis*
 *H. mollis* 'Brevipetala'
 *H. mollis* 'Coombe Wood'
 *H. mollis* 'Pallida'
 *H. vernalis* f. *carnea*
 *H. virginiana*
*Hydrangea macrophylla* subsp. *serrata*
 'Preziosa'
 *H. quercifolia*
 *H. quercifolia* 'Snowflake'
 *H. quercifolia* 'Snow Queen'
*Ilex* 'Harvest Red'
*Lagerstroemia* 'Acoma'
 *L.* 'Hopi'
 *L.* 'Pecos'
 *L.* 'Zuni'
*Leucothoe axillaris*
 *L. davisiae*
 *L. fontanesiana* 'Scarletta'

*L. keiskei*
*Lindera angustifolia*
*Mahonia aquifolium*
 *M. aquifolium* 'Apollo'
 *M. aquifolium* 'Atropurpurea'
 *M. aquifolium* 'Compacta'
 *M. aquifolium* 'Golden Abundance'
 *M. aquifolium* 'Mayhan Strain'
 *M. aquifolium* 'Moseri'
 *M. nervosa*
 *M. repens*
 *M. trifoliata*
*Punica granatum*
 *P. granatum* 'Emperior'
 *P. granatum* 'Hizakuru'
 *P. granatum* 'Nana'
 *P. granatum* 'Peach Princess'
 *P. granatum* 'Toyosho'
 *P. granatum* 'Shiro Botan'
 *P. granatum* 'Twisted Trunk'
 *P. granatum* 'Wonderful'
*Rhamnus frangula* 'Asplenifolia'
*Rhus aromatica* 'Gro-low'
 *R. chinensis* 'September Beauty'
 *R. copallina*
 *R. glabra* var. *cismontana*
 *R. trilobata*
 *R. trilobata* 'Autumn Amber'
 *R. typhina* 'Dissecta'
 *R. typhina* 'Laciniata'
*Rubus odoratus*
*Salix gracilistyla*
*Sorbus reducta*

*Spiraea* × *cinerea* 'Grefsheim'
 *S. fritschiana*
 *S. japonica* 'Shibori'
*Stachyurus praecox*
*Syringa patula* 'Miss Kim'
*Ungnadia speciosa*
*Viburnum* × *bodnantense* 'Dawn'
 *V.* × *bodnantense* 'Deben'
 *V.* × *burkwoodii* 'Mohawk'
 *V. carlcephalum* 'Cayuga'
 *V. carlesii* 'Aurora'
 *V. carlesii* 'Charis'
 *V. carlesii* 'Compactum'
 *V.* 'Chesapeake'
 *V.* 'Chippewa'
 *V. dilatatum* 'Catskill'
 *V. dilatatum* 'Erie'
 *V. dilatatum* 'Iroquois'
 *V. dilatatum* 'Michael Dodge'
 *V.* 'Huron'
 *V. nudum* 'Winterthur'
 *V. plicatum* f. *tomentosum* 'Shasta'
 *V. plicatum* f. *tomentosum* 'Shoshoni'
 *V. plicatum* f. *tomentosum* 'Summer Snowflake'
 *V. rufidulum*
 *V. sargentii* 'Flavum'
 *V. sargentii* 'Onondaga'
 *V. sargentii* 'Susquehanna'
 *V. setigerum* 'Aurantiacum'
*Xanthorhiza simplicissima*
*Zenobia pulverulenta*

# APPENDIX IV

# List of Authorities

Synonyms are enclosed in brackets.

*Abelia chinensis* R. Brown
*Abelia floribunda* (M. Martens & Galeotti) Decaisne
*Abelia* × *grandiflora* (Andre) Rehder (*A. chinensis* R. Brown × *A. uniflora* R. Brown)
*Abelia schumannii* (Graebner) Rehder
*Abeliophyllum distichum* Nakai
*Acanthopanax sieboldianus* Makino [*A. pentaphyllus* (Siebold & Zuccarini) Marchal]
*Adina rubella* Hance
*Aesculus californica* (Spach) Nuttall
*Aesculus parviflora* Walter
*Aesculus parviflora* Walter f. *serotina* Rehder
*Amelanchier ovalis* Medicus
*Aralia cordata* Thunberg [*A. edulis* Siebold & Zuccarini]
*Aralia elata* (Miquel) Seemann
*Aralia spinosa* L.
*Arctostaphylos bakerii* (Eastwood) J. E. Adams
*Arctostaphylos densiflora* M. S. Baker
*Arctostaphylos stanfordiana* Parry
*Ardisia crenata* Sims [*A. crenulata* Loddiges]
*Ardisia crispa* (Thunberg) A. de Candolle
*Aronia arbutifolia* (L.) Persoon
*Aronia melanocarpa* (Michaux) Elliott
*Azara dentata* Ruiz & Pavón
*Azara petiolaris* (D. Don) I. M. Johnson
*Azara serrata* Ruiz & Pavón
*Bauhinia lunarioides* (Britt & Rose) Lundell [*B. congesta* A. Gray ex S. Watson]
*Berberis darwinii* Hooker
*Berberis* × *gladwynensis* E. Anderson (*B. verruculosa* Hemsley & E. H. Wilson × *B. gagnepainii* Schneider)
*Berberis koreana* Palibin

*Berberis linearifolia* Philippi
*Berberis thunbergii* A. de Candolle
*Berberis verruculosa* Hemsley & E. H. Wilson
*Berberis* × *wisleyensis* Ahrendt (*B.* × *carminea* Ahrendt × *B.* × *rubrostilla* Chittenden)
*Berberis triacanthrophora* Fedde
*Brugmansia arborea* (L.) Lagerheim [*Datura arborea* L.]
*Brunfelsia australis* Bentham
*Brunfelsia latifolia* (Pohl) Bentham
*Brunfelsia pauciflora* (Chamisso & Schlechtendal) Bentham
*Brunfelsia pauciflora* (Chamisso & Schlechtendal) Bentham var. *calycina* (Bentham) J. A. Schmidt
*Buddleia alternifolia* Maximowicz
*Buddleia davidii* Franchet [*B. variabilis* Hemsley]
*Buddleia fallowiana* Balfour f. & W. W. Smith
*Buddleia globosa* Hope
*Buxus microphylla* Siebold & Zuccarini
*Buxus microphylla* Siebold & Zuccarini var. *japonica* (Mueller-Argoviensis) Rehder & E. H. Wilson
*Buxus microphylla* Siebold & Zuccarini var. *koreana* Nakai
*Buxus sempervirens* L.
*Buxus sinica* (Rehder & Wilson) M. Cheng
*Callicarpa americana* L.
*Callicarpa americana* L. var. *lactea* (F. J. Mueller) Rehder
*Callicarpa bodinieri* Léveillé var. *giraldii* (Hesse ex Rehder) Rehder
*Callicarpa dichotoma* (Loureiro) C. Koch
*Callicarpa japonica* Thunberg
*Calluna vulgaris* (L.) Hull
*Calycanthus fertilis* T. Walter
*Calycanthus floridus* L.
*Camellia chrysantha* (Hu) Tuyama
*Camellia euryoides* Lindley
*Camellia hiemalis* Nakai

*Camellia japonica* L.

*Camellia oleifera* Abel [*C. oleosa* (Loureiro) Y. C. Wu]

*Camellia rosaeflora* Hooker

*Camellia sasanqua* Thunberg

*Camellia sinensis* (L.) O. Kuntze

*Camellia* × *williamsii* W. W. Smith (*C. japonica* L. × *C. saluenensis* Stapf ex Bean)

*Caragana aurantiaca* Koehne

*Caragana frutex* (L.) K. Koch

*Caragana pygmaea* (L.) A. de Candolle

*Carissa macrocarpa* (Ecklon) A. de Candolle [*C. grandiflora* (E. H. Meyer) A. de Candolle]

*Carpenteria californica* Torrey

*Caryopteris* × *clandonensis* A. Simmonds ex Rehder (*C. incana* (Thunberg ex Houttuyn) Miquel × *C. mongholica* Bunge)

*Ceanothus impressus* Trelease

*Ceanothus* x *pallidus* Lindley (*C. delilianus* Spach × *C. ovatus* Desfontaines) var. *roseus* (Spach) Rehder

*Cephalotaxus harringtonia* (Forbes) K. Koch

*Cercis canadensis* L.

*Cercis canadensis* L. subsp. *mexicana* (Rose) Murray

*Cercis chinensis* Bunge

*Cercis reniformis* Engelmann

*Chaenomeles japonica* (Thunberg) Lindley ex Spach

*Chaenomeles speciosa* (Sweet) Nakai

*Chaenomeles* × *superba* (Frahm) Rehder (*C. japonica* (Thunberg) Lindley ex Spach × *C. speciosa* (Sweet) Nakai)

*Chamaecyparis obtusa* (Siebold & Zuccarini) Endlicher

*Chamaecyparis pisifera* (Siebold & Zuccarini) Endlicher

*Chimonanthus nitens* Oliver

*Chimonanthus praecox* (L.) Link

*Choisya ternata* Humboldt, Bonpland & Kunth

*Cistus laurifolius* L.

*Cistus* × *purpureus* Lamarck (*C. ladanifer* L. × *C. villosus* L.)

*Cistus salvifolius* L.

*Cistus* × *skanbergii* Lojacono-Pojero (*C. monspeliensis* L. × *C. parviflorus* Lamarck)

*Cistus villosus*

*Clerodendrum bungei* Steudel

*Clerodendrum trichotomum* Thunberg var. *fargesii* (Dode) Rehder

*Clerodendrum ugandense* Prain

*Clethra alnifolia* L.

*Clethra acuminata* Michaux

*Clethra barbinervis* Siebold & Zuccarini

*Comptonia peregrina* (L.) J. Coulter

*Comptonia peregrina* (L.) J. Coulter var. *asplenifolia* (L.) Fernald

*Cornus alba* L.

*Cornus mas* L.

*Cornus sericea* L. [*C. stolonifera* Michaux]

*Correa alba* Andrews

*Correa backhousiana* Hooker

*Correa* × *harrisii* Paxton (*C. pulchella* Mackay ex Sweet × *C. reflexa* (La Billardiere) Ventenat)

*Correa reflexa* (La Billardiere) Ventenat

*Corylopsis glabrescens* Franchet & Savatier

*Corylopsis pauciflora* Siebold & Zuccarini

*Corylopsis platypetala* Rehder & E. H. Wilson

*Corylopsis sinensis* Hemsley

*Corylopsis sinensis* Hemsley f. *veitchiana* (Bean) Morley & Cheo

*Corylopsis spicata* Siebold & Zuccarini

*Corylopsis willmottiae* Rehder & E. H. Wilson

*Cotoneaster adpressus* Bois

*Cotoneaster apiculatus* Rehder & E. H. Wilson

*Cotoneaster conspicuus* Marquand

*Cotoneaster dammeri* C. K. Schneider

*Cotoneaster horizontalis* Decaisne

*Cotoneaster racemiflorus* (Desfontaines) K. Koch var. *soongoricus* (Regel & Herder) Schneider

*Cotoneaster rotundifolius* Wallich

*Cotoneaster* × *watereri* (*C. frigidus* Wall × *C. salicifolius* Franchet × *C. rugosus* E. Pritzel ex Diels)

*Cryptomeria japonica* (L. f.) D. Don

*Cyrilla racemiflora* L. [*C. parviflora* Rafinesque]

*Cytisus battandieri* Maire

*Cytisus* × *praecox* Bean (*C. purgans* (L.) Spach × *C. multiflorus* (Aiton) Sweet)

*Cytisus scoparius* (L.) Link

*Danae racemosa* (L.) Moench

*Daphne* × *burkwoodii* Turrill (*D. caucasica* Pallas × *D. cneorum* L.)

*Daphne caucasica* Pallas

*Daphne cneorum* L.

*Daphne genkwa* Siebold & Zuccarini

*Daphne giraldii* Nitsche

*Daphne* × *mantensiana* T. M. C. Taylor & F. Vrugtman (*D.* × *burkwoodii* Turrill × *D. retusa* Hemsley)

*Daphne mezereum* L.

*Daphne mezereum* L. f. *alba* (Weston) Rehder

*Daphne odora* Thunberg

*Daphne retusa* Hemsley

*Daphne tangutica* Maximowicz

*Decaisnea fargesii* Franchet

*Dendromecon rigida* Bentham

*Deutzia chunii* H. H. Hu

*Deutzia gracilis* Siebold & Zuccarini

*Deutzia* × *hybrida* Lemoine (*D. discolor* Hemsley × *D. longifolia* Franchet)

*Deutzia scabra* Thunberg

*Deutzia scabra* Thunberg var. *candidissima* Froebel

*Diervilla rivularis* Gattinger

*Diervilla sessilifolia* Buckley

*Diervilla* × *splendens* (Carrière) Kircher (*D. lonicera* Miller × *D. sessilifolia* Buckley)

*Dipelta floribunda* Maximowicz

*Disanthus cercidifolius* Maximowicz

*Duranta repens* L.

*Duranta stenostachya* Todaro

*Elaeagnus* × *ebbingei* Boom (*E. macrophylla* Thunberg × *E. pungens* Thunberg)

*Elaeagnus pungens* Thunberg

*Elliottia racemosa* Muhlenberg

*Embothrium coccineum* J. R. Forster & G. Forster

*Enkianthus campanulatus* (Miquel) Nicholson

*Enkianthus campanulatus* (Miquel) Nicholson var. *palibinii* Bean

*Enkianthus cernuus* (Siebold & Zuccarini) Makino var. *rubens* (Maximowicz) Ohwi

*Enkianthus chinensis* Franchet

*Enkianthus deflexus* (Griffith) C. K. Schneider

*Enkianthus perulatus* (Miquel) C. K. Schneider

*Escallonia bifida* Link & Otto [*E. montevidensis* (Chamisso & Schlechtendal) A. de Candolle]

*Escallonia* × *exoniensis* Veitch (*E. rosea* Grisebach × *E. rubra* (Ruiz & Pavón) Persoon)

*Escallonia laevis* (Villars) Sleumer

*Escallonia rubra* (Ruiz & Pavón) Persoon

*Escallonia virgata* (Ruiz & Pavón) Persoon

*Euonymus alatus* (Thunberg) Siebold

*Euonymus europaeus* L.

*Euonymus oxyphyllus* Miquel

*Exochorda giraldii* Hesse var. *wilsonii* Rehder

*Exochorda* × *macrantha* (Lemoine) C. K. Schneider (*E. korolkowii* Lavallee × *E. racemosa* (Lindley) Rehder)

*Feijoa sellowiana* O. Bergius

*Forsythia europaea* Degen & Baldacci

*Forsythia* × *intermedia* Zabel (*F. suspensa* (Thunberg) Vahl × *F. viridissima* Lindley)

*Forsythia mandshurica* Uyeki

*Forsythia ovata* Nakai

*Forsythia suspensa* (Thunberg) Vahl var. *sieboldii* Zabel

*Forsythia viridissima* Lindley var. *koreana* Rehder

*Fothergilla gardenii* J. Murray

*Fothergilla major* (Sims) Loddiges

*Fouquieria splendens* Engelmann

*Fremontodendron californicum* (Torrey) Coville

*Fremontodendron mexicanum* A. Davidson

*Gardenia taitensis* A. de Candolle

*Garrya elliptica* Douglas

*Garrya* × *issaquahensis* Nelson (*G. elliptica* Douglas × *G. fremontii* Torrey)

*Genista aethnensis* (Bivona) A. de Candolle

*Genista lydia* Boissier

*Genista pilosa* L.

*Genista sagittalis* L.

*Grevillea alpina* Lindley

*Grevillea banksii* R. Brown

*Grevillea bipinnatifida* R. Brown

*Grevillea juniperina* R. Brown

*Grevillea lavandulacea* Schlechtendal

*Grevillea rosmarinifolia* A. Cunningham

*Grevillea tridentifera* (Endlicher) Meissner

*Grevillea victoriae* F. Mueller

*Grewia occidentalis* L.

*Hamamelis* × *intermedia* Rehder (*H. japonica* Siebold & Zuccarini × *H. mollis* D. Oliver)

*Hamamelis macrophylla* Pursch

*Hamamelis mollis* D. Oliver

*Hamamelis vernalis* Sargent f. *carnea* Rehder

*Hamamelis virginiana* L.

*Heptacodium miconioides* Rehder [*H. jasminoides* Airy Shaw]

*Heteromeles arbutifolia* (Aiton) M. J. Roemer

*Hibiscus paramutabilis* Bailey

*Hibiscus rosa-sinensis* L.

*Hibiscus syriacus* L.

*Hippophae rhamnoides* L.

*Hydrangea arborescens* L.

*Hydrangea aspera* D. Don subsp. *aspera* D. Don [*H. villosa* Rehder]

*Hydrangea macrophylla* (Thunberg) Seringe

*Hydrangea macrophylla* (Thunberg) Seringe subsp. *serrata* (Thunberg) Makino

*Hydrangea paniculata* Siebold

*Hydrangea quercifolia* Bartram

*Hydrangea sargentiana* [*H. aspera* D. Don subsp. *sargentiana* (Rehder) McClintock]

*Hypericum calycinum* L.

*Hypericum forrestii* (Chittenden) N. Robson

*Hypericum frondosum* Michaux

*Hypericum hookeranum* Wight & Arnott

*Hypericum kalmianum* L.

*Hypericum patulum* Thunberg

*Hypericum prolificum* L.

*Ilex amelanchier* M. A. Curtis

*Ilex aquifolium* L.

*Ilex* × *aquipernyi* Gable

*Ilex ciliospinosa* Loesener

*Ilex cornuta* Lindley & Paxton

*Ilex crenata* Thunberg

*Ilex decidua* Walter

*Ilex glabra* (L.) A. Gray

*Ilex integra* Thunberg

*Ilex* × *meserveae* S. Y. Hu

*Ilex opaca* Aiton

*Ilex pernyi* Franchet

*Ilex rugosa* Schmidt

*Ilex serrata* Thunberg

*Ilex verticillata* (L.) A. Gray

*Ilex verticillata* (L.) A. Gray f. *chrysocarpa* Robinson

*Ilex vomitoria* Aiton

*Illicium anisatum* L.

*Illicium floridanum* Ellis

*Illicium floridanum* Ellis f. *album* Meyer & Mazzeo

*Illicium henryi* Diels

*Illicium mexicanum* A. C. Smith

*Illicium parviflorum* Michaux

*Indigofera kirilowii* Maximowicz ex Palibin

*Itea ilicifolia* D. Oliver

*Itea virginica* L.

*Ixora chinensis* Lamarck

*Ixora finlaysoniana* Wallich ex G. Don

*Ixora nienkui* Merrill & Chun

*Ixora odorata* Hooker

*Juniperus chinensis* L. [*J. sphaerica* Lindley]

*Juniperus × media* Van Melle

*Juniperus squamata* D. Don

*Juniperus virginiana* L.

*Kalmia angustifolia* L.

*Kalmia angustifolia* L. f. *candida* Fernald

*Kalmia latifolia* L.

*Kerria japonica* (L.) A. de Candolle

*Kolkwitzia amabilis* Graebner

*Lagerstroemia fauriei* Koehne

*Lagerstroemia indica* L.

*Leiophyllum buxifolium* (Bergius) Elliott

*Leiophyllum buxifolium* (Bergius) Elliott var. *hugeri* (Small)
  C. K. Schneider

*Leptodermis oblonga* Wallich

*Leptospermum rotundifolium* (Maiden & Betche) Domin

*Leptospermum scoparium* J. R. Forster & G. Forster

*Lespedeza thunbergii* (A. de Candolle) Nakai

*Leucophyllum frutescens* (Berlandier) I. M. Johnston

*Leucospermum cordifolium* (Salisbury ex Knight) Fourcade
  [*L. nutans* R. Brown]

*Leucospermum reflexum* Buek ex Meissner

*Leucothoe axillaris* (Lamarck) D. Don

*Leucothoe davisiae* Torrey ex A. Gray

*Leucothoe fontanesiana* (Steudel) Sleimer

*Leucothoe keiskei* Miquel

*Leucothoe populifolia* (Lamarck) Dippel [*Agarista populifolia*
  (Lamarck) Dippel]

*Leycesteria formosa* Wallich

*Lindera angustifolia* Cheng

*Lindera benzoin* (L.) Blume

*Lindera obtusiloba* Blume

*Lonicera pileata* D. Oliver

*Lonicera tatarica* L.

*Lonicera xylosteum* L.

*Loropetalum chinensis* (R. Bron) D. Oliver

*Mahonia aquifolium* (Pursh) Nuttall

*Mahonia bealei* (Fortune) Carrière

*Mahonia fortunei* (Lindley) Fedde

*Mahonia japonica* (Thunberg) A. de Candolle

*Mahonia lomariifolia* Takeda

*Mahonia × media* Brickell (*M. japonica* A. de Candolle ×
  *M. lomariifolia* Takeda)

*Mahonia nervosa* (Pursh) Nuttall [*Berberis nervosa* Pursh]

*Mahonia repens* (Lindley) G. Don

*Mahonia trifoliata* (Moricand) Fedde

*Medinilla magnifica* Lindley

*Michelia figo* (Loureiro) Sprengel

*Myrica cerifera* L.

*Myrica cerifera* L. var. *pumila* Michaux

*Myrica gale* L.

*Myrica pensylvanica* Loiseleur-Deslongchamps

*Nandina domestica* Thunberg

*Neillia affinis* Hemsley

*Neillia sinensis* D. Oliver

*Neillia thibetica* Franchet

*Neviusia alabamensis* A. Gray

*Osmanthus americanus* (L.) A. Gray

*Osmanthus delavayi* Franchet

*Osmanthus × burkwoodii* (Burkwood & Skipwith) P. S. Green
  (*O. delavayi* Franchet ×*Phillyrea decora* Boissier &
  Balansa)

*Osmanthus fragrans* (Thunberg) Loureiro

*Osmanthus heterophyllus* (G. Don) P. S. Green [*O. ilicifolius*
  Hasskarl ex Carrière]

*Pachystachys lutea* Nees [*Jacobinia lutea* Nees ex Moricand]

*Paeonia suffruticosa* Andrews

*Paeonia suffruticosa* subsp. *rockii* S. G. Haw & L. A. Lauener

*Pernettya mucronata* (L. f.) Gaudichaud-Beaupré

*Philadelphus coronarius* L.

*Philadelphus inodorus* L.

*Philadelphus × virginalis* Rehder (*P. × lemoinei* Lemoine × *P. ×
  nivalis* Jacques)

*Physocarpus opulifolius* (L.) Maximowicz

*Picea abies* (L.) Karsten

*Picea omorika* (Pančić) Purkyne

*Picea pungens* Engelmann

*Pieris floribunda* (Pursh ex Sims) Bentham & Hooker f.

*Pieris formosa* (Wallich) D. Don var. *forrestii* (Harrow ex
  W. W. Smith) Airy Shaw

*Pieris japonica* (Thunberg) D. Don ex G. Don

*Pieris phillyreifolia* (Hooker) A. de Candolle

*Pieris taiwanensis* Hayata

*Pinus densiflora* Siebold & Zuccarini

*Pinus mugo* Turra

*Pinus sylvestris* L.

*Potentilla fruticosa* L.

*Prostanthera ovalifolia* R. Brown

*Prostanthera rotundifolia* R. Brown

*Punica granatum* L.

*Pyracantha angustifolia* (Franchet) C. K. Schneider

*Pyracantha coccinea* M. J. Roemer

*Pyracantha coccinea* M. J. Roemer var. *pauciflora* Andre

*Pyracantha crenulata* (D. Don) M. J. Roemer

*Pyracantha crenatos errata* (Hance) Rehder

*Pyracantha fortuneana* (Maximowicz) Li

*Pyracantha koidzumii* (Hayara) Rehder

*Pyracantha rogersiana* (A. B. Jackson) Bean

*Rhamnus frangula* L.

*Rhodotypos scandens* (Thunberg) Makino

*Rhus aromatica* Aiton

*Rhus chinensis* Miller

*Rhus copallina* L.

*Rhus glabra* L. var. *cismontana* (Greene) Cockerell

*Rhus trilobata* Nuttall

*Rhus typhina* L.

*Ribes alpinum* L.

*Ribes aureum* Pursh

*Ribes odoratum* H. L. Wendland

*Ribes sanguineum* Pursh

*Ribes speciosum* Pursh

*Robinia hispida* L.

*Robinia pseudoacacia* L.

*Rosa* × *alba* L. (*R. canina* L. × *R. damascena* Miller)

*Rosa arkansana* T. Porter

*Rosa* × *borboniana* Desportes (*R. chinensis* Jacquin × *R. damascena* Miller)

*Rosa canina* L.

*Rosa centifolia* L.

*Rosa centifolia* L. f. *muscosa* Miller

*Rosa chinensis* Jacquin

*Rosa damascena* Miller

*Rosa damascena* Miller var. *bifera* Persoon

*Rosa foetida* Hermann

*Rosa gallica* L.

*Rosa gallica* L. var. *officinalis* Miller

*Rosa gigantea* Colla ex Crépin

*Rosa glauca* Pourret [*R. rubrifolia* Villars]

*Rosa hugonis* Hemsley

*Rosa* × *kordesii* Wulfen (*R.* × *jacksonii* Willkom 'Max Graf')

*Rosa moyesii* Hemsley & E. H. Wilson

*Rosa* × *odorata* (Andrews) Sweet

*Rosa phoenicea* Boissier

*Rosa pimpinellifolia* L. [*R. spinosissima* L.]

*Rosa pimpinellifolia* L. var. *altaica* Willdenow

*Rosa rugosa* Thunberg

*Rosa xanthina* Lindley

*Rubus cockburnianus* Hemsley

*Rubus deliciosus* Torrey

*Rubus odoratus* L.

*Rubus trilobus* Seringe

*Ruscus aculeatus* L.

*Salix fargesii* Burkhill

*Salix gracilistyla* Miquel

*Salix lanata* L.

*Salix melanostachys* Makino

*Sambucus racemosa* L.

*Sarcococca confusa* Sealy

*Sarcococca ruscifolia* Stapf

*Shepherdia argentea* (Pursh) Nuttall

*Shepherdia canadensis* (L.) Nuttall

*Skimmia japonica* Thunberg

*Skimmia reevesiana* Fortune

*Sorbaria aitchisonii* (Hemsley) Hemsley ex Rehder

*Sorbaria sorbifolia* (L.) A. Braun

*Sorbus reducta* Diels

*Spiraea* × *bumalda* Burvenich (*S. albiflora* (Miquel) Zabel × *S. japonica* L. f.)

*Spiraea* × *cinerea* Zabel (*S. cana* Waldstein & Kitaibel × *S. hypericifolia* L.)

*Spiraea fritschiana* Schneider

*Spiraea japonica* L.

*Spiraea nipponica* Maximowicz

*Spiraea* × *vanhouttei* (Briot) Zabel (*S. cantoniensis* Loureiro × *S. tribolata* L.)

*Stachyurus praecox* Siebold & Zuccarini

*Stephanandra incisa* (Thunberg) Zabel

*Streptosolen jamesonii* (Bentham) Miers

*Syringa* × *henryi* C. K. Schneider (*S. josikaea* Jacquin f. ex Reichenbach × *S. villosa* Vahl)

*Syringa* × *hyacinthiflora* (Lemoine) Rehder (*S. oblata* Lindley × *S. vulgaris* L.)

*Syringa* × *josiflexa* Preston (*S. josikaea* Jacquin f. ex Reichenbach × *S. reflexa* C. K. Schneider)

*Syringa laciniata* Miller

*Syringa meyeri* C. K. Schneider

*Syringa microphylla* Diels

*Syringa oblata* Lindley var. *dilatata* (Nakai) Rehder

*Syringa patula* (Palibin) Nakai

*Syringa* × *prestoniae* McKelvey (*S. reflexa* C. K. Schneider × *S. villosa* Vahl)

*Syringa reflexa* C. K. Schneider

*Syringa villosa* Vahl

*Syringa vulgaris* L.

*Tabernaemontana divaricata* (L.) R. Brown [*Ervatamia divaricata* (L.) Burkhill]

*Taxus baccata* L.

*Taxus* × *media* Rehder (*T. baccata* L. × *T. cuspidata* Siebold & Zuccarini)

*Tecoma stans* (L.) Humboldt, Bonpland & Kunth

*Tecoma stans* (L.) Humboldt, Bonpland & Kunth var. *angustata* Rehder

*Thevetia thevetioides* (Humboldt, Bonpland & Kunth) K. Schumann

*Thujopsis dolabrata* (L. f.) Siebold & Zuccarini

*Tsuga canadensis* (L.) Carrière

*Ungnadia speciosa* Endlicher

*Viburnum* × *bodnantense* Aberconway (*V. farreri* Stearn × *V. grandiflorum* Wallich)

*Viburnum* × *burkwoodii* Burkwood & Skipwith (*V. carlesii* Hemsley × *V. utile* Hemsley)

*Viburnum* × *carlcephalum* Burkwood ex Pike (*V. carlesii* Hemsley × *V. macrocephalum* Fortune)

*Viburnum carlesii* Hemsley

*Viburnum dilatatum* Thunberg

*Viburnum farreri* Stearn

*Viburnum japonicum* (Thunberg) K. Sprengel

*Viburnum lobophyllum* Graebner

*Viburnum lantana* L.

*Viburnum macrocephalum* Fortune

*Viburnum nudum* L.

*Viburnum plicatum* Thunberg f. *tomentosum* (Thunberg) Rehder

*Viburnum* × *pragense* (*V. rhytidophyllum* Hemsley × *V. utile* Hemsley)

*Viburnum* × *rhytidophylloides* Suringar (*V. lantana* L. 'Mohican' × *V. rhytidophyllum* Hemsley)

*Viburnum rufidulum* Rafinesque

*Viburnum sargentii* Koehne

*Viburnum setigerum* Hance

*Viburnum utile* Hemsley

*Vitex agnus-castus* L.

*Vitex negundo* L. var. *heterophylla* (Franchet) Rehder

*Vitex rotundifolia* L.

*Weigela florida* (Bunge) A. de Candolle

*Xanthorhiza simplicissima* Marshall

*Zenobia pulverulenta* (Bartram) Pollard

# Index of Botanic Names

# Index of Common Names